THE PAPERS OF WOODROW WILSON
Volume 47:
March 13-May 12, 1918

ARTHUR S. LINK, EDITOR

DAVID W. HIRST, SENIOR

ASSOCIATE EDITOR

JOHN E. LITTLE AND

FREDRICK AANDAHL,

ASSOCIATE EDITORS

The nine weeks covered here are a transitional period in Wilson's conduct of the war and see the emergence of the War Industries Board, the so-called War Cabinet, and the National War Labor Board. Administration forces rally behind the Overman bill. Wilson quiets an outcry against the Aircraft Production Board and deals with problems such as the fixing of prices of basic commodities; requests for federal assistance from farmers and livestock growers; the transportation system; leasing of public lands to oil companies; and alleviation of the housing shortage in Washington. He also blocks a bill for the trial by special military tribunals of persons charged with disloyalty.

Meanwhile, peace with Austria-Hungary is discussed, but Wilson believes that Germany is not prepared for a general settlement. In late March, the Germans begin their long-awaited spring offensive on the western front. The Allies turn to Wilson for help, and a compromise among Americans and Allies grants Pershing some control over his forces, while postponing the formation of an independent American army in France. France and Britain want an intervention in Siberia by Japan, but Wilson is resolute in his opposition to this move.

THE PAPERS OF

WOODROW WILSON

VOLUME 47

MARCH 13–MAY 12, 1918

SPONSORED BY THE WOODROW WILSON
FOUNDATION
AND PRINCETON UNIVERSITY

Portrait by John Singer Sargent

THE PAPERS OF

WOODROW WILSON

ARTHUR S. LINK, *EDITOR*

DAVID W. HIRST, *SENIOR ASSOCIATE EDITOR*

JOHN E. LITTLE, *ASSOCIATE EDITOR*

FREDRICK AANDAHL, *ASSOCIATE EDITOR*

MANFRED F. BOEMEKE, *ASSISTANT EDITOR*

PHYLLIS MARCHAND AND MARGARET D. LINK,

EDITORIAL ASSISTANTS

Volume 47
March 13–May 12, 1918

PRINCETON, NEW JERSEY
PRINCETON UNIVERSITY PRESS
1984

Publication of this book has been aided by a grant
from the National Historical Publications and Records
Commission.

Printed in the United States of America
by Princeton University Press
Princeton, New Jersey

INTRODUCTION

THE nine weeks covered in this volume are a transitional period in Wilson's conduct of the war. On the home front, the War Industries Board replaces the Council of National Defense as the agency primarily charged with the mobilization and allocation of industrial resources. Administration forces in Congress rally behind the Overman bill, which gives Wilson almost unlimited authority to reorganize all executive and administrative departments and agencies. Wilson takes additional steps to assure a greater degree of harmony and cooperation in the prosecution of the war effort. On March 20, he creates his so-called War Cabinet or War Council, which meets with Wilson regularly on every Wednesday. Next, Wilson moves toward the establishment of a unified labor policy and, to promote industrial peace, establishes the National War Labor Board as the supreme arbiter of labor disputes.

Although the war machinery is thus getting into ever higher gear, numerous perplexities remain. The sculptor, Gutzon Borglum, hurls accusations of "disloyalty, graft and conspiracy" against the Aircraft Production Board. Wilson quickly quietens the public and congressional outcry by ordering appropriate investigations. Other problems, such as the fixing of the prices of various basic commodities; requests for federal assistance from farmers and livestock growers; the efficient use of the nation's transportation system; the leasing of public lands to oil companies; and the alleviation of the chronic housing shortage in Washington are constant concerns to Wilson. In addition, Wilson blocks consideration of a bill, introduced by Senator Chamberlain of Oregon, for the trial by special military tribunals of persons charged with disloyalty. Wilson also keeps up his steady support of the woman-suffrage amendment; gets involved in several Democratic preprimary campaigns; and discourages the League to Enforce Peace from advocating a detailed constitution for a league of nations.

Meanwhile, peace between Austria-Hungary and the United States and the Allies seems possible, as talks among Vienna, London, and Washington continue, and Emperor Charles suggests to Wilson the inauguration of a "direct oral discussion" between Austrian and American representatives. While Wilson is receptive to these Austrian overtures, he believes that the peace of Brest-Litovsk clearly shows that Germany is not prepared for a general settlement based upon liberal principles. And Wilson tells an audience in Baltimore on the first anniversary of the entry of the United States into the war that there can be but one response to Germany's imperialism in eastern Europe: "Force, Force to the utmost, Force without stint or limit, the righteous and triumphant Force which shall make Right the law of the world, and cast every selfish dominion down in the dust."

In late March, the German army delivers its answer to any discussion about peace with its long-awaited spring offensive on the western front. The British army reels under the tremendous German onslaught. A decisive German victory seems possible, and Allied leaders, in despair and panic, turn to Wilson for help. They request the immediate dispatch of large numbers of American reinforcements, particularly infantry and machine-gun units, and they insist upon the amalgamation of these ill-trained and inexperienced forces with Allied divisions. Wilson and Secretary Baker are sympathetic to these demands and agree, in the face of the present emergency, to postpone the formation of an independent American army in France. However, General Pershing continues to resist any plans for the wholesale brigading of his troops with French and British divisions. The ensuing acrimonious dispute among American and Allied political and military leaders is solved only when a shaky compromise grants Pershing some measure of control over the disposition of his forces.

French and British leaders seize upon the German offensive in the West as another argument in their ongoing attempt to persuade Wilson to sanction an intervention in Siberia by Japan in order to reestablish an eastern front. The documents in this volume amply demonstrate the tenacity and perseverence of the Allied governments on this question. Still, Wilson is not impressed by any of the arguments advanced. He believes that the military advantage gained by an intervention would be negligible and that it would alienate the Bolshevik government and drive the Russian people into the arms of the Germans. Thus, although Wilson quite readily agrees to cooperate with the Allies in a limited action in northern Russia, as this volume ends, he is as resolute as ever in his opposition to any move into Siberia.

"VERBATIM ET LITERATIM"

In earlier volumes of this series, we have said something like the following: "All documents are reproduced *verbatim et literatim*, with typographical and spelling errors corrected in square brackets only when necessary for clarity and ease of reading." The following essay explains our textual methods and review procedures.

We have never printed and do not intend to print critical, or corrected, versions of documents. We print them exactly as they are, with a few exceptions which we always note. We never use the word *sic* except to denote the repetition of words in a document; in fact, we think that a succession of *sics* defaces a page.

We usually repair words in square brackets when letters are missing. As we have said, we also repair words in square brackets for clarity and ease of reading. Our general rule is to do this when we, ourselves, cannot read the word without having to stop to puzzle out its meaning. Jumbled words and names misspelled beyond recognition of course have to be repaired. We correct the misspelling of a name in a document in the footnote identifying the person.

However, when an old man writes to Wilson saying that he is glad to hear that Wilson is "comming" to Newark, or a semiliterate farmer from Texas writes phonetically, we see no reason to correct spellings in square brackets when the words are perfectly understandable. We do not correct Wilson's misspellings unless they are unreadable, except to supply in square brackets letters missing in words. For example, he consistently spelled "belligerent" as "belligerant." Nothing would be gained by correcting "belligerant" in square brackets.

We think that it is very important for several reasons to follow the rule of *verbatim et literatim*. Most important, a document has its own integrity and power, particularly when it is not written in perfect literary form. There is something very moving in seeing a Texas dirt farmer struggling to express his feelings in words, or a semiliterate former slave doing the same thing. Second, in Wilson's case it is crucially important to reproduce his errors in letters which he typed himself, since he usually typed badly when he was in an agitated state. Third, since style is the essence of the person, we would never correct grammar or make tenses consistent, as one correspondent has urged us to do. Fourth, we think that it is very important that we print exact transcripts of Charles L. Swem's copies of Wilson's letters. Swem made many mistakes (we correct them in footnotes from a reading of his shorthand books), and Wilson let them pass. We thus have to assume that Wilson did not read his letters before signing them, and this, we think, is a significant fact. Finally, printing typed letters and documents *verbatim et literatim* tells us a great deal about the educational level of the stenographic profession in the United States during Wilson's time.

We think that our series would be worthless if we produced unreliable texts, and we go to considerable effort to make certain that the texts are authentic.

Our typists are highly skilled and proofread their transcripts carefully as soon as they have typed them. The Editor sight proofreads documents once he has assembled a volume and is setting its annotation. The Editors who write the notes read through documents several times and are careful to check any anomalies. Then, once the manuscript volume has been completed and all notes checked, the Editor and Senior Associate Editor orally proofread the documents against the copy. They read every comma, dash, and character. They note every absence of punctuation. They study every nearly illegible word in written documents.

Once this process of "establishing the text" is completed, the manuscript volume goes to our editor at Princeton University Press, who checks the volume carefully and sends it to the printing plant. The galley proofs are read against copy in the proofroom at the Press. And we must say that the proofreaders there are extraordinarily skilled. Some years ago, before we found a way to ease their burden, they queried every misspelled word, absence of punctuation, or other such anomalies. Now we write "O.K." above such words or spaces on the copy.

We read the galley proofs at least three times. Our copyeditor gives them a sight reading against the manuscript copy to look for remaining typographical errors and to make sure that no line has been dropped. The Editor and Senior Associate Editor sight read them against documents and copy. We then get the page proofs, which have been corrected at the Press. We check all the changes three times. In addition, we get *revised* pages and check them twice.

This is not the end. The Editor, Senior Associate Editor, and Assistant Editor give a final reading to headings, description-location lines, and notes. Finally, our indexer of course reads the pages word by word. Before we return the pages to the Press, she comes in with a list of queries, all of which are answered by reference to the documents.

Our rule in the Wilson Papers is that our tolerance for error is zero. No system and no person can be perfect. There may be errors in our volumes. However, we believe that we have done everything humanly possible to avoid error; the chance is remote that what looks at first glance like a typographical error is indeed an error.

With the publication of this volume, our long association with Judith May comes to an end. Mrs. May became our editor at Princeton University Press in May 1977 and quickly became involved in all stages of production of Volumes 27 through this one. She was efficient, watchful, and ever helpful. We congratulate her upon her new and important responsibilities with Princeton University Press. We take this occasion to welcome our new editor, Alice Calaprice.

We are very grateful to Professor Thomas Fischer of the Ruhr-Universität Bochum, for making available to us a valuable collection of Wilson letters to Professor Fischer's grandfather, Dr. Richard

Ludwig Enno Littmann. They appear in the Addenda to this volume. Professors John Milton Cooper, Jr., William H. Harbaugh, Richard W. Leopold, and Betty Miller Unterberger read this volume carefully, and we thank them for their unflagging enthusiasm and helpful suggestions. Finally, for all their fine assistance over the years, we wish to thank Earle Coleman, University Archivist, and the staff of the Photographic Services, particularly John Leypoldt and Donald D. Breza.

THE EDITORS

Princeton, New Jersey
February 14, 1984

CONTENTS

Collateral Materials

ILLUSTRATIONS

Frontispiece

ABBREVIATIONS

ALI	autograph letter initialed
ALS	autograph letter signed
ASB	Albert Sidney Burleson
CC	carbon copy
CCL	carbon copy of letter
CCLS	carbon copy of letter signed
CL	copy of letter
CLS	Charles Lee Swem
CLSsh	Charles Lee Swem shorthand
EBW	Edith Bolling Wilson
EMH	Edward Mandell House
FKL	Franklin Knight Lane
FLP	Frank Lyon Polk
FR	*Papers Relating to the Foreign Relations of the United States*
FR-LP	*Papers Relating to the Foreign Relations of the United States: The Lansing Papers, 1914-1920*
FR-WWS 1917	*Papers Relating to the Foreign Relations of the United States, 1917, Supplement, The World War*
FR-WWS 1918	*Papers Relating to the Foreign Relations of the United States, 1918, Supplement, The World War*
FR 1918, Russia	*Papers Relating to the Foreign Relations of the United States, 1918, Russia*
Hw, hw	handwriting, handwritten
HwI	handwritten initialed
JD	Josephus Daniels
JPT	Joseph Patrick Tumulty
JRT	Jack Romagna typed
L	letter
MS, MSS	manuscript, manuscripts
NDB	Newton Diehl Baker
RG	record group
RL	Robert Lansing
T	typed
TC	typed copy
TCL	typed copy of letter
TCLS	typed copy of letter signed
TI	typed initialed
TL	typed letter
TLI	typed letter initialed
TLS	typed letter signed
TS	typed signed
TWG	Thomas Watt Gregory
WBW	William Bauchop Wilson
WCR	William Cox Redfield
WGM	William Gibbs McAdoo
WHP	Walter Hines Page
WW	Woodrow Wilson
WWhw	Woodrow Wilson handwriting, handwritten
WWsh	Woodrow Wilson shorthand

WWT	Woodrow Wilson typed
WWTL	Woodrow Wilson typed letter
WWTLI	Woodrow Wilson typed letter initialed
WWTLS	Woodrow Wilson typed letter signed

ABBREVIATIONS FOR COLLECTIONS
AND REPOSITORIES

Following the National Union Catalog
of the Library of Congress

AFL-CIO-Ar	American Federation of Labor-Congress of Industrial Organizations Archives
CSt-H	Hoover Institution on War, Revolution and Peace
CtY	Yale University
DLC	Library of Congress
DNA	National Archives
FFM-Ar	French Foreign Ministry Archives
FMD-Ar	French Ministry of Defense Archives
FO	British Foreign Office
HPL	Hoover Presidential Library
ICHi	Chicago Historical Society
InNd	University of Notre Dame
IOR	India Office Library and Records
JDR	Justice Department Records
JFO-Ar	Japanese Foreign Office Archives
LDR	Labor Department Records
MH-Ar	Harvard University Archives
MSCV	Connecticut Valley Historical Museum
Nc-Ar	North Carolina State Department of Archives and History
NDR	Navy Department Records
NFM-Ar	Netherlands Foreign Ministry Archives
NjP	Princeton University
OClWHi	Western Reserve Historical Society
PHi	Historical Society of Pennsylvania
PPAmP	American Philosophical Society
PRO	Public Record Office
RSB Coll., DLC	Ray Stannard Baker Collection of Wilsoniana, Library of Congress
ScCleU	Clemson University
SDR	State Department Records
WC, NjP	Woodrow Wilson Collection, Princeton University
WDR	War Department Records
WHi	State Historical Society of Wisconsin
WP, DLC	Woodrow Wilson Papers, Library of Congress

SYMBOLS

[March 13, 1918]	publication date of published writing; also date of document when date is not part of text
[*April 16, 1918*]	composition date when publication date differs
[[May 4, 1918]]	delivery date of speech if publication date differs
**** ***	text deleted by author of document

THE PAPERS OF

WOODROW WILSON

VOLUME 47

MARCH 13–MAY 12, 1918

Remarks to Representatives of Livestock Growers[1]

[March 13, 1918]

I want to express my appreciation, gentlemen, of what has just been said about me. I have never had the slightest doubt that you are behind me. Gentlemen come to me, gentlemen who frequent clubs, go out to dinner frequently, and tell me that the people of this country don't know what the war is about. My reply is invariably "rats." I know the people of the United States very much better than these gentlemen do, and I believe that, on the farms and in all the remote districts, the war is just as well understood as it is in Washington—a great deal better than it is understood in Washington by some people. So that, if they have had any doubt about that, we are engaged in an enterprise now that is, quite certainly, I must say, the most momentous in history. We are saving for the world the institutions that America first made distinguished by setting up this great republic, and everything will go by the board if we don't win. I hate even to use the word "if," even in a sentence like that, because there is no "if" about that.

I am trying to draw out from the Central Powers some distinct statement of what they are fighting for. I can't get it, but it doesn't make any difference whether we get it or not, we are going to finish this war. Of course, we will be glad to finish it now, if they will give us what is right, but if they won't give us what is right, we have only begun, and we will see it through. And I know, just as well as we stand here, that you will, and all the people of the United States, with humble peoples, will stand for that and will support it.

And that being the case, I feel just as much obliged as a man could feel to stand by you wherever I can. I can't, I am obliged to admit, understand all the problems that are put up to me. I use the brain I have, and all I can borrow, every day, and then sometimes feel a little confused with myself with some of the problems that spring up in such manifold ways all around us. But if there is any way in which I can help, which you will make clear to me, of course I will do so.

The fact of the matter is that there has got to be a burden all around. I don't see any way to escape that. And one of the things that we must not increase, if we can possibly avoid it, is the burden which the United States Treasury is now carrying, because the business of the world is upset by this war, and financial operations are very much more abnormal and difficult than they would be in other circumstances. Therefore, we must see to it that we don't overtax the instrumentalities that we have. But, of course, everything that is necessary must be done, and I want to help do it if I can.

I have no doubt that Mr. Hoover will be kind enough to bring to me the problems that you have stated to him, and if I can assist him in any way, you may be sure I will be glad to do it. I like to share this work, too.

JRT transcript (WC, NjP) of CLSsh (C. L. Swem Coll., NjP).
 [1] Wilson spoke at 5:30 p.m. at the White House to a delegation of some twenty-five persons from Missouri, Illinois, and Nebraska, who were introduced by Representative William W. Rucker of Missouri.

To the Council of the American Philosophical Society

My dear Sirs: The White House 13 March, 1918

I take the liberty of writing to suggest that Marshal Joffre be elected a member of the American Philosophical Society. I believe that Marshal Joffre's scientific and professional acquirements would in themselves justify this election, and I believe that the additional argument for his election is irresistible, namely, our desire to manifest in this way our very high regard for one of the most honored representatives of the French Nation.[1]

Very respectfully yours,   Woodrow Wilson

TLS (PPAmP).
 [1] Joffre was elected to membership in the American Philosophical Society on April 20, 1918.

To David Lawrence

My dear Lawrence: [The White House] 13 March, 1918

I have been thinking a great deal about your proposal for an article about my executive work,[1] and I find that I can't for the life of me think it out in any way that would be striking or effective. That is my trouble. The day seldom sounds impressive when summed up, because most of the questions which I have decided come to me in the form of memoranda to which I reply in writing. My interviews and consultations are chiefly with people who need not

have taken my time, and lead to nothing except the gratification
on the part of those who see me that they have had their say.

Had you sketched out an article at all?

In haste   Faithfully yours,   Woodrow Wilson

TLS (Letterpress Books, WP, DLC).
¹ Wilson was probably replying to an oral suggestion. There is no letter from Lawrence
on this subject. Lawrence undoubtedly had suggested that it was time for a sequel to
his earlier article, "The President and His Day's Work," *Century Magazine*, XCIII (March
1917), 641-52.

To Frank Lyon Polk

My dear Polk: [The White House] 13 March, 1918

When I was president of Princeton, I had as my secretary for a
couple of years Mr. Gilbert F. Close, who is now serving as Secretary
Daniels' confidential secretary. He is one of the most loyal and
trustworthy men I have ever had the good fortune to be associated
with, and I am anxious to find for him a place which will make it
less difficult for him to maintain his little family. I am, therefore,
venturing to ask if there is not some confidential work in the State
Department to which it would be wise and practicable to assign
him?

The one thing that stands in Close's way is his lack of initiative.
He does the tasks assigned him with the greatest intelligence and
thoroughness, and is always utterly to be trusted, but he has no
other sort of executive ability, so far as I was able to test him. The
State Department has so much work of an entirely confidential
nature in connection, for example, with coding and decoding that
it has occurred to me that there might be some place open for Close
there which would pay him a living salary. I wonder if there is, and
if you would need such a man?

Cordially and sincerely yours,   Woodrow Wilson

TLS (Letterpress Books, WP, DLC).

To Edward Nash Hurley

My dear Hurley: [The White House] 13 March, 1918

I wish I could think of some man whom all the country would
recognize as just the right man for what you suggest in your letter
of yesterday,¹ but before putting my mind to it I would like to have
just a little further light.

Your suggestion of Albert Shaw would seem to indicate that you do not want a man accustomed to directing cost accounting or technically qualified to judge of the results of such accounting, but only somebody whose character and public spirit and intelligence would be evident to everybody. Is that your idea?

Another question: How much time would the man have to devote to the work? Would he have to give his whole time to it?

I am greatly interested and will help all I can.

Cordially and sincerely yours,   Woodrow Wilson

TLS (Letterpress Books, WP, DLC).
  [1] E. N. Hurley to WW, March 12, 1918, Vol. 46.

To Joseph R. Wilson, Jr.

Dear Joe: [The White House] 13 March, 1918

I am as much annoyed as you are by the report which you tell me is being circulated in Tennessee by Senator Shields' friends.[1] Of course, you may be sure that Senator Shields will get no letter from me, but to send Cates[2] a letter from me to that effect would be to do the very thing which I think would be inexcusable, namely, personally intervene as between two Democrats. If I did it in this case, I would be beseeched to do it in others and would bring down upon myself a degree of unpopularity which would be a very serious handicap. The best I can think of is that you should yourself personally assure Cates that he need have no apprehension that any such letter will be given Senator Shields, at the same time warning him not to bring me into the case.

In haste   Affectionately yours,   Woodrow Wilson

TLS (Letterpress Books, WP, DLC).
  [1] The letter to which Wilson was replying is missing.
  [2] Charles Theodore Cates, Jr., lawyer of Knoxville and a former Attorney General of Tennessee. He was a supporter of Governor Thomas Clarke Rye, who ran, unsuccessfully, against Shields in the Democratic primary election for United States senator in 1918.

To William Gibbs McAdoo

Personal and Private.

My dear Mac: [The White House] 13 March, 1918

There is a persistent rumor being spread by the friends of Senator Shields of Tennessee that you and I are going to give him letters of support of some sort. Shields is one of the men whom I would dearly like to see left out of the Senate, because I don't like either his attitude or his principles which seem to me thoroughly selfish, and I am merely writing this line to express the hope that you will not give him any countenance in his fight in Tennessee for renomination. Our only hope of success as leaders of the party is in confining our support to genuine out-and-out friends.

I dare say this is quite unnecessary, but I thought I would let you know what is being promised by friends of Senator Shields who don't care whether their promises are true or not.

Affectionately yours,   Woodrow Wilson

TLS (Letterpress Books, WP, DLC).

To Charles Spalding Thomas

My dear Senator: [The White House] 13 March, 1918

I have been both puzzled and considerably distressed by the question of the price of coal in the Colorado district.[1] I have now twice gone over the matter very thoroughly with the Fuel Administrator, who has shown me figures collected, not by amateurs but by men who have every right to be regarded as experts and who have had sufficient experience in that particular kind of work to entitle their conclusions to the greatest respect. Going through the matter up and down and left and right, I cannot convince myself that any essential injustice has been done. I do not understand why the mines should be closing down. I hope with all my heart that it is not in order to exercise a certain degree of pressure. I honestly do not see how they can justify their closing.

You yourself saw the figure sheets, Mr. Garfield tells me, and I have not only seen them but have gone over a considerable part of the data upon which they are founded. I believe, therefore, that it is absolutely necessary for me, acting in a judicial capacity in this matter, to confirm and abide by the decision of the Fuel Administrator.

What I particularly regret about this is the distress it has evidently caused you.

Cordially and sincerely yours,   Woodrow Wilson

TLS (Letterpress Books, WP, DLC).
[1] Wilson was replying to C. S. Thomas to WW, March 9, 1918, printed as an Enclosure with WW to H. A. Garfield, March 11, 1918, and to C. S. Thomas to WW, March 12, 1918, all printed in Vol. 46.

To Albert Sidney Burleson

My dear Burleson: The White House 13 March, 1918

What sort of reply would you advise me to make to this letter?[1] Shall I merely accept the resignation, or shall I go on to express some hope with regard to the fortunes of the election in Wisconsin? I should very much value your advice.

Cordially and sincerely yours,   Woodrow Wilson

TLS (A. S. Burleson Papers, DLC).
[1] That is, J. E. Davies to WW, March 12, 1918, Vol. 46.

To Harry Augustus Garfield

My dear Garfield,   The White House 13 March, 1918

I have just heard of your mother's death.[1] My heart goes out to you, my dear friend, in profound sympathy. It was my great pleasure to know her, and, having had some taste of her quality, I can understand that you have lost a noble friend and counsellor as well as a beloved mother. The news of her death came to me as a great shock. May comfort come to you from the only source it can come from when such a sorrow is to be borne!

Your sincere friend   Woodrow Wilson

ALS (H. A. Garfield Papers, DLC).
[1] Lucretia Rudolph (Mrs. James Abram) Garfield had died of pneumonia in South Pasadena, California, on March 13, at the age of eighty-five.

From William Howard Thompson

My dear Mr. President: Washington March 13, 1918.

I desire to respectfully call attention to the necessity of the government taking over, controlling and operating, the packing industries of the country during the war.

The investigation now being carried on by the Federal Trade Commission, the hearings conducted by the Senate Agricultural Committee of which I am a member, and other Congressional Committees, as well as the bitter experience of the people of the country in endeavoring to provide themselves with the necessities of life, together with the immense requirements of the army and navy, clearly demonstrate the great importance of such action. Meat, eggs, canned goods, and other necessities of life, handled by these industries, have already reached such unreasonably high prices as to make it impossible for a man of limited means, or a laboring man who works for daily wages, to purchase. In my judgment, it is clearly established in these proceedings that these packing concerns are violating the laws in restraint of trade and should be prosecuted to the limit of the law, yet such legal proceedings would avail nothing during the war as it is food the people need, as well as the government, to carry on the war. Unless these packing plants are taken over much suffering among the people will result and our fighting power in the war will be greatly diminished.

Very respectfully,   Wm. H. Thompson

TLS (WP, DLC).

From William Cox Redfield

My dear Mr. President: Washington March 13, 1918.

As you know the Director General of Railroads has taken up, through a special committee for the purpose, the matter of transportation on our waterways. Another phase of the transportation problem is forcing itself rapidly to the front and should, I think, be included within the scope of the Railroad Directorate as having supervision of all transportation. I refer to the use of the motor truck which is rapidly coming into service in interstate traffic and is for such traffic being utilized by the War Department.

May I ask that you kindly read the enclosed copy of letter recently sent the Governor of Maryland which gives my views on the subject from the standpoint of commerce?[1]

The Council of National Defense has an able and active committee on this subject called the Highways Transport Committee. They desire to work in cooperation with the Railroad Directorate and, I know, would appreciate the assistance that would be given if the Director General of Railroads could assign some officer of his service to give his special thought and effort to this matter of highways transportation.

The matter has come to me normally from its commercial relations but an active share in it does not lie within my scope and I am assured by the Director General of Railroads in a letter dated the 5th instant that he will be glad to assi[s]t in the matter, which I therefore lay before you for such action as you may think it to merit.   Yours very truly,   William C. Redfield

TLS (WP, DLC).
[1] WCR to E. C. Harrington, March 9, 1918, CCL (WP, DLC).

From Franklin Knight Lane

My dear Mr. President: Washington March 13, 1918.

I have been importuned by Mr. Untermyer, representing a Mr. Hamon of Oklahoma,[1] and by Mr. Bertron, to give oil leases to large quantities of land in the Osage territory. Mr. Untermyer's proposition was to take the whole of the undeveloped portion of the territory, something over 800,000 acres, and give him a blanket lease to this upon liberal terms to the Indians. Mr. Bertron's request was for 4800 acres.

The first proposition had the assent of the Indian Council. I have declined to approve it, however, upon the ground that we would not make any leases in private, that our policy was to put everything up at private auction, for competitive bidding,—let the world know what was for sale—and I frankly stated the danger that would arise from what might be termed a "Star Chamber" lease. I think the country would rise up in high indignation if it was known that we had leased nearly a million acres of land without giving any but one company an opportunity to get a portion of it. If this grant were made it would create a monopoly very much larger than any monopoly that has existed. Even the Standard Oil Company has never held any such amount of possible producing land.

The right to develop these lands as community lands and have all of the revenue divided among all of the Indians expires in 1931, and the Indians are very anxious that this period should be extended, because if not extended the oil will go to the surface land owners, many of whom are whites, who have no right to it whatever and who bought the land upon the assumption that they were getting only the surface. I have told the Indians that if we could not get the time extended beyond 1931 that we would open up this property, and if by the end of this session this is not done I think we must take steps to develop it so that all of the Indians may have the benefits of the proceeds. But if this is done it should be done only in the most public manner possible, and for tracts certainly not exceeding 4800 acres.

I send you a letter of instructions that I have sent to Mr. Wright, our agent in the Osage who is handling these matters,[2] and if there is any correction in this policy that you think should be made I will be glad if if [sic] you will let me know.

Cordially yours,   Franklin K Lane

TLS (WP, DLC).

[1] Jacob ("Jake") L. Hamon, wealthy oil operator and railroad builder of Ardmore, Oklahoma; long-time leader of the Republican party in Oklahoma.

[2] FKL to J. George Wright, Feb. 7, 1918, TCL (WP, DLC). Wright was superintendent of the Osage Indian Agency at Pawhuska, Oklahoma.

From Edward Mandell House, with Enclosures

Dear Governor: New York. March 13, 1918.

I am enclosing a cable which has just come from Balfour.

It looks as if the Austrians were in earnest in their endeavors for peace. I think conditions are very bad in many directions there. I doubt whether General Smuts is a good man to meet Czernin. Lord Robert Cecil would seem to me a better choice. Smuts is an able man but has not the international touch sufficiently to deal with the Austrians.

I am sorry that I was not able to go to Washington on Monday. I am still having fever each day, although I am around the house and doing some work. I doubt whether it will be wise for me to leave before next week.

Affectionately yours,   E. M. House

TLS (WP, DLC).

E N C L O S U R E   I

March 13, 1918.

Urgent.

No. 64. Following from Mr. Balfour for Col. House:

Our messenger[1] telegraphs that Austrian omens seem favourable. Through illness Austrian agent has not yet been seen. If, as is hoped, he indicates that Austrian Minister for Foreign Affairs is prepared to discuss terms apart from Germany with English Cabinet Minister, we should like to take an opportunity to talk over situation with Italian President of the Council,[2] who arrives here tomorrow. If latter does not object, we should then send out General Smuts to meet Austrian Minister for Foreign Affairs.

I know this is in full accordance with President's policy. I will keep him fully informed.

TC telegram (WP, DLC).

[1] Philip Henry Kerr, private secretary to Lloyd George, whom the British War Cabinet sent to Bern in early March 1918. About this ill-fated mission, see Sterling J. Kernek, *Distractions of Peace during War: The Lloyd George Government's Reactions to Woodrow Wilson, December, 1916-November, 1918* (Philadelphia, 1975), pp. 82-84.

[2] That is, Vittorio Emanuele Orlando.

ENCLOSURE II

Sidney Edward Mezes to Edward Mandell House

Dear Edward,   New York March 12, 1918.

As you have no doubt guessed, I have been really worried about the diplomatic situation. For the first time I have wondered whether even the President could deal with it adequately. But his message to the Russian people[1] is a wonder. In view of the complex difficulties of the situation, the brevity and straightforward ease with which he avoids every pitfall, and attains every objective, is unexampled in diplomacy—certainly in the testing field of open diplomacy. If there is any capacity for understanding in the Soviets, the simple sincerity of his sympathy and assurance of support will reach them; nor can the warnings that his words carry, and have a right to carry, fail to reach and impress the enemies of Russia, and of democracy, or those whose friendship and backing both sorely need and should have. And the thing is done in three short paragraphs! In nice and precise adjustment of means to complex and lofty aims I consider it his masterpiece.

Hoping this will find you all right again,

Fraternally,   S. E. Mezes.

TLS (WP, DLC).
[1] That is, Wilson's message to the Fourth All-Russian Congress of Soviets, March 11, 1918, printed at that date in Vol. 46.

From Benedict Crowell, with Enclosure

My dear Mr. President: Washington March 13, 1918.

Please find enclosed an interesting letter from General Bliss to Secretary Baker, together with a newspaper clipping to accompany it.   Very truly yours,   Benedict Crowell

ENCLOSURE

Tasker Howard Bliss to Newton Diehl Baker

My dear Mr. Secretary: Versailles. February 21, 1918.

I inclose herewith a clipping from the Daily Mail, an English newspaper which has a Paris edition.[1] Doubtless by the time this reaches you the controversy in the House of Commons, arising out of the displacement of the British Chief of Staff, General Robertson, will be an old story to you.

The passage in Mr. Lloyd-George's speech which I have marked,[2] relates to the paper which I submitted at the last meeting of the Third Session of the Supreme War Council,—Saturday, February 2. I am pleased that he made this public statement, because you may be wondering whether the Americans are having any influence on the Supreme War Council. I am sure that we have had such influence, unless both the political and military representatives have gone out of their way to tell me things which they did not believe, (and this I know to be not the case), and an influence for good.

The thing that amazes me is that after the Third Session of the Supreme War Council, which was perfectly harmonious and unanimous in its decisions, the subsequent controversy over General Robertson could have arisen, but on reflection, I think there is only one explanation. You know what my original views were as to the presence of political representatives on the Supreme War Council. I do not mean *any* political representatives, but those of such great importance as the Prime Ministers of our three Allies who, in reality, are the heads of their Governments quite as much as President Wilson is the head of our Government. They are three lightning-rods erected over Versailles to attract the attacks of men and women, (and, unfortunately, the latter perhaps most of all), who want to attack not the Supreme War Council but one or another of the Prime Ministers who constitute it;—because, you must always remember, that it is the three Prime Ministers, and they alone, who constitute the Supreme War Council, while the military men and all others are simply their advisers. The controversy over General Robertson has been carried on not by people who care a turn of their hand about him but by people who are seeking the downfall of Mr. Lloyd-George and his Government.

And, in such matters, it is astonishing the amount of trouble that results from the political intrigues of women of high position. Every such English woman is openly and frankly a politician; and every such French woman is covertly a politician.

I think there is no doubt that the wealthy people of England are, as a class, opposed to Mr. Lloyd-George. They recognize in him the man best fitted to head the Government for the purposes of this war. For these purposes they require a man with the driving energy which he has more than any other English man, apparently, in public life. But they dread what he will do when the war is over. These are the people who have attempted to use General Robertson as a club with which to assail Mr. Lloyd-George. I do not think that they have had the idea of driving him from power now but of making it easier to do so at a later time. I think General Robertson has allowed himself to play into their hands by listening to their insinuations until he has convinced himself that he has a real grievance. I am surprised at his doing so because I have admired him increasingly from the time when I first met him, as a very able man and, apparently, with no other ambition than to serve his country to the best of his ability. I am sure that he will regret the use that has been made of him.

I think that our government should do all in its power to sustain the existing governments, especially in England and France. A change now would be disastrous, and the people who want a change in the future are secretly convinced that it would be disastrous were it to come now. There is some real unity of action being developed in military matters, and it would be criminal if just at this time the political governments were to show the reverse.

Mr. Clemenceau is just such another man as Mr. Lloyd-George;— a man of tremendous energy, afraid of nothing, with no other purpose just now than to force the war to a successful termination, and holding in abeyance, apparently, all his very radical political and social ideas; a man of impulse and, therefore, a man of action at a time when action is the one thing required, and when it is almost impossible for an ordinarily sane man to misdirect his action.

Both he and Mr. Lloyd-George may be unsafe administrators in time of peace, (I do not know), but for present purposes they are the men for their places. The common people and the Army,— which now mean the same thing,—have confidence in them, notwithstanding the efforts of a certain clique to undermine the confidence of the English Army in Mr. Lloyd-George. Our motto should be, as the Irish say, "More power to their elbow."

Cordially yours,   Tasker H. Bliss.

TLS (WP, DLC).
¹ "Supreme War Council: Mr. Lloyd George's Statement," London *Daily Mail*, Paris edn., Feb. 20, 1918, clipping (WP, DLC). This article was a lengthy paraphrase of Lloyd George's speech in the Commons on February 19 in which he defended his role in the resignation of General Sir William R. Robertson as Chief of the Imperial General Staff (about which see EMH to WW, Feb. 15, 1918, n. 3, Vol. 46).
² This passage (included in the clipping cited in n. 1 above) referred to a "very cogent document" submitted by the American delegation to the Supreme War Council which argued against the creation of still another war-policy-making body in the form of a proposed "Council of Chiefs of Staff."

From Jean Jules Jusserand

Dear Mr. President,   Washington March 13, 1918.

I sent yesterday, by order of my Government, an important letter to the Department of State concerning the question of a Japanese action in Siberia. A copy will be, I believe, placed to-day before you by care of the acting Secretary.

I take the liberty of calling your attention to the facts and reasons which cause my Government to earnestly desire that you might now favor a plan, the usefulness of which seems to be demonstrated by the more recent news received from those regions and from Japan.

From Japan we have the confirmation that the Government is ready to proclaim in emphatic terms its desinterestedness, which would go a long way to allay Russian misgivings. The Japanese Government is ready to work in agreement with the United States and their co-belligerents, hoping moreover that America might assist them with the kind of supplies they may need.

We are informed that Mr. Krupensky, Russian Ambassador to Tokio,[1] is of opinion that, provided the declaration of desinterestedness be positive, Japanese help will be welcome, and that he is ready to assist in making the object and limitations of that action better understood by his own compatriots.

From Irkoutsk, the information comes that the Japanese would be welcome.

No undertaking of such importance in these troublous days, can of course go without some drawbacks. But, in the eyes of my Government, they are not to be compared with the advantages, the chief of which is the keeping open for us all and the shutting to the enemy, of the trans-siberian route, for us henceforth the only means of access to Eastern and Southern Russia.

Such military forces as may exist in those regions being small, composite and ill trained, the probabilities are that the one of the two parties which may first occupy the line would not meet much difficulty. It seems, therefore, exceedingly desirable that the first to do so be one of us.

Commending the whole situation to your wise consideration, I beg you to believe me, dear Mr. President,

Very sincerely and respectfully yours,   Jusserand

TLS (WP, DLC).
[1] Vasilii Nikolaevich Krupenskii.

From Alexander Jeffrey McKelway

Dear Mr. President: [Washington] March 13, 1918.

I have just read Colonel Harvey's output in this month's North American Review,[1] and Richard Washburn Child's article on "The President" in this week's Collier's,[2] neither of which is worthy of your perusal. I sometimes relieve my mind, in such cases, by giving a piece of it to author or editor, as the case may be. But, of course,

Harvey is hopeless, and I take it that Child, like Hard, Chambers, Wister, Dunne, Ogden Reid, Von Valkenburg, Whigham, and the Abbotts,[3] is still a victim of the Roosevelt obsession; so I thought I would write you a letter instead.

I wish sometimes that you could put on a Bolsheviki beard, or other suitable disguise, and get out among the real folks to hear what they say about you. A few weeks ago I paid a visit to my old home at Charlotte Court House, Va., and I wish that you could have been there to hear and to see. Everybody is working, with the winning of the war as the foremost object. Women are knitting and raising money for the Y.M.C.A. and Red Cross work in astonishing amounts; preachers are preaching; school teachers are lecturing; the young men are all at the front, and the city fathers sit around the drug-store sawdust box, when the day's work is done, and encourage themselves by expressing their faith and confidence in you, and Daniels, and Baker, and all the rest of them.

On this visit, I looked up a little family history on my mother's[4] side, and I find that my two boys who are in the service,[5] one in the Army and the other in the Navy, belong to the sixth generation of the descendants of Colonel Isaac Read of the War of the Revolution, whose son of the same name was in the War of 1812, whose son, Isaac Read, had five sons in the Confederate Army, and that the descendants of the first Isaac have distinguished themselves in all the later wars of the Republic, though I do not believe that a single member of the connection has ever been at West Point. I mention this just because it is rather typical of the older families of this section who are essentially non-military, and yet have never failed their country in the hour of its need.

I spent last week in Richmond in the closing days of the session of the Virginia Legislature. I was astonished at the character and capacity of the members of the House of Delegates, elected last fall, and therefore since the declaration of war. I have suffered many things of many Congressmen in both Houses here in Washington, but I sat hour after hour in the gallery of the Virginia House of Delegates, listening to the debates. There was a singleness of mind with reference to all matters relating to the war which was most inspiring, and the speeches, in grammar, diction, and real eloquence, were, I should say, above the average of those of the House of Representatives in Washington, if not of the Senate. Certainly there were no Reeds, or Hitchcocks, or Gores, or Hardwicks, to discourage the patriotic heart.

Among the leaders of the House of Delegates was Major William A. Anderson,[6] of Lexington, formerly Attorney-General of the state, and one of its ablest lawyers. I have no doubt he returned to the Legislature for the sole purpose of serving his country in time of war. And there were numerous younger men of surprising ability, it seemed to me. It gave me new hope for the progressiveness of the old state.

Senator Robertson,[7] of Rockbridge County, was dressed in khaki with a First Lieutenant's shoulder bars, and he was invariably applauded and cheered when he brought, according to the ancient custom, a message from the Senate to the House. A member of the House, "the gentleman from Amherst,"[8] was also in khaki. Matters presented by the Council of Defense were considered privileged, and the three consecutive readings on three consecutive days required by the Constitution were dispensed with by unanimous consent.

But what I started to say was that everybody I talked with in Richmond seemed to believe that every citizen's first duty is to follow wherever the President leads. There is no need for the expression of intolerance against slackers and traitors, for there seemed to be none left against whom indignation could be turned.

I must confess that I played rather a mean trick on the Virginia Legislature. I was interested in a child labor bill, bringing up the standards of the Virginia law to those of the Federal Child Labor Act, and, when the Senate Committee met to consider the bill, I demolished opposition by reading your letter to me of December 20th last.[9] The passage of the bill was delayed in the Senate partly through the agency of Rorer James,[10] Chairman of the Virginia Democratic Committee, the same man who was misguided enough to run against Carter Glass for National Committeeman. I understand he is interested in the Danville cotton mills. We finally got the bill through the Senate, however, and upon its third reading in the House, the day of adjournment. It could not have been passed except by unanimous consent under the rules then prevailing, and, under ordinary circumstances, that would have been hopeless. So I had printed above your letter the words—"Pass the Child Labor Bill! (Senate Bill No. 43)," and had the document distributed among the members of the House, and no one had the face to object to its passage.

I hope you will pardon such a use of your letter in a good cause.

Cordially yours,   [A. J. McKelway]

CCL (A. J. McKelway Papers, DLC).

[1] [George B. M. Harvey], "Wanted: A Leader" and "Coordination at the Top," *North American Review*, CCVII (March 1918), 321-34. The first editorial attacked Wilson for his alleged failure to appoint a cabinet capable of waging war effectively and for his failure to provide leadership to the Allied nations. The second editorial criticized the quarreling over war policy between Congress and the White House and asserted that Wilson was to blame for it because he was autocratic and secretive.

[2] Richard Washburn Child, "The President," *Collier's: The National Weekly*, LXI (March 16, 1918), 6-8, 41-42. Child portrayed Wilson as a man of far-seeing vision and fine ideals but with little or no ability to cooperate with practical managers who could transform these ideals into reality. Child viewed Wilson as a person increasingly isolated

from all contact except with a few favored colleagues such as Baker, who shared his outlook. Meanwhile, according to Child, the American war effort floundered in utter confusion which might lead to a disaster. Child said that the solution lay in the creation of a war cabinet with real power to get things done; however, he added, the chief obstacle to the formation of such a body was Wilson himself. Despite his inability to manage the war machine himself, Wilson would not delegate the necessary authority to anyone else.

[3] That is, William Hard, James Julius Chambers, Owen Wister, Finley Peter Dunne, Ogden Mills Reid, Edwin Augustus Van Valkenburg, Lawrence Fraser Abbott, and Lyman Abbott. Henry James Whigham was editor and publisher of *Metropolitan Magazine*.

[4] Catherine Scott Comfort (Mrs. John Ryan) McKelway.

[5] Lt. Benjamin Mosby McKelway, with the A.E.F. in France, and Ens. Alexander Jeffrey McKelway III, a naval aviation pilot.

[6] William Alexander Anderson.

[7] Absolam Willis Robertson.

[8] Peyton Randolph Evans.

[9] WW to A. J. McKelway, Dec. 20, 1917, Vol. 45.

[10] Rorer Abraham James, also editor and publisher of the *Danville Register*.

Lord Reading to Arthur James Balfour

[Washington, March 13, 1918]

Your tel. No 1388.[1] Upon receipt yesterday I immediately saw Polk in absence of Lansing and verbally communicated text of message. His view was that Frazier would be attending proceedings for purpose of reporting to the President. Polk has just sent message that U.S.G. are instructing Bliss and Frazier to attend and report. Polk added that time was too short to permit of the designation of any person to represent the President. Your cablegram did not ask for representation.   R.

HwI telegram (FO 115/2475, p. 9, PRO).
[1] A. J. Balfour to Lord Reading, March 12, 1918, T telegram (FO 115/2475, p. 8, PRO).

To Breckinridge Long

My dear Mr. Long: The White House 14 March, 1918

After several days' delay I have had the opportunity at last to read carefully your memorandum of March fourth about Russia.[1] It has interested me very much, but in view of what seems to me the necessary limitations of our action over there I do not think that it would be practicable to carry out your suggestion. I mean that we have not the instrumentalities through which to act alone, and cooperation where alone it is possible cuts in many directions.

Cordially and sincerely yours,   Woodrow Wilson

TLS (B. Long Papers, DLC).
[1] B. Long to WW, March 4, 1918, Vol. 46.

To Rudolph Blankenburg

[The White House] 14 March, 1918

Will you not be kind enough to convey to the meeting over which you are to preside tomorrow evening[1] an expression of my very sincere sympathy in the cause represented by the Friends of German Democracy? I do not feel that any country is at liberty to dictate the institutions and policy of another, but it is nevertheless clearly our privilege to express the most cordial sympathy with everything that legitimately makes for liberty and democracy throughout the world.   Woodrow Wilson.

T telegram (Letterpress Books, WP, DLC).
    [1] A meeting of the Philadelphia branch of the recently formed Society of Friends of German Democracy, an organization intended to promote a democratic form of government in Germany. Some 500 persons, mostly either German-born or of German descent, attended the meeting held in the Germantown Branch Library on March 15. Blankenburg presided and read Wilson's message. Philadelphia *Evening Bulletin*, March 16, 1918.

To William Squire Kenyon

Personal.

My dear Senator Kenyon: [The White House] 14 March, 1918

I have your letter of March ninth[1] and need hardly say that I am anxious to help in any way that it would be possible to help the farmers, not only those who produce the cereals but those who produce the meats of the country.
The matter of taking over the packing business has engaged my thought a good deal, and I must admit that my judgment is not yet prepared for it. It would be a very big undertaking for which we have no adequate preparation and in which it might be we could not get the cooperation which would permit an uninterrupted continuation of what is, of course, an indispensable function.

Your letter, however, fixes my attention upon the matter again, and you may be sure I shall think it out.
              Cordially and sincerely yours,   Woodrow Wilson

TLS (Letterpress Books, WP, DLC).
    [1] W. S. Kenyon to WW, March 9, 1918, Vol. 46.

To Washington Gladden

My dear Doctor Gladden: [The White House] 14 March, 1918

My heart often turns to you in these days of your illness, and I hope sincerely that you are mending with a real intention to get well again and support us as of old with your indomitable spirit. This is just a message of affectionate sympathy.

Cordially and sincerely yours,   Woodrow Wilson

TLS (Letterpress Books, WP, DLC).

To Franklin Knight Lane

My dear Mr. Secretary: [The White House] 14 March, 1918

I am sincerely glad that you disapproved the action of the Indian Council with regard to leasing the oil lands. I think that such leases as Mr. Untermyer and Mr. Bertron are proposing would be clearly against the public interest.

I hope that it will be possible to extend the policy of community lands to which you refer as expiring in 1931, but I dare say it is a little too early to propose it to the Congress.

Cordially and sincerely yours,   Woodrow Wilson

TLS (Letterpress Books, WP, DLC).

To David Franklin Houston

My dear Houston: [The White House] 14 March, 1918

I should very much value your advice in this matter.[1]

Cordially and sincerely yours,   [Woodrow Wilson]

CCL (WP, DLC).
  [1] Wilson referred to J. M. Baer to WW, March 13, 1918, TLS (WP, DLC). Baer asked Wilson to say a word to the leaders of the House of Representatives on behalf of his bill (H.R. 7795), which authorized the Secretary of Agriculture to make loans to farmers for the purchase of seed grain and to advance funds for the transportation of farm laborers for the crop year 1918. The bill appropriated $7,500,000 for the former purpose and $2,500,000 for the latter. Baer said that the bill would have to be enacted within the next fifteen days if it was to have any effect upon seeding for the current year. He enclosed a copy of the printed report on the bill (65th Cong., 2d sess., *House Report No. 364*). Houston's response to Wilson's note of March 14 was that, while he was not sure of the actual need for the bill, he nevertheless would urge its passage in order to guarantee a large wheat crop for the current year. C. Ousley to WW, March 16, 1918, TLS, enclosing D. F. Houston to F. R. Harrison, March 15, 1918, TC telegram, both in WP, DLC. For the fate of the Baer bill, see D. F. Houston to WW, March 28, 1918, n. 2.

From Frank Lyon Polk, with Enclosure

My dear Mr. President: [Washington] March 14, 1918.

I enclose, for your information, a translation of a letter, dated March twelfth, from the French Ambassador on the subject of Japanese Intervention in Siberia. As you will notice, it advances arguments in favor of such action and at the end asks whether the United States Government, upon a re-examination of the question, will concur in the views expressed by the French Ambassador and join in the action they have taken. When the Ambassador spoke to me about this matter on Tuesday, I told him I felt sure this Government would not be disposed to change its position, certainly not at the present time. Will you please let me know whether it is satisfactory to you for the Department to state, in answering the Ambassador's letter, that we see no reason for a change of opinion at this time.   Yours faithfully,   Frank L Polk

March 15, 1918 Pres. told Secy at Cabinet to ans. as suggested FLP

TLS (SDR, RG 59, 861.00/1676, DNA).

E N C L O S U R E

Jean Jules Jusserand to the Secretary of State

Mr. Secretary of State: Washington, D. C. March 12, 1918.

By order of my Government I have the honor to impart to Your Excellency the latest intelligence that has reached it on the question of Japan's intervention in Siberia and to point to the consequences which we deem it proper to draw therefrom in the interest of the common cause.

In a general way, Japan, as Your Excellency knows, must and will intervene in Asia in defense of her present position and of her future. If she does so without our assent she will do it against us and there is some likelihood of her later arriving at an understanding with Germany. This of itself we would regard as a decisive consideration.

But it must be remarked, in addition, that an agreement of the Allies with Japan affords the only means of obtaining from her declarations expressly stating that she is acting as an ally of the moral person represented by Russia and is resolved not to encroach in the least on Russia's right of self determination in selecting this or that form of Government, that she desires to help Russia out of the political and economic control of Germany and to assist in reconstituting Russia's national unity which necessarily implies the restoration of order which the Russians, in their present state of anarchy, are no longer able to achieve.

Negotiations with the Japanese Government will, in the second place, make it possible to call on it for public guarantees of territorial disinterestedness, which will go much farther than a mere reservation that the fate of the countries occupied by Japan shall be determined by the Peace Congress.

Lastly, with respect to the extent and effectiveness of Japan's action, it also depends on us to have its reality clearly defined and to secure pledges in this respect. That is one of the main objects of the pending negotiations in Tokyo. In our opinion that action may be far reaching.

Japan, a great power with a population of 56 millions, an active army numbering 600,000 men and a reserve army of equal strength, has largely increased her wealth during the war; she is enjoying full prosperity and at the present time commands considerable financial resources. Even if it were not so, the Allies could if needed furnish the financial means she might need, although Japan did declare that she proposed the act unassisted and assumed the burdens and responsibilities of the undertaking.

Taken as a whole the plan, the adoption of which by Japan we are seeking and the scope of which would justify and effectuate her intervention, embraces the following points: First, occupation of the Trans-Siberian Terminals at Vladivostock and Karbin [Harbin] for the preservation of our stocks and the maintenance of the regular ways of communication, both military and economic, with Russia; next, to secure the control of the Trans-Siberian Railway by occupying the Tchita pass, the key to the several railroads of Northern Asia; to reinstate at Irkoutsk and Tomsk the Siberian Governments that have been driven out by the anarchists with the help of the German prisoners; to establish in Siberia a center of resistance and attraction for the sound parts of Russia with which relations may be entered into in Southern Russia; to keep out of the reach of the Germans the stores of grain hoarded in Asiatic Russia as the yield of three crops, the fats which are there in large quantities, to prevent the outgoing of Turkestan cotton, that is to say, to bring into play an economic action that can be speedily exerted and the immediate importance of which is almost greater than that of political action.

Furthermore, this action would be complemented by shipping to Russia American and Japanese manufactures that are so urgently needed by our Russian allies.

This is the first part of the program which we believe to be to the interest of the Allies to propose to Japan, which the Russians, if enlightened by means of public declarations and of an explanatory propaganda to be plied on Russian opinion by the Entente and local newspapers, cannot but recognize as beneficial and disinterested.

The resistance that may be offered by certain hostile Russian elements that are not qualified to represent the allied nation, or by indifferently trained and armed prisoners, is not likely to check for any length of time the methodical dash of the Japanese troops.

As for a more extensive and direct intervention of Japan against Germany in European Russia, of such a nature as to cause more concern to the Central Empires and compel them entirely to re-constitute their Eastern military front, the question presented is obviously more complex and remote. It does not as such appear to be impossible of execution, but while it is advisable to consider it without delay, it would be inexpedient to burden the present ne-gotiations with it.

In the opinion of my Government which hopes that it will be shared by that of the United States, in dealing with a country as sensitive as Japan, it is of great importance to avoid in the pending negotiations any step that might create an impression that there exists a feeling of mistrust, of apprehension that that country will not live up to its engagements or harbors intentions other than those it declares. I know from a remark recently made by Your Excellency that you fully appreciate the punctiliousness with which Japan strives to keep her promises and abide by her engagements.

I will add in conclusion that the Allies have conscientiously weighed the pros and cons of a Japanese intervention, in the light of all the available information gathered from the most reliable sources. They have come to the conclusion that the advantages outweigh the drawbacks by far and that it was important to act as quickly as possible in the indicated sense and to cast aside any hesitation or regret apt to delay or restrict such action and thereby hamper its effectiveness without in the least lessening the apprehended ob-jectionable contingencies.

Convinced that Japan's cooperation which circumstances make desirable to us may be secured under conditions of security and effectiveness in keeping with the general interests of all the Allies, Russia and the United States included, the Government of the Republic would be particularly glad to hear that the United States Government upon a reexamination of the question will concur in our views and join in our action.

Be pleased to accept, etc.   Jusserand.

T MS (SDR, RG 59, 861.00/1676, DNA).

From Frank Lyon Polk, with Enclosure

My dear Mr. President: Washington March 14, 1918.

I sent a telegram to Berne asking for the information you require in connection with the matter discussed with you today by the Dutch Minister.[1] It occurred to me that you might care to look over all the telegrams we have on file on the subject, now the matter is fresh in your mind, and I am therefore sending over the originals.[2]

Yours faithfully,   Frank L Polk

TLS (R. Lansing Papers, NjP).
[1] See A. Philips to WW, March 20, 1918.
[2] The only enclosure filed with this letter is the one printed below.

E N C L O S U R E

Paris Jan. 10, 1918

3016. Strictly confidential. I have received a letter under date of December 29th from Professor George D. Herron temporarily residing at Geneva, in which, after stating that he had recently had two or three experiences in German mentality and method, indicting that country's determination to secure a peace that would be to her advantage before America can reach Europe in adequate force, he writes as follows: "A former Dutch Minister of Justice, Doctor B. Dejong Van Beekendonk[1] now settled at Berne and equipped with everything necessary for his work is carrying on an urgent propaganda for a German peace. He asked a British Military Attache who is also my intimate friend for an introduction to me and made an appointment at my house. When he sent up his card I went down to find him accompanied by Mr. Haussman[n] the leader of the Progressive or Liberal Party of Germany and for thirty years a member of the Reichstag and one of the most influential German politicians; also by Mr. Meinn[2] one of the most powerful financiers of the Austrian Empire and very close to the Emperor Charles. I let them speak for an hour without interruption."

Professor Herron then goes on to say that his callers had announced at the outset that Germany and Austria were very anxious for peace. They had learned many lessons from the war and now wanted to resume normal relationships with the world, and enter a league of nations; that, on account of Germany's strong position at the present time, with every reason to expect still further military gains, too many concessions should not be expected; that America is naturally a pacifist nation, engaged in a war that is unnatural to her people and ought to be the first to persuade the Allies to come to terms with Germany. Mr. Herron then states that he replied that if Germany really wanted peace all she had to do was to openly transmit her request to the Allies through any neutral agency acceptable to them, and to state specifically and unreservedly her terms, that the Allies might consider them; that Germany did not need to be undermining the world with subterranean intrigues nor besieging unofficial individuals such as himself; that if she wants peace she can never obtain it by assuming the role of victor or seeking it by her present indirect methods; that she was laboring under a delusion as regards America, that though it was a pacifist nation, having once drawn the sword it would never sheath it until either the thing called Germanism or we ourselves were destroyed. Mr. Herron also states that after considerable further talk, the discussion finally resolved itself into this quest on the part of his visitors: (Blue) "If Germany now takes the initiative, if Germany makes a great beaugeste proposing what she would regard as definite and generous terms of peace what would be the attitude of President Wilson and the Government at Washington? Germany might be ready now to take this initiative, so they said, if she knew in advance that she would not be turned down by America." Mr. Herron states that he told the gentlemen that there was only one way to ascertain the attitude of America and that was to make their proposition; that he himself was only a private citizen, did not know the attitude of Washington and had no authority to express any opinion. Some other talk was indulged in by him along the same lines.

The callers then wanted to know if he would undertake to find out the probable American attitude to which he replies that such a proposition was absurd, saying in substance that if Kaiser William and Chancellor Hertling wished to know what President Wilson and Secretary Lansing would think, under certain circumstances, their business was to transmit their inquiry directly to our President and our Secretary of State.

Mr. Herron said that they left with him this last interrogation: (Blue) "Suppose we do come back to you with a mandate signed by either the Kaiser or Chancellor Hertling a confidential mandate, of course *predicting* a confidential answer, inquiring as to the probable attitude of Washington if Germany should take the initiative in proposing definite and generous terms of peace, would you take or transmit that imperially signed and confidential question."

Mr. Herron adds. "I submit the whole interview to you asking your immediate and urgent judgment about the matter. If the utterly incredible thing should happen as the Americans say 'call my bluff' should I transmit the question to you or should I flatly refuse to receive both the question and the men. I certainly should have refused to see them in the first place had I known they were coming as they did or what they had to propose.

I suppose they sought me out rather than some other American for the reason that I have written so much for the European Press in defense and interpretation of President Wilson and America's action that I am to their minds an available or obvious person to see unofficially; possibly they imagine that I possess some personal power or authority which I do not in the least possess." (Green) I have not answered Mr. Herron's letter and of course could only say that I have no authority whatever to give him advice concerning the matter which he writes me. I am transmitting in the next pouch a copy of the letter in full which covers seven pages.

Professor Herron had written me undoubtedly because having called to see me while he was in Paris during the stay of Mr. House. He told me many interesting things regarding the situation existing in Germany and Austria, as he learned it, at short range.

Concerning one of his interviews with Professor Foerster,[3] having to do with that gentleman's negotiations with Emperor Charles of Austria, I wired the President on December one.[4]

All the straws now blowing from the direction of Germany and Austria would seem to indicate that there is a greatly accentuated desire on the part of the German Government to bring about a speedy cessation of the war. But great as is this desire every sign points to the fact that it has been much more intensified among the masses of the German people. How to effectuate these desires, by what methods and through what channels voice can be given to them without facing danger of too much loss of prestige at home or rejection of their concessions by the Allies is the problem now acutely facing those governments.   Sharp.

T telegram (R. Lansing Papers, NjP).
    [1] That is, Jonkheer Benjamin de Jong van Beek en Donk, about whom see H. R. Wilson to RL, Jan. 31, 1918, n. 3, Vol. 46.
    [2] That is, Julius Meinl, about whom see WW to RL, Jan. 1, 1918, n. 1, Vol. 45.
    [3] That is, Friedrich Wilhelm Foerster, about whom see H. R. Wilson to RL, Jan. 31, 1918, n. 2, Vol. 46.
    [4] W. G. Sharp to RL, Dec. 1, 1917, *FR-WWS 1917*, 2, I, 332-34. The interview between Foerster and Charles is summarized in the Enclosure printed with the letter cited in n. 2 above. The only new point made in Sharp's dispatch was that Charles had been eager to find the best means of communicating with the Allies concerning a separate peace.

From Frank Lyon Polk, with Enclosure

My dear Mr. President: Washington March 14, 1918.

General Marsh has just read me a message from General Bliss, reporting that the Supreme War Council considered the recom-

mendation of the Interallied Naval Council on the subject of requisitioning the Dutch ships, and the Supreme War Council decided,
in spite of the objection presented by the Naval Council, to approve
the policy of requisitioning the Dutch ships. The Secretary had left
the Department, but I got in touch with him on the telephone and
he suggested that possibly you would prefer not to send the telegram to London based on Simms' report, and asked me to see if I
could stop the telegram prepared and communicate with you.

I was able to stop the telegram to London on Simms' report, and
will have it held pending your instructions. I enclose a copy of it
for your information.

It would seem that, in view of the action of the Supreme War
Council, Page would not understand the purpose of this message,
particularly as the objection in the Naval War Council seems to
have been put forward in the first instance by the French.

Yours faithfully,   Frank L Polk

TLS (WP, DLC).

E N C L O S U R E

AmEmbassy, London.   March 16, 1918.[1]

Despatch has been received from Simms stating that the Inter-
allied Naval Conference had strongly recommended that the Dutch
ships be not requisitioned for military reasons. Bliss reported same
and added that matter would be considered by the Supreme War
Council on the fifteenth. Department is amazed and embarrassed
at the attempt to reconsider the matter at this late date. Original
suggestion of requisitioning the ships came from the British Government and this Government then gave reluctant assent to the
plan. Last week British Government sent what appears to have
been an ultimatum to the Dutch Government that unless the agreement was signed on the eighteenth the ships would be requisitioned, and added for the information of the British Minister in
Holland[2] that this Government had acquiesced. This latter statement was made before this Department or the War Trade Board
had given its formal assent.

Later the ultimatum was given to the press by the British Government and telegraphed here. It was then necessary for this Government also to state its position, namely, that it was prepared to
requisition ships if the agreement was not signed. It should also
be added that the Interallied shipping authorities and military authorities had stated that it was absolutely necessary for military
reasons that ships be taken. It was natural for this Government to

assume the whole matter had been considered from every angle by the Allies, and for that reason it is all the more difficult to understand why the subject should be reopened again, particularly in view of the fact that publicity had been given to the ultimatum and subject had been thoroughly discussed in the neutral and German press.

The ill effects, if any, have already begun to work in Holland, and absolutely to reverse our position at this time could not but create a more unfavorable impression abroad and indicate a lack of firmness and indecision, which would make negotiations with other neutrals most difficult.

Department awaits with interest a full report from you on the situation. No communication has been received from the British Government, and until that Government states that it agrees with the views of the Interallied Naval Council, Department assumes that British Government has not altered its position. Nevertheless the belated recommendation of the Naval Council is most disquieting, as a change of policy, if contemplated, cannot but injure prestige of the Governments concerned.[3]

CC MS (WP, DLC).
   [1] This copy postdated.
   [2] Sir Walter Beaupré Townley.
   [3] Wilson, on March 20, requisitioned Dutch ships in American harbors. His proclamation and statement concerning the seizure of the ships are printed in the *Official Bulletin*, II (March 21, 1918), 1-2.

From Royal Meeker

My dear Mr. President: [Washington] March 14, 1918.

I understand that a bill is now in process of being drawn to provide for the functional and vocational rehabilitation of wounded soldiers and sailors discharged from the service and their reemployment in industry.[1] I have had a good deal to do with this subject ever since we entered the war. It is most important that the men injured in the service of the country should be rehabilitated as completely and quickly as possible and reemployed at real work where they can give real service for just compensation. I am fully aware of the great importance of taking care of war cripples, but, as important as this work is, it is insignificant compared to the vastly greater problem of providing for the rehabilitation and reemployment of industrial cripples. It is my desire to effect an organization to take care of our war cripples, which would be permanent in character and would be the beginning of a permanent organization to take care of the vast army of industrial cripples which we have always with us, despite all our safety work. The vocational retraining and reemployment of cripples, whether military or industrial, is an industrial problem. This is why I have opposed from the beginning putting this work under either of the military arms of the Federal Government. I have also strenuously opposed putting this important work into the hands of an "Interdepartmental Commission." My experience with such organizations is that they are bound by their very nature to be clumsy and ineffective. I have likewise opposed the appointment of a special commission to administer the rehabilitation and reemployment work for crippled soldiers and sailors because the functions of such a commission would, of course, be confined to war cripples and would inevitably cease to exist with the termination of the war.

It seemed to me all along that the Federal Board for Vocational Education was the proper existing agency to take care of the functional retraining of men disabled either in war or industry. Functional retraining for cripples is merely a part of the job this Board was created to perform. It belongs to this Board by right of its organic act. The Board is a permanent body and will continue to exist long after the war and its special problems have become things of the past. The Vocational Education Board is a thoroughly competent and representative body which sufficiently safeguards the interests of both employer and employee. After the men have been functionally retrained by the proper medical and surgical agencies and have been vocationally trained under the supervision and control of the Vocational Board, their reemployment in industry would naturally come under the jurisdiction of the Department of Labor. As I have said above, the work of functional retraining and reemploying crippled men is an industrial problem. It would be most unfortunate if we confine our efforts along these lines to men crippled in the military service of our country. The present war emergency makes it possible, it seems to me, for us to organize our rehabilitation work as it should be organized on a national basis and to include in this organization provision for men crippled in industry. The compensation commissions of the various States have done practically nothing toward giving industrial cripples any adequate medical and surgical treatment, much less have they accomplished in the way of functional restoration of disabled members. They have done less than nothing to provide suitable employment for men so disabled. If the work of reclaiming men disabled in industry is to be given the attention which its importance deserves, it can be done only through the Federal Government's bringing pressure to bear upon the State compensation commissions so as to encourage them—compel them voluntarily, so to speak—to provide for the restoration of industrial cripples to industry.

The opportunity is now ripe. I think an amendment to include industrial workers is now being drafted and will be submitted to you. I trust that you will find it possible in the midst of your multitudinous duties and responsibilities to give this matter attention and to insist that the bill, providing for the rehabilitation of injured soldiers and sailors, shall also provide the same service to disabled industrial workers.   Sincerely yours,   Royal Meeker

TCL (WP, DLC).
¹ Senator Hoke Smith, on April 8, introduced an administration-sponsored bill (S. 4284) for the vocational rehabilitation of disabled persons discharged from the army or navy. Following extensive hearings in joint meetings of the Senate Committee on Education and Labor and the House Committee on Education, Smith introduced a revised bill (S. 4557) on May 20. It was this latter bill which, after further debate and amendment, was finally enacted as Public Law 178 on June 27, 1918. *Cong. Record*, 65th Cong., 2d sess., pp. 4754-57, 6764-65, 8394.

From Franklin Knight Lane

My dear Mr. President: Washington March 14, 1918.

I think I should call to your attention the following letter which I have sent to Senator Hoke Smith, Chairman of the Senate Committee on Education and Labor, and to Representative Sears,¹ Chairman of the House Committee on Education.

"I believe that the time has come when we should give serious consideration to the education of those who cannot read or write in the United States. The war has brought facts to our attention that are almost unbelievable and that are in themselves accusatory. There are in the United States (or were when the census was taken in 1910) 5,516,163 persons over ten years of age who were unable to read or write in any language. There are now nearly 700,000 men of draft age in the United States who are, I presume, registered, who cannot read or write in English or in any other language. Over 4,600,000 of the illiterates in this country were twenty years of age or more. This figure equals the total population of the States of California, Oregon, Washington, Montana, Idaho, Wyoming, Colorado, Utah, Nevada, Arizona, New Mexico and Delaware. The percentage of illiterates varies in the several States, from 1.7% in Iowa to 29% in Louisiana. More than 10% of it was in thirteen States. Half of the illiterates were between twenty and forty-five years of age. It has been estimated by one of those concerned with this problem that if these five million and a half illiterate persons were stretched in a double line of march at intervals of three feet and were to march past the White House at the rate of twenty-five miles a day, it would require more than two months for them to pass. Over 58% are white persons, and of those 1,500,000 are native born whites.

"I beg you to consider the economic loss arising out of this condition. If the productive labor value of an illiterate is less by only fifty cents a day than that of an educated man or woman, the country is losing $825,000,000 a year through illiteracy. This estimate is no doubt under rather than over the real loss. The Federal Government and the States spend millions of dollars in trying to give information to the people in rural districts about farming and home-making. Yet 3,700,000, or 10% of our country folk, cannot read or write a word. They cannot read a bulletin on agriculture, a farm paper, a food pledge card, a Liberty Loan appeal, a newspaper, the Constitution of the United States, or their Bibles, nor can they keep personal or business accounts. An uninformed democracy is not a democracy. A people who cannot have means of access to the mediums of public opinion and to the messages of the President and the acts of Congress, can hardly be expected to understand the full meaning of this war, to which they all must contribute, in life or property or labor.

"It would seem to be almost axiomatic that an illiterate man cannot make a good soldier in modern warfare. Until last April the regular army would not enlist illiterates, yet in the first draft between 30,000 and 40,000 illiterates were brought into the army, and approximately as many near illiterates.

"They cannot sign their names.
They cannot read their orders posted
    daily on bulletin boards in camp.
They cannot read their manual of arms.
They cannot read their letters or write
    home.
They cannot understand the signals or
    follow the signal corps in time of
    battle.

"There are 700,000 men who cannot read or write who may be drafted within our army within the next year or two. Training camps for soldiers are not equipped for school work, and the burden of teaching men to read the simplest English should not be cast upon the officers or others in the camps. We should give some education to all our men before they enter the army.

"There is even a larger problem than this that challenges our attention, and that is the teaching of the English tongue to millions of our population. Dr. John H. Finley, President of the University of the State of New York, in a recent speech, presented this picture which he found in one of the cantonments:

"How practical is the need of a language in this country, common to all tongues, is illustrated by what I saw in one of the great cantonments a few nights ago. In the mess hall, where I had sat an hour before with a company of the men of the National Army, a few small groups were gathered along the tables learning English under the tuition of some of the comrades, one of whom had been a district supervisor in a neighboring State and another a theological student. In one of those groups one of the exercises for the evening consisted in practicing the challenge when on sentry duty. Each pupil of the group (there were four of Italian and two of Slavic birth) shouldered in turn the long-handled stove-shovel and aimed it at the teacher, who ran along the side of the room as if to evade the guard. The pupil called out in broken speech, 'Halt! Who goes there?' The answer came from the teacher, 'Friend.' And then, *in as yet unintelligible English* (the voices of innumerable ancestors struggling in their throats to pronounce it), the words, 'Advance and give the countersign.' So are those of confused tongues learning to speak the language of the land they have been summoned to defend. What a commentary upon our educational shortcomings that in the days of peace we had not taught these men, who have been here long enough to be citizens (and tens of thousands of their brothers with them), to know the language in which our history and laws are written and in which the commands of defense must now be given! May the end of this decade, though so near, find every citizen of our State prepared to challenge, in one tongue and heart, the purposes of all who come, with the cry, 'Who goes there?' "

"What I have said here leads to a respectful request that you give early consideration to House Bill 6490, which provides for a modest appropriation for the Bureau of Education to begin and conduct a vigorous and systematic campaign for the eradication of adult illiteracy. If the bill can be passed soon special attention can be given to teaching illiterate men of draft age, and especially those who are classified in Class A."

Cordially and faithfully yours,   Franklin K Lane

TLS (WP, DLC).
[1] William Joseph Sears, Democrat of Florida.

From Charles Spalding Thomas

My dear Mr. President: [Washington] March 14, 1918.

I am in receipt of your decision of the 13th instant regarding the schedule of prices for Colorado coal and sincerely regret your inability to modify or overrule the Commissioner's order. It is true that I went over the charts to which Dr. Garfield refers, and that the order was probably based upon their disclosures. But, Mr. President, charts, however carefully prepared, should not alone determine such a vastly important subject. The gentlemen who made them, unless I am misinformed, would not have reduced prevailing prices if the subject had been left to them. On the other hand, the carefully prepared statements of the operators submitted to the Commissioner seem to have been disregarded, if indeed, any but subordinates ever saw them. They know what they are making, and I am sure that they have not, and would not dare to present false figures or doctored statements.

I hope you will not impugn the good faith of those who have closed their mines consequent upon the order. They are the little fellows, generally speaking, who need the protection of the Government most of all. The big ones may be able to get through in some fashion. If I thought for a moment that a single one of the suspended mines was closed to exercise pressure, as you intimate, I would wash my hands of the entire matter.

I sincerely hope that your final decision may not become the occasion of greater suffering. As the matter stands, I see no escape from the resort by these people to the protection of the Courts. With that, however, I have no concern.

Very respectfully,
                    Your most obedient servant,   C. S. Thomas

TLS (WP, DLC).

From Joseph R. Wilson, Jr., with Enclosure

My dear Brother: Baltimore, Maryland March 14, 1918.

I am enclosing for your approval or revision as you may deem best a draft of a letter to General Cates. Please return it to me with such alterations as your desire to make, so that I may forward it at once. There is some doubt in my mind as to whether I should make the last statement contained in my letter, giving Cates authority to use my communication as he sees fit. I will leave this to your judgment.   Your affectionate brother,   Joseph R. Wilson

TLS (WP, DLC).

ENCLOSURE

My dear friend: Baltimore, Maryland

The report now being circulated in Tennessee by the friends of
Senator Shields to the effect that he has the promise of a letter
from the President commending him for re-election is certainly very
annoying, and, I am positive, is entirely without foundation. You
may be sure, as I wired you, that Senator Shields will receive no
such letter, it being the President's policy not to intervene as between two Democrats. I am familiar with the President's attitude
in all such matters, and I know he will not take sides in the pending
Tennessee senatorial campaign, or in any other contest between
Democrats.

I am not writing as the official spokesman of the President, of
course, but for the purpose of personally acquainting you with the
situation as I know it to exist. You are at liberty to use this letter
as you see fit.

With personal regards,   Sincerely yours,

T MS (WP, DLC).

From Joseph Patrick Tumulty

Dear Governor: The White House 14 March 1918.

In the matter of suffrage: We will need two more votes. Senator
Hollis was in to see me this morning and said he had made a poll;
the Republicans have 34, and the Democrats 28; 64 votes are necessary.

I got your note[1] last night about your embarrassment with reference to Senators Trammell and Fletcher and told Senator Hollis
just how you felt. He made this suggestion which really emanates
from Senator Ransdell,—that you send for Senators Fletcher and
Ransdell, both of whom are members of the Committee on Commerce, which Committee has recently been investigating the Shipping Board and Hog Island. Senator Hollis understands that you
have not talked over shipping matters with Fletcher and Ransdell
for some time and that they will be able to give you some valuable
information that may speed up the shipping programme. They are
both great friends of the Administration and are anxious to serve.
You might very properly send for them at once to discuss the speed-
ing up of the shipping programme. If you do this, Senator Ransdell
will call your attention to the situation in connection with suffrage
and will give you a most excellent chance to discuss it with Senator
Fletcher. Senator Trammell has stated that if Senator Fletcher votes

for suffrage, he will also. This will enable us to put the matter over this week.[2]   Sincerely yours,   Tumulty

TLS (WP, DLC).
  [1] He meant WW to JPT, March 12, 1918, Vol. 46.
  [2] There is nothing in the Executive Appointment Diary, the Head Usher's Diary, or in any other documents in WP, DLC, to indicate that Wilson saw, or was in communication with, either Trammell or Fletcher at this time. However, Carter Field, Washington correspondent of the *New York Tribune*, in a signed article in that paper on March 14, 1918, stated that Wilson had "swung over" two Senate votes which, with those already in favor, would provide the two-thirds majority needed for passage of the suffrage amendment. Field said that he could not name the two senators because of possible embarrassment to them, but he did say that both were from the same southern state. If this statement referred to Fletcher and Trammell of Florida, either it was incorrect at the time or the two men soon changed their minds again. Not only did both Florida senators vote "no" on a motion to bring up the amendment for consideration on May 6, 1918, but they also voted against the amendment itself on October 1. *Cong. Record*, 65th Cong., 2d sess., pp. 6097, 10987.

From Harry Augustus Garfield

Dear Mr. President: Washington D. C. March 14, 1918

I need not assure you with how grateful an appreciation I read your note of sympathy. That you knew Mother—perceived the fine quality of her mind & heart, & that she accepted your leadership, seeing with clear & unprejudiced eye the nature of the great issue to be faced, adds something to your message which is peculiarly comforting just now. Thank you from the bottom of my heart for your expression of friendship & believe me as always, With warmest regard,   Faithfully yours,   H. A. Garfield.

ALS (WP, DLC).

Sir William Wiseman to Sir Eric Drummond

[New York] March 14th. 1918.

SECRET No. 77. The President, who, while he wishes to support Allied plans to meet German advance into Russia, wants to avoid danger he sees of driving Russia into Germany's power by Japanese intervention, is now endeavouring to find a way both to reconcile American people to need for intervention and to allay Russian fears of it. He is studying feasibility of a joint Japanese American enterprise whereby the United States would collaborate with Russians in reorganization of Russian elements with Japanese military assistance. A Japanese military expedition would be accompanied by American Civil Missions, headed by known sympathizers with Russian revolution, to take up relief, Red Cross, propaganda and recruiting work, and prepared to assist Russians in reorganization.

The President's message to Russian people was sent at my suggestion as a preliminary step in elaboration of above scheme. Here it has already produced good effect and will undoubtedly serve to reduce American opposition if Japanese intervention, with or without American civil participation, is agreed to by U.S.G. It depends on reception of message in Russia whether he will pursue the whole idea further. It is most unlikely that he will take it up officially unless the message produces a sympathetic reply from some body of opinion in Russia.

T telegram (W. Wiseman Papers, CtY).

To Frank Lyon Polk, with Enclosure

Dear Polk,   [The White House, c. March 15, 1918]

I have no objection to Mr. Pachitch's making the statement he suggests   W.W.

ALI (SDR, RG 59, 763.72119/1546, DNA).

E N C L O S U R E

Corfu Mar. 8, 1918.

Premier Pachitch requests me to telegraph that the Parliamentary opposition seriously complains that he failed to inform the Allies regarding Servia's national aspirations and that they declare that consequently the President of the United States and Lloyd George's speeches did not mention realization Servia's vital national aspirations but only her restoration and access to the sea. Premier inquires whether the Government of the United States would have any objection to his stating in Parliament if necessay that the President of the United States speeches did not describe detailed programme of war aims but only briefly summarized them and that if Servia's Allies won the war they would meet Serbo Croat national aspirations as far as possible. Although if the Government of the United States found such a statement opportune he would be greatly obliged and thought that it would quiet the opposition and strengthen them to resist the enemy to the end. He did not wish to ask for anything which the Government of the United States would not care to grant. He had made similar request to the British Minister.[1] Premier referred to reports from the Hague of peace offers made by Servia to the Central Powers indignantly denying them. Crown Prince[2] also emphatically denied them to the British Minister. Deadlock regarding formation of a cabinet mentioned in my February 27, 10 p.m. continues, all the opposition groups showing greatest irritation against Pachitch.   Dodge.[3]

T telegram (SDR, RG 59, 763.72119/1546, DNA).
  [1] Sir Charles Louis Des Graz.
  [2] Alexander, Prince Regent of Serbia.
  [3] Henry Percival Dodge, special agent of the Department of State in Serbia.

To Joseph R. Wilson, Jr.

Dear Joe: The White House 15 March, 1918

I am taking the liberty of sending you a revised copy of the letter you thought of sending to Mr. Cates.[1]

The fact of the matter is we are threading [treading] on very dangerous and delicate ground in this matter and cannot be too careful. I hope you will approve of the revision.

In great haste   Affectionately yours,   Woodrow Wilson

TLS (received from Alice Wilson McElroy).
  [1] It is missing.

To Charles Spalding Thomas

My dear Senator: [The White House] 15 March, 1918

I have your letter of March fourteenth. I see that you are distressed about the Colorado coal decision, and that gives me a great deal of concern, I assure you. You may be certain that if I had any fear that any of the mines were being closed down for the impression it would make, it was a very indefinite one and will certainly not be expressed publicly. I hope with you that it is entirely unfounded.

I beg you to believe that you are mistaken in supposing that I was going entirely by charts or anything so "scientific" as that. I had been over the figures from many sources upon which the charts were founded, and you may be sure if I could have found in those figures any sufficient justification for a change of decision, I would have been glad to find it.

Cordially and sincerely yours,   Woodrow Wilson

TLS (Letterpress Books, WP, DLC).

To Louis Brownlow

My dear Brownlow: [The White House] 15 March, 1918

Thank you for your letter of yesterday about the housing problem.[1] I am afraid from what I have learned that there is not a very good prospect of getting the words back into the House bill which you desire to see restored and which I think it would be very desirable to restore,[2] but I will, of course, avail myself of any opportunity I have to help in the matter.

May I not suggest this: Chairman Swagar Sherley of the House Committee on Appropriations is sincerely and most intelligently interested in this whole subject and if you have not had a conference with him, I wish very much that you would have one. I know he has plans in mind, particularly for the housing of the women employees of the Government, which seemed to me when he mentioned them to me to be comprehensive and excellent, and we ought all, of course, to work to the same end and have as small a variety of plans as possible.

Cordially and sincerely yours,   Woodrow Wilson

TLS (Letterpress Books, WP, DLC).
[1] L. Brownlow to WW, March 14, 1918, TLS (WP, DLC). Brownlow once again called Wilson's attention to the critical shortage of housing for government workers in the District of Columbia. Some 15,000 new civilian employees, as well as many industrial workers and army and navy officers, were expected to come to Washington by July 1. The only way to bring quick relief to the housing crisis was to include civilian employees in the housing bill then before Congress (see n. 2 below).
[2] A bill (H.R. 9642) to provide housing for war needs, introduced in the House on February 7, had included a phrase which made such housing available "for employes of the government." This phrase had been struck out by the House Committee on Public Buildings and Grounds and thus left the projected housing in the District of Columbia available only to industrial workers. Brownlow desired to have the phrase restored in H.R. 10265, the new bill introduced on February 26 which covered much the same ground as the earlier bill.

To Benedict Crowell

My dear Mr. Secretary: [The White House] 15 March, 1918

Your letter of March twelfth about Monticello, Mr. Jefferson's one-time home,[1] lays a great temptation before me. For years I have been exceedingly anxious to see that beautiful property bought by the Government of the United States, but I am afraid that I could not rightly spend any part of the fund at my disposal for that purpose. I know the location of Monticello so well that the situation and character of the property does not seem to me to make it at all suitable for use as a hospital, and your letter itself states that the Surgeon General thinks it hardly necessary to have that site for that purpose at present.

I take great credit to myself in resisting the temptation, but I feel that I must.

Cordially and sincerely yours,   Woodrow Wilson

TLS (Letterpress Books, WP, DLC).
¹ B. Crowell to WW, March 12, 1918, TLS (WP, DLC).

To Morris Sheppard

Personal.

My dear Senator: [The White House] 15 March, 1918

I need not say that I share with you the feeling that the most systematic and effective organization should be given to our whole effort in the department of aeronautics,¹ but I have in recent months seen so clearly the danger, the fatal error indeed, of setting up any department which would have to do with the vital interests of other departments, that my judgment is that it would be very unwise indeed to create a Department of Aeronautics. It would, you observe, straddle the Army and Navy Departments, taking things which directly affect them out of their hands and putting them under another direction entirely. I am convinced that that would be a practical blunder.

Our line of development should undoubtedly, I think, run along the line of perfecting the machinery we have already in part created, and I want you to know that I am now engaged through a disinterested commission of three in giving the whole programme a thorough going over.² I have not thought it wise to speak of this, because I do not want it to be generally talked about. I find the most satisfactory results are obtained by going into the newspapers afterwards instead of contemporaneously.

I value your confidence most highly and thank you very warmly indeed for consulting me about this all-important matter.

Cordially and sincerely yours,   Woodrow Wilson

TLS (Letterpress Books, WP, DLC).
¹ Wilson was replying to M. Sheppard to WW, March 14, 1918, TLS (WP, DLC).
² See WW to G. Borglum, March 15, 1918, n. 2.

To David Lawrence

My dear Lawrence: [The White House] 15 March, 1918

I am hopelessly useless for publicity purposes. I have long been convinced of that, but your letter of the thirteenth¹ makes me more certain of it.

It is true that I am constantly playing a part in the formation of all the important decisions which are formed in every branch of the Government's war activities, and its peace activities, too, for that matter, but after the work is done I necessarily forget its details. If you were to sit down with me and pump me, I could not recall the particulars or the conferences or the methods, and I am afraid that the plan is on that account "no go."[2]

I do not think that the articles in Colliers'[3] and the others to which you refer do any particular harm. I think the people of the country are satisfied that I am keeping hold of as much of the job as is humanly possible.

In haste   Faithfully yours,   Woodrow Wilson

TLS (Letterpress Books, WP, DLC).
   [1] It is missing.
   [2] Despite Wilson's misgivings, Lawrence did produce an article on Wilson's working methods: "Okeh W.W.," *Saturday Evening Post*, CXC (May 4, 1918), 5, 93-94, 97.
   [3] In addition to the article discussed in A. J. McKelway to WW, March 13, 1918, n. 2, Wilson probably referred to such articles as Carl Snyder, "The 'Why' of the Tie-Up," *Collier's: The National Weekly*, LX (Feb. 23, 1918), 7, which discussed the interrelated crises in the nation's supplies of coal and available railroad cars; Mark Sullivan, "Wake Up!," *ibid.* (March 2, 1918), pp. 5-7, which dealt with the critical shortage of ships; and Mark Sullivan, "Was Baker Right?," *ibid.*, LXI (March 23, 1918), 5-7, which was about the alleged deficiencies of the Secretary of War. The latter article was available by March 15.

To Thomas Riley Marshall

My dear Mr. Vice President: [The White House] 15 March, 1918

I am ashamed of myself that I overlooked the fact that yesterday was your birthday. May I not congratulate you very sincerely? I hope that you feel the real affection with which you are regarded by all of us who really know you, and I want you to know that my own feeling for you constantly grows warmer and more intimate.

I have no doubt that you have been following, as I have, with a good deal of anxiety the critical Senatorial contest in Wisconsin. The attention of the country will naturally be centered upon it because of the universal feeling against Senator La Follette and the question which will be in every patriotic man's mind whether Wisconsin is really loyal to the country in this time of crisis or not.

Personally, I do not doubt that the great body of the citizens of Wisconsin are thoroughly loyal, but there is some danger of the issues being obscured. The election of Mr. Lenroot[1] would, I am afraid, by no means demonstrate that loyalty, because his own record has been one of questionable support of the dignity and rights of the country on some test occasions. It is, therefore, of the utmost importance, I think, that we should secure the election of

Davies, and I am wondering if you would not add to your many generous acts in such matters by going out there to make some speeches for him. It would greatly hearten everybody and I am sure would be most effective.

With warm regards,

Cordially and sincerely yours,   Woodrow Wilson

TLS (Letterpress Books, WP, DLC).
[1] Wilson obviously thought that Lenroot would win the Republican nomination in the special primary election to be held on March 19, as indeed he did, to select candidates to run for the vacancy created by the death of Paul O. Husting.

To Houghton, Mifflin & Company

My dear Sirs: [The White House] 15 March, 1918

I thank you sincerely for your letter of March eleventh[1] with its enclosure, a copy of your letter to Messrs. Harper & Brothers about the rights to CONGRESSIONAL GOVERNMENT and MERE LITERATURE.

I must say that I think the position you have taken is entirely fair. As I wrote the other day to Messrs. Harper & Brothers,[2] Houghton Mifflin & Company have always been so considerate of my interests and rights that I have a very warm place in my heart for them, particularly as they accepted and brought out my first book when I was an unknown youngster, and I certainly would not urge anything that was contrary to the interests of the house.

At the same time, I would very much like to have all that I have published brought together in something like a uniform edition, and I had thought that the plan of Messrs. Harper & Brothers was the most promising that had been presented.

Cordially and sincerely yours,   Woodrow Wilson

TLS (Letterpress Books, WP, DLC).
[1] F. Greenslet to WW, March 11, 1918, Vol. 46.
[2] See WW to EMH, Feb. 26, 1918, *ibid.*

To Gutzon Borglum

My dear Mr. Borglum: The White House 15 March, 1918

I have your letter of March eleventh[1] and thank you for it. I am writing in great haste to say that the whole aircraft matter is undergoing a very thorough review.[2]

In haste   Sincerely yours,   Woodrow Wilson

TLS (G. Borglum Papers, DLC).
[1] It is missing. A White House memorandum indicates that Borglum reiterated his belief that the Aircraft Production Board had been "frankly and flatly a promoter's enterprise." He recommended that, of the members of the original board, only Howard

E. Coffin be retained and that a "Department of Approved Design" be created at once.
    ² The War Department had announced on March 12 the appointment of a three-man committee to "make a broad survey of the Government's aeronautical program with particular relation to the industrial phases of the work." The members of the committee were Hudson Snowden Marshall, United States Attorney for the Southern District of New York, 1913-1917; Edward Hubbard Wells, president of Babcock & Wilcox Co., manufacturers of boilers; and Gavin McNab. *Official Bulletin*, II (March 14, 1918), 4; *New York Times*, March 13, 1918. The committee's preliminary report, which was addressed directly to Wilson, is printed as an Enclosure with B. Crowell to WW, April 12, 1918.

From Joseph Patrick Tumulty

                                                                      The White House.
Memorandum for the President: March 15, 1918
    Mrs. Potter of the Texas Equal Suffrage Association telephoned that she is just in receipt of a telegram from Texas that the suffrage amendment has passed the House by a large majority and is certain of passage in the Senate. She thought the President would be glad to know of the result of the letter he was good enough to write her.¹

TL (WP, DLC).
    ¹ WW to Elizabeth H. Potter, March 8, 1918, Vol. 46. "Please convey to Mrs. Potter my thanks for her message and my warm congratulations on the result." WW to [JPT], c. March 16, 1918, TL (WP, DLC).

From Bainbridge Colby

My dear Mr. President: Washington March 15, 1918.
    I was fortunate enough to be able to arrange an interview today with the gentleman whom I regard as the most influential in the matter about which you spoke to me yesterday.¹ I am now confident that the approaching meeting² will be conducted along lines that are entirely in accord with your wishes.
    If you desire to see me and to have a more detailed account of our very interesting interview, I am, of course, entirely at your call.
    The matter of nitrate I have in hand and hope to be able to report to you shortly.   Very sincerely yours,   Bainbridge Colby

TLS (WP, DLC).
    ¹ About this interview, see the memorandum by William Howard Taft printed at March 29, 1918.
    ² A meeting of the League to Enforce Peace, to be held in Philadelphia (not New York, as Wilson later writes) on May 16, 1918.

To Bernard Mannes Baruch

My dear Baruch: The White House 16 March, 1918

I wonder if it would be possible for you to make it convenient to meet me at the White House next Wednesday at 2:30 to discuss a number of matters which I would like to discuss with you and the following gentlemen, whom I am also inviting:

Mr. McAdoo, Mr. Hurley, Mr. McCormick, Mr. Hoover, and Doctor Garfield.[1]   Faithfully yours,   Woodrow Wilson

TLS (B. M. Baruch Papers, NjP).
[1] Wilson wrote the same letter, *mutatis mutandis*, to H. C. Hoover, March 16, 1918, TLS (H. Hoover Papers, HPL); E. N. Hurley, March 16, 1918, TLS (E. N. Hurley Papers, InNd); H. A. Garfield, March 16, 1918, TLS (H. A. Garfield Papers, DLC); V. C. McCormick, March 16, 1918, TLS (Letterpress Books, WP, DLC); and W. G. McAdoo, March 16, 1918, TLS (Letterpress Books, WP, DLC). The meeting on March 20 was the first of the weekly meetings of the "War Cabinet," about which see n. 2 to the extract from the House Diary printed at Feb. 25, 1918, Vol. 46.

To Samuel Reading Bertron

My dear Mr. Bertron: [The White House] 16 March, 1918

I have your letter of March fifteenth[1] and appreciate your interest in the Russian situation and your desire to counsel with me about it. I would be very glad to see you if you could come in next Wednesday afternoon at 5:00.   Sincerely yours,   Woodrow Wilson

TLS (Letterpress Books, WP, DLC).
[1] It is missing.

To Bainbridge Colby

My dear Colby: The White House 16 March, 1918

Your letter of yesterday about your conference concerning the meeting in New York gratifies me very much. You have done me a service which I warmly appreciate. I hope some time soon we may have a talk about the conference with our friend and what you gathered from it.

In haste
                    Cordially and faithfully yours,   Woodrow Wilson

TLS (B. Colby Papers, DLC).

To Robert Lansing, with Enclosure

My dear Mr. Secretary,   The White House. 16 March, 1918.

It is a most distressing decision to be forced to, but I fear I must concur in your judgment that these amounts must be limited, and I have no doubt that you are in a much better position than I to say to what figures they should be restricted. I think, however, that it would not be wise or just to make the restriction retroactive.

Faithfully Yours,   W.W.

WWTLI (SDR, RG 59, 860c.48/12, DNA).

E N C L O S U R E

From Robert Lansing

My dear Mr. President: Washington March 15, 1918.

In November you authorized the continuance of monetary relief to the destitute in occupied Poland and also to the subject races in Turkey, but the question of the amount of the relief funds to be transmitted has never definitely been fixed, either by the War Trade Board or by the Department of State.

I enclose a brief report for the period from November, 1917 to March, 1918, inclusive,[1] which illustrates the amounts which the War Trade Broad has licensed to forward to both Poland and Turkey. The February and March remittances have, however, not all been transmitted as yet. It is deemed desirable to set a limit, if possible, on the monthly remittances. At the present rate at which we are asked to transmit money to Poland, the annual total would not be less than eight and a half million dollars, taking $700,000 as the monthly average. For Turkey, not under British occupation the annual remittances would total between four and five millions.

It seems to me that these amounts are altogether too high and that we should limit the funds for Poland not to exceed $300,000 per month—$200,000 to be for General Relief and $100,000 for individual remittances. An appropriate figure for Armenian and Syrian relief might be placed at $150,000 per month, most of which is for general relief.

The Polish Relief Committee, the Joint Distribution Committee, and the other organizations will naturally criticize the limiting of these relief funds as these charitable organizations are deeply interested in getting as much relief as possible to the destitute in those countries, and they have very large resources in the United States upon which to draw for this purpose. I believe, however, it is the duty of the Government, in view of recent military developments in Russia and Turkey, to restrict the amounts sent to those countries for relief purposes.

I should be grateful for an expression of your views on this question, and, if you approve of the limiting of the remittances, whether you think it advisable to make the limit retroactive so as to include certain of the sums totalling about one and one half million dollars, which have not yet actually gone forward but for which licenses have been granted by the War Trade Board.

In this connection it should be pointed out that, to supplement this monetary relief, it is proposed to permit second hand clothing to be purchased in neutral European countries and shipped to Poland for the relief of the destitute.

I am, my dear Mr. President,

Very sincerely yours,   Robert Lansing

TLS (SDR, RG 59, 860c.48/12, DNA).
[1] Not printed.

From William Kent

Dear Mr. President: Washington March 16, 1918.

In response to your request, and the reference to me for comment of the letters of Secretary Houston and Mr. Hoover,[1] first let me refer to the general live stock situation as I see it, and as it comes to me from honorable, loyal and unselfish men engaged in the business of live stock production.

There is clear recognition on their part of their obligation to sustain the Government in so far as is possible to sustain it, by providing needed meat supplies. That they may work to this end, there must be confidence not only in the existence of a coherent Government policy but a belief that the policy is sensible and considers doing justice to production. The best intentions cannot pay continuing losses.

As a matter of fact, there is among live stock people a lack of confidence in the Government's policy, or absence of policy, which, coupled with serious losses due to stimulated output, and curtailed demand, will without question result in a disastrous diminution of meat supplies, unless there shall be a change.

Only by a frank, intelligent statement of needs, with the assurance of Government recognition of the service rendered, can this confidence be restored.

[1] WW to W. Kent, March 5, 1918, Vol. 46. See also WW to H. C. Hoover, Feb. 19, 1918 (second letter of that date); H. C. Hoover to WW, Feb. 21, 1918; and DFH to WW, March 1, 1918, all printed in *ibid.*

I had contemplated sending you a statement in great detail answering the various propositions urged in the letters. I find that such a report would require a compilation of figures and statistics which would require a large amount of clerical labor, and which would probably be more voluminous than you would care to consider. I therefore submit in broader outline the facts of the situation as I see them.

Neither of these two gentlemen answer at all the last two paragraphs of the memorial handed you, which, in the interest of future production, carry the crux of the situation:

"We believe it is essential to our national success that a national live stock policy be promptly adopted, just to both the producer and consumer, and based on such sound economic principles as will stimulate production and at the same time put us in a position to meet the critical readjustment period which is bound to follow the conclusion at this world conflict.

"In developing and putting into execution such a national live stock policy, we believe that production and distribution should be considered as one problem, involving cooperation between the Department of Agriculture and the Food Administration, and that a joint committee of these two Departments should promptly formulate and present to the country their program. While the full responsibility must rest with the Government, we can assure the disinterested support and assistance of the Nation's live stock producers."

The task, as I understand it, was divided between the Secretary of Agriculture, who was to stimulate production of meat by every means in his power, while the distribution of that meat was to be made through the Food Asminstration [Administration]. Although positive assurances of recognition of cost have not been made in definite terms, there have been implied and loosely stated assurances that meat producers would find the business remunerative. Figures showing a world shortage were quoted, and production was urged on the largest possible scale.

The price of feedstuffs, corn, cottonseed meal, and hay, have participated in the rise, due to demand in an open and uncontrolled market. Meat consumption, on the other hand, has been cut down by every possible appeal to the patriotism of the people. And now, the patriotic response to the request for "meatless" days, and diminished use of meat on other days, to the end of furnishing supposedly needed supplies to our Allies and our own troops, has resulted in over-supply and congestion which should have been for[e]seen, and which is now admitted by the Food Administration, and which seemingly will lead to further lowering of prices and consequently added losses to the producers of meat. This congestion necessitates the borrowing of vast sums by the packers, and tremendous unnecessary expense which must be paid by someone. The packers are in position to shift this burden.

It is now admitted that mutton is not used in recognizable quantities for export, and yet mutton has been part of our "meatlessness." Under present conditions, it is admitted that only about five percent of our beef output can go abroad for our own and Allied uses combined. This percentage may be increased somewhat by an increase in shipping space.

The Food Administration has urged, through speakers that have had large audiences and enthusiastic reception, that the "blood of starving children in the Allied countries, of our own and Allied armies, and of people far back of the lines would be on our heads" if we consumed any portion of the pork produced in this country. As a matter of fact, the export possibilities of pork at the present time are not more than 25 percent of our output.

It is of interest here to remark, in view of statements of Mr. Hoover that beef, perishable in its nature, cannot be put into a reserve, that there is now on hand something like 275,000,000 pounds of frozen beef, which is 128 percent of the fresh meat exported for the entire calendar year of 1917, besides large quantities of fresh pork and lamb. There are admittedly large supplies of fat cattle and lambs now being carried in feed lots at continuing and serious losses to those who must provide hay and grain.

As concerns the losses accruing, it is but fair to state that meat animals and "feeder" steers were sold by the range cattlemen during the summer and fall of 1917 at fairly remunerative prices. Although the expenses of ranch operation have greatly increased, there has been no increase in grazing costs at all comparable with costs of hay and grain.

Moreover, "feeder" steers were sold in open competitive market, where their price was bid up by the farmers and feeders who were urged to turn them into meat.

Both Secretary Houston and Mr. Hoover seemingly fail to comprehend the great proportionate part played in meat production by "feeders." Cattle fit for beef do not reach the market from the range or other grazing places during more than five months of the year, and then not in quantities that aggregate any large proportion of the supply. During seven months of the year, beef animals come mostly from the feed lots and farms where certain amounts of hay and grain or cottonseed and hay must be used to keep them in condition and to improve their quality.

It is idle to attempt to segregate the "feeding farmers" from the "feeders." But few farmers who handle beef animals provide all the corn and hay necessary from their own tillage, and few of them have adequate pasturage to raise their own cattle. Even such small units as two carloads usually require the purchase of part of the animals and part of the feedstuffs.

If there is any reason why we can expect farmers to sell their grain more cheaply through the laborious and risky process of feeding it to live stock rather than in cashing it as grain, that reason is difficult to fathom, and yet Secretary Houston expresses the opinion that the farmer who feeds has not shared in the admitted losses of the "feeders." It may take the farmer longer to learn his loss, because he may not keep books on his diversified performances.

It is beyond question that at the present time the use of grain for feeding should be cut to the practical minimum, and that fancy cattle are a luxury which the nation cannot afford. Some grain, however, is needed for the larger proportion of stock carried through the non-grazing period. That grain is always fed at a loss in so far as calculations are based on resultant increases in weight. The return must always be found in the improved quality of the original weight of the animal fed. When Mr. Hoover attributes this situation to war conditions, he shows a lack of understanding of the business of meat production.

Roughly speaking, the value of a bushel of corn as used in the corn belt will produce about four pounds of meat. It requires little calculation to demonstrate the accruing loss, if there be no recognition of quality in terms of price. Nor can there be any question as to the relative food value of well-conditioned and ill-conditioned beef.

This leads us to a consideration of the statistics of meat animals quoted by both Mr. Hoover and Secretary Houston, which do not carry the same content as those put forth when the producers were asked last summer to do their utmost to increase supplies.

If it be true that there is an actual increase in the number of meat animals, that statement does not at all mean an increase in the amount of meat. Discouragement of feeding will tend to cause light weight and a loss of quality in the animals marketed, and an undoubted decrease in the pounds of meat produced. The only exception to this would be beef produced on the range, where much increase is improbable from the fact that the range is fully occupied and forage on much of it is being depleted. There must necessarily be a larger marketing of under-weight, inferior stock, and a continual decrease in the number of head, if present conditions continue.

Mr. Hoover sets forth that there has been a slight increase in the value of the bulk of sales, as opposed to the great increase in the price of the better quality of cattle. This does not mean that during the winter months these animals were profitably sold, but does mean that they were sold unripe at relatively smaller losses.

It would be interesting to know how much benefit the laboring people or anyone else is getting from the retail price of the meats which are purchased from live stock producers at lower prices, on account of inferior quality. Wholesale quotations show a diminishing margin between the lowest and highest grades of carcases. The packers doubtless absorb a part of this, the retailers doubtless take their toll, the consumer may benefit a little, but the burden that falls on the producer of good meat is intolerable.

The average grade of animals customarily known as "canners," consisting of thin and ill-conditioned cattle, has been improved, for the reason that there was not enough of such "poor stuff" to meet the demand, and I understand that this improvement in average quality is recognized by higher prices.

Mr. Hoover admits packer control to a limited extent. This extent is really limited only by the placing of prices of meat so high that the consumer curtails his purchases, or the prices of live stock so low that the producer cannot afford to make meat. The admission of such control from day to day, or as concerns discrimination between the sellers of live stock, is sufficient to work ruin to the individual or to the industry. The control is broader than this, for, although the packers may not handle to exceed fifty percent of the cattle slaughtering of the country, they are so placed strategically as to have absolute control of market prices. Their control is exerted on central and focal points, and what has always been known but not proven, that they can destroy all troublesome competitors, has recently been demonstrated from their own files. Mr. Durand, of the Food Administration,[2] last January informed the packers that they must keep cattle prices down, in order to protect the price on a large British contract for future delivery. Whether or not this was justifiable, two things were demonstrated: first, that the Food Administration recognized the control of the packers over purchase prices of live stock; and second, that the packers actually did as suggested and held prices down to a point of serious loss to live stock producers. This while Mr. Hoover in his letter states that he has been attempting to keep packing plants running by securing foreign orders. His request of the Federal Trade Commission for assistance in the examination of the packers' books is a request for

[2] Edward Dana Durand.

tremendous service. I am informed that, first and last, there are
1800 people employed in the bookkeeping department of Swift and
Company. There can hardly be such a thing as an overhauling of
books kept as the packers know how to keep them. This was shown
by the exonerating report of the Garfield Commission.[3] This is merely
mentioned as an aside, but leads to the suggestion that, if Mr.
Hoover desires to know what the packers are doing, his Department
should have the authority, if it does not possess it at the present
time, to inaugurate a system whereby the facts of the situation are
made clear.

Mr. Hoover states that "cattle," obviously meaning beef, is a most
perishable commodity, and that it must be marketed within ten to
twelve days, and that there is no means of preserving it in adequate
quantities to create a reserve. This statement ignores the frozen
meat trade, which certainly offers possibilities of reserve. But if, in
a measure, his statement is correct, then the only way to keep up
a continuing steady supply of meat throughout the major portion
of the year is by feeding grain, and there must be recognition of
the fact that the feeder, whether a farmer or not, is a manufacturer
and a necessary factor.

It would be but fair to ask of Secretary Houston what he would
have the feeder do. Suppose that the feeder has equipment in pas-
ture land, in feed lots, in elevators, in capital, for the carrying of
three thousand cattle and three thousand hogs per year, to the end
of converting meat animals into meat. What would Secretary Houston have him do? Should he be permitted to take his chance in a
packer-ridden market, as in the past, only asking that Governmental
agencies should not depress his product? Should he be called upon
to operate with the chances of such artificial depression and consequent inevitable loss? Should he, as an unnecessary factor, quit
his business altogether? Or should he be induced to furnish meat
with an assurance of a reasonable margin of profit, in consideration
of average current prices of feeder cattle and feedstuffs? This question, asked by the large feeder, is the question asked by the feeder
farmer. Where [There] are many thousand people who are looking for an answer which does not appear to be coming from an
unorganized national live stock policy.

Mr. Hoover states that there is no such thing as standardizing
cattle qualities. As a matter of fact, there are few cattle sold in the
central markets where the minds of experienced, competent, buy-

[3] That is, the report on the so-called "beef trust" issued by the United States Bureau
of Corporations in March 1905, about which see n. 1 to the news report printed at Feb.
27, 1905, Vol. 16.

ers, sellers, and commission men do not practically meet on this question of quality.

Granted that with the present prices and demand for corn, a minimum of grain should be used, and that the highly finished cattle of former times are at present an economic waste, it would not be difficult to identify by a system of arbitration such grades as would fairly represent food values and average cost of production.

Yours truly,   William Kent

TLS (WP, DLC).

Herbert Bayard Swope to Joseph Patrick Tumulty

[Washington] Sunday night

My dear Tumulty: [March 17, 1918].

From what I gathered from your talk with the President I was under the impression that I was to have the reports that Borglum made. They are essential to a comprehensive story. It is not possible to make answer to charges that do not appear. In going through the letter files, I got copies of the President's notes referring to the reports but the reports themselves are not yet turned over. The papers that Coffin's man gave me Saturday night, after I explained the situation to you, were not, as I had thought, the reports but letters from B. to the President. Today I find the reports are in the hands of Mr. Crowell. I had a talk with him and he said he would be glad to give them to me if he heard from you to that effect. Will you tell him to let me have them? If I do not get the originals I shall be compelled to use B's own abstracts, and they are far more severe than the actual reports. No names are mentioned in the reports while in the abstracts that Borglum prepared he takes shots at Baruch and Meyer and others.

I am trying to help as best I can but I'm finding it a hard job. And then, to cap the climax, after holding off New York on publishing the story at their end, I find that somebody has leaked to the AP, and a story is sent out that was printed this morning which really takes the edge off of what I had purposed doing.[1] I have armed myself with facts and figures to refute and deny the allegations made by Borglum but, obviously, I can't refute charges that aren't made. I talked to Baruch about the plan and he agrees that the one I have in mind is easily the best way of handling the situation. You agreed, too, and probably thought you were giving me everything when you gave me access to the files but the most important material is missing—the reports. Will you call me up about eleven-thirty at The Willard and let me know what you can do? You can take my word that the best course is for me to condense the reports and write a story about them. Otherwise B. will break loose in New York with his own version and he will declare that his findings were so startling that they dare not be published.

With regard,   Swope[2]

I dictated a story tonight[3] to cover over until the real story is told tomorrow. Please read it.

TLS (WP, DLC).
    [1] Swope referred to a news report which appeared, with variations in detail, in several newspapers on March 17. This story indicated that Borglum had made a report on the aircraft-production program to Wilson. The exact nature of the report was unknown, the story said, but it was understood that it pointed out serious delays in the program as well as the possibility of profiteering by some of the contractors involved. The story also discussed briefly the forthcoming investigation of the aircraft program by the committee of three recently appointed by Wilson. See, for example, the *New York Times*, the *New York Herald*, and the New York *World*, March 17, 1918.
    [2] "Will the President advise the Secretary if he will agree to this?" [JPT to WW], March 18, 1918, TL (WP, DLC).
    [3] H. B. Swope, "Aerial Estimate Cut 40 Per Cent," New York *World*, March 18, 1918. Swope reported that administration officials were revising downward their earlier estimate that 20,000 American aircraft would be in France by July 1918. These officials now believed that the actual figure would be about 40 per cent below the original estimate. Swope noted also that a new investigation by the committee of three was under way.

To Joseph Edward Davies

My dear Mr. Davies: [The White House] 18 March, 1918

This acknowledges your letter of March twelfth.[1] It is with sincere regret that I accept your resignation as a member of the Federal Trade Commission, but I must commend the patriotic impulse which urges this action on your part. May I not express to you my warm appreciation of your sympathetic cooperation during the early part of this administration in bringing about the adoption of all those measures of reform which we had promised the people and which I have an abiding confidence will ultimately redound to their lasting benefit? May I also add a word of thanks to you for your steadfast loyalty and patriotism during that trying period before we were thrust into the war, while to avoid becoming involved therein every effort was being made aggressively to assert and fearlessly to maintain American rights.

The McLemore Resolution, the Embargo Issue, and the Armed Neutrality Measure presented the first opportunities to apply the acid test in our country to disclose true loyalty and genuine Americanism. It should always be a source of much satisfaction to you that on these crucial propositions you proved true.

Assuring you of my high regard, and with hearty good wishes
for your success in whatever you may undertake, I am

Cordially yours,   Woodrow Wilson

TLS (Letterpress Books, WP, DLC).
¹ J. E. Davies to WW, March 12, 1918, Vol. 46.

To Charlotte Everett Wise Hopkins

My dear Mrs. Hopkins: [The White House] 18 March, 1918

I was sincerely sorry to disappoint you about an interview, but I
am sure you will understand that interviews are often practically
impossible for me.¹

The housing problem has come to me again and again and I
think in every phase, and I am helping in every way that I can.
The elimination of the words "for government employees" from the
bill to which you refer² was due, I believe, to an attitude which is
quite general in the House of Representatives and based upon some
serious considerations, and I fear that it will not be possible to get
the words restored.

I hope that you know the plans which Chairman Sherley of the
House Appropriations Committee has in mind with regard to housing. I am exceedingly anxious to get all minds engaged upon this
subject together.

As to the alley legislation, will you not be kind enough to send
a brief memorandum of just its status and whom I should resort
to in the House of Representatives to get the proper legislation
considered. I need not tell you my deep interest in that.

In haste

Cordially and sincerely yours,   Woodrow Wilson

TLS (Letterpress Books, WP, DLC).
¹ Wilson was replying to Charlotte E. W. Hopkins to WW, March 16, 1918, TLS (WP,
DLC).
² See WW to L. Brownlow, March 15, 1918, n. 2.

To Vance Criswell McCormick, with Enclosure

My dear McCormick,   The White House. 18 March, 1918.

Here is a letter from Colver of the Trade Commission which I
wish you would very carefully consider. I believe he is right, and
I am willing to ask Lind to undertake the candidacy if you think
well of the suggestion.

A letter purporting to be from me was published some time ago in Minnesota recommending, in effect, the re-election of Senator Nelson, but I never wrote it, of course. I have not denied its authenticity because of my warm feeling for the Senator himself, whom I greatly esteem and because it was never brought to my attention in any way that made it necessary for me to say whether I wrote it or not. I did not want to go out of my way to do the Senator a disservice. But Colver is right about his political analysis.

Faithfully Yours,   Woodrow Wilson

WWTLS (V. C. McCormick Papers, CtY).

E N C L O S U R E

From William Byron Colver

My dear Mr. President:

Washington March Eighteenth
Nineteen Hundred Eighteen

It is only because I am certain that the matter I wish to bring to your attention is of the highest importance, that I add this note to your burdens.

I beg to direct your attention to the general political situation in Minnesota and to suggest that Mr. McCormick counsel with the local people before an immediate program shall be confirmed.

A definite movement is on foot for a fusion by the Minnesota Democrats with the Minnesota Republicans and especially as to the candidacy of Senator Nelson.

This would be a disaster to progressive development in the northwest.

The coalition would be one of the reactionary elements in both old parties and would leave that fine young spirit of democracy without a means of expression. It would drive many over to the extreme movements represented by the Socialists and the Non-Partisan League.

In the name of "loyalty"—which nowadays is being made to cover a multitude of sins—reaction seeks to regain control. These very men themselves are responsible far more than the intemperate radicals whom they condemn, for the growth of extreme radicalism, discontent and unrest among the masses in that section.

The Non-Partisan League will make a supreme effort to capture the Minnesota primaries this spring. They may succeed in many instances but they cannot defeat Senator Nelson's renomination.

I urge that while the extreme reactionaries and the extreme radicals contest the control of the Republican party, the Democrats, under democratic leadership, can offer a medium for political expression to the great body of sane and progressive citizens who will not be delivered by any political bargain that may be attempted.

The only man who can unite democrats of all parties is John Lind. He does not want to make the contest[.] Nothing short of a personal request made by you will persuade him. If he goes in he stands a good chance to win and, win or lose, he will furnish a rallying point for progress and democracy.

All the familiar forces of reaction of all parties are busy on the fusion scheme. It will mean the submergence of a fine young Democracy, the halt of progressive political expression and the growth of extreme and non-constructive radicalism. It is suicide for Democracy in the state. It leaves the state organization little more than a medium for the distribution of federal patronage.

If you shall deem it wise to request Mr. Lind to run he will do so. The effect will be to give new life and new hope to democracy and to progress and to stem the rising tide of revolutionary radicalism.

The enclosed clipping[1] is a "feeler" that was put out Saturday a week ago. The reaction was distinctly unfavorable so far as the democracy of the state is concerned.

Time is short and the course to be adopted within the next few days will have a great and lasting effect upon future political history throughout the middle west.

If I can aid in any way I shall be happy.

With all respect, I am,

Yours very truly,   William B. Colver

TLS (V. C. McCormick Papers, CtY).
    [1] The undated clipping, from an unidentified Minneapolis newspaper, contained a report about a meeting of the executive committee of the Minnesota Democratic State Central Committee at which resolutions were adopted praising Senator Knute Nelson for his "loyalty" and support of the Wilson administration in the war emergency. The article suggested that this action might foreshadow a formal endorsement of Nelson for reelection by the State Democratic Conference at its meeting in St. Paul on March 27.

From Robert Lansing, with Enclosure

My dear Mr. President: Washington March 18, 1918.

I enclose herewith, for your information, a translation of a further note received from the French Ambassador regarding the question of Japanese intervention in Siberia.

The Ambassador's previous note of March 12, which you have seen, was answered by the Department, according to your instructions, to the effect that this Government is unable at the present time to alter its opinion and attitude towards this question.

With assurances of respect, etc., I am, my dear Mr. President,
Faithfully yours,   Robert Lansing.

TLS (WP, DLC).

E N C L O S U R E

Jean Jules Jusserand to Robert Lansing

Mr. Secretary of State: Washington. March 14, 1918.

Referring to my note of the 12th of this month, I have the honor to inform Your Excellency that it would appear from later information received from Tokyo by my Government that the Japanese Government is ready to make even now the necessary arrangements for important action in Siberia if it can rest assured not only that the plan meets with no real objection on the part of the United States and that the United States not only would not look askance at the considerable effort to be put forth but would extend material assistance in the matter of resources and products that may be wanting.

Viscount Motono gave express assurance to our Ambassador[1] in this connection that he was ready unhesitatingly and unreservedly to declare that the Japanese Government would, as a friend of Russia, present itself in Siberia without any other desire than that of ridding that country from German domination and oppression, that it will establish no protectorate and *a fortiori* annex no Russian territory. Such a declaration solemnly made and published cannot fail to reassure public opinion in Russia proper and in Siberia.

These affirmations, from a statesman whose past is a warrant for the faith to be reposed in his word are, in my Government's opinion, highly important in that they show, at once, that Japan contemplates a far reaching action and proposes to act in Siberia as the deputy of its co-belligerents and the ally of Russia and forego any territorial advantage.

My Government hopes that these new facts may incline the President of the United States to bring his views nearer to our own in regard to a plan which from the standpoint of the outcome of the war it is so important to carry out and that he will see fit to take into account the circumstances, worthy of his attention, that their reluctance to launch into the undertaking without being assured of his assent, is evidence of the loyalty and sincerity of purpose of the Japanese.

Delaying the action would seem furthermore very unfortunate, because delay would hamper and impair that action and again because a revulsion harmful to our cause in the Japanese opinion and Government may be apprehended.

Under the conditions now surrounding the contemplated undertaking, it seems to my Government that that of the United States by granting such material assistance as may be needed would secure a supervisory right over the Japanese intervention which would thereby be put in closer connection with the general conduct of the war by the Allies, while Japan would be thoroughly pledged to the defense of the common cause. The Siberian people would in another aspect doubtless be thankful to the United States for the efforts made by its industry to supply them with the manufactures of which they are almost entirely deprived.

It may not be amiss to put together with the foregoing considerations the reports received by my Government from various sources which hold out a hope that a Russian Government will be constituted at Irkoutsk, particularly through the action of Prince Lvoff, former President of the Zemtsvos [Zemstvos] Assembly. The importance that would attach to the creation of such a Russian center of government capable of bringing together all the sound elements of the country; its establishment would signify that Russia can, partly by herself, emerge from the state of anarchy which threatens to throw her, a huge and profitable prey, upon the mercy of our enemies.

I should be glad if the American Government, taking these various considerations into account, would kindly join in our action at Tokyo to the full extent that is required to secure from Japan that cooperation which she alone is in position to bring us in halting the German progress toward the East.

Be pleased to accept, Mr. Secretary of State, the assurances of my high consideration.   Jusserand.

T MS (WP, DLC).
¹ That is, Eugène Louis Georges Regnault.

From Thomas Riley Marshall

My dear Mr. President: Washington. March 18, 1918.

I am very sorry that you gave yourself a moment's uneasiness in overlooking, as you put it, the fact that I had a birthday. I did not expect you to remember it nor did your failure to remember it lessen at all my regard for and loyalty to you. I am expecting nothing of you in these hours save that which I am sure you are giving,—the very best of yourself to the winning of this war and the preservation of the institutions which have made our country prosperous and yourself illustrious.

I am going to comply with your request and am leaving next Monday for Madison, Wisconsin, where I shall present as best I can your cause.

Believe me to be,

Regardfully and loyally yours,   Thos. R. Marshall

TLS (WP, DLC).

From Louis Brownlow

My dear Mr. President: Washington March 18, 1918.

Permit me to thank you for your letter of the 15th relative to the housing problem. I had already had several conversations with Representative Sherley on the housing problem, and I agree with you that his plans for the housing of the women employes of the Government are excellent. He had told me, however, that there were some serious difficulties in the way of his taking up the matter in the appropriations committee on account of the attitude of certain other committees of the House. After I received your note, I again talked with him and found that the situation had not changed.

On Saturday, the Secretary of Labor made arrangements for a conference this morning with the House Committee on Public Buildings and Grounds, at which he was represented by Mr. Watson, and the Secretary of War by Mr. Dorr.[1]

As a result of this conference, I am very glad to say that the committee agreed to a committee amendment restoring the words to the housing bill which will provide for the Government employes in the District of Columbia, and also approved another amendment adding ten million dollars to the appropriation to take care of the necessary building program here in the District.

As the bill already has been reported, these committee amendments must, of course, be adopted on the floor but as the committee has changed its attitude and will heartily support the amendments, I have very high hope that they will be adopted.

If these amendments can be incorporated in the Department of Labor housing bill, I believe that the whole matter can be well cared for under the Department of Labor.

Very sincerely yours,   Louis Brownlow

TLS (WP, DLC).
[1] Robert Watson, Assistant to the Secretary of Labor, and Goldthwaite Higginson Dorr, Assistant to the Secretary of War.

Gordon Auchincloss to Edith Bolling Galt Wilson, with Enclosure

My dear Mrs Wilson: Washington March 18th, [1918]

Mr House has asked me to let you know that he has seen telegram No 19 March 16 11 A.M. from Frazier in London reporting a part of the proceedings of the Supreme War Council and to tell you that he has not changed his opinion of the subject thereof

Faithfully yours   Gordon Auchincloss.

I thought you might want this while you were talking to Reading E[1]

ALS (WP, DLC).
[1] EBWhw.

E N C L O S U R E

London March 16, 1918.

19 For the President.

Meeting of Supreme War Council extended its session from fifteenth to sixteenth so that political * did not take place until yesterday afternoon. It was held at Number 10 Downing Street, following were present: Mr. Lloyd George and his military secretary Colonel Hankey, M. Clemenceau, Signor Orlando, Mr. Balfour, M. Pichon, M. Bissolati,[1] Lord Hardinge, General Spiers who acted as interpreter, and myself.

The subjects discussed were the question of Japan in Siberia, a declaration regarding the German-Russian and German-Ukraine peace, and a Polish declaration.

Mr. Balfour began the Debate on the first subject by saying that the United States after consenting to act with the Allies was now apparently drawing back, evidently influenced by the stream of telegrams from Russia and fezrful [fearful] of public opinion in America. Unless the United States intervened in Siberia he did not think Japan would act alone as the latter did not wish to risk incurring the ill will of the United States upon whom she counted for financial and material help, but he said do we ourselves believe in the policy sufficiently to ask the Department of State to accept the gamble, and it is a gamble, of persuading the Japanese to intervene in Siberia. Mr. Pichon thought that Mr. Balfour had very well stated the case and agreed with him in the main, he believed that Great Britain, France and Italy should reach a thorough understanding on this subject and put the case before the United

States in an Identic telegram, this telegram to consist of two questions. First. Do you believe intervention necessary? Second. If you do to what extent can you help Japan? Signor Orlando agreed with Mr. Pichon. He felt that the intervention of Japan was desirable, the only question was to what extent it was desirable. It was evident that the United States thought that Japanese intervention in Siberia would arouse opposition in Russia and put Russia against the Allies. Mr. Balfour asked Mr. Clemenceau whether his Government had any late telegrams from Petrograd, because he said Lockhart who was in daily touch with Trotsky reported the latter as being opposed to Japanese intervention and as having said that the Bolcheviks were quite prepared to fight the Germans in the west and the Japanese in the east and that he saw no advantages which would co[u]nterbalance the serious disadvantages which such a policy would entail. Mr. Balfour admitted that the best information he had received from Russia was rather against than for intervention, he was therefore of opinion that it would be wiser to await the action of the Soviet Conference at Moscow on March 17, rather than to take any precipitate step. M. Pichon was strongly in favor of no time being wasted. Mr. Lloyd George stated that he did not think anything would be lost by waiting as the Japanese he was informed were proceeding with their preparations. M. Pichon objected, that opposition in Japan to intervention was gaining ground and that delay would give this opposition time to grow. M. Clemenceau was all for intervening without delay, by acting now pledges of disinterestedness could be obtained from the Japanese Government. If the latter acted independently later on the Allies could bring no pressure to bear on them. He thought President Wilson was pursuing an extraordinary policy. He is willing to fight side by side with us, but does not wish to be our political ally, he wishes to reserve his action in Europe and Asia; so far as Europe is concerned I understand the President's attitude because there are shades of policy unintelligible across the Atlantic; I am nevertheless not uneasy as I have great confidence in the President; in Asia however things are different and we have no right to hesitate, therefore I request Mr. Balfour to draft a telegram for the three governments represented to send to Mr. Wilson asking him to act, I see no reason for deferring intervention any longer and I think a great error will be committed if we do not act. Mr. Balfour said he did not believe in identic telegrams and thought each government should instruct its representative in Washington independently. M. Clemenceau retorted what will President Wilson think of three Ministers who have come from three capitols to confer and who cannot agree on identic telegram, it would give him an additional reason for not following the policy recommended. He said President Wilson was present, that is to say some one was listening for him, which placed him in a singularly position, but he added we have nothing to hide. Mr. Lloyd Geor[g]e believed that Japan should not be treated as an inferior at this moment, guarantees should not be exacted of her which no one would dream of asking from the United States, that in the telegram to President Wilson the Allies should indicate that they had confidence in Japan as the latter was much less likely to make a demand for territorial compensation fi [if] her pride was not injured. It was thereupon agreed that Mr. Balfour should draft a telegram to President Wilson in the name of all the powers represented at the conference.

It was quite obvious that the French and Italians on the one hand and the English on the other regarded the subject of discussion from different points of view, the French and Italians were all for prompt action and inclined to make light of the danger of antagonizing Russia, both Mr. Balfour and Mr. Lloyd George had evident misgivings as to the wisdom of the policy and the former especially was in favor of delay in the hope that possibly the invitation for Japanese intervention might come from the Russians themselves.

A further conference will be held this afternoon at three oclock. The other matters discussed at the conference of yesterday will be reported in separate telegrams. This telegram enciphered by me.

Frazier.   Page.

T telegram (WP, DLC).
  [1] Leonida Bissolati (sometimes known as Bissolati Bergamaschi), leader of the Italian Reformist Socialist party and Minister for Military Aid and War Pensions in the Orlando government.

From Arthur James Balfour

British Embassy [March 18, 1918].[1]

Message for the President from Mr Balfour.

At a conference with the Prime Ministers and Foreign Ministers of France Italy and Great Britain held on 15th of this month in London, I was deputed to lay before the President of the United States of America their views on the expediency of allied intervention in Eastern Russia for the purpose of checking the complete penetration of that country by enemy influences.

Danger in opinion of conference is both great and imminent. Russia has utterly destroyed both her army and her navy; and she will never be permitted by Germany to reconstitute them. Her territory swarms with hostile agents; such energies as she still possesses are expended in internal conflicts; and no power of resistance

is left her against German domination. Her sole protection is to be
found in vast distances which invaders must traverse before obtaining complete military occupation of her Empire.

Unfortunately however complete military occupation is quite unnecessary. What Germany desires is that Russia should be impotent
during war, subservient after it, and in meanwhile to supply food
and raw material to Central Powers. All this can be effectually
accomplished in present helpless condition of the country without
transferring great bodies of troops from West to East.

Such is disease. What is remedy? To the conference it seemed
that none is possible except through allied intervention. Since Russia cannot help herself she must be helped by her friends. But
there are only two approaches through which such help can be
supplied: Northern ports of Russia in Europe and Eastern frontiers
of Siberia. Of these Siberia is perhaps the most important and is
certainly most promptly available for forces of Entente Powers. Both
from point of view of man-power and of tonnage, Japan is in a
position to do much more in Siberia than France Italy America and
Britain can possibly do in Murmansk or Archangel. It is therefore
to Japan that in the opinion of the conference appeal should be
made to aid Russia in her present helpless condition.

The conference was well aware that there are weighty objections
to this course. Though Russia has gladly availed herself of Japanese
assistance during whole course of war, there are many observers
who think, if that assistance now took the form of a Japanese army
operating on Russian soil, it would be regarded with distrust and
even with aversion. If this be so it is doubtless due in the main to
fear that Japan would treat Russia in the East as Germany is treating
her in the West, would rob her of her territory, and cover her with
humiliation. No such suspicion can be entertained by those associated with Japan in the present war. If she intervenes at present
juncture it will be as the friend of Russia and the mandatory of
Russia's other allies. Her object would not be to copy the Germans
but to resist them: and without doubt this would be made abundantly clear to all the world before any action was undertaken by
Japan.

This in brief is the argument for Japanese intervention which
the Conference desired me to lay before the President. I have only
to add, that in its view, no steps could usefully be taken to carry
out this policy which had not the active support of the United States.
Without that support it would be useless to approach the Japanese
Government and even if Japanese Government consented to act on
the representation of France, Italy and Great Britain, such action,

without the approval of the United States Government, would lose half its moral authority.

I earnestly trust therefore that favourable consideration will be given to a policy which with all its admitted difficulties seems required by the dangerous situation which has recently arisen in Eastern Europe.

T MS (WP, DLC).
[1] This was the date on which Reading handed this document to Wilson. The "originals" of this telegram are the Foreign Office to Lord Reading, March 16, 1918, No. 1515, T telegram (A. J. Balfour Papers, FO 800/205, PRO), and A. J. Balfour to Lord Reading, March 16, 1918, No. 1515, T telegram (FO 115/2445, pp. 156-61, PRO).

Two Telegrams from Lord Reading to Arthur James Balfour

[Washington] March 18th, 1918.

Very Secret.

Your cablegram No. 576 to Paris[1]

I informed the President at interview to-day of Vatican enquiry. He agreed entirely with your view and observed that it was not even suggested for what purpose an armistice should take place. If for further peace proposals they must be definitely stated. The President treated the suggestion as quite out of the question before I had even stated your reasons for rejection.[2]   Reading.

T telegram (FO 115/2427, p. 76, PRO).
[1] The British Chargé d'Affaires at the Vatican had been approached by the Cardinal Secretary of State as to whether the French, United States, and British governments would accept a proposal from the Pope for an armistice on the western and Italian fronts for one or two weeks at Easter. If not, the Holy See would not make the proposal, which should remain secret. His Majesty's Government believed that the proposal should be rejected because the enemy was preparing for an offensive on the western front, and the Allies could not depend upon any undertaking by him not to proceed with preparations for the offensive. Moreover, aerial reconnaissance could not continue during the armistice, and the enemy could therefore complete his arrangements unobserved and unhindered in any way. "Please inform Govt. to which you are accredited and ask their views." A. J. Balfour to Lord Reading, Washington, No. 1524, March 17, 1918, T telegram (FO 115/2427, p. 72, PRO). This telegram was addressed to Paris as No. 576.
[2] The French government also rejected the proposal. A. J. Balfour to Lord Reading, March 19, 1918, No. 1582, T telegram (FO 115/2427, p. 75, PRO).

Washington. March 18th. 1918.

Very Secret.

I delivered your letter upon Italy[1] to the President who stated that he hoped when the time came that Italy would modify her demands. He thought some arrangement might eventually be made that Trieste should be constituted a free port as the term was understood in olden times and that the Italian wish for an university there might be gratified. Some suggestion to this effect had recently been made to him.

T telegram (A. J. Balfour Papers, FO 800/202, PRO).
  ¹ A. J. Balfour to WW, Jan. 31, 1918, Vol. 46.

Pleasant Alexander Stovall to Robert Lansing

Pontarlier (Berne) March 18, 1918

2886. Strictly confidential. Department's 1619 March 14, 6 p.m.[1] I have questioned Herron again concerning conversation with Jong. Herron assures me in the most categorical fashion that nothing whatever was said that could have been considered as a pledge as to the attitude in which American Government would receive proposal from Holland. Herron states that if such idea was conveyed to Dutch Minister for Foreign Affairs, it was distortion by Jong, not only of his words, but of the tone of his conversation.

He had informed Jong that the matter in question was one which had no business being treated in Switzerland and belonged exclusively between Dutch Government and American Government and had even spoken most pessimistically of what he thought would be reception by Washington of this message and he had pointed out to Jong frankly that in view of past attitude of Dutch, prevalent opinion in America was that country was Pro-German and therefore any steps they took in this connection would probably be looked on with suspicion by Americans. He informed Jong that beyond reporting these conversations to Washington he could not see that this Legation had any interest whatsoever in the matter. He added that he begged Jong to leave no doubt in the mind of the Dutch Foreign Minister that there was no promise, intimation, or hint of what America's action on this matter would be.

Conversation originated as follows: When Montgelas (see my 2757 March 1, 7 p.m.)[2] was talking with Herron, Jong called at the house and heard Montgelas's remarks about America calling Germany's bluff.[3] Jong said nothing at that time but returned later and asked Herron whether Herron thought Switzerland might call the bluff. Herron replied he was sure this country would take no such action. Jong then asked what if Holland should take such a step. Herron gave the same answer. Without further conversation on this subject, Jong left and telegraphed his Government as reported in my 2816, March 9, 11 a.m.[4]

I know that Jong is acquainted with various members of Austrian Legation but he does not appear to associate much with any official persons. Those closest to him in Switzerland are Muehlon, Prince

Hohenlohe, Doctor Fried⁵ and men of this stamp. While the possibility of his action being inspired by Austrian influences is not
excluded, evidence obtainable seems to point to personal initiative.

Jong is considered by most people to be honest but not particularly intelligent, a busybody and a man who may be carried away
by his desire for peace.

Herron will endeavor to discreetly obtain copies of despatches
which Jong submitted to The Hague.   Stovall.

T telegram (SDR, RG 59, 763.72119/8732, DNA).
¹ In this telegram, Polk had asked whether anything had been said in Herron's conversation with Jong which would justify the Netherlands government in believing that
the United States desired or would be willing to receive the proposed communication
described in Stovall's telegram No. 2816 (see n. 4 below). Polk also asked for full
information as to how the matter started and who Jong's associates were. FLP to P. A.
Stovall, March 14, 1918, T telegram (SDR, RG 59, 763.72119/10777, DNA).
² In this telegram, Hugh R. Wilson reported that Maximilian Maria Karl Desiderius,
Count von Montgelas, had called upon Herron. Montgelas, a retired German general,
was the brother of Count Adolf von Montgelas of the German legation in Bern and
came to Herron highly recommended by Muehlon and the German democrats in Switzerland, who said that he opposed the German government and sought the redemption
of the Fatherland. Wilson reported further that Maximilian von Montgelas affirmed,
"with profoundest feeling and deliberate conviction" based upon knowledge of German
purposes and secret weapons, that a "complete European catastrophe" was coming, and
that Prussia would be in practical possession of Europe unless some "moral or political
initiative" of the United States intervened. Montgelas believed that Austria was helpless
in German hands but nonetheless urged that no effort be spared to try to "build a bridge
between Washington and Vienna." Montgelas said that President Wilson should instantly respond to the speech in which Hertling had accepted the four principles of
peace. H. R. Wilson to RL, March 1, 1918, T telegram (SDR, RG 59, 763.72119/8188,
DNA). For an account of related contacts in December 1917 between Herron and Adolf
von Montgelas, with the consent of the German Foreign Office, see Wolfgang Steglich,
Die Friedenspolitik der Mittelmächte 1917/18 (Wiesbaden, 1964), pp. 276-79.
³ That is, by asking how Hertling's acceptance of Wilson's principles of peace would
actually be applied to all territorial questions and to the separate peace treaties which
had already been signed.
⁴ Stovall reported that Herron had told H. R. Wilson that Jong had asked whether it
would be desirable for the Netherlands to call Hertling's bluff and whether the President
would be offended or pleased by such a step. Herron had said that he could not answer
such a question, but that the American legation might perhaps submit the matter to
Washington. Jong had then sent to the Netherlands Foreign Minister the following
draft:
"The Dutch government has learned with satisfaction that the German Chancellor
declares his readiness to accept the four principles proclaimed by President Wilson, and
to be willing to discuss peace on that basis.
"The Dutch Government, assuming that also the other belligerents accept these
principles, hopes to address itself to the belligerents, suggesting that they enter into a
general peace discussion on that basis.
"Before doing so, however, the Dutch government feels obliged to try to make clear,
beyond a shadow of a doubt, that it is also the conviction of the Central Powers that at
those discussions, aiming at a general peace, all problems raised by this war ought to
be a matter of consideration, including those concerning which the Central Powers
have just concluded separate peace treaties. It seems evident that to bring about a real
durable general peace, the last mentioned questions have to be reconsidered by the
World Conference where all interests will be represented.
"The Dutch Government therefore begs to ask the Governments of the Central Powers
to be willing to affirm that this [affirm this] conception of the scope of a possible general
conference on the basis of President Wilson's four principles, presumably agreed to by
the Central Powers."
Jong had indicated to Herron that the Netherlands government was "thoroughly
disposed" to present this note to Germany if it knew that the President would not be
displeased. Herron and H. R. Wilson had discussed the matter thoroughly and agreed

that the former should inform Jong that he (Herron) had no official status, that the American legation would submit a full statement for the President's consideration, that the Netherlands Minister in Washington should submit to Wilson the note as the Netherlands government proposed to send it, and that no assurances of any sort could be given as to how he would receive it. Stovall concluded the telegram by stating his own view that such a note would strengthen sympathy for the Entente among the neutrals and that its rejection (which he considered certain) would have a "very serviceable effect" on the masses in Germany. P. A. Stovall to RL, March 9, 1918, T telegram (SDR, RG 59, 763.72119/10777 DNA).
   5 Alfred Hermann Fried, an Austrian pacifist and publicist, corecipient of the Nobel Peace Prize for 1911.

To Benedict Crowell

My dear Mr. Secretary: [The White House] 19 March, 1918
   The situation connected with the shipment of coal to New England is so critical that I feel justified in calling your attention to the fact that the Ship Control Committee, of which Mr. Franklin is chairman,¹ acted absolutely against instructions in assigning to the War Department the steamship NEWTON, now lying at Lambert Point, I believe, in Hampton Roads. The ship was constructed for the special use of coal shipments to New England, and it seems to me imperatively necessary that she should be released. I hope that you will apprise the Ship Control Committee of this memorandum of mine and that the proper officer of the War Department will see that the NEWTON is restored to her former service.
   I am sure that you will realize that I would not send you this request if I did not feel that it was justified by a peculiar exigency.
                    Cordially and sincerely yours,   Woodrow Wilson

TLS (Letterpress Books, WP, DLC).
   ¹ Philip Albright Small Franklin.

To Louis Brownlow

My dear Brownlow: [The White House] 19 March, 1918
   I am glad to get your letter of yesterday and to hear that the House Committee on Public Buildings and Grounds has reversed its action.
   In haste   Sincerely yours,   Woodrow Wilson

TLS (Letterpress Books, WP, DLC).

To Gutzon Borglum

My dear Mr. Borglum: [The White House] 19 March, 1918

I believe I have already acknowledged the receipt of your last communication, conveying to me a supplementary report with regard to your inquiries into the execution of the aviation programme and telling me that you have now gone as far as you can in the circumstances, but I wish, besides expressing my sincere thanks for the diligence and care of your inquiry, to say that I have put the reports you have been kind enough to make to me in the hands of a thoroughly competent and impartial committee of investigation with the instruction to institute a thorough-going inquiry into all the aspects of the programme and its execution. I hope that what you have sent me will be of direct service to them. I am sure that nothing will be overlooked or omitted.

Very sincerely yours,   Woodrow Wilson

TLS (Letterpress Books, WP, DLC).

To the White House Staff

[The White House, March 19, 1918]

Please ask the State Department to send this cable:

"The President deeply appreciates the kind desire of the Institution of Naval Architects of Great Britain to place his name on the list of honorary members of the Institution, but regrets that he cannot accept. The people of the United States have usually required of their Chief Magistrate that he should not accept honors of this sort while in office."   The President.

T MS (WP, DLC).

From Robert Lansing, with Enclosures

My dear Mr. President: Washington March 19, 1918

I am sending you herewith a memorandum together with some telegrams showing evidence of a considerable body of opinion unfavorable to intervention in Siberia by Japan.[1] A large number of the telegrams are from mass meetings and from individuals in this country; others are from our Ambassador and Consular officers. There is also a telegram from the American Military Attache at Petrograd and another from the Manager of the National City Bank at Petrograd.[2]

No doubt the report of Admiral Knight from Vladivostok may already have been brought to your attention. A copy of it is nevertheless included as the telegrams bear directly on some of the Admiral's observations.

Faithfully yours,   Robert Lansing.

TLS (WP, DLC).
   [1] These telegrams are missing in WP, DLC.
   [2] These telegrams are also missing in WP, DLC.

E N C L O S U R E   I

Washington March 18, 1918.

MEMORANDUM.

Effect of Japanese Intervention on Public Opinion in Russia.

Attached are miscellaneous telegrams to the President, protesting for one reason or another, against intervention by Japan as a menace to the Russian democracy. Most of these telegrams emanate from different organizations of Russian citizens in the United States; some of them are from individual Americans. The written protests are, for the most part, from socialists and workmen assembled in mass meetings.

Supplementing these telegrams, reports from the Ambassador and the Consuls in Russia, seem to indicate quite clearly that while the more intelligent classes might favor and be heartened by international intervention in Siberia, there is no support for the intervention of Japan alone.

Several American citizens, business men, arriving from Russia have called at my office. They all tell the same story. For example, Mr. Draper, a consulting engineer, who tells me he has been in the copper, smelting and mining business in the Urals and Western Siberia for six years in close touch with several thousands of Russian workmen,[1] confirms the universal reports that the Russian peasants and workmen are, first of all, keenly jealous of their new-found liberty. They have also an ingrained suspicion and hostile feeling toward the Japanese. If the Japanese intervened alone they would, perhaps, turn to the Germans for assistance to eject them. The Russian peasants and the proletariat have not yet got to the point where they want any uninvited help from the outside.

We have a report from official sources that about twenty Japanese were either killed or wounded at Blagoveschensk last week.[2] It is to be noted that these were not peaceful citizens but volunteer members of the local militia, who tried and succeeded in preventing a number of Bolshevik soldiers from seizing certain supplies of powder. The press reports put quite a different face on this incident.

Basil Miles

TS MS (WP, DLC).
¹ Draper cannot be further identified.
² The "report" on this clash between Bolsheviks and anti-Bolshevik "volunteers" is Willing Spencer to RL, March 12, 1918, *FR 1918, Russia*, II, 77-78. In a telegram on March 17, 1918, Spencer reported that two hundred "Japanese volunteer militia" had participated in the fighting, of whom six had been killed and twelve wounded. *Ibid.*, pp. 80-81. The details of this affair, especially the composition and origins of the "volunteers," remain obscure to this day. Spencer's report to the contrary notwithstanding, the Bolsheviks did emerge victorious and took control of Blagoveshchensk. See George F. Kennan, *The Decision to Intervene* (Princeton, N. J., 1958), p. 58.

ENCLOSURE II

Paraphrase of a telegram Admiral Knight to the Navy Department, received March 18th.

Wish to submit following preliminary report.

There exists a possibility that part of munitions may be destroyed, as they are scattered in armories over many miles, making it impracticable to guard all sections efficiently but that for the same reason it is impossible that any great quantity could be destroyed if such an attempt were made and were at all successful. There is, moreover, absolutely no danger at present that munitions now here (Vladivostok) will reach the Germans. German agent, Kudriasheff,¹ reported as having been sent to the Far East to arrange for destroying munitions, was arrested and hanged by cossacks several weeks ago and his funds diverted to support of Colonel Semenoff, leader of the forces operating near Chita. I am collecting detailed information concerning location of individual items of munitions and preparing chart which will make it possible to keep general oversight of them without antagonizing. Do not consider danger great, but will be on the alert.

There is no doubt that German influences are at work in Siberia— in some cases supported by Bolshevik elements, in others opposed. No evidence of a substantial progress in Eastern Siberia.

Very difficult to obtain reliable information from other parts Siberia, but will continue efforts. Many conflicting reports concerning Bolshevik attitude toward Germans. My belief that attitude varies at different times and different places and that individual influences of cooperation cannot be accepted as indications of a general policy. Undoubtedly many Bolsheviks are German agents, but many others are honest and hate Germany. Opinion is wide-spread that Lenine is an idealist, but that Trotzky is in pay of Germany.

¹ Unidentified.

Reports that German and Austrian prisoners have been armed are not at present true but appear to have some foundation in other parts of Siberia. Wounded men arrived Harbin March 8th from Colonel Semenoff, who had been engaged in battle with Bolsheviks near Manchuria Station on railroad, were well interviewed by my aide de camp, Patterson,[2] and stated positively that they had been engaged at close quarters by men whom they recognized as Germans. One of these witnesses was a Servian, who stated that he had fought Germans on Russian front and could not be mistaken regarding their identity. I think this to be true, but do not regard it as proving that prisoners are being generally armed and shall endeavor to clear this point. Reports apparently trust-worthy that large number prisoners in Irkutsk have been armed and that they are prepared to destroy bridges and tunnels on Trans-Baikal Railroad.

Referring to report in Japan that German military forces are likely to appear in Eastern Siberia and along coast and waters of Pacific Ocean, I regard these reports as preposterous. One great danger to be feared is that German power will reach area immediately east of the Ural Mountains where immense supplies of grain exist. I am not in a position to estimate the probability of this, but if the military situation, as known to the United States, does not indicate it as a real danger, it is safe to say that no real *necessity* (?) exists for armed intervention in Siberia unless such intervention is desirable for the establishment of law and order.

At present existing conditions in most parts of Siberia under local Bolsheviki (groups garbled) are recognized as intolerable and this quite as much by friends of Russian democracy as by its enemies. The resulting dissatisfaction among all classes is finding expression in more or less active resistance at many points and may result in a reaction towards imperialism. This tendency can only be checked by modifying the conditions out of which it is developing, but I do not believe the hope of checking it lies in intervention from the outside. It lies, I believe, in the growing recognition by the Russian people themselves of the distinction between liberty and license and in their support of the forces standing for the establishment of order and the protection of life and property. While the evidence on the subject is contradictory and confusing I believe that upon the whole the power of the extreme radical faction is declining and that of the constitutionalist increasing and that order will gradually be established by the people of the country themselves. There are

[2] Lt. Comdr. David Calvin Patterson, Jr.

several movements in progress looking to this end through the establishment of a temporary government for Siberia. At present these movements lack unity, but efforts are being made to get together for the common good. One of the most promising of these movements centers about the available membership of the Siberian Provincial Conference elected by all provinces of Siberia, which convened at Tomsk in December, 1917, and was broken up by the Terrorists.

If, for any reason, armed intervention in Siberia is decided upon, it is of the first importance that Japan should not be permitted to act alone. This is the one point upon which everybody who knows conditions and sentiment in Russia is absolutely agreed. It is universally believed by Russians that Japan desires to take over a large part of Siberia and no arguments can shake this belief. On the other hand Japan's military men state that they will not operate with the forces of any other power, having had experience of this in the Tsing Tau China Campaign. Thus a very difficult situation is created and one which probably arranged only by compromise.

I venture to suggest the following for consideration as a possible compromise if intervention ultimately becomes necessary to check the German advance. American, British, French and Italian forces to take control in Vladivostok and the Amur Railway as far as its junction with the direct line at Karymskaya. China to continue to hold Chinese Eastern Railway through Manchuria. Japan with large force to operate westerly from Karymskaya with line of communication through their own railway (i.e. the South Manchurian Railway) and via Harbin not through Vladivostok. The occupation of Vladivostok and neighboring territory to be a naval operation and the Amur Railway to be held by military forces of the powers above mentioned to the number of about ten thousand. Whatever plan is adopted should be preceded by a proclamation to the Russian people signed by all the powers concerned solemnly promising that no territory or privileges of any kind will be retained. A full understanding should be reached that the westerly advance should not stop short of the Ural Mountains where Germans must be held if the purpose of the campaign is to be accomplished. It should be made clear also that the movement is not one of antagonism to any part[y] in Russia, even though it may be necessary to assume temporarily an attitude of this antagonism in order to break through * * * with which the weakness, disorganization and, perhaps, treachery now existing are covering the advance in German central * * * the eastern and especially towards the rich grain areas of west Siberia already referred to.

The following have seen this message and entirely agree with it, Senior British Naval Officer, American and British Consuls.[3]

Signed: KNIGHT
Commander-in-Chief, Asiatic Fleet.[4]

TC telegram (WP, DLC).
[3] That is, Capt. Christopher Russell Payne, commander of the British cruiser *H.M.S. Suffolk*; John K. Caldwell, the American consul at Vladivostok; and Robert MacLeod Hodgson, the British consul at Vladivostok.
[4] At Wilson's and House's request, Wiseman sent a paraphrase of this telegram to the Foreign Office in W. Wiseman to E. Drummond, March 21, 1918, No. 82, CC telegram (W. Wiseman Papers, CtY), with the following advice: "HOUSE and PRESIDENT WILSON consider this message gives a very interesting and sane view of the situation."

From Bertrand Hollis Snell[1]

Dear Mr. President: Washington, D. C. March 19, 1918.

There is a request before the Rules Committee for special rule to provide for immediate consideration of bill appropriating $10,000,000 to be used for loans to farmers to buy seed grain.

This is asked on the ground that it is an urgent war measure. Would you consider this an important war measure?

Your opinion would be very highly appreciated.

Obediently yours,   Bertrand H. Snell

TLS (WP, DLC).
[1] Republican congressman from New York.

From Benedict Crowell

Sir: Washington. March 19, 1918.

Pursuant to the instructions of the Secretary of War, I beg leave to send you herewith a draft of an Executive Order designating the types of military service to be recognized as noncombatant in character, and setting forth the procedure with regard to the treatment of men drawn for military service who are members of religious faiths opposed to combatant warfare, and of others professing conscientious scruples of the same character. This draft was prepared by Mr. Baker personally, and has been examined by the Acting Chief of Staff and the Judge Advocate General.[1]

Respectfully,   Benedict Crowell

TLS (WP, DLC).
[1] The Executive Order issued on March 20, 1918, stipulated that persons who had been certified by local draft boards as members of religious organizations whose creeds did not permit participation in war, and persons who objected to such participation because of conscientious scruples but who had failed to obtain certification, should be assigned to noncombatant military service. Service in the Medical Corps and certain

duties in the Quartermaster Corps and the Corps of Engineers were classified as non-combatant service. Persons so assigned were to receive certificates to that effect, which would prevent their future transfer to any combatant service. The order further stipulated that commanders were to report monthly to the Adjutant General the names of all persons who rejected assignments to noncombatant services for religious or conscientious reasons and their reasons for so doing. The Secretary of War would, from time to time, classify these persons and give further instructions as to their disposition. Pending such directions from the Secretary of War, all persons who did not accept assignments to noncombatant service should be segregated and placed under the command of a "specially qualified officer of tact and judgment," who was to impose no punitive hardship upon them. In the event that courts-martial were ordered, these persons should be tried for willful disobedience of a lawful order or command, but the sentences should prescribe confinement in United States disciplinary barracks, not in penitentiaries. *Official Bulletin*, II (March 22, 1918), 1-2, and the *New York Times*, March 22, 1918.

From Edward Nash Hurley

My dear Mr. President: Washington March 19, 1918.

You expressed my thought better than I could express it. What I have had in mind is precisely the sort of man you indicate—one whose character and public spirit and intelligence would be evident to the public.

Expert accountants, because of the character of their work, seldom win fame. We will have experts whose integrity and ability will be well established, but in appointing a man to take charge of the work, I thought we should have someone whom the public knows—someone whose connection with the work will be eloquent of its impartiality and correctness.

It would not be necessary for such a man to give his whole time to the task. I merely had Dr. Shaw in mind as a type. You may know of someone else. The accuracy of the work is already assured, but if we are able to get the right man, he will be able in a very brief time to familiarize himself with the method we are pursuing, and his mere presence on the job, especially for occasional conferences with the accountants, will be the main requirement.

I appreciate the interest you are taking in this matter.

Faithfully yours,   Edward N. Hurley

TLS (WP, DLC).

Two Telegrams from Arthur Hugh Frazier

Paris, Mar. 19, 1918.

26. For the President. At the political conference on the 15th instant, Sir Eric Geddes[1] was summoned to make a report on the mercantile shipping losses. He stated that the net loss in the world's tonnage was only two and one half millions out of forty-two million

tons. Germans had greatly exaggerated them; their exaggeration varied from forty-five per cent to seventy per cent in the month of January last, therefore if the truth were told the Germans would be depressed and not elated. He personally had been opposed to the publication of the figures until the production of tonnage had approached the losses. During the fourth period 1917 the loss was one million two hundred thousand tons and nine hundred thousand tons had been obtained, that is to say a net loss one hundred thousand tons per month. The British and American Governments both believed that since one hundred thousand tons deficit per month could easily be made good if the men realized what the position was. If the standard of the last quarter of 1917 had been maintained the output would have exceeded the losses before June.

M. Clemenceau said that he was somewhat alarmed when he heard that the British had decided to publish the losses. He pointed out that British and French public opinion were not quite the same thing. England wanted to get more work out of her workers and consequently statements must be pessimistic. In France while they wished to have the truth they required an optimistic note to be sounded. He therefore requested that before publication, Sir Eric Geddes exercise great caution about the form in which statements were to be made as all depended on this.

Signor Bissolati drew attention to the bad effect which the publication of the losses would have on Italian public opinion. The Italian morale, he said, was easily depressed.

M. Clemenceau said that he was willing to agree to this publication in order to give the English the means of increasing their output. Signor Bissolati also withdrew his opposition. It was therefore agreed that Sir Eric Geddes should draft the announcement taking steps to lay special stress on the exaggerated figures of submarine losses published in Germany, the announcement not to be made before March 21. Frazier.   Sharp.

[1] First Lord of the Admiralty.

Paris, March 19, 1918.

28. For the President and the Secretary:
Conference of the sixteenth instant. Mr. Lloyd George made the statement that the Allied Governments might soon expect a demand from the Socialist and the Labor Party for an international conference where the Allied representatives could meet those of the enemy. As the last Socialist Conference at London had reached an agreement regarding the war aims of the Allies[1] it was probable that the Socialists would make a definite request to proceed perhaps to Berne for the purpose of discussing peace terms with enemy

Socialists. He thought it highly important that the Allied Governments should all make the same reply to such a demand.

M. Clemenceau said he would reply by a frank explanation; the question had often arisen in France, but all Governments of all shades of opinion had consistently opposed Allied Socialists to meet and discuss peace terms with the Germans. Inasmuch as there existed in Great Britain, France and Italy, Governments which were the sole proper organs to discuss terms of peace and war it would imply a tendency to substitute some Socialist representatives for the Governments if the request of the Socialists were granted. There were also moral obligations; peace conversations would mean discussion with the enemy and this might prove a serious danger to the Allied nations in view of the enormous effort made and the long duration of the war. M. Clemenceau said he dreaded these discussions for although they would be entered into in good faith by French and British Socialists the German Socialists would not enter them with equally good faith. He went so far as to say that under the present conditions no reasonable basis for a discussion of peace terms existed, only yesterday in Berlin at the bi-election the Socialist vote was given for the imperialistic candidate.[2] He deemed it the duty of the Governments to try to make their Socialists understand the position without actually discouraging them, in fact he thought that, at the present time, any proposal for an International Socialist Conference would be premature.

Signor Orlando said that it was a very difficult and delicate question; he was opposed to any conference, he agreed with M. Clemenceau that the Allied Socialists might enter the conference in good faith while the Germans would enter it in bad faith. No one could say, however, that a resolution taken at the present time could be final for all time.

Signor Bissolati pointed out that the London Socialist Conference had thrown out every proposal against the cause of the Allies. He considered, as far as Italy was concerned, that it would be dangerous to allow a meeting to take place with enemy Socialists, the refusal of the Government to allow such a meeting would be well received by all except the Pacifists; since the Brest-Litovsk treaty of peace, there was a general feeling in Italy that it would not be right to meet the enemy.

Mr. Balfour thought that it would be easy to refuse the Socialists without annoying them by replying in the sense that it was not an occasion when a discussion was desirable with German Socialists who were the tools of their Government, and Russian Socialists who lived in the clouds. Mister Lloyd George said he would refuse on the ground that it was an affair of the Government and not of parties. He himself in addressing the British Labor Party had asked what answer he should give if English Liberals desired to meet German Liberals and if English Conservatives wished to meet German Conservatives. He had pointed out that the Socialists themselves had protested at the idea of British financiers meeting German financiers and yet if one party were allowed to confer with the enemy other parties should have the same right. Such a reply however would be inconsistent with Mr. Clemenceau's suggestion that the proposal was premature. Mr. Clemenceau said, having expressed the whole of his idea on the subject he wished to leave himself a loophole of escape because he felt that, if at any time he found a party or a group in France capable of engaging serious ideas of peace with a corresponding party in the enemy country, he would not have the courage to oppose it.

Mr. Lloyd George stated that certain Socialist delegates consisting of Messrs. Jouhaux and Cachin for France,[3] Canopa for Italy,[4] and Camille Huysmans for Belgium,[5] desired proceed to the United States to confer with Mr. Gompers and the Socialist party of that country. They had approached the Shipping Comptroller for permission to sail for New York.

Mr. Balfour suggested that the United States should first be asked whether they desired that permits should be issued to these men.

M. Clemenceau said there was a great difference between associating themselves with permits to an International Socialist Conference and those to proceed to America. He himself was quite ready to consider the French delegates permits. He has been informed by one of M. Tardieu's assistants that Socialist delegates could do no harm in America, and would not be listened to by individual. Recommended that the Allies send real working men to America, men who were not only practical workers, but also sound about the war. M. Clemenceau said that he had at once acted on this suggestion and had sent one working man from Lyons, who is a Socialist, and another man from Nancy, who although not a Socialist, was a miner and has been working in the zone of fire for some time; he thought that [if] the British and Italian Governments were to do the same thing; excellent results might follow.

Signor Orlando accepted this suggestion which he thoroughly approved of.

The Conference decided that Mr. Balfour telegraph to the United States to ascertain if the American Government desired permits to be given to the Socialist Deputation. Frazier.   Sharp.

T telegrams (WP, DLC).
[1] Lloyd George referred to the "Memorandum of War Aims," adopted by the Inter-Allied Labor and Socialist Conference at London on February 23, 1918. Based upon an

earlier "Memorandum on War Aims" adopted by the British Labour party and the Trades Union Congress on December 28, 1917, the later document was also influenced by Wilson's Fourteen Points Address of January 8, 1918. The memorandum of February 23 is printed in *FR-WWS 1918*, I, I, 155-67. For a discussion of the background and content of both memoranda, see Arno J. Mayer, *Political Origins of the New Diplomacy, 1917-1918* (New Haven, Conn., 1959), pp. 315-21, 388-89.

[2] In an election held on March 14 in the Potsdam-Niederbarnim district to fill a vacancy created by the death of the incumbent, the Majority Socialist candidate, Rudolf Karl Wissell, defeated the Independent Socialist candidate, Rudolf Breitscheidt, by 28,850 votes to 18,892. *Schulthess' Europäischer Geschichtskalender*, LIX (1918), Part I, pp. 116-17.

[3] Léon Jouhaux, secretary general of the Confédération Générale du Travail, and Marcel Cachin.

[4] Giuseppe Canepa, leader of the Reformist Socialist party.

[5] Secretary general of the Labour and Socialist International Bureau in Brussels.

Roland Sletor Morris to Robert Lansing

Tokio March 19, 1918

Advisory Council of Foreign Affairs[1] met on Sunday morning. This afternoon Minister for Foreign Affairs handed me the following confidential memorandum:

"The Japanese Government have submitted to the most serious consideration the memorandum of the American Embassy under date of March seventh bearing on the question of the situation in Siberia.[2] They highly appreciate the sentiments of friendship and confidence manifested to them in that memorandum and the absolute frankness with which the views of the American Government on this important question have been communicated to them.

It will be clearly understood that the intervention now proposed by the Allied Governments to arrest the sinister activities of Germany in Siberia did not originate from any desire expressed or any suggestion made by the Japanese Government. At the same time the Japanese Government have viewed with grave concern the chaotic conditions prevailing in Siberia and they fully realize the serious danger of the German aggression to which those regions are exposed. Desiring at all times to contribute whatever lies at their disposal towards the common end of the Allies they are prepared to entertain, as far as possible and with all sincerity, any plan of action with which they may be approached by the Allied Governments to meet the exigencies of the situation.

They, however, feel that the success of such undertaking will depend largely upon the whole-hearted support of all the great powers associated in the war against German confederation. Accordingly, it is their intention to refrain from taking any action on which due understanding has not been reached between the United States and the other great powers of the Entente.

It will hardly be necessary to add that should the hostile activities in Siberia develop to such a degree as to jeopardize the national security or vital interests of Japan she may be compelled to resort to prompt and efficient measures of self protection. The Japanese Government are confident that in such event they can count on the friendly support of the American Government in the struggle which may be forced upon them.

In all cases they are happy to assure the Government of the United States that whatever action they might be called upon to take in the Russian territory it will be wholly uninfluenced by any aggressive motives or tendencies and that they will remain unshaken in the profound sympathy towards the Russian people with whom they have every desire to maintain the relations of cordial friendship."   Morris.

T telegram (SDR, RG 59, 861.00/1335, DNA).
    [1] About which, see R. S. Morris to RL, March 12, 1918, Vol. 46.
    [2] See WW to R. S. Morris, March 5, 1918, *ibid.*

Lord Reading to Arthur James Balfour

Washington, 19 March 1918.

No. 1159. *Very Secret.*
Your cable No. 1515[1] received 17 March.
I have had interview today of an hour and a half duration with the President and discussed at length the Japanese question.

I presented the message forwarded by you textually reproduced and I added verbally some observations in support which I summarize as follows.

(1) Assuming the Japanese intervention did not take place Germany would work her will in Russia and gradually under German domination and direction would evolve order out of the present chaos. Russians would be driven to work for their bread and would be made to till the soil and work the mines and oil fields for the benefit of the Germans. Probably a few hundred thousand well disciplined and well equipped German troops would suffice to carry on German policy. If not Austria is free of enemies except on the Italian frontier and could send further troops to establish order in Russia.

Moral force would doubtless have its effect in stimulating Russia to resist German domination but a long time must elapse before Russia could organize resistance to the German yoke, more particularly with German military power controlling Russia. If Germany

[1] A. J. Balfour to WW, March 18, 1918.

was allowed to carry out her policy in the East unmolested by the Allies she could concentrate upon attacks on the western front.

The President observed that doubtless the results would be as indicated if no steps were taken against Germany in the East, but the Russians themselves would object to the German domination and would be difficult to manage and control and eventually would rise against Germany. To my observation that a long time must first elapse and that meanwhile the war might be over, the President said that according to their information the happenings in Russia were tending to consolidate the Bolsheviki elements against the Germans and propertied classes in Russia, which would give the Germans much trouble.

(2) In all probability Japanese intervention will take place with or without the assent of the Allies. It might take place in one of three ways:

(a) With the mandate or assent of the Allies and America. This would be the best safeguard against German propaganda or Russian suspicion of the objects of intervention. America's assent was of the utmost importance because she alone appeared to be trusted by the Russian people at the present time.

(b) With the mandate or assent of the Allies without that of America. German propaganda would make the most of America's non-participation and Russia might turn a more friendly eye towards Germany.

(c) Without the mandate or assent of the Allies or America. This course would probably raise strong suspicions of Japanese intentions and would have a greater tendency to drive Russia toward Germany.

The President agreed that if it were possible (a) would undoubtedly be the safest of these courses and agreed in substance with the views above expressed. He added however that he feared the Russian trust of America was held by a very slender thread. He said that Trotsky and Lenin evidently had a notion that the American Administration existed for the benefit of capitalists. I think this was a reference to the Soviets answer to the President's message.[2]

[2] Wilson's message to the Fourth All-Russian Congress of Soviets, March 11, 1918 (printed at that date in Vol. 46), was read to that body on March 15. The congress then adopted by acclamation a resolution in reply, drafted earlier by the Central Executive Committee, which read as follows:

"The Congress expresses its gratitude to the American people, above all the laboring and exploited classes of the United States, for the sympathy expressed to the Russian people by President Wilson through the Congress of Soviets in the days of severe trials.

"The Russian Socialistic Federative Republic of Soviets takes advantage of President Wilson's communication to express to all peoples perishing and suffering from the horrors of imperialistic war its warm sympathy and firm belief that the happy time is not far distant when the laboring masses of all countries will throw off the yoke of

(3) I referred to our combined forces in the trenches and said that every opportunity should be seized to relieve them from the pressure of Germany and that Japanese intervention according to the opinion of our military advisers would have the effect of causing some withdrawal of German troops from the Western front.

(4) If nothing was done in Russia was there not possibility of Germany offering terms of peace which would be attractive but for advantages and increase of power which Germany would obtain in Russia. ⟨Was it quite certain that if favourable terms were offered the war would be continued by all the Allies? Would there be the same unity in America if such offers were made?⟩

(5) Will not the effect of America holding aloof be discouraging to the French and Italians?

Lastly I asked what possible alternative could be suggested and whether we could be satisfied with doing nothing at the present moment to counteract the German victorious procession into Russia.

The President said he was very conscious of the perplexities of the situation and although I had only indicated various points for consideration it was unnecessary to elaborate them as his mind had travelled in the same direction and had considered these various points. He avowed himself ready to take risks provided he was convinced that there was a fair prospect of successful result of the venture but his main difficulty was that he could not see how the Japanese intervention would so seriously affect Germany as to cause German troops to be withdrawn from the western front. Even if there was a considerable opinion against taking the risk he would not hesitate to take it if convinced of its wisdom but his own mind must be satisfied that it was right to take the course. He was not convinced that any sufficient military advantage would be gained. The distances were so great that he did not see how the Japanese forces available to enter Siberia could be so spread as to guard the trans-Siberian railway. He understood the proposal was that the Japanese were to proceed as far as Lake Baikal and then later if necessary to proceed as far as the Ural mountains but Lake Baikal was a long way from the Urals. According to the reports received from the American commission the railway was broken up in many places and there were no means of repairing available and there were difficulties with rolling stock. Viewing these facts his mind

capitalism and will establish a socialistic state of society, which alone is capable of securing just and lasting peace as well as the culture and well-being of all laboring people." M. Summers to RL, March 15, 1918, *FR 1918, Russia,* I, 399-400. For a brief commentary on the significance of the Russian reply, see George F. Kennan, *Russia Leaves the War* (Princeton, N. J., 1956), pp. 512-13.

was not convinced that Germany would [be] require[d] to move troops from the western front because of the intervention. He agreed with my observation that the Germans had always been taught to be apprehensive of the Yellow peril and that their population would probably require security against the menace even if it were remote but that the protection afforded by the German troops already there could be supplemented if necessary by additional Austrian troops & would give all the safeguards required. The President much regretted that America should be standing out against the views of the Allies on this question. He felt the force of the argument that the American abstention would cause disappointment to the Allies but he could not think that the situation here was completely understood by them. Daily he was receiving opinions from those whose views were the most thoughtful and had most influence upon America and all those contained expressions of satisfaction that the President had not joined in backing the Japanese intervention. He again reverted to the doubtfulness of a military result of the intervention. I suggested that further material might be submitted to him for the purpose of convincing him of the soundness of the opinion of our military advisers. He said he would be glad to consider any further data if I could get fuller information to show that military advantage would be gained by the proposed course. If this could be established it would help him very much. He added confidentially that General Bliss had expressed very serious doubts upon the military aspect of the question.

He considered that at some later stage Germany might begin to overrun Siberia and that the situation would then require reconsideration.

Substantially the President's view is that no sufficient case has been made by the military authorities to cause him to change the views he had hitherto held and expressed. The military aspect is the one that has troubled me most as I have no knowledge of the reasons of the allied military advisers views except the obvious ones above indicated. The President had received yesterday a full report of the proceedings of the war council[3] and referred to it in the conversation with me. It was evident that he had definitely formed his conclusions before I saw him. These were based so far as I could gather upon this report and the doubtful character of the military advantage which would result. Balancing it against the political disadvantages which he sees with great conviction and which in his view are of the utmost importance in helping him to carry on the war with the full support of the nation he is not disposed to take a course which would rouse so much opposition.

[3] The Enclosure printed with G. Auchincloss to EBW, March 18, 1918.

I asked what was the alternative suggestion. He answered that the decision must be on western front and to my observation that it would mean twelve or eighteen months before sufficient numbers of American troops were there to make big attack he replied that in May or June this year America would be sending assistance in aeroplanes and would be supplying more ships and from that time onwards would be increasing strength of Allies which would give continuous encouragement until all was ready.   R.

TI telegram (FO 115/2445, pp. 172-78, PRO).

From the Diary of Josephus Daniels

March Tuesday 19 1918

Cabinet. Talked of ships & nitrates & need of priority. There are not enough ships & I must decide how to employ them first said WW. "We must feed the world" Therefore the pledge to bring nitrates to farmers must be kept. McAdoo said coal must go to New England & President agreed we should commandeer no more ships from N.E. coal trade.

After Cabinet talked to WW. He had had long talk with Lord Reading who urged encouraging Japan to go into Russia to fight Germany. What military advantage? It is 6,000 miles from Vladivostok to where Germans are fighting with a single rail and Japan does not propose at the most to go further than Ural mountains. He told Lord R to get what military men expected to accomplish. He did not trust their wisdom Thought it most unwise

Bound diary (J. Daniels Papers, DLC).

To the Democrats of New Jersey[1]

My dear Mr. Toastmaster: The White House 20 March, 1918.

I sincerely regret that matters of pressing importance will prevent my taking part in the reorganization banquet to which you have generously invited me. It is my feeling, as I am sure it will be the feeling of those present, that my clear duty is to stay here on the job. My work can be properly done only if I devote my whole thought and attention to it and think of nothing but the immediate task in hand.

At the same time it is clear that in the present posture of affairs in New Jersey I cannot overlook my responsibility as leader of a great party, and that it is my privilege to point out what I believe to be the duty of the Democrats in New Jersey, now and in the months to come, in order that the exigency of a great hour of crisis may properly be met.

During the months that I had the privilege of serving the people of New Jersey in the office of Governor we sought to accomplish this definite purpose, namely, to open the processes of government to the access and inspection of every citizen, in order that the people might feel that the Government of New Jersey represented their hopes, their impulses, and their sympathies. It was with this great purpose in mind that we succeeded in establishing electoral machinery which took away from selfish political leaders the power to hold the mass of the party voters in the State in subjection to themselves. In the matter of employers' liability we substituted for the cold letter of the old law the warm and wholesome tonic of humane statute. In every act of legislation we cut a clear pathway of public service and achieved a record remarkable for its variety and humanity, in every way comprehensive in character and touching no vital interest in the State with a spirit of injustice or demagogy. We gave the people, after many tedious and discouraging years of waiting, a government which they could feel was their own, free and unhampered by special privilege.

A time of grave crisis has come in the life of the Democratic Party in New Jersey—a time when its friends and supporters must face the facts of the situation if they would serve the cause of free government in New Jersey. Every sign of these terrible days of war and revolutionary change, when economic and social forces are being released upon the world whose effect no political seer dare venture to conjecture, bids us search our hearts through and through and make them ready for the birth of a new day—a day, we hope and believe, of greater opportunity and greater prosperity for the average mass of struggling men and women, and of greater safety and opportunity for children.

The old party slogans have lost their significance and will mean nothing to the voter of the future, for the war is certain to change the mind of Europe as well as the mind of America. Men everywhere are searching democratic principles to their hearts in order to determine their soundness, their sincerity, their adaptability to the real needs of their life, and every man with any vision must see that the real test of justice and right action is presently to come as it never came before.

The men in the trenches, who have been freed from the economic serfdom to which some of them have been accustomed, will, it is likely, return to their homes with a new view and a new impatience of all mere political phrases, and will demand real thinking and sincere action.

Let the Democratic Party in New Jersey, therefore, forget everything but the new service which they are to be called upon to render. The days of political and economic reconstruction which are ahead of us no man can now definitely assess, but we know this, that every program must be shot through and through with utter disinterestedness; that no party must try to serve itself, but every party must try to serve humanity, and that the task is a very practical one, meaning that every program, every measure in every program, must be tested by this question, and this question only: Is it just; is it for the benefit of the average man, without influence or privilege; does it embody in real fact the highest conception of social justice and of right dealing without respect of person or class or particular interest? This is a high test. It can be met only by those who have genuine sympathy with the mass of men and real insight into their needs and opportunities, and a purpose which is purged alike of selfish and of partisan intention.

The party which rises to this test will receive the support of the people because it deserves it.

Very sincerely yours,   Woodrow Wilson.[2]

Multigraphed CL (WP, DLC).
   [1] Wilson's letter was read to a "reorganization" or "harmony" dinner at Krueger Auditorium in Newark on March 20, attended by some 2,000 persons. The aim of the meeting was to reunite the Wilson and Nugent factions of the Democratic party in New Jersey. Tumulty was the chief speaker at the dinner, and James F. Fielder, Robert S. Hudspeth (the toastmaster), and Representative Scott Ferris of Oklahoma also spoke. Earlier in the day, the Democratic State Committee, meeting in Newark, had accepted the resignation of Edward E. Grosscup as state chairman and had elected Charles F. McDonald of Englishtown, a person acceptable to both the Wilson and Nugent factions, to replace him. *New York Times*, March 21, 1918.
   [2] There is an undated WWsh outline of this letter in WP, DLC.

To the Most Reverend Cosmo Gordon Lang[1]

My dear Archbishop: [The White House] 20 March, 1918

I am very glad that you have found it possible to pay a visit to Washington, and Mrs. Wilson joins me in the hope that you will give us the pleasure of having you take dinner with us on Monday evening, the first of April, at eight o'clock. I hope sincerely that your engagements will permit.

I am, with deep respect,
            Cordially and sincerely yours,   Woodrow Wilson

TLS (Letterpress Books, WP, DLC).
   [1] Archbishop of York.

To Robert Lansing

My dear Mr. Secretary,   The White House. 20 March, 1918.

I do not see how I could very well decline this[1] after having accepted a similar honour from the University of Bologna.[2] I would, therefore, be very much obliged to you if you would be kind enough to have the following message sent to Page:

The President accepts with deep appreciation
the honour so generously proposed by Cambridge
University.[3]

Faithfully Yours,   W.W.

WWTLI (SDR, RG 59, 811.001 W69/348, DNA).
  [1] The University of Cambridge desired to confer, in absentia, the honorary degree of Doctor of Laws upon Wilson and wished to know whether he would accept the degree. WHP to RL, March 18, 1918, T telegram (SDR, RG 59, 811.001 W69/348, DNA).
  [2] The University of Bologna had conferred the degree of Doctor of Laws upon Wilson in July 1917.
  [3] This message was conveyed in RL to WHP, March 20, 1918, T telegram (SDR, RG 59, 811.001 W69/348, DNA).

To Bertrand Hollis Snell

My dear Mr. Snell: The White House 20 March, 1918

I am very glad to reply to the inquiry of your letter of yesterday. I do regard the bill appropriating $10,000,000 to be used as loans to farmers to buy seed grains as a measure of pressing necessity which will lose its value if not passed at once.

Cordially and sincerely yours,   Woodrow Wilson

TLS (A. F. Lever Papers, ScCleU).

To Edward Mandell House, with Enclosure

My dear House,   The White House. 20 March, 1918.

We have been greatly distressed by your illness, and beg that you will take no risks, but come only when you feel entirely fit. We hope with all our hearts that you are mending fast now.

The thing I wanted particularly to see you about when I sent the message through Gordon was the folly of these League to Enforce Peace butters-in. We must head them off one way or another. Bainbridge Colby is on rather cordial terms with Mr. Taft and he saw Mr. T. for me and thinks he has prevented the particular thing I feared, that they would insist upon a discussion now of the *constitution* of the league of nations; but Mr. T. never stays put. I had before that written to Mr. Marburg, of Baltimore, one of the principal woolgatherers, stating my position very flatly.[1]

I enclose a message which Henderson, the British labour leader, has just sent me. I believe you will think it as interesting as I do; but I do not know just what reply to make. It opens, of course, a channel of influence which may upon some occasion be very useful indeed; but, if I meet Mr. Henderson half way and, so to say, get into confidential relations with Henderson, is that not likely to embarrass my dealings with Lloyd-George and the rest of the Ministry, to whom Henderson is now in opposition?

You are in direct communication with Frazier, are you not? It occurs to me that you might ask Frazier to convey to Henderson an expression of my very warm appreciation of his confidence and the assurance that I would be very glad to avail myself of it if occasion should arise or if Henderson should wish my advice on any particular matter. If you think that all right, will you do it for me?

By the way, Frazier's report of the conference of prime ministers where the Siberian matter was debated made the impression on my mind that Clemenceau was irritated that I should be present 'listening' by deputy when I was unwilling to actually take part in their counsels and join them in their actions. Do you not think that it might be well to instruct Frazier to withdraw if that is his own impression, making some excuse that would give no offence, or else frankly stating his impression and saying that he knew that I would not wish him to be present if it caused the least embarrassment, and that, at the same time, he knew that I would quite understand and would feel not in the least hurt?

Mrs. Wilson joins me in most affectionate messages and in the renewed injunction that you take care of yourself. Please give our love to Mrs. House.

Affectionately Yours,   Woodrow Wilson

WWTLS (E. M. House Papers, CtY).
  [1] WW to T. Marburg, March 8, 1918, Vol. 46.

ENCLOSURE

FOR THE PRESIDENT.   Paris, March 18, 1918.

Before I left London Buckler, Special Agent at the Embassy in London, transmitted to me a message from Henderson, the British labor leader, to you to the effect that he was prepared to follow any course suggested by you; that you had only to signify your wishes and he would endeavor to comply with them. Henderson's influence with British labor is said to be very great at the present time.

This telegram enciphered by me. Frazier.   Sharp

T telegram (E. M. House Papers, CtY).

From August Philips

My dear Mr. President: Washington, D. C. March 20, 1918

I have the honor to inform you that I have now received from Mr. Loudon, our Minister of Foreign Affairs, the information for which you asked at our last interview,[1] and about which I promised you that I should cable to the Hague.

If, as I expect, you wish to see me again about this matter, I trust that you will let me be informed when I may have the honor of another audience.[2]

I thought it right to adopt this way of writing to you direct, as the whole matter was treated by Mr. Loudon in such a specially confidential way.

May I avail myself of this opportunity, my dear Mr. President, to renew to you the assurances of my highest consideration.

Aug Philips

TLS (WP, DLC).
[1] Wilson had seen Philips at the White House on March 14. For a report of this interview, see A. Philips to J. Loudon, March 24, 1918.
[2] Wilson saw Philips again on March 25. For a report of this meeting, see A. Philips to J. Loudon, March 25, 1918.

From Arthur Charles Townley

St Paul, Minn., March 20, 1918.

Delegates representing the 45,000 patriotic farmers of Minnesota who are affiliated with the National Non-Partisan League assembled in joint convention with the organized workers in this city indorse wholeheartedly your statement of the war aims of the United States and unequivocally pledge you our [un]limited support until those aims are accomplished and a lasting and democratic peace is assured. We have urged all farmers and workers to keep up their splendid efforts at increased production and conservation of food supplies and to generously support the liberty loans and all other war activities calculated to aid our boys at war. Patriotism demands service of all according to their capacity and we wish to assure you that the farmers and workers appreciate your efforts to protect their interests. Do not be misinformed by politicians. The farmers of the Northwest cheerfully acquiesce in your decision fixing the price of wheat on the basis of the 1917 crop, only asking in return that Congress enact legislation that will enable you to carry out your price fixing program so that other commodities may be dealt with upon a like basis and the people relieved of the extortionate profiteering which still largely contributes to the burdensome cost of living. The heart of America beats loyal and strong and we know that you believe in us despite the vile slanders of a subsidized press.

National Non-Partisan League,
A. C. Townley,   Prest.[1]

T telegram (WP, DLC).
[1] "I do not know how really representative the body referred to in this telegram is. I wish you would find out from the Department of Agriculture. I don't feel at all safe in the hands of Mr. Townley or the Non-Partisan League and would like to proceed rather carefully in dealing with them." WW to JPT, c. March 20, 1918, TL (WP, DLC).

From Morris Sheppard

My dear Mr. President: [Washington] March 20, 1918.

I have been considering for some time the advisability of introducing the bill for complete war-time prohibition. I recall that when the Food Control measure was pending, you did not consider it advisable to insert a clause for complete prohibition, on account of the fact that the brewery interests threatened to delay the measure indefinitely.

I now have in mind introducing an independent measure without any connection with any other proposition. I do not wish to do this, however, if it will interfere with your general plan for the conduct of the war, etc., as I realize that you are in position to know better how a measure of this kind fits in with the general situation.

Kindly return the bill with your reply,[1] and rest assured that it will be kept entirely confidential, and that I will abide by your decision.

With every expression of regard, I am
Yours very sincerely,   Morris Sheppard

TLS (WP, DLC).
[1] Wilson returned the enclosure.

From Harry Augustus Garfield, with Enclosure

Dear Mr. President: Washington, D. C. March 20, 1918

For your information, I enclose copy of a letter I am sending Senator Thomas concerning the Colorado situation.

Faithfully yours,   H. A. Garfield.

TLS (WP, DLC).

E N C L O S U R E

Harry Augustus Garfield to Charles Spalding Thomas

Dear Senator Thomas: [Washington] March 20, 1918

Referring to your letter of March 15th, I beg to quote you from a report made to me this morning by Mr. Cyrus Garnsey, Jr., Mr. R. V. Norris and Mr. James H. Allport, the Committee of Engineers advising me in the matter of mining costs. The Committee, at my request, examined the statements contained in your letter to me and the numbered paragraphs refer to your letter.

"In relation to Senator Thomas' letter of the 15th, referred to us, we have the honor to state in reply—

First—The reduction of prices in the summer months to encourage storage, was made at the request of the Colorado Operators' Committee, who stated that this reduction was a trade custom of many years standing, the amount of the reduction for each month, as named, was made exactly as requested, and allowance was made in the price to fully reimburse the operators for this reduction.

Second—Senator Thomas has been misinformed as to the relative prices in the Trinidad and Bituminous Domestic fields. The prices fixed on Domestic coal show an average realization on a weighted average of all sizes produced of $2.6825 per ton mined, while for Trinidad the average realization is but $2.265, a realization 41¾ cents less, not ten cents more than that of the Bituminous Domestic field.

You will note that but 17% of the Trinidad coal is shipped as prepared as compared with 53% of the Domestic. The Trinidad coal is essentially a steam coal and the Run of Mine and Slack used for steam purposes are properly priced higher than the same grades of Domestic coal which are less desirable for this purpose, while in the prepared sizes the Domestic coal is properly priced higher than the Trinidad which is less desirable for domestic use.

Third—The Utah prices are Prepared $3.30, Run of Mine $2.65,

Screenings $1.50, with the percentage of sizes produced the realization per ton mined is $2.66, slightly less than the realization in the Colorado Domestic region, while the operators' reports show that the mining costs are practically identical.

Fourth—The statements made by the operators were most carefully considered and their representatives had numerous conferences with your Committee, and the costs upon which you based the prices were taken from all the reports of the operators filed with the Federal Trade Commission; if any small mines were omitted from the charts it was because the operators of such mines had not filed their cost statements with the Federal Trade Commission."

I have examined the costs reported by 13 of the mines reported by Mr. Nash[1] to have shut down; the sheets of the others, apparently, have not been turned in to the Federal Trade Commission. The costs reported reveal the fact that not in a single instance did the August costs reported by the mine exceed the price fixed. Indeed, the highest cost for August allowed a profit of 2¢ per ton, and the lowest 80¢ per ton. In September two of these mines reported costs slightly in excess of the price fixed. In one case only was the cost excessively high and that was of a mine which produced only 298 tons. This mine reported $1.69 less cost per ton on a still smaller tonnage for August.

An examination of the costs available of these mines does not warrant the assumption that they have closed down because of inability to produce at a profit.

Sincerely yours,   H. A. Garfield

TCL (WP, DLC).
[1] Harry Fletcher Nash, of Denver, Colo., general manager of the Oakdale Coal Co.

From James Alexander Hudson and William Hirth

Columbia, Missouri, March 20, 1918.

During recent weeks the Missouri Farmers Association appealed to the United States Food Administration for relief from ruinous prices on live stock. In conversation recently with a prominent member of the Missouri delegation in Congress Mr. Hoover expressed the view that the true remedy was to reduce the price of corn and other feeds rather than to increase the price of pork, beef and mutton, and from the tremendous drop in corn prices during the last few days it would seem that some powerful influence is being exerted to this end. During our recent visit to Washington we protested that such a procedure would merely seek to rectify one wrong by committing a still greater wrong against thousands of farmers who through lack of farm help and cars in which to ship still have much of last year's crop on hand. Again such a remedy will not help cattle feeders, the most of whom purchased their corn months ago unless something is done to protect corn prices immediately the situation is certain to greatly reduce the corn acreage which is about to be planted and we therefore trust you will take a hand in matters without a moment's delay. In view of the large extent to which corn must be substituted for wheat the raising of a maximum corn crop this year is imperative and the only way in which this can be assured is to see that farmers receive not less than a dollar and fifty cents per bushel for all the good corn left from last year. Unless steps to this end are taken immediately the corn producer is destined for the same fate which has already overtaken the hog and cattle feeder. Surely as food is as important as it is said to be the hour is at hand when we must have a more sympathetic cooperation from the government than we have thus far received. The situation could hardly be more critical and we trust you will look into matters immediately.

J. A. Hudson,   Chairman Executive Board
Missouri Farmers' Association;
William Hirth,   Publisher The Missouri Farmer.

T telegram (WP, DLC).

Robert Lansing to Roland Sletor Morris

Washington, March 20, 1918.

Please take the first suitable opportunity to say confidentially to the Minister of Foreign Affairs that this Government most earnestly hopes that the Japanese Government understands that our attitude in regard to Japan's sending an expeditionary force into Siberia is in no way based upon suspicion of the motives which would induce the Japanese Government to take such action in the event that it seems advisable. On the contrary we have implicit faith in the loyalty of Japan to the common cause and in her sincere desire to bear unselfishly her part in this war.

The attitude of this Government rests upon the fact, first, that, from the information which we have received from various sources, we must conclude that the moral effect of such action upon the Russian people would be bad and would undoubtedly work to the advantage of Germany; and, second, that the evidence, which we possess, is insufficient to show that the military effect of that action would be great enough to compensate for the moral loss which it would entail.

You will especially impress upon His Excellency our full reliance upon the good faith of his Government and our sincere hope that the reasons for our policy are not misconstrued.[1]   Lansing

TS telegram (SDR, RG 59, 861.00/1360b, DNA).
  [1] It seems very likely that Wilson participated in the drafting of this telegram.

The Foreign Office to Lord Reading

F.O. 20th. March 1918

Private

Sir J. Jordan's tel: No. 255 of March 18 which we are repeating to you.

Please communicate it to the President at once.[1]

Hw telegram (A. J. Balfour Papers, FO 800/209, PRO).
  [1] It is printed as Enclosure I with RL to WW, March 21, 1918.

From the Diary of Josephus Daniels

1918 Wednesday 20 March

Knight telegraphed about helping to set up government in Siberia.[1] WW said telegraph him that Siberians must settle their own government & for K. not to take any steps until directed by his Government.[2] Also K. cabled he & English would resist by force any attempt to move munitions from V. No. K had not conferred with Japs. Asked: Why not?

Many wires clamoring for Japs to go in. Lansing called. Said Japs were acting in best possible way and that they did not wish to go in unless it was agreed that it was best.

  [1] A. M. Knight to Chief of Naval Operations, March 20, 1918, T telegram (NDR, RG 45, Naval Records Coll., Telegrams—Incoming, Nov. 2, 1917-June 1, 1918, DNA). The most important paragraphs follow:
  "07019 In my judgement the recent ratification peace by Bolsheviki authorities materially modifies situation previously existing and calls for corresponding modification of policy by United States and Allies and prompt announcement of policy decided upon period. Sentiment through Siberia is crystallizing in favor of autonomous government. Such government would be strongly pro-ally and if established promptly and supported effectively should be able defend whole Siberia against any force that Germany seems likely send East of Ural Mountains. There are now in Siberia large numbers delegates duly elected by Siberian people as representatives to the all-Russian constituent assembly which met at Petrograd December and was broken up by Bolsheviki authorities period. As this assembly was never dissolved by proper authority the delegates retain their characters as representatives of the people, entrusted with mission to form a government.
  "It is suggested that United States and allies issue Proclamation inviting the Siberian delegates of this assembly to meet at Vladivostok under protection naval forces and

organize provisional government for Siberia to act until a new cons[t]ituent assembly can be elected and convened. If the number of delegates who gather at Vladivostok in answer to this call should prove too small to be effective the members might be requested by the allies to embody in their members the delegates elected to the all-Siberian assembly which met at Tomsk in February and was also broken up by the Bolsheviki. The proclamation calling the assembly should state that this step is designed to give effect to the will of the people of Siberia as expressed by their vote and to provide protection for Siberia from the powers which are outrageously running and dominating western Russia. It should promise protection for the assembly, the assistance financial, economic and military including loans and such commercial arrangements as may be necessary to provide the people of Siberia through liberal commercial arrangements with the essential articles of daily life of which they are in such urgent need. The Proclamation should specifically announce over the signature of all the powers acting that they jointly and severally promise to retain no territory concession or other advantage after the present war is ended by a satisfactory peace. To insure the stability of the government, guarantee its operation along sane and conservative lines, and protect the interests of the powers supporting it, there should be provided an advisory body of several members representing the powers concerned, with authority to act, under instructions from their governments in any matter where such action may be necessary. Senior Officer Present could act temporarily.

"Military forces should be organized by assembly assisted by advisory council, consisting primarily of Russians but including such forces furnished by powers as may be found necessary to insure a vigorous and successful campaign. Question military command to be settled by the powers. This plan does not necessarily conflict with that suggested for Allied cooperation in 11017. Developement of transportation should be pushed under guide Americans already engaged in this work."

² JD to A M. Knight, March 21, 1918, T telegram (NDR, RG 45, Naval Records Coll., Telegrams—Outgoing, Feb. 6, 1917-May 31, 1919, DNA): "Unwise to take the action proposed in that dispatch Paragraph Your Zero seventy nineteen Any movement for an independent government in Siberia must originate from within period When such a situation arrives [arises] the course of action of this government will be determined and you will be instructed accordingly Acknowledge 18021 Wire daily all information. Josephus Daniels"

To Herbert Bayard Swope

My dear Swope: The White House 21 March, 1918

Thank you for your letter of yesterday,[1] but I am afraid that you do not realize what irritation and, perhaps I might say, even resentment would be created if I were to institute a process of constant inquiry into the efficiency with which the innumerable jobs of the Government were being carried through. Inasmuch as I deal with sensibilities every day, I know how much, as a rule, they play in efficiency itself, and I do not think it would be wise to risk ruffling them all the time.

Besides, it would mean a very big piece of machinery indeed and one which would attract a great deal of public attention to keep such inquiries up-to-date with regard to the whole range of our present work. Don't you think so?

In haste

Cordially and sincerely yours,   Woodrow Wilson

TLS (received from Bruce Gimelson).
[1] It is missing.

To Lee Slater Overman

My dear Senator: [The White House] 21 March, 1918

May I not say how gratified I am that the bill giving me authority to effect the necessary readjustments in administrative machinery to secure efficient action has been reported out with the approval of so substantial a majority of your committee?[1] And may I not express the hope that the Senate will see its way to a prompt passage of the measure? Senator after Senator has appealed to me most earnestly to "cut the red tape." I am asking for the scissors.

Cordially and sincerely yours,   [Woodrow Wilson]

CCL (WP, DLC).
[1] That is, the Senate Judiciary Committee, which on March 20 had voted eleven to seven to report out S.3771, the so-called Overman bill. *New York Times*, March 21, 1918. Overman had introduced the measure on February 6. According to the *New York Times*, February 7, 1918, it had been handed to Overman on the day before by Burleson, at Wilson's request. The *Times* also reported that the Democratic floor leader, Senator Martin, had earlier refused to present the bill on the ground that it was too sweeping in nature. Nothing is known about the drafting of this legislation. However, it was clearly the administration's response to the agitation in Congress for the creation of a "War Cabinet" and/or a minister of munitions.

The Overman bill authorized the President, for the duration of the war and one year thereafter, "to make such redistribution of functions among executive agencies as he may deem necessary." He was empowered "to coordinate or consolidate any executive commissions, bureaus, agencies, offices, or officers, to transfer any duties or powers from one existing department, commission, bureau, agency, office, or officer to another, to transfer the personnel thereof, or any part of it, either by detail or assignment, together with the whole or any part of the records and public property belonging thereto, and to employ by Executive order any additional agency or agencies and to vest therein the performance of such functions as he may deem appropriate." Moreover, he was authorized to divert monies already appropriated, or to be appropriated, for any existing department, commission, bureau, agency, office, or officer to finance such new arrangements as he might make. Any existing law or regulation which conflicted with the exercise of the new presidential authority was to be considered suspended during the life of the new law. The bill as introduced is printed in full in the *New York Times*, February 7, 1918.

The bill as reported by the Judiciary Committee included two changes. First, monies could be used only for the purposes for which they had been appropriated, even if they were expended by a different agency acting under the President's direction. Second, upon the termination of the Act, all executive and administrative agencies and departments would exercise the same functions, duties, and powers as before, unless changed by law. *Cong. Record*, 65th Cong., 2d sess., p. 3815.

The Overman bill had created a furor among congressional opponents of the administration. Many of them argued that Congress would abdicate its own powers and responsibilities if it adopted the measure.

To Thomas Staples Martin

My dear Senator Martin: [The White House] 21 March, 1918

Thank you for letting me see the telegram from the Reverend James Cannon, Jr.[1] He makes a suggestion which has been repeatedly made and which I have thought about rather carefully. I have been inclined rather to discourage speakers going to England, because the effectiveness of what they did would depend rather upon what the least wise and discreet of them said than upon what the best of them said, and the men suggested who can be spared have not seemed to me likely to make the impression that would be most useful. In brief, I think there is more risk than certainty of gain in the proposition, much as it might accomplish if it could be ideally done.

Cordially and faithfully yours,   Woodrow Wilson

TLS (Letterpress Books, WP, DLC).
¹ Wilson returned Cannon's telegram.

To Royal Meeker

My dear Mr. Meeker: [The White House] 21 March, 1918

Thank you for your letter of March fourteenth about the functional and vocational rehabilitation of wounded soldiers and sailors. It seems to me to contain some very sound suggestions indeed, and I am putting it in the hands of those who are just now considering the matter.

In haste

Cordially and sincerely yours,   Woodrow Wilson

TLS (Letterpress Books, WP, DLC).

To Josephus Daniels

My dear Daniels: [The White House] 21 March, 1918

I believe you are acting just now as Chairman of the Council of National Defense, and I know that the matter of providing for the functional and vocational rehabilitation of wounded soldiers and sailors is now being considered by the Council of National Defense. I am sending the enclosed letter from Mr. Royal Meeker because it seems to me to contain some very sound suggestions, and I know that those who are considering the matter will read it with interest.

Faithfully yours,   Woodrow Wilson

TLS (Letterpress Books, WP, DLC).

From Atlee Pomerene

Dear Mr. President: [Washington] March 21, 1918.

The Senate this afternoon adopted the G   amendment, fixing the minimum price of wheat at $2.50 per bushel, by an overwhelming vote. I am at a loss to understand it. We hope to produce this

year 750,000,000 bushels of wheat. By the vote of this afternoon
we have increased the cost of bread to the consumer at the rate of
50¢ per bushel of wheat over the price fixed by statute last year,
or to an amount of $375,000,000. Or, if we count the increase of
this Bill over the $2.20 rate, which you recently named in your
proclamation, we have increased the price of the bread in the nation
30¢ per bushel, or $225,000,000.

I dislike profiteering of all kinds, but profiteering in bread stuffs
by legislation is in its worst form, and for one I indulge the hope
that you may see your way clear to veto this Bill if it is presented
to you as it passed the Senate.

Very sincerely,   Atlee Pomerene

TLS (WP, DLC).

From Robert Lansing, with Enclosures

My dear Mr. President: Washington March 21, 1918.

I saw Lord Reading this afternoon. He handed me paraphrases
of two telegrams which the Foreign Office had received relative to
the situation in eastern Siberia.

As you should see them immediately I am not taking time to
have them copied and I will appreciate it if you will kindly return
them after you have considered them.

Faithfully yours,   Robert Lansing

TLS (SDR, RG 59, 861.00/1432½, DNA).

E N C L O S U R E   I

Handed me by Lord Reading
Mch 21/18 RL

Paraphrase of Telegram received by the Foreign Office
from Peking, dated March 18, 1918.

The following is a telegram which the British Consul at Harbin[1]
sent to me yesterday and which appears to me to sum up the
situation from a local point of view with fair accuracy.

Begins.

I have had numerous interviews during the past few days at
which my American, French and Russian colleagues,[2] the French
Military Attaché at Peking,[3] and Colonel Pichon,[4] a French staff

[1] Henry Edward Sly.
[2] Charles Kroth Moser and Mikhail Konstantinovich Popov. The French consul at
Harbin unidentified.
[3] Unidentified.
[4] Jean Pichon, attached to the French military mission in Russia.

officer who recently arrived here from Siberia where he spent two
and a half months and who is employed in Intelligence work, and
I have discussed the present situation in Northern Manchuria and
Siberia.

The state of affairs in Siberia as described by Colonel Pichon is,
briefly, as follows.

Anarchy reigns supreme. Germany has already virtually secured
the economic conquest of Siberia. Of the original two million Austrian and German prisoners quartered in Siberia only about half a
million remain and complete freedom is enjoyed by a large proportion of these. The Austrian prisoners greatly exceed the Germans
in numbers. There are 12,000 rifles in the arsenal at Irkutsk, which
is protected by armed Austrians, and the camp of enemy prisoners
at that place is similarly guarded. There is no desire for further
fighting amongst the Austrian prisoners, but the rigid discipline
imposed by their officers on the German rank and file is respected
by the latter, and if the Germans should make an attempt to organise
an ordered armed force it is thought they would carry many of the
Austrians with them. Large numbers of Hungarian prisoners are
already working on the land. These men have either co-habited
with or married the peasant women, who greatly prefer them to
the Russian men, who are dirty and rough. The better class of
prisoners are employed as shop assistants and clerks, but factories,
industries, banks, and mines are, generally speaking, at a standstill,
and complete control has been obtained by the Bolsheviks of all
communal and municipal councils and public institutions. Colonel
Pichon finally gives it as his opinion that the fixed policy of the
Bolsheviks, which is prompted by the Germans, is one of complete
demolition of authority. This would lead to a passive German conquest of Siberia, as German merchants and others would enter into
relations with the inhabitants of the country and find it an easy
task to convince the latter that they can and will re-establish order
and bring about a return of prosperity.

My own personal opinion agrees with that of Col. Pichon and is
supported by the following shortcomings of the Russian people:
want of application, lack of capacity to co-ordinate, want of constructive power, distrust of one another and jealousy, also individual
selfishness, aided by the present demoralized and impoverished
condition of the whole nation. Money is the only thing which at
present counts in Russia, for even where patriotism exists it is
unable to find a hearing.

It would appear then that there is a great danger that if a speedy
termination is not put to the present Bolshevist or German movement in Siberia, it will grow in intensity and spread further and
further east. The Germans will thus find themselves masters of a

huge stretch of territory extending from the West of Europe to the Pacific Ocean. Such a prospect, when viewed alone, is of sufficiently alarming a nature, but it becomes still more so when consideration is given to it in conjunction with a German movement to the Caucasus.

I do not think that there can be any doubt that the Japanese are prepared to intervene to an extent at least sufficient to safeguard their own country, which, as it is stated, would be menaced by aeroplane and submarine attack even if the Bolshevist or German ascendancy in the extreme East did not go beyond the control of the Amur, Trans-Baikal, Chinese Eastern and Usuri Railways. In the opinion of some the idea of submarine attacks against Japan is nothing but a chimera so long as it is possible for an Allied naval force to operate at Vladivostock and Nicolaievsk at the mouth of the Amur. I am unable to judge whether this is or is not so, but it would not appear that the same arguments could apply to the case of aeroplanes, which need not be transported to a seaport and which could at least be a menace to Manchuria and Korea. Furthermore there is the consideration that if the Bolshevists controlled these railways the passage, if nothing worse, of enemy agents into China will be facilitated and this will lead to the undoing of a great deal, if not all, of what has been done with the object of counteracting the influence of the enemy in that country. I rely very little upon Chinese opposition to the Bolshevists as I am convinced that the Chinese are in their heart of hearts greatly afraid of the Germans, and are seriously alarmed as to the consequences in the future should the Germans emerge victorious from the present war. Had they been left to themselves, for example, the prohibition imposed on exports from Northern Manchuria into Russia would never have been made effective by the Chinese, this prohibition being only made possible by the executive control which the foreign staff of the Chinese Maritime Customs exercises.

I gather that the United States Government do not regard the intervention of the Japanese in Siberia with favour as they fear that the Japanese may require an unduly large reward for any assistance which may be rendered by them. It is possible that there may be good grounds for this apprehension, but on the other side it must be considered that if we win the war with the assistance of Japan, the United States and Great Britain will be very strong powers, which Japan as an Island Empire would hardly wish to antagonize. If, moreover, we oppose Japan when the latter is rightly or wrongly convinced that the time for action has arrived, there is a danger that such opposition may result in an alliance between Japan and Germany and Russia as a vassal of Germany.

The feeling exists here that as a result of the loss of valuable time Seminov will not now be able to hold Karimskai and Chita without aid, even should he succeed in taking them. The members of the Far Eastern Committee[5] and other Russians of influence here, though in many cases they are anxious to save their country and are exerting themselves to that end in varying degrees, suffer from the defects of their race; the progress made so far has, therefore, fallen very considerably short of what should have been accomplished by this time.

On March 14th General Horvat[6] and my Japanese colleague,[7] who was accompanied by Japanese military and railway officials, held a conference, and the French Military Attaché is of opinion that at this conference the question of the transportation of troops was discussed.

I am informed by the Russian Consul-General that each pair of machine guns supplied to Seminov by Japan will be accompanied by a Japanese gunner. I do not think it possible to keep secret the fact that we are also giving assistance to Seminov, though I understand that such secrecy is desirable until His Majesty's Government have decided whether they intend openly to oppose the Bolshevists or not.

It is clear that any appreciation of the Russo-Japanese position in Manchuria which fails to take into account inter-Allied interests in the Southern and Northern Railway systems must be imperfect. It is neither the desire of the Russian nor of the Japanese Railway authorities that their influence and position shall be weakened by the Chinese, and the fact that the Chinese Eastern Railway have now appointed a Chinese President, a post which has been left vacant since 1900, must be distasteful to both. In my opinion the Chinese would have been better advised had they postponed this appointment until a later stage.

According to a telegraphic report received yesterday from a reliable source from Pogram Chnaya large numbers of Bolshevists were advancing upon that place. In recent fighting at Blagovestchensk some Japanese were killed.

[5] The Far Eastern Committee for the Defense of the Fatherland and the Constituent Assembly, an anti-Bolshevik group organized in Harbin in late January or early February 1918. This body, organized by Popov and other former czarist officials, was receiving some military aid from the Japanese government. See the index references in James W. Morley, *The Japanese Thrust into Siberia, 1918* (New York, 1957).

[6] Dmitrii Leonidovich Horvat (or Horvath), general manager of the Chinese Eastern Railway and *de facto* governor general of the area of northern Manchuria adjacent to that railway line.

[7] That is, the Japanese consul general at Harbin, Naotake Satō.

ENCLOSURE II

Handed me by Lord Reading
Mch 21/18 RL

PARAPHRASE OF A TELEGRAM from the BRITISH CONSUL AT HARBIN.
(Received March 21, 1918. via Peking.)

I have received the following information as to conditions in Siberia from the Acting British Vice-Consul at Irkutsk[1] and from the British Embassy at Petrograd. The information is based upon statements made to the Vice-Consul by Colonel Jakovlef,[2] who was recently in command at Irkutsk of the prisoners of war camp. The information was brought to Harbin by an American Secretary of the Y.M.C.A. whose journey from Blagovestchensk took six days.

"There is a movement of German soldiers to Irkutsk from Tomsk, where maxims, ammunition and shells are being concentrated. A composite army corps is now being formed under Stenberg,[3] who is a Swede, at Irkutsk. One division is two-thirds German and one-third Austrian and the other division is Russian. German officers are adopting Russian names and a German chief of general staff is now on his way from Petrograd. Up to date 4000 Cossacks have joined under the command of Lazo,[4] and Cossacks are offered pay of 21 rubles a month. Small lots of prisoners dressed as civilians are arriving in Irkutsk, and ammunition is being forwarded as ordinary baggage by passenger trains. There are now 58 aeroplanes in store at Krasnoyarsk and 36 motor cycles and 12 armoured cars have been sent from Petrograd.

"The number of German prisoners now in Siberia is 80,000 and Jakovlef was recently asked how many he could accommodate at Irkutsk; he replied that he could accommodate 10,000, and he was informed that this number, all of German nationality, would be sent in a few days. In the event of the Manchurian frontiers remaining closed, all foreign consuls and diplomatic officers will be detained and if the Japanese undertake active operations the Japanese Consular representative at Irkutsk[5] will be executed. Orders have been given to destroy all tunnels and bridges as soon as information is received that forces are approaching from the East. Enemy prisoners are now guarding the Arsenal at Irkutsk, which contains 10,000 rifles and a good supply of ammunition and small arms.

[1] Unidentified.
[2] Nikolai Nikolaevich Ikovlev (or Yakovlev), president of the Central Executive Committee of the All-Siberian Congress of Soviets.
[3] Or Strenberg, the Soviet military commander of the Irkutsk district. He cannot be further identified.
[4] Sergei Georgievich Lazo, leader of the Bolshevik military force in Transbaikalia in pursuit of Gregorii M. Semenov. Lazo became a Soviet hero after his execution by the Japanese in 1920.
[5] Unidentified.

"The Germans are generally believed to have started the rioting at Irkutsk. In order to enable Austrian soldiers to return to Austria, an office has been opened with the special object of supplying them with false passports."

Lazo is in command of the Bolsheviki forces who were engaged with Semenov lately, and only included 250 cossacks. The information given in other respects is generally in accordance with that given in my most recent messages.

I learn that the French Consul-General at Irkutsk[6] has telegraphed to the French Consular agent his intention of departing shortly and the Intelligence Officers under Colonel Pichon are being withdrawn. The authorities of the local Y.M.C.A. are recommending to the State Department that their organization should at once leave Siberia.

The casualties of the Japanese in the fighting at Blagovestchensk amounted to 4 killed and about 10 wounded and 8 missing. There was Japanese militia present, and I hear that the Commanding Officer was a regular Japanese Colonel passing as a civilian merchant. I hear also that the conflicts already reported arose owing to the attempt of the Bolsheviki to disarm the Japanese militia.

All the information in our possession as to conditions in Siberia indicate the urgent need of an occupation in strength of at least Karchinskaya. This, however, I fear seems to be beyond the power of Semenov alone and the moment appears to have come when considerable danger must arise if there is any further delay in deciding the question of Japanese intervention.

TC telegrams (SDR, RG 59, 861.00/1432½, DNA).

[6] Gaston Bourgois.

From Edward Mandell House, with Enclosures

Dear Governor: New York. March 21, 1918.

I am enclosing you a copy of a letter from Lawrence Lowell. I do not think there will be any difficulty in getting these League to Enforce Peace people to do anything you desire. So far, I have succeeded in keeping them from doing anything and I have no doubt it will be easy to have them continue that policy.

The only thing I have suggested is that they unofficially and independently formulate their ideas from time to time so that when the peace conference comes, you may have the benefit of their thoughts—if they have any. This is as near as one can get to an innocuous policy. If an attempt is made to go further than that, they might become unruly.

The Archbishop of York is to take lunch with me on April 11th and I had thought to ask Mr. Taft, Lowell and Root to join us. Root, as you know, belongs to a different group. His is the "World Court." He, too, expresses a desire to confrom [conform] to your wishes. If I get them all together I believe I can bring about a definite understanding that nothing be done further than I have indicated.

Please let me know if you disagree with this.

I received your message through Gordon about Henderson and I shall do nothing until I hear from you. I would suggest that I send a despatch to Frazier asking him to express to Henderson your thanks and warm appreciation for his message. Simply that and nothing more.

As to Frazier's sitting in the Supreme War Council, that, I think, had better be left until Wiseman arrives on the other side. He is leaving in a week. He promises to get both from the British and French their feeling about Frazier and without saying anything further than that we have expressed a doubt to him, Wiseman, as to whether it was the proper thing to do.

Wiseman is going over to get the lay of the land and is to return immediately to report. I wish you could see him before he sails. I think it would be of value. He will be in Washington on Monday.

I am still feeling the effects of grip and am not very well, although I am perfectly able to go to Washington at any time if it is necessary. I have a bad cough and am not altogether a desirable companion.

Affectionately yours,   E. M. House

P.S. I also enclose a copy of a letter from Lord Robert Cecil.

TLS (WP, DLC).

E N C L O S U R E   I

Abbott Lawrence Lowell to Edward Mandell House

Dear Colonel House: Cambridge. March 13, 1918.

I am afraid that I did not make the object of my last letter clear. I had no idea of proposing that the Entente Powers should start during the war a League of Nations with the hope of getting the Central Powers and the Neutrals to join later; and if the first paragraph of the draft I sent you gave that impression it certainly was not so intended. In deference to some English opinion, this first paragraph was drawn so as to provide that the League, when formed at the close of the war, should consist prima facie of the Entente Powers; but I think it would be better to change it so that any of the Central Powers that were admitted would be admitted as primary members on the formation of the League. A plan for an immediate league has been proposed by some members of our organization, but I have always opposed it.

Last night I was talking with the Archbishop of York, and the ideas of his group and ours in the League to Enforce Peace seem to agree very closely. He tells me that he is to see you again before he sails.

I sent you the extract from Lord Bryce's letter because he thought it would be better to have a joint commission appointed by the governments of the two countries. As you are virtually such a commission on the part of our Government, I want to coordinate the work of the League to Enforce Peace with yours. I gathered from your letter that you think it is better not to have a governmental joint commission, but to have plans made independently, though keeping in touch with one another.

The essential point in the plan we are drawing up in the League to Enforce Peace is that the executive authority of the League, so far as executive action is needed, should be in the hands of the rulers, or the direct representatives of the rulers, of the governments whose action in matters of peace and war will be decisive. The experience of the English House of Lords shows that a body, however great the personal distinction of its members may be, cannot have any considerable authority if it does not represent political forces.

The plan also provides for a position in the League of small permanently neutral states, which I believe necessary for their preservation and for a state of peace.

I should be glad if you would make any suggestions to keep us in touch with your work.

Very truly yours,   A. Lawrence Lowell.

E N C L O S U R E   I I

Lord Robert Cecil to Edward Mandell House

Dear Colonel House: London. February 16, 1918.

I write to you because I know that you have been specially charged by the President with the superintendence of all questions which need preparation in connection with the Peace Conference.

I think you will agree with me that the "League of Nations" will be one of those questions, and we have therefore appointed a Committee[1] to enquire, particularly from a juridical and historical point of view, into the various schemes for establishing, by means of a league of nations or other device, some alternative to war as a means of settling international disputes, to report on their practicability, to suggest amendments, or to elaborate a further scheme if on consideration it should be deemed possible and expedient.

We do not at present intend to publish the fact of the formation of this Committee. The Chairman is Sir Walter Phillimore lately Lord Justice of Appeal, and a well known authority on International Law, and the author of a recent work entitled "Three Centuries of Treaties of Peace," a copy of which I hope you will accept from me.[2]

I do not know whether your staff is also engaged on a similar task, but if they are it has occurred to me that if we could establish cooperation, it would be a mutual benefit to us. If you share this view would you be inclined to let me know, for our confidential information, the lines on which you are working, and I will undertake to keep you similarly informed.

Yours very sincerely,   Robert Cecil.

TCL (WP, DLC).
  [1] About this committee and its work, see George W. Egerton, *Great Britain and the Creation of the League of Nations: Strategy, Politics, and International Organization, 1914-1919* (Chapel Hill, N. C., 1978), pp. 65-69.
  [2] Sir Walter George Frank Phillimore, *Three Centuries of Treaties of Peace and Their Teaching* (London, 1917).

From Elizabeth Herndon Potter

New York, March 21, 1918.

Glorious suffrage victory in Texas Senate, Governor's signature certain. You help a lot. Hotel McAlpin.

Elizabeth H. Potter.

T telegram (WP, DLC).

From George H. Slater

San Antonio, Texas, March 21, 1918.

The following resolution was unanimously adopted by Texas Federation of Labor and voices sentiment organized wage earners of Texas:

WHEREAS organized labor affiliated with the Texas State Federation of Labor has evidenced its loyalty to our Government by its men in trenches and the opening of its treasuries in the support of the war against autocracy, and

WHEREAS, in spite of all we have done and are doing the enemies of labor would have the public believe that organized labor is not doing its full duty in this hour of our nation's crisis, be it

RESOLVED, as further evidence of our loyalty that the Texas State Federation of Labor in its 21st annual convention assembled in the City of San Antonio, March 18, 1918, pledge its members to any sacrifice needed, be it our lives, that lives of our loved ones, or our treasuries and in the conduct of our affairs to exhaust every means to avoid cessation of labors that our members are loyal to President Woodrow Wilson and his Administration, fully realizing the responsibility resting upon organized labor.

Geo. H. Slater,   Secretary.[1]

T telegram (WP, DLC).

[1] "Please refer this to Mr. Gompers. I am not familiar with the circumstances referred to in the second 'Whereas' and would very much value advice from Mr. Gompers as to a reply." WW to [JPT], c. March 21, 1918, TL (WP, DLC).

To Edward Mandell House

My dear House,   The White House. 22 March, 1918.

Yes, indeed, I think your lunch with Taft, Lowell, and Root is most wise and should be most helpful, if they have any sense among them,—which I sometimes seriously doubt.

My own conviction, as you know, is that the administrative *constitution* of the League must *grow* and not be made; that we must *begin* with solemn covenants, covering mutual guarantees of political independence and territorial integrity (if the final territorial agreements of the peace conference are fair and satisfactory and *ought* to be perpetuated), but that the method of carrying those mutual pledges out should be left to develop of itself, case by case. Any attempt to begin by putting executive authority in the hands of any particular group of powers would be to sow a harvest of jealousy and distrust which would spring up at once and choke the whole thing. To take one thing, and only one, but quite sufficient in itself:

The United States Senate would never ratify any treaty which put the force of the United States at the disposal of any such group or body. Why begin at the impossible end when there is a possible end and it is feasible to plant a system which will slowly but surely ripen into fruition?

As for the message to Henderson, I suggest this, in view of an interview I had yesterday with Samuel Gompers: Express my sincere appreciation of the confidence he generously reposes in me and say that I would like to convey to him the intimation that it would make a bad impression in this country if any group of men were to visit it who would be understood to represent a party, whether that party be national or international, the people of this country being just now intolerant of parties and impatient of special missions, and this qwite [quite] irrespective of the welcome they might in other circumstances wish to extend to the individuals composing this group.

I suggest this in view of the fact that there is a plan afoot to have a group of Socialist-Labour Party leaders (English, French, Belgian) visit the United States "to confer with the American Federation of Labour," to whom their visit would be unwelcome, for the purpose of making interest among them in favour of an international Socialist-Labour conference, at Stockholm or Berne or some other neutral city, to which German Socialists would be invited to discuss peace! The whole plan is outrageous and fraught with the greatest mischief.

When you feel wholly fit, come down (we shall not need more than an hour's notice) and we will have one of our clearing talks, which I stand in much need of.

We are happy that you are getting well, and all join in affectionate messages.   Affectionately Yours,   Woodrow Wilson

WWTLS (E. M. House Papers, CtY).

To Robert Lansing

My dear Mr. Secretary,   The White House. 22 March, 1918.

I am much obliged to you for sending these papers[1] to me so promptly, but I do not find in them sufficient cause for altering our position. They still do not answer the question I have put to Lord Reading and to all others who argue in favour of intervention by Japan, namely, What is it to effect and how will it be efficacious in effecting it? The condition of Siberia furnishes no answer.

Faithfully Yours,   W.W.

WWTLI (SDR, RG 59, 861.00/1433½, DNA).
[1] The Enclosures with RL to WW, March 21, 1918.

To Morris Sheppard

My dear Senator: [The White House] 22 March, 1918

It is certainly generous of you to consult me about the bill[1] which I am returning with this letter, and I know that you really desire my frankest opinion.

My feeling is, therefore, that the introduction and discussion of such a bill, at any rate at the present session of the Congress, might operate seriously to disturb and delay the necessary business of this session, and that I should very much deplore.

Besides, my dear Senator, it would undoubtedly introduce a new element of disturbance in the labor situation which I should dread, because I would know of no way in which it could be quieted. I have received delegations of working men who, apparently speaking with the utmost sincerity, have declared that they would regard it as a genuine hardship if they were deprived of their beer, for example. There is no arguing with feelings of that sort, and just because there is no arguing with them there would be no way of handling them in this time of crisis.

With warm appreciation of your consideration,

Sincerely yours,   Woodrow Wilson

TLS (Letterpress Books, WP, DLC).
¹ See M. Sheppard to WW, March 20, 1918.

From Benedict Crowell

My dear Mr. President: Washington, March 22, 1918.

I am enclosing herewith copy of an important cablegram just received from General Bliss,¹ with the recommendation of the War Department that the American Government concur in the recommendations of Generals Foch, Rawlinson and Tasker H. Bliss as given in paragraph 3 of the cablegram.

Sincerely,   Benedict Crowell

TCL (WDR, RG 407, World War I Cablegrams, DNA).
¹ T. H. Bliss to RL et al., No. 55, Very Confidential, March 21, 1918, received March 22, 1918, 4:18 a.m., T telegram (WDR, RG 407, World War I Cablegrams, DNA). This telegram reported on the recommendation, in paragraph 3, of Generals Foch, Rawlinson, and Bliss to transfer two Italian, two French, and one British division from the Italian front to the western front. "In order to reach harmonious agreement it is very desirable that American Government should immediately concur in the recommendations of Generals Foch, Rawlinson and Tasker H. Bliss as given in paragraph three above. The prompt concurrence of American government will probably settle the matter at once. Please telegraph me decision."

To Benedict Crowell

My dear Mr. Sec'y,   [The White House] 22 March, 1918.

I do not feel that I am qualified to form an independent judgment on the question here submitted to me and I am glad to concur in the judgment of Gen'l Bliss.

Faithfully Yours,   Woodrow Wilson

TCL (WDR, RG 407, World War I Cablegrams, DNA).

From Robert Lansing, with Enclosure

My dear Mr. President: Washington March 22, 1918.

I enclose for your consideration a telegram which I prepared to send to Ambassador Sharp stating our position in reference to unofficial international conferences, which is in response to the statements made at the meeting of the Supreme War Council, or, rather, of the premiers of the Allied Governments on the 16th instant.

In case you approve of the telegram will you kindly return it, and also inform me whether you think it desirable to repeat it to London and Rome?   Faithfully yours,   Robert Lansing.

Approved as altered W.W.

TLS (SDR, RG 59, 763.72119/1529½B, DNA).

ENCLOSURE

Washington, March 22, 1918.

Frazier's No. 28. FOR FRAZIER.

You may communicate to the Minister of Foreign Affairs, in substance the following, as a statement of the attitude of this Government in regard to unofficial international conferences such as the proposed conference of representatives of the Socialist and Labor Parties of the countries at war.

The discussion of international questions of a political character by representatives of a political party or group with similar representatives from other countries can accomplish no good purpose and may seriously embarrass the Governments which are solely responsible to their people for the conduct of international affairs. The success of a democratic government depends upon submission to the will of the majority which finds expression in the popular election of public agents authorized to exercise the sovereign power. Until those agents are replaced by the people their policies, so far as other nations are concerned, are the policies of the nation, and no course of action by individuals, except through the channels of internal politics, should be permitted when it tends to weaken or affect a government's international policies.

Unofficial international conferences upon political subjects, since they do not and cannot express the popular will of the nations from which the delegates come, are liable to cause confusion and create false impressions which may work irreparable harm in carrying out the national policies of the responsible authorities, and this is especially true if the conferees represent minority political parties *and include representatives of enemy nations.*[1]

It would, therefore, in the opinion of this Government, be unwise and dangerous to the vital interests of a nation to permit, and much less to encourage, such unauthorized conferences ⟨particularly⟩[2] during the progress of war when the national safety demands unity of purpose and undivided loyalty to the government chosen by the people.[3]   Lansing

TS telegram (SDR, RG 59, 763.72119 SO, DNA).
  [1] WWhw.
  [2] Wilson's deletion.
  [3] This was sent as RL to W. G. Sharp, March 22, 1918, TS telegram (SDR, RG 59, 763.72119 SO, DNA).

From Lee Slater Overman

My dear Mr. President: Washington, D. C. March 22, 1918.

I beg to tender you my sincere appreciation of your very kind letter. I had a hard fight in the Committee, but am proud the administration was sustained by even a larger majority than I expected.

Now as to the question of proceeding with the consideration of the bill upon the floor of the Senate permit me to say, my dear Mr. President, that in my judgment it will be best to allow the bill to soak for about a week or ten days, as I believe the sentiment in favor of its passage will grow stronger and stronger every day. Let the Senators consider it and talk about it in the cloak room, and I think we will stand a better chance of passing it without a filibuster.

I gave notice in the Senate yesterday that I would call up the bill immediately upon the passage of the Indian Appropriation Bill, which is next in order upon the Calendar. However, my dear Mr. President, if it is your desire that we proceed with it at once I will endeavor to get the consent of the Senate to allow me to take it up right away. But I feel sure the wise thing to do is to delay its consideration for a few days.

        Most cordially and sincerely yours,   Lee S. Overman

TLS (WP, DLC).

To Lee Slater Overman

My dear Senator: [The White House] 22 March, 1918

I have just been handed your kind letter of this morning. I did not at all intend to have any judgment of mine about the passage of the bill overrule or conflict with your own. I am quite ready to put myself entirely in your hands with regard to the time at which its passage is to be pressed. I thank you sincerely for advising me with regard to the situation. I am sure you will keep in close touch with it and act at the proper moment.

Cordially and sincerely yours,   [Woodrow Wilson]

CCL (WP, DLC).

From Grosvenor Blaine Clarkson, with Enclosure

My dear Mr. President: Washington 22 March, 1918

Mr. Rosenwald has told me of your fine letter to him of the other day[1] and of your desire, as I recall it, to obtain from him thoughts on the future life of the Council and Advisory Commission. I am not Julius Rosenwald, than whom I know of nobody with more of the genius of common sense, but perhaps you will find something of use in the enclosed memorandum. If it has value it is possibly because in the thirteen months I have been down here I have dealt far more with the outside than with the official world.

If you will permit me a personal expression I would like to say that, as in the case of a good many men these changing days, I was a man without a party when I came to Washington, my early affiliations through family tradition having been with the old order in the Republican ranks. But it gives me the most genuine and sincere pleasure now to offer you the assurance of my loyal regard and adherence.   Faithfully yours,   Grosvenor Clarkson

TLS (WP, DLC).
[1] WW to J. Rosenwald, March 7, 1918, Vol. 46.

E N C L O S U R E

22 March, 1918

A memorandum on the past and future
functions of the Council of National
Defense, by Grosvenor B. Clarkson,
Secretary of the Council and of the
Advisory Commission.

The Council of National Defense, in its present form, was born almost overnight to meet the nation's need. Created by act of Congress in August, 1916, it was then designed to be a body for peace-time effort—an agency primarily for the coordination of industries and resources for the national security and welfare before war should come upon the land. It would seem, however, that the Pres-

ident and the authors of the enabling act had almost an inspirational
insight into what was to be America's task, for when we finally
entered the war the embryo organization of the Council constituted
the only available mechanism whereby on a large scale to rally and
to utilize the industrial, engineering, and scientific genius of the
country for the Union's defense.

The Council, its Advisory Commission, and their subordinate
bodies were not permanently organized until early in March, 1917.
At no time has the Council had mandatory power in carrying out
its purpose, yet after twelve months of war it has, almost solely
through its initial vision of seizing upon and translating into action
the theory of voluntary cooperation, become a unique body in governmental affairs and put behind it a volume of pioneer and fruitful
work probably not to be equalled in the history of federal administration. That is a pretty strong statement, but let us examine the
facts.

The Call to Industry

The Council has made three chief contributions to America's part
in the war. By summoning to Washington the unquestioned leaders
of industry, engineering, and science, and putting these men to
work with no other persuasion than that of the most poignant of
appeals, love of country, it opened new paths along which government and industry have come to a better understanding each of
the other, and encouraged those eminent in industrial and professional life to bend their energies to the common effort. And the
country knows the foregoing to be the fact.

Secondly, through the principle of voluntary cooperation, the
Council has very largely eliminated profiteering in connection with
the war making of the United States, and in doing so has undoubtedly raised a higher standard both of industry and of government.
It is this same principle (and perhaps only this principle) which
has made it possible for one division alone of the Council, that of
raw materials, minerals, and metals, under Bernard M. Baruch of
the Advisory Commission, to save to the nation sums running into
hundreds of millions of dollars through the reduction of prices on
iron and steel as against the pre-war prices for those commodities.
It is obvious that such cooperation should bring a new philosophy
into American governmental affairs, and make all of us realize anew
that the American nation, properly appealed to and justly dealt with,
is simply a partnership of one hundred million persons seeking,
sometimes blindly, sometimes with irritation, sometimes with undue sentimentality, but still always fundamentally seeking, to fuse
their interests, material and spiritual, into a national unity.

Thirdly, the Council has performed a well-nigh priceless function in acting as a sort of official incubator for new ideas necessary to win a war under modern conditions. Few people realize to what an extent the Council has either conceived or adopted such ideas, passed them through the crucible of investigation and research, vitalized them with the touch of organization, and moved them on to one or another of the executive departments of the government. Witness, among other instances, the Aircraft Production Board, the Committee on Coal Production, and the Industrial Service Section. The Council created these vital bodies, and then allowed them, or the fruit of their labors, to be allocated to their proper and permanent abiding places in the government. (Many of the specific accomplishments of the Council are detailed in the opening pages of its first annual report.) In closing this thought, which could easily be developed into a volume, I cannot refrain from pressing farther afield and thinking of Pan-Germany and its brilliant and terrible success in the application of political science to modern war—the study, as M. Andre Cheradame has put it,[1] of geography, ethnology, political economy, and national psychology in the pursuance of Germany's dreams of conquest, dreams that have come true, for Central Pan-Germany is now a fact almost trite.

A National Clearing House

Particularly when war comes to a democracy in these days with all the tremendous organizing ability which modern conflict relentlessly demands of nations, there must be a head-center as well as a central germinating point for the conception and analysis of the ideas and needs brought forward by the hour—a clearing house of national problems, if you please. Through the irresistible force of circumstances the Council has been made this common focus. The extent to which the truth of this, consciously or unconsciously, has sunk into the mind of the country may be gained by a perusal of the thousands of newspaper and magazine editorials on the work of the Council which are on file in my office and which show a tacit or affirmative realization of the role that the Council has played during the epic twelve months through which we have just lived, and a complete acceptance of it as an organic (I am tempted to write a paternal) body of the government. I am particularly familiar with this angle of the matter since a part of my work here for thirteen months has been to act as the official mouthpiece of the Council in dealing with the newspapers of the country. The indisputable fact is—and those who have been wise enough to keep their vision projected out of Washington into the country at large

[1] That is, André Chéradame, *The United States and Pangermania* (New York, 1918).

will admit the truth of it—that the Council has seized upon the imagination of the nation to such a thoroughgoing extent that it would be administrative homicide to permit its annihilation to any radical degree. The Council and its works were thrust into the consciousness of the people at a time when the country's receptivity was at white heat, and it would probably mean years of effort on the part of the government to raise up another similar body possessing in equal measure the hold which the Council has gained upon the public. There are those who keep their minds immovably fixed here in Washington, allowing their perspective to be increasingly blunted by the loose and superficial criticisms that are the chief disease of this city, who will question the truth of the foregoing statements; but nobody can do so who will examine into the full picture on the canvas, who will listen more to the voice of the small American town than to the voice of the hotel lobbies of Washington.

Hence in the mutability of things it has been necessary for the Council of National Defense to hold itself essentially a flexible organization. War today is primarily a conflict of the mechanic and the machine, and the direction of the vast and delicate mechanism of American industry demands great administrative elasticity. The Council is and can be in no sense a fixed institution, but must continue its evolution swiftly enough to move parallel with the current of the times and yet with equal wisdom must maintain a conservatism sufficient to avoid lack of correlation and the cohesion of purpose and action synonymous with sane and scientific government.

Reconstruction Questions

The time is approaching, if not at hand, when we must consider squarely the problems of reconstruction. Is it not reasonable to assume that all of the hard-won experience that the Council has gathered in touching the life of the country so intimately at almost every point cannot be dispensed with when this new task is thrust before us? Is not the Council the proper central quarter for this work? There has been accumulated through its activities fresh knowledge of America and its potentialities that it would be almost criminal not to apply in considering the post-war problems of the republic.

Finally, while a great deal of interpretation of the work of the government to the people is going on through authorized news channels, the fact is too often ignored—indeed it seldom occurs to anybody—that the Council is the chief medium through which to procure for the government information concerning the varied life of the country. It is as vital to have a sentient channel along which shall be carried the moods and aspirations of a people at war to those who are fusing and directing the efforts of that people, as it is to keep the public informed as to what is afoot at the seat of government. There is no other agency under the government which in a broad way begins to approach the contribution of the Council in this respect. A writer in the New York Tribune, to whom I gave some of these thoughts the other day, published an article in which appear the following sentences:

"* * * Even its critics will unite in asking that its new life be recognized as valuable and necessary in a unique sense to the nation at war. Certainly it is difficult to deny value to any agency that reaches out from the capital to almost every county in the states in a manner that is particularly personal, particularly close to the lives of the people who must fight the war and who must pay for it in blood and money. The Council of National Defense is not at Washington. It only comes to Washington.

"There may be even another day, when soldiers return and men try to pick up the broken ends and take up their wonted ways, when the Council of National Defense, a living framework touching the United States wherever they are living and sensitive, will be the chief agency for drawing the nation out of the hypnotisms of war into the even progressions of peace."

For my own part, I feel that the Council and the Advisory Commission would be a great deal better off if they were divorced entirely from the War Industries Board and permitted to go back to their original and invaluable function of investigation and research, and to "the creation of relations which will render possible in time of need the immediate concentration and utilization of the resources of the nation." There would still remain the very vital and fruitful Commerical Economy Board, the function of which in essence is to clear business for action, and which, in my judgment, should remain precisely where it is, since its absorption by another organization would rob it decidedly of many things through which it has made a success; the State Councils Section, which has done a fine work in unifying state defense activities, and which in itself is a considerable organization; the Committee on Women's Defense Work, which is gradually coming into its own; the Highways Transport Committee, the Committee on Education, the National Research Council, acting as the department of science and research of the Council, and the highly valuable Medical Section with its general medical board and thirty-five active sub-committees. The final disposition of the Committee on Labor under Mr. Gompers is of course an open question which I purposely do not discuss here.

Here then would be a compact and motive body nowhere in conflict with the executive departments of the government, and yet a body with a distinct and logical reason for existence. I also venture the suggestion that the Council of National Defense is the rational center from which *to direct a close-knit and concentrated secret service* organization, than which there are few greater needs under this government today. Thus would the Council emerge from its present more or less nebulous state and thus would be obtained the sharp line of demarcation which it is elementary to have for clean-cut and efficient administration. Of the need for such a definite agency, whether in war or in peace, there can be no question. There is still one further need, however: That the Council in the future content itself not merely with the mobilization and scrutiny of material things, but in far greater measure give heed to the spiritual sense of America, the sense that in the long run must pay the bills of this war and make endurable the sacrifices that are now just around the corner of our common life.

T MS (WP, DLC).

From George Wylie Paul Hunt

My dear Mr. President: Phoenix, Arizona March 22, 1918.

I am in receipt of your confidential letter of the 11th instant[1] and that you took the time to give my telegram the careful personal consideration that your letter evidences is a source of much satisfaction to me and places me under one more obligation to you.

I am very briefly going to take advantage of your very kind suggestion of further communication on the subject, not through any personal considerations because looking at the matter from the personal viewpoint of Captain Wheeler's appointment I would now consider the incident closed if I had ever opened it on that basis. But it is from the aspect of industrial peace in our State, in the United States and, I believe without any exaggeration, in all of the Allied nations that I view the matter. In that connection, I want to make two quotations from the stenographic report of the proceedings of your Mediation Commission during the sessions held at Bisbee, November first to fifth of last year. In addressing Sheriff Wheeler, then on the stand, Secretary Wilson, Chairman of the Commission, said:

"It is being used over there and used against us with the Russian workmen and Russian peasants, trying to make them think we are not a democratic government, that, in fact, we are a plutocratic government, and these things are cited as instances that this is an autocracy, and so on, all of which we know is not true, but the instance is used and we cannot deny it, and so it puts us in an embarrassing situation."

As Sheriff Wheeler was leaving the stand Commissioner Walker said to him:

"I believe this thing that has been done here has injured our government more than any one thing that has been done in years."

If these things were true then how much more emphatic they are now that Sheriff Wheeler has been commissioned. The report of the Commission that I have quoted from contains some six hundred and fifteen pages. Of course it has been impossible for me to review it thoroughly but it contains much that is germane to the present matter.

The thought has occurred to me that the letters of commendation that Sheriff Wheeler had from Senators Ashurst and Smith ante-dated the time of the Bisbee deportations. It is of course impossible for me to verify this belief without violating the confidence of your letter. I have entertained this possibility because last year when Sheriff Wheeler first thought of securing a commission he secured a letter from me recommending him. At that time I really believed that he possessed the three qualifications that has been my understanding the War Department considered paramount: military training and experience; general training and experience; character. Since July 12th I would credit Sheriff Wheeler with the first qualification only.

I realize that Sheriff Wheeler and his friends would consider that I am highly prejudiced in the matter. To that and as a final suggestion I would urge that you consult Secretary Wilson of the Department of Labor if you entertain any idea of going further into the matter of Sheriff Wheeler's qualifications and fitness as an officer of the United States Army in its great struggle for the safety of the world.   Very respectfully yours,   Geo. W. P. Hunt

TLS (WP, DLC).
    [1] WW to G. W. P. Hunt, March 11, 1918, Vol. 46.

From Lord Reading

My dear Mr. President,   Washington March 22nd/18

I thank you very cordially for your kind letter received this morning inviting Lady Reading and myself to dinner on April 1st.

Lady Reading and I appreciate the friendly thought of yourself and Mrs. Wilson and we shall have much pleasure in availing ourselves of your invitation.

I am forwarding your letter to the Archbishop and have also the honour to accept the invitation for him.

I have the honour to be

     My dear Mr President

          Yours with the highest respect   Reading

ALS (WP, DLC).

Two Letters from Robert Somers Brookings

My dear Mr President: Washington March 22, 1918.

Some two or three weeks ago, Secretary Houston requested Mr Baruch and myself to meet him in consultation with Mr Lever (Chairman of the Congressional Committee on Agriculture) for the purpose of making such changes in the original Price Fixing Bill prepared by Judge Lovett as would eliminate its application to agricultural products. This would have practically reduced its operations to metals, chemicals and their components, which through our war needs and existing commandeering laws, we have more or less in hand. Mr Baruch and I both argued that as the railroads have been taken over by the Government, and all building construction practically ceased, the only interest the civilian population has looking to stabilizing the cost of living is in agricultural products. Cotton, wool and leather, representing our clothing and of course the food products speak for themselves.

However, we arranged a subsequent meeting which included Judge Lovett in an endeavor to frame up something in the way of a bill meeting the views of Secretary Houston and Mr Lever, yet simplifying and improving our present methods of handling metals, chemicals, etc. After considerable discussion, Judge Lovett agreed to prepare something in the way of a bill which he thought would cover our needs. Meanwhile, however, he became interested in his new duties under the Director of Railroads, and finally asked to be relieved of having anything to do with it. Mr Baruch also, absorbed by his new responsibilities, and assuming that my enlarged interests in the matter of price fixing would, to some extent, qualify me for the work, requested me to personally look after it. Our Legal Department and Judge Parker[1] are now in consultation with me, and we hope in the near future to produce something that will meet with Secretary Houston and Mr Lever's approval. I cannot, however, Mr President, refrain from an earnest expression of opinion that the fundamental economic health of this country depends upon our stabilizing the cost of living with a view of preventing its rising above the present level or above what is generally termed double pre-war or normal base.

We have now what is known as a "runaway market" in manufactured cotton goods out of all proportion to even the high price of cotton. The manufacturers themselves, realizing the bad effect of this and possibly fearing some drastic legislation to regulate it, have requested our committee to meet them in conference Tuesday of next week with a view of our entering into some arrangement similar to that with the steel people. While the Government is, of course, using a much smaller proportion of cotton manufactured products than of steel, our needs have been sufficiently large to be mainly responsible for the present wild market condition. Of course, in meeting the cotton goods manufacturers, we face an utterly different condition in the initial raw material from that of steel, where by commandeering the ore, we had a pretty clearly defined method of enforcing control. This would not be the case with cotton, but, in my judgment, it would not be necessary as the conversion price which we could control by agreement would probably be all that is necessary.

As the initiative is taken by the cotton manufacturers, I could see no reason for our objecting to meet them next Tuesday with a view of hearing what they have to say, when we could take the matter up more directly with you before in any way committing ourselves.

I am writing you thus fully thinking you may wish to communicate with me further before the proposed meeting.

Awaiting your commands in the premises, believe me

Most respectfully yours,   Robt. S. Brookings

[1] Edwin Brewington Parker, corporation lawyer of Houston, Tex., at this time priorities commissioner of the War Industries Board.

My dear Mr. President: Washington March 22, 1918.

I herewith enclose an abstract of the minutes of a meeting of the steel manufacturers and the Price Fixing Committee, which completed its session yesterday, the 21st.[1]

You will notice that we have finally been able to place the larger manufacturers fairly on record approving a system by which production may be maintained without the necessity of advancing prices to the high level necessary for the protection of small producers through some method of the strong integrated companies assisting those less favored. We have also, by reducing the price of pig iron and scrap steel, inaugurated a reduction in the raw materials which are fundamental in fixing finished values.

The steel people showed a fine feeling throughout the meeting which encourages me to believe that (sustained by your authority) we will be able to exert through agreement with manufacturers, a stabilizing influence on many other industries.

I enclose the usual statement to be given to the press if our recommendations meet with your approval.[2]

Respectfully yours,   Robt. S. Brookings

TLS (WP, DLC).
[1] "Abstract of Minutes of Steel Meeting," c. March 21, 1918, T MS (WP, DLC). In addition to the decisions summarized by Brookings above, the participants in the meeting had agreed to extend the prices previously fixed for ore, coke, steel, and steel products for another three months to July 1, 1918.
[2] Wilson returned this enclosure.

From Bainbridge Colby

My dear Mr. President: Washington March 22, 1918.

I am in receipt of the inclosed letter from ex-President Taft[1] and, by a later mail, of the letter of Mr. W. H. Short,[2] Secretary of the League to Enforce Peace, which I also inclose, together with some accompanying data.

I have underscored two sentences in Mr. Taft's letter which bear directly on the point,[3] and have indicated in brackets on the prospectus of the convention the sections which seem to warrant particular attention. I am of opinion that Mr. Taft thoroughly understands your point of view and that the situation requires nothing further than an acknowledgment by me of his letter and, possibly, a renewed expression of confidence in his ability to carry out the assurances given in his interview with me.

Very sincerely yours,   Bainbridge Colby

TLS (WP, DLC)
[1] W. H. Taft to B. Colby, March 19, 1918, CCL (W. H. Taft Papers, DLC). Taft sent Colby a copy of the tentative program of the national meeting of the League to Enforce Peace to be held in Philadelphia in May.
[2] The Rev. William Harrison Short, Congregational minister active in the peace movement in the United States.
[3] The sentences underscored by Colby were probably these (they followed Taft's statement that he was enclosing a copy of the tentative program for submission to Wilson): "Mr. Short will, however, send you tomorrow a statement of the commitments that we have made in respect to the May Convention and the well-nigh universal approval that we have received in editorial comment of the purpose of the Convention and of its being held. Of course there will be no difficulty in curbing any of our speakers in the subject matters they discuss or the opinions they may express, if there is a particular phase of the subject which the President would like to have omitted."

From Vance Criswell McCormick

Dear Mr. President: Washington March 22nd, 1918.

I have just heard that Mr. Colby is hesitating about speaking in the Wisconsin campaign on account of the opposition of some of the members of the Shipping Board.

We all think it very important that he keep the engagements we have made for him the end of next week, and will appreciate your urging him to go, if you think proper.

Sincerely yours,   Vance C. McCormick

TLS (WP, DLC).

From Herbert Clark Hoover

Dear Mr. President: Washington 22 March 1918

Please find enclosed a letter which I have dispatched today to Lord Reading on cereal supplies during the next three months.[1] Our office has worked out the most constructive method that we can think of to give further relief to the Allies. The problem revolves in fact on shipping, because if enough ships were placed at once at the disposal of the Allies, with sufficient pressure upon the Argentine, it appears to me that we could be relieved of pressure here by the end of May. The following figures will indicate to you approximately our present situation:

Wheat on Farms March 1st				111,000,000
" in Mills	"	"		36,700,000
" in Elevators	do			47,500,000
Flour Mills	do			10,000,000
				205,200,000
Less—				
Seed		30,000,000		
Farms Reserve		20,000,000		
Allies		50,000,000	100,000,000	
			105,200,000	

Five months to go at 21,000,000 = 105,000,000

In addition to the above we have a reserve of the floating stocks of flour in transit and in wholesalers' and retailers' hands which might be worked down to somewhat smaller dimensions, but this is but a small marginal reserve.

We are confronted with four serious matters. The first is that a compilation of the wheat marketed by farmers to March 1st, added to the existing wheat on the farms according to the Department of Agriculture reports, indicates that last year's crop was 40,000,000 to 50,000,000 bushels lower than the estimate. This is not an abnormal difference in estimate as all crop estimates are necessarily 10 to 15 per cent speculation, but, unfortunately, the difference is against us this year and adds to the seriousness of the whole position. We really had no export surplus at all, and we will by the end of March have exported about 100,000,000 bushels.

The second difficulty we are confronted with is the fact that in order to even carry out this programme, we must secure a further marketing of 60,000,000 bushels from the farmer, and I am afraid there is a great deal of hoarding, stimulated by the agitation in Congress. I have recently sent out a strong appeal to farmers to market their wheat before May 1st, and I feel that if we have not secured it by that date it may be necessary that I should propose to you that we should requisition all outstanding wheat. All of the loyal farmers will have marketed by that time and such a requisition would be received favorably by the majority of those.

The third difficulty lies in the fact that although we are getting a gradually increased substitute milling capacity by the conversion of wheat mills, we may have difficulty in keeping pace with the demand.

The fourth difficulty is our total lack of adequate authority to impose a competent control of distribution, that whatever we do must be based to a large degree on voluntary action and, to a secondary degree, on remote interpretation of the Food Bill.

A fifth difficulty lies in the present location of our wheat, we having dangerously exhausted those milling sections that must supply the industrial population. The programme outlined in my letter to Lord Reading supplies 800,000 tons per month from North America, against a total demand of about 1,500,000 tons. Their actual need by careful conservation and gradual expansion of stocks is probably 1,200,000 tons.

For all these reasons I feel we are not only taking great risks but asking the last mite from our own people.

Faithfully yours,   Herbert Hoover

TLS (WP, DLC).
¹ H. C. Hoover to Lord Reading, March 21, 1918, TCL (WP, DLC), in which Hoover stressed the necessity for Canada to make up its shortages in supplying large amounts of wheat to the United States to replace American grain shipped to the Allies, as had been previously agreed upon by the Inter-Allied Conference in November 1917.

From Edward Mandell House, with Enclosure

Dear Governor: New York. March 23, 1918.

I am enclosing you a cable which has come from Balfour and which explains itself.

I will send a cable to Frazier asking him to give your message to Henderson as you have outlined it. I think it important enough for Frazier to go to London and deliver it in person.

I think I can now definitely say that I will be down the early part of next week as I am feeling today, for the first time, something like my normal self.

I am glad to hear through Gordon that you were able to play golf today. I was afraid that you, too, might have this detestable grip.

Affectionately yours,   E. M. House

TLS (WP, DLC).

E N C L O S U R E

Dated March 22, 1918.
Received March 22, 1 p/m

Following for Col. House from Mr. Balfour:

No. 66. My telegram of March 12th.[1] Our messenger[2] reports interview with Austrian Agent and change of attitude on the part of Czernin, who no longer proposed meeting with British statesman on alleged ground that Allies are not so much interested in coming to real settlement with Austria-Hungary as in manoeuvring to detach her from Germany. Our messenger explained that H. M. Government's whole object in the war was not peace manoeuvre but final settlement of European problems on the principle of justice to all peoples, which was the only possible foundation for a lasting peace. He added that if H. M. Government were to agree to a meeting it would not merely be to discuss abstract principles, but their practical application to question at issue between Austria-Hungary and Entente, and mentioned especially cases of Italy, Serbia, Roumania, to all of which Austria-Hungary would have to make concessions in accordance with above principles. He added further that while British Government did not wish to interfere with internal affairs of other countries, it was impossible to draw absolute line between internal and external problems, and that internal questions could not be entirely excluded from discussion.

He finally made it clear that inasmuch as the German Government stood for exactly opposite principles of settlement, Allies would not consent in existing circumstances to be drawn into discussion of peace with Germany.

Austrian Agent thought this statement valuable and of interest to Czernin. He was very anxious to avoid any statement or suggestion that purpose of a meeting should be settlement of conditions of a separate peace and he would have liked our messenger to commit himself in this sense.

Our messenger definitely refused this and suggested only course was to leave matter open.

Position appears to be that if Czernin again proposes a meeting it will be for the purpose of arriving at settlement of all questions outstanding between Austria-Hungary and Allies—principle being, no bargaining of territory, but that of justice for all peoples in South Eastern Europe.

TC telegram (WP, DLC).
  [1] Printed as Enclosure I with EMH to WW, March 13, 1918.
  [2] That is, Philip Kerr.

From the White House Staff

                                          The White House.
Memorandum for the President: March 23, 1918

Former President Taft called on the telephone from New Haven to ask if the President could see President Lowell of Harvard and himself on Wednesday, Thursday or Friday of next week, if possible, concerning the forthcoming meeting of the League to Enforce Peace. Mr. Taft stated that the President had asked Mr. Colby to see him concerning the matter, and that he had sent some letters to Mr. Colby about it, but that Dr. Lowell and he thought it would be wise if they could have a personal conversation with the President.[1]

Mr. Taft asked if we would telegraph the President's decision to him at New Haven tonight or tomorrow.

T MS (WP, DLC).
  [1] Again, see the memorandum by William Howard Taft printed at March 29, 1918.

From Josephus Daniels

My dear Mr. President: Washington. 23rd of March, 1918.

I thank you for your letter of the 21st of March, enclosing one from Mr. Royal Meeker, with reference to providing for the functional and vocational rehabilitation of wounded soldiers and sailors which is now under consideration by the Council of National Defense. The Council meets next Monday afternoon and I will bring Mr. Meeker's letter up for consideration.

Sincerely,   Josephus Daniels

TLS (WP, DLC).

Count Ottokar Czernin von und zu Chudenitz to Prince zu Fürstenberg

MOST SECRET   Vienna 23.3.18.

With reference to the answer of H. M. the Emperor to the President's despatch so graciously transmitted by the King of Spain,[1] the Emperor forwards King Alfonso the following message for Mr. WILSON:

I. German Text.

"The reply made by the President to my communication respecting the fundamental principles of a just and lasting peace, strengthens me in the conviction that between those principles on the one hand and my own views on the other, such a degree of harmony exists as is necessary to start a successful discussion of the conditions of that peace which is so heartily longed for by all States. The President's reply contains nothing that deprives me of the hope that we may agree in the application of these principles. I am still of the opinion that the best method of procedure would be by means of direct oral discussion between one of my representatives and one appointed by Mr. Wilson. This would avoid a delay of many weeks. I believe that by so doing the President would be convinced that on the various special points mentioned by him we too are seeking a settlement from which, to use his own words, 'there is most probability of securing a lasting peace.' In this connection I can give the assurance that the satisfaction of the righteous national aspirations of those Slav peoples residing in such close proximity to my own territory, must be my earnest desire in the permanent interest of my country, because those populations are so intimately related to large masses of my subjects, as the President rightly points out. If the President on his part is prepared for similar propositions, we shall gladly stretch out our hand and do all in our power to improve the conditions of their existence, their progress and trade, without allowing them to be bartered about from one sovereignty to another. At the same time, we cannot permit populations to be transferred against their wishes from one State to another in the interest of one particular race, as this cannot be done without infringing the rights of other States. Such a discussion would furnish proofs that we are not pursuing any policy with reference to the Adriatic coast which conflicts with any of Mr. Wilson's principles, or have we any desire to alter the balance in this region in our favour. But if we do not wish to introduce new elements of discord calculated to disturb the peace of Europe in accordance with Mr. Wilson's intentions, we must avoid securing to any State such a preponderance which might lead to * * * , this would arise e.g. if Italy were to seek territorial aggrandisement in that quarter. The rivalry in the Balkans is due to the fact that up to the present there has been no final territorial settlement, but such can, however, be attained if an earnest endeavour is made to solve these questions in favour of the populations, as Mr. Wilson manifestly desires. I have already suggested in this connection that the relation of (?Bulgars) living in * * * with the mother country, the granting of the necessary commercial facilities to Serbia, etc., are questions for which a solution is to be sought and can be found by mutual agreement. Nor have I any doubt that, with regard to the protection of non-Turkish populations included in the Turkish Empire, a solution can be discovered which accords with the President's pronouncements and takes into full consideration the just claims of Turkey.

The President inquires further what definite concessions to Italy I should regard as just. In my opinion, I should regard as just those concessions which are in harmony with the principles enunciated by him. Now the territorial aspirations of the Italian State, as openly proclaimed in this war, do not agree in the slightest with the principles laid down by the President. Italy demanded that the whole of the territory as far as * * * and almost to LAIBACH,[2] should be ceded on strategical grounds. Those are the demands of a war of aggression. They are in contradiction with the President's principles. The population of the districts in question are in overwhelming majority German or Slav and both peoples have regarded it as a grave injustice to be subjected by force to a foreign State with which they have no community of interests, sentiment or ideas. If then I understand the President's question as it only can be understood in the light of his pronouncements—How far the definite wishes of Italy can be fulfilled 'not as part of a mere adjustment or compromise of rival States' (in this case Austria and Italy) but 'in the interests and in favour of the peoples concerned'—it is not possible to regard any concession as just. Italy is striving for the possession of territory inhabited by a larger number of Slavs and Germans than Italians. As the Italian minority has with difficulty maintained itself for more than 400 years in Austrian * * *, how can it aspire to the CARSO region,[3] the population of which is entirely Croatian and totally distinct from the Italians? Hence Italy desires to dominate a foreign people for whom the separation from Austria would mean commercial ruin. It would compel them to start a new existence. This would not be any solution in accordance with the President's large principles, according to which [']all territorial questions raised by this war must be adjusted in the interests and in favour of the populations affected.' The President will be convinced after what I have said that I, like himself, am honestly anxious to discover for the war settlement such a basis which will meet just claims and which consequently will contain the elements of permanence* * * * He will be convinced that I believe I have discovered such a basis in similar principles to those laid down by him. What remains to be established is whether, as I firmly believe and hope, we can agree as to the application of these principles in definite cases. The direct discussion proposed by me would have as its object to ascertain this and to supply each of us with the necessary information on this head. I hold that it is incumbent upon us to leave no avenue unexplored which offers any hope of restoring the vanished peace to our countries. In short, all belligerent States alike should pledge themselves to refrain from annexing foreign States and I can only repeat that, if the President will endeavour to influence his Allies in this direction. Austria too will do her utmost to induce her Allies to similar action. There is only one obstacle to peace that cannot be solved in open discussion, and that is the French and Italian lust of conquest. If the President can induce both these States to renounce their plans of annexation, he will render the cause of universal peace the greatest service.

    II. French translation in vieux c[h]iffre francais.

CZERNIN.

TC telegram (SDR, RG 59, 763.72119/8735, DNA).
    ¹ See Prince zu Fürstenberg to Count Czernin, March 5, 1918, Vol. 46.
    ² Later Ljubljana, the capital city of Slovenia, located seventy miles west, northwest of Zagreb.
    ³ The region which included Trieste, Ciceria, and Fiume.

Samuel Gompers to Joseph Patrick Tumulty

My dear Mr. Tumulty: Washington, D. C. March 23, 1918.

    Permit me to acknowledge receipt of your favor of the 22d instant with enclosed resolution adopted by the Texas State Federation of Labor and transmitted to the President by Mr. Geo. H. Slater, its Secretary. The language employed in the second Whereas, is that well known to the men in the labor movement, and hence when many bodies employ these terms they erroneously imagine that all are familiar with the situation.

Perhaps the recital of a few instances may be helpful. For years the Los Angeles Times and a few newspapers of the same caliber have attacked, abused, and denounced the labor movement and its men, stigmatizing both in vilest terms and opposing every species of legislation asked by the workers at the hands of the government of the United States, of the several states, and municipalities. Not a measure demanded or method employed but has received the same treatment at the hands of these publications.

The magazine American Industries later The Square Deal, issued monthly by the National Association of Manufacturers, pursued the same course as did the Los Angeles Times and other newspapers of that ilk.

The National Erectors' Association is founded principally upon antagonism to union labor and its activities are directed to the accomplishment of that purpose.

The National Association of Manufacturers conducted a system of espionage and secret lobbying against the workers' interests, the expose of which you know at least in part through the Congressional Committees.

The National Industrial conference declared by themselves to be an Eight Billion Dollar concern, started last year upon a campaign of "extermination" of organized labor.

The United States Steel Corporation is pronouncedly and openly anti-labor, and is closed to the employment of any worker who may be a member of an organization.

The overwhelming preponderance of the work of the various detective agencies throughout the country is a system of espionage upon workers who may join unions, to report them to the employers for dismissal, and in many instances where organization has not been entirely prevented, to provoke the workers to premature strikes and to defeat them and to trump up charges against innocent defenseless workers.

I am just reciting a few of these instances. They will give an insight of what workers of Texas in the State Federation convention know by experience and by authentic information they have.

Of course the President in his reply will express in the warmest terms his appreciation of the resolution of loyalty and devotion. He could make some reference of his understanding and gratitude for this position of the workers that they need fear no enemies or antagonists as to what hurt or injury they could do to the great humanitarian cause of labor, so long as they pursue the course which American labor has outlined for itself and that the efforts of the enemies of labor must and will prove abortive so long as the rational, natural and loyal course is faithfully adhered to and that he is persuaded and convinced that the toilers in this crucial time will give a good accounting of themselves.

With kindest personal regards, I am,

Sincerely yours,   Saml. Gompers

TLS (WP, DLC).

Pleasant Alexander Stovall to Robert Lansing

Pontarlier (Berne) March 23, 1918.

2920. Strictly Confidential. My 2886, March 18.

Herron has transmitted me copy Jong's telegram to The Hague after interview with Herron. Telegram follows: "Our plan, to which was added for explanation literal text of my scheme for note which I sent you by letter, was cabled officially today, Friday morning, to principal himself, together with Dressel-Huyse[1] telegraphic reply and accompanied by warm recommendation on the part of both Herman and his Berne chief. In order to *achieve* that not a single day be lost and because initiative from principal himself is scarcely conceivable and not even desirable, the two latter urgently recommend that your representative take the initiative by paying personal visit to principal and by further (?) plan by letter. Herman and his Berne chief have already cabled to principal prospect of similar visit which they recommend as desirable. They assure me that step in question will in no way be interpreted as unfriendly act now and that even in case proposal were repudiated absolute discretion will be guaranteed. Signed Jong."

The principal refers to President Wilson and Herman to Herron.

In transmitting Imperial Government text[2] Herron writes that he does not know whether Jong utterly failed to grasp the points presented to him with precision and emphasis or whether he deliberately distorted the matter. Herron then reiterates the points which he made to Jong which I have transmitted in previous telegrams. Herron believes that Jong was so eager to initiate something that might lead to peace that he was ready to make himself believe anything.

Herron concurs in my belief that no further communications or discussion should be held with Jong in this matter or in any other matters of importance.   Stovall.

T telegram (WP, DLC).

[1] Dr. Hendrick Coenraad Dresselhuys, former secretary general of the Department of Justice and member of Parliament in the Netherlands. He was the Netherlands member of the executive committee of the Central Organization for a Lasting Peace, which had its headquarters in The Hague.

[2] This text has not been identified. The reference may be to the text which Jong had proposed be sent by the Netherlands government to the governments of Germany and Austria-Hungary.

William R. Hollister[1] to Josephus Daniels

My dear Mr. Secretary: Washington, March 23rd, 1918

Our mutual friend Davies told me some days ago that he thought you would be willing to come to Wisconsin and make at least one speech for him next week. I have not bothered you until now about this matter because I wanted to wait until the situation had cleared somewhat. If you can go to Wisconsin and speak Friday or Saturday night I wish you would let me know and I will arrange a big meeting for you. If you desire to take this up with me in person I will come to the department and see you.

Very truly yours,   W. R. Hollister[2]

TLS (WP, DLC).
[1] Assistant Secretary of the Democratic National Committee.

[2] "The Secretary begs to call the President's attention to this letter addressed to Secretary Daniels. He thinks that Mr. Daniels should not go to Wisconsin." JPT to WW, c. March 27, 1918, TL (WP, DLC). "On the whole I agree with the Sec'y W.W." WWhw on *ibid*.

Peyton Conway March to Joseph Patrick Tumulty, with Enclosure

My dear Mr. Tumulty: Washington March 23, 1918.

I am enclosing herewith a copy of an important dispatch just received from General Bliss, for the information of the President. This in the absence of the Acting Secretary of War.

The town "Ham," referred to in the dispatch, is thirteen miles in a straight line in rear of the British line as it was when the German attack began.   Sincerely,   P. C. March

TLS (WP, DLC).

ENCLOSURE

Received at the War Department March 23, 1918, 6:30 P.M.

Rush. Number 59. For Acting Chief of Staff. Confidential and not to be made public.

Paragraph 1. Telephone despatches just received from both British and French General Headquarters state that Germans have taken town of Ham on the River Somme and have crossed the river at that place. If not promptly checked this creates grave situation as it will turn the British position along that river. Three French divisions are now arriving in accordance with agreement to extend French lines to Peronne.

Paragraph 2. Before foregoing news was received the Executive War Board unanimously passed following resolution which is now being carried into effect: "In view of the proportion reached by the battle now being fought the Executive War Board decides that it is absolutely necessary to bring back at once from Italy: two French divisions, four brigades of British field artillery, (not in divisional cadres), one British division. As any delay might have the most serious results the Executive War Board directs the execution of this movement."   Bliss

TC telegram (WP, DLC).

Arthur James Balfour to Lord Reading

[London] March 23 1918

No. 1711. Very Urgent.

Following from Lord Derby[1] begins.

You should appeal to President that we are engaged in what may well prove to be decisive battle of war. Germans are concentrating greater part of their available forces against British front and are pushing their attacks with greatest determination. We have every hope of checking him but our losses have been very heavy and will be heavier. This is only beginning of campaign of 1918 and we have to look to future. In present state of our manpower resources we cannot keep our divisions supplied with drafts for more than a short time at present rate of losses and we shall be helpless to assist our allies if as is very probable enemy turn against them later. We have divisional cadres ready with all necessary services and what we require is men to help us keep them filled. You should appeal to President to drop all questions of interpretation of past agreements and send over infantry as fast as possible without transport or other encumbrances. Situation is undoubtedly critical and if America delays now she may be too late.

Hw telegram (FO 115/2461, pp. 93-94, PRO).
[1] Edward George Villiers Stanley, 17th Earl of Derby, at this time Secretary of State for War but soon (in April) to become British Ambassador to France.

From Edward Mandell House

Dear Governor: New York. March 24, 1918.

Because of the great offensive now in progress Wiseman and I think it best for him not to go to Europe for the present. He will therefore not be in Washington tomorrow.

What would you think of sending a message to Field Marshal Haig, either through Pershing or Bliss, expressing our warm admiration for the courage and tenacity which the British troops are maintaining, and the high hope we have of their ultimate victory? It would please the people in this country and it would please the Allies to have you take this notice of the gallant defence which is now being made in Flanders.

I am sure this would be a good move.[1]

Affectionately yours,   E. M. House

TLS (WP, DLC).
[1] EMHhw.

From Robert Lansing

My dear Mr. President: Washington March 24, 1918.

If the reports, which persist, that the military prisoners in Siberia are being organized under German officers and have succeeded in occupying Irkutsk are confirmed, we will have a new situation in Siberia which may cause a revision of our policy. It would seem to me, therefore, that we should consider the problem on the hypothesis that the reports are true and be prepared to act with promptness.

The occupation of important points in eastern Siberia by a German military force and the helpless state of the Russians to resist the extension of the German power place the situation on an entirely different basis from the one presented by the chaotic state caused by quarreling Russian factions. The presence of the Germans and the possibility of their control of Siberia becomes a real menace to the peace of the Far East. The situation of Irkutsk is such that the Germans, if masters of the place, might invade Manchuria and obtain control of the Trans-Siberian Railway.

In view of these facts I do not see how Japan could be expected to refrain from taking military measures to resist further extension of the German power, nor do I think we could reasonably oppose their resistance to the German advance in that region. In fact I believe that in the circumstances Japan will act whether we approve or not. Would it then be the better policy to approve or to be in opposition to Japanese intervention?

With the actual control by the Germans of so important a place as Irkutsk the question of the moral effect upon the Russian people of an expedition against the Germans is a very different thing from the occupation of the Siberian Railway in order to keep order between contending Russian factions. It would seem to be a legitimate operation against the common enemy. I do not see how we could refuse to sanction such a military step.

The question presented, if intervention in Siberia seems advisable, is whether Japan alone or the Powers arrayed against Germany acting jointly should constitute the expeditionary force employed to overthrow the German power. I think that we must concede that in any event the burden of this task must fall upon Japan. No Power has forces available for this undertaking sufficiently strong to be a real factor in achieving the end desired. Furthermore Japan seems to be opposed to joint action. In the circumstances are not Japan's sensibilities more important than the sensibilities of the Russian people?

If the reports turn out to be correct will we lose anything by making Japan the manditory of the Powers, and giving approval to her sending an expeditionary force into Siberia to oust the Germans and to restore Russian authority in that region?

Ought we not to adopt this policy in the event that Irkutsk is actually controlled by the Germans?

I think that the situation requires careful consideration and a policy should be adopted in advance because no time ought to be lost to meet and offset the German activities in Siberia, if the reports prove to be correct.   Faithfully yours,   Robert Lansing.

This was returned to me 3/26/18 by the Prest who said that he quite agreed by [but] did not think the situation yet warranted change of policy RL[1]

TLS (SDR, RG 59, 861.00/1433½A, DNA).
  [1] RLhw.

A Translation of a Telegram from August Philips to Jonkheer John Loudon

No. Bf 108   Washington, D. C., March 24, 1918
Peace Negotiations

In Your Excellency's telegram No. 311,[1] received by me on March 14, 1918, I was instructed to ascertain President Wilson's opinion concerning an idea that was offered through the American Consul at Geneva,[2] and which, with the approval of the American Minister at Bern—as was already known to Your Excellency—was transmitted to the President, that the moment seemed to have come to bring about, through Your Excellency, talks between the belligerents concerning a general peace, as set forth further in Your Excellency's telegram 311.[3]

On the occasion of my visit to the President on March 14, I carried out these instructions. Mr. Wilson began by expressing his appreciation of Your Excellency's intentions, but emphasized that he never wished to see a peace conference in the spirit of the Congress of Vienna take place; that he would not permit Germany to enter into negotiations over the relinquishment of conquests in the West while retaining advantages in the East; that a peace conference seemed acceptable only if Germany would openly declare in advance that, as far as the East was concerned, it would also submit to the decisions of the conference. He expressed more such general ideas which, however, he did not wish to be considered as an answer to Your Excellency's question, but rather, as he said, as "thinking aloud." Before giving an answer, he wished to think about the idea for some days. At the end, he asked whether it was known to me by whom the idea that Your Excellency should, at this time, take the initiative was first brought up. I had to reply to this that nothing else was known to me other than the fact that the idea was voiced by the American Consul at Geneva, but that I did not know whether it had been conceived by him or by someone else. The President then asked whether a "Baron de Jong" was involved in it, whereupon I said that nothing was known to me of that. In reply, Mr. Wilson asked me whether I would object to inquiring of Your Excellency with whom the idea, as far as it is known to Your Excellency, had originated, which I promised I would do. Thus, my telegram 405, sent on March 14 last.[4] After Your Excellency's answer No. 351,[5] from which it seemed to me that it also was not known to Your Excellency with whom the idea had first originated, but that, in any event, Your Excellency was not approached directly or indirectly by the Central Empires, I asked for a new audience, which was promised to me for Monday, March 25.

The Minister.

CC T telegram (Washington, P-8, Vredesonderhandelingen, 1918-1919, NFM-Ar).

¹ J. Loudon to A. Philips, No. 311, March 14, 1918, Hw telegram (Washington, P-8, Vredesonderhandelingen, 1918-1919, NFM-Ar).

² Lewis Wardlaw Haskell.

³ "Pourparlers among belligerents based on the four principles recently set forth by the President, subject to engagement in which the Central Powers, in case of negotiations general peace, would consent to revise the separate peace treaties which they have just concluded." (Our translation.)

⁴ A. Philips to J. Loudon, No. 405, March 14, 1918, Hw telegram (Washington, P-8, Vredesonderhandelingen, 1918-1919, NFM-Ar): "President greatly appreciates your démarche but asks several days before giving reply. He asks that you inform him if you know from what side idea to arrange pourparlers has been suggested."

⁵ J. Loudon to A. Philips, March 19, 1918, No. 351, Hw telegram (Washington, P-8, Vredesonderhandelingen, 1918-1919, NFM-Ar). This telegram said that the person involved was a highly placed Hollander who had been in Switzerland for several months. It was not clear who had had the first idea of having conversations. If the President had any doubt on the subject, Philips should inform him that the idea had not come, directly or indirectly, from the Central Powers.

To Sir Douglas Haig

The White House March 25, 1918

May I not express to you my warm admiration of the splendid steadfastness and valor with which your troops have withstood the German onset, and the perfect confidence all Americans feel that you will win a secure and final victory?   Woodrow Wilson

TC telegram (WP, DLC).

To George Creel, with Enclosure

My dear Creel   The White House 25 March, 1918

The enclosed letter from the Attorney General (which I would be very much obliged if you would be kind enough to return when you have read it) puts a very different face on the case of the young Swedes about whom you spoke to me,¹ and I thought you ought to see it.

In haste   Faithfully yours,   Woodrow Wilson

TLS (G. Creel Papers, DLC).
¹ G. Creel to WW, Feb. 26, 1918, Vol. 46.

From Thomas Watt Gregory

My dear Mr. President: Washington, D. C. [c. March 24, 1918]

I respectfully acknowledge your letter of the 27th ultimo[1] enclosing letter addressed to you by Mr. Creel, under date of February
26th in which he called attention to the cases of about one hundred
young Swedes of Rockford, Ill., who in July 1917 were sentenced
by United States District Judge Landis[2] to one year in the House
of Correction, for failure to register; and in which Mr. Creel suggested the informal appointment of some trusted man to talk with
the prisoners and make recommendations to you based upon the
careful investigation of each individual case. My reply has been
delayed somewhat by the difficulty of obtaining light on this request
from the local authorities in Illinois.

In view of the facts forwarded here by the United States Attorney
for the Northern District of Illinois,[3] who prosecuted these men, I
am constrained to oppose the granting of Mr. Creel's request. Briefly
the facts stated by the United States attorney are these: These
defendants are members of a group of one hundred and eleven men
who pleaded guilty June 26th, 1917 for failure to register—a violation of the Selective Service Act. They were sentenced on the 5th
and 6th of July and their terms, with allowance for good behavior,
will expire on or about May 6th next. Although indicted separately
on the technical charge of having failed to register, these men in
fact were guilty of conspiracy. On the day prior to the date for
registration, they and others met together in the Socialist Hall at
Rockford, and agreed to evade registration and by united effort to
defy the law. On the following day they failed to register and three
of them were arrested. That night they again met at the Socialist
Hall and by agreement made a demonstration by marching in a
body to the jail, demanding the release of the three men arrested
and in the alternative that if the three were not released all should
be locked up. They carried a banner with a slogan of the I.W.W.
and were led by the local organizer of the I.W.W. At the jail where
they were arrested and imprisoned, they tore down a United States
emblem, smashed one of the radiators and all of the windows in
the part of the jail where they were imprisoned and announced
their purpose of wrecking the jail. This was prevented by the sheriff
separating them and sending them to other institutions. On ar-
raignment each defendant was separately interrogated by the United
States District Judge, with the aid of an interpreter in cases where
the defendant did not speak English. They were practically unan-

imous in telling the court that they would not serve in the army or that they preferred to serve in jail rather than to fight for the country.

It would be necessary for you in exercising Executive Clemency either to treat all of these men as of one class and at the same time include the cases of some seventeen other defendants who are not Swedes, or in the alternative to pass upon each individual case. The procedure suggested by Mr. Creel would be in effect to review the discretion exercised by Judge Landis and I should not wish this undertaken unless the representatives of my Department could be present or could simultaneously investigate each individual case. Entirely apart from the objections that I have already outlined, this last mentioned proceedure could not be properly put through in the short time that remains before the term of these men will expire, namely May 6th.

In giving this subject most careful consideration I have also in mind a telegram recently received by me in another connection from the Governor of Illinois[4] in which he calls attention to the difficulty at the present time of putting down sedition and disloyalty in that State and urgently asks that I make special and extraordinary arrangements to aid him in impressing on local authorities throughout the State the seriousness of the situation and the necessity for their co-operation.

In the light of all these circumstances, I respectfully express the opinion that no intervention should be made by you in the cases referred by Mr. Creel.   Respectfully,   T. W. Gregory

TLS (WP, DLC).
  [1] WW to TWG, Feb. 27, 1918, Vol. 46.
  [2] Kenesaw Mountain Landis.
  [3] Charles Francis Clyne.
  [4] Frank O. Lowden.

To Thomas Watt Gregory

[The White House]

My dear Mr. Attorney General: 25 March, 1918

You may have learned that the United States Gas Mask Plant, recently established at the corner of Jackson Boulevard and Second Avenue, Borough of Queens, New York, has been obliged to dismiss 143 employees who were detected in purposely puncturing with pins or needles the masks which the company was making.[1] I am wondering whether no criminal action lies against such rascals? Is dismissal all that they must undergo? This is merely an inquiry.[2]

In haste
                    Cordially and faithfully yours,   Woodrow Wilson

TLS (Letterpress Books, WP, DLC).
¹ This was sent in response to WGM to WW, March 21, 1918, CCL, enclosing Malcolm Ross McAdoo to WGM, March 18, 1918, TLS, both in W. G. McAdoo Papers, DLC.
² For the substance of Gregory's reply, see WW to WGM, March 28, 1918.

To Herbert Clark Hoover

My dear Mr. Hoover: The White House 25 March, 1918

Thank you for your letter of March twenty-second. I see how serious the situation is, but there is no choice, I believe, but to go forward as best we can.

Cordially and sincerely yours,   Woodrow Wilson

TLS (H. Hoover Papers, HPL).

Two Letters to Bainbridge Colby

My dear Colby: The White House 25 March, 1918

Thank you warmly for letting me see the enclosed letter from Mr. Taft. You have done all that it was possible to do, and I am glad to say that I am going to have an opportunity on Thursday of having a little conference with Mr. Taft, Mr. Root, and President Lowell, which may still further help to simplify matters.

Cordially and sincerely yours,   Woodrow Wilson

My dear Colby: The White House 25 March, 1918

I understand that some of your colleagues on the Shipping Board are expressing the opinion that it would not be wise for you to take part in the campaign in Wisconsin. I am heartily sorry for that. Your assistance there would be invaluable, and I must say that I cannot see any impropriety in your going, because I am sure that there would be nothing personal in anything that you would say, but, of course, I am always ready to abide by your judgment.

Cordially and faithfully yours,   Woodrow Wilson

TLS (B. Colby Papers, DLC).

To the Right Reverend Alfred Harding

My dear Bishop Harding: [The White House] 25 March, 1918

Mrs. Wilson and I are expecting to have the pleasure of entertaining the British Ambassador and Lady Reading and the Archbishop of York at dinner next Monday evening, the first of April, at eight o'clock, and Mrs. Wilson joins me in the hope that you will find it possible to dine with us also at that time.

No other guests than those that I have mentioned have been invited. The dinner is not a "function" of any kind. We have arranged it merely in order that we might have the pleasure of meeting the Archbishop and extending an informal welcome to him.

Cordially and sincerely yours,   Woodrow Wilson

TLS (Letterpress Books, WP, DLC).

To Lord Reading

My dear Mr. Ambassador: The White House 25 March, 1918

When I wrote to you the other day, inviting you to dine with us on Monday night next, I said that nobody else was invited except the Archbishop of York. I do not know how I came to forget that I was inviting also the Bishop of Washington. As soon as I recollected my blunder, I felt that I ought to correct my statement to you. I am sure you will understand how a busy man has slips of memory.

I am, my dear Lord Reading,

Cordially and sincerely yours,   Woodrow Wilson

TLS (Reading Papers, Add. MSS Eur. F 118/117, IOR).

Two Letters to Robert Somers Brookings

My dear Mr. Brookings: [The White House] 25 March, 1918

Thank you for your letter about the price of cotton goods. I think you are pursuing the right course undoubtedly, and am glad that the manufacturers are willing to confer in the spirit indicated.

Let me also express my gratification that you hope to be able to frame a bill with regard to price fixing which will meet the views of Secretary Houston and Mr. Lever.

Cordially and sincerely yours,   Woodrow Wilson

My dear Mr. Brookings: [The White House] 25 March, 1918

I have cheerfully approved the enclosed statement with regard to the prices of steel.

I have just had a message from Mr. Goltra[1] of St. Louis begging that if any change were made in the price of pig iron, it might be made operative only in the regions east of the Mississippi, but I do not feel that such an arrangement is justified by all the circumstances. Is it your own feeling, I wonder, that there is any unfairness in the $32.00 price to the producers of pig iron on the other side of the Mississippi?

Cordially and sincerely yours,   Woodrow Wilson

TLS (Letterpress Books, WP, DLC).
  [1] E. F. Goltra to WW, March 22, 1918, TLS (WP, DLC).

To Atlee Pomerene

My dear Senator: [The White House] 25 March, 1918

I have your letter of March twenty-first, and I need not say that I agree with you absolutely with regard to the Gore amendment fixing the price of wheat at $2.50 per bushel. Nothing more distinctly against the public interest has been put into a bill in many a month, and I fail to see any need for it, from the point of view even of the farmer. You may be sure that I will do all that I can to convince those who are handling the bill of the fatal inadvisability of the provision.

Cordially and sincerely yours,   Woodrow Wilson

TLS (Letterpress Books, WP, DLC).

To Curtis Brown

My dear Sir: [The White House] 25 March, 1918

I appreciate very much the inquiry contained in your courteous letter of March ninth[1] but feel obliged to say in reply that, while there is no authorized biography of myself now available for publication or for translation for sale on the Continent, I do not feel that I would be justified in encouraging the preparation of one. All judgments are in solution just now, and I do not feel that my career has reached a stage which would make the task of a biographer a feasible one.

Cordially and sincerely yours,   Woodrow Wilson

TLS (Letterpress Books, WP, DLC).
  [1] C. Brown to WW, March 9, 1918, Vol. 46.

To Mary Eloise Hoyt

Confidential.

My dear Cousin Mary: The White House 25 March, 1918

I don't wonder that you were concerned by what Miss Gould told you about the trend of things in Spain.[1] I have known about it and have watched it with not a little anxiety, but, unfortunately, I have seen no way in which the influences at work there could be successfully offset, and I believe that the military danger of Spain is in fact very slight. There has in recent years been such complete disorganization and demoralization in Spain from the administrative point of view that she can do very little.

I am not minimizing the dangers, I am only explaining that there has been no feasible way to guard against them. The court circles of Spain have never been favorable to the Allies, the King is a weak intriguer, so far as I can make out, and there has never been any real foothold for Entente influences there. This is, in short, one of the many risks it is inevitable we should take, but I am none the less obliged to you for conveying to me the information which I know to be substantially true.

I echo your wish that we might see you occasionally, but just now there doesn't seem to be any private life left for any of us. We must fight our way out of this jungle and then be normal human beings again.

In haste   Affectionately yours,   Woodrow Wilson

TLS (received from William D. Hoyt, Jr.).
  [1] Wilson was replying to Mary E. Hoyt to WW, March 17, 1918, ALS (WP, DLC). She had reported on a recent conversation with Alice Gould, an old friend from Boston. Miss Gould had just returned to the United States after a number of years spent in Spain, first in historical reseach and, more recently, as secretary to Capt. Benton Clark Decker, the Naval Attaché in the American embassy in Madrid. Miss Gould feared that Spain would enter the war on the side of the Central Powers.

From Robert Lansing, with Enclosure

My dear Mr. President: Washington March 25, 1918.

I forward you a dispatch from Colonel Ruggles[1] which possibly you have seen but which I am sending you because I think if you have not seen it you should read it.

Faithfully yours,   Robert Lansing

TLS (R. Lansing Papers, NjP).
  [1] Lt. Col. James A. Ruggles, Military Attaché in Russia.

E N C L O S U R E

Vologda (Petrograd) March 12, 1918.

Received today message from Martin[1] at Murmansk dated March 7 to the effect that Marines have been landed there from British battleships, more to follow from battle cruiser just arrived. A French force to arrive soon. These forces to cooperate with red army in defense of Murmansk and Murmansk railroad line. Committee on military organization Murmansk formed of three officers British, French and Russian for protection in that port and railroad lines from threatened German or pro-German attack. Martin (?) conferred with local Soviet, with British and French upon (?) Allied officers and soviet. Local soviet wired central soviet at Petrograd for authority to enter into cooperation with Allies. Reply was received from Trotsky authorizing acceptance all Allied aid. This resulting landing of Allied forces in compliance with request of local soviet.

Soviet committee expressed regret that United States had not had representative there to enter into similar agreement as was signed by British and French, that any American aid would be most welcome and that American troops would be accepted upon same terms as British and French namely, military organization to be placed under committee of three officers hereinbefore mentioned, this committee to be under control of executive committee of the local soviet. England and France agree not to interfere in internal affairs of Murmansk district.

Stated (?) that he was not authorized to make any statement nor take any action in present situation but upon their request attend S. conference to keep in touch.

Have wired approval of Ambassador and myself of Martin.

Report from north front states that the soldiers and staffs ask Allied aid and officers.

Trotsky stated to me in interview that he proposed organizing new army not less than 1,000,000 under "iron discipline" and that groups of Allied officers in Russia would be most welcome also American railroad men. Presence of Allied officers would encourage Russian officers to return to service. No definite plan of action yet suggested by Trotsky. Believe this may (*) Moscow convention March 13 he greatly fears Japanese army control in Siberia and of Siberia railroad as army would be organized east of Urals. Moscow is to be seat of government, transfer now being made.

If practicable please outline American policy. Recommendation referred until later.   Ruggles.

(*) apparent omission.

T telegram (R. Lansing Papers, NjP).
  [1] Lt. Hugh S. Martin, Assistant Military Attaché in Russia.

From Richard Melancthon Hurd[1]

New York, March 25, 1918.

The American Defense Society urges you to exert your influence toward the suppression of the German press, the German language and for the revocation of the charter of the German-American alliance. These three agencies are the three most pernicious influences working against a thorough Americanization of the Germans in this country and serve only one purpose, the promulgation of German ideas and German propaganda in this country.

> Richard M. Hurd, Chairman Board of Trustees,
> American Defense Society, New York

T telegram (WP, DLC).
  [1] President of the Lawyers Mortgage Company of New York since 1903.

A Translation of a Telegram from August Philips to Jonkheer John Loudon

No. Bf 111   Washington, D. C., March 25, 1918.
Peace Negotiations

In continuation of my report of yesterday, I have the honor to inform Your Excellency that today I have had the audience which I mentioned at the end thereof. During this audience, I informed the President of the fact, which was contained in your telegram No. 351, and which mainly amounted to this, that it was not known to Your Excellency with whom the idea of your possible moves had first originated. President Wilson said that he, for one, also had inquiries made, and that he had been told that the idea had originated with Mr. de Jong van Beek en Donk, who, on his part, had discussed it with the American Consul at Geneva.

Under repeated assurances of his great appreciation of Your Excellency's intentions, the President was of the opinion that, for three reasons, he ought not to pursue the idea at the present time.

In the first place, the circumstances had changed too much since the idea was first suggested: the conduct of the Central Powers in the East was, according to him, already an actual rejection of the four principles which the President had declared in his last message to Congress.

Secondly, there seems no reason to have great expectations from any initiative by Your Excellency, now that the idea thereof seemed to have originated from an entirely private side, even though it was, to be sure, with excellent intentions.

In the third place—and on this the President put the emphasis—he believed that he had to abstain from anything which, in the present circumstances, already so extremely painful for Your Excellency, would make matters even more difficult for you. He made this clear by saying that he deeply regretted the difficult condition which our country had got into by the measures taken against our ships, and he was afraid that the relations of Your Excellency vis-à-vis the Central Powers would become even thornier, if, at the present time, steps were taken by Your Excellency as discussed in Bern.

When the President began to speak about matters concerning the ships, I asked him urgently not to pursue that subject any further at the moment, since I was still without instructions as to the position which I should assume on this point. His answer was that he also did not intend to deal with the matter any further than in connection with his answer to the question posed, namely as one of the reasons why he believed that he should not pursue the Bern idea at this time.

I gave you a short report of this conversation in my telegram No. 472 of today.[1]   The Minister.

CC T telegram (Washington, P-8, Vredesonderhandelingen, 1918-1919, NFM-Ar).
[1] A. Philips to J. Loudon, No. 472, March 25, 1918 (Washington, P-8, Vredesonderhandelingen, 1918-1919, NFM-Ar).

To Grosvenor Blaine Clarkson

My dear Mr. Clarkson: [The White House] 26 March, 1918

Mr. Forster has handed me your letter of March twenty-second and the accompanying memorandum on the past and future functions of the Council of National Defense, and I have given both a very careful reading.

I am very much impressed by your discussion of the subject and find myself in substantial accord with you. Indeed, it has been my hope and expectation all along that the investigating and advisory functions of the Council of National Defense would proceed in the fullest vigor, because they are perhaps needed now more than ever and I cannot foresee any situation in which they would not be needed and would not be of the highest value. The War Industries Board is practically now under its reorganization divorced from the Council of National Defense. By my recent letter to Mr. Baruch, I have practically made it a direct administrative agency and, indeed, I so regard it, feeling that I am very much indebted to the Council of National Defense for having created the board in the first place and made it ready for such separate and independent uses.

I shall be very glad to keep your suggestions in mind, and want to thank you very sincerely for your generous references to myself in your letter.

Cordially and sincerely yours,   Woodrow Wilson

TLS (Letterpress Books, WP, DLC).

To George H. Slater

My dear Mr. Slater: [The White House] 26 March, 1918

I hope that you will say to your associates of the Texas Federation of Labor that I very deeply and sincerely appreciate the resolution of loyalty and devotion which you were kind enough to embody in your recent telegram. I think that I can assure the workers of Texas, as well as the workers of all the rest of the country, that no enemies or antagonists can do any great or serious hurt or injury to the great humanitarian cause of labor so long as the laborers of the country pursue the fine course which American labor has outlined for itself, and that the efforts of the enemies of labor which your telegram refers to must and will prove abortive, so long as the rational, natural and loyal course is faithfully adhered to which such resolutions as yours embody. I am confident that the toilers of the nation will at this crucial time give in every respect a good and loyal account of themselves.

Cordially and sincerely yours,   Woodrow Wilson

TLS (Letterpress Books, WP, DLC).

To Minnie Fisher Cunningham[1]

[The White House] 26 March, 1918

Please accept my warmest congratulations on the adoption of the primary suffrage bill by the Legislature of the State.[2]

Woodrow Wilson

T telegram (Letterpress Books, WP, DLC).
  [1] Mrs. Beverly Jean Cunningham, president of the Texas Equal Suffrage Association.
  [2] Governor William Pettus Hobby had just signed into law an act which permitted women to vote in primary elections in Texas. Since Texas was then a one-party state, this meant in effect that women were enfranchised in state elections. A. Elizabeth Taylor, "The Woman Suffrage Movement in Texas," *Journal of Southern History*, XVII (May 1951), 208-11.

From Benedict Crowell, with Enclosure

Dear Mr. President: Washington. March 26, 1918.

I am sending you a very important resolution of the War Council together with a report on which it is based.

May I have the opportunity of discussing this matter with you?

Respectfully yours,   Benedict Crowell

TLS (WP, DLC).

ENCLOSURE

Washington. March 26, 1918.

At its seventy-eighth meeting, held on March 26, 1918, the War Council adopted unanimously the following resolutions:

RESOLVED, That the War Council approves of the following memorandum and recommends that it be brought to the attention of the President of the United States:

The Report of the Director of Storage and Traffic,[1] dated March 21, 1918, relative to the minimum military program of the United States, as defined by the Supreme War Council, reveals a condition so grave that it should be brought at once to the attention of the President.

Several difficulties must be overcome in order to carry out the movement of two complete divisions per month, commencing April 1, 1918. Latest information discloses that with the single exception of tonnage, the Army will successfully overcome these obstacles, either through its own efforts or with the assistance accorded in France by the Allies. Unless drastic action is taken as to the tonnage deficit, however, the realization of the project will be defeated.

There are now in trans-Atlantic army service cargo ships aggregating approximately 800,000 deadweight tons. The requirements for April are 1,576,000 deadweight tons. Thereafter the requirements increase rapidly until September when they amount to 2,916,000 deadweight tons. After allowing for the new ships which may be delivered by the Emergency Fleet Corporation there remains a deficit of 684,000 deadweight tons in April, which increases rapidly to 1,208,000 deadweight tons in August. The Council is unable to secure any dependable assurances that these deficits will be met; in fact it is of the opinion that no such assurances can be given so long as the present procedure for the allocation of ship tonnage continues. On the other hand, if an authoritative plan of allocation is adopted at once, the Council believes that the necessary tonnage can be secured.

The Council, therefore, recommends:

1. *In order to secure immediate relief*:

The adoption of the recommendations made by the Director of Storage and Traffic, as follows:

(a) That in order that the United States shall live up to its military obligations, the President direct that all American tonnage suitable for trans-Atlantic service shall be set aside for use of the Army.

(b) That hereafter no ship built under the direction of the Emergency Fleet Corporation and suitable for army service shall be assigned to any other service.

2. *As a permanent plan for the allocation of ships.*
   (a) That the Ship Control Committee with the utmost dispatch ascertain and report to the President its conclusions with regard to the minimum tonnage needs of the United States requisite
      (1) To move absolutely necessary imports, exports and coast wise cargoes;
      (2) To maintain and equip our now existing military expeditionary forces and meet the requirements of the Navy;
      (3) To carry the materials and supplies due the British and French Governments to replace materials and supplies furnished by them to the American Expeditionary Forces.
   (b) That all United States tonnage in excess of that required for the foregoing specific national and military needs of the United States as approved by the President be made a part of an Inter-Allied Shipping pool.
   (c) That authority to recommend the allocation of the tonnage comprising this Inter-Allied Shipping pool be vested in the Supreme War Council.
   (d) That a cable message be sent to the Premiers of England, France and Italy apprising them of our tonnage requirements to meet the present minimum military program of the United States and urging their serious consideration of the above plan for effecting a redistribution of tonnage which will more completely meet military and other needs of the United States and the Allies.

The Supreme War Council has now machinery for classifying and analyzing all Inter-Allied tonnage needs and is in a position to distinguish between the absolute essentials and those less essential items which under the present stress can be stricken from the schedule of requirements.

If such a plan is made operative, the United States would at all times have under its control tonnage requisite for the maintenance of its forces abroad, but the determination of the rate at which such forces should be reinforced would be based on the recommendations of the Supreme War Council upon which all the allied nations have equal representation.

The preservation of our lines of communication can be provided for automatically through assigning to the permanent use of the United States the additional tonnage which will be required from time to time for the reinforcements added to our present expeditionary forces.

In no other way can the United States be placed in the right light with regard to its position in the war; failing this, misunderstand-

ings and contentions developing possibly into national embarrassment, are certain to arise.

For the War Council: P. C. March

T MS (WP, DLC).
¹ Maj. Gen. George Washington Goethals, whom Baker had appointed to this post in
the General Staff in February 1918.

From Bainbridge Colby, with Enclosure

My dear Mr. President: Washington March 26, 1918.

I beg to inclose a letter received this morning from Mr. Taft. I
would have liked to save you from an unnecessary interview, and
thought my telegram brought the incident to a period. However, I
can well understand the desire of Mr. Taft and Mr. Lowell to see
you personally, and their call may afford you an opportunity to bring
about, through the meeting of the League, an expression of the
nation's unflinching spirit, which may be of far reaching effect.

My attention has been called to a meeting of the United States
Chamber of Commerce, on April 10th. I wonder if you deem it
advisable to consider the possibilities that this occasion may hold
for a clear expression of our determination and resolve, and whether
it calls for anything in the way of guidance or suggestion.

Very sincerely yours,   Bainbridge Colby

E N C L O S U R E

William Howard Taft to Bainbridge Colby

My dear Mr. Colby: New Haven, Conn March 24th, 1918.

I have your telegram as follows: "Many thanks for your letter
nineteenth, also Mr. Short's letter of twentieth. Both duly submitted
and entire reliance is felt in your attitude and assurances given at
our interview. Would appreciate receiving program with topics and
speakers if entirely agreeable to you. With much appreciation."

I received your telegram when in conference with President Lowell and other members of the Executive Committee, and we concluded that the best thing for us to do was to send a little Committee
of Mr. Lowell and myself to have a personal conference with the
President. Accordingly I called you up and found that you were
out-of-town. So I called up the White House with the hope of speaking to Mr. Tumulty. He was not in, and I spoke to Mr. Forster, the
Assistant Secretary. He told me that he would communicate my
wishes to the President and advise me what day of this week, either

Wednesday, Thursday or Friday, when Dr. Lowell and I could see the President. We can talk the matter over with him and get his ideas of the limitations upon the subject and the speakers in order to conform to his wishes.   Sincerely yours,   Wm H Taft

TLS (WP, DLC).

From Bainbridge Colby

My dear Mr. President: Washington March 26, 1918.

I am leaving for Wisconsin. Your note of today, very happily to me, resolves any doubts I have felt on the subject. My hesitation was really due to a fear that you might not entirely approve of my going out there, and some of my associates over here felt that possibly a conservative course was the better one. I am very much pleased that you approve of my going and all of my colleagues are deeply interested in the outcome of the fight and keenly alive to the importance of the issue. I am heartily in favor of the candidacy of Mr. Davies, and when you pledge him your support, he is sure of mine.

With great appreciation of your kindness in giving me your thought on this matter, I am

Very sincerely yours,   Bainbridge Colby

TLS (WP, DLC).

From Franklin Knight Lane

My dear Mr. President: Washington March 26, 1918.

Sometime ago I made inquiry regarding the Mooney case, when I first heard you speak of the effect in Petrograd of his conviction. While I have not communicated with Governor Stephens, I found that the feeling among his friends was that he was committed to the proposition that whatever the courts decided he would abide by. There are a lot of men whom I could name in California who are his friends, but in my judgment there will be no use in appealing to him through them. If you cannot by your direct personal telegram cause him to take the course which you advise, there is nothing that can be done.

Cordially and faithfully yours,   Franklin K. Lane

TLS (WP, DLC).

From Herbert Clark Hoover, with Enclosure

Dear Mr. President: Washington March Twenty-Sixth *1918*.

I am sending you, herewith, a letter on the whole meat problem, in amplification of my conversation on Friday in asking for the appointment of a commission to study this subject.

As you have seen by the number of deputations to Washington, there is a great deal of discontent amongst the animal growers in the country, and I believe the appointment of such a commission would go far to quiet this matter and develop some constructive policy.

I feel that it would do a lot of immediate good, if you find yourself in accord with the proposal that I make, that I should issue the accompanying letter to the press, together with your approval of the appointment of such a commission; and my excuse for writing at such length is to set out with all the care that may be the whole problem to public view, as there is the greatest misunderstanding throughout the country as to the Government's activities in this instance.   Faithfully yours,   Herbert Hoover

TLS (WP, DLC).

E N C L O S U R E

Dear Mr President: [Washington] *26 March 1918*

I feel that we have reached a position with regard to the whole meat industry of the country that requires a reconsideration of policy. The situation is one of the most complex with which the Government has to deal, by virtue of the increasing influence that the Government purchasing has upon prices, by the necessity of providing for increasing supplies for the Allies, and the consequent reduction of civilian consumption and, with all, the due protection of the producer and the civilian consumer. This change of policy may take the form of more definite and systematic direction of the larger packers as to the course that they are to pursue from month to month, or may even take the form of operation of the packing house establishments by the Government.

The General economic forces bearing on the situation appear to me to be—

1. The Allied purchases for both civilian and military purposes in meats, as in many other commodities, have been consolidated by necessity of shipping conditions and by necessity of the Treasury arrangement for advances to the Allies until private trading has been of necessity eliminated.

It is also becoming necessary for the Government to coordinate these purchases with those of our Army and Navy in order to prevent conflict in the execution of orders. This great consolidation of buying has to some extent, and will increasingly, dominate prices.

We have, since last September, recognized that the export purchase of pork products would affect prices and after consultation with important committees of swine growers we last autumn gave a rough assurance to the swine producer of a minimum price which we felt that we could maintain from the export buying and this has been maintained although with considerable difficulties and has been beneficial in stimulating production. The indications are that these purchases will now be further increased.

The beef purchases have not, up to the present time, been sufficient in volume to more than temporarily affect price, but the present indications are that for some time in the future they will be greatly increased and to a point where they may affect prices materially.

2. The increased quantities required for export must be obtained by either increased production or by reduction in civilian consumption—probably both.

The reduction in civilian consumption can be obtained much the most equitably by voluntary reduction by the consumer and by moderate restraints such as meatless days, et cetera, and while it may be contended by some that a reduction in consumption may be obtained by increase in price, such conservation is obtained by the elimination of that section of the community with the least purchasing power. In other words, conservation by price becomes conservation for the rich and not for the poor; whereas an extension of the conservation policy now in force places reduction in consumption where it rightly belongs—on those who can save from plenty, not upon those who save from nourishment.

It appears to me also of the utmost national importance that we shall maintain through the country a complete sense in voluntary reduction in the consumption of all commodities if we are to provide the necessary surpluses either in money, man-power, or material, necessary to winning the war. On the other hand, the adjustment of conservation measures of this type and the surplus required from time to time is extremely difficult without these measures themselves affecting price and developing discontent and criticism in sections of the producing community.

I recognize fully the well-founded objection to any theory of price-fixing, but where the purchases of war necessities in a given commodity have reached such a volume that the purchase of these commodities trench into the domestic consumption, the operation of this purchasing power becomes a condition of price-fixing and, to my mind, all theories go by the board.

3. The Government is thus faced with three alternatives in the matter of control of meats:

a. To free the Government from all interest in price by abandoning direction of war purchases and to abandon conservation measures because these may also affect price.

This would be a relief to the Government but with growing volume of purchases the price influence will be transferred to uncontrolled agencies who are themselves price-fixing and carries the following dangers:

It will stimulate profiteering and speculation. Prices in the season of the year of large production can be manipulated downward and in the sparse season will ascend to the point where some classes will be eliminated from consumption. The cost of living thus subjected to abnormal fluctuation will reflect in wage discontent and instability. It will destroy systematic saving of the commodity by individuals and this saving in consumption is a vital national policy. The producer will go through erratic periods of discouragement and of stimulation which must undermine any systematic policy of national or individual increase in production, for every period of discouragement cuts off production of animals, which cannot be recovered.

b. To continue as at present the direction of these large purchases with a mixture of partial national policy in production and day to day dealing with emergency.

This is an almost intolerable situation for any Government official in criticism from both producer and consumer and with the growing volume of purchases this criticism must increase. It permits of no constructive policy in production.

c. To stabilize prices based upon cost of production at a fair and stimulative profit to the producer and with stabilization to eliminate speculative risks and wasteful practices and thus some gains for the consumer.

If such a policy is adopted it also follows that it will have a most important bearing on and relation to policies of agricultural production and a long view can be taken and supported in assuring the producer of fair returns.

This course is also fraught with dangers. It leads either to a voluntary agreement with the packers as to prices to be paid producers and charged to consumers from time to time: or, to actual operation of the packing plants by the Government. In either case the Government will need to take some financial responsibility in speculative business. In such situation the Government will be under constant pressure from the producers for enhancement of price and from the consumer for reductions. It necessitates the constant action of a commission to determine such prices. It will mean that all the complaints of trade fall upon the Government. The choice of alternatives is one of determination of the maximum contribution to winning the war and the choice of the lesser economic evil between such alternatives.

4. The legal ability of the Government to give authority to such measures lies in the power to direct contracts for war necessities, to take over and operate plants and to make voluntary agreements to carry out a definitive and constructive policy. When purchases are so large as to cut into civilian consumption, it becomes possible to insure manufacturers a complete market, thus eliminating their risk and thereby eliminating some of the margin that they must take in the conduct of a speculative business and it also gives sound reason for directing their policies.

5. For these very reasons it has been necessary to set up partial or complete arrangements of this character in iron, steel, copper, explosives, wheat, sugar and some other commodities. None of these arrangements have evolved out of any governmental policy of price-fixing, or any desire to interfere with the operation of natural trade laws, but are simply the result of the Government being forced into the issue of becoming the dominant purchaser and thereby, willingly or unwillingly, the price determiner in particular commodities.

We have been struggling as intelligently as possible with the situation in the meat industries with entire inadequacy of definite national policy. Our purchases hitherto have been sufficient to influence the market at times and in the case of pork products have been sufficient to preserve a minimum price. We have been, however, powerless hitherto to properly protect all branches of the cattle industry with its constantly changing economic situation, or to give intelligent direction or assistance to cattle production. As you know, I have never felt that when we arrived at a point to determine the broad policy with respect to a commodity that this should be determined at the opinion of any single individual, no matter how sincere and earnest the application of intelligence might be.

I would therefore like to recommend to you to extend the policy which you have already initiated in the matter of many commodities, by early appointment of a board to study the entire situation with regard to the meat industry and the steps that should be taken with regard thereto. I would suggest that, following the precedent that you have already established, a committee should be set up embracing, either the following gentlemen or their delegates directly responsible to them.—

The Secretary of Agriculture as representing the producer.

The Chairman of the Federal Trade Commission as representing trade conditions.

The Chairman of the Federal Tariff Board as representing economic thought.

The Secretary of Labor as representing the civilian consumer.

The Food Administrator as having to carry out any given policy determined upon.

This commission should at once exhaustively consider the entire situation in all of its aspects and determine a positive national policy in meats.

I apologize for writing at such length but the subject permits of little brevity.

I am   Your obedient servant,   Herbert Hoover.

Mimeographed L (WP, DLC).

From Josephus Daniels

My dear Mr. President: Washington March 26, 1918.

I brought Mr. Meeker's letter which you enclosed with your letter of March 21st, to the attention of the Council of National Defense at its meeting yesterday.

It is the Council's view that the functional and vocational rehabilitation of wounded soldiers and sailors is properly a war measure, but that the rehabilitation of industrial cripples is not. The Council does not question the desirability of rehabilitation of industrial cripples, but feels that for the present it would be most wise to confine the scope to wounded soldiers and sailors with the thought that a strong and effective organization created to take care of war cripples could and probably would, when the war is over, be continued by Congress for the rehabilitation of industrial cripples.

The Council agrees with Mr. Meeker in his opinion that the Federal Board for Vocational Education is the proper agency for carrying out the vocational rehabilitation, and a bill which is now being drawn for submission to the Council for its approval so provides.   Sincerely yours,   Josephus Daniels

TLS (WP, DLC).

From Jessie Woodrow Wilson Sayre

Dearest, dearest Father,   Cambridge, Mass. March 26, 1918

Your beautiful, lovely, dearest letter[1] was awaiting me here when I returned home and made me feel as if I were still with you all. I shall treasure it always and I feel now as if I could never be blue with such a letter to read and re-read whenever the absorbtions of war roll between us again and prevent communications. It will be my rainbow in the sky, that and my memory of this perfect little visit. It was so blessed to see you all.[2] One gets in the way of thinking that all these burdens *must* be crushing you physically and to see you and be assured again of the wonderful spirit, and the power of God, that are keeping you physically fit, as well as so marvellously fit every other way, is so comforting, to your little daughter up here.

I had a pleasant trip up with no more than a fair share of banging, and Frank surprised me by getting on at Back Bay station. He is over his cold and the children are bright and well so that we had a most happy reunion. Spring has just put out a few feelers even here and a certain gladness and sunshine are perceptible.

I miss the bulletins of the fighting! The Boston papers are so rotten and the New York papers don't come till afternoon, but if this is to be another four months battle I might as well have patience now at once.

Give a whole heartful of love to dear, dear, Edith from us both, and thank her again for her lovely and loving generosity and sweetness to me. With deepest love and pride,

Your daughter Jessie.

ALS (WP, DLC).
   [1] It is missing.
   [2] Jessie had visited the Wilsons on Saturday and Sunday, March 23 and 24.

From Brent Dow Allinson[1]

Mr. President: Washington, D. C. March 26, 1918.

A group of liberal-minded men and women desire to call upon you for a few moments on Friday afternoon or Saturday of this week or Monday to express to you their gratitude and appreciation of your recent executive order defining the meaning of the word "non-combatant" in the Selective Service Law and offering certain forms of service to men, whether members of well-recognized religious sects or not, who are unwilling, from reasons of judgment and conscience, to participate in the destructive horrors of war and who have been living for many months in confinement and idleness at the army cantonments.[2]

The men and women, whose names are indicated below, desire also to make to you a constructive suggestion concerning the further disposition of such men as may be unwilling to accept any service directly under the military, but who are able to render national service of much value and significance under the civilian arm of the Red Cross, in the Friends' Reconstruction Unit, or in agriculture.

If you cannot arrange at this time to meet a group of persons will you receive their message through the under-signed?

Those who hope to be received by you include the following:

Dr. John L. Elliott of New York City,

Prof. Rufus Jones of Haverford College, Chairman of the Friends' Reconstruction Unit,

Mr. Samuel J. Bunting, Secretray [Secretary] of the Reconstruction Unit,

Professor Manley Hudson of New York City,

Mrs. Glendower Evans of Boston

Mrs. Anna N. Davis of Boston,

Mr. Oswald G. Villard of New York,

Mr. Robert Dunn of Yale College,

Mr. George Hallett of the University of Pennsylvania,

Mr. Roger Baldwin, Secretary of the National Civil Liberties Bureau,

Dr. and Mrs. George Nasmyth of Washington,

Miss Leonore Flint of Washington,

Mr. Arthur Fisher of Washington.[3]

I remain, Mr. President,

Very respectfully,   Brent D. Allinson

TLS (WP, DLC).

[1] A former accounting officer for the Fuel Administration for Illinois and an associate editor of *War?*, a pacifist magazine published by the Collegiate Anti-Militarism League. Allinson had been appointed clerk at the American legation in Bern on February 9, 1918. However, on February 23, the day of his intended departure for Switzerland, he was summoned to Washington and dismissed from the Foreign Service because a lengthy article in the *New York Tribune* of February 22 had "exposed" him as a pacifist and a firm opponent of the draft. See the *New York Tribune*, Feb. 22, 1918; see also B. D. Allinson to WW, March 4, 1918, TLS (WP, DLC).

[2] About this Executive Order, see B. Crowell to WW, March 19, 1918, n. 1.

[3] Those persons who can be identified and who have not hitherto been identified in this series were Manley Ottmer Hudson, Professor of Law at the University of Missouri, secretary of the Missouri Peace Society, and an associate of The Inquiry; Robert Williams Dunn, an undergraduate student at Yale University active in pacifist and civil-rights movements, later an associate director of the American Civil Liberties Union; George Hervey Hallett, Professor of Mathematics at the University of Pennsylvania; George William Nasmyth, sociologist, executive secretary to the United States Fuel Administrator; Florence Nasmyth; Arthur Fisher, a law student at Harvard University, later president of the American Civil Liberties Committee of Chicago; and Anna Norwood Hallowell (Mrs. Horace Andrew) Davis.

Two Telegrams from Sir Eric Drummond to Sir William Wiseman[1]

[London] March 26, 1918.

URGENT. *No.* 67. I send a copy of a telegram which I propose despatching to TOKIO. But before doing so I should like to know confidentially whether COL. HOUSE has any comments to make upon it. If it would cause embarrassment at Washington I will not let it go.

I have always present in my mind probability that JAPAN may in her own interest intervene without our concurrence. In that case we should suffer all the evils consequent on intervention and reap none of the advantages.

DRAFT TELEGRAM.

(Begins). Situation as I understand it is as follows:

America feels the risk turning on Russian sentiment against Allies through Japanese intervention is too serious to be run at present moment. The three European Allies while admitting the risk think that the advantages of intervention outweigh its dangers. None of these four Powers have the smallest mistrust of Japan: all are well convinced that any action she may take in Siberia at present juncture will be for protection of Russia not its exploitation. But it is not easy to see how this can be brought home to Russians. Yet if they realize for a moment they can no longer help themselves and that no one can help them on a large scale except Japan, they should welcome its intervention provided they could be convinced that their former enemies were now coming as disinterested friends.

Our main problem therefore is to devise means by which this may be accomplished. Clear declarations of intentions such as those contained in my telegram No. 198[2] would do much. But many Russian observers as well as Government of United States of America doubt if it will do enough and in these circumstances I am forced to reconsider a plan which has already been considered and rejected, plan I mean of inter-allied cooperation.

To this as I am well aware Japanese have a rooted objection. On more than one occasion I have discussed it with Japanese Ambassador[3] and he has never left me in any doubt as to views of his Government on the subject. I gather, however, that objection was in no small degree founded on idea that Allied Powers desired to be associated with a Japanese expedition because they or some of them mistrusted Japanese. If therefore Japanese Government realised that the only object of such cooperation was to reassure Russians and thus facilitate Japanese efforts they might be disposed to modify their views.

If there were the least hope of such a result I have little doubt Allied Governments including America would be prepared to consider favorably any plan for cooperation which Japanese Government might themselves suggest. Such a plan need not interfere with Japanese control in military matters; it might even be confined to a civilian mission working in harmony with Japanese military authorities. All that seems required is some Far East external evidence that intervention was undertaken not as enterprize of a single Power taking advantage of Russia's weakness, but on joint responsibility of all the Great Powers, who like the Russians are fighting against German domination.

My telegram No. 198 to TOKIO was repeated to Washington, numbered 1235.

[1] The copy retained by the British embassy in Washington (FO 115/2445, pp. 212-14, PRO) states that this telegram was "sent to Wiseman for Colonel House from Mr. Balfour."

[2] A paraphrase of this telegram is printed as an Enclosure with FLP to WW, March 5, 1918, Vol. 46.

[3] That is, Viscount Sutemi Chinda.

[London] March 26, 1918.

No. 68. FOLLOWING FOR COLONEL HOUSE FROM MR. BALFOUR:

PRIME MINISTER and I saw MR. BAKER this morning and earnestly pressed upon him the urgency of obtaining from the proper authorities assent to the three following suggestions:

First: That four American divisions should be used at once to hold the line and relieve further French divisions.

Second: We understand that transport is available for bringing six complete American divisions to this country. We strongly urge that, in present crisis, this tonnage would be more usefully employed if it were not used to carry complete divisions with their full complement of artillery et cetera but if it were used in main for transport of infantry of which at this moment we stand in most pressing need.

Third: That as temporary expedient American engineer units in France now engaged in preparing base and line of communication of future American Army and said to include many skilled engineers should be diverted from present occupation and utilized as extemporized engineer units for construction of defences et cetera in rear of our armies.

Four: That one of American displacement divisions which is reported to be complete with transport should also be employed in the line either as a separate division or to increase infantry in combatant divisions.

T telegrams (W. Wiseman Papers, CtY).

Sir William Wiseman to Sir Eric Drummond

[New York] March 26, 1918.

Following for Drummond: for Mr. Balfour from Col. House:

No. 86. Your No. 68 received and has been handed to the President with my urgent recommendation that orders be at once issued as suggested.

Although anxious we have such faith in the courage and tenacity of the British troops that we feel confident of the final outcome.

T telegram (W. Wiseman Papers, CtY).

To Gordon Auchincloss

My dear Mr. Auchincloss,   The White House. 27 March, 1918.

Will you not be kind enough to telephone the following to Mr. House as a basis for his Answer to Mr. Balfour:

In view of Mr. Balfour's message I have been expecting a cable from Baker, but none has come. I think the reason plain. All the decisions asked for can be much better and more wisely made on the other side of the water than on this and Baker, Bliss and Pershing have full authority to make them,—acting, of course, as they should act, under the authority of the Executive Committee or Board of the Supreme War Council. I wish them to make these decisions and will accept any plan they determine. The possible execption [exception] is the suggestion about sending only infantry from this country instead of full-quota divisions; but even with regard to that I shall act upon the advice of Baker and Bliss in consultation with the Executive Board of the Supreme War Council.

Mr. House will know how to put this in his message.

In haste,   Faithfully Yours,   W.W.

WWTLI (E. M. House Papers, CtY).

To Herbert Clark Hoover

My dear Mr. Hoover: The White House 27 March, 1918

I have your letter of yesterday about the arrangements proposed with the Western Grain Exchanges,[1] and in reply must frankly say that I have no judgment of my own about the matter. I do not feel that I am qualified to form one. I am quite willing to leave the decision in your own hands. I think it a very satisfactory feature of what is proposed that room is left for reconsideration and for checking speculation whenever it goes too far.

Cordially and sincerely yours,   Woodrow Wilson

TLS (H. Hoover Papers, HPL).
    [1] H. C. Hoover to WW, March 26, 1918, TLS (WP, DLC). Hoover reported that he had called a conference of the representatives of the western grain exchanges in order to work out a plan to increase the efficiency of the exchanges and, at the same time, to prevent speculators from using them to their own advantage.

To Herbert Bayard Swope

My dear Swope: The White House 27 March, 1918

Thank you for sending me Sidney Webb's little book.[1] I knew of his connection with the programme of the British Labor party and shall be glad to go through this little volume. Webb gives me thoughts even when I do not accept his own.

Cordially and sincerely yours,   Woodrow Wilson

TLS (received from Bruce Gimelson).
    [1] Sidney Webb, *The Restoration of Trade Union Conditions* (London, 1917). A copy of this book is in the Wilson Library, DLC.

To Bernard Mannes Baruch

My dear Baruch: The White House 27 March, 1918

I think there is a great deal of serious force in what the Director General of Railroads urges in the enclosed letter,[1] and I am sending the letter to you in the hope that you may see your way to guide the purchases of the War and Navy Departments in accordance with the policy which McAdoo suggests. It may for all I know be too late to build up the instrumentalities necessary in the congested region, but it is obviously wise and pressingly necessary to do so if it is possible.   Faithfully yours,   Woodrow Wilson

TLS (B. M. Baruch Papers, NjP).
    [1] WGM to WW, March 25, 1918, TLS (B. M. Baruch Papers, NjP). McAdoo proposed the establishment and enforcement by all governmental departments and agencies of a policy which would discourage the creation of new industrial enterprises and the enlargement of existing ones in New England and the Northeast. Instead, all possible new industrial developments should be diverted into the territory south of the Potomac and Ohio rivers. Such a policy, McAdoo argued, was imperative, since it had become evident that the eastern railroads could not adequately take care of the already existing amount of traffic. Uncontrolled industrial development in the Northeast would further increase the burden upon these railroads and inevitably result in a progressive slowing down of traffic. It would, moreover, force a growing aggregate of war traffic and other export traffic through the North Atlantic ports, which were already congested and which could only with great difficulty be supplied with the necessary bunker coal for trans-Atlantic steamers. Since additional facilities could not be provided fast enough, the only

solution, McAdoo concluded, was for the government to "establish and enforce the definite policy that its various departments and agencies shall, in making purchases and other contracts, do everything possible to avoid the enlargement of traffic already being created in New England and Eastern Territory and to throw the development of further traffic into those parts of the country where the railroads and ports are able to take care of it."

To William Dennison Stephens

[The White House] March 27, 1918

With very great respect I take the liberty of saying to you that if you could see your way to commute the sentence of Mooney it would have a most helpful effect upon certain international affairs which his execution would greatly complicate.[1]

Woodrow Wilson

CC telegram (WP, DLC).
[1] The California Supreme Court, on March 1, 1918, had denied Mooney's appeal, filed a year before, and reaffirmed his conviction and death sentence.

From Sir Douglas Haig

[The White House] Received March 27, 1918

Your message of generous appreciation of the steadfastness and valour of our soldiers in the great battle now raging has greatly touched us all. Please accept our heartfelt thanks. One and all believe in the justice of our cause and are determined to fight on without counting the cost until the freedom of mankind is safe.

Douglas Haig.

T telegram (WP, DLC).

From Newton Diehl Baker

Paris March 27, 1918.

For the President. Had decided to postpone visit to Italian front. Next few days are critical with regard to the German offensive. I will go to General Pershing's headquarters at Chaumont as my being at either Paris or Versailles might suggest my having political rather than purely military object here. Will report military developments to you from Chaumont. General Foch has been chosen Supreme Commander,[1] acting under Mr. Clemenceau. General Pershing will visit him tomorrow and arrange to cooperate fully.

This arrangement is everywhere regarded as most happy and will probably mean a Supreme Commander for the rest of the war.

Baker

T telegram (WP, DLC).
[1] Ferdinand Foch, chief of the French General Staff, had been appointed to this post on March 26.

From Josephus Daniels, with Enclosure

My dear Mr. President: Washington. March 27, 1918.

I enclose herewith copy of a cablegram just received from Admiral Sims giving the best impressions he can of the situation in Great Britain, which I thought would interest you.

Sincerely yours,   Josephus Daniels

TLS (WP, DLC).

E N C L O S U R E

PARAPHRASE

From: Vice Admiral Sims
To: Opnav

Urgent. Following is from reliable source in close touch with prominent Englishmen both in public and private life. English fully realize that they have suffered an extremely grave reverse and there is general feeling of depression without despair. Consolation is derived from consideration: first, British Army losses relatively light in proportion number engaged; Second, German losses undoubtedly very high, estimated from twenty to thirty percent of the six hundred thousand enemy troops engaged. Later figures regarded as too high by more conservative judges who place enemy losses at about one hundred thirty five thousand for first four days; Third, although British front has been pushed back it has not broken; Fourth, War Office official announcement all British losses thus far in men and all have been made good. General expectations British retirement will be as far as line held July first nineteen sixteen possibly further, but high military authorities say Haig is confident of preventing enemy from driving wedge between British and French Armies. Same authorities profess assurance Amiens will not fall. They also point out that further west and south British retirement nearer they approach their great reserve area with consequent automatic strengthening of their capacity for resistance German drive.

A pleased impression has been caused every where in England by President Wilson's warm message of commendation to the British Commander-in-Chief. In private conversation a note of bitter disappointment or worse is sometimes heard because of American troops were not thrown in heavy numbers to help resist German attack. No such criticism known to have been uttered in any responsible British quarters, but men in streets know troops are in France in considerable numbers but knowing where wonder in vague way quote They are not helping us in the hour of our supreme trial.

My own information is to the effect that British troops are being sent to France at the rate of twenty thousand daily which is fast as they can be assimilated in France. Reliable reports to day indicates English have retreated to Albert and enemy has bombed and wrecked railroad station at Amiens.   Sims

TC telegram (WP, DLC).

From Josephus Daniels

My dear Mr. President: [Washington] March 27, 1918.

I am enclosing you copy of a message received from Admiral Knight.[1] You will observe that the British and Japanese Admirals have been instructed by their Governments to prevent the sending of munitions from Eastern Siberia into the interior. Admiral Knight has assumed that his part was to protect these munitions in cooperation with the British and Japanese, to whom the munitions belong, and especially to prevent them reaching Germans or being used in internal warfare between Russian factions. Admiral Knight wishes instructions. Will you please advise me what instructions you wish forwarded to him?[2]

                    Sincerely,   [Josephus Daniels]

CCL (J. Daniels Papers, DLC).
[1] A. M. Knight to JD, March 26, 1918, No. 02026, T telegram (NDR. RG 45, Naval Records Coll., Telegrams—Incoming, Nov. 2, 1917-June 1, 1919, DNA).
[2] JD to A. M. Knight, March 29, 1918, No. 20028, T telegram (NDR. RG 45, Naval Records Coll., Telegrams—Outgoing, Feb. 6, 1917-May 31, 1919, DNA).
"You say the munitions belong to British and Japanese period Under International law they can protect property belonging to them but it is not clear why this Government should take any action with reference thereto period During disturbed conditions in Russia this Government most anxious that nothing be done that could in any way affect the confidence of the Russian people in our sincere desire to help them establish and maintain government of their own choosing period Keep Department advised daily of conditions so that instructions can be given
"Be careful to proceed upon the principle that we have no right to use armed force except for the protection of American or distinct American interests period Take no action unless instructed by Department period Keep Department fully advised daily 17029 Acknowledge 20028 Secnav"

From Robert Lansing, with Enclosure

My dear Mr. President: Washington March 27, 1918.

I beg to enclose herewith a copy of Ambassador Fletcher's confidential report No. 838 of March 13, 1918, regarding the attitude of President Carranza and his Government with respect to the war. I think you will be interested in reading this despatch.

Faithfully yours,   Robert Lansing

TLS (SDR, RG 59, 763.72/9243, DNA).

E N C L O S U R E

Henry Prather Fletcher to Robert Lansing

No. 838 STRICTLY CONFIDENTIAL

Sir: Mexico, March 13, 1918.

I have the honor to report for your strictly confidential information, the following impressions as to the attitude of President Carranza and his Government, with respect to the Great War.

As to the Mexican official attitude toward the war before our entry thereinto, I can only speak in a general way, as I did not arrive in Mexico until after we had severed diplomatic relations with Germany. From what I have gathered in conversations with colleagues and others, and from a study of the official documents, it seems that the Mexican Government regarded the war as a purely European quarrel, growing out of the economic and imperialistic rivalries of Germany and England, with the sympathies of the Carranza army chiefs enlisted on the side of Germany.

The effects of the war before our entry into it were not severely felt in Mexico. Trade with Germany was never an important or controling factor. The German merchants and manufacturers, and mining concerns continued their business, transferring their base from Germany to the United States. But with our entry all this was changed. Politically, the effect was felt almost immediately; economically, it has been more gradual as our measures of preparation have developed.

President Carranza remains unchangeable in his belief that neutrality is the true policy of Mexico. I think he would sooner abandon power than change his position in this respect. From his general attitude, and from his remarks made in private conversation, as well as from inspired editorials in the newspapers maintained by his Government, it is abundantly clear that he does not believe that the United States entered the war in pursuance of the aims and ideals so clearly and ably stated by President Wilson, and in spite of all that has been done by the Government of the United States to help him to consolidate his position and power, he feels that the President and Government of the United States are not friendly disposed to him.

The presence of American troops in Mexican territory following Villa's raid on Columbus, and the conflicts and clashes with the Carranza authorities arising therefrom, were then and still are deeply resented.

In Carranza's refusal to accept the recommendations of the American-Mexican Commission, the withdrawal of the Pershing expedition and the exchange of Ambassadors, he felt that he had scored another diplomatic victory over the United States. The Department will recall (see my despatch number 17 of March 13, 1917)[1] that the attitude of Carranza and Aguilar in connection with the Zimmermann telegram, was neither frank nor friendly, and evidence now in the possession of the Department shows clearly, in spite of official denials, that the subject matter of the said telegram had been brought to their notice by the German minister and the Japanese Legation sounded by Aguilar in regard to it. One of the effects of the said telegram was to flatter Mexican national pride, and supplemented by German propaganda and arguments, it still operates as an encouragement to the Mexican Government to hope for substantial aid and assistance from Germany, if not indeed an actual alliance, against the further extension of American influence South of the Rio Grande.

In the fear of the gradual extension of this American influence in Mexico, I think, will be found the master-key of Mexico's present attitude in the great world war.

The fact that the United States Government refused to permit the Mexican Government to secure arms and ammunition in the United States, was deeply resented by Carranza and his Government. This having been arranged to their satisfaction, the next complaint brought to my attention was their inability to secure financial assistance in the United States, which the President himself intimated to me was due to the attitude of the United States Government. After it was made abundantly clear that our Government would not impose obstacles to such a loan, and that his failure to secure it was due to his own lack of credit, the restrictions which our Government was obliged to place upon its foreign commerce,

[1] H. P. Fletcher to RL, March 13, 1917, No. 17, TLS (SDR, RG 59, 862.20212/119, DNA).

and especially the exportation of gold, gave the Mexican Government another grievance against the United States.

From the conversations I have had with President Carranza, it is apparent that he thinks because Mexico allows the free exportation of practically all her products to the United States, that she is deserving of similar treatment at our hands, irrespective of war conditions, and while he is willing that some exceptions may be made in the matter of foodstuffs and other articles, the exportation of which must necessarily be curtailed on account of the war, he cannot and will not accept that we should not allow Mexico to receive in gold the trade balances in her favor.

These difficulties with the United States have afforded the Germans an opportunity to keep alive the smouldering embers of Mexican distrust and dissatisfaction, which they have taken advantage of to the full.

As the Department is aware, there is good reason to believe that future, if not indeed present, financial assistance has been offered by Germany to Mexico. It is the German aim to keep Mexico not only neutral in the war, but constantly irritated against the Allies and especially against the United States, in the hope of finding in Mexico a rich field for commercial, economic, and political exploitation after the war. This policy, under Carranza, is succeeding.[2]

In this connection, it is a significant fact that in the year that I have been here, none of the men in public life in Mexico have approached me as to ways and means for increasing the good relations between the two countries, and few, in fact, have cared to discuss the subject, except by way of complaint of actions of the United States Government. They have remained aloof, and for a public man to advocate a policy of friendship for the United States is considered unpatriotic. "Yancófilo"—friend of the Yankees—is a term of reproach.

I am convinced that President Carranza—and this means Mexico to-day—desires correct rather than cordial relations with the United

[2] Throughout 1917, the possibility of a large German loan to Mexico had repeatedly been discussed among German officials. This idea had gained new momentum with the breakdown of negotiations between the Mexican government and private American bankers in the autumn of 1917, and, in January 1918, the German government had requested that Mexico immediately send a representative to Germany to negotiate a loan. At the same time, German industrialists and bankers had begun to show an increasing interest in Mexican raw materials, particularly oil, and had considered plans for a large-scale economic expansion in that country. Even though the Mexican government was sympathetic toward a more active German involvement in Mexican affairs, neither the plans for financial assistance nor the ambitious economic projects were ever realized. For a detailed discussion, see Friedrich Katz, *The Secret War in Mexico: Europe, the United States and the Mexican Revolution* (Chicago and London, 1981), pp. 387-411.

States, and hopes to find in the victory or non-defeat of Germany in the great war, a defense or counterbalance of the moral and economic influence of the United States in Mexico.

I have the honor to be, Sir,

Your obedient servant,   Henry P. Fletcher

TLS (SDR, RG 59, 763.72/9243, DNA).

From Newton Diehl Baker

Paris March 27, 1918.

For the President I have returned to Paris and leave tonight for visit to Italian headquarters Will sail for home April first The situation here is very grave but seems better this morning than at any time since the offensive began The French have taken over a substantial part of the British line and reserves of both armies are now concentrated near chief point of attack which seems to be Amiens which is rail head for supplies of British front. Its capture would be serious. A part of the German plan is to drive in between the French and British forces and for a while they were out of touch with one another. Contact was reestablished last light [night] and the line of defense is now unbroken. General Pershing is in full accord with General Pétain and General Haig and is placing all our men and resources here at their disposal. Our engineer troops are being brought up from the line of communications to aid Haig in the construction of new defensive positions and Pétain in placing four of our divisions in the line[1] thus freeing French divisions for use as battle reserves. This is the best use to be made of them all agree. They will be in action but not as a corps as they have not had corps experience except in association with French divisions and under French Corps Commanders. Both British and French people calm but serious. British have control of air but enemy is still able to use air service effectively.   Baker.

T telegram (N. D. Baker Papers, DLC).
[1] They were the First, Second, Twenty-sixth, and Forty-second Divisions. See *Final Report of Gen. John J. Pershing* (Washington, 1920), p. 32.

From Winthrop More Daniels

My dear Mr. President: Washington Marcy [March] 27, 1918.

This refers to your communication of November 22nd last, in re forcible deportations from Bisbee, Ariz., addressed to Hon. Henry C. Hall,[1] the then Chairman of this Commission, and with which was transmitted copy of the report to you of the President's Mediation Commission.[2]

Among the recommendations made was one that:

> In so far as the evidence before the (Mediation) Commission indicates an interference with interstate lines of communication, the facts should be submitted for appropriate attention by the Interstate Commerce Commission. A memorandum for submission to the Interstate Commerce Commission is herewith appended. (Appendix C.)

I have been instructed by my colleagues to report to you that the Appendix C referred to has been carefully examined, together with the testimony submitted to us by the Mediation Commission, and that after due consideration, and at the advice of our Chief Counsel, we are of the opinion that the only possible ground for legal intervention on our part would be in respect to the free transportation of these unwilling passengers. Beyond that somewhat doubtful ground of proceeding nothing in the papers submitted appears to us to warrant any action on our part, especially under the conditions now existing. The other matters to which attention is called, such as alleged interference with interstate telephonic and telegraphic communication, are beyond the jurisdiction of the Interstate Commerce Commission and perhaps properly come within the province of the Department of Justice.

Very sincerely yours,   W. M. Daniels

TLS (WP, DLC).
[1] WW to H. C. Hall, Nov. 22, 1917, TLS (WP, DLC).
[2] That is, WBW *et al.* to WW, Nov. 6, 1917, Vol. 44.

Two Letters from Robert Somers Brookings

My dear Mr President: Washington March 27, 1918.

Replying to your inquiry, would say that, in my judgment, there was absolutely nothing unfair to the pig iron manufacturers west of the Mississippi River in the reduction of the price of basic pig iron one dollar per gross ton.

As for Mr Goltra, I cannot see that he was very much injured. I explained to him over the telephone that the reduction did not affect foundry pig, which is more than half his product. Where the manufacturer does not sell his basic pig iron, but converts it into steel (which I think is largely the case with Mr Goltra) of course the reduction in price of pig iron does not affect him. As the steel mills use about 50% of pig iron to 50% of scrap steel, of which scrap steel they produce themselves probably half and purchase the balance on the market, the reduction in scrap steel has been to their advantage. I further explained to Mr Goltra that the Price Fixing Committee was now making a careful study of every steel plant in the country in order that we may acquire the necessary detailed information with which to study the steel problem before our next meeting with the manufacturers.

Respectfully yours,   Robt. S. Brookings

My dear Mr President: Washington March 27, 1918.

At the meeting of the Price Fixing Committee with a representative committee of the cotton manufacturers yesterday, it developed that their committee represented something like fifteen million of the thirty million spindles in the country, or one half the industry, largely the more refined or New England half, although many southern mills were represented.

Without burdening you with details, the unanimous expression of opinion upon the part of the cotton people was to the effect that, if some governmental influence was not brought to bear upon the situation, the speculators in finished products and raw materials could, owing to the short supply, do pretty much as they pleased with the cotton price. As manufacturers, they declared that no immediate profit to them would offset the demoralizing influence of a runaway market, which involved labor problems and a commercial relation to the other markets of the world which, after the war, would make their position impossible. They expressed the opinion that, if the Government would enter into the same arrangement with them as with the steel and copper people, by which the President would announce the fixing of price on at least their leading staple products, which price was to be agreed upon as with the steel people, it would enable them to make a considerable reduction below the present market and so stabilize the industry as to prevent any very great fluctuations. While it was thought by some that the raw cotton of the country should be practically commandeered by the Government at the present high market price to prevent it from going higher, it was argued by others that the simple announcement of the price being fixed by the President, based upon the present market price of cotton with a fair compensation only to manufacturers, would be all that was necessary to prevent speculators from advancing the price. They further argued that, in addition to the fixing of a mill price by the President, if a wholesale and retail price was announced at the same time, regardless of the lack of any price fixing laws applicable to the case, the mere announcement of the President would be as effective as any number of enabling acts by Congress.

I explained to them that, while we recognized the danger of the present situation and were glad to receive an expression of their views as to a remedy, when the President assumed the responsibility for fixing public prices, it was necessary that he should be first fully informed regarding the nature and need of protection for the public, and that of course until we had discussed the matter with you, we did not feel at liberty to even express an opinion regarding it.

Now, in conclusion, Mr President, I think it is the judgment of our committee that something should be done to stabilize the cotton textile market, and, if you see no objection to using your authority as above outlined, we will take the matter up with a properly constituted committee of the cotton manufacturers (representing the entire industry) with a view of submitting something to you later for your consideration and approval.

Hoping to have an expression of opinion from you at your convenience, believe me most

Respectfully yours,   Robt. S. Brookings

TLS (WP, DLC).

From George Creel

My dear Mr. President,   Washington, D. C. March 27, 1918

I return herewith the letter of the Attorney General, with which I agree, as a matter of course. It was not justice that I asked, however, but clemency. As over a month has passed since I wrote the letter, the Attorney General is right when he says that it is too late for an investigation such as I asked.

Respectfully,   George Creel

TLS (WP, DLC).

From Gutzon Borglum

Detroit, Mich., March 27, 1918.

Please instruct Mr. Coffin to get in touch with me at Hotel Pontchartrain, Detroit, at once and arrange to go over the factories and to return with me to Buffalo and Dayton. I have been over the ground completely with two associate experts. (We must drive these troubles into their hole.)

Am returning to Washington with comprehensive remedy. Conditions are worse than I put before you two months ago and something must be done immediately. I should be glad to have Henry

Ford accompany me with whom I have conferred, if agreeable wire him. I only indicated to you in my report the sources of trouble, analyzed mainly from official records in Washington, I find not a single department of airplane production has escaped what I believe to be worse than ignorance, engine production, ignition, self-starter instruments, spruce, general plan, variety of machines, fitted and unfitted for Liberty motor, who should build, when deliver, designs, release of designs, inspection, and even the gauges have not escaped attention of either gross ignorance or trouble makers.

Gutzon Borglum.

T telegram (WP, DLC).

Sir William Wiseman to Sir Eric Drummond

MOST URGENT.   [New York] March 27th 1918.

Following for Drummond from Wiseman:
No. 87 Following for Mr. Balfour from Col. House:
With reference to your No. 68 of the 25th. The President agrees with practically every suggestion that you make regarding the disposition of our army. I am glad to inform you that Secretary Baker after consultation with Generals Bliss and Pershing has given orders making effective the recommendations set forth in your message. I will confer with the President personally to-morrow regarding your No. 67 of the 26th. which you propose sending to the British Ambassador at Tokio.

T telegram (W. Wiseman Papers, CtY).

Lord Reading to Sir Eric Drummond

[New York] March 27, 1918.

Following for Mr. BALFOUR *from* LORD READING:
No. 89. Reference to your Cable No. 67 of 26th March to WISE-MAN for HOUSE:
I have discussed this matter with COL. HOUSE, who goes to Washington tomorrow, and will take the matter up with the President.

Undoubtedly the present battle has modified their views on this as on other subjects. House is inclined to agree that, apart from the intrinsic value of the scheme, it may be advisable, and even necessary, to put it into effect for the sake of the Allied morale. At the same time he remains unconvinced as to the real value of the expedition, and believes the President will be the same. House points out that his real objection to the scheme is his firm belief that in the end it will prove of far more value to Germany than to ourselves. He foresees the danger that the Germans by means of skilful propaganda will be able to arm and organize considerable Russian forces to oppose the Japanese, and acting thus as "saviours of the country" obtain an influence which they otherwise could not have over large parts of Russia. He asks what practical effect a comparatively small Japanese army in Northern Siberia can have on the main theatre of war in France? Unless the Japanese can put in a really big force he doubts whether they can advance far enough to have the slightest moral effect. He says that no estimate has yet been given as to what maximum force the Japanese could or would employ, and how far they themselves estimate such a force could push along the Trans-Siberian railroad. Also it is evident the Japanese will require financial and material assistance from the United States. No estimate has been given as to what amount of assistance they will require. In his opinion a great deal depends on the answers to these two questions. If you can give us some information on these two points we will press the matter strongly with the President. The argument that will probably most appeal to him is the necessity of helping the Allied morale at the present moment and the danger of refusing the Japanese assistance even though we doubt the actual effect such assistance will have on the military operations of the enemy. I pointed out to him that now the German morale was so high it would damp their enthusiasm to know that America will redouble her efforts to help in the West and that Japan with America and Allies is intervening in the East. He agreed that it would show the Germans that the struggle was not finished. He wondered whether it would be possible to get even unofficially some expression of Russian assent to Japanese and American and Allied intervention and whether Lockhart would be a useful channel to obtain assent. I promised to ask your view but expressed strong doubt as to Lockhart's suitability for such a mission. This question shows disposition always to revert to making assent of Russia indispensable feature of American policy. Nevertheless I do not think it hopeless at this moment to press for American cooperation without this assent.   Reading.

T telegram (W. Wiseman Papers, CtY).

From the Diary of Josephus Daniels

March Wednesday 27 1918

The Presidents Council,[1] including McAdoo Crowell & myself met at White House. Talked nitrates & decided to allocate ships to bring enough from Chili.

Shall all shipping of allies be pooled? England asked if we would give up 50-50 of Dutch & Norwegian ships? Will Engld give us 50 50 of all? Geddes said she had net loss of only 2½ mil. tons. Where is her 40 mil. tons left? McCormick thought we should pool. WW doubted until Stevens² assured us that the suggestion of Engld was just.

Shall RR get usual low rates given to RRs? Or pay like others? McAdoo wants to furnish cars & get low rate. Garfield no. WW seemed to favor equal price to all even if RRs lost money

¹ That is, the so-called War Cabinet.
² That is, Raymond B. Stevens.

To John Joseph Pershing¹

[The White House, March 28, 1918]

Please convey to the officers and men of our Expeditionary Forces my warmest greetings on this the anniversary of the entrance of the United States into this great war for liberty, and say to them that we all not only have greatly admired and been very proud of the way they have so far accounted for themselves, but have the utmost confidence that in every test they will prove to be made of the finest mettle of free men.   Woodrow Wilson.

T telegram (WP, DLC).
¹ Wilson sent the following message for publication in the official weekly newspaper of the A.E.F., *Stars and Stripes*, at the request of its editor and general manager, Capt. Guy Thomas Viskniskki. See J. J. Pershing to H. P. McCain, March 18, 1918, T telegram (WP, DLC), and B. Crowell to WW, March 20, 1918, TLS (WP, DLC). Wilson's message was published in *Stars and Stripes* on April 5, 1918.

To William Gibbs McAdoo

My dear Mac: The White House 28 March, 1918

You may remember that you sent me the other day a letter from your brother calling attention to a factory where gas masks are being manufactured where he had been told that a very large number of men, I think he said 124, had been detected in purposely puncturing the masks with pins or needles. I wish, if possible, you would get from your brother all the details of this, together with such evidence as we would be able to make something of. The Attorney General advises me that if we can really establish these facts with regard to any of such employees, we can indict them for treason, and he is very anxious to get hold of any evidence of that sort. In his letter to me is the following:

"No information regarding any such situation is in the hands of either the military or naval intelligence services, and inquiry at New York indicates that, while a few persons have been dismissed from day to day for incompetency and various other causes, no one, so far as can be learned by the brief inquiry thus far made, has been discharged for any deliberate injury to the masks. The percentage of rejections has been reduced from seven to four per cent. The rejections, I am informed, are usually due to small holes which are caused by bubbles and which cannot be entirely eliminated. I am also informed that there is no chance that any imperfect mask shall be actually sent to our forces for use in the field."

Cordially and affectionately yours,   Woodrow Wilson

TLS (W. G. McAdoo Papers, DLC).

To Robert Somers Brookings

My dear Mr. Brookings: [The White House] 28 March, 1918

Thank you very much for your letter of yesterday about the meeting of a representative committee of the cotton manufacturers. In reply, let me say that I hope you will take the matter up with a properly constituted committee of the cotton manufacturers representing the entire industry, with a view to submitting something to me for my consideration and approval. I should not hesitate to exercise such authority as I have in these matters if it seems, on the whole, possible and effectual to do so.

Cordially and sincerely yours,   Woodrow Wilson

TLS (Letterpress Books, WP, DLC).

To Robert Lansing

My dear Mr. Secretary: [The White House] 28 March, 1918

The Secretary of the Treasury and I have been searching for some time, as I believe you know, for a proper official designation for Mr. Crosby, now at the head of the Allied Commission on Finance. At present, of course, he ranks, in English parlance, merely as an under secretary and, though chairman of the commission, is associated on the commission itself with men who have the highest rank in the British Civil Service. The title which the Secretary of the Treasury suggests is that of "High Commissioner of Finance." I hesitated to accept that designation before asking you whether it had in usage any diplomatic implication. I would be very much obliged to you for a suggestion of your own.[1]

Cordially and faithfully yours,   Woodrow Wilson

TLS (Letterpress Books, WP, DLC).
    [1] There is no further correspondence on this subject. Crosby was never designated high commissioner.

To Gutzon Borglum

The White House Mar 28 1918

Am sorry to say I cannot act upon the advice of your telegram of March twenty seventh I have put the whole matter in other hands and I am sure that nothing will be left uncoilded [uncoiled] about the process and needs of the service   Woodrow Wilson

T telegram (G. Borglum Papers, DLC).

Two Telegrams from Newton Diehl Baker

Paris March 28, 1918.

URGENT. A joint resolution of the advisors of the Supreme War Council will reach you today with my recommendation appended. It seems important for us not to insist upon carrying out an ideal program at a moment when all agree that the greatest need here is infantry and the use of shipping for other personnel decreases the number of infantry possible to be transported. Nevertheless I agree with General Pershing that we should keep constantly before the British and French that all our plans are ultimately in that direction. This for the two reasons, first—we do not want either nation to rely upon us for replacements, and, second—we want the Germans to know that we are augmenting the present allied forces and not merely making good its losses. Moreover (American?) sentiment must be satisfied. After full consideration I believe you should approve the joint resolution in the manner suggested in my note attached to the copy sent you by General Bliss. General Pershing will then be free to make necessary stipulations with French and British commanders for the use and ultimate return of these units and General Pershing's judgment of the military situation will determine when they can safely be reincorporated in American forces.

Baker.

T telegram (WP, DLC).

Versailles. March 28th [1918].

Number 67 Confidential.

Paragraph 1. The Secretary of War this morning directed this telegram be sent direct to the President with copies for Secretary of State and Acting Secretary of War and Chief of Staff. Following joint note eighteen of the permanent military representatives with the Supreme War Council is transmitted for the action of the President. Following the text of the joint note are the recommendations of the Secretary of War dictated by him this morning.

Paragraph 2. The following joint note eighteen was adopted by the permanent military representatives March 27th, 1918 "(1) In paragraph four of joint note number twelve dated twelfth January 1918 the military representatives agreed as follows: 'After the most careful and searching inquiries they were agreed on the points that the security of France could also be assured *them* but in view of the strength of the attacks which the enemy able develop on this front, an attack which, in the opinion of the military representatives could reach a strength of ninety-six divisions (excluding reenforcements by roulement[1]); they feel compelled to add that France will be safe during 1918 only under certain conditions, namely; (A) That the strength of the British and French troops in France are continuously kept up to their present total strength, and that they receive the expected reenforcements of not less than two American divisions per month.' (2) The battle which is developing at the present moment in France and which can extend to the other theaters of operations may very quickly place the Allied armies in a serious situation from the point of view of effectiveness, and the military representatives are from this moment of opinion that the above detailed condition (A) can no longer be maintained and they consider as a general proposition that the new situation requires new decision. The military representatives are of opinion that it is highly desirable that the American Government should assist the Allied armies as soon as possible by permitting, in principle, the temporary service of American units in Allied army corps and divisions, such reenforcements must however be obtained from other units than those American divisions which are now operating with the French, and the units so temporarily employed must eventually be returned to the American army. (3) The military representatives are of opinion that, from the present time, in execution of the foregoing, and until otherwise directed by the Supreme War Council, only American Infantry and machine gun units, organized as that government may decide, be brought to France, and that all agreements or conventions hitherto made in conflict with this decision be modified accordingly."

Paragraph 3. The following is the action recommended by the Secretary of War. "To the President: The foregoing resolutions were considered by General Tasker H. Bliss General Pershing and me. Paragraph three proposes a change in the order to shipment of American troops to France and necessarily postpones the organization and training of complete American divisions as parts of an independent American Army. This ought to be conceded only in view of the present critical situation and continued only so long as that situation necessarily demands it. The question of replacements will continue to embarrass the British and French Governments, and efforts to satisfy that need by retaining American units assigned to them must be anticipated, but we must keep in mind the formation of an American army, while, at the same time, we must not seem to sacrifice joint efficiency at a critical moment to that object. Therefore I recommend that you express your approval of the joint note in the following sense; 'The purpose of the American Government is to render the fullest cooperation and aid and therefore the recommendation of the military representatives with regard to the preferential transportation of American Infantry and machine gun units in present emergency is approved. Such units when transported will be under the direction of the Commander in Chief of the American Expeditionary Forces and will be assigned for training and use by him in his discretion. He will use these and all other military forces of the United States under his command in such manner as to render the greatest military assistance, keeping in mind always the determination of this government to have its various military forces collected as speedily as their training and the military situation will permit, into an independent American Army, acting in concert with the armies of Great Britain and France and all arrangements made by him for their temporary loss of time and service will be made with *these* ends in view.['] Baker."[2]

Bliss.[3]

T telegram (WDR, RG 407, World War I Cablegrams, DNA).
    [1] That is, by rotation.
    [2] In Bliss' retained copy (WDR, RG 120, Records of the American Section of the Supreme War Council, 1917-1919, File No. 315, DNA) the end of this sentence reads "for their temporary training and service will be made with that end in view."
    [3] This telegram was received at the War Department at 9:17 p.m. on March 28.

From Walter Hines Page

London, Mar. 28, 1918.

9268, Most Secret. For the Secretary and the President.

My 8910, March 6.[1] In the absence from England of Admiral Hall I have only just received a copy of King Alfonso's message of

March 5 to the Emperor Charles, transmitting the President's reply as handed to Riano, and also of the Emperors rejoinder to the President dated March 23rd, which I do not telegraph as I assume it has now been received in Washington.

In the message of the fifth instant, after communicating the text of the President's reply to the Emperor, the King of Spain added:

"The President received the Ambassador with the usual cordiality. He told him that in order to maintain secrecy he had himself typed on the typewriter the message which he handed him. My Ambassador gave expression to his delight that the President had found in your message something that might form a basis for future understanding, and which might in some way open the possibility of negotiation, a statement to which the President assented. At the same time he remarked that in spite of his (wireless groups jammed) he was of opinion that after direct conversations had taken place he would (further undecipherable group) inform his Allies. The Ambassador's impression is if not optimistic nevertheless fairly favorable for he thinks that if you are willing to answer the peace questions in detail the goal of all our proposals will be brought nearer. It is my private impression that the delegate proposed by you should have as chief (to strive ?) to clear up those points which Wilson regards critical. This would not (imply ?) complicated and formal negotiations and in this manner you could avoid pledging yourself by the direct reply desired of you. In all these matters my services are ever at your disposal. With royal greetings. Alfonso."

Page.

T telegram (WP, DLC).
[1] WHP to RL, March 6, 1918, T telegram (SDR, RG 59, 763.72110/7700, DNA). Page summarized the telegram from Alfonso to Charles of March 1, which described Wilson's reaction to Charles' message contained in Alfonso's letter printed at February 26, 1918, Vol. 46. According to the Spanish Ambassador, who delivered the communication, Wilson showed an "enormous surprise" but apparently welcomed the King's intervention. Wilson characterized Charles' message as "transcendental" and stated that its receipt had placed him in a somewhat embarrassing situation, since he had expressed himself as opposed to secret negotiations.

From David Franklin Houston

Dear Mr. President: Washington March 28, 1918.

Your personal inquiry regarding the representative character of the National Nonpartisan League, of which Mr. A. C. Townley is president, was received during my recent absence.[1] It seems that there is a strong suspicion that the League is not at all a representative body. It operates under a secret caucus system. No public election of officers has been held so far as we have been able to learn. Mr. Townley has been its president since its inception, and also appears to have designated not only his associates in office, but the candidates for the public offices within the State of North Dakota.

The rank and file of its membership are hard-working, honest, well-intentioned, and for the most part, loyal farmers. Well-informed people in the Northwest question seriously the loyalty of a number of the officers of the League. Mr. Townley himself is a radical Socialist, as are most of his associates. He registered as a voting member of the Socialist party under the North Dakota registration laws. I am enclosing a clipping from the Washington Post of March 13, 1918, indicating that Mr. Townley has been indicted by the Martin County, Minnesota, grand jury, on the charge of "issuing and circulating a seditious pamphlet tending to discourage enlistments." I have no information regarding the further developments in this matter.

The League appears to have thriven largely through the cultivation of class hatred of one kind or another to convince the farmer of the Northwest that he has not and can not secure a square deal through existing political parties.

At a meeting in St. Paul last week, one of the organizers of the League told his farmer audience at the St. Paul Auditorium, "You are outside the law and the courts won't protect you. The only way the farmers can meet the existing conditions is to dislodge corporation-owned legislators from their entrenched positions."

The League conducts a daily newspaper, The Courier News, at Fargo, North Dakota, and a weekly magazine, The Nonpartisan Leader, which until January 1 was printed at Fargo, North Dakota, but since that date has been published at St. Paul, Minnesota. How carelessly these official organs deal with fact is well illustrated by the full-page cartoon with its legend in the issue of March 18 of the Leader. You will recall, not only your own helpful attitude concerning the so-called Baer Bill, H.R. 7795, but my own recommendations with respect to it from time to time; also the favorable report of the Committee on Agriculture of the House. The legend of the full-page cartoon referred to states as follows:

"Baer's bill to help drouth-stricken farmers of the United States by providing loans for them at reasonable rates, looked as though it would pass. The agricultural committee of the house of representatives seemed to be for it. Food Administrator Hoover indorsed and urged it. But Secretary of Agriculture Houston, who evidently thinks nothing is good for the farmers unless it originates with him, opposed it and swung a majority of one on the committee against the bill. The committee refused to report it out for passage."[2]

As stated above, I believe the rank and file of the farmer membership are loyal and honest in their beliefs, though grossly misinformed by their leaders.

Should you desire further and more detailed information, I will be glad to secure it from reliable sources in the Northwest.

Sincerely yours,   D. F. Houston

TLS (WP, DLC).
[1] A. C. Townley to WW, March 20, 1918, had been referred to Houston on March 22.
[2] As Houston points out, this was, indeed, a gross misrepresentation of his position on the Baer bill. Houston had endorsed the measure before the House Committee on Agriculture on February 25. At the same time, however, he had denied the existence of a severe food shortage in the United States. This statement had apparently convinced the committee, which had been about to report the bill, that there was no urgent need for such a measure. See the *New York Times*, Feb. 26, 1918.
Contrary to the assertion of the *Nonpartisan Leader*, the committee had reported the bill on March 8, and Houston continued to recommend its immediate adoption. See, e.g., DFH to Floyd R. Harrison, Assistant to the Secretary of Agriculture, March 15, 1918, TC telegram (WP, DLC). For Wilson's support of the bill, see WW to B. H. Snell, March 20, 1918; WW to G. M. Young, March 18, 1918, TLS (Letterpress Books, WP, DLC); and WW to J. S. Sherley, March 28, 1918, TLS (Letterpress Books, WP, DLC).
The House adopted an amended version of the Baer bill on March 29 by a vote of 250 to sixty-seven. However, the Senate failed to take any action on it. See *Cong. Record*, 65th Cong., 2d sess., pp. 4297-98.

From Thomas Watt Gregory

Dear Mr. President: Washington, D. C. March 28, 1918.

Immediately on leaving the last Cabinet meeting I called on the Pardon Attorney[1] for a list of the men convicted in what is known as the Indian[a]polis Dynamiters Case[2] who were still in prison, for a statement of how long each of them had served and how much longer they would be required to serve under their sentences. I also told him to attach a short memorandum indicating the connection of each of these men with the conspiracy charged.

This memorandum I herewith enclose and I believe it furnishes what you desired.[3] While I have not again gone over the voluminous papers in this case, I am satisfied that Mr. Finch's statement is accurate.   Faithfully yours,   T. W. Gregory

TLS (WP, DLC).
[1] James A. Finch.
[2] About which see E. M. Nockels *et al.* to WW, Dec. 4, 1916, n. 1, printed as an Enclosure with S. Gompers to WW, Dec. 5, 1916, Vol. 40.
[3] James A. Finch, "Memorandum for the Attorney General. In re Indianapolis Dynamite Case," March 27, 1918, TS MS (WP, DLC). Finch pointed out that three of the defendants were still in prison: Frank M. Ryan, former president of the International Association of Bridge and Structural Iron Workers; Eugene A. Clancy, a former vice-president of the union; and Michael J. Young, a former member of its executive board. Ryan had been sentenced to seven years and Young and Clancy each to six years. Since they had been released on bond for varying periods during earlier applications for pardon, they had not served equal time. Ryan had served three years and ten months, with fifteen months remaining; Clancy had served three years and nine months, with six

months remaining; and Young had served four years and three months, with only seven weeks left until the expiration of his term. Finch also briefly reviewed the evidence in the case and concluded that the guilt of the defendants was beyond doubt.

From William Bauchop Wilson

My dear Mr. President: Washington March 28, 1918.

The Children's Bureau of this Department and the Woman's Committee of the Council of National Defense are desirous that the second year of the war be signalized by special effort for the protection of the American Child.

Beginning April 6th, sixty days will be devoted to a nation-wide test of the weight and measurement of children under school age. This is proposed because of the understanding that one-third of the rejections of soldiers for physical defects in the first draft were for causes many of which could have been removed if recognized and treated in early childhood.

May I not, therefore, ask that you address a communication to me along the lines of the accompanying paragraphs, and I will then be in a position to give the necessary publicity to the matter.[1]

Faithfully yours, W B Wilson

TLS (WP, DLC).
[1] WW to WBW, March 29, 1918, is a paraphrase of W. B. Wilson's suggested letter. The latter is a T MS in WP, DLC.

From Bernard Mannes Baruch

My dear Mr. President: Washington March 28, 1918.

I have your letter of March 27th enclosing one from Mr. McAdoo. He is absolutely correct in the views he expresses and position he takes. We are exerting every effort to discourage, not only new developments in Eastern territory, but we are endeavoring to force the placing of additional orders out of the congested area.

There is more business offered than can be taken care of by labor, transportation and facilities. Business not necessary to the conduct of the War will have to give way.

I have taken this position for some time and am persisting in it. The results will be slow but sure.

Faithfully yours, Bernard M. Baruch

TLS (WP, DLC).

From Gutzon Borglum

Detroit, Mich., March 28, 1918.

Your telegram has been received. I cannot understand its meaning, as I am wholly uninformed of the situation; however, I cannot question your sincerity nor purpose.   Gutzon Borglum.

T telegram (WP, DLC).

David Lloyd George to Lord Reading

Paraphrase of a Telegram from the Prime
Minister to Lord Reading, dated March 28th 1918.

Please see the President immediately and beg him to approve the action proposed in this telegram.

A great success has been won by the German forces and although, largely as a result of exhaustion, their advance has been stayed for the moment, there can be no doubt that they will make another terrific onslaught as soon as they possibly can with the object of capturing Amiens, the great railway centre, and effecting a separation between the French and British Armies. It is impossible to say that they will not succeed in their object although we are hurrying reinforcements with all possible speed to the crucial point.

It has unfortunately not proved possible to achieve through the machinery set up at Versailles the perfect co-operation between the British and French Armies which is essential, in spite of all the efforts that have been made to that end. This had been due to the inherent difficulty of welding into a single whole the armies of two or three different nationalities, and in no way to a lack of desire on the part of one Government or the other. In these circumstances a meeting took place yesterday between the British and French Governments and they decided, with a view to this grave defect being remedied, that General Foch should be entrusted with the co-ordinating authority over all the dispositions of the Allies on the Western Front. The arrangement is actually worded as follows:

"General Foch has been entrusted by the British and French Governments with the task of co-ordinating the action of the Allied Armies on the Western Front. He will consult for this purpose with the Commanders-in-Chief who are requested to furnish him with all necessary information."

We feel sure that the President will realise that the extreme urgency of the situation made it impossible to delay action for the purposes of consultation, and we are confident that he will approve the decision which does no more than carry out the policy of unity of control which it had been intended to secure by the Versailles agreement and to which he gave his strong approval. The action of General Foch is of necessity confined for the moment to the co-ordination of the movements of the British and French Armies, but it is earnestly hoped that the President will agree to the same authority being exercised by him in regard to the movements of the American Army which it is desired shall come into the fight.

Further, it is of paramount importance that American troops should be sent to France with the utmost speed possible and I wish you to urge this on the President. Should the present object of the enemy, viz: the separation of the British and French Armies, prove successful, the second operation will certainly be an attempt completely to destroy one of these armies while the other is being held. If this second operation also succeeds, he will turn upon the remaining one with the whole of his strength. If, on the other hand, the Allies now succeed in holding the enemy, my military advisers are of opinion that he will go off and help the Austrians to smash Italy, returning afterwards with Austro-Hungarian forces in an attempt to seize the Channel ports before our armies can again be made up to their fighting strength. The late Spring or early Summer of this year is, in any case, certain to see further fighting of the most desperate nature. France has no further reserves at her disposal. We are scraping men from every possible side. Our military age is being raised to 50 and possibly to 55, and we are considering whether conscription shall not be applied to Ireland. As we have already raised over five millions of men it is inevitable, however, that the further numbers we can get by this scraping process will be small. It is, therefore, of vital importance that American troops of all arms should be poured into France as rapidly as possible, whatever may be the outcome of the present battle. I beg you to press this fact upon President Wilson with all the force you can. For the present it is not material which is required, but man power to make good the losses in killed, wounded and missing.

Finally, there is the question as to how to make available in the quickest possible time the American forces now in France and those which may arrive later on. I am advised that it is not possible to use many of the American divisions in active operations in their present state of training. As regiments they are, however, excellent. Arrangements for the use of a great part of this force have already been made with General Pershing, and we should like to know if the President would agree to the brigading, during the crisis, of all other units that may become available with French or British divisions, as regiments are fit for incorporation into experienced divisions long before they can be formed into divisions by themselves. We most earnestly trust that he will agree. Before this battle is over every man may count who is capable of fighting, and American troops may be of inestimable service if they can be employed in whatever way they may be of most use. I can see no other way of utilising this splendid material which should be made available for fighting in France this summer when the whole war may be decided one way or the other.[1]

T MS (WP, DLC).
    [1] Other versions of this telegram are A. J. Balfour to Lord Reading, No. 1793, March 28, 1918, T telegram (Reading Papers, FO 800/224, PRO), and A. J. Balfour to Lord Reading, No. 1793, March 28, 1918, T telegram (FO 115/2461, pp. 131-33, PRO).

Lord Reading to David Lloyd George

Washington, 28th March 1918.

Very Urgent. Personal. For the Prime Minister. Very Secret. Your Cablegram No. 1793.

I have just returned from interview with the President. As regards the appointment of General Foch the President had had this news from Secretary Baker and also that General Pershing would meet Secretary Baker next day with a view to arranging cooperation with General Foch. The President approved the appointment and said as you indicated in your cablegram that he has always believed in such unity of control. As regards the other two matters he expressed the strong desire to assist in any way that was practicable but added that he had given power to Secretary Baker and General Pershing to decide all such questions and must rely upon their judgment.

The President had received a cablegram from Secretary Baker which had not yet been completely decoded but as appeared from the passage he read to me it deals with the very subjects you raise.

I impressed upon the President the gravity of the situation and urged him to agree to your second and third proposals. He answered that there was no need to press these matters upon him as he was only anxious to do all he could but that in such matters as brigading of American infantry with British and French divisions he would be guided by his military advisers who must decide whether it was practicable. He said he would consider your requests after he had received and studied the full message from Secretary Baker. I told him I should send you immediate answer as above stated because I knew you would be anxious to learn his views.[1]

T telegram (Reading Papers, FO 800/224, PRO).
    [1] A. J. Balfour to D. Lloyd George, March 28, 1918, T telegram (FO 115/2461, p. 138, PRO), is another copy of this telegram. A slightly different version is Lord Reading to D. Lloyd George, March 29, 1918, T telegram (A. J. Balfour Papers, FO 800/209, PRO).

Sir William Wiseman to the Foreign Office

Washington [c. March 28, 1918].

Following for Mr. Balfour. Very secret.

It may be useful to explain to you the attitude of the President towards the present crisis.

The President never believed that the Germans would attempt the much advertized offensive.

He thought the morale of their troops was low and the influence of the military party waning.

The success of their present attack has been a great shock to him and necessitates a readjustment of opinions and hopes to which he has stubbornly clung in spite of much advice to the contrary.

The first effect here of the recent news has been to let loose a storm of criticism against the Administration which has been brewing for some time.

The events of the past week seem to justify the Republican charge that the American army would not be ready in time to take its proper share in the war.

Possibly the War Department is open to criticism but it [is] only natural that the Presidents mind should be alert to meet these charges—and refute them—feeling, as he honestly does, that everything possible has been done in the face of enormous difficulties.

It will be hard for you to realize that anyone should be concerned with the credit of an Administration at a time like this, but we are very far from the great struggle in France. The President, at any rate, regards his critics here as little better than traitors to America and the Allied cause.

The immediate consideration is, I take it, not what the U. S. might have done but what they can do now.

The authority of the President is so supreme that we must have his cordial personal co-operation if we are to secure the last ounce of American effort.

Expediency demands that we should help the President in order that he will help us. Our public statements, then, should be directed to strengthening the authority and prestige of the President and the unification of the war effort of America.

At the same time we are entitled to observe that the criticisms of the Administration in the American Press are most useful stimulants and providing they do not undermine the Presidents authority, must be regarded as definitely assisting the Allied cause.

Moreover, so long as our public attitude is entirely sympathetic we need not hesitate in diplomatic communications and interviews to point out to the President the exact truth even though it may carry with it criticism of the administration's shortcomings. But we should confine ourselves to insisting firmly on definite points to which we want him to agree rather than general appeals for greater efficiency.

It is also important that when we intend to insist on something to which we think the President may have objections, we should always make joint representations with the French.

It should not always be the duty of the British to lay unpleasant truths before the President.

It is my firm conviction that the President is determined to stand by the Allies whatever may occur with all the resources of the United States and to meet any demands which he considers practically possible.

Col House is staying in Washington, at the Presidents request, during the crisis and is in the closest touch with Lord R.

Hw telegram (W. Wiseman Papers, CtY).

From the Diary of Colonel House

The White House, March 28, 1918.

I came to Washington this morning with Janet and David Miller on the 11.08 train. The trip was without incident. I was really not able to travel but I had put off coming so long and the President was so insistent that I decided to make the effort.

I came directly to the White House. The President was not in but I had tea with Mrs. Wilson and a confidential chat before he appeared. After dinner he and I went into executive session and cleared up our budgets. As I anticipated, he was much annoyed at Lloyd George's cable to Reading and at Reading's lack of judgment in reading it.[1] I told him the circumstances, and tried to smooth the matter over, both as to Lloyd George and the Ambassador. I told him George had been requested to send the cable because of Reading's proposed speech, but that Reading did not give him any intimation as to what to say.

The President's point was that it was a most discourteous and unusual, as well as an undiplomatic thing, for an ambassador to give out publicly a message from his government directly to the people of another country without addressing it to the head of that Government. He said it was sufficient cause to send an ambassador home.

We had this conversation when I first saw him this afternoon. Strangely enough, Reading had an appointment with the President within the hour, and he expressed his intention of telling Reading how he felt. I dissuaded him from this, saying it was all meant in good part, and that Reading himself had had no diplomatic experience. I thought we ought not to be critical since he was our sincere friend and doing the best he knew.

The main work we did tonight was to outline the speech we decided he should make soon. The opportunity will be given him when he reviews the Camp Meade troops at Baltimore on April 6th, which is the anniversary of our entrance into the war. It is to [be] the occasion of opening the Third Liberty Loan.

We had no difficulty in agreeing as to what the speech should contain, for we were practically of one mind. In talking of our ambassadors, he showed me a cable from Sharp,[2] remarking that he considered him altogether the most satisfactory ambassadorial appointment he had made. He thought Sharp had "judicial turn of mind," and he expressed a desire to give him a Federal judgeship, should an opportunity occur. He was surprised to hear me say he was not a lawyer but a business man.[3]

T MS (E. M. House Papers, CtY).
[1] During a speech at a dinner given in his honor by the Lotos Club of New York on March 27, 1918, Reading had read a telegram from Lloyd George to the American people which he had received that same day. The war, Lloyd George wrote, had reached the crisis stage with the recent German onslaught, and he urged the United States to hasten reinforcements to Europe as soon as possible. *New York Times*, March 28, 1918; see also *"Across the Flood." Addresses at the Dinner in Honor of the Earl of Reading at the Lotos Club, New York, March 27th, 1918* (New York, 1918).
[2] It was probably W. G. Sharp to RL, Jan. 10, 1918, printed as an Enclosure with FLP to WW, March 14, 1918.
[3] Sharp had in fact earlier practiced law.

To Ferdinand Foch

[The White House] March 29, 1918.

May I not convey to you my sincere congratulations on your new authority? Such unity of command is a most hopeful augury of ultimate success. We are following with profound interest the bold and brilliant action of your forces.   Woodrow Wilson.

Printed in the *New York Times*, March 30, 1918.

To Newton Diehl Baker

[The White House, March 29, 1918]

The President concurs in the joint note of the permanent military representatives with the Supreme War Council in the sense formulated in your No. 67 March 28 and wishes you to regard yourself

authorized to decide all questions of immediate cooperation or replacement.[1]

WWhw telegram (WDR, RG 407, World War I Cablegrams, DNA).
[1] This was sent as H. P. McCain to T. H. Bliss, March 29, 1918, No. 39, T telegram
(WDR, RG 407, World War I Cablegrams, DNA).

To George Wylie Paul Hunt

Confidential.

[The White House]
My dear Governor: 29 March 1917 [1918]

After the receipt of your letter of March twenty-second, I again
went into the case of Captain Wheeler, and I want to say now very
frankly that I think more harm would be done by attempting to
undo what has occurred than by letting it alone. No doubt the
suggestions you make in your letter are very true with regard to
the circumstances attending the appointment of Wheeler, but his
military qualifications are undoubted and it would be clear to everybody that only his military qualifications ought to be considered in
an appointment such as he has just received, and that to draw in
the other matter, however grave the other matter might be, would
be to introduce very disturbing elements into the whole question
of army appointments.

I warmly hope that your own judgment will jump with mine in
this matter, for you may be sure that I am not minimizing the
considerations which you have urged upon me, and that I set a
high value on your own opinion.

Cordially and sincerely yours,   Woodrow Wilson

TLS (Letterpress Books, WP, DLC).

To Winthrop More Daniels

Dear Daniels: The White House 29 March, 1918

Thank you for your letter of March twenty-seventh about the
Bisbee, Arizona, cases. I have very little doubt in my own mind
that your conclusions are quite right.

Cordially and faithfully yours,   Woodrow Wilson

TLS (Wilson-Daniels Corr., CtY).

To David Franklin Houston

My dear Mr. Secretary: [The White House] 29 March, 1918

Thank you very much for your letter about the Non-partisan League. It gives me just the sort of estimate of the association that I wanted.

Cordially and faithfully yours,   Woodrow Wilson

TLS (Letterpress Books, WP, DLC).

To William Bauchop Wilson

My dear Mr. Secretary: [The White House] 29 March, 1918

Next to the duty of doing everything possible for the soldiers at the front, there could be, it seems to me, no more patriotic duty than that of protecting the children, who constitute one-third of our population.

The success of the efforts made in England in behalf of the children is evidenced by the fact that the infant death rate in England for the second year of the war was the lowest in her history. Attention is now being given to education and labor conditions for children by the legislatures of both France and England, showing that the conviction among the Allies is that the protection of childhood is essential to winning the war.

I am very glad that the same processes are being set afoot in this country, and I heartily approve the plan of the Children's Bureau and the Woman's Committee of the Council of National Defense for making the second year of the war one of united activity on behalf of children, and in that sense a children's year.

I trust that the year will not only see the goal reached of saving one hundred thousand lives of infants and young children, but that the work may so successfully develop as to set up certain irreducible minimum standards for the health, education and work of the American child.

Cordially and sincerely yours,   Woodrow Wilson

TLS (Letterpress Books, WP, DLC).

To William Bauchop Wilson, with Enclosure

My dear Mr. Secretary: [The White House] 29 March, 1918

I don't like to send this memorandum to you and bring up again the perplexing Minneapolis situation,[1] but I do so only because I

would like you to tell me whether there is anything that you see
that I could personally do to straighten out this situation which
ought never to have arisen.

One of the statements in the memorandum puzzles me. It seems
to assume that the Federal Government has the right to take over
the street railways of Minneapolis, but that is not true, is it?

Cordially and sincerely yours,   Woodrow Wilson

TLS (Letterpress Books, WP, DLC).
  [1] About which see, L. F. Post to WW, Dec. 10, 1917, Vol. 45, and n. 2 thereto.

E N C L O S U R E

MINNEAPOLIS SITUATION

The President's Mediation Commission has been unable to affect
settlement of the street car controversy in Minneapolis and St. Paul
Minnesota. The status of the case now is as follows:

The Mediation Commission, after a thorough investigation there
and then careful consideration of all of the facts in connection with
the matter, and after a further interview with the President of the
Company, Horace Lowry, here in Washington, finally made findings which were to the effect that the men who were idle were to
be given the preference in going back to work over any newcomers
making applications for jobs. They were to go back at whatever
work the Company had at the old rate of pay they had been getting
previous to the time they were locked out, and once they were back
at work they were to get credit for the service they rendered previous
to the time they were locked out in their seniority rating, which
gave them according to the length of time of service, preference in
the choice of desirable runs that became vacant, with the right to
belong to the organization if they wanted to, no discrimination
either way. The Company was willing to take the men back as new
employes and give them the preference, let them start on the night
runs, or undesirable runs as new beginners and work themselves
up just as if they had never worked for the Company at all.

The Commission submitted its findings to the National Council
for Defense and they approved of them and requested the State
Safety Council of Minnesota, Governor of which state[1] is chairman
of that Council, to use their power and influence in carrying its
provisions into effect. The Secretary of War also asked the Minnesota State Safety Council to carry the provisions of the Mediation
Commission's findings into effect. The State Safety Council refused
to do so. The President's Mediation Commission then went back
to Minnesota and took the matter up directly with the Company

and with the Governor representing the Public Safety Commission. While the Governor did not refuse outright to use his influence in that direction, he absolutely failed to do so and there was no question but what he decided not to do so. The Company utterly refused to agree to take the men back on the basis of the President's Mediation Commission's findings. They agreed to everything with the exception of letting the men, when they went back, have their old standing and seniority which meant the same rate of wages they were getting prior to their being locked out and the right of choice of new runs in accordance with the length of time of their actual service prior to the time they were locked out.

The attitude of the men on strike and the labor movement in the Twin Cities has been everything the government could desire. In the beginning at the request of the President's Mediation Commission they withdrew their order for a sympathetic strike and by motion agreed to abide by whatever decision the President's Mediation Commission would render in settlement of the dispute. They reiterated that position when the Commission went back the second time notwithstanding in their judgment they felt they were not getting what they were entitled to in the decision that had been rendered.

At the present time over five hundred men are still idle. The rest of the labor movement are very much perturbed about the situation and there is great likelihood of serious and large industrial disturbances taking place which might affect at least some of the industries engaged in the production of supplies and equipment for war needs.

Mr. O. P. Briggs[2] of Minneapolis, one of the men active in the Citizens' Alliance, the purpose of which, so far as the union men are concerned we understand, has been to prevent organization of workers, has had a good deal to do in determining the attitude of the Company in this matter and also the Minnesota Public Safety Commission. He made the statement to the Commission just prior to leaving Minneapolis that if the President, or the National Council for Defense would issue an order for them to comply with the findings of the Mediation Commission they would do so.

There is no question but what the enemies of the government from a war point of view (pacifists and German sympathizers) are using this situation to create sentiment detrimental to the government in the prosecution of the war not alone in the Twin Cities but in the entire State and in a considerable number of other places.

If anything can be done to get the matter settled it should be done. The Twin City Rapid Transit Street Railway Company is not a very large concern comparatively. Their paper valuation is forty five million dollars, and their actual valuation, on pretty reliable information, is something like ten million dollars, and as this is the first company that has defied the United States Government, the National Council for Defense, the Secretary of War, and the President himself, through the President's Mediation Commission, the Government might be justified in taking over the industry and operating it. In fact it may be necessary if settlement of disputes by moral influences through such agencies as the President's Mediation Commission is to be of any value in the future, and particularly when it is such a small concern and can be handled easily without inconveniencing the government. It seems desirable that it should be done.

Congressman Van Dyke[3] has been working in cooperation with the Commission in trying to settle this matter and he is now in St. Paul trying to bring about an adjustment on the basis of the Mediation Commission's findings.

T MS (WP, DLC).
[1] That is, Joseph Alfred Arner Burnquist, a Republican.
[2] Otis P. Briggs, chairman of the executive committee of the Citizens' Alliance and chief negotiator for the transit company.
[3] That is, Carl Chester Van Dyke, Democrat from St. Paul.

To William Charles Adamson[1]

My dear Judge: [The White House] 29 March, 1918.

Thank you for your letter of the twenty-eighth.[2] I unaffectedly hope that the movement to name the Mussel [Muscle] Shoals Dam after me will not go very far, because I frankly hate to have things named after me,[3] but you may be sure that I none the less appreciate, and appreciate very deeply, the generous sentiment that lies behind the movement. I am, and have been as you know, greatly interested in the work at the Shoals and rejoice that it is now being pushed forward.

With the best wishes,
            Cordially and sincerely yours,   Woodrow Wilson

TLS (Letterpress Books, WP, DLC).
[1] Adamson had resigned from the House of Representatives in December 1917 upon his appointment to the Board of General Appraisers in the Customs Service in New York.
[2] It is missing.
[3] Actually, it was named Wilson Dam.

To Edward Thomas Brown

Personal.

My dear Colonel: [The White House] 29 March, 1918.

The talk that I had with Harris yesterday leads me to ask if you will not be kind enough to see Clark Howell[1] and Major Cohen,[2] if that is agreeable to you, and tell them that I have asked you to say to them that I am warmly in favor of the election of Harris to the Senate.

Let me explain that Harris tells me that in order to save their faces Clark Howell and others are asking, and perhaps for all I know promising, a letter from me conveying a public endorsement of Harris. Unless such a letter were framed more skillfully than I can now work it out in my mind, it might have a very serious reaction, if put in the wrong light by Hardwick in his usual unscrupulous manner, and my present judgment is that it would not be wise, but I am perfectly willing that this direct message should be carried to Howell and Cohen, if you are willing to carry it.

We all join in the most affectionate messages.

Faithfully yours,   Woodrow Wilson

TLS (Letterpress Books, WP, DLC).
   [1] Owner and editor in chief of the *Atlanta Constitution*.
   [2] John Sanford Cohen, editor of the *Atlanta Journal*, and president of the Atlanta Journal Co.

To Herbert Clark Hoover

My dear Mr. Hoover: The White House 29 March, 1918

I have read the enclosed letter,[1] which I take the liberty of returning, and believe that it would be all right to publish it[2] and to proceed with the plan for the appointment of a commission.

Cordially and sincerely yours,   Woodrow Wilson

TLS (H. Hoover Papers, HPL).
   [1] That is, H. C. Hoover to WW, March 26, 1918, printed as an Enclosure with H. C. Hoover to WW, March 26, 1918.
   [2] It was published in the *Official Bulletin*, II (April 1, 1918), 1, 6.

To Ben Johnson[1]

My dear Mr. Johnson: [The White House] 29 March, 1918

I hesitate to write you about a matter to which I have not been able to give any direct personal attention, but I have learned that it is the opinion of those who have been most seriously interested, and most intelligently interested, in the work of reclaiming the alleys of Washington that it would be advantageous to the work if the operation of the legislation recently passed in that matter should be postponed until the expiration of a brief period after the war.[2] I am, therefore, taking the liberty of asking if you will not be kind enough to look into the matter with a view to meeting that opinion, if you can do so.

Cordially and sincerely yours,   [Woodrow Wilson]

CCL (WP, DLC).

[1] Democratic congressman from Kentucky and chairman of the House Committee on the District of Columbia.

[2] Wilson was referring to the so-called Washington alley bill (H.R. 13219), which had been adopted with Ellen Axson Wilson's earlier strong support in September 1914. This measure laid down minimum standards with regard to space, light, and sanitary facilities for houses in the alleys of the District of Columbia and prohibited the use and occupation, after July 1, 1918, of those dwellings which did not meet stipulated requirements. 38 *Statutes at Large* 716.

To Gutzon Borglum

My dear Mr. Borglum: [The White House] 29 March, 1918

In view of your telegram of yesterday, I am very glad to explain to you what my telegram to you meant. It meant this, that I have now instituted a very systematic inquiry into the whole aviation situation and think it wise that all processes of investigation should be in the charge and under the direction of the gentlemen to whom I have committed this task. I have placed at their disposal the material you were kind enough to furnish me with and can assure you that they will go to the bottom of it all.

I know your own judgment will approve of this.

Sincerely yours,   [Woodrow Wilson]

CCL (WP, DLC).

To Joseph Patrick Tumulty

Dear Tumulty: [The White House, March 29, 1918]

Will you not be kind enough to send a telegram over your own name to Townley substantially as follows:

"The President has asked me to express to you the pleasure which he has derived from the assurances conveyed by your telegram of March twentieth. He begs me to say, also, that he would greatly value the assistance of the League in correcting the many serious misrepresentations which have gone abroad from time to time with regard to the action of the Department of Agriculture whose earnest work in the interest of the farmers he can himself personally vouch for."   The President.[1]

TL (WP, DLC).
  [1] As it turned out, this message to Townley was not sent. Tumulty held it until the following day, when he forwarded to Wilson a telegram from E. H. Nicholas, county attorney of Jackson County, Minn. Nicholas protested against the decision by the Committee on Public Information to furnish a speaker for a meeting to be held at Lakefield, Minn., under the auspices of the Nonpartisan League. Nicholas pointed out that officers of the league had either been convicted of or indicted for disloyalty in Minnesota. E. H. Nicholas to WW, March 29, 1918, T telegram (WP, DLC).
  Tumulty also sent to Wilson a clipping from the *Washington Post* of March 13, 1918, which reported that Townley was under indictment in Martin County, Minn., for issuing and circulating a "seditious" pamphlet. Wilson thereupon canceled the telegram to Townley. See JPT to WW, March 30, 1918, TL (WP, DLC). See also Robert L. Morlan, *Political Prairie Fire: The Nonpartisan League, 1915-1922* (Minneapolis, 1955), pp. 159-71.

From Simon Julius Lubin[1]

Dear Mr. President: Washington, March 29, 1918.

Complying with the request you made this afternoon, permit me to submit herewith as briefly as I can, matters that we think should be called to your personal attention.

Several months ago, Mr. George L. Bell, attorney and executive officer of our commission, called upon you in the name of the governors of Oregon, Washington, Arizona, Nevada, Idaho, Utah, Colorado and California, for the purpose of obtaining federal aid in the matter of the I.W.W. menace which then was threatening the West.[2] As a result of that conference, you asked Mr. Bell to carry back to each governor a message involving substantially these suggestions:

(1) That the governor request public peace officers to redouble their efforts in enforcing all laws, and to report to the governor rumors or evidence of plots to cripple industry, anything approaching treasonable talk, threats to lynch or deport agitators; to suppress any unnecessary publicity regarding the I.W.W; that when these officials feel warranted in making arrests, they shall not make public that the men apprehended are members of that organization.

(2) That the governor ask large employers to keep close watch upon possible agitation within their plants.

(3) That the governor request his industrial commission to make a survey of working and living conditions, with the object in view of removing factors that might serve as pretexts for uprising.

  [1] Founder and president of the California State Commission of Immigration and Housing.
  [2] About Bell's mission to Washington and his meeting with Wilson, see WW to JPT, July 20, 1917, n. 1, Vol. 43, and the memorandum by G. L. Bell printed at July 25, 1917, *ibid*.

(4) That the governor direct his board of health to clean up camps used by migratory workers.

(5) That the governor direct his immigration board or other appropriate department to send among foreigners men who speak their languages, to explain the war situation and their security as long as they behave, to urge them not to affiliate with lawless associations, to urge them to learn English and to become citizens.

(6) That the governor do not call for troops until he feels troops are absolutely necessary.

(7) That the governor supplement the secret service force of the communities.

(8) That no publicity be given to this program or to its carrying out.

Immediately after Mr. Bell's return to the Coast, the governor of Oregon called a conference of far Western governors. Advantage was taken of that conference to present your program as outlined above. (In addition to the above states, Montana was represented at that conference.) The governors assembled unanimously accepted the program, and promised to put it into effect.

We believe that it is not sufficient that the matter be permitted to rest there; but that you should follow up by repeated visits through trustworthy representatives. For this service, the Commission, or its executive officer, is subject to your command.

Reports that come to us daily show clearly that I.W.W. activity is still very much alive in the far West. We are expecting trouble at any moment, especially in the lumber [camps] and in the copper mines. As one piece of evidence, we submit this attached sticker,[3] of which many thousands are now being spread throughout the West. Our investigators report that the men in the jungles are not backward about giving a very obvious interpretation to it. If the many more than one hundred thousand migratory workers burn their blankets on May the First, 1918, and demand that their employers supply them with new blankets, that would manifestly reduce the supply for the "yellow-legs," or soldiers. Again, if the faithful rebel is not too careful about his selection of a spot for the ceremony, the forests will take fire; but that will not be his fault. Of the scores of similar posters that have come to our attention during the past four years, this is by far the boldest, and the most outspoken.

Permit us to suggest, Mr. President, that you authorize this commission, or some other equally competent body, to investigate any serious I.W.W. outbreaks or movements in these states, in order

[3] It was captioned "May the First 1918" and depicted a migrant worker pouring oil on his burning blanket.

that we may report to you upon the fundamental underlying causes, and advise you as to the proper federal action in the premises.

Let us cite one recent happening where such foresight might have anticipated a very unpleasant existing situation. Several months ago, there was an attempt made to blow up the governor's mansion. The local police in Sacramento, to make a showing, rounded up some sixty men in and around the I.W.W. headquarters. Then, they did not know what to do with them. At first the police appealed to the special agent in charge of the bureau of investigation of the Department of Justice to take the men over; but he refused. A committee of local citizens then in some way got in touch with certain authorities here, who, we are told, instructed the United States Marshall in San Francisco to hold the prisoners. A little later, they were brought before the federal grand jury, which, upon the advice of the federal deputy attorney, an irresponsible man, found inditements against the men. The State was placarded with the enclosed sheet (Exhibit A),[4] in the hope that some one would come forward with incriminating evidence against the men. From what we learned in the grand jury room, and from what the federal attorney told us, we doubt that they have any stronger evidence against fifty-five of the sixty men than this: that they swore and blasphemed and pounded upon the cell walls, *after they were arrested*.

The situation at this moment is bad. If the men are now released, it is more than likely that some of them will be lynched, or at least very badly handled. If they are held, there is more than good ground for agitation to gain their release; and we doubt whether any jury would bring in a conviction.

To give you just one bit of evidence of the feeling in our community, let us submit the enclosed clipping from the Sacramento Bee of March 16, this year (Exhibit B).[5] The spokesman was formerly lieutenant-governor of the State. He was recently appointed by the governor to the chairmanship of a committee of the State

---

[4] It showed police photographs of the fifty-nine men who had been arrested. Two accompanying letters from Don S. Rathbun, a special agent of the Department of Justice in San Francisco, called on the postmasters, sheriffs, and police officers of California to display the photographs, to make inquiries with ranchers and contractors about the men, and to search the records of all fingerprints and photographs to determine whether any of the men had been arrested earlier.

[5] "Throw I.W.W. in River, Says Labor Committee," *Sacramento Bee*, March 16, 1918. This article reported at length on a meeting of the Farm Labor Committee of the California State Council of Defense and summarized certain recommendations by that committee to alleviate the shortage of farm labor in California. However, it placed particular emphasis on the need to suppress the propaganda and activities of the I.W.W. It quoted a statement by Alden Anderson, the chairman of the committee, who advised the citizens of California: "If you encounter one of them preaching his doctrine, have him arrested, if you can; if not, take him by the neck and drown him in the river."

Council of Defense, which committee is entrusted with the task of solving the farm labor problem of California.

We submit, Mr. President, that if when the appeal referred to above had been made to Washington by the committee of local citizens, the authorities had gotten the unprejudiced opinion of an informed body similar to our commission, the government would not be in the unpleasant position in which it now finds itself. With the facts in the case known, the authorities undoubtedly would have refused to act, and the burden would have been left upon the shoulders of the local police, where it belongs.

When Mr. Bell was here, he presented to you the following suggestions for a federal program, which we desire to submit again for your further consideration:

(1) That members of the I.W.W. against whom there is evidence of intrigue or activity, not merely to agitate for better conditions, but to commit acts of treason and treasonably to hinder the operation of industry or the harvesting of crops necessary to the prosecution of the war, be not arrested after charges, but that they be interned during the period of the war,—preferably in camps at some distance from the place of apprehension. This plan would effectively mystify and frighten them; would avoid making heroes of them; would deprive them of their best material for propaganda, besides avoiding rash action by citizens. The federal government has the secret service machinery to discover such evidence, while the states have none.

(2) That the national censorship board urge upon the press to suppress all mention of the I.W.W. in any connection. This would deprive them of their best means of publicity; and would deprive them of their best and almost only material used in increasing their membership by appealing to the dissatisfied to join the "ONE, big, effective, fighting, organized movement."

(3) That the Department of Justice, or the Department of War, as a war measure, and after thorough, secret investigation, request employers who are threatened with strikes, quietly to remedy, during the period of the war, all conditions against which there is reasonable cause for objection, and that may give pretext for the usual I.W.W. agitation. This would be more effective than attempts to recognize and to conciliate with an organization that desires no conciliation, and that does not feel bound by any contract or agreement under an economic, or employing system that is contrary to their fundamental theories of industry and society.

(4) That the federal government might have secret agents scattered throughout the country as members of the organization, to attempt to discover if German money is being used, and to start a

counter-agitation within the organization against the acceptance of such aid,—pointing out how it will eventually injure the organization and defeat its real aims.

By way of summary:

We believe that there should be a follow-up of your programs suggested to the several far western states by a personal representative.

We believe that you should have on the ground a representative who could report difficulties as they arise, or, better, before they arise; a representative in whose knowledge of the general I.W.W. situation and in whose ability to report accurately and faithfully you have confidence.

To perform both of these functions, we put at your disposal the Commission of Immigration and Housing of California, or any one of its five members, or its attorney and executive officer.

If you desire that I should take up any of the matters referred to above with any of the members of your cabinet, please command me. I expect to remain in Washington, Hotel Raleigh, until Thursday, April 4.   Respectfully yours,   Simon J. Lubin.

TLS (WP, DLC).

A Memorandum by William Howard Taft

[c. March 29, 1918]

Memorandum concerning a Conference held with President Wilson by President A. Lawrence Lowell, of Harvard University, and Chairman of the Executive Committee of the League to Enforce Peace, and William H. Taft, President of the League to Enforce Peace.

The Executive Committee of the League to Enforce Peace had announced publicly its intention to hold a convention of the League in Philadelphia on May 16th, 17th and 18th, 1918. On March 14th, 1918, I spent the night at the Bellevue-Stratford in Philadelphia, expecting to leave for Washington the next morning. I received a telegram at the Bellevue-Stratford from Bainbridge Colby, as follows:

"Washington, D. C., March 14, 1918.

Hon. William H. Taft,
Hotel Bellevue-Stratford,
Philadelphia, Pennsylvania.

There is a matter of pressing moment about which I have been asked to speak to you at the earliest opportunity. Could you arrange to see me for three or four minutes upon reaching Washington tomorrow noon? If you will send me word, I can come to Miss Boardman's[1] house very promptly. Please address me care United States Shipping Board. Bainbridge Colby."

I wired Mr. Colby that I would see him at Miss Boardman's on Friday, March 15th, at noon. He came there and told me that he had come to see me at the instance of President Wilson, who had visited him in person at his office in the Shipping Board, for the purpose of asking him to see me and request me to stop the holding of the Convention, as announced. He said the President said he was afraid that at the Convention, details of the proposed League would be discussed by men of prominence, and that it would embarrass him in such communications as he might wish to make for peace when the time arrived. I told Mr. Colby that the object of the Convention was not to discuss the details of the League—that those we had been considering in a confidential way in a Study Committee. I told him the great purpose in holding the Convention was to support the Government in carrying through the war, to the defeat of Germany, on the ground that no League to Enforce Peace could be useful until we defeated Germany; that I would have Mr. Short, the Secretary of the League, send him the tentative program of the League, to be submitted to the President, and that if there was any part of it that seemed objectionable, we would cut it down. I also told him that we intended to have a meeting of part of the Executive Committee on Saturday, March 23rd, in New Haven, and that I would bring the matter of the President's request before the sub-committee, and would be glad to hear from Mr. Colby before that meeting if he had anything further to say. I saw Mr. Short on Monday, March 18th, in New Haven, and he handed me the tentative program, which I forwarded to Mr. Colby. Mr. Short also wrote Mr. Colby advising him of the extensive preparations that had been made to hold the Convention and spoke of the inadvisability of giving it up. On Saturday, March 23rd, at the meeting of part of the Executive Committee, the matter came up for discussion, and while we were in session, a telegram was handed me from Mr. Colby, as follows:

"Washington, D. C., March 23, 1918.
Hon. William Howard Taft,
Hotel Taft,
New Haven, Conn.

Many thanks for your letter nineteenth, also Mr. Short's letter of 20th. Both duly submitted and entire reliance is felt in your attitude and assurances given at our interview. Would appreciate receiving

[1] That is, Mabel Thorp Boardman.

program with topics and speakers, if entirely agreeable to you. With much appreciation.   Bainbridge Colby.''

It was then deemed wise, in order to clarify the matter and have a distinct understanding with the President, that President Lowell and I should seek an interview with the President the following week and discuss with him the proposed convention. Accordingly, through Mr. Tumulty, Secretary to the President, I secured for us an appointment to see the President at half past four Thursday afternoon, March 28th. President Lowell and I drove to the main White House entrance, were shown into the Green Room, and there we were greeted by the President at the appointed time. I began the conversation by thanking the President for giving us this interview, and explaining our reasons for it by reference to Mr. Colby's conversation. He said he was glad to see us—that his fear had been there would be an effort to formulate officially the plans for the League to Enforce Peace. He said the discussion and framing of such plans by the persons who would take part in the Convention, whose names and opinions would carry weight with the public, he deprecated. He said it might embarrass him thereafter in dealing with the subject. He said that the Minister for Foreign Affairs of France, M. Ribot, had consulted him about the appointment of a French Committee to consider the subject, and that he (the President) had advised against it.[2] President Lowell referred to the suggestion of Lord Bryce that there might be an informal conference between persons selected by the President and an English Committee to discuss the plans for the League, and he (President Lowell) assumed that the President's view with respect to that was the same as in respect to M. Ribot's suggestion. Indeed he understood that from Mr. Marburg, and the President said "Yes." The President then took up the subject of what could be done by the nations after the war. He said he though[t] the nations might guarantee to one another their integrity and territory, and that if any violations of these were threatened or occurred, special conferences might be called to consider the question. He said he knew that this would be slow, but that the common law was built up that way, and he thought that by a series of such conferences it would be possible ultimately to reach some form of machinery which experience would suggest; that this might be done by precedents and procedure which custom would formulate. He gave it as his opinion that the Senate of the United States would be unwilling to enter into an agreement by which a majority of other nations could tell the United States

[2] See J. J. Jusserand to RL, July 20, 1917, printed as an Enclosure with FLP to WW, July 25, 1917, and FLP to J. J. Jusserand, Aug. 3, 1917, both printed in Vol. 43.

when they must go to war. To this minimizing statement of the President, President Lowell invited his attention to his speech at the dinner of the League to Enforce Peace,[3] and his reference to the League in his subsequent messages, and said that he had thus brought the subject before foreign countries and had had great commendation for it the world around. He asked the President if he did not think that it was often possible in a critical time to accomplish more in definiteness of agreement and its extent than the negotiating parties thought possible, and referred to the formation of the Constitution of the United States as an instance in which the men who had gathered to adopt it had gone much further than anyone except Hamilton had intended to go when they entered the Convention. President Lowell said that Hamilton was greatly assisted by the fact that he had a plan before entering the Convention, although his plan was not ultimately adopted.

The President said that the compelling circumstances in respect to the Federal Constitution were very different from those that would control a League of Nations, in which President Lowell acquiesced, but said he thought there was enough of an analogy between the two cases to justify the view that it was wise to adopt a definite program even more comprehensive and detailed than would probably be adopted. The President said it was very necessary to look after the smaller countries and secure protection of their integrity and that any plan should have that in mind.

President Lowell said we had been considering the part to be played by the smaller nations in the League, and suggested that there might well be given representation to smaller nations in any legislative action of the League, while the greater nations with their greater armies and navies might better be given control of the executive. The President acquiesced in this but pointed out that the selection of the executive evoked always many jealousies. He instanced the fact that there had been much difficulty in securing united action by the military forces of the Alli[e]s. He said he had pressed its necessity upon the Allies and had secured the military joint council, but that Haig had made a great fuss because report of its action had not been transmitted through him to the English Government and had been sent direct. How he (the President) felt greatly pleased to hear that a commander-in-chief of the allied forces had been agreed upon. President Lowell asked who it was. President Wilson answered that it was a Frenchman, as it ought to be, because the fighting was on French soil. He said that the officer chosen was one whose name he had not heard before and

[3] It is printed at May 27, 1916, Vol. 37.

it had escaped his memory. I said the French seemed better strat-
egists than the English which would be important if this drive
which was giving us such concern finally brought the fighting out
into the open. The President agreed to this and said he shared the
concern over the drive but that he had not seen the afternoon
papers. We told him of the afternoon despatches. The conversation
then turned on the War. He said that as we doubtless understood
his messages defining our attitude were intended to call the bluff
of Germany and Austria in professing to desire to negotiate a peace
and he had succeeded in showing it was a bluff, and that instead
of announcing specific terms, their answers were vague and unintelligible. He said he greatly deprecated Lloyd George's declaration that we must fight this war to a knockout of Germany.[4] He
said he did not think it was possible and he thought such a statement showing a desire to punish the German people would keep
them solidly behind the Kaiser, and in sympathy with the military
party, whereas he thought it was important to separate them from
such influence and control and have them believe that we were
ready to make a reasonable and just peace, as he was. He said they
knew that the Austrian situation was a desperate one. I said I did
not think we could trust the present military dynasty of Germany
to make a peace that would bind Germany to anything. He said he
thought the German people would be near a break if this drive
failed. To this I replied that of course if the dynasty was broken a
treaty would be worth while. He said that if this drive was not a
success ultimately and the Allies by a counter attack forced the
Germans back, the German people would know they were beaten
and would insist on peace and negotiations to that end. He said
the peoples of the Allies were war weary. He did not believe that
either the British people or our own would insist on fighting the
war merely to restore Alsace-Lorraine to France and if that was all
that stood between peace and continued war, Germany would be
allowed to retain them.

We then referred again to the League Convention by way of
conclusion. President Lowell said we understood that he had no
objection to the Convention if its speeches and resolutions were
confined to the slogan of "Win the War" as a necessary basis of
the League. He said this was true.

Mr. Lowell then handed him the tentative detailed plan for a
League which our Study Committee had agreed upon.[5] We then
withdrew.[6]   Wm. H. Taft.

T MS (W. H. Taft Papers, DLC).

[4] See RL to WW, Sept. 30, 1916, n. 1, Vol. 38.
[5] It is missing in WP, DLC, but a carbon copy was enclosed in A. L. Lowell to W. H.

Taft, March 25, 1918, TLS (W. H. Taft Papers, DLC). It was a draft of a treaty for a league of nations, which defined the league's scope, functions, and terms of membership. The heart of the proposal provided for joint diplomatic and economic pressure against any nation which threatened war against a member of the league, and which had not first sought international conciliation or arbitration. This was to be followed by the joint use of military force in the event that an actual act of hostility had been committed. Membership in the league would be divided into three groups: states which would share all the responsibilities of the league, including the use of economic and military power against a common foe; states which would be compelled to apply economic sanctions only; and "neutralized states," which would not take part in any enforcement but would be defended by the league.

The organs of the league were to consist of a Court of the League, a permanent tribunal to which all justiciable questions between members of the league were to be submitted and whose decisions were binding; a permanent Council of Conciliation, which would recommend settlement of all nonjusticiable questions between members of the league not settled by conciliation or arbitration; a Court of Conflicts, which would decide whether a particular question was justiciable; a Court of Claims, which would adjudicate claims by any persons or corporate bodies; the Congress, which would be composed of representatives of all members and would discuss and recommend on questions concerning international law, the reduction of armaments, and any other matter affecting international relations; and the executive body of the league, which would be composed of representatives of the states of the Court of the League and which would decide upon the existence of a state of war and call upon the members of the league to use their economic and military forces against an aggressor. A slightly revised version of the proposed treaty is printed in John H. Latané, ed., *Development of the League of Nations Idea: Documents and Correspondence of Theodore Marburg* (2 vols., New York, 1932), II, 791-94.

[6] A. L. Lowell, "Memorandum of Conference with President Wilson, March 28, 1918," T MS (W. H. Taft Papers, DLC), is a briefer version of Taft's memorandum and adds nothing to it by way of detail.

Sir William Wiseman to Sir Eric Drummond

[Washington] March 29th 1918.

No. 90. Following for Balfour from House.

In reply to your No. 67 of the 26th. I have discussed the matter with the President, and he hopes that nothing will be done for the moment because the situation is so uncertain. There seems no need for immediate action and the situation may possibly clear itself a little later and we would know better what to do.

T telegram (W. Wiseman Papers, CtY).

David Lloyd George to Lord Reading

PARAPHRASE OF A TELEGRAM FROM THE PRIME
MINISTER TO LORD READING.
Dated March 29/18
Recd.   ″   30/18

It has now been possible for us to go in a more detailed fashion into the military problem. While there are good hopes that the present effort of the enemy may be checked, it is possible that

Amiens will be lost, and the events of the immediate future will prove whether the enemy can reach this point or not. If Amiens falls we shall have to face a very grave military situation. In any event, the enemy has certainly shown his ability to break through the Franco-British front over a wide area, and it is certain that if the German high command cannot secure all their aims in the present battle, they will at once commence preparing their forces to deliver a further attack at the earliest possible date. The point at which this attack will be delivered must depend to a great extent on the eventual result of the operations now proceeding. The entire military position in the future must depend on whether we can re-constitute and re-inforce our armies in sufficient time to check the next blow, and, in the light of the last week's fighting, it is clear that the problem of man power is the fundamental question with which the Allies are faced.

The present battle has lasted only a week and our losses so far have reached about 120,000 men. We can barely make good these losses by bringing in our whole resources of partially and fully trained men, and we shall be obliged to use all our trained reserves in doing so. In these circumstances we are immediately taking action to increase the number of our troops by taking in youths of 18 and by raising the age limit to 50, and we are also again "combing out" our industrial establishments to a large extent, a proceeding which will cause serious hardship and dislocation to our industries. Furthermore, we are ready to run the risk of serious difficulties in Ireland, as we regard it as absolutely essential that we should during the summer of this year be in a position to show ourselves more powerful than the Germans. These drastic measures will, we hope, give us 400,000 to 500,000 men as reinforcements, but they cannot be given sufficient training to enable us to employ them in France for another four months at least. There is, therefore, the risk of a shortage during the period of May to July next, and this is the very time at which the next great effort by the Germans is to be antic-ipated.

Thus, in order to be certain of checking the enemy during these months, and making it impossible for him to reach a military de-cision on the West front, it will be necessary to make good the deficiency during this period by the use of American troops. In this way alone is it possible to secure the position of the Allies.

The shipping experts in London have estimated that the tonnage which we can provide by heavier sacrifices in other ways will be able to embark about 60,000 men in the United States during April, and, according to an estimate by Admiral Sims, 52,000 men per month can be carried by the American trooping fleet. There is also a certain volume of Dutch shipping which could be used by the United States, and the use of certain further Italian tonnage is being secured by us. We think that in all it is possible to embark 120,000 from the United States during April, a number which could be somewhat increased in the following months.

I would therefore wish you to urge formally on the President, on behalf of His Majesty's Government, that orders may be issued to embark and send to Europe 120,000 infantry monthly from now on to the end of July; the battalions of the American regiments thus embarked to be brigaded with French or British divisions in the same way as that proposed for the six divisions. The troops forwarded, as indicated in the resolution adopted by the military representatives at Versailles on March 27th, in which General Pershing has concurred, should consist solely of infantry and machine gun units. The battalions, after training, can be re-constituted into regiments and forwarded to General Pershing as required, in the same way as agreed in the case of the six divisions.

I should be glad if you could discuss this with the President immediately. That is the only way in which the thousands of trained and partially trained men now in the United States can be made use of in this crisis, since it is impossible to organize them into separate units sufficiently quickly for them to be of use. If the struggle should be decided against us without these troops being employed, it is quite possible that the war may be terminated and the cause lost, for which the President has pleaded so eloquently, without the United States having received a chance of making use of anything but a small fraction of her forces.

The whole future of the war will, in our opinion, depend on whether the enemy or the Allies can be first to repair the losses which have been incurred in this great struggle, and it is certain that there will not be a moment's delay on the part of the Germans. They are in possession of sufficient man power to repair what they have lost, and there is also the Austrian army 250,000 of which are, according to statements made by the German press, already in the West. If we cannot refit as rapidly as the enemy, this will give the enemy the opportunity to secure the definite military decision by which the German leaders hope to terminate the war as a German victory.[1]

T MS (WP, DLC).
[1] This was a paraphrase of D. Lloyd George to Lord Reading, March 29, 1918, No. 1828, T telegram (FO 115/2461, pp. 102-104, PRO). There is a different version of this paraphrase in FO 115/2461, pp. 105-108, PRO.

From the Diary of Colonel House

March 29, 1918.

I called on Reading at the British Embassy. I told him of the President's feeling regarding the Lloyd George message and his speech. I thought it advisable to do this in order to make him more careful in the future. He expressed his regret and hoped I had smoothed the matter over. He suggested that the President make a statement as to what the United States had done for the Allies since the war began, and what we were doing now. I thought that he, Reading, or his Government, were the ones to make such a statement and not the President. The thought flashed over me while we were talking that it would be a *coup d'etat* for the President if he could get the British Government committed to the assertion that his administration had done everything in the past, and was doing everything now, that could be done to help.

In discussing the matter later with Wiseman, he fully shared this view, and said that Lloyd George at any time, in order to save himself, might blame the result of the failure in France on the President.

Reading did not know what he could do in this direction, but he said he would try to frame a despatch to send the Prime Minister, which the Prime Minister would be requested to give to the Press.

It was afterwards determined, under Sir William's guidance, to write a message to Lloyd George and ask him to give it out as his own. Sir William helped Reading frame the cable. He sat at his elbow, pushing him along in the right direction until it was done. When I told the President about it he was pleased beyond measure, and wondered whether it would be successful. We shall see in a day or two.

From the Diary of Josephus Daniels

March Friday 29 1918

Cabinet. I presented telegram from Knight[1] saying he might have to land at Vladivostok in view of presence of German officers & [men] present and shipment of munitions from that place to interior for fear it would fall into Japanese [German?] hands. Should [we and] Japan go into Russia? Lane & B thought it would be better than for Japanese to go in alone WW & Lansing thought not. WW said, What military advantage. Japan has only 400,000 troops, regular & reserved—& is not keen to go in. Might drive resentful Russia into hands of Germany.

[1] A. M. Knight to JD, March 28, 1918, T telegram (NDR, RG 45, Naval Records Coll., Office of Naval Records and Library, Telegrams—Incoming, Nov. 2, 1917-June 1, 1919, DNA).

To George Creel

My dear Creel: The White House 30 March, 1918

My attention has been called to this release.[1] Had it received your own personal inspection and approval? The statements about hundreds being shipped and perfection finally having been obtained are, I am afraid, very questionable as to accuracy, though I am having the whole aeroplane situation looked into in a way which will enable me to know in a very short time. I am merely calling your attention to this statement at this time because I think it a great mistake, as I am sure you do, to create any degree of baseless optimism about this important programme.

Cordially and faithfully yours,   Woodrow Wilson

TLS (G. Creel Papers, DLC).
[1] It is missing. However, it consisted of the captions of four photographs issued by the Division of Pictures of the C.P.I., which described the building and shipment of American airplanes to France. The captions contained some blatant misinformation about the progress of American airplane production. While, in fact, only a single airplane built in the United States had been sent to France, the captions said that "hundreds" had already been shipped and that "thousands upon thousands" would soon follow. The captions maintained, moreover, that scientists and engineers had finally perfected the planes and that factories had been put on a "quantity-production basis."

A hearing before the Senate Committee on Military Affairs on March 27 had revealed that the photographs did not show actual battle planes, but rather depicted training planes for American pilots. On that occasion, the senators severely attacked the C.P.I. for spreading falsehoods and misstatements. As a result, Lawrence Rubel, the head of the Division of Pictures, promised to withdraw the captions and sent out telegrams to newspapers not to use them. In spite of this assurance, the captions were still published in the *Official Bulletin*, II (March 28, 1918), 8. See also the *New York Times*, March 28 and 30, 1918.

To Samuel Gompers

My dear Mr. Gompers: The White House 30 March, 1918

I am very much obliged to you for sending me the paper containing the action of the officers of the Amalgamated Association of Street and Electric Railway Employees of America.[1] It is in admirable spirit and shows a thoughtful realization of the present situation and a thorough-going patriotism which is very heartening and reassuring. I hope that you will have some opportunity of conveying to the gentlemen concerned an expression of my admiration and appreciation.

Cordially and sincerely yours,   Woodrow Wilson

TLS (S. Gompers Corr., AFL-CIO-Ar).
¹ Gompers' letter and its enclosure are missing in WP, DLC. Gompers had written to Wilson on March 27, 1918, and had enclosed a copy of a "patriotic letter" from the union to its locals. White House memorandum, March 27, 1918, T MS (WP, DLC).

To Frank William Taussig

My dear Taussig: [The White House] 30 March, 1918

I am heartily sorry that you feel that you have not time to continue to serve upon the price-fixing committee of the War Industries Board,¹ because I know that Mr. Baruch and his associates regard the work you are doing as of the greatest importance, but I readily understand that it must be a very considerable burden and that it may be impossible for you to do all three things that have been put upon you.

May I not, before accepting your resignation from the price fixing committee, to which I attach the highest importance, ask you to answer confidentially this question: Do you think that the work on the price fixing committee is less important than the work of the committee of inquiry upon the Milling Division of the Food Administration? I ask this, as you will understand, because in every such case we must make the frankest and most cold-blooded choice. Don't you think so?

Cordially and sincerely yours,   Woodrow Wilson

TLS (Letterpress Books, WP, DLC).
¹ See F. W. Taussig to WW, March 29, 1918, TLS (WP, DLC).

To Samuel Reading Bertron

My dear Mr. Bertron: [The White House] 30 March, 1918

Thank you for your letter of March twenty-ninth with the enclosure, which I return.¹

My feeling is that the association² to which your letter refers, while it may do some excellent and admirable things, is of the sort which easily runs after impracticable ideas and purposes, and my judgment is that it would not be wise for you to associate yourself with it.

I am cordially obliged to you for doing me the honor of consulting me in this important matter.

Cordially and sincerely yours,   Woodrow Wilson

TLS (Letterpress Books, WP, DLC).
¹ Bertron's letter and enclosure are missing.
² Probably the League to Enforce Peace.

To Albert Sidney Burleson

My dear Burleson: The White House 30 March, 1918

I dare say you know Pat Harrison. You can readily see how embarrassing it is for me to answer the enclosed letter.[1] Would you do me the very great favor of consulting Harrison with regard to it? I am relieved to find that a plurality does not determine in the Mississippi primary for a Senator, and, of course, it has been my principle in all cases that I will not interfere as between Democrats, but I don't know just how to answer this letter without doing some incidental injury to Harrison.

Faithfully yours,   Woodrow Wilson

TLS (A. S. Burleson Papers, DLC).
[1] It is missing.

From Newton Diehl Baker

[Paris] March 30, 1918.

I have just been shown a copy of a message from Lloyd George to you with regard to General Foch and American troops.[1] The situation seems to be that Lloyd George is personally in favor of a Supreme Commander but fears British opinion will be the other way because such a Commander could sacrifice the Channel ports to the defense of Paris. The arrangement therefore is that General Foch is to be supreme enough to coordinate but without being called Supreme Commander. General Pershing will, of course, act under General Foch as Pétain and Haig have agreed to do. I venture to suggest that in replying to that part of Lloyd George's message you might go further than he asks and say that we are willing to accept a general Supreme Command whenever the French and British are. Perhaps the relative smallness of our present forces and our having no immediate defensive object in France would make it unwise for us to urge the point though the present events would seem to have demonstrated the need. * * * General Pershing's prompt and fine action with regard to the use of our troops and facilities here in the emergency has won enthusiastic commendation from French and British. Our 1st Division will shortly be withdrawn from trenches and used in battle.   Baker.

Printed in John J. Pershing, *My Experiences in the World War* (2 vols., New York, 1931), I, 372.
[1] That is, D. Lloyd George to Lord Reading, March 28, 1918.

From William Dennison Stephens

Los Angeles, California, March 30-31, 1918.

Your wire of March twenty seventh forwarded me here. Time in which Supreme Court can order rehearing about over. You can rest assured Mooney case will have careful consideration.

William D. Stephens,   Governor.

T telegram (WP, DLC).

From Robert Lansing

My dear Mr. President: Washington March 30, 1918.

Referring to our conversation of yesterday in regard to the possible visits to this country of delegates of socialist groups in the Entente countries I enclose for your consideration and comment telegrams to our Embassies at London and Paris setting forth the attitude of this Government in relation to the reception by you of such unofficial delegates.[1]

Please return the telegrams indicating your wishes in the matter.

Faithfully yours,   Robert Lansing.

Approved and authorized W.W.

TLS (SDR, RG 59, 763.72119/1531½A, DNA).
  [1] RL to WHP, April 2, 1918, TS telegram, and RL to W. G. Sharp, April 2, 1918, TS telegram, both in SDR, RG 59, 763.72119.So/3, DNA. In these identical telegrams, Lansing pointed out that it was a punishable offense for an American citizen to have any unauthorized dealings with a foreign government with the intent to influence its conduct to the detriment of the United States. It would be contrary to the principle of reciprocity in international relations and inconsistent with the traditional policy of the United States, Lansing concluded, for the President to receive citizens of a foreign state and discuss with them international questions which involved the policy of their government, unless their government had authorized them to do so.

From Robert Wickliffe Woolley

Dear Mr. President: Washington March 30, 1918.

I have had the pleasure, in the last few days, of discussing with Justice Brandeis the present delicate labor situation and the probable attitude of labor following the return of peace.

It is hardly conceivable that any thought advanced by either of us has not already occurred to you and received your most careful consideration. With great respect, however, I beg to suggest an act on your part which in our humble opinion would stimulate labor to its best effort while hostilities last and minimize the danger of serious unrest in days to come.

This suggestion is that you issue, at the earliest suitable moment, a statement setting forth that the rights of the man or woman who works by the day or piece are recognized as equal to and are to be safeguarded along with those of the salaried person, that there is to be full-time employment throughout the year in all shipyards and other industrial plants under Government control.

The reassuring effect on those immediately concerned would be instant. The increased efficiency which would follow their removal from the twilight zone of uncertainty would be so noticeable that private industries, practically all of which are in active competition with the Government for labor, would soon find it necessary to give like assurances of protection. May I not cite the fact that thousands of employes of the Postoffice Department, for instance, could earn more money elsewhere, but the knowledge that they are serving, that they are secure in their positions and can rely upon a certain income binds them to the Government? Of course, there is no more loyal or efficient body of men.

There can be no doubt that much of the slowing down of which we hear a great deal is chargeable to poisonous propaganda insidiously spread by German agents, but much is also due to a feeling that high speed in production may result all too soon in a dearth of work. The long-established practice of cutting down the hours of employment or reducing the number of persons employed on time and piece work so soon as the least slackening in demand is evident hangs over the head of the laboring men like the sword of Damocles. He feels that, no matter how much he gives of his heart and his brain, so long as he is not on a salary he is not a part of the permanent organization and that appreciation ends when he is handed his pay envelope. On the other hand, his outlook on life is more wholesome and he is a more efficient workman and a better citizen when he knows that "his feet are under the table."

If the idea appeals to you, I would respectfully suggest that the statement be made prior to the issuance of the impending report of the Railroad Wage Commission. The sum total of the increases to be recommended in the latter document will be so large that it may cause further uneasiness among those employed on a wage or piece basis in Government industries. Reassuring them first seems to me to be highly desirable.

To my mind no single achievement of your Administration has proven so momentous from a social standpoint as the enactment and application of the War Risk Insurance Law. Every insured soldier feels that he has a stake in the game, that a government that will do such a thing for him and his heirs is worth dying for; and it gives those who stay at hime [home] an exalted feeling such as I am confident was never excelled in any previous like period. What a wonderful thing for the war and for the Government it would be if this act only embraced all Government employees, all workers in shipyards and other Government-controlled industries and all railroad employees while the carriers are in the hands of the Government!

Mr. Roosevelt talked in Maine Thursday of what the Reds and the Proletariat might do after the war. The thought of Justice Brandeis and myself is that if the psychology of the situation is properly dealt with now there will be no Proletariat after the war.

With kindest regards and great respect, I am,

Faithfully yours,   R. W. Woolley

TLS (WP, DLC).

From Francis Patrick Walsh

My dear Mr. President: Washington, March 30, 1918.

I feel that I must again trespass upon your priceless time in behalf of my friend, Frank M. Ryan. His story, of course, is familiar to you. He is the former President of the Structural Iron Workers' organization, now confined in the Federal Prison at Leavenworth.

His eligibility for parole was reached many months ago. His transgression, if any there was, has certainly been expiated by him to the last degree. He is a man of very fine sensibilities, has loyal friends among all classes of people, and a man sincerely devoted to his home and family. His confinement has already extended over a period of almost four years. This matter, I understand has been presented to you from many sources, and my information is that the Attorney General has withdrawn whatever objection he may have heretofore had and the entire matter is ready for your action.

Mr. Ryan is a man quite well advanced in years, his two sons are in the Army, and unless he secures his liberty very shortly they must go abroad either without seeing their father or must visit him in the prison. The whole situation is charged with the greatest pathos, so that I am venturing to suggest that the cause of justice having been fully vindicated, you pass upon his case favorably and at the earliest moment possible.

With assurances of my continued great regard, I am

Faithfully yours   Frank P. Walsh

TLS (WP, DLC).

Two Telegrams from Lord Reading to
David Lloyd George

Washington, March 30th. 1918.

No. 1360. *Very Secret*.

Following for Prime Minister:

I had an interview with the President today. He began by referring to the two requests in your cablegram No. 1793. On the 28th of March I cabled a report to you of my interview with him and stated that he would give an answer after he had received the full message from Secretary Baker. The President informed me that he had now received it and he had yesterday instructed Secretary Baker to cooperate with you in respect of (1) sending American troops to France with the utmost speed and (2) the method of making American forces now in France available. The President said that Secretary Baker had proposed a formula which was not identical with yours but was substantially the same. The President had cabled to Secretary Baker to act in accordance with the proposals submitted by him to the President.

I delivered a paraphrase of your cablegram No. 1828 to the President with the exception of the part marked confidential.[1] He requested me to inform you that he would issue instructions to the proper authorities to act in accordance with your request and desired me to assure you that, in every respect in which it was possible for him, he would co-operate with the Allies in meeting the necessities of the situation. Accordingly he will direct that 120,000 infantry be embarked for transport to Europe in each of the months of April May June and July, making a total of 480,000 always provided the ships and necessary equipment would be available and of which he had not the details. In principle he approves the employment of the troops in the manner desired but leaves details to his military chiefs.

This decision is in accordance with the willingness of the President repeatedly expressed to me to send more men to Europe provided proper and sufficient transportation and terminal facilities could be given. He said that the difficulty hitherto had been that although the United States Government had been ready to fulfil the programme arranged at the Paris conference it could not be carried out owing to insufficient accommodation facilities at the French ports. With regard to the use of the American forces the President, as I informed you early in February, had given the fullest powers to General Pershing to dispose of the American troops in an emergency or otherwise as he thought best. The President is

ready to send even a larger number of troops than requested if only
sufficient transport and other facilities can be found. He desires
me to inform you that it is only the limitations of shipping and port
and railway capacity in Europe which prevents him sending a larger
number of troops than requested by you.[2]

T telegram (Reading Papers, FO 800/224, PRO).
    [1] "Confidential. We believe that shipping of this number of men can be managed from
America but that chief difficulty will be in transportation and terminal facilities. We
rely on you to see that these obstacles are not allowed to hinder transportation of these
vital troops otherwise consequences may be disastrous. In view of what President said
to you in your last interview I am informing Baker and Pershing and Bliss of general
substance of this communication and asking them to support proposals we are making."
D. Lloyd George to Lord Reading, March 29, 1918, No. 1828, T telegram (FO 115/2461,
pp. 102-104, PRO).
    [2] Another copy of this telegram is Lord Reading to D. Lloyd George, March 30, 1918,
T telegram (FO 115/2461, pp. 139-40, PRO).

Washington March 30th 1918.

No. 1361 Very Secret.
    My immediately preceding telegram.
    It would be very useful if you could make public that you have
received this report from me of the President's determination and
willingness to co-operate with the Allies. Doubtless you will not care
to give numbers of troops but otherwise I suggest to you that the
substance of the whole of the preceding cablegram might be made
public.[1] I suggest for your consideration that it would hearten our
people at home to have a statement by the President of the assistance that the United States will give, and further it would, in my
judgement, be an advantage if your public statement were cabled
verbatim for use in the press on this side. I am in a position to
judge of the advantage of publication on this side but it can hardly
take place until published first on yours. There is some tendency
to use your message to me for the Lotus Club dinner as a means
of attack upon the Administration. I am convinced that the Lotus
Club message has produced a good effect in stirring the American
people to a better understanding of the situation and what will be
required of them. Nevertheless any use of it by political opponents
of the President is a disadvantage to us.
    From all I have seen and learnt during my stay here I fear that
any serious disturbance in Ireland consequent upon an attempt to
enforce conscription may cause recrudescence of anti-British feeling among some sections of the American community and may
disturb the unanimity of the war spirit now prevailing. I do not
presume to judge the effect upon Ireland of any measures you may
wish to take but I must tell you the effect that may be produced
in this country.

T telegram (FO 115/2461, pp. 144-45, PRO).

[1] The British government issued a statement on April 1, 1918, which announced the American promise to send immediate reinforcements to France and concluded: "President Wilson has shown the greatest anxiety to do everything possible to assist the Allies, and has left nothing undone which could contribute thereto. . . . The Prime Minister feels that the singleness of purpose with which the United States have made this immediate, and, indeed, indispensable contribution towards the triumph of the Allied cause should be clearly recognized by the British people." London *Times*, April 2, 1918.

From the Diary of Colonel House

March 30, 1918.

This has been a busy day. I saw Lord Reading again. He is very nervous and anxious and Wiseman and I have to be constantly around in order to cheer him. All through this terrible offensive Sir William has never lost his self possession. As a matter of fact, outside of the President, Sir William and myself, there seems to be a general inclination to be "rattled." All the despatches we are receiving from the other side indicate it, and the most demoralizing feature of the situation, as the President and I see it, is the poise which seems to be failing the French and British Governments at this time. This is especially true of the English with whom we are in closer touch. The President remarked today that he hoped the British military men were not panicy, for if they were, it would communicate itself to the men and disaster would be sure to follow.

March 31, 1918.

I spent most of the day at Janet's. We had the Attorney General and Nelson Perkins to lunch. Sir William Wiseman and John Hays Hammond were among the callers.

I began to feel badly again in the afternoon. I went to the White House around six o'clock and told the President I was in for another spell. He immediately sent for Dr. Grayson who confirmed my view. I insisted upon going to Janet's, but both the President and Grayson vetoed this proposal so vigorously that I had nothing to do except to pick the most convenient room to be ill in, have my things moved from the Yellow Room, which I usually occupy when I am well, and go to bed.

To George Creel, with Enclosure

My dear Creel: The White House 1 April, 1918

I must say this is a pretty convincing telegram. I am afraid we are getting into deep water in that part of the country. Whatever we may think of the intentions of Townley and his associates, they are certainly getting "in bad" with the communities in which they are most active, and I think it will be your judgment, as it is mine, that we had better pull away from them.[1]

Cordially and faithfully yours,   Woodrow Wilson

TLS (G. Creel Papers, DLC).
    [1] "Dear Tumulty: Please acknowledge this telegram; say that I appreciate its gravity. The President." WW to JPT, c. April 2, 1918, TL (WP, DLC).

ENCLOSURE

From James C. Caldwell and Christian H. Wendt[1]

Lakefield, Minn., March 31, 1918.

WHEREAS, as the Non-Partisan League has sent agents into Jackson County, not only taliing [talking] and stirring up class dissension, but talking disloyalty in public speeches in behalf of the League and in private conversation in soliciting members for the League and,

WHEREAS, in consequence of such work on the part of the officials of said League, the officials charged with the enforcement of the laws of the State of Minnesota in said Jackson County and the representative of the Safety Commission in said County backed by loyal citizens of said county notified the officers of said League that they would not be permitted to further carry on such work and such meeting in said County, and

WHEREAS, in open defiance of such express notification the officers of said League did attempt to hold further meetings of such character and one JOSEPH GILBERT, Secretary of said League was duly arrested while making disloyal statements to one of such meetings and was thereafter, duly brought to trial following such arrest before a jury of twelve men each one whom was declared satisfactory to the defendant and was duly convicted by said jury as charged and was sentenced to three months in jail and,

WHEREAS, an appeal was taken to the District Court of Jackson County and said Gilbert was duly released on bail and said matter is now pending in said County and,

WHEREAS, A. C. TOWNLEY, President of said League has been arrested in said County on disloyalty charges and is awaiting the action of the grand jury of said County soon to sit therein[2] and,

WHEREAS, the Chief Executive of the State of Minnesota and the head of the Safety Commission of said State has publicly branded the officers of said League as disloyal and indictments have been found against various officers and [members] thereof in other counties of this State and,

WHEREAS, the said League officers through their publications and otherwise have been carrying on an active propaganda to create prejudice among the citizens of this and other counties with a view to influencing the future action of the courts and jurors of such counties in said matters,

WHEREAS, it is the opinion of the citizens of Lakefield, that the plan of having a representative of the Federal Government speak at Lakefield under the auspices of said League [w]as conceived with the purpose not of furthering loyalty but of furthering the propaganda above referred to and of advancing the political interests of the said political organization known as THE NON-PARTISAN LEAGUE, and

WHEREAS, the citizens of said village deem it highly injurious to the best interests of the Government at this time as well as improper in view of the impending trials that the United States Government should impliedly put its stamp of approval upon the disloyal activities heretofore referred to, now therefore, be it

RESOLVED, by the citizens of the village of Lakefield in mass meeting assembled that said village of Lakefield does hereby invite the Information Bureau of the National Government to send loyal and patriotic speakers to said village as often as it may see fit so to do said speakers to come under the auspices of the United States Government, and be it further

RESOLVED, that we are unalterably opposed to said Bureau sending speakers furnished by the Government at public expense or otherwise under the auspices of the Non-Partisan League or under the auspices of any other political party or political organization of whatever name to Lakefield or to any other community whatsoever.

                                 J. C. Caldwell,   Chairman
                                 C. H. Wendt,   Secretary

T telegram (WP, DLC).
    [1] Caldwell was president of the First National Bank of Lakefield, Minn., and active in several farmers' cooperative societies; Wendt owned a restaurant in Lakefield, Minn.
    [2] In fact, Townley had never been arrested in Jackson County. Although several newspapers announced that a warrant for his arrest had been issued in connection with Gilbert's conviction, the action did not then materialize. However, Townley had been arrested and indicted in neighboring Martin County. See Morlan, *Political Prairie Fire*, pp. 160-61 and 167-71.

To Sterling Galt[1]

My dear Friend: [The White House] 1 April, 1918

I think that if any mourning is to be worn, your suggestion[2] is much the best that I have heard, but my own feeling is that no emblems of mourning should be worn, that the whole effect would be depressing and that if, on the contrary, mourning were left off, the grief would in a certain sense have a stimulating effect just because of the added element of personal steadfastness and courage which it would involve.

In any case, my judgment is that it would be a mistake to give official sanction to any badge of mourning, particularly at this time, because it would seem to be in anticipation of heavy losses which must indeed come, but which need not be so explicitly anticipated.

Don't you think that, on the whole, this is the wisest attitude?

We are all well, had a quiet Easter, and all unite in affectionate messages and best wishes to you all.

Cordially and sincerely yours,   Woodrow Wilson

TLS (Letterpress Books, WP, DLC).
  [1] Brother-in-law of Mrs. Wilson, who lived in Emmitsburg, Md. He was the publisher of the *Emmitsburg Chronicle*, a one-time member of the Maryland State Board of Education, and active in Democratic politics in Maryland.
  [2] S. Galt to WW, March 30, 1918, ALS (WP, DLC).

To William Fellowes Morgan[1]

My dear Mr. Morgan: [The White House] 1 April, 1918

Allow me to acknowledge the receipt of your letter of March twenty-ninth.[2]

My own impression is quite different from yours. Every mail, almost every newspaper, daily brings me evidence that the particular need to which the opinion of the country is awaking is the need for ships. I think the people of the country would be very much surprised to receive a message from me on that subject.

I would be very much interested to know how you got the opposite impression. Here in Washington nothing is talked about so much and, as I have said, the country is vocal with the acknowledgment of the same need.

I, of course, appreciate your courtesy in proposing a meeting of the Merchants' Association of New York at which I could deliver the message you suggest, and I hope you will convey to the officers of the Association my sincere appreciation, but my present duty is to stay here and help see that the shipping programme is carried through.   Sincerely yours,   Woodrow Wilson

TLS (Letterpress Books, WP, DLC).
  [1] President of the Merchants' Association of New York.
  [2] It is missing.

To Francis Patrick Walsh

My dear Mr. Walsh: [The White House] 1 April, 1918

I have your letter of March thirtieth about Frank M. Ryan. It came just as I was looking into the case again with the hope that I might act upon the suggestion you make.

Cordially and sincerely yours,   Woodrow Wilson

TLS (Letterpress Books, WP, DLC).

To Thomas Watt Gregory

[The White House]

My dear Mr. Attorney General: 1 April, 1918

You may remember that the other day at Cabinet I spoke of the case of Frank M. Ryan, one of the men involved in the McNamara dynamiting cases. Will you be kind enough to have Finch send me a brief memorandum concerning the men condemned in connection with that trial who are still left in the penitentiary.

In haste

Faithfully and cordially yours,   Woodrow Wilson[1]

TLS (Letterpress Books, WP, DLC).
[1] TWG to WW, April 2, 1918, TLS (WP, DLC) is a reply to this letter. Gregory wrote that he had already sent the requested memorandum, and he went on to quote his letter to Wilson of March 28 and enclosed another copy of Finch's memorandum.

From Ferdinand Foch

[Clermont-sur-Oise, April 1, 1918]

En pleine confiance grace à la parfaite Union des Alliés et en particulier au noble élan de l'Armée Americaine demandant a entrer immediatement dans la bataille, je vous addresse mes vifs remerciements pour votre télégramme de félicitations.   Foch.

Printed in Pershing. *My Experiences in the World War*, I, 366.

From Robert Lansing

My dear Mr. President: Washington April 1, 1918.

I do not know whether these War Department telegrams have been called to your attention.[1] In the event they have not I think you should read them as they indicate a serious condition of affairs in Switzerland. I am at a loss to see how we can overcome the

German influence there and yet I feel that something ought to be done.

Kindly return the telegrams to me after you have read them.

Faithfully yours,   Robert Lansing

TLS (SDR, RG 59, 763.72111/7358C, DNA).
    [1] Lt. Col. William Frederick Holford Godson, American Military Attaché in Bern, to the Military Intelligence Staff, March 25, 1918, No. 39, and March 26, 1918, No. 40, T telegrams, both in SDR, RG 59, 763.72111/7358c, DNA. In the first telegram, Godson pointed out that conditions in Switzerland were growing increasingly delicate. There were rumors of a general mobilization. The Swiss General Staff was in close touch with Berlin, and an understanding was supposed to have been reached for German assistance in the defense of Switzerland. Public opinion, too, was distinctly pro-German, and German propaganda was encouraging disbelief in the good will of the United States. Moreover, Godson concluded, Germany's submarine warfare against all shipping had had the effect of starving Switzerland and forcing it to accept German terms for trade between the two countries.
    Godson's second telegram reported that the Swiss Minister of War had assured the Allied military attachés that the chief of the Swiss General Staff and the Federal Council intended resolutely to maintain Switzerland's neutrality. However, Godson cautioned, everything was ready for a general mobilization, and, in his judgment, Swiss action would depend upon the outcome of the present German offensive. Godson then elaborated on the food shortage in Switzerland, which, he pointed out, was becoming more serious every day. The German authorities in Bern constantly emphasized the fact that the Allies were either unable or unwilling to supply foodstuffs to Switzerland. It seemed only a matter of time, Godson concluded, before the Swiss would have to accept German aid and thus become a silent ally of Germany.

From Raymond Blaine Fosdick

My dear Mr. President: Washington April 1, 1918

"Turn to the Right," one of our Smileage companies,[1] is playing this week at Camp Meade, in the government theater. I wonder if you would care to run over some night and see it, preferably Wednesday night. A first class company is playing it—the same company that played it on Broadway last year—and I am confident that you would enjoy the experience of seeing not only the show but a soldier audience of 3,000 men.

I should be delighted to make the necessary arrangements, if you are free to go.

With warm personal regards,

Cordially yours,   Raymond B. Fosdick

TLS (WP, DLC).
    [1] Fosdick was at this time chairman of the Commission on Training Camp Activities, which had been appointed in May 1917 to check the problems of drinking and prostitution in and near army and navy training camps and to provide facilities for "wholesome" recreational activities. One of the commission's projects involved the building and operation of forty-two "Liberty theaters," which featured leading actors and actresses from Broadway in well-known plays and musicals. To raise funds for the operation of the theaters, the commission launched the so-called Smileage Book campaign. Booklets with coupons exchangeable for tickets to the Liberty theaters were sold to persons who would send them on to relatives and friends in camps and provide them free admission to the shows. See Raymond B. Fosdick, *Chronicle of a Generation: An Autobiography* (New York, 1958), pp. 143-48 and 152-53.

From Herbert Clark Hoover

Dear Mr. President: Washington *1 April 1918*

In extension of your note of 29th March approving of the appointment of a commission to consider the meat policy, would you be so good as to address a note to the Secretary of Agriculture, Chairman of the Federal Trade Board, Federal Tariff Commission and Secretary of Labour, asking them if they will sit in this capacity or select a representative for that purpose? Might I suggest that in such note you throw out the suggestion that whoever may be selected should have no personal interest in either production or distribution.

These gentlemen would probably understand the nature of the problem better if they had copies of the letter which I addressed to you and in case you should desire to adopt this suggestion I enclose herewith some copies of it to save clerical work.

I beg to remain

Your obedient servant,   Herbert Hoover

TLS (WP, DLC).

David Lloyd George to Lord Reading

[London] 1 Apl. 1918.

No. 1869. Following from Prime Minister begins.

Please convey to President at once sincere thanks of War Cabinet for his instant and complete response to appeal of British and French Govts. It has come as the greatest relief to all those who have the immediate responsibility for dealing with this crisis to know that, thanks to the President's prompt co-operation allied armies are to receive an indispensable reinforcement of men during the next few vital months.

Private and confidential.

In accordance with your request we are issuing a statement to the Press tonight. I shall send you a longer telegram tomorrow in regard to the practical measures which we propose for carrying out this decision. I feel that unless you can give your personal attention to the measures taken to carry out the President's undertaking the men will not be forthcoming. We have been let down badly once or twice before. In fact we are largely suffering now because the Americans have fallen egregiously short of their programme. They promised to have 17 divisions in France by March; they have actually only 4 and these 4 have only just gone into the line. It is vital, and I emphasize this, that this time promise should be redeemed otherwise there may be irretrievable disaster.

T telegram (FO 115/2461, p. 147, PRO).
  [1] Reading conveyed Lloyd George's thanks to Wilson in Lord Reading to RL, April 2, 1918, CCL (FO 115/2461, p. 148, PRO). Reading also issued a statement on April 2, which thanked Wilson for his "prompt co-operation." *New York Times*, April 3, 1918.

To Raymond Blaine Fosdick

My dear Fosdick: The White House 2 April, 1918

You ask me to "run over" some night this week to see "Turn to the Right" played at Camp Meade, but on what can I "run over?" The roads are destroyed between here and Camp Meade, and it would be a veritable adventure to attempt them at night. To go by train is really rather difficult and, worse than all, I never can be sure long enough ahead that I can get away.

I admire the work you are doing and wish sincerely that I could do what you suggest.

Cordially and faithfully yours,   Woodrow Wilson

TLS (WP, DLC).

To David Franklin Houston

My dear Mr. Secretary: [The White House] 2 April, 1918

May I not take the liberty of calling your attention to the enclosed letter recently addressed to me by Mr. Herbert Hoover, the Food Administrator,[1] and ask you to read particularly the recommendation on Page 7 as to the appointment of a committee to deal with the important matter of the meat industry?

I would be very much gratified if you felt at liberty to cooperate with Mr. Hoover in this important matter. I am not assuming, of course, that it will be possible for you personally to take part in the deliberations of the committee, though that, of course, would be the most desirable thing, but I sincerely hope that it will be possible for you to suggest or delegate someone who may act as your representative and keep in touch with you about this business.

Cordially and sincerely yours,   Woodrow Wilson[2]

TLS (Letterpress Books, WP, DLC).
  [1] That is, a copy of the Enclosure printed with H. C. Hoover to WW, March 26, 1918.
  [2] Wilson sent the same letter, *mutatis mutandis*, as WW to WBW, April 2, 1918; WW to W. J. Harris, April 2, 1918; and WW to F. W. Taussig, April 2, 1918, all TLS, Letterpress Books, WP, DLC.

To William Bacon Oliver[1]

My dear Mr. Oliver: [The White House] 2 April, 1918

I have not had time to read thoroughly, I am sorry to say, the report of the sub-committee of the Committee on Naval Affairs, as a result of its investigation of the conduct and administration of the Navy,[2] but I have seen enough of it to realize how thorough and candid it is, and I want to give myself the pleasure of expressing to you and to your colleagues on the sub-committee my admiration for the work you have done and the spirit in which you have done it.   Cordially and sincerely yours,   Woodrow Wilson

TLS (Letterpress Books, WP, DLC).
  [1] Democratic congressman from Alabama.
  [2] "Report of the Subcommittee for Investigation of Conduct and Administration of Naval Affairs," *Annual Report of the Secretary of the Navy for the Fiscal Year 1918* (Washington, 1918), pp. 145-57.

To Francis Patrick Walsh

My dear Mr. Walsh: [The White House] April 2, 1918.

I have been so much and so deeply gratified, in common I believe with the great body of our fellow-citizens, by the outcome of the conferences of the War Labor Conference Board[1] that I cannot deny myself the privilege and pleasure of writing you at least a line to say how highly serviceable I believe the result attained will be to the country and how fine an example it is of the spirit of cooperation and concession which is drawing our people together in this time of supreme crisis.

               Cordially and sincerely yours,   Woodrow Wilson[2]

TLS (Letterpress Books, WP, DLC).
  [1] The board had concluded its conferences on the formulation of a national labor program and had sent its recommendations to Secretary Wilson on March 29, 1918. The report is printed as Enclosure II with WBW to WW, April 4, 1918. About the formation of the War Labor Conference Board, see WBW to WW, March 8, 1918, Vol. 46.
  [2] Wilson sent the same letter, *mutatis mutandis,* to the other members of the War Labor Conference Board: WW to W. H. Taft, April 2, 1918; WW to T. J. Savage, April 2, 1918; WW to T. A. Rickert, April 2, 1918; WW to V. A. Olander, April 2, 1918; WW to C. E. Michael, April 2, 1918; WW to L. F. Loree, April 2, 1918; WW to W. H. Van Dervoort, April 2, 1918; WW to B. L. Worden, April 2, 1918; WW to L. A. Osborne, April 2, 1918; WW to F. J. Hayes, April 2, 1918; and WW to W. L. Hutcheson, April 3, 1918, all TLS, Letterpress Books, WP, DLC.
  Worden was now vice-president and general manager of the Submarine Boat Corporation and general manager of the Newark Bay Shipyard. The members not previously identified in this series were Thomas A. Rickert, president of the United Garment Workers of America, and Thomas J. Savage, a member of the general board of the International Association of Machinists.

To Herbert Bayard Swope

My dear Swope: The White House 2 April, 1918

Thank you warmly for your memorandum of yesterday afternoon.[1] Might I suggest this in your formula, that America's non-assent to the suggestion of Japanese intervention in Siberia seems to have checked the original plan and that it is not likely that anything will be done along that line until there is actual military necessity for the step, leaving out the words, "in which case America will give her consent." I should like to leave that idea out, in view of the many impressions which are beginning to cluster around this extremely difficult and delicate subject.

Cordially and appreciatively yours,   Woodrow Wilson[2]

TLS (WP, DLC).
[1] H. B. Swope to WW, [April 1, 1918], TLS (WP, DLC): "To clear up doubt arising from contradictory reports of our attitude on the Japanese-Siberian situation, and in the hope that the publication may show that we are still the controlling force in international developments, I purpose printing an article to this effect: That America's non-assent to the suggestion of Japanese intervention in Siberia checked the original plan and that nothing is to be done along that line until there is actual military necessity for the step, in which case America will give her consent. Such necessity is to be demonstrated by Russia's invitation to give her our help or through German operations extending into Siberian territory. Is this outline sufficiently accurate to justify publication?"
[2] As it turned out, this letter was not sent. Tumulty recommended, and Wilson agreed, that it be destroyed, and that he, Tumulty, convey its contents to Swope orally. As Tumulty pointed out: "I suggest this not because I distrust Swope but letters sometimes get lost!" JPT to WW, April 2, 1918, TL (WP, DLC).

From Frank William Taussig

My dear Mr. President: Washington April 2, 1918.

I have considered the situation in cold blood, as you asked, and am bound to say that the price fixing business is more important than the inquiry about the Milling Division.

I state this conclusion with great reluctance, because I have the strongest desire to be of service to Mr. Hoover. You know what spirit of sympathy and loyalty he stirs, and I have promised to be of service to him so far as I can. I will endeavor at least to initiate the milling inquiry, and see what happens.

As regards the Price Fixing Committee, much would be gained if its operations could be conducted with despatch. You know what the difficulties of the situation are, and I fear it is indispensable to overcome them in some way, if the committee is to be permanently of service.

You have done me the honor to delegate me for service on the committee that is to formulate a policy upon the meat and packing industries. I hope that I am right in inferring from the terms of

Mr. Hoover's letter on this subject that a delegate or representative, suggested by me, will be able to serve in my place. I have in mind at least one person who would fit. I fear it is quite impossible for me to do any active work at all on this third task.

With high respect and esteem,

Sincerely yours,   F. W. Taussig

TLS (WP, DLC).

To Herbert Clark Hoover

My dear Mr. Hoover: The White House 2 April, 1918

I feel selfish to ask the question that I am about to ask, but I feel bound in duty to ask it. Mr. F. W. Taussig, the Chairman of the United States Tariff Commission, has been acting not only in the important matter of the inquiry you have been conducting in connection with the Milling Division of your Administration, but also as a member of the Price Fixing Committee of the War Industries Board. He feels that it is inconsistent with his duties on the Tariff Commission to undertake both of these duties and, indeed, impossible to perform them in addition to his regular work and inasmuch as I feel that so many things in so many departments turn upon the determinations of the Price Fixing Committee, I am going to be bold enough to ask if you think you could replace Mr. Taussig in the milling industry.

I know this is asking a great deal, but I feel bound to suggest "priorities" in a case of this importance and I am sure you will pardon me.

Cordially and faithfully yours,   Woodrow Wilson

TLS (H. Hoover Papers, HPL).

From Robert Lansing

My dear Mr. President: Washington April 2, 1918.

There were two matters concerning which I intended to speak to you after Cabinet this afternoon but, unfortunately, the memoranda[1] did not reach my desk in time. I am therefore enclosing them for your consideration and decision.

Faithfully yours,   Robert Lansing

TLS (F. L. Polk Papers, CtY).
[1] They are printed as Enclosures with WW to RL, April 4, 1918.

From George Creel

My dear Mr. President: Washington, D. C. April 2, 1918.

With regard to the attached telegram, I have never at any time had any connection with the Non-Partisan League. None of our regular speakers have ever appeared under its auspices, nor have we ever paid the expenses of a special speaker. This League wanted to hold some loyalty meetings, and asked us to suggest speakers. We put the League in touch with a Mr. Dickson Williams,[1] of Chicago, but explained to him that Townley and Gilbert had been indicted, and that there was a good deal of feeling against the League, and that if he went, the decision must be his own.

Even this indirect effort has been stopped, however, and while I deeply resent this terrorism, we cannot afford an open break with the State authorities. This League has been loyal absolutely, and is loyal now, and the Safety Commission is willing to drive it into disloyalty in order to further its own mean political end.

Respectfully,   George Creel

TLS (WP, DLC).
  [1] That is, Dixon C. Williams, president of the Chicago Nipple Manufacturing Co. Williams had been nominated in 1916 as Postmaster of Chicago but had been rejected by the Senate. See J. H. Lewis to JPT, Sept. 5, 1916, n. 1, Vol. 38.

Frank Lyon Polk to Robert Lansing, with Enclosure

Dear Mr. Secretary: [Washington] April 2, 1918.

The attached memorandum has to do with sending a warship to Murmansk. Several of the high military officers are strongly in favor of this step. I will be very much obliged if you will let me have your views.   FLP

TLI (F. L. Polk Papers, CtY).

E N C L O S U R E

Washington April 2, 1918.
MEMORANDUM.
American Warship for Murmansk

The attached telegrams from the Embassy at Vologda[1] show the following:

1. The Ambassador and also Military Attaché recommend presence of American war vessel at Murmansk to join British and French who are cooperating with Soviet there; they believe effect would be good.

2. In addition to four British ships at Murmansk a French cruiser is now there and has landed two hundred troops in barracks; British cruiser has landed field pieces and marines.

3. Murmansk Railway is reported threatened by Finnish White Guards drilled by German officers.

It is to be noted that the British Embassy requested this Government to send a warship to Murmansk about two weeks ago.[2] The Department is informed that the original landing of the British at Murmansk was made with the full consent and approval of Trotsky.[3]   Basil Miles

TS MS (F. L. Polk Papers, CtY).
[1] D. R. Francis to RL, March 28 and 31, 1918, printed in *FR 1918*, *Russia*, II, 471.
[2] A. Robertson to FLP, March 14, 1918, printed in *ibid.*, pp. 470-71.
[3] This memorandum was sent to Wilson. See B. Miles to FLP, c. April 2, 1918, T MS (F. L. Polk Papers, CtY).

Sir Eric Drummond to Sir William Wiseman

[London, April 2, 1918]

No. 72. From Mr. Balfour to Col. House.

The President's message with regard to the sending of American troops to France has been received with very great satisfaction and its effect on the general situation will be most important.

The problem of increasing our man-power presents considerable difficulties and our perplexities are great as they involve Irish problems which necessarily affect American politics.

The Case may be briefly set forth as follows: Great Britain can only raise more men: 1. by causing the ruin of all such industries which are not required for the conduct of the war as still remain; 2. By making, say, 50 th[e] age limit.

The severity of both the above measures is obvious and to impose them on England and Scotland thereby increasing the burden on this island while Ireland is not even called upon to bear the burden of conscription is tantamount to offering them insult.

Ireland's sufferings, at this moment, are not only less than those of any of the European nations now at war, they are less than those of the European nations which have remained neutral. Is it probable that England and Scotland will stand for the prolongation of so unfair a distinction to say nothing of its serious aggravation?

On the other hand the practical objections to the inclusion of Ireland in a measure of conscription are obvious. The enforcement of the law will only be obtained at the cost of serious disorder and possibly, even, of bloodshed. This is certain. It is not certain that the troops to be obtained, numbering, say, 150.000 will turn out to be reliable or useful. The priests, Parliament, the Nationalists and Sinn Feiners will unite to oppose conscription, and the only plan we can devise to reduce their opposition will probably alienate Ulster and all that Ulster, Belfast and her shipyards mean where the effective conduct of the war is concerned.

For this plan implies the association of a Bill to give immediate effect to the report which the Irish Convention is about to submit[1] with the Bill which will extend conscription to Ireland. The report will be published within the week. It may prove acceptable to England & Scotland, but whether it will be equally acceptable to Ulster is uncertain. There is even a doubt whether it will be satisfactory to the Irish Nationalists as the Nationalist minority at the Convention, which includes all the Roman Catholic Bishops, is very powerful. The Bishops want more than is given to them by the report.

Therefore if the association of the measures leads to a quarrel with the North of Ireland over one of them and with the South of Ireland over the other, or over both, the war situation, to express it mildly, will not be bettered.

I am troubling you with this long exposition of difficulties which are apparently purely domestic as I fear that they may prove to affect you also. I have never considered myself able to gauge the exact part that Irish question takes in American politics and now less than ever do I feel competent to do so. I will, therefore, be most grateful if you will inform me of your opinion of the policy which I have outlined above and of its effect on the conduct of the war viewed from America, and I beg you to do so with the same amplitude and freedom that I have used in this message.[2]

T telegram (E. M. House Papers, CtY).

[1] The report of the Irish Convention was submitted by its chairman, Sir Horace Plunkett, on April 8, 1918. The delegates formulated a number of proposals for home rule but failed to agree on an over-all scheme for the self-government of Ireland. The recommendations included the creation of an Irish Parliament with full powers over internal legislation and administration. However, the supreme power of the imperial Parliament over Irish affairs was to remain unaffected, including decisions on war and peace, treaties and foreign relations, and the army and navy. The executive power would be vested in the King and would be exercised through a Lord Lieutenant. One of the major issues which divided the delegates was the question of Irish fiscal autonomy and the control over customs and excise. The Southern Unionists and the Ulster Unionists insisted that all imperial services, including customs, should be left in the hands of the imperial Parliament. The Nationalists, on the other hand, considered complete fiscal autonomy an essential symbol of national independence. While the Southern Unionists and a majority of the Nationalists had, at one point, been prepared to work out a compromise on this issue, the Ulster Unionists and a minority of the Nationalists, which included the Roman Catholic bishops, remained adamant in their positions. The report glossed over these differences by suspending a final decision on the question until after the war. *Report of the Proceedings of the Irish Convention* (Dublin, 1918). See also R. B. McDowell, *The Irish Convention, 1917-18* (London and Toronto, 1970), pp. 179-84.

[2] WWhw on verso of page 2 of this letter: "Would accentuate the whole Irish and Catholic intrigue which has gone hand in hand in some quarters in this country with the German intrigue." House added in handwriting: "W.W. April 3/18."

David Lloyd George to Lord Reading

[London] 2, April 1918.

No. 1887. URGENT.

Secret and Confidential. Following from Prime Minister begins.

I want to impress on you in order that you may press it upon President Wilson and the administration supreme importance of time in the matter of American reinforcements. This battle is only at its first stage. We have survived the first crisis but there is bound to be another attack very shortly but if we defeat the second there will be a third and so on until one side or the other is exhausted or winter puts an end to the fighting. Closest analogy to present is Battle of Verdun but fought on a vastly larger scale and with whole Western front from Flanders to Venice as theatre. In stage of 1918 campaign now beginning enemy probably reckons for his success on refitting his divisions faster than the Allies and on outlasting them in man power. He will therefore go on delivering blow after blow until he has got a decision or is exhausted.

It is very difficult for you at this distance without being in close touch with realities of position to realise how success or disaster in this battle will be decided by exertions which America puts forth in next few weeks or even days. I believe German chances now depend mainly on whether or not America can get her troops effectively in the line in time. Difference of even a week in date of arrival of troops may win a battle and delay of a week may lose it. And remember that no troops can be put into battle line for at least a month after they land. They must be put through final training by men acquainted with conditions at first hand and this I understand is alone possible in France.

We have so often had large promises in past which have invariably been falsified in result that I am sincerely apprehensive that this last undertaking may not be carried out in actual practice. In the circumstances everything depends upon your going beyond ordinary province of an Ambassador and exercising personal supervision over carrying out of pledge. War Mission of which you are the head will enable you to find out where delays are occuring. Immediately a hitch does occur we rely on you to bring pressure to bear in right quarter to secure its immediate removal. In particular we depend greatly on Colonel House and hope that he will devote his great influence and energy to this question until it is certain that 120,000 American infantry are going, in fact and not merely on paper, to arrive in Europe in April and in each succeeding month afterwards. If you can get more so much the better. We can do with all you can send. I am told that there are barely 400,000 infantry in all in whole of U. S. with which to enable President

Wilson to redeem his pledge of sending 480,000 men. If so it is essential that there should be an immediate fresh draft on a large scale.

In order to facilitate your task I am sending over Mr Graeme Thomson by first boat. Since war began he has been at head of our sea transportation and has moved millions of troops to France Egypt Mesopotamia and Salonika and in fact all over the world. He is undoubtedly foremost and ablest organizer of sea transportation in the world. In order to assist in equally important task of getting reinforcements from Camps into transports we are sending by same boat General Hutchinson[1] of Adjutant Generals Department. You will find him very intelligent and experienced officer.

Finally I give you herewith a time table of transportation of American troops, so far as our shipping is concerned. It is vital that we should work to an agreed schedule if we are to get men across in time.

Estimates which follow relate to all troops other than those arriving under ordinary American War Office programme but they include the six divisions which it was arranged at last Supreme War Council should be sent over to be brigaded with us and French. Of these I understand that only 1700 men have so far started.

It is estimated that 61,000 troops can be embarked in British tonnage in April in accommodation becoming available apart from unforeseen contingencies at rate of 16,000 in each first and third week 12,000 in each second and 17,000 in fourth week of month. This does not include two Italian ships which will also be available. Practically all the men carried in British tonnage will be brought to England and transported to Northern French ports by us. This leaves Brest and Bayonne ports free to deal with men carried direct to France by American shipping. Please obtain from American authorities at once similar estimate of numbers which can be carried in tonnage provided by America during four weeks, including such of Dutch ships or other allied tonnage as are suitable and available. It is vital that we should have this time table as soon as possible in order that we may complete arrangements with Pershing in regard to reception training and brigading with allied forces.

It is also very important that vessels of American Line be fitted and used to carry full number of men of which they are capable. Up to present they have been carrying less than 1,000 men per voyage. If they were fitted up as our troopships they could carry 2,000 to 2,500. Mongolia and Manchuria could carry from 2,500 to 3,000.

T telegram (FO 115/2461, pp. 109-12, PRO).
  [1] Maj. Gen. Robert Hutchison, not Hutchinson, director of organization at the War Office.

From the Diary of Josephus Daniels

April Tuesday 2 1918

Cabinet discussed situation.

WW read letter from Ambassador Sharp[1] of the destruction of church in Paris by 90 mm gun & 100 killed including Swiss Secy of Legation.[2] Wife of minister was violent in denunciation of conduct of Germans

Pres. decided to issue Proclamation requesting all parties to abide by action of Labor Adjustment Board[3]

[1] W. G. Sharp to RL, April 2, 1918, T telegram (WP, DLC).
[2] Henri Stroehlin.
[3] It is printed at April 8, 1918.

To Robert Lansing

My dear Mr. Secretary   The White House 3 April, 1918

The people who send these papers to me are very persistent and I do not know whether they are trustworthy or not.[1] I wish you would have someone who has followed the Costa Rican business advise you and me through you what action, if any, is feasible or proper. Of course, it goes without saying that they must not be allowed to draw us into any of the miserable intrigue down there, and our course is unchangeably fixed with regard to the usurper no matter what the character or intrigues of his predecessor. All of that I am sure you will agree with me is none of our business. Apparently Mr. Field and his associates wish us forcibly to intervene down there. If so, I think we can better tell them in the plainest terms that we will not consider such suggestions, but I don't want to make any answer until I am sure I know the whole case.

Cordially and faithfully yours,   Woodrow Wilson

TLS (SDR, RG 59, 818.00/398½, DNA).
[1] W. H. Field to R. Forster, March 27, 1918, enclosing W. H. Field to A. B. Bielaski, March 27, 1918, both TCL (SDR, RG 59, 818.00/398½, DNA); "MEMORDANDUM OF W. H. FIELD," T MS dated March 26, 1918, same file number as above; W. H. Field to Julius Klein, March 27, 1918; and W. H. Field to Marshall Morgan, March 27, 1918, both TCL, same file number.
About Woolsey Hopkins Field and the background of the Costa Rican situation, see the Enclosure printed with RL to WW, Feb. 7, 1917, Vol. 41, and index references to Costa Rica in Vol. 41 and following volumes. A White House memorandum (T MS, WP, DLC) summarizes the aforementioned documents as follows:
"Encloses copy of letter which he has sent to Mr. Bielaski, as well as a memorandum, copies of which have been sent to State Department and Department of Commerce. States the 'Latin-American colony in New York have given up hope in regard to the American government having sufficient backbone to right wrongs committed in the name of American capital and commerce. They realize the pressure under which the President is working and the many more important matters.'
"In the accompanying memorandum Mr. Field refers to Costa Rica and states that Manual Castro Quesada sailed today (March 26th) without taking leave at Washington, and will proceed to Central America to prepare the various groups of Costa Ricans for

an armed resistance against the Secretary of War Tinoco who has seized the reigns [reins] of government in Costa Rica and with the assistance of other Latin-American countries hopes to re-establish law and order. States he did not go to Washington for the reason that the State Department had requested him that no arms be used or blood shed while at the same time reports arrived from Costa Rica bringing further news of friends, who were men of standing in Costa Rica, and who have been shot down in cold blood by the traitor, Secretary of War Tinoco. A report also was received of a statement made by the representative of the State Department residing in San Jose, Costa Rica, who is in charge of the American Legation, that if the people would rise up in arms United States ships would come and help them take Tinoco from the office that he has seized. The people in Costa Rica, therefore, took up arms relying upon the diplomatic word of honor of the United States, and when no ships arrived and Tinoco had a short time, he seized the children of the leaders of the movement against him and sent word to them that he would mutilate their children if their fathers did not voluntarily surrender, which in most cases they have done to save their children. States the reported promise of the diplomatic representative of the United States has caused Tinoco to make the statement that if the United States Government were to inform him that he must vacate the office of President he would turn the government over unconditionally to constitutional designate Aguilar Barquero. He has already offered to turn the presidency over to Barquero provided he could retain the office of Secretary of War or name the said Secretary and have complete control over the armed forces of Costa Rica, but Barquero refused to accept unless the Government was turned over to him unconditionally. It seems to Mr. Field that it might be of value to send such a message to Tinoco but if he refused force would have to be used for which there is no precedent."

Two Letters to Thomas Watt Gregory

My dear Gregory: [The White House] 3 April, 1918

I was very stupid in writing to you twice for information about the Ryan case.[1] I beg that you will pardon me. The first request had clean gone out of mind.

The more I think about the case of Ryan, the more I think it would be timely and justifiable to pardon him, and I am going to ask you if you won't be kind enough to have Finch prepare the pardon for me.[2] This is a case which, like yourself, I have gone over so often that I seem to know my way about it in the dark, and all I wanted to know was the relative terms of the men still in prison. Thank you very much for sending it.

Cordially and faithfully yours,   Woodrow Wilson

[1] Actually, Wilson had *written* only once to Gregory about this matter, in WW to TWG, April 1, 1918. As that letter reveals, Wilson had first asked Gregory for information on the case at the cabinet meeting on March 26. Gregory had sent the required information in TWG to WW, March 28, 1918, and its Enclosure.
[2] Wilson commuted Ryan's sentence to expire at once on April 6, 1918.

My dear Gregory   [The White House] 3 April, 1918

You will remember that a Mr. Bell came here with great excitement from the Pacific Coast, delegated by certain of the Western Governors to propose some rather radical things to us for the purpose of suppressing the I.W.W.'s who certainly are worthy of being suppressed. He has been followed now by a Mr. Lubin, who came to me with a letter of introduction from Lane and who has at my request sent me this memorandum.[1] Will you not be kind enough to have it carefully read in your department with a view to seeing whether anything is proposed which it is feasible and wise for us to do?   Cordially and faithfully yours,   Woodrow Wilson

TLS (Letterpress Books, WP, DLC).
  [1] That is, S. J. Lubin to WW, March 29, 1918.

To Frank William Taussig

My dear Mr. Taussig: [The White House] 3 April, 1918

Your letter of today,[1] I need hardly tell you, gives me the greatest gratification, but I must, nevertheless, beg that you will not undertake more than you feel justified in undertaking, because the last thing I want to do is to overburden and break down the most valuable men about me.

It goes without saying that I shall be delighted to see you continue all the activities to which we have perhaps selfishly called you, but you mustn't do so at the sacrifice of your health and strength.
                Cordially and sincerely yours,   Woodrow Wilson

TLS (Letterpress Books, WP, DLC).
  [1] He meant Taussig's letter of April 2.

From Edward Nash Hurley

My dear Mr. President: Washington April 3, 1918.

I think you will be interested in reading the telegram which I sent to all the shipbuilders yesterday. I am enclosing a copy of it.[1]

Probably it will bring some brisk replies from the yards that maintained their schedule and eloquent excuses from those that did not. Both classes of replies will be useful, in checking up.

My own feeling has been that the owners of the yards are not fighting as they should be fighting for increased production. It seemed to me that the only way to change the situation was to put the situation squarely before them, letting the public know where the blame lies. If we can make them feel that we are holding them responsible, and intend to fix the blame where it belongs, I believe that greater progress can be made.

If any of the replies reveal any fault at our end, we can be guided accordingly. We have worked night and day to straighten out their labor situation and to get them their materials.

I hope you will make any suggestions that occur to you with reference to the telegram.

Sincerely yours,   Edward N. Hurley

TLS (WP, DLC).

¹ E. N. Hurley and C. Piez to "all Managers of shipyards now engaged in work for the U. S. Shipping Board and Emergency Fleet Corporation," [April 2, 1918] TC telegram (WP, DLC). Hurley and Piez stated that they were "keenly disappointed" by the amount of tonnage delivered by American shipyards during the month of March, which had been significantly lower than that promised by the shipbuilders. Hurley and Piez demanded that a special effort be made in April to compensate for previous losses. Moreover, they requested full information about the causes of the delay, asked for detailed statements on the efficiency of the shipyards, and invited realistic estimates of the expected production during April. The Emergency Fleet Corporation, Hurley and Piez concluded, would hold the managers of the shipyards personally responsible for meeting the schedule of production since the American people wanted ships, not excuses.

From Gutzon Borglum

My dear Mr. President: Washington, D. C. April 3, 1918

I am back after a trip of inspection of the important factories engaged in plane and engine production, and I find here the aeronautic situation the topic of general discussion, and hasten to give you the enclosed data to date.

You should know that I have met in public places Mr. Franklin D. Roosevelt, General Leonard Wood, and Senator Hitchcock, among others, and I learn from these gentlemen that they are to a considerable extent familiar with the situation, and Monday I called upon Mr. Polk whom I have known for some years and expressed quite frankly and privately to him my fears regarding conditions and delays.

There seems little to do now but to wait upon events unless there is a real desire which I feel there is an absolute need of, a thoroughly informed enquiry into the sources of the trouble I have indicated by especially trained men. In closing I want to say that whatever there has been of an unhappy nature in this unfortunate business, it has not wanted conscientiousness and sacrifice nor can I more than indicate this, but I believe you know, or at least must feel that I have sacrificed everything to make my work searching and impartial though hindered and unaided, and even if I seem to have hurt you, you must also know that I have desired most to protect.

We face the gravest scandal that a Government could have and must go through, and it is a misfortune, personally, that I, who am a creative man purely and simply, should be compelled to play the part that has been necessary.

I want to thank you for the confidence, the very great confidence, that you have placed in me, which I shall carry away with me as the single reward in it, and trust you believe me,

Faithfully and sincerely,   Gutzon Borglum

Tomorrow you *will* receive a *small* package of very important facts from factories—with some other data

TLS (WP, DLC).

Gutzon Borglum to Joseph Patrick Tumulty

My dear Mr. Tumulty: Washington, D. C. April 3, 1918.

I am sending herewith in your care a few remaining papers covering my examination of the chief factories engaged in engine and plane production. Will you kindly see that the President receives these as promptly as possible. They are important and he may wish to refer them to some one.[1]

I hope you are very well.

Sincerely yours,   Gutzon Borglum

TLS (WP, DLC).
[1] See WW to G. Borglum, April 5, 1918.

From Dixon C. Williams

Democratic National Committee
Dear Mr. President: Washington, D. C. April 3, 1918

At the suggestion of Mr. George Creel, I beg to submit to you a report on a visit just made to Minnesota. At Mr. Bestor's[1] instance, Mr. John Thompson of St. Paul representing the National Non-Partisan League, invited me to make a number of loyalty speeches in Minnesota and the Dakotas.

I arrived at St. Paul Saturday morning, March 30, reporting to Mr. Arthur LeSueur[2] as instructed, expecting to be at once furnished with the itinerary. To my vast astonishment, he informed me that after repeated efforts by wire to the sheriffs of the various counties, in which the towns of Windom, St. James and Fairmount are located, he had finally received from sheriffs O. G. Peterson, O. C. Lee and A. E. Lindquist,[3] emphatic refusal to allow the National Non-Partisan League to hold any meeting whatever in the counties they represented, no matter who the speaker might be or who might stand sponsor for him, that loyalty speakers if approved by local patriotic societies could speak provided a local loyal man presided, but no known representative of the Non-Partisan League would be tolerated on the platform. The reason ascribed for this was the declaration that the League was disloyal.

Upon observing this situation I wired Hon. James E. Blythe, former chairman of the State Republican Committee[4] at Mason City, Iowa, where I had spoken the previous night to wire Governor Burnquist vouching for my loyalty. His wire to the Governor was as follows:

"Last night Dixon C. Williams delivered the most wonderful patriotic speech in support of the Administration and Third Liberty Loan yet heard in Mason City. Audience large and enthusiastic. Our people feel that we have been greatly helped. Everyone should hear this powerful and convincing argument."

The effect of this was an invitation from C. B. Mills, Chairman of local Liberty Loan Speakers Bureau and from Mr. Libby of the Commission on Public Safety,[5] to speak under their auspices, both invitations being accompanied with the proviso that I should not at any future time speak under the auspices of the Non-Partisan League. I went to the Capitol and talked with Mr. Libby and Mr. Henke,[6] the publicity man of the Public Safety Commission, and showed them a very excellent and prudent letter written me by Mr. Bestor, stating the reasons for furnishing speakers to patriotic organizations, but without effect so far as changing their declared purpose to prevent any meeting the League might attempt. As justification, they contended that the League was a political organization, a disturber of the established order and absolutely pro-German and disloyal.

With this view I do not agree. I do believe at one period, perhaps in the earlier stages of existence of the League, they were radical and did allow organizers to work for the League who were to say the least, indiscreet, and some of them perhaps worse. The League officials do not deny this but claim that as fast as such individuals were reported to them, dismissal immediately followed and that no known disloyal utterance oral or written is tolerated. All of their speech to me and all of their printed announcements breathe the highest degree of loyalty to the Administration and particularly the Administration's war policies. I have read much of their literature.

The organization claim a membership among the farmers of over 50,000 and are affiliated with organized labor. They have bitterly attacked the policies of what they call Big Business in the North West and the profiteer. The League submit a long list of alleged grievances the farmers have suffered and are now indeed almost desperate at this latest attack on what they feel is their inalienable right of free speech.

They point to Liberty Bonds and War Savings Stamps they have helped to sell and to their purpose to push the Third Liberty Loan, now in danger of being thwarted by an order prohibiting them to sell bonds, savings stamps or even take collections in support of Y.M.C.A. activities. The situation seems indeed serious and to me presents some danger phases particularly in view of our foreign complications and the drastic course the state authorities seem determined to pursue. After conversing with the adherents of both sides, my judgment is that anxiety to crush out disloyalty is not the sole factor in the aggressive and uncompromising attitude of the state authorities. I fear politics is at least one moving consideration. It is difficult after all one hears from the opponents of each to escape the conviction that Governor Burnquist stands in great fear of what the League may do to his ambition to succeed himself and anticipates if he cannot crush the League absolutely or cast a doubt on the loyalty of the organization, the loss to his party of four or five Congressional candidates this next election. The leaders of the League do not hesitate to declare that it is to their best interest to join the Democrats in their efforts to elect Congressmen in certain districts.   Very sincerely,   Dixon C Williams

TLS (WP, DLC).
    [1] That is, Arthur Eugene Bestor, the director of the Speaking Division of the C.P.I.
    [2] A former member of the executive committee of the Socialist party; at this time president of the People's College, Fort Scott, Kansas, and an attorney and legal adviser of the Nonpartisan League.
    [3] They were the sheriffs of Jackson, Cottonwood, and Watonwan counties, respectively. The Editors have been unable to discover their full names.
    [4] Blythe was a lawyer and former member of the legislature of Iowa.
    [5] Charles B. Mills, vice-president of the Midland National Bank of Minneapolis, and Henry W. Libby, secretary of the Minnesota Public Safety Commission and an insurance agent and prominent church leader of St. Paul.
    [6] Charles W. Henke, a newspaper editor.

Tasker Howard Bliss to Peyton Conway March

Versailles. April 3rd [1918].

Number 76
    For Acting Chief of Staff.
    Confidential and not to be made public.
    Paragraph 1. French and British Great Headquarters report only local actions to noon today. No important changes in lines. Junction of British and French forces has been moved northward to a point 1,300 meters southeast of Thennes.
    Paragraph 2. For the President, Secretary of War and Acting Chief of Staff. In the conference at Doulens on March 26th General Foch was charged with the responsibility of coordinating the mil-

itary action of the Western front but he was not specifically given full power to do this. The result has been what might have been expected. He has been obliged to persuade the allied commanders when he ought to have had the power to give them orders. Yesterday General Pershing and myself were requested by Mr. Lloyd George and Mr. Clemenceau to attend a conference at Beauvais at about noon today. There were present Mr. Lloyd George, Mr. Clemenceau and Generals Haig, Petain, Foch, Wilson, Pershing and Bliss. The following agreement was made with perfect unanimity and cordiality. "General Foch is charged by the British, French and American governments with the duty of coordinating the action of the allied armies on the Western front; and with this object in view there is conferred upon him all the powers necessary for its effective accomplishment. For this purpose the British, French and American governments entrust to General Foch the strategic direction of military operations. The Commanders in Chief of the British, French and American armies *shall* exercise in full the tactical conduct of their armies. Each Commander in Chief shall have the right to appeal to his government if in his opinion his army finds itself placed in danger by any instructions received from General Foch. Signed by Mr. Lloyd George, Mr. Clemenceau, Petain, Foch, Haig, Wilson, General Bliss and General Pershing." I was not in favor of the right of appeal of any Commander in Chief to his own government. Nevertheless there was cordial agreement by all to the above quoted document.

Paragraph 3. The English and French at above conference expressed belief that Germans are about to deliver another heavy attack north of Arras.   Bliss.

TC telegram (WDR, RG 407, World War Cablegrams, DNA).

Edward Mandell House to Arthur James Balfour

The White House, April 3, 1918.

In reply to your No. 72, I am not able to advise intelligently as to the effect of conscription upon your own domestic situation, but I feel certain that it would accentuate the whole Irish and Catholic intrigue which has gone hand in hand in some quarters in this country with the German intrigue.   Edward House.

TC telegram (E. M. House Papers, CtY).

Arthur James Balfour to Sir William Wiseman

[London] April 3d. 1918.

No. 76. Following for Col. House from Mr. Balfour:

I quite agree that ideal arrangement would be for Bolsheviki to request Japanese American allied assistance against German aggression. We have already instructed Mr. Lockhart to do all he can to bring this about and he does not altogether despair of ultimate success.

It seems possible that Bolsheviki will be able to collect men but not to train them, organize them or equip them sufficiently to enable them to meet a modern army with the smallest chance of success.

With Japanese American aid position might be entirely altered and Bolshevik Army turned into an effective weapon to save Russia. Germans no doubt realize this and will probably endeavour to destroy Bolshevik forces at an early date and I fear they cannot but succeed unless Japan America and the Allies are already giving help. Time therefore is of essential importance both to Allies and to Bolsheviki. Ought we not to do all we can to hasten an invitation? I understand that Col. Robins is on excellent terms with Bolshevik leaders and I venture to suggest he might be asked to second Mr. Lockhart's endeavours.

Sir Eric Drummond to Sir William Wiseman

[London] April 3, 1918.

No. 73. Following from BALFOUR:

(Begins): Please inform Col. House that we have received through an intermediary a memorandum drawn up by Austrian Minister for Foreign Affairs dealing with recent conversations between our messenger and Austrian Agent. Following is a translation of the memorandum:

"Austrian Minister for Foreign Affairs finds it difficult to believe declarations of British messenger really tend towards a general peace based on justice, since they leave aside the one difficulty in way of a just and lasting peace, i.e. the desire for annexation on the part of France and Italy. Central Empires will never recognize this desire, which appears to them unjustified. So long as Italy wishes to annex Austrian territory, and France declares that she cannot make peace without acquiring Alsace-Lorraine, peace with those Powers is impossible. If, however, they abandon their aims of conquest, Austrian Minister for Foreign Affairs sees no obstacle to conclusion of peace at once. So long as England supports her allies in their annexationist schemes no one in Central Empires will believe she seeks a just and lasting peace. Central Empires have not the slightest desire to interfere with internal affairs in Allied countries neither do they wish for others to interfere in theirs.

"Austrian Minister for Foreign Affairs feels reproach with regard to peace with Roumania is unjustified and proof of this is that Roumanian people wish for nothing more than formation of a Marghiloman Ministry[1] such as will allow them to draw closer to Central Powers in a profitable manner. Roumanian people feel benefits which a rapprochement will confer will be greater than sacrifices which peace imposes on them.

"As regards after war, Count Czernin declares he is resolutely decided to adhere to a programme which will aim at preventing future wars.

"But first, present war must be brought to an end which will only be possible when France and Italy no longer speak of conquests. It will be possible then to discuss future."

After delivering this message Austrian Agent, evidently under instructions, explained to an intermediary views of his Government on Alsace-Lorraine and Trentino questions. He said there could be no question of surrendering Trentino which had never been Italian territory. Since the year 1400 it had formed part of Holy Roman Empire and in 1804 Austria incorporated it. Towns on coast live on tourists and peasants on their vines and oranges. If Trentino were to belong to Italy it would be ruined. Its deputies in the Reichsrath had always urged maintenance of a strong customs barrier against Italian wines and adoption of measures to hinder Austrian tourists from going southward to Italy.

There would, however, be no difficulty in establishing an Italian University at Trieste after the war if inhabitants want it. Land owners and peasants were all for Austria and Irredentists are all lawyers, doctors, and intellectuals who engage in politics and have no money. Italy has many ports already and ought not to deprive Austria of her only outlet to sea.

As regards Alsace-Lorraine, German Government are convinced except in and around Metz a referendum would result in their favor. In Lorraine German villages are far richer and healthier than French and have therefore lost nothing by annexation

If Allies had occupied Alsace-Lorraine, Trieste or Trentino new position might have arisen.

Our Minister at Berne points out that above bears evident traces of German inspiration and shows either that Austrian Agent has been exaggerating Count Czernin's attitude or that latter is an opportunist and awaiting result of present fighting.

Austrian Agent hinted at possibility of further interviews but was told in reply that there was no common ground and that manner in which Count Czernin had shifted his ground betrayed weakness of Austrian Government.

Agent seemed visibly embarrassed.

In general evidently nothing more to be done at present.

T telegrams (W. Wiseman Papers, CtY).
    [1] Alexandru Marghiloman, head of the Conservative party and of the Rumanian Red Cross, was appointed Prime Minister of Rumania by King Ferdinand on March 20, 1918, for the express purpose of signing a peace treaty with the Central Powers. Marghiloman, who was known for his hostility to the Entente cause, had remained in Bucharest during the German occupation and had close personal relations with German and Austrian officials. See R. W. Seton-Watson, *A History of the Roumanians from Roman Times to the Completion of Unity* (Cambridge, 1934), pp. 514-15.

From the Diary of Josephus Daniels

1918 Wednesday 3 April

War Council met with President. First took up the question of getting men to France. Hurley reported could send over 90,000 a month but this would require reduction of imports used in Japan and Brazilian trade. President said "Tell Great Britain how many we can send not taking out Japan Brazil tonnage and then ask England and France to furnish ships for balance"

John Skelton Williams brought up buying coal for RRs at less figure than public pays—said operators were making unconscionable big profits, but were willing to continue practice of selling to RR cheaper if cars are furnished. Garfield opposed drop in price & said RR should pay same as public & Navy, & the practice of furnishing 100% cars to certain RRs was indefensible. Williams said G's prop. made giving 40 mil. dollars to operators & no benefit to anybody else. I asked why not commandeer? WW said the RR did not belong to the Government & we could not commandeer.

WW—Not let cars go to certain mines but divide in zones, & require better prices for RR because coal to them is essential to keep all industries going.

To Robert Lansing, with Enclosures

My dear Mr. Secretary,   The White House. 4 April, 1918.

I must say that none of these memoranda has anything in it that is at all persuasive with me. I hope that you feel the same way.

Faithfully Yours,   W.W.

WWTLI (SDR, RG 59, 861.00/1439½, DNA).

E N C L O S U R E   I

Handed me by Lord
Reading Apr. 2/18 RL

Washington, April 1, 1918.

MEMORANDUM

No: 352 The British Embassy have received instructions to communicate to the Department of State the following summary of telegraphic reports which have been received with regard to the situation at Vladivostok at the end of last month.

The employees of the Post and Telegraph Offices have refused to accept control by the Bolsheviki, and as a result the offices have been taken over by the Red Guard, on the instructions of the Soviet: the senior postal officials have been placed under arrest, and communication abroad and with the interior is at present suspended. The Zemstvo and Municipal authorities have made a strong protest against these proceedings.

Subsequent to these transactions various officials of the volunteer fleet, including the manager, were arrested on March 26, and it seems clear that the Bolsheviki party are confident that no action will be taken by the Allies and that, acting on this belief, they mean to seize the control of all the local institutions one by one. The local British representatives report that present indications lead them to believe that, in the absence of active opposition on the part of the Allied Governments, the extreme party will be able to acquire full control at Vladivostok, as the movement against them at Blagovestchenk has completely collapsed, and it is, owing to the failure of this movement, impossible to count on any effective action by the Ussuri Cossacks. Orders are being given to forward enemy prisoners of war from the Vladivostok district to Irkutsk.

In opposition to the proceedings of the Bolshevists the employees of the volunteer fleet, the telegraph offices and the supply ships have declared a strike, and a further strike is planned by the employees of the Government offices, with the exception of the Customs and Treasury, while the shops and business houses are also contemplating joining the movement. There is however no force which would be able to resist the Red Guards: the extremists are encouraged by their success at Blagovestchenk: and there is reason to anticipate that the strike movement will be unsuccessful unless its promoters can definitely expect allied support. The Bolshevists believe that, in the present political situation, the men of war in the port will not take any action except, possibly, to act for the protection of the foreign Consulates, and they realise that these vessels cannot afford any protection to the city without definite orders to that effect. They are increasing the armament of their troops, and are seizing stocks, and, while they anticipate Japanese intervention some time or another, they expect to be able to gain complete local control by immediate violent action.

In view of the situation outlined above His Majesty's Government have sent instructions to the Commander of His Majesty's Ship "SUFFOLK" to act in concert with the commanders of the American and Japanese ships now in the harbour with a view to preventing the removal of stores from Vladivostok, if the local Bolshevist authorities should contemplate taking such a step.

In view of the instructions sent to His Majesty's Ship "SUFFOLK" the British Embassy would be much obliged if they could be informed in due course whether the United States Government propose to issue any similar instructions for joint action by the ships of war of the countries concerned in the event of attempts being made to remove from Vladivostok the warlike stores now lying at that place.   Reading

TS MS (SDR, RG 59, 861.00/1435½, DNA).

ENCLOSURE II

Handed me by Lord
Reading Apr. 2/18 RL

Washington, March 29, 1918.

PARAPHRASE of telegram dated March 29, 1918.

The Germans now have complete liberty of action in all other theatres of war except the West front, and for this reason it has been possible for them to bring about a critical situation in the West. We have every hope that the British and French armies may be able to check the advance in France for the present moment, but further German divisions can be transferred from Russia to the West front, and further Austrian divisions from Russia to the Italian front, and Germany is thus still capable of making still further efforts in the West.

It will be many months before the American forces can bring their weight and influence to bear, but the Japanese army is capable of immediate use. While it has not yet been used it can be used; if it were employed at once it might be turned to great advantage, and it is even possible that immediate action by the Japanese army, though it would only produce a moral effect at first, might prove to be the deciding factor.

As regards the moral effect, if Japanese forces were to land in

Siberia and occupy the railway the result might well be that Germany would cease withdrawing her forces from the Eastern front: furthermore it is in the East that the German Government are now taking steps to overcome the effects of the blockade, to upset the security of British India, and to carry the war down to Afghanistan and Persia, incidentally giving the Turks a free hand in Armenia.

The lessons of history show that it is absolute folly to expect that a resolute and well-disciplined enemy can be resisted by armies called into existence by appeals to patriotism or by proclamations, unless such armies can be grouped round a nucleus of reliable and experienced troops. Any views to the contrary have been set forth only by civilians lacking in military knowledge and taken in by the irresponsible promises of enthusiasts ignorant of the questions at issue. The British General Staff consider the Japanese Army as constituting the sole reliable nucleus round which the loyal sections in Russia could unite for the purpose of combating domination of their country by Prussia: the Japanese are ready and even anxious to assume this role and also to accept the service of allied officers and assistance from the allies in the way of material. For success in such an operation time is the vital factor. Assuming that Japan were immediately to start embarking a force consisting of eight or ten divisions they should, if material assistance is given from the United States, be in a position to control the railway as far as the Tomsk area before it has been possible for the enemy to arm and organise the enemy prisoners in Siberia, to provide them with good leaders, and to destroy the railway tunnels and bridges. In order to defeat the German propaganda which urges that Japan will either retain any occupied districts or will throw in her lot with Germany it would be necessary to give an international character to the expedition in Siberia. The control of the force should however, for reasons of efficiency, remain wholly with Japan.

T MS (SDR, RG 59, 861.00/1436½, DNA).

ENCLOSURE   III

Handed me by Lord
Reading, Apr. 2/18 RL

Washington, April 1, 1918.
PARAPHRASE of telegram from the British
Ambassador at Tokyo, dated March 28/18.

The General Staff have today informed the British Military Attache that Semenov has received the arms furnished for him by Japan. Semenov is now in a comparatively satisfactory position.

The Bolshevists are now in control of the situation at Vladivostok and have forwarded a considerable quantity of the war stores lying there via the Amur Railway to Irkutsk for the German Bolshevist force which is now being formed there. The stores sent include guns. The Bolshevist force at Krasnoyarsk has also been successful in obtaining arms and rolling stock. A number of enemy prisoners have proceeded to the Western Provinces of China where they are being used to incite the local Mohammedans against the allied countries.   Reading

TS MS (SDR, RG 59, 861.00/1437½, DNA).

ENCLOSURE IV

Handed me by Lord
Reading, Apr. 2/18 RL

Washington, April 2, 1918.
PARAPHRASE of telegram from Mr. Lockhart,
Moscow: Dated March 28th, 1918.

On March 27 I had a very satisfactory discussion with Trotsky, who again mentioned the possibility of allied troops being sent via Siberia to Russia. Trotsky confirmed the remarks made by the Minister of Foreign Affairs,[1] and said that Russia would welcome help from the allied countries, now that she is involved in a life and death struggle, even if to obtain this help it should become necessary for the socialist forces to fight in cooperation with the army of the imperialists, Provided that the allies would give guarantees on certain points and that *other allied forces were present*[2] he thought there was no objection to the use of Japanese troops. I do not doubt that it is more than possible to come to an arrangement in this question, but in order to do so we must act with caution.

As regards the army: Trotsky informs me that he is fully supported by Lenine on the questions of the suppression of the Committees, stern discipline, and the death sentence. He says he is convinced that he will be able to carry out his own policy and that he will give up his post if he cannot. Orders have been given to Nitrinor to behave in a more tactful manner and to stop all peace propaganda:[3] possibly another man may be appointed in place of him.

The attitude of the Bolsheviks towards the Allies is completely changed and it is most important that this should be realised. The change is of course due to the necessity for fighting. But it must also be remembered that allied interests in Russia would be disastrously prejudiced by a counter-revolution at the present moment.

Trotsky is confronted with a hard task in organising any fighting force, even a small one, and in carrying out this task we should, I am strongly of opinion, give him all the support we can. The political situation will be completely overshadowed by the military situation if once war recommences and as soon as a Russian army of any sort is actually engaged in hostilities against the Germans.

T MS (SDR, RG 59, 861.00/1438½, DNA).
  [1] That is, Georgii Vasil'evich Chicherin.
  [2] Wilson's emphasis.
  [3] Maksim Maksimovich Litvinov, not "Nitrinor," at this time the "provisional" Bolshevik "ambassador" to Great Britain. Litvinov had for several months conducted a vigorous propaganda campaign in Britain and had urged workers to demand the conclusion of an immediate peace. See Richard H. Ullman. *Anglo-Soviet Relations, 1917-1921: Intervention and the War* (Princeton, N. J., 1961), pp. 59-61 and 78-81.

Two Letters to Robert Lansing

My dear Mr. Secretary,   The White House. 4 April, 1918.

I have read this report[1] with careful attention and, of course, with a good deal of concern; but I do not see that there is anything that Mexico can do that will seriously embarrass us,—do you?

Faithfully Yours,   W.W.

WWTLI (SDR, RG 59, 763.72/9243, DNA).
  [1] H. P. Fletcher to RL, March 13, 1918, printed as an Enclosure with RL to WW, March 27, 1918.

My dear Mr. Secretary,   The White House. 4 April, 1918.

I am willing that a warship should be sent to Murmansk, if there is one available near those waters, and I am willing to have its commander cooperate there; but I think it would be wise to ask the Secretary of the Navy to caution him not to be drawn in further than the present action there without first seeking and obtaining instructions by cable from home.

Faithfully Yours,   W.W.

WWTLI (photostat in F. L. Polk Papers, CtY).

To Herbert Clark Hoover

My dear Mr. Hoover: The White House 4 April, 1918

I do not know whether the Federal Trade Commission has supplied you with a copy of the enclosed report.[1] If not, it certainly ought to be in your hands, and I take pleasure in sending it to you.

Cordially and sincerely yours,   Woodrow Wilson

TLS (H. Hoover Papers, HPL).

¹ It is missing in WP, DLC. However, it was a report by the Federal Trade Commission on the cost of flour milling and flour jobbing and was part of the general food investigation then being undertaken by the commission. See W. J. Harris to WW, April 4, 1918, TLS (WP, DLC). The report is printed as *Food Investigation. Report of the Federal Trade Commission on Flour Milling and Jobbing* (Washington, 1918).

To Gutzon Borglum

My dear Mr. Borglum: The White House 4 April, 1918

Thank you very much for your letter of yesterday. You may be sure that the whole matter will be and is being gone into to the bottom.   Cordially and sincerely yours,   Woodrow Wilson

TLS (G. Borglum Papers, DLC).

From William Bauchop Wilson, with Enclosures

My dear Mr. President: Washington April 4, 1918.

I am submitting to you herewith draft of the proposed proclamation relative to the establishment of a National War Labor Board.

I am also inclosing you copy of memorandum of appointment and copy of the report of the War Labor Conference Board setting forth the plan of mediation and arbitration. You will observe from paragraph (g) on page 2 that provision is made that "The National Board shall refuse to take cognizance of a controversy between employer and workers in any field of industrial or other activity where there is by agreement or Federal law a means of settlement which has not been invoked." That paragraph is inserted to prevent friction through interference with the operation of trade agreements and to make it clear that there is no intention to substitute this Board for the Labor Adjustment Boards of the Director General of Railroads, the Shipping Board, or other agencies already established by law or agreement.   Faithfully yours,   W B Wilson

TLS (WP, DLC).

E N C L O S U R E   I

Washington April 2, 1918.

WHEREAS, the Secretary of Labor appointed a War Labor Conference Board for the purpose of devising some method of labor adjustment for the period of the war which would be acceptable to employers and employees; and

WHEREAS, said Board has made a report recommending the creation for the period of the war of a National War Labor Board of the same number and to be selected by the same agencies that created the War Labor Conference Board, whose duties shall be to adjust labor disputes in the manner and in accordance with certain conditions set forth in the report.

NOW, THEREFORE, in accordance with the recommendation contained in the report of said War Labor Conference Board to the Secretary of Labor under date of March 29, 1918, I do hereby appoint Hon. William Howard Taft and Hon. Frank P. Walsh as representatives of the General Public of the United States; Messrs. Loyall A. Osborne, L. F. Loree, W. H. Van Dervoort, C. E. Michael and B. L. Worden as representatives of the employers of the United States; and Messrs. Frank J. Hayes, William L. Hutcheson, Thomas J. Savage, Victor A. Olander and T. A. Rickert as representatives of the employees of the United States, as members of the National War Labor Board.

The duties of the National War Labor Board shall be as defined in the report above referred to.   W B Wilson
                                                    Secretary of Labor.

TS MS (WP, DLC).

ENCLOSURE II

For Release Sunday Papers, March 31.

The following report and recommendations are presented by the WAR LABOR CONFERENCE BOARD, representing employers and employees appointed in accordance with the suggestion of Secretary of Labor William B. Wilson, to aid in the formation of a National labor program for the period of the war:

                              Washington, D. C., March 29, 1918.
Honorable William B. Wilson,
        Secretary of Labor.
Sir:

The Commission of representatives of employers and workers, selected in accord with the suggestion of your letter of January 28, 1918, to aid in the formulation, in the present emergency, of a National labor program, present to you, as a result of their conferences, the following:

(a) That there be created, for the period of the war, a National War Labor Board of the same number and to be selected in the same manner and by the same agencies as the commission making this recommendation:

(b) That the functions and powers of the National Board shall be as follows:

1. To bring about a settlement, by mediation and conciliation of every controversy arising between employers and workers in the field of production necessary for the effective conduct of the war.

2. To do the same thing in similar controversies in other fields of national activity, delays and obstructions in which may, in the opinion of the National Board, affect detrimentally such production.

3. To provide such machinery by direct appointment, or otherwise, for selection of committees or Boards to sit in various parts of the country where controversies arise, to secure settlement by local mediation and conciliation.

4. To summon the parties to the controversy for hearing and action by the National Board in case of failure to secure settlement by local mediation and conciliation.

(c) If the sincere and determined effort of the National Board shall fail to bring about a voluntary settlement, and the members of the Board shall be unable unanimously to agree upon a decision, then and in that case and only as a last resort, an umpire appointed in the manner provided in the next paragraph shall hear and finally decide the controversy under simple rules of procedure prescribed by the National Board.

(d) The members of the National Board shall choose the umpire by unanimous vote. Failing such choice, the name of the umpire shall be drawn by lot from a list of ten suitable and disinterested persons to be nominated for the purpose by the President of the United States.

(e) The national Board shall hold its regular meetings in the city of Washington, with power to meet at any other place convenient for the Board and the occasion.

(f) The National Board may alter its methods and practice in settlement of controversies hereunder, from time to time as experience may suggest.

(g) The National Board shall refuse to take cognizance of a controversy between employer and workers in any field of industrial or other activity where there is by agreement or Federal law a means of settlement which has not been invoked.

(h) The place of each member of the National Board unavoidably detained from attending one or more of its sessions may be filled by a substitute to be named by such member as his regular substitute. The substitute shall have the same representative character as his principal.

(i) The National Board shall have power to appoint a Secretary, and to create such other clerical organization under it as may be in its judgment necessary for the discharge of its duties.

(j) The National Board may apply to the Secretary of Labor for authority to use the machinery of the Department in its work of conciliation and mediation.

(k) The action of the National Board may be invoked in respect to controversies within its jurisdiction, by the Secretary of Labor or by either side in a controversy or its duly authorized representative. The Board, after summary consideration, may refuse further hearing if the case is not of such character or importance to justify it.

(l) In the appointment of committees of its own members to act for the Board in general or local matters, and in the creation of local committees, the employers and the workers shall be equally represented.

(m) The representatives of the public in the Board shall preside alternately at successive sessions of the Board or as agreed upon.

(n) The Board in its mediating and conciliatory action, and the umpire in his consideration of a controversy, shall be governed by the following principles:

PRINCIPLES AND POLICIES TO GOVERN RELATIONS BETWEEN WORKERS AND EMPLOYEES IN WAR INDUSTRIES FOR THE DURATION OF THE WAR

THERE SHOULD BE NO STRIKES OR LOCKOUTS DURING THE WAR

RIGHT TO ORGANIZE

1. The right of workers to organize in trade unions and to bargain collectively, through chosen representatives, is recognized and affirmed. This right shall not be denied, abridged or interfered with by the employers in any manner whatsoever.

2. The right of employers to organize in associations of groups and to bargain collectively, through chosen representatives, is recognized and affirmed. This right shall not be denied, abridged or interefered with by the workers in any manner whatsoever.

3. Employers should not discharge workers for membership in trade unions, nor for legitimate trade union activities.

4. The workers, in the exercise of their right to organize, shall not use coercive measures of any kind to induce persons to join their organizations, nor to induce employers to bargain or deal therewith.

EXISTING CONDITIONS

1. In establishments where the union shop exists the same shall continue and the union standards as to wages, hours of labor and other conditions of employment shall be maintained.

2. In establishments where union and non-union men and women now work together, and the employer meets only with employees or representatives engaged in said establishments, the continuance of such condition shall not be deemed a grievance. This declaration, however, is not intended in any manner to deny the right, or discourage the practice of the formation of labor unions, or the joining of the same by the workers in said establishments, as guaranteed in the last paragraph, nor to prevent the War Labor Board from urging, or any umpire from granting, under the machinery herein provided, improvement of their situation in the matter of wages, hours of labor, or other conditions, as shall be found desirable from time to time.

3. Established safe-guards and regulations for the protection of the health and safety of workers shall not be relaxed.

WOMEN IN INDUSTRY

If it shall become necessary to employ women on work ordinarily performed by men, they must be allowed equal pay for equal work and must not be allotted tasks disproportionate to their strength.

HOURS OF LABOR

The basic eight hour day is recognized as applying in all cases in which existing law requires it. In all other cases the question of hours of labor shall be settled with due regard to governmental necessities and the welfare, health and proper comfort of the workers.

MAXIMUM PRODUCTION

The maximum production of all war industries should be maintained and methods of work and operation on the part of employers or workers which operate to delay or limit production, or which have a tendency to artificially increase the cost thereof, should be discouraged.

MOBILIZATION OF LABOR

For the purpose of mobilizing the labor supply with a view to its rapid and effective distribution, a permanent list of the number of skilled and other workers available in different parts of the nation shall be kept on file by the Department of Labor, the information to be constantly furnished:

1. By the trade unions;
2. By state employment bureaus and federal agencies of like character;
3. By the managers and operators of industrial establishments throughout the country.

These agencies should be given opportunity to aid in the distribution of labor, as necessity demands.

CUSTOM OF LOCALITIES

In fixing wages, hours and conditions of labor regard should always be had to the labor standards, wage scales, and other conditions, prevailing in the localities affected.

THE LIVING WAGE

1. The right of all workers, including common laborers, to a living wage is hereby declared.
2. In fixing wages, minimum rates of pay shall be established which will insure the subsistence of the worker and his family in health and reasonable comfort.

(Signed) Loyall A. Osborne   Frank J. Hayes
         L. F. Loree   Wm. L. Hutcheson
         W. H. Van Dervoort   Thomas J. Savage
         C. E. Michael   Victor A. Olander
         B. L. Worden   T. A. Rickert
         Wm. H. Taft   Frank P. Walsh

STATEMENT OF EX-PRESIDENT WILLIAM H. TAFT,
REPRESENTING THE PUBLIC.

I am profoundly gratified that the conference appointed under the direction of Secretary Wilson has reached an agreement upon the plan for a National Labor Board to maintain maximum production by settling obstructive controversies between employers and workers. It certainly is not too much to say that it was due to the self-restraint, tact and earnest patriotic desire of the representatives of the employers and the workers to reach a conclusion. I can say this with due modesty, because I was not one of such representatives. Mr. Walsh and I were selected as representatives of the public. Personally it was one of the pleasant experiences of my life. It brought me into contact with leaders of industry and leaders of Labor, and my experience gives me a very high respect for both. I am personally indebted to all of the Board, but especially to Mr. Walsh, with whom as the only other lawyer on the Board, it was necessary for me to confer frequently in the framing of the points which step by step the conference agreed to. Of course the next question is "Will our plan work?" I hope and think it will if administered in the spirit in which it was formulated and agreed upon.

STATEMENT OF FRANK P. WALSH, REPRESENTING THE PUBLIC.

The plan submitted represents the best thought of capital and labor as to what the policy of our Government with respect to industrial relations during the war ought to be. Representing capital were five of the largest employers in the nation, but one of whom had ever dealt with trade unions, advised and counselled by Ex-President Taft, one of the world's proven great administrators and of the very highest American type of manhood. The representatives of the unions upon the Board were the national officers of unions engaged in war production and numbering in their ranks considerably over one million men and women.

The principles declared might be called an industrial chart for the Government securing to the employer maximum production, and to the worker the strongest guaranty of his right to organization and the healthy growth of the principles of democracy as applied to industry, as well as the highest protection of his economic welfare while the war for human liberty everywhere is being waged. If the plan is adopted by the Government, I am satisfied that there will be a ready and hearty acquiescence therein by the employers and workers of the country so that the volume of production may flow with the maximum of fruitfulness and speed. This is absolutely essential to an early victory. The industrial army, both planners and workers, which are but other names for employers and employees, is second only in importance and necessity to our forces in the theater of war. Their loyal cooperation, and enthusiastic effort, will win the war.

T MS (WP, DLC).

From Joseph Patrick Tumulty

Dear Governor: The White House 4 April 1918.

It is true, as the Newark News says in its editorial of last evening, that insufficient attention has been paid your letter to the New Jersey Democrats. Speaking of this letter, the New Republic says, "His letter to the New Jersey Democrats indicates for the first time the direction in which his mind is working and the burden of radicalism which in his opinion a responsible political leader can afford to carry."

The New York World of yesterday, discussing the programme of the new National Party,[1] says, "But what is revealed in many of the assaults upon the Administration, and especially upon the President, is the line of cleavage that is to mark the future political division of the American people. *Men are beginning to take sides instinctively*. It is an old and irrepressible conflict, *and even the greatest war of all time is impotent to stifle it*. The deep note in all this criticism of the President is the sound of the preliminary artillery fire in an economic battle of tremendous proportions. The old regime is digging in under the protection of its heavy guns preparatory to making its last fight for existence when the American people turn from the problems of war to the problems of peace. *Special privilege has mobilized to gain for itself the fruits of humanity's suffering and sacrifice.*"²

In discussing the New Jersey letter, the New Republic says, "Up to date Mr. Wilson stands alone among responsible American statesmen in anticipating radical changes in domestic political issues and in adjusting his mind to deal with them; but he need not hesitate or draw back on that account. He will have the facts on his side. *The more expressly and sharply he can create an issue between himself and the frank or furtive defenders of the status quo ante, the surer he will be to attain ultimate success.*"³

The whole point of this note is to try to impress upon you the importance of repeating the idea to which you gave expression in your New Jersey letter,—of changes that are bound to take place after the war and of the necessity of considering in all these changes the interests of the men, women and children of the country. If you will read the editorial from the New York World, entitled, "Special Privilege Mobilizes"; the one from the Newark News, entitled, "Asleep at the Switch"; and the one from the New Republic,⁴ you will see how important this idea is.

Sincerely yours,   Tumulty.

Will you please return these enclosures? T.

TLS (WP, DLC).
¹ The National party was founded in March 1918 by prowar Socialists who had left the Socialist party at the St. Louis convention in April 1917 and by former members of the Progressive party, prohibitionists, single-taxers, and left-wing Democrats and Republicans. The new party held its first annual convention in Chicago from March 6 to March 8, 1918, and elected David C. Coates, a former lieutenant-governor of Colorado and a member of the Labor Advisory Committee of the Council of National Defense, as its chairman. Other officers included John Appleton Haven Hopkins, the chairman of the executive committee; John Spargo, a member of the executive committee; and Upton Sinclair, a member of the advisory board. The party platform, which was adopted at the convention, included a variety of traditional progressive and socialist demands, such as equal suffrage, freedom of speech, nationwide prohibition, public ownership of public utilities, federal loans and insurance for farmers, restriction of immigration, shorter working hours, enforcement of child-labor laws, and rigorous inspection of factories. In international politics, the party advocated as its ultimate goal the establishment of a "republic of the world" and called, among other things, for the abolition of secret diplomacy, the abolition of discriminatory tariffs, and the freedom of the seas. It endorsed wholeheartedly the prosecution of the war and urged its followers to support the great democratic ideals of President Wilson. See the *New York Times*, March 6, 7, 8, 9, and 11, and April 7, 1918.
² Emphasis WW's.
³ *Ibid.*
⁴ Tumulty enclosed clippings of these editorials with his letter. They were from the New York *World*, April 3, 1918, the *Newark Evening News*, c. April 3, 1918, and *The New Republic*, XIV (March 30, 1918), 246, 248.

From Bernard Mannes Baruch

My dear Mr. President: Washington, April 4, 1918.

The morning papers say that the Senate Committee will call upon you in reference to the shipping program.

If they bring up the matter of steel, you can refer them to me and, if you do refer them to me, they will be convinced of the necessity of the Overman Bill and the wisdom of your recent action.[1]

Very truly yours,   Bernard M Baruch

TLS (WP, DLC).
[1] That is, Wilson's sweeping grant of authority to Baruch over priorities, etc., when he appointed him chairman of the War Industries Board on March 4, 1918.

From Frank William Taussig

My dear Mr. President: Washington April 4, 1918.

I much appreciate your goodness in communicating with Mr. Hoover concerning my release from the Committee of Inquiry on the Milling Division. I find, however, that I simply must continue, at least in the initial stages, on that Committee. Apart from my wish to be of service, there are personal grounds. I find that those who were to be associated with me in the inquiry feel that the inquiry must virtually cease if I withdraw, and I had committed myself to some of these gentlemen so far that I must go on.

I will do my best to serve on the Price Fixing Committee.

As regards the Committee on the Meat Industry, I hope to be able to make suggestions for a delegate, or representative, who will be able to serve acceptably.

With much appreciation of your kind consideration, I am, with high respect and regard,   Sincerely yours,   F. W. Taussig

TLS (WP, DLC).

From Ben Johnson

My dear Mr. President: Washington, D. C. April 4, 1918.

Answering your note of several days ago, relative to the alley houses, I wish to say that I shall be glad, indeed, to be instrumental in having your suggestions carried out.[1]

Most respectfully yours,   Ben Johnson

TLS (WP, DLC).
[1] On April 23, 1918, Johnson introduced a bill (H.R. 11628) which was designed to alleviate the severe housing shortage in Washington by extending the date after which it would be unlawful to occupy certain houses in alleys from July 1, 1918, until one

year after the end of the war. The Committee on the District of Columbia reported the bill favorably on May 10, and the House passed it on May 15. The Senate adopted the measure on the following day, and Wilson signed it on May 23. See *Cong. Record*, 65th Cong., 2d sess., pp. 5538, 6360, 6564-65, 6575-76, 6882, and 7043.

From Edward Beale McLean

My dear Mr. President,   Washington, D. C. April 4, 1918.

Illness has prevented me from sooner answering your kind letter.[1] Never-the-less I have given a great deal of thought to the subject.

Please believe that as a life long Democrat, I am keenly interested in the success of your administration, and deeply anxious, to be of real service to it.

In order to best facilitate this, I would like to have occasional suggestions from you, as to how best I can be helpful.

Very truly yours   Edward McLean.

TLS (WP, DLC)
[1] "I value your letter of yesterday very highly. It is generous and public-spirited and I thank you for it very warmly." WW to E. B. McLean, March 5, 1918, CCL (WP, DLC).

Lord Reading to David Lloyd George and Arthur James Balfour

Washington April 4th. 1918.

Urgent.

Personal. Following for Prime Minister and Mr. Balfour.

Urgent. Secret and confidential.

I have just heard from House that President was very pleased with statement you issued[1] and it has had an excellent effect.

Preparations for shipment of troops are proceeding with remarkable vigour.

Nothing will be allowed to stand in the way of carrying out the promised troops (sic). Arrangements have been made for shipment of 60,000 monthly in American ships and United States Government are relying implicitly upon us to carry our part.

My impression is that they will call up more men and will energetically prepare for sending of further reinforcements.

In view of definite expression of wishes from high quarter that Wiseman should go to England to discuss matters with you I have arranged accordingly with him and he will leave within next three days. He will give you full information. Should you wish anything special please cable immediately.

T telegram (D. Lloyd George Papers, F/60/2/52, House of Lords Record Office).
[1] See Lord Reading to D. Lloyd George, March 30, 1918 (second telegram of that date), n. 1.

From Robert Lansing, with Enclosure

Dear Mr. President: Washington April 5, 1918.

I enclose a translation of a telegram which the President of France has sent you on the anniversary of our entry into the war. M. Jusserand ventures to express the hope that your reply may be received in Paris to-morrow before three o'clock P.M., at which time the President of France opens a very important French celebration in honor of this event. He adds that the President of France would be happy to read your reply on this occasion.

You may care to consider the enclosed draft reply.

With assurances of respect, etc., I am, my dear Mr. President,
                    Faithfully yours,   Robert Lansing

TLS (WP, DLC).

E N C L O S U R E

Paris [April 4, 1918]

One year has passed since the United States of America, under your high and generous direction, took with splendid enthusiasm the resolution to participate in the majestic struggle which the free nations are waging against the unchained furies of imperialism.

The gallant Americans arrive, without interruption, on the theatre of war and their distinguished chief has already claimed for them the honor to serve on the field of battle where the fate of the world is being decided. Allow me, Mr. President, to seize the opportunity on this moving anniversary to tell you, once again, how near in these grave and solemn hours the heart of France feels itself to the heart of America.

Our two great countries know that together they fight for justice and liberty against the hypocritical and brutal spirit of conquest.

They see clearly before them the noble objectives which you have immortally defined and they are decided, not like their enemies who pretend to adopt the better to dispel them, to make of them shining realities for the ages to come.

Side by side, therefore, we pursue untiringly unto victory this war of liberation which must determine the destinies of humanity.

R. Poincaré.[1]

T MS (WP, DLC).
[1] The original of this telegram is S. Pichon to J. J. Jusserand, April 4, 1918, T telegram (Guerre 1914-1918, États-Unis, Vol. 510, p. 222, FFM-Ar).

To Raymond Poincaré[1]

Washington, April 5, 1918.

I thank Your Excellency for the gracious telegram which you have done me the honor to send on the occasion of this anniversary of the entry of the United States in the war. We are proud to be associated with noble and heroic France in the struggle to overcome the iniquitous aggressions of imperial militarism, and to obtain the recognition of liberty, self government and undictated development of all peoples; and if in the year that has past we have not accomplished all that we anticipated or would wish, I trust that what we have done will be accepted by France as an earnest of our strong determination to continue and enlarge our efforts until right shall triumph and wrong be overthrown. The objects for which we are fighting we see with clear vision and to their obtainment our full resources are dedicated. The heroic defense, which the valiant sons of France are making for their beloved country fills ⟨me⟩ *us* with admiration and it is ⟨my⟩ *our* sincere hope that in the glory of final victory that shall come the sons of America will have their full share of pride.   Woodrow Wilson

TS telegram (SDR, RG 59, 763.72/9495, DNA).
[1] Words in angle brackets deleted by Wilson; words in italics added by him.

To John St. Loe Strachey

Personal.

My dear Mr. Strachey: The White House 5 April, 1918

I very much appreciate your kind letter of March twelfth,[1] and am very glad indeed to open my mind to you, in confidence, with the greatest frankness about the League of Nations as I have conceived it.

I have all along been of the opinion that it would be impossible to effect an elaborate and active organization. To attempt a "constitution" for a league of peace would raise all the points of jealousy and put them so at the front as to obscure the essential objects of the league itself and perhaps prevent their achievement. I have thought of the plan in very elementary and simple form. I have thought only of a mutual guarantee of political independence and territorial integrity, and also, as you suggest, of the binding and sacred force of treaty agreements.

Of course, the territorial guarantee I have always thought of as conditioned upon the assumption that the final peace arrangements would be substantially just in character and therefore likely to remain undisturbed if thus guaranteed until altered by international agreement.

The league for peace means, as I conceive it, in no case simply an alliance or a group formed to maintain any sort of balance of power, but must be an association which any nation is at liberty to join which is willing to cooperate in its objects and qualify in respect of its guarantees.

I feel the full weight of your fear that after this terrible war no nation will care to take up arms upon the occasion of any obscure or relatively unimportant boundary dispute or minor aggression of nation upon nation, but it seems to me that the effects of this war may just as reasonably be expected to operate in the other direction. We shall henceforth feel that any quarrel, however small, however limited the questions it involves, may again, if carried to the point of war, kindle a flame throughout the world. I think the particular thing that nations will exert themselves about in the future is the prevention of the provocations which bring about war, at any rate for a long time to come, and until the action of the league of peace had been illustrated in a sufficiently large number of cases to indicate what strengthening or alteration was necessary, I believe that this motive would operate.

Certainly no apology was needed for your interesting letter.

With much respect,   Sincerely yours,   Woodrow Wilson

TLS (J. St. L. Strachey Papers, Beaverbrook Library).
¹ J. St. L. Strachey to WW. March 12, 1918, Vol. 46.

To Gutzon Borglum

My dear Mr. Borglum: The White House 5 April, 1918

I have your note of April third with its accompanying document, and am taking the liberty of placing the information in the hands of the committee of which I have several times spoken.

In haste   Sincerely yours,   Woodrow Wilson

TLS (G. Borglum Papers, DLC).

To Benedict Crowell

My dear Mr. Secretary: The White House 5 April, 1918

Here is the last, at least I hope the last, from Mr. Borglum. I would be very much obliged if you would place it in the hands of the gentlemen who are making this investigation for us.

Cordially and sincerely yours,   Woodrow Wilson

TLS (B. Crowell Papers, OClWHi).

To Joseph Patrick Tumulty, with Enclosure

Dear Tumulty: [The White House, c. April 5, 1918]

This is politics, pure and simple, or rather impure and simple, and in order that you may know all that I know I am sending you the enclosed memorandum from George Creel[1] attached to another telegram which I got from an excited community. My own feeling is that it is not wise to answer these inquiries. As a matter of fact, as Creel says, this League has been rendering what certainly appeared to be the most patriotic support of the Government and I don't like to send a message which would undoubtedly be used as a slap in the face to the whole organization.

The President.

TL (WP, DLC).
  [1] See G. Creel to WW, April 2, 1918.

E N C L O S U R E

Mineola, Texas, April 5, 1918.

Non-partisan League active in this section. They claim endorsement from President Wilson for their league. Wire us collect if this is true. Patriotic rally Saturday, April sixth. Want answer by twelve this date.   R. J. Gaston.[1]

T telegram (WP, DLC).
  [1] Roy James Gaston, president of the First National Bank of Mineola, Texas, and chairman of the War Savings Committee of Wood County.

Peyton Conway March to Tasker Howard Bliss

Washington, April 5, 1918.

Number 43 Confidential.

Paragraph 1. Acting upon the call of the Inter-Allied Supreme War Council for the fullest possible immediate American military participation the President has decided after consultation with representatives of England and France and heads of Government departments to increase our military effort as follows: (1) A minimum of 91,000 troops will be shipped oversea monthly commencing April 1st. Every available American transport, the transports loaned by the British, and American and British liners will be used for this movement. We understand England to have guaranteed besides sufficient additional tonnage to carry at least 29,000 additional troops per month. This makes a total of 120,000 troops per month as a minimum. (2) A cargo movement will be carried out consisting of the necessary engineering material for ports and lines of communication, such part of the Aviation and Ordnance programs as will be ready for shipment including replacement materials 438,000 tons for France and 50,000 tons for England, and Quartermaster, medical and miscellaneous supplies for monthly increments of 91,000 men, plus maintenance of our troops now in France and the establishment of reserves. Great Britain to furnish the materials and supplies for the additional troops according to her agreement as fully stated in Pershing's cablegrams number 596 dated Feb. 12th[1] and number 705 dated March 10th.[2]

Subparagraph A. After careful study of all tonnage requirements of the United States it is clear that this movement can be carried out, but only with the greatest difficulty. The execution of the undertaking is subject to the provisions that we retain all neutral tonnage now employed in the service of the United States, that the submarine sinkings do not develop to an unusual extent above the present losses, that the emergency fleet corporation's promised delivery of ships be carried out, and that the import reduction now planned be not impeded. All tonnage owned or controlled by the United States will be required by the shipping board to meet the military programs and other imperative needs and commitments. Ships loaned to France and Italy will not now be disturbed but we must utilize all Dutch ships requisitioned in our harbors to meet our present program. We cannot divert any additional tonnage without imparing the military program to which we are thus definitely committed. British and French Ambassadors notified. Send copy of this cable by officer to Pershing. March   McCain

TC telegram (WDR, RG 407, World War I Cablegrams, DNA).
[1] J. J. Pershing to Chief of Staff, Feb. 12, 1918, printed as an Enclosure with NDB to WW, Feb. 13, 1918, Vol. 46.
[2] J. J. Pershing to Chief of Staff, No. 705, March 10, 1918, printed in Historical Division, Department of the Army, *United States Army in the World War, 1917-1919* (17 vols., Washington, 1948), Vol. 3, pp. 57-58. This telegram was a report on the arrangements which Pershing had made with the British concerning American divisions which were to be sent to the British front for training.

Two Telegrams from Newton Diehl Baker

Paris April 5, 1918.

For the President. Returned from Italy Thursday. Spent one day at the front and one in Rome as Mr. Page feared misunderstanding if I failed to visit Capital after having been in Paris and London.

Military situation continues stationary with very heavy artillery duel more or less continuously. Believed here that the Germans have still thirty divisions of fresh troops and plan another attack in force near Arras. Plans for defence along the whole line are made and allies have much larger and better placed reserves than on March 21. If estimate of thirty divisions is correct Germans have used up more than half of their first quality attack troops. Our first division begins to move out of the trenches tomorrow to become a part of the battle reserve and will probably be in action in a week or ten days. This division about equals two British divisions in numbers and is regarded as fully trained. The men are full of enthusiasm and pride. They are also completing one of the replacement divisions so that we will have four in the trenches and one in battle. Period. Our four because of larger numbers release six French for reserve. Our contribution is thus important and helpful. Counter attack in preparation which may modify whole recent situation.

The original appointment of General Foch was hesitating and powers given him largely advisory. At meeting yesterday whole matter was reviewed and practically supreme command given him over British, French and American armies on West front. Paragraph.

So far as I can see there is nothing else for me to do here now and unless you advise otherwise I will leave on Tuesday, April ninth, for home. No available ship sails earlier. Reply will reach me care Ambassador Sharp.   Baker.

T telegram (N. D. Baker Papers, DLC).

                                        Versailles April 5th Midnight [1918].
Tres urgent CONFIDENTIAL Number 79

Paragraph 1. The Secretary of War directs that you hand his following message to the President as early as practicable and cable his reply direct to me for the Secretary: The reply should reach here by Saturday evening April sixth.

Paragraph 2. "To the President: Mr. Lloyd George read to General Bliss and General Pershing on Wednesday April three a cablegram from Lord Reading which reported that in an interview with him you agreed to the transportation, in American and British ships, of infantry and machine gun units to the extent of one hundred and twenty thousand a month for four months.[1] I have Maj. Gen. Peyton C. March's cablegram number thirty-nine[2] informing me of your approval of resolutions of Supreme War Council as recommended by me in General Bliss' cablegram number sixty seven March 28th, but no numbers of troops are stipulated in those resolutions. As I am to confer with British and General Pershing on Sunday morning to arrange details it would be helpful if I could have particulars of

any agreements reached with Lord Reading and particularly numbers of infantry and machine gun units per month and for how
many months, if such details were definitely arranged. Baker."

                                                              Bliss.

TC telegram (WDR, RG 407, World War I Cablegrams, DNA).
 ¹ Lord Reading to D. Lloyd George, March 30, 1918 (first telegram of that date).
 ² P. C. March to NDB, No. 39, March 29, 1918, T telegram (WDR, RG 120, Records
of the American Section of the Supreme War Council, 1917-1919, DNA): "The President
concurs in the Joint Note(s) of the Permanent Military Representatives of the Supreme
War Council in the sense formulated in your Number 67 March 28th and wishes you
to regard yourself authorized to decide questions of immediate cooperation or replacement."

From Josephus Daniels

My dear Mr. President: Washington. 5 April, 1918.

   Referring to your letter of 4 April, 1918 to the Secretary of State,
the only vessels which are available to send to Murmansk are those
operating in European waters. These vessels are all occupied actively in scouting, patroling and convoying. If a vessel should be
taken from the escorting of Overseas Transportation, it would seriously interfere with this most important service.

   If, however, it is considered that the presence of our flag at that
point would have sufficient international political influence to warrant this action, a vessel will be sent.

                      Faithfully yours,   Josephus Daniels

I am enclosing two dispatches just received from Admiral Knight.¹
JD

TLS (WP, DLC).
 ¹ Flag Brooklyn to Secnav, No. X-8, April 5, 1918, and Flag Brooklyn to Secnav, No.
X-9, April 5, 1918, both TC telegrams (NDR, RG 45, Naval Records of the Office of
Naval Records and Library, Subject File, 1911-1927, WA-6 Russia: Siberia, Conditions
in Vladivostok, 1917-1919, DNA). These telegrams reported that the Japanese had
landed a force to protect Japanese nationals in Vladivostok following the killing of a
Japanese subject and the wounding of another. In addition, the British had decided to
land a force of fifty men to protect their consulate. In his first telegram, Knight said
that he would land men only if necessary to protect the American consulate. In his
second telegram, Knight said that he would only land a force "if our interests are
threatened which is not the case at present."

From Eleuthérios Venizélos

                                          Athens. April 5, 1918.

   It is with a profound emotion that the Hellenic nation salutes the
anniversary of the entrance of the United States in the great struggle for the defense of liberties threatened by the Central Powers
and their allies. The magnificent enthusiasm which brings on the

battlefields of France the flower of the American youth and the gallantry with which the first American contingents participate in the liberation of the French soil can leave no doubt as to the final triumph of our cause. Greece is proud of participating in the sacrifices so generously consented to by the democratic peoples of the world in order to assure to all the nations the right to their free development for the greatest benefit of humanity[.] she thence nourishes with reliance the hope that at the end of the present struggle thanks to the support of her powerful allies not only will she recover the integrity of her territory but will also see guarantees of existence according to their legitimate aspirations granted to those of her congenitors who will not yet have been included in her frontiers.   Venizelos.

T telegram (WP, DLC).

From Arthur Everett Shipley[1]

My dear Mr President,   Cambridge 5 April 1918.

I am writing on behalf of this ancient University to say how pleased we all feel at the acceptance of the Honorary Degree which the University wishes to confer upon you. It is the highest we can award and it is, in a way, making history, as Cambridge has hitherto never granted an Honorary Degree *in absentia*. I need not say how honoured we feel by your acceptance.

I should like to add that it is a very peculiar pleasure to me that I should be Vice-Chancellor at this time, as I think it is already thirty years ago since I first met you at Princeton.

We are in terrible straits—the Colleges & University are practically ruined and more than half of our young men are killed. Each day adds to the toll. The past ten days has been simply appalling.

With the kindest regards,

Believe me to be, Dear Mr President,

Yours very sincerely,   A E Shipley

TLS (WP, DLC).
[1] Master of Christ's College, Cambridge, and Vice-Chancellor of Cambridge University.

From Albert Sidney Burleson

My dear Mr. President: Washington April 5, 1918

I enclose herewith the Crowder Bill, the proposed regulations thereunder and the argument in support thereof.[1] I think it extremely important that you should give these careful reading, and I hope you will find time to do so.

Sincerely yours,   A. S. Burleson

TLS (WP, DLC).

¹ E. H. Crowder, *Selective Draft and Adjustment of Industrial Man Power*, printed copy, signed (WP, DLC). The purpose of the proposed bill, which Crowder suggested as an amendment to the Selective Service Act, was the efficient mobilization of available manpower in order to increase industrial production. The measure would compel all men between the ages of eighteen and fifty, who were not exempted from the draft, to engage in "useful" employment. Any person of draft age who, without a reasonable excuse, was found idle or engaged in an occupation which the President had designated as not necessary to the national interest, would be summoned before his local draft board and would have either to find suitable employment or be subject to induction into the army.

Crowder's proposed regulations outlined the administrative procedures which were to be followed in implementing the bill; defined the occupations which would be considered nonuseful (for example, bartenders, fortune tellers, gamblers, pool-room attendants, etc.); and listed a number of excuses for nonuseful employment which would be considered reasonable by the draft boards. Sales clerks, domestic servants, ushers, and waiters were in a marginal category.

Crowder also included a detailed discussion in support of his proposed bill, which argued, among other things, that there was a popular demand for mobilization of manpower, but that public opinion would not agree to a direct industrial draft; that the measure would avoid the wasteful draft into military service of men who were effectively employed; and that his plan would lead to the establishment of an effective system of control over all available manpower which would be sufficient for any eventuality of the war.

From Lord Reading, with Enclosure

My dear Mr President,   Washington, April 5, 1918

I have the honour to forward to you by the King's command the message herein enclosed from His Majesty.

May I be permitted to express to you my own deep sense of gratification that I should be entrusted with the presentation of this message to you.

I have the honour to be, My dear Mr President, With the highest respect,   Your obedient servant,   Reading

TCL (FO 115/2472, p. 354, PRO).

E N C L O S U R E

[London] 5 April 1918.

No. 1939 Urgent

Please convey following message from the King to President which will be published on April 6th.

On the occasion of the anniversary of momentous decision of United States to enter this war for guarding of international right and justice I desire to convey to you Mr. President and through you to the American people the friendly greetings of the entire British nation.

At this critical hour when our enemies are sparing no sacrifice and counting no cost to the achievement of victory the French and British troops stand united as never before in their heroic resistance to these endeavours. They are buoyed up with the thought that the great democracy of the West in the same spirit and with the same objects as their own is putting forth every effort to throw its supreme force into the struggle which will once for all decide destinies of free nations of the earth.

The deeds of Americans on land and sea have already indicated to the enemy that his hope is vain. Every day that passes as American troops pour in ever-increasing numbers into France diminishes the chances of his success.

The American people may rest assured that the British Empire now tried by nearly four years of war will cheerfully make yet further sacrifices. The thought that U. S. under your leadership are with us heart and soul emboldens us in the determination with God's help finally to destroy the designs of the enemy and to re-establish on earth rule of right and justice.   George R.I.

T telegram (FO 115/2472, pp. 352-53, PRO).

Sir William Wiseman to Sir Eric Drummond

[Washington] April 5, 1918.

No. 95. In reply to your No. 78 of the 5th:[1]

Col. HOUSE's reply to MR. BALFOUR's enquiry represents accurately the views of the PRESIDENT though I do not think either he or HOUSE feel very strongly about the matter. As you ask me to give my own impression, I will venture to disagree with them. In the first place, the Administration naturally do not want to risk any anti-war agitation in this country which would dissipate American energies. It is true that conscription in Ireland, accompanied by disturbances and armed force, might create very bad situation here, but I do not think it is by any means certain that it would. In my opinion it would depend very largely on the manner in which conscription was carried out; and on the statements made by the British Government as to the necessity for the measure; all of which should be done with an eye on public opinion in America as well as elsewhere. The vast majority of people in America think the British Government made a mistake in not putting the Home Rule Bill into operation, regret that the Convention has not yet reached more definite results, and might be described as supporting the Redmond policy,[2] but certainly having little patience with Sein Fein. Of course, there would be an outcry from Irish extremists here, but it would depend on the reasons given for the step and manner in which it was carried out as to how far that was taken up by the general public. In this connection the International News Service is of some importance. If you could persuade the French to agree to reinstatement at once (or, failing that, if we could reinstate them without the French), I am positive that would modify, though not entirely alter, Hearst's attitude towards conscription in Ireland. I would urge it as the most obviously expedient step to reinstate I.N.S. before announcing any decision of the Government on this question. A good deal would depend here on the attitude of the Roman Catholic leaders. In short, I consider that America's view would depend largely on how the case is presented through the Press, and I do not believe the possibility of bad effects here should influence your decision.

T telegram (W. Wiseman Papers, CtY).

[1] "No. 78. Personal. Most urgent. You have seen Balfour's message to Col. House about Ireland and conscription and latter's reply. Has House expressed views to you on the subject and what are your own impressions? Reply most urgent. Above is, of course, for yourself alone." E. Drummond to W. Wiseman, April 5, 1918, T telegram (W. Wiseman Papers, CtY).

[2] That is, John Edward Redmond, M.P., chairman of the Irish party and leader of the Nationalist majority at the Irish Convention, who had died on March 6, 1918. Redmond had been convinced that it was imperative for the convention to work out a generally accepted scheme for Irish home rule. Thus, he had endorsed a compromise on the question of Irish fiscal autonomy, which had been offered by Lord Midleton, the leader of the Southern Unionists. It proposed that the Irish Parliament should have control over internal taxation, including excise duties, but that customs duties should remain under the control of the imperial Parliament. See McDowell, *The Irish Convention*, pp. 129-30, 145-50.

An Address[1]

Copy used in delivery, Balto. 6 April, 1918. W.W.[2]

Fellow Citizens: This is the anniversary of our acceptance of Germany's challenge to fight for our right to live and be free, and for the sacred rights of free men everywhere. The nation is awake. There is no need to call to it. We know what the war must cost, our utmost sacrifice, the lives of our fittest men and, if need be, all that we possess. The loan we are met to discuss is one of the least parts of what we are called upon to give and to do, though in itself imperative. The people of the whole country are alive to the necessity of it, and are ready to lend to the utmost, even where it

[1] Wilson spoke on the occasion of the opening of the third Liberty Loan campaign at the Fifth Regiment Armory before a capacity crowd of 15,000 people. Phillips Lee Goldsborough, former Governor of Maryland, introduced Wilson.

[2] WWhw.

involves a sharp skimping and daily sacrifice to lend out of meagre earnings. They will look with reprobation and contempt upon those who can and will not, upon those who demand a higher rate of interest, upon those who think of it as a mere commercial transaction. I have not come, therefore, to urge the loan. I have come only to give you, if I can, a more vivid conception of what it is for.

The reasons for this great war, the reason why it had to come, the need to fight it through, and the issues that hang upon its outcome, are more clearly disclosed now than ever before. It is easy to see just what this particular loan means because the Cause we are fighting for stands more sharply revealed than at any previous crisis of the momentous struggle. The man who knows least can now see plainly how the cause of Justice stands and what the imperishable thing is he is asked to invest in. Men in America may be more sure than they ever were before that the cause is their own, and that, if it should be lost, their own great nation's place and mission in the world would be lost with it.

I call you to witness, my fellow countrymen, that at no stage of this terrible business have I judged the purposes of Germany intemperately. I should be ashamed in the presence of affairs so grave, so fraught with the destinies of mankind throughout all the world, to speak with truculence, to use the weak language of hatred or vindictive purpose. We must judge as we would be judged. I have sought to learn the objects Germany has in this war from the mouths of her own spokesmen, and to deal as frankly with them as I wished them to deal with me. I have laid bare our own ideals, our own purposes, without reserve or doubtful phrase, and have asked them to say as plainly what it is that they seek.

We have ourselves proposed no injustice, no aggression. We are ready, whenever the final reckoning is made, to be just to the German people, deal fairly with the German power, as with all others. There can be no difference between peoples in the final judgment, if it is indeed to be a righteous judgment. To propose anything but justice, evenhanded and dispassionate justice, to Germany at any time, whatever the outcome of the war, would be to renounce and dishonour our own cause. For we ask nothing that we are not willing to accord.

It has been with this thought that I have sought to learn from those who spoke for Germany whether it was justice or dominion and the execution of their own will upon the other nations of the world that the German leaders were seeking. They have answered, answered in unmistakable terms. They have avowed that it was not justice but dominion and the unhindered execution of their own will.

The avowal has not come from Germany's statesmen. It has come

from her military leaders, who are her real rulers. Her statesmen
have said that they wished peace, and were ready to discuss its
terms whenever their opponents were willing to sit down at the
conference table with them. Her present Chancellor has said,—in
indefinite and uncertain terms, indeed, and in phrases that often
seem to deny their own meaning, but with as much plainness as
he thought prudent,—that he believed that peace should be based
upon the principles which we had declared would be our own in
the final settlement. At Brest-Litovsk her civilian delegates spoke
in similar terms; professed their desire to conclude a fair peace and
accord to the peoples with whose fortunes they were dealing the
right to choose their own allegiances. But action accompanied and
followed the profession. Their military masters, the men who act
for Germany and exhibit her purpose in execution, proclaimed a
very different conclusion. We cannot mistake what they have done,—
in Russia, in Finland, in the Ukraine, in Rumania. The real test of
their justice and fair play has come. From this we may judge the
rest. They are enjoying in Russia a cheap triumph in which no
brave or gallant nation can long take pride. A great people, helpless
by their own act, lies for the time at their mercy. Their fair profes-
sions are forgotten. They nowhere set up justice, but everywhere
impose their power and exploit everything for their own use and
aggrandizement; and the peoples of conquered provinces are invited to be free under their dominion!

Are we not justified in believing that they would do the same
things at their western front if they were not there face to face with
armies whom even their countless divisions cannot overcome? If,
when they have felt their check to be final, they should propose
favourable and equitable terms with regard to Belgium and France
and Italy, could they blame us if we concluded that they did so
only to assure themselves of a free hand in Russia and the East?

Their purpose is undoubtedly to make all the Slavic peoples, all
the free and ambitious nations of the Baltic peninsula, all the lands
that Turkey has dominated and misruled, subject to their will and
ambition and build upon that dominion an empire of force upon
which they fancy that they can then erect an empire of gain and
commercial supremacy,—an empire as hostile to the Americas as
to the Europe which it will overawe,—an empire which will ultimately master Persia, India, and the peoples of the Far East. In
such a programme our ideals, the ideals of justice and humanity
and liberty, the principle of the free self-determination of nations
upon which all the modern world insists, can play no part. They
are rejected for the ideals of power, for the principle that the strong
must rule the weak, that trade must follow the flag, whether those
to whom it is taken welcome it or not, that the peoples of the world

are to be made subject to the patronage and overlordship of those who have the power to enforce it.

That programme once carried out, America and all who care or dare to stand with her must arm and prepare themselves to contest the mastery of the World, a mastery in which the rights of common men, the rights of women and of all who are weak, must for the time being be trodden under foot and disregarded, and the old, age-long struggle for freedom and right begin again at its beginning. Everything that America has lived for and loved and grown great to vindicate and bring to a glorious realization will have fallen in utter ruin and the gates of mercy once more pitilessly shut upon mankind!

The thing is preposterous and impossible; and yet is not that what the whole course and action of the German armies has meant wherever they have moved? I do not wish, even in this moment of utter disillusionment, to judge harshly or unrighteously. I judge only what the German arms have accomplished with unpitying thoroughness throughout every fair region they have touched.

What, then, are we to do? For myself, I am ready, ready still, ready even now, to discuss a fair and just and honest peace at any time that it is sincerely purposed,—a peace in which the strong and the weak shall fare alike. But the answer, when I proposed such a peace, came from the German commanders in Russia, and I cannot mistake the meaning of the answer.

I accept the challenge. I know that you accept it. All the world shall know that you accept it. It shall appear in the utter sacrifice and self-forgetfulness with which we shall give all that we love and all that we have to redeem the world and make it fit for free men like ourselves to live in. This now is the meaning of all that we do. Let everything that we say, my fellow countrymen, everything that we henceforth plan and accomplish, ring true to this response till the majesty and might of our concerted power shall fill the thought and utterly defeat the force of those who flout and misprize what we honour and hold dear. Germany has once more said that force, and force alone, shall decide whether Justice and peace shall reign in the affairs of men, whether Right as America conceives it or Dominion as she conceives it shall determine the destinies of mankind. There is, therefore, but one response possible from us: Force, Force to the utmost, Force without stint or limit, the righteous and triumphant Force which shall make Right the law of the world, and cast every selfish dominion down in the dust.[3]

Printed reading copy (WP, DLC).

[3] There is a five-page WWT outline of this address and a WWT draft (which Wilson sent to the Public Printer) in WP, DLC.

To George V

The White House, April 6, 1918

Permit me to express the warm gratification with which your generous message has been received and to assure you that it is with the greatest satisfaction that the people of the United States find themselves side by side in this final war for free self-government with such steadfast and indomitable associates. Permit me also to assure Your Majesty that we shall continue to do everything possible to put the whole force of the United States into this great struggle.   Woodrow Wilson

T telegram (WP, DLC).

To Tasker Howard Bliss

[Washington] April 6th [1918]

Number 45 Confidential

With reference to your number 79[1] following received from President: "Please cable to the Secretary of War that I agreed upon no details whatever with Lord Reading. I told him that I had agreed to the proposition of the Supreme War Council in the formula proposed to me by the Secretary of War by cable and that I could assure him that we would send troops over as fast as we could make them ready and find transportation for them. That was all. The details are left to be worked out and we shall wish the advice of the Secretary of War as the result of his consultations on the other side. Woodrow Wilson."[2]   March

TC telegram (WDR, RG 407, World War I Cablegrams, DNA).
    [1] NDB to WW, No. 79, April 5, 1918 (second telegram of that date).
    [2] The quoted sentences are from WW to B. Crowell, April 6, 1918, WWTLS (B. Crowell Papers, OClWHi).

To Eleuthérios Venizélos

The White House [April 6, 1918].

May I not acknowledge with the deepest appreciation your generous message and convey through you to the oldest of the western nations the fraternal greetings of the young Republic of the West, at the same time expressing our confidence that the valour and devotion of the armies of Greece will play an important and distinguished part in the final triumph. May I not also convey to you personally my own cordial assurances of friendship and tell you of the warm admiration your unselfish devotion to the cause of liberty has excited among our people.   Woodrow Wilson.

WWT telegram (WP, DLC).

Two Letters from William Bauchop Wilson

My dear Mr. President: Washington April 6, 1918.

Referring to my statement yesterday relative to the National War Labor Board, I took the matter up with Mr. Gompers and now have a communication from him nominating for appointment the five representatives of labor who were on the War Labor Conference Board. I also took the matter up with Mr. Alexander,[1] President of the National Industrial Conference Board, and have a telegram from him naming the same men as representatives of employers who were on the War Labor Conference Board. Mr. Walsh informed me several days ago that the selection of Mr. Taft and himself as representatives of the public was the desire of both elements. William H. Johnston,[2] President of the International Association of Machinists, was a member of the Board as originally constituted. He was sent to England by Mr. Gompers as one of the labor delegation. Mr. T. J. Savage was appointed to fill the vacancy. It is Mr. Gompers' desire that Mr. Johnston be appointed a member of the National War Labor Board and that Mr. Savage act as his substitute until his return. I therefore recommend that the name of William H. Johnston be substituted for that of T. J. Savage in the proclamation. As the difficulty has now been straightened out, I suggest that the proclamation be issued at as early a date as possible.

The incident, however, has impressed upon me the advisability of making a slight amendment to the draft of the proclamation, by inserting after the word "Labor," in line 2, the words "upon the nomination of the President of the American Federation of Labor and the President of the National Industrial Conference Board," which would make the first paragraph read:

"WHEREAS, in January nineteen hundred and eighteen, the Secretary of Labor, upon the nomination of the President of the American Federation of Labor and the President of the National Industrial Conference Board, appointed a War Labor Conference Board for the purpose of devising for the period of the war a method of labor adjustment which would be acceptable to employers and employees."   Faithfully yours,   W B Wilson

[1] That is, Magnus Washington Alexander, chief designing engineer of the General Electric Co.
[2] That is, William Hugh Johnston.

My dear Mr. President: Washington April 6, 1918.

I have your letter of March 29th, inclosing memorandum relative to the Minneapolis situation. It is now practically assured that there will be no sympathetic strike, although the presence of five hundred striking street car men in the community creates a continuous source of irritation that will need to be closely watched. Large numbers of men engaged in the production of war material have to travel to and from work on these lines. That is what gives it a national significance.

We were advised by influential citizens of Minneapolis and St. Paul that if the Council of National Defense would indorse the recommendation made by the President's Commission, the street car company would accept it and the incident would be closed. The Council of National Defense did indorse the recommendation and communicated its indorsement through Secretary Daniels, Acting Chairman of the Council, to Governor Burnquist, Chairman of the Committee on Public Safety of Minnesota. It had no effect. You do [no] doubt know that the Committee on Public Safety did not take very kindly to the Mediation Commission looking into the case, although we approached it as diplomatically as we could. There is consequently the possibility that they might refuse to give heed to such suggestions as you might make. If the case were of vital importance, I would advise that you nevertheless go ahead. It does not seem to me to be of such importance, however, as to warrant taking the chances of a refusal where we have not the power to compel. Congressman Van Dyke is making a further effort to bring about an adjustment.

So far as taking over the street railways of Minneapolis and St. Paul is concerned, I do not know whether the war powers that have been conferred extend to the commandeering of properties of this character, but even if it did it would not be well to exercise it. In our trip through the western country, we found a sentiment expressed amongst strikers generally, in such uniform language that it gave us the impression that it must have emanated from some central source somewhere, to the effect that the Government needs were so great that if the employers did not yield the Government would commandeer the plants. We found it in the oil fields of Texas and California, in the copper mining sections of the mountain region, in the street car situations of San Francisco and Minneapolis, in the telephone strike on the Pacific Coast, in the lumber producing sections of the Pacific Northwest, and in the packing industry. Our method of meeting it was to say that even though one believed in Government ownership, he must realize that it was an experiment. No one could tell in advance whether it would result in success or failure; that the taking over of one industry would result in tremendous pressure for the taking over of others; that the taking over of the industrial plants of the country would mean the building up of a great organization to handle them; that we were rapidly organizing a large army and extending our industries into new lines to defeat the common enemy in the field; that tremendous reorganization of our manpower was necessary to meet the crisis, and that it would be folly to add to the difficulties of the situation by Government ownership of our industrial plants unless it became absolutely necessary for the common defense.

That argument usually had the desired effect, and I have the same viewpoint with regard to taking over the Twin City street car system.

The memorandum which you inclosed is returned herewith.

Faithfully yours,   W B Wilson

TLS (WP, DLC).

From John Marshall Harlan[1]

My Dear Mr. President: Princeton, N. J., April 6, 1918.

I am writing to you in the hope that you, in the midst of your arduous duties, may be able to send a message to the members of Princeton University, at this beginning of the Third Liberty Loan.

The undergraduate body responded to the last two loans with patriotic eagerness and a message at this time from you, Princeton's most distinguished graduate, would be an inspiration and a means of spurring the undergraduate to still further effort in this noble cause.

I hope, sir, that I have not taken too great a liberty in writing to you and trust that you may be able to send a message to us at Princeton.

Believe me, Mr. President,

Yours very sincerely,   John M Harlan

TLS (WP, DLC).
[1] Princeton 1920, a future Associate Justice of the United States Supreme Court (1955-1971).

From William Truman Drury[1]

Dear Sir: Morganfield, Ky., April 6th, 1918.

In our town there lives a naturalized German-American, who until our country entered the war was very warm in his advocacy of the German cause, but when this nation became a belligerent all was changed. He is a widower, he has no children of his own, but has two children whom he has raised, a neice and a nephew, this niece, his foster daughter, is married and lives with him and her husband, an expert mechanic, has made application for service in the aviation corps, and this nephew, his foster son, is in the navy, and the old man has bought $1,000.00 of the third Liberty Loan, yet in spite of all this many of our native born Americans remembering his former advocacy of Germany are disposed to criticize this man and to boycott his business, yet these same critics have moved heaven and earth to get exemption or deferred classification for their sons and kindred, and have never bought a bond.

This old man is August Friedreich, he is our town butcher, and a good citizen, and I know I am asking a great deal but I hope you will write this old man and commend his course. I want this done that he may shame some of these hypocrites, who are always standing on the street corners, boasting of their descent from Revolutionary stock, thanking God they are not like other men, and yet never buy a bond. I want to show them that patriotism is measured in service.   Yours very truly,   W. T. Drury[2]

TLS (WP, DLC).
[1] Lawyer of Morganfield, Ky., and chairman of the Liberty Loan Organization of Union County, Ky.
[2] "Dear Tumulty: You will see the delicacy of this case on reading Mr. Drury's letter. It would perhaps be imprudent for me to do this sort of thing, and yet a case like this greatly excites my sympathy because I have no doubt that there are hundreds of cases like it. It occurs to me that you might, if you will, write a letter to Mr. Drury telling him how much interested I have been in hearing of the contributions and sacrifices Mr. Friedreich has made and asking him if he will not himself convey an expression of my appreciation to Mr. Friedreich. The President." WW to JPT, c. April 10, 1918, TL (WP, DLC).

From William Bayard Hale

Mr. President: New York April 6, 1918.

Once more—not without very keen appreciation indeed of the value of your time—I venture to address you personally, even though there is reason to believe that it would be easily possible to persuade a Senator or two to ask more of your working hours than the reading of this letter will consume.

You have constituted a Custodian of Enemy *Property*.[1] Is it not more necessary to have a Custodian of Enemy LIFE, or a Commissioner for Enemy Life and Safety, or Enemy Welfare, or something of the sort?

The amount of Alien *property* in the United States is very great indeed; but, Mr. President, is not the value of Alien LIFE far greater?—worthy of far more attention?

Would not a conscientious humanitarian organization, occupied with safeguarding the lives and ordinary welfare of the millions of Germans, Austrians, Hungarians, Bohemians, while preventing them from assisting the enemy, reflect the highest credit upon a Government which concerned itself with it?

Last night a young man (a stranger to me) called upon me, saying that he had a scrap-book of several hundred cases of unlawful violence against Teutonic American persons. This morning's papers recorded four or five. No doubt some of these were really due to the absence of Federal Supervision of Aliens and Suspects.

This morning Mr. Taft is reported as making a speech deploring these "outrages," as bringing disrepute upon democracy.[2] This morning is generally republished Mr. Creel's *Independent* article ascribing these occurences to German spies.[3] The Socialist papers are printing conspicuously stories which, one may fear, may get across and receive too much attention in Germany.

The whole subject of the oversight of the millions of Enemy Aliens resident in the United States would certainly seem to be one worthy of particular study and direction, under a special Commission.

I am, dear Mr. President,

Yours sincerely,   Wm. Bayard Hale[4]

TLS (WP, DLC).
   [1] Wilson, on October 19, 1917, had appointed A. Mitchell Palmer as Alien Property Custodian under Section 6 of the Trading with the Enemy Act.
   [2] Hale was referring to an editorial in the *New York Times*, which denounced the recent lynching of Robert Paul Prager, a German citizen, in Collinsville, Ill., about which see H. C. Peterson and Gilbert C. Fite, *Opponents of War, 1917-1918* (Madison, Wisc., 1957), pp. 202-207. The editorial quoted from a speech by Taft to the Muskogee, Okla., Chamber of Commerce on April 3, 1918, in which Taft had advocated that spies be court-martialed and shot but had maintained that "mob violence such as practiced in certain parts of the United States should be everywhere condemned, that the United States may not sink to the lawless savagery of the Germans." *New York Times*, April 6, 1918; see also *ibid.*, April 4, 1918.
   [3] George Creel, "Unite and Win," *The Independent*, XCIV (April 6, 1918), 5-6. This was the eighth article in a series written by Creel under the general title of "Message from the United States Government to the American People," which appeared in *The Independent* from February 9, 1918 to May 11, 1918. Creel maintained that German sympathizers were taking advantage of every social, racial, religious, and political dissension in the United States to divide the American people. He charged, among other things, that German agents were inciting racial violence and were leading mobs to tar and feather the innocent victims of their propaganda of social unrest.
   [4] "Dear Tumulty: For some reason, I don't like to write to Hale, and I would be very much obliged to you if you would yourself acknowledge this letter. Tell him how I deplore the acts of violence to which he refers and how much I should like to know the best means of protecting innocent men, and that the matter has and will have my serious attention. The President." WW to JPT, c. April 9, 1918, TL (WP, DLC).

From Walter Stowell Rogers[1]

Dear Mr. President: New York City April 6, 1918.

Your receiving the foreign correspondents next Monday afternoon is a notable event. These men are really ambassadors from millions of newspaper readers to the United States.

This Division has tried to help these correspondents follow events in America and to sense the country's underlying purposes and determination. The correspondents have been taken about and shown ship yards, munition plants and so forth. They have been encouraged to organize and become acquainted with each other and through such association and our efforts to see the larger aspect of their work.

It is only fair to say that their despatches reflect our friendly attitude and their own growth in vision. Almost to a man they are responding. We ask no favors of them, merely that they should be patient and understand.

Your seeing them as a group will further their growing respect for their chosen work.[2]   Respectfully,   Walter S Rogers

TLS (WP, DLC).
  [1] At this time, director of the Division of Foreign Cable News Service of the C.P.I.
  [2] Wilson's remarks to the foreign correspondents are printed at April 8, 1918.

A Translation of a Telegram from
Georges Clemenceau

Washington. April 6, 1918.

The first anniversary of the entry into war of the United States affords me the high privilege of rendering to you in a solemn hour the salute of the French Democracy.

We should all, you said to the American people nine days after the declaration of war, act and serve together. The native land of Washington and of Lincoln has heard you, has understood you, follows you. She follows you for the maintenance in the world of the most precious boon of humanity, and with her immense resources she springs forward as the disinterested champion of the independence of peoples. Determined on the defense, not of interest but of right, she has taken her place, august and serene, at the side of the Allies to assure the triumph of their cause. To your doctrine as pure and resplendent as your star-spangled banner is opposed that of force, supreme and sole argument of princes; but the force which is incapable of absolving our enemies from the bloody responsibilities they have assumed is powerless against the eternal fortress of right.

Leaning on these noble conceptions, you have led the people of the United States toward its destinies. Already its blood has bathed the land of France, already its heroes have mingled their laurels with our own. Receive, Mr. President, at a time when no longer, as too often before, covetousness struggles with ambition, but when justice and iniquity themselves contend, the ardent protestation of the friendship of France which sustained your native land at her birth, which has always been attached to her throughout the glorious course of her history, and which now, united to her by the indissoluble pact entered into for the safety of liberty, welcomes on her soil famed by so many combats, the invincible legions of the citizens of America.[1]

T MS (WP, DLC).
   [1] The "original" of this telegram is Foreign Ministry to J. J. Jusserand, April 5, 1918, T telegram (Guerre 1914-1918, États-Unis, Vol. 510, p. 223, FFM-Ar).

A Translation of a Telegram from Victor Emmanuel III

Italian General Headquarters [April 6, 1918].

One year now has passed since the great Republic of America under your enlightened guidance, Mr. President, entered the sanguinary struggle maintained by the free peoples united in a common ideal of justice and democracy against the threatening yoke of autocracy and militarism. While the valiant American troops are exposing themselves in the glorious land of France on the bulwarks of the freedom of nations and while fresh legions are preparing to cross the ocean, and the powerful assistance of the United States is strengthening our resistance, the people and soldiers of Italy, full of confidence in the justice of the common cause and the sanctity of Italy's national aspirations, await with a stout heart the enemy's onslaught and join me in sending, on this auspicious anniversary, a fervent greeting to you Mr. President and to the American people and army.   Victorio Emanuele.

T MS (WP, DLC).

John J. Spurgeon[1] to Joseph Patrick Tumulty

Dear Mr. Tumulty: Philadelphia April sixth 1918

On account of this newspaper's support of the President in his sympathetic attitude toward the Russian people, some of our contemporaries are circulating the report that the PUBLIC LEDGER is pro-German.

A prominent citizen of Philadelphia has also stated that in government circles in Washington "the PUBLIC LEDGER is regarded as one of the doubtful papers of the country." As I assume that the PUBLIC LEDGER comes under your notice, may I ask if in your

opinion such a criticism is warranted? As an important representative of the government, do you regard the PUBLIC LEDGER as "one
of the doubtful papers"?

Would it be possible to secure an expression from the President?[2]

I assure you that your reply[3] will be held in the strictest confidence and is merely for the guidance of Mr. Curtis[4] and myself.

Respectfully yours,   John J. Spurgeon.

TLS (WP, DLC).

[1] Executive director of the Philadelphia *Public Ledger*.

[2] "Dear Tumulty: I think it would be perfectly wise for you to make the frankest sort of answer to this. I do not read the Public Ledger and can form no opinion. It is being edited, as I understand it, by Brougham and Colcord, two very progressive fellows. The President." WW to JPT, c. April 9, 1918, TL (WP, DLC).

[3] "As a daily reader of the Ledger, I feel free to answer your inquiry. While the Ledger has not always agreed with all the Admn. pol & with reg[ard] to the conduct of the war there is no question in my mind, of its patr. & good faith.

"So far as her assos. with me at the White House are concerned, the Ledger has never been accused of doubtful loyalty.

"The President had asked me to write you in this frank [manner] & you may consider this expression of opinion as representative of his views." JPT to J. J. Spurgeon, c. April 9, 1918, Hw draft (WP, DLC).

[4] That is, Cyrus Hermann Kotzschmar Curtis, head of the Curtis Publishing Co.

Peyton Conway March to Tasker Howard Bliss

[Washington] April 6, 1918, 12.50 A.M.

Number 44, Very Confidential.

The actual monthly cargo movement involved in the military
program of the United States as approved by the President April
3rd and set forth in cablegram Number 43 to you is estimated as
follows: In thousands of long tons April 407, May 463, June 488,
July 633, August 747, September 710, October 727, November 743,
December 748, making a total movement April to December inclusive of 5,687. Total shipments by departments will be in thousands
of long tons Engineers 1,783, Quartermaster 1,853, Ordnance 1,648
including about 480 replacements, Signal 278, Medical 64, miscellaneous 62. Recent and possible changes in composition and
disposition of expeditionary force may change above departmental
estimates but will not reduce total. Send copy to Pershing.

March

TC telegram (WDR, RG 407, World War I Cablegrams, DNA).

To Victor Emmanuel III

[The White House, April 7, 1918]

Your Majesty's message to the American people on the anniversary of the entrance of the United States of America into the war has been received with the deepest and sincerest appreciation. The American people have felt the most sincere and active sympathy with the Italian people in this great struggle and are with one mind desirous of lending all the aid that is within their power to the cause in which your people have joined. They count with the utmost confidence upon the steadfastness and bravery of the Italian armies to carry the common cause to complete victory against those who have invaded your own territory and disregarded your rights. It is their confident hope that in the final settlement the interests of Italy may be once for all securely safeguarded.

Woodrow Wilson.

T telegram (Letterpress Books, WP, DLC).

Lord Reading to David Lloyd George

Washington. April 7, 1918.

No. 1471. SECRET & CONFIDENTIAL.

Following for the Prime Minister.

Your telegram 1887 of 3rd April.[1]

I have made inquiry as to your information that there are only 400,000 Infantrymen in all U. S. The Chief of Staff has assured me this is not so. We need have no fear that the 480,000 will not be sent according to programme. Confidentialy from other sources I learn that the 480,000 represent all there are now in U. S. and that unless fresh drafts are made this number of Infantrymen will be exhausted but each month it is intended to call up 150,000 men at least and the first call is now made for April 26th.

Confidential. Some question was raised with me yesterday by Counsellor Polk as to the conversation between the President and me on 30th March reported in my telegram No. 1360 to you:[2] Secretary Baker has asked President whether he ever agreed to the Brigading of the 480,000 with French and British. President has replied that he agreed in principle that there should be brigading but did not commit himself to the total and reserved the details for Generals Bliss and Pershing.

I do not find any substantial difference between this and my report to you which I quote:

"In principle he approves the employment of the troops in the manner desired but leaves details to the Military Chiefs."

Only difference, if any, is that President had in mind that the Generals might not wish to brigade total of 480,000, although nothing was said about it in terms. Nevertheless I quite understood that any such question was left open if his Military Chiefs wished it as the President was careful to leave all Military details to them.

I send you this full statement in case any question should arise about it.

T telegram (FO 115/2461, pp. 118-19, PRO).
    [1] D. Lloyd George to Lord Reading, April 2, not April 3, 1918.
    [2] Lord Reading to D. Lloyd George, March 30, 1918 (first telegram of that date).

Lord Reading to Arthur James Balfour

Washington. 7th April 1918.

No. 1474. No action has been taken by American warship at Vladivostock and no instructions have been issued from here to American Naval Commander to cooperate with Japanese and British warships in landing a party. Tomorrow I shall try to induce Administration to take action in cooperation but much fear that they will abstain unless American property is in their view in such danger as to require armed protection. The statement issued in press here that Trotsky has given orders "to resist the invasion"[1] will serve to harden the American view. My definite impression is that the Administration receives with some reluctance statements coming from our or Allies representatives of attacks upon Japanese or their property or of the arming of prisoners near Irkutsk.

The President is I believe more confirmed than ever in his opinion that America should not assent to or take part in intervention of Japanese unless there is at least something in nature of request from Russian Government for this assistance. Most if not all of the reports reaching the U. S. Government from its own representatives strongly emphasise that without such request the effect of Japanese intervention will be to throw the Russians into German arms. Even members of Administration who were at first inclined to favour American assent to or cooperation with Japanese intervention are now inclined the other way.

The absence of further information as to the military advantage to be gained by the intervention which the President has been expecting to receive if there were further information in existence is also hardening his mind. You will remember that at my interview with him reported in my telegram No. 1159 of March 19th[2] I was to obtain further data as to military advantage and substantially none have been supplied. There is also impression in State Department that it is the French who are pressing at the Councils for this intervention and that we are supporting it largely because we do not wish to differ from them.

I am sending you this last information in order that you may correct it if you wish. The impression is I believe gathered to some extent from their reports of Supreme Council meetings which I have not seen. When I press our view I have observed this tendency to doubt whether we are as anxious for Japanese intervention as my instructions and consequent representations to them would convey.   R.

T telegram (FO 115/2445, p. 261, PRO).
    [1] Following the shooting of three Japanese civilians by Russian soldiers in Vladivostok on April 4, 1918, a party of 500 Japanese marines had landed the following day, ostensibly for the purpose of protecting the lives and property of Japanese subjects in the city. The British had followed suit by putting ashore fifty men to guard the vicinity of their consulate.
    According to a semiofficial dispatch from Moscow quoted in the *New York Times*, the Council of People's Commissars had immediately ordered all the soviets in Siberia to "offer armed resistance to an enemy incursion into Russian territory." *New York Times*, April 7, 1918. For a detailed discussion of this incident, see Kennan, *The Decision to Intervene*, pp. 99-106.
    [2] Lord Reading to the Foreign Office, March 19, 1918.

A Proclamation

[April 8, 1918]

BY THE PRESIDENT OF THE UNITED STATES OF AMERICA.

Whereas, in January, 1918, the Secretary of Labor, upon the nomination of the president of the American Federation of Labor and the president of the National Industrial Conference Board, appointed a War Labor Conference Board for the purpose of devising for the period of the war a method of labor adjustment which would be acceptable to employers and employees; and

Whereas, said board has made a report recommending the creation for the period of the war of a national war labor board with the same number of members as, and to be selected by the same agencies, that created the War Labor Conference Board whose duty it shall be to adjust labor disputes in the manner specified, and in accordance with certain conditions set forth in the said report; and

Whereas, the Secretary of Labor has, in accordance with the recommendation contained in the report of said War Labor Conference Board dated March 29, 1918, appointed as members of the

National War Labor Board Hon. William Howard Taft and Hon. Frank P. Walsh, representatives of the general public of the United States; Messrs. Loyall A. Osborne, L. F. Loree, W. H. Van Dervoort, C. E. Michael, and B. L. Worden, representatives of the employers of the United States; and Messrs. Frank J. Hayes, William L. Hutcheson, William H. Johnston, Victor A. Olander, and T. A. Rickert, representatives of the employees of the United States;

Now, therefore, I, Woodrow Wilson, President of the United States of America, do hereby approve and affirm the said appointments and make due proclamation thereof and of the following for the information and guidance of all concerned:

The powers, functions, and duties of the National War Labor Board shall be: To settle by mediation and conciliation controversies arising between employers and workers in fields of production necessary for the effective conduct of the war, or in other fields of national activity, delays and obstructions which might, in the opinion of the National Board, affect detrimentally such production; to provide, by direct appointment or otherwise, for committees or boards to sit in various parts of the country where controversies arise and secure settlement by local mediation and conciliation; and to summon the parties to controversies for hearing and action by the National Board in event of failure to secure settlement by mediation and conciliation.

The principles to be observed and the methods to be followed by the National Board in exercising such powers and functions and performing such duties shall be those specified in the said report of the War Labor Conference Board dated March 29, 1918, a complete copy of which is hereunto appended.

The national board shall refuse to take cognizance of a controversy between employer and workers in any field of industrial or other activity where there is by agreement or Federal law a means of settlement which has not been invoked.

And I do hereby urge upon all employers and employees within the United States the necessity of utilizing the means and methods thus provided for the adjustment of all industrial disputes, and request that during the pendency of mediation or arbitration through the said means and methods there shall be no discontinuance of industrial operations which would result in curtailment of the production of war necessities.

In witness whereof, I have hereunto set my hand and caused the seal of the United States to be affixed.

Done in the District of Columbia, this eighth day of April, in the year of our Lord one thousand nine hundred and eighteen, and of the independence of the United States the one hundred and forty-second.   Woodrow Wilson.

(SEAL.)

By the President:
  ROBERT LANSING, *Secretary of State.*

Printed in the *Official Bulletin*, II (April 10, 1918), 3.

Remarks to Foreign Correspondents[1]

8 April, 1918

Mr. Creel and gentlemen: I am very glad to have this opportunity to meet you. Some of you I have met before, but not all. In what I am going to say, I would prefer that you take it in this way, as for the private information of your own minds and not for transmission to anybody, because I just want, if I may in a few words, to create a background for you which may be serviceable to you. I speak simply in confidence.

I was rendered a little uneasy by what Mr. Lloyd George was quoted as having said the other day, that the Americans have a great surprise in store for Germany.[2] And I don't know in what sense he meant that, but there is no surprise in store. I want you to know the sequence of resolves and of actions. Some time ago, it was proposed to us that we, if I may use the expression, feed our men into the French and English armies in any units that might be ready—companies or regiments or brigades—and not wait to train and coordinate the larger units of our armies before putting them into action. My instinctive judgment in the face of that proposition was that the American people would feel a very much more ardent interest in the war if their men were fighting under their own flag and under their own general officers. But at that time, a long time ago, that is to say, some months ago, I instructed General Pershing that he had full authority, whenever any exigency that made such a thing necessary should occur, to put the men in any units or in any numbers or in any way that was necessary—

---

[1] Creel had written to Wilson on April 2 that there were about thirty correspondents of foreign newspapers in the United States who were eager to come to Washington "for the inspiration" of a sight of him. Creel said that they had been very cooperative and that an interview with Wilson would "buck them up tremendously" at a time when the administration needed them most. G. Creel to WW, April 2, 1918, TLS (WP, DLC). Wilson received a group of twenty reporters at the White House on April 8 at 2 p.m.

[2] In a message read at a luncheon given by the Lord Mayor of London on April 7, 1918, to commemorate the anniversary of the entry of the United States into the war, Lloyd George had stated that, during the next few weeks, America would "give the Prussian military junta the surprise of their lives." *New York Times*, April 7, 1918.

just as he is doing. So that what I wanted you to know was that that was not a new action, that General Pershing was fully instructed about that all along.

Then, similarly, with regard to the impression that we are now going to rush troops to Europe. Of course, you cannot rush any faster than there is means of rushing, and what I have said recently is what I have said all along—that we get men there just as fast as we can get them ready and as quickly as we can find the ships. Now, we are doing that now, and we have been doing it all along. Now let me point out some of the circumstances: our first program was to send over ninety thousand men a month, but for several months we were sending over only thirty thousand—one third of the program. Why not? Not because we didn't have the men ready, not even because we didn't have the means of transportation, but because—and there is no criticism of the French government involved in it—because the ports assigned to us for landing couldn't take care of the supplies that we had shipped. We had to send materials and engineers and workmen, even, over to build the docks and the piers that would be adequate to handle the number of men we sent over, because this was happening: we began with the ninety-thousand program, and the result was that cargo ships that we needed were lying in those ports for several weeks together without being unloaded, as there was no means of unloading them. And it was bad economy and bad practice from every point of view to have those ships lying there during a period when they could have made two or three voyages. There is still this difficulty, which I am afraid there is no means of overcoming rapidly at all, that the railroad communication between those ports and the front is inadequate to handle very large bodies of men. You may notice that General Pershing recommended that Christmas boxes should not be sent to the men. That sounded like a pretty hardhearted piece of advice, but if you could go to those ports and see those Christmas boxes which are still there, you would know why he didn't want them sent. There was no means of getting them to the front. Vast accumulations of these gifts were piled up there with no means of storing them adequately, even.

I just wanted to create for you this picture—that the channels have been inevitably choked. And now we believe that, inasmuch as the impediments on the other side are being largely removed, we can catch up, or catch up by resuming the original program and add to it in proportion as the British can spare us the tonnage, and they are going to spare us the tonnage for the purpose. And that is what makes the extra tonnage which the British are going to spare us and which will take the men, not to France but to Great

Britain, and send them to the front through the Channel ports. You see, that makes a new line where the means of handling are already established and where they are more abundant than they are at the French ports. Now, I want to say again that none of this involves the least criticism of the French authorities, because I think they did their very best in every respect. But they couldn't make ports out of hand, they couldn't build new facilities suddenly, and their manpower was being drawn on very much more and in a far larger proportion than our manpower. Therefore, it was perfectly proper that we should send them over there and send materials to make the means of handling the troops and the cargoes more expeditious.

But I wanted you gentlemen to realize, if you could, that there wasn't any wave-like motion in this thing so far as our purpose and preparation are concerned, that we have met with delays, of course, in production, some of which might have been avoided and ought to have been avoided, and which are being slowly corrected, but, apart from that, the motive power has been back of this thing all the time. And it has been the means of action that has oscillated— sometimes been greater and sometimes less than was necessary for the program.

I, for my own part, don't like the idea of having surprises. I would like people to be surprised that we didn't do our duty, but not surprised that we did. Of course, I don't mean that Mr. Lloyd George meant that we would surprise anybody by doing our duty, but I don't just know how to interpret his idea of it, because I have said the same thing to the British representatives all along, as I informally expressed it to Lord Reading—that we had been and always would be doing our damndest, and there could not be a more definite American expression of purpose than that.

So I wanted you gentlemen, therefore, to get out of your minds, if it has been there, the idea of any difference of speed that resulted from differences of purpose or plan, or of pressure from this end, because there have been no such differences. I have said the same thing so often to the official representatives of the Allies that I have been ashamed to say it again, because I thought it was better to have something. And I am sure they have understood the circumstances. They have never been disturbed as to what we intend to do.

Now, as to another matter—I am just giving you things to think about and not things to say, if you will be kind enough to take it that way. That speech I made on Saturday I hope was correctly understood. We are fighting, as I understand it, for justice to everybody and are ready to stop just as soon as justice to everybody is everybody's program. I have the same opinion privately about, I won't say the policy, but the methods of the German government that some gentlemen have who see red all the time, but that is not a proper part of my thought. My thought is that, if they insist that the thing shall be settled unjustly, that is to say by force, then of course we accept that and will settle it by force. Whenever we see sincere symptoms of their desire to settle it by justice, we will not only accept those suggestions, but we will be glad and eager to accept them, as I said in my speech. I would be ashamed to use the knock-down and drag-out language; that is not the language of liberty, that is the language of braggadocio. For my part, I have no desire to march triumphantly into Berlin. If they oblige us to march triumphantly into Berlin, then we will do it if it takes twenty years. But the world will come to its senses some day, no matter how mad some parts of it may be now, and this is my feeling—that we ought, when the thing is over, to be able to look back upon a course which had no element in it which we need be ashamed of. And so it is so difficult in any kind of speech—this kind or any other—to express two things that seem to be going in opposite directions. I wasn't sure that I had succeeded in expressing them on Saturday: the sincere willingness to discuss peace whenever the proposals are themselves sincere and yet, at the same time, the determination never to discuss it until the basis laid down for the discussion is justice. Now, by that I mean justice to everybody. Personally, if I were in a peace conference right now, I would say, "Gentlemen, I am here to say for the United States that I don't want anything out of this. And I am here to see that you don't get anything out of it."

Now, I am showing the inside of my mind, gentlemen, and I am trusting to your confidence to preserve it, and that is my premise. Nobody has the right to get anything out of this war, because we are fighting for peace if we mean what we say—for permanent peace. No injustice furnishes a basis for permanent peace. If you leave a rankling sense of injustice anywhere, it will not only produce a running sore presently, which will result in trouble and probably war, but it ought to produce war somewhere. The sore ought to run. It is not susceptible to being healed except by remedying the injustice. Therefore, I, for my part, wouldn't want to see a permanent peace which was based upon compelling any people, great or little, to live under conditions which it didn't willingly accept.

So that if I were just a sheer Machiavellian and didn't have any heart but had brains, I would say: "If you mean what you say and are fighting for permanent peace, then there is only one way to get it, whether you like justice or not." It is the only conceivable intellectual basis for it, because this is not like the time, a hundred years ago, of the Congress of Vienna. Peoples were then not willing, but so speechless and unorganized and without the means of self-expression, that the government could sit on their necks indefinitely. They didn't know how to prevent it. But they are wide awake now, and nobody is going to sit comfortably on the neck of any people, big or little, and the more uncomfortable he is if he tries it, the more I am personally pleased. So that I am in the position in my mind of trying to work out a purely scientific proposition: "What will stay put?"

I have all my reading days been very fond of quoting a sentiment of Burke, but I can't quote the language as he said it: "If any man asks me what is a free government, I reply 'A government which those living under it will guard.' " It is the only possible definition of a free government. There may be all sorts of free governments, but the fundamental and essential element of it is that people like it and believe in it. The amazing thing to my mind is that a lot of German people that I know like the government they have been living under. It took me a long time to believe it; I thought they were bluffing. But I found some Germans whom I had to believe who really liked it and thought all nations ought to live under that kind of government. Now, there isn't any one kind of government under which all nations ought to live. There isn't any one kind of government which we have the right to impose upon any nation. So that I am not fighting for democracy except for the peoples that want democracy. If they want it, then I am ready to fight until they get it. If they don't want it, that is none of my business. In the Virginia Bill of Rights, which is the original of our bills of rights, and which follows substantially along the lines of the original English Bill of Rights, there is—and I can't quote the language—a sentiment to this effect, that the people have the right to make any kind of government it pleases and change the government it makes in any way that it pleases, and the implication is that it is nobody else's business how they change it.

That was the principle that I acted on in dealing with Mexico. I said that Mexico was entitled, so far as we were concerned, if she did not interfere with us, to have any kind of order or any kind of disorder that she pleased—that it was none of our business. I couldn't get that into the heads of some of the gentlemen who visited me. I found out the truth about Mexico, by the way, by a very interesting process—by hearing a large enough number of liars tell me all about it. Because the interesting thing about the truth is that it matches and about lies that they don't match. And no man has invention enough to invent everything he tells you. So that if you hear a large number of people, you will get a large body of information, and the statements that match all through you will know to be so. Those that do not match you will know are not so. So I found out a good deal about Mexico by that very tedious and trying process.

But the moral is perhaps more vividly fixed by the case of Mexico than any other I could refer to, because the idea of many American capitalists, the idea of many American public men, was that we had a right to insist that Mexico do this and that in order that our people might go into Mexico and make money. Now that proposition I utterly reject, and I will never stand for it. There is the acid test, because, goodness knows, Mexico was in a most unhappy and impossible state and hasn't got thoroughly out of it yet, but that is none of our business.

A peace is not going to be permanent until this principle is accepted by everybody, that, given a political unit, it has the right to determine its own life.

Now, gentlemen, I believe that is all I have to say to you, but it is the real inside of my mind, and it is the real key to the present foreign policy of the United States which, for the time being, is in my keeping. And therefore I thought it might be useful to you, as it is welcome to me, to have this occasion of telling you what I really think and what I understand we are really doing. We are very much obliged to you.

T MS (WP, DLC), with corrections and additions from a reading of the CLSsh notes in the C. L. Swem Coll., NjP.

A Press Release

[c. April 8, 1918]

President Wilson held a conference at the White House proper Monday Afternoon at 4:30, with a number of persons deeply interested in the little black Republic of Liberia.

Those who presented Liberia's claims for consideration at this time, when it is being so hard pressed, economically and otherwise, were: Dr. R. R. Moton, Principal of the Tuskegee Normal and Industrial Institute, Tuskegee, Alabama; Dr. Ernest Lyon, Liberian Counsul-General to the United States; Attorney William H. Lewis, of Boston, Mass., former Assistant Attorney-General of the United States;[1] Dr. James H. Dillard, President of the Slater and Jeanes Fund Boards of Trustees;[2] Dr. Thomas Jesse Jones of the Phelps Stokes Fund[3] and Mr. Emmett J. Scott, who was a member of the

American Commission to Liberia in 1909 and at present is serving as Special Assistant in the War Department.

President Wilson greeted the party most cordially, and expressed interest in the cause as presented by his callers.

CC MS (WDR, RG 407, Adjutant General's Office, Emmet J. Scott Papers, DNA).
    [1] That is, William Henry Lewis.
    [2] James Hardy Dillard, who had long been involved in the promotion of education in the South. He was also a trustee of the General Education Board and the General Theological Seminary and the rector of the College of William and Mary.
    [3] A sociologist and educational director of the Phelps Stokes Fund.

To Josephus Daniels

My dear Daniels: The White House 8 April, 1918

With regard to sending a vessel to Murmansk, I am anxious to do so if it can be done without sacrificing more important objects, but, of course, not unless it can be done without that sacrifice. I had hoped that there might be some vessel on this side that could be sent over that would be sufficient force to command respect and afford real cooperation without taking any vessel from the overseas convoy business, but if there is not, that is an end of it. I feel perfect confidence in your advice in the matter.[1]

    Cordially and faithfully yours,   Woodrow Wilson

TLS (J. Daniels Papers, DLC).
    [1] The vessel selected was Admiral George Dewey's former flagship, *U.S.S. Olympia*, then in American waters. *Olympia* arrived off Murmansk on May 24, 1918.

To Jean Jules Jusserand, with Enclosure

My dear Mr. Ambassador: [The White House] 8 April, 1918

I take pleasure in enclosing a copy of the reply I am today sending to Monsieur Clemenceau, in answer to his splendid message of Saturday.

May I not thank you for bringing the Prime Minister's message to me in person?

    Cordially and sincerely yours,   Woodrow Wilson

TLS (Letterpress Books, WP, DLC).

E N C L O S U R E

[The White House, April 8, 1918]

Your gracious and generous message of the sixth of April has been received with the greatest pleasure and appreciation. It is delightful to have one who knows America so thoroughly as you do interpret its spirit and purpose so admirably. I am sure that I can say that it adds greatly to the zest of the people of the United States in the prosecution of the war for their own rights and the rights of free men everywhere that they should be associated in the great undertaking with the people of France, whom they so much admire and for whom their admiration has been so confirmed and increased during this war in which the French people have exhibited to all the world an example of spirited action and a valor that knows no discouragement or dismay. The warmest greeting of our people goes with my own across the sea with this message to our trusted comrades and associates.   Woodrow Wilson.

T telegram (Letterpress Books, WP, DLC).

To Robert Wickliffe Woolley, with Enclosure

My dear Woolley: The White House 8 April, 1918

I was so much interested in the suggestion contained in your letter of March thirtieth that I asked the advice of the Secretary of Labor about it, and I am now taking the liberty of enclosing to you a copy of his letter. I am afraid that you will find it as wise and conclusive as I did. I say "afraid" because, of course, I should like to do what you suggest. It would have a fine effect.

            Cordially and sincerely yours,   Woodrow Wilson

TLS (R. W. Woolley Papers, DLC).

E N C L O S U R E

From William Bauchop Wilson

My dear Mr. President: Washington April 5, 1918.

I am in receipt of your letter of April 1st,[1] inclosing one from Mr. Woolley, relative to issuing a statement giving assurance that there is to be full-time employment throughout the year in all shipyards and other industrial plants under Government control.

There can be no doubt that it would add materially to the efficiency of the workers if they could have definite assurance of steady and continuous employment. The difficulty lies in being able to carry out such an assurance once it is given. Some large employers in seasonal occupations, such as the needle trades, have solved the problem to advantage by using a larger working capital and storing the production during the off season so as to keep their working force steadily employed throughout the year. In the present state of industrial activity for war purposes it is a very difficult thing to do. It would require very careful planning, with a definite knowledge of what the needs are going to be in each particular line during the war, and then coordinating the industrial activities to produce the things required in proper proportion. I understand that Mr. Baruch is undertaking a general survey with this object in view. Such a survey is a tremendous task, and the coordination of the industries to a proper balance with each other is still a bigger one. Even after it is completed extraordinary demands will arise for greater production in certain lines than had been anticipated, while in other lines the needs will be less. In war emergencies an immense amount of work must of necessity be temporary.

Under these circumstances it would be very difficult to carry out the assurance when given, and unless the War Department, the Navy Department and the Shipping Board can work out plans by which it can be put into practical operation, it would be well to withhold any statement for the present.

Faithfully yours,   W B Wilson

TLS (WP, DLC).
 ¹ WW to WBW, April 1, 1918, TLS (received from Mary A. Strohecker).

To William Bauchop Wilson

My dear Mr. Secretary: The White House 8 April, 1918

I warmly appreciate your kindness in writing me so fully about the present situation in Minneapolis. I think your conclusions are as wise as they are conservative.

Cordially and sincerely yours,   Woodrow Wilson

TLS (received from Mary A. Strohecker).

To Edward Beale McLean

My dear Mr. McLean: [The White House] 8 April, 1918

I am distressed that you should have been so long ill, and sincerely glad to infer from your letter of April fourth that you are better and at your desk again.

You may be sure that I value your hint about suggestions very much indeed, and that I shall be glad to avail myself of it at times. That I have not done so frequently has been due to the fact, and only to the fact, that I am so absorbed from day to day that I have not leeway of thought enough apparently to originate suggestions.

Sincerely yours,   Woodrow Wilson

TLS (Letterpress Books, WP, DLC).

To Joseph Patrick Tumulty

Dear Tumulty: [The White House, c. April 8, 1918]

Please refer these gentlemen to the War Department[1] and be kind enough to send a note to Mr. Crowell saying that we have made the reference in order that he may bring these gentlemen in touch with the committee that is conducting the investigation if he thinks it best to do so. Please warn him at the same time that this Aero Club is in my judgment seeking to get control, as it did in the beginning, of the aircraft business and must be dealt with with suspicious caution.   The President.

TL (WP, DLC).

[1] A White House memorandum attached to the above document reveals that Alan Ramsey Hawley of New York, president of the Aero Club of America, had sent telegrams to Wilson and Tumulty on April 6, urging that the President see Frank G. Diffin, chairman of the Aircraft International Standardization Board, who had just returned from Europe with much new information on the "aircraft situation, some of which was given him in confidence for transmission to the President alone."

From Herbert Clark Hoover

Dear Mr. President: Washington 8 April 1918

The War Council of the War Department has apparently decided that no shipping can be afforded to the Belgian Relief Commission. I fully appreciate the extreme gravity of the present situation yet I have the feeling that this decision was taken without consideration of the whole of its bearings and it does seem to me that it should be reviewed.

The Belgian Relief Commission has a fleet untouched by this decision which is able to transport to the population of Belgium and Northern France an average of under 60,000 tons of food per month. The amount of food which we have always considered as the minimum on which this population could be maintained in even reasonable health is about 120,000 tons of food per month. We have felt latterly that under this great shipping stringency and with the approaching spring, we could reduce it to 90,000 tons of food a month temporarily without bringing about a disaster; thus leaving 30,000 tons to be carried monthly by new shipping—needing, say, 65,000 tons deadweight.

In the original Dutch agreement we were to have 100,000 tons of Dutch shipping. Upon the failure of this agreement, Mr. Hurley undertook to do his utmost to supply the Relief Commission with some 70,000 tons of shipping at once and three Norwegian steamers have been assigned but under this last direction there is some uncertainty as to whether even these will not be taken away and no more be provided.

Aside entirely from its deep humanatarian aspects, the Relief problem has very great political importance. So great has the political aspect been regarded by the Allied governments that during the whole of these years they have not only supported it in shipping and money but at the recent Inter-Allied Council in Paris it was decided to be of such extreme importance that the Belgian Relief was given a priority in shipping, money and food, over all Allied needs. This political importance hinges around:

1st. The prevention of an agreement between the Flemish population and the Germans as to the establishment of a separate and independent government under German tutelage.

2nd. The fact that the Belgian government itself and the Belgian Army may consider the cost in sacrifice of life of their civilian population too great to pay for constancy in the war.

3rd. The loss of morale to the French people and the French Army by a debacle amongst their own civilians in the North of France. The French Premier has expressed himself vigorously on this point.

5th [4th]. There are some 2,000,000 workmen in Belgium who have, with the most extraordinary constancy, refused all these years to work for the Germans and even under the terrible suffering of actual forced labor they have so resisted as to give the Germans no adequate return for the measures they adopted in this manner.

I believe we can maintain the Relief and the whole of its objectives if we can have (a) No interference with our present fleet, including the three ships already assigned by the Shipping Board. (b) The assignment of five more ships promptly for April loading and four further ships for May loading.

The whole matter seems to me of such importance that it should at least be referred to the Supreme War Council in Europe for decision before any action of the nature proposed is taken here.

Yours faithfully,   Herbert Hoover

TLS (WP, DLC).

From David Lawrence

PERSONAL

My dear Mr. President: [Washington] April 8, 1918.

I wonder if, in the little time you get for reading, you have observed the policies pursued by some of our leading magazines.
Many of them have openly dedicated themselves to a win-the-war
policy and are doing splendid work, but I want to draw your attention particularly to one of the most subtle and yet most effective
kinds of pro-American propaganda that the war has brought out.
It is reaching right into the hearts of millions of people and is
making an appeal that I know is measurable every day by results.
You probably do not get much time to read magazines, but I think
Mr. George Horace Lorimer, Editor of the Saturday Evening Post
has undoubtedly developed an unusually effective policy—putting
over not merely in special articles but in realistic fiction some of
the main principles of the war, such things as food conservation,
liberty bonds, war savings stamps, etc. There is nothing in the outer
aspect of the magazine to indicate that its pages are filled with
material about the war, but there is not a fiction story or a special
article that hasn't some bearing on the war. You can readily imagine
how the millions of people who read the Post from week to week
follow their favorite authors who still write as entertainingly as
before but whose theme is the central thought of American life
today—the war. Unfortunately it is only the spectacular kinds of
service that attract attention, and appreciation does not always reach
the men who most deserve it. But if there is one man who is using
his business to win the war—in spite of the discouragements and
embarrassments of transportation, white paper, postal troubles, and
similar obstacles—that man is the editor of the Saturday Evening
Post. I did not know until I got into this thing so deeply in the last
few months what a wonderful work was being done. That is why
I think you should know of it.

Sincerely yours,   David Lawrence

TLS (WP, DLC).

From William Bowyer Fleming[1]

Dear Mr. President: Washington April 8, 1918.

May I be permitted humbly to join in the enthusiastic approval
being accorded your great message delivered at Baltimore? This
approval will be universally found wherever the love of liberty still
lives.

Like yourself, I was reluctant to renounce the Hope that somehow around the Council Table Reason might sit enthroned and a way found to hasten Peace by some other means than Force of Arms, but the course of the Kaiser and his military satraps has shown them lost to reason and has shut the door to that hope. No alternative is left save the exercise of the supremest Physical Force.

The time had come for you to sound the note rung out at Baltimore, and gloriously has it been done.

Mr. President, God has inspired you to rise to every occasion.

The whole world recognizes and acclaims you its Mighty Leader.

MAY THE LORD OF HOSTS BLESS AND KEEP YOU!

Your Baltimore speech will live side by side with Lincoln's immortal address at Gettysburg.

Most cordially,   W. B. Fleming

TLS (WP, DLC).
[1] Lawyer and Democratic politician from Kentucky; foreign trade adviser to the Department of State since October 1, 1913; adviser on commercial treaties since January 31, 1916.

From Benedict Crowell

My dear Mr. President: Washington. April 8, 1918.

Enclosed please find a resolution of the War Council,[1] which should have been sent to you before, but through a misunderstanding, has been held here.

You will observe that this plan, if adopted, will have a far-reaching effect, and is really outside of the scope of the War Department.

Yours very truly,   Benedict Crowell

TLS (WP, DLC).
[1] War Department, Office of the War Council, Resolution, March 20, 1918, TS MS (WP, DLC). In this resolution, the War Council approved Crowder's plan for the mobilization of industrial manpower and urged its immediate adoption. The resolution also provided a detailed rationale for the measure and outlined various steps to implement it. For a summary of Crowder's proposed bill, see ASB to WW, April 5, 1918, n. 1.

From Gutzon Borglum

Dear Mr. President: [New York] April 8 1918

The New York World continues its daily alternating statements of half truths and paliations, injecting names into possible control of the Aircraft and direct statements corroborating this come from associates of the investigating committee, all of which is extremely disturbing. To place the bankrupt program into the hands of Deeds'

appointees or of his bankers, or into the hands of people who have
financed Curtis, Fisher Body or Dayton Wright or several other
concerns will be the signal for real alarm. No change is intended
by Wall Street and no names are mentioned that do not come out
of the same financial hole in Wall Street.

Is it possible no man of the Assistant Secretary of the Navy's
standing, ability and loyalty can be found?

Mr. President, I've gone too deeply into this miserable business
to be a silent partner in a patched up arrangement to further deceive
this nation and the world and I cannot do it.

Immunity from subsequent military abuse, proclaimed by you,
would bring a hundred Signal Corps officers to your door in a day,
with stories of disloyalty, graft and conspiracy that would shock the
nation.

I'm sending this by messenger from New York as I do not dare
expose it to the wire.   Sincerely yours,   Gutzon Borglum

I would like not to further disturb you with this business, but
the interests are raising heaven and hell to save their division of
this nation's appropriations   G.B.

TLS (WP, DLC).

Philip Whitwell Wilson[1] to the London *Daily News*

Washington, D. C. April 8, 1918.

Important message opens for release Thursday morning President Wilson has just received foreign correspondents accredited to
this country. At the White House this afternoon there gathered
representatives of Britain, France, Italy, Scandinavia, Australia, Japan and other countries. We met in the Green Room, a stately yet
simple salon which well illustrates the architecture of a mansion
designed under eye of Washington with the ducal residence of the
Leinsters for model. We stood in a semi-circle while President entered. Stenographer sat at little table and George Creel of Public
Information Committee introduced us. This was the only ceremony,
and we were all in touring clothes. Wilson is a lightly built yet alert
man evidently in buoyant health. He is very erect, of medium height
and carefully dressed, though not in formal style. His face is tanned
with the open air, and his attitude when addressing us sometimes
suggested his known fondness for golf. Many of his portraits do
him an injustice. Not only are his eyes direct and kindly, but his
smile is singularly open and engaging, nor is the firmness of his
mouth on which so much has been written nearly as prominent as

we have been led to believe by photographers and caricaturists. The head is fuller and longer than perhaps one had expected, while the hair is turning grey and is possibly scantier than in earlier years. For a man of his build he has a large and masterful hand, of which, when speaking, he makes most excellent use, emphasising his points with delightful gestures which are occasionally as persuasive as the words used. He spoke quietly for twenty minutes, without notes of any kind, yet without hesitation. His voice is round and musical. In many ways the accuracy of his diction recalls Asquith, and beyond all question he has to perfection what we in England call a Parliamentary style. But the flow of dignified phrases is illuminated by ripples of genuine humor and even by a touch of delicately chosen colloquialism so that quotations from Burke and ancient statutes are mingled in the texture of the speech with hints of Americanism. A great portrait of Abraham Lincoln looked down on us and not one word passed which would have been unworthy of that illustrious man. The speech though strictly confidential was obviously of importance, but to me at any rate the one sustaining reflection was that amid all this tragic chaos I had met a statesman with a mind at ease within itself who was first and foremost and all the time a leader of every liberal impulse. Mentally measuring the President by the many British Ministers whom I have known and watched, despite his long career as professor and lecturer, he shows not a trace of the pedagogue but is a man with a rare gift of charm. And this charm is fully consistent with his known quality of stiff decision and almost obstinate determination. But behind and beyond all this is the supreme background of reverence by this one man for all other men. Autocratic he may be, but only as representing those for whom such autocracy is a necessary protection. His rhetoric is at times brilliant but it is held subservient to his ethical meaning and is never obtruded for display. His self revelation came as a surprise to many who heard him. Having thus listened to him I cannot say that I wish to alter anything of the messages interpreting his policy which I have sent you from time to time. Some of the things he said will live long in the memory. All of them will serve as an immediate guide and inspiration in a dark time. The occasion did not seem to be one on which any questions should be directed to the President who shook hands with each of us cordially as we passed out. As I stood in the hall I saw him walking back to his study, calm, erect, grave, a man who, with Irish blood in his veins, has strong emotions which a Scottish ancestry enables him to keep under stern control. Whether President Wilson will repeat the privilege conferred today upon us remains to be seen. In the interests of the cause one may express the hope that he will do so at some future date for the press needs not only the intimacy of his ideals but also the personal appreciation of his faith. Ends.   P. W. Wilson.[2]

TC telegram (WP, DLC).
   [1] American correspondent of the London *Daily News*.
   [2] The foregoing document is enclosed in EMH to WW, n.d., TLI (WP, DLC).

Lord Reading to the Foreign Office

Washington. 8th April 1918.

No. 1477 Your telegram No. 1997.[1]

American Naval commander has not landed a party. I have impressed upon State Department the vital importance of this landing taking place to prevent even an appearance of difference of policy of American and British Governments.

Secretary Lansing stated that U.S.G. were waiting for further reports. His inclination was to take no steps with a desire to preserve relations between Bolsheviks and U.S.G. because he feared effect in Russia of allied intervention at this moment.

I urged upon him in consequence of your above mentioned telegram that the U.S.G. should act with us in this matter which was purely of a defensive character and that if they refrained it would leave us in the position of having cooperated with the Japanese notwithstanding that the Americans refrained.

His first inclination was to treat the withholding of American cooperation as of no importance as American warship was there, but I think I convinced him that though small in itself the incident might have very important consequences and would be used to establish that there was dissension between U.S.G. and the British Government. I expect to hear later from him after communications which I have sent to him have been shown to the President and his directions taken. If necessary I shall see President but at the moment should receive merely answer that they must await the news which is coming to them before taking any steps.

T telegram (FO 115/2445, pp. 271-72, PRO).
   [1] Foreign Office to Lord Reading, April 7, 1918, T telegram (FO 115/2445, p. 254, PRO).

Two Letters to Benedict Crowell

My dear Mr. Secretary: The White House 9 April, 1918

I have your letter of yesterday with its enclosure, the minute and resolution of the War Council with regard to the confidential memorandum of the Provost Marshal General proposing a plan which seeks to correct the defect of the draft by providing a method for organizing and adjusting the man power of the nation to the needs of agriculture and industry during the present emergency, and write to beg that this whole proposal may be kept in confidence until I shall have had time to consider it more maturely. My present judgment is that it would make a very unfavorable impression upon the country to propose to extend the registration to all men between eighteen and fifty, because, while the object would not be to draw older men than are now being drawn into the military service, very much more explanation than would be taken in would be required to remove that impression from the country.

I am sure you agree with me that it is very important that proposals of this sweeping character, and indeed all proposals of general legislation, should be proposed to the Congress only by those who are directing the general policy of the nation, and I take it for granted that the War Council is acting on that principle.

Cordially and sincerely yours,   Woodrow Wilson

TLS (B. Crowell Papers, OClWHi).

My dear Mr. Secretary: [The White House] 9 April, 1918

The enclosed case[1] has particularly attracted my attention, and I have given a great deal of thought to it, not because I have any sympathy with the young man's request to be exempted from service, but because I know so well the impression that will be made upon the community from which young Herink comes.[2] They are a peculiar people. They are perfectly willing to do their legal duty, indeed, would feel it a disgrace if they did not, and yet they are legalists and feel a sense of injustice if more than the law requires is exacted of them. From the point of view of the moral effect of insisting upon not correcting the mistake as to the man's age which was evidently made, I am of the opinion that we should at once give him an honorable discharge, and I beg that you will direct that this shall be done.[3]

I would not express this confident opinion if I had not studied the peculiar social aspects of this case very thoroughly.

Cordially and sincerely yours,   Woodrow Wilson

TLS (Letterpress Books, WP, DLC).

[1] It concerned the application for a discharge from the army by Pvt. Albert Herink, a farmer from Cuba, Kansas, and a son of Bohemian immigrants. Without knowing his exact age, Herink had registered for the draft in June 1917 and had been drafted in September 1917. Since then, he had found out that, at the time of his registration, he had been above the draft age (he was born in January 1885) and was not obliged to serve. See G. T. Helvering to WW, March 19, 1918, TLS (WP, DLC).

[2] The town of Cuba, Kansas, was an agricultural community with a population of about 500 people, the majority of whom were homesteaders and immigrants from Bohemia.

[3] Herink was given an honorable discharge. See B. Crowell to WW, April 10, 1918, and NDB to WW, April 25, 1918, both TLS (WP, DLC).

To William Bowyer Fleming

My dear Mr. Fleming: [The White House] 9 April, 1918
   I deeply appreciate your kind letter of yesterday. It has brought me real cheer and encouragement, and I beg you to accept my very warm and sincere thanks.
                    Cordially yours,   Woodrow Wilson

TLS (Letterpress Books, WP, DLC).

To David Lawrence

My dear Lawrence: [The White House] 9 April, 1918
   Thank you for calling my attention to the methods by which the Saturday Evening Post is making the country aware of all that is involved in the war. I am going to give myself the pleasure of dropping Mr. Lorimer a word of appreciation.
                Cordially and sincerely yours,   Woodrow Wilson

TLS (Letterpress Books, WP, DLC).

To George Horace Lorimer

My dear Mr. Lorimer: The White House 9 April, 1918
   Public affairs press upon me so constantly that I seldom get a chance to look about me and see what is being said and done and consequently it is only just now that my attention has been drawn to the admirable way in which you have been filling the Saturday Evening Post with matter which interprets and emphasises the objects and meaning of the great struggle we are engaged in. The method you have adopted is all the more admirable because it is not carried in headlines but runs like an essence through the whole contents of the weekly. Will you not accept my sincere expression of admiration?
                Cordially and sincerely yours,   Woodrow Wilson

TLS (PHi).

To Mary Pickford[1]

My dear Miss Pickford: [The White House] 9 April, 1918
   It was very delightful to receive the beautiful roses, and you may be sure that I was sincerely gratified that you should have wished

me to receive such a token of your friendship. It was a pleasure to meet you and my best wishes follow you.[2]

Cordially and sincerely yours,   Woodrow Wilson

TLS (Letterpress Books, WP, DLC).
[1] Actress and famous Hollywood motion-picture star.
[2] Wilson received Mary Pickford, Douglas Fairbanks, Charles Chaplin, and Marie Dressler at the White House on April 5, 1918, to ask for their support for the third Liberty Loan campaign.

To Ripley Hitchcock

My dear Mr. Hitchcock: [The White House] 9 April, 1918

Colonel House has told me of the limited edition of the Documentary Edition of my HISTORY OF THE AMERICAN PEOPLE which you are planning to issue, and I will, of course, be willing to sign the sheets, though I hope that you can indulge me in signing them slowly, because it will be possible for me to sign only a few each day until they are finished. I sincerely hope that the edition will yield the margin for the Red Cross to which you refer.

In great haste

Cordially and sincerely yours,   Woodrow Wilson

TLS (Letterpress Books, WP, DLC).

From William Howard Taft

My dear Mr. President: New Haven, Conn April 9th, 1918.

On my return from a trip to the far West, I find your letter of April 2nd.[1] I am very glad to know that you approve the result of the War Labor Conference Board, and I sincerely hope that the machinery and the principles recommended by that Board may result in securing the elimination of obstructive differences between employers and employees at a time when the vital interests of the country require maximum production.

Sincerely yours,   Wm H Taft

TLS (WP, DLC).
[1] That is, the letter cited in WW to F. P. Walsh, April 2, 1918, n. 2.

From Edward Mandell House, with Enclosure

Dear Governor: New York. April 9, 1918.

Reading has a cable from his Government saying that Pershing is strongly opposed to our sending over what infantry we have under the plan agreed upon. Baker and Bliss, he is told, take a contrary view. The British Government is worried lest Pershing's view may prevail.

The situation in France must be even more critical than we think, for the nervousness of both the French and British Governments cannot otherwise be explained.

Before Sir William left, he gave me a cable which came from his Government to Reading. I am enclosing you a part of what it contained. I am not sure that Reading knows that I have seen this and it would be best not to refer to it.

Reading wanted to see you today, but I advised waiting until tomorrow, knowing that you had a Cabinet meeting on.

Outside of the general gravity of the situation, I have still further anxiety because of the effect which a grave disaster in France would have upon your Administration. If the German offensive fails, no one can lift a voice in criticism of what America has done. But if it succeeds, then, there will be no end to the denunciations from such as Roosevelt, Wood and their kind. Pershing's feeling that an American army under his command should be established and made as formidable as possible is understandable. Nevertheless, the thing to be done now is to stop the Germans, and to stop them it is evident that we must put in every man that is available.

Affectionately yours,   E. M. House

P.S. Cobb telephoned today that he thought the Senate would make an adverse report on the aircraft investigation and he was wondering whether or not it would be well for you to beat them to it and say whatever you have in mind to say about that situation.

TLS (WP, DLC).

ENCLOSURE

The battle now being fought on the Western front is only in its first stage. The crisis which we have just survived will most certainly be soon followed by another strong attack. If we are able to defeat this second attack we may be sure that it will be followed by others until one side or the other is exhausted or until the winter renders further fighting impossible. The present battle can be compared to that of Verdun, but on a vastly larger scale, extending from Flanders to Venice. The enemy's hopes of success are probably based chiefly on his belief that he will be able to refit his divisions faster than the Allies and that he can dispose of a superior manpower which will enable him to outlast them. He will, therefore, deliver blow after blow until he either forces a decision or is exhausted.

At so great a distance and beyond close touch with the realities of the situation it is very difficult for you to realize how evident it is that the extent and effectiveness of America's exertions during the next few weeks, or even days, will practically decide whether this great battle is to end in success or in disaster. I believe that Germany's chances depend mainly on America's ability to send her reinforcements in time for them to take their place in the line effectively. A difference of even a week in the date of arrival of American troops may win or lose a battle. It should be remembered that all troops must be put through a final training by men with first hand experience before they can be put into the line of battle. I understand this training can only be given properly in France and, as it requires at least a month, at least that time must elapse between the arrival of troops and their actual employment at the front.[1]

T MS (WP, DLC).
    [1] The foregoing is a paraphrase of and extract from D. Lloyd George to Lord Reading, April 2, 1918.

John R. Mott to Ethan Theodore Colton[1]

Dear Colton: London, April 9th, 1918.

. . .[2] Your cablegram in which you sent such a reassuring word from the leading representatives of the American Government in Russia has overtaken us here and affords the keenest satisfaction. I am glad to report that all the members of the Root Mission, the representatives of the Red Cross Mission who have returned, the members of the Stevens Railway Mission so far as they have returned, and General Judson all agree as to the wisdom of the Association keeping as many as possible of its men in Russia and devoting itself to serving Russian young men and boys wherever the opportunity presents itself. Shortly before I left home I went to Washington to sound leading members of our Government on the same subject. I had an unhurried interview with the President and asked him whether he would advise us to call out the men whom we had sent to Russia, now that it was apparent that they could not do the kind of work for which we sent them, but rather would have to devote themselves largely to work for men wherever men might be found. He agreed with me absolutely and emphatically that we should not call out our representatives, save the comparatively few who were subject to the draft when they left America. The men who had been exempted on any ground, he gave me to understand, need not be in any hurry. He recognized the great desirability of our country being in evidence among the Russian people in such a fruitful and unselfish ministry. He agreed with me as to the wisdom of our men not participating in politics, but devoting themselves exclusively and impartially to serving the men of all classes and parties. I also had interviews while in Washington with representatives of the State Department, the War Department, the Treasury Department, the Interior Department, the Navy Department—most of them members of the Cabinet—and also with other men prominent in the Government. Without exception, they unqualifiedly favor this policy which I have just indicated. From the point of view of accomplishing the purpose of the Allies in this war, what could be more important than through our work to give the Russian people such unmistakable evidence that America has not forgotten or deserted them, but is more deeply interested than ever in their welfare and destiny? . . .[3]

Very cordially yours,   John R. Mott

CCL (Russian Materials, Y.M.C.A. Library, New York).
  [1] Associate general secretary of the Y.M.C.A. and organizer of the Y.M.C.A. service in Russia and Siberia. Mott wrote to him in care of the United States consulate in Samara (later Kuybyshev).
  [2] The deletion is the first paragraph of this letter. It describes Mott's itinerary until about May 15, 1918.
  [3] This deletion describes Mott's activities in England from about April 2 to April 9.

David Lloyd George and Arthur James Balfour to Lord Reading

Washington, April 9th. 1918.

Paraphrase of Telegram from the Prime Minister and Mr. Balfour to Lord Reading dated April 8th. 1918.

General Hutchinson had an interview in Paris on April 7th. with Mr. Baker and General Pershing and the tenour of the conversation which passed causes us much uneasiness.

It appears from what took place that General Pershing is of the opinion that no understanding has been given by the United States to transport 120,000 infantry and machine gun units monthly for four months for the purpose of brigading them with French or British troops.

The only arrangement recognised by General Pershing is that under which British vessels during April are to transport 60,000 infantry and machine guns belonging to the six divisions, for the purpose of brigading with British troops as they reach this side during the present month. You will remember that this arrangement had practically been arrived at before the beginning of the present enemy offensive and before the President had received the appeal made by Mr. Lloyd George.

It is further evident from what passed at the interview in question that General Pershing contemplates passing these six divisions rapidly through the British Army and then withdrawing them for addition to the American Army in process of formation. His intention is no doubt that, on the withdrawal of the infantry forming the six divisions, a like number of troops from the United States will be used to replace them.

From this summary of the interview it is plain that the views held by General Pershing are in no way consistent with the broad lines of policy which we understand to have been accepted by the President. The principal point of difference is that in our view the promise given meant that, in the course of the four months April, May, June and July, 480,000 infantry and machine guns are to be brigaded with British or French troops. This obligation is not admitted by General Pershing who clearly disapproves of the adoption of such a policy.

A further and lesser discrepancy is that the British Government, while quite in agreement with General Pershing's view as to the ultimate withdrawal of the troops brigaded with the British and French for the formation of an American Army, consider that this process cannot and should not be attempted before about October or November next at the end of this year's season for active military operations.

The President has shown such a firm grasp of the situation that we are most unwilling to cause him any possible embarrassment by criticising his officers. It is however essential to have the question cleared up, as the repeated indications of the difference between the view taken by General Pershing and what we understand to be the policy decided upon by the President show that these differences are of fundamental importance and closely affect the issues of the whole war.

Mr. Baker who took part in the interview between General Hutchinson and General Pershing leaves today for the United States. Broadly speaking, we believe that he and General Bliss sympathise with the point of view which we have taken in this matter.[1]

T MS (WP, DLC).
[1] The foregoing is a paraphrase of A. J. Balfour to Lord Reading, April 8, 1918, No. 2017, T telegram (FO 115/2461, pp. 153-54, PRO). There is a copy of Balfour's telegram in the Reading Papers, FO 800/224, PRO. There is a copy of the paraphrase in FO 115/2461, pp. 155-57, PRO.

David Lloyd George to Lord Reading

[London] 9. April 1918.

Very Urgent.

No. 2049. Secret. Following from Prime Minister. Begins.

Mr. Balfour's tel. No. 2017 of Apr. 8th.[1]

I hope you will see there is no misunderstanding about brigading of 480,000 Americans with Allied units. Another tremendous battle is impending and we are relying on American reinforcements to make good gaps which it will make in Allied ranks. Allied plans depend on 120,000 American troops being available per month for brigading with Allied forces. In no other way can we make good losses or equal German reserves of man power. If Americans do not arrive or if hesitation or misunderstanding makes difficulties over brigading we cannot answer for consequences. I am sure that the President means to make good his undertakings but if so I think that he must issue explicit instructions to his subordinates that they must throw themselves heart and soul into this business of transporting and brigading 480,000 American troops with Allied units and that all questions of building up an independent American Army in Europe must come second to this imperative necessity whilst crisis lasts.[2]

T telegram (Reading Papers, FO 800/224, PRO).
  [1] That is, the telegram paraphrased in the preceding document and mentioned in n. 1 thereto.
  [2] There is a copy of this telegram in FO 115/2461, pp. 158-59, PRO.

From the Diary of Colonel House

[New York] April 9, 1918.

I have had a miserable time since this diary was broken off. I had fever the night of the 31st and all during the following day, nausea and everything disagreeable that could happen to one.

The President came in repeatedly to sit by my bedside. I had arranged for him to see Sir William Wiseman Monday afternoon and he hoped to bring him to my bedroom so we might talk matters over together, but, unfortunately, both high fever and the state of my stomach prevented. It has been definitely arranged for Wiseman to go to Europe at once. Reading objected, but the President agrees with me that he should go, and while I cannot use the President's name to the Ambassador, I have pressed it upon him as my desire until Reading was compelled to yield. I had to promise to look out for him during Sir William's absence, and he was finally content when he was told that he could keep in touch with me through Gordon as closely as he had through Sir William.

The message to Lloyd George turned out just as planned. He gave out to the press the cable that Reading sent him, practically as it was written.[1] The President was delighted. He remarked, "that pockets Mr. Lloyd George for the moment." I told him it not only pocketed Lloyd George, but it pocketed Mr. Roosevelt, General Wood and a few other critics. I was not well enough to feel happy over anything, but if I could have been braced up, the success of this maneuver would have done so. It is in these ways that I constantly try to help and protect the President, and he appreciates such things keenly. He shows it in every way possible, and I could not ask for greater consideration.

I got out of bed on Wednesday but was miserable all the week. The President would not go to the theater a single night, although he usually goes two or three times. I do not believe this was wholly on my account, for I went to bed so early that his remaining added but little to my pleasure.

He wrote something on his speech almost every night and we would then talk it over. He would come in with the speech in sections to discuss it. He made such eliminations as occurred to me as being advisable without argument. There were but few. He outlined the speech first in paragraphs and it was admirably done. Each paragraph was afterwards enlarged. We agreed that it should be short, and that it should leave the door open for peace and yet strike a note that the German Military Party would clearly understand. We both hoped that what he said about our meeting force with force would allay something of the panicy feeling in England and France. I notice by the press dispatches that it has done so.

The President received a Greek lady[2] who very much desired him to send a message to Venizelos. She thought Greece had been neglected and that the Greeks felt the slight. The President asked what I thought of sending a message to Venizelos upon the anniversary of our entering the war, saying that the newest republic sent greetings to the oldest western nation, etc. etc. I thought it would seem like dragging it in by the heels. I wondered whether he could not use Veniselos' birthday as a pretext if it should happen to fall in the near future. We looked in Who's Who and found he

[1] See the extract from the House Diary printed at March 29, 1918; also Lord Reading to D. Lloyd George, March 30, 1918 (second telegram of that date), n. 1.
[2] Wilson had met the Greek-American author and journalist, Demetra Vaka (Mrs. Kenneth) Brown at the White House on April 3, 1918. He had just written to thank her for sending him a copy of her book, Demetra Vaka, *In the Heart of German Intrigue* (Boston and New York, 1918): "I shall look forward with the greatest interest and pleasure to reading it just so soon as I can command a little leisure for the purpose." WW to Demetra Vaka Brown, April 1, 1918, TLS (Letterpress Books, WP, DLC).

was born in 1864 but it gave no date. He then called his office and asked them to find from the Greek Legation the date of Venizelos' birth. Strangely enough, no one knew. Irving Hoover was finally appealed to, and in order to beat the State Department and the Executive Offices, he took the trouble, after exhausting every other resource, to telephone a Greek newspaper in New York where he found that Venizelos was born in January, the third I think. This closed that avenue. Before we finally decided upon a method of procedure, a cable came from Venizelos himself congratulating the President upon the United States' entry in the war.[3] The President thought it a very strange coincidence—something almost miraculous. I suggested that the Greek lady was a very clever personage and seeing that he hesitated to send the message without some proper excuse, she probably sent a cable to Venizelos, or had the Legation do so, suggesting his action. The President finally accepted this theory rather than that of a miracle or coincidence.

A message came from King George apropos of the anniversary.[4] I suggested the form of the President's reply, which he accepted.[5] I thought the State Department should answer such cables for him. He replied that there was no one there to do it. This is largely his fault because he does not keep in touch with them or use them as he should.

There was an intimation from the French quarter that the French were sensitive because the President had sent a cable to Haig congratulating him upon holding the lind [line] and had said nothing about the French. The President had a weary smile and asked what should be done. I suggested that he use Foch's appointment as Generalissimo as the occasion to congratulate the French, saying something about their courage etc. This he did,[6] and seemed much relieved with such an easy way out. . . .

One night, I think it was Saturday, we were sitting around playing games. Someone suggested getting out the ouija board. This was done and Mrs. Wilson and her brother tried to see what success they would have. It was a rather remarkable demonstration, but it did not convince me. I observed afterward that those using it should be blindfolded. A message came from what purported to be a soldier in France. He gave his name as Lieutenant Robert Fisher, of a certain infantry regiment, claiming that he knew miss Helen Bones,

[3] E. Venizélos to WW, April 5, 1918.

[4] George V to WW, April 5, 1918, printed as an Enclosure with Lord Reading to WW, April 5, 1918.

[5] WW to George V, April 6, 1918.

[6] Wilson did so in his messages to Poincaré and Clemenceau: WW to R. Poincaré, April 5, 1918, and WW to G. Clemenceau, April 8, 1918. Wilson did not send a new message to Foch at this time.

and that the message was for the President. It was, "please send us food, men and guns as rapidly as possible." He also sent a message to "Colonel House" which read "God bless him. Ask him to get well soon." This in view of the fact that I was sick would have been more interesting if the operators had been blindfolded.

On sunday afternoon the President dropped into my bedroom to see me. Mrs. Wilson soon followed, then came McAdoo, Mrs. McAdoo, and while they were there Dr. Grayson brought in Ned McLean of the Washington Post, who was not shown into the room until the others left.

McLean wished to say that the Post and Cincinnati Enquirer were at the disposal of the Administration if we would use them. I promised to see what could be done. I have a notion to write an editorial which, if they will publish it, will put them as safely in our pocket as Lloyd George placed himself when he sent the message prepared by Reading and Wiseman.

I had the President, Mrs. Wilson, Dr. Grayson and the entire household to oppose when I announced I would leave on Monday morning for New York. I was confident that getting home and the change would do me good. They were confident that I should remain there another week. However, I felt as if I could not stand being away from home longer and I determined to go come what may.

I was right in my conclusion for I improved from the moment I left Washington and I am feeling better today than since my relapse.

I showed the President while in Washington the lurid advertisements which nearly all the papers are carrying on the forthcoming book, "The Real Colonel House," which is syndicated throughout the country.[7] I told him they were advertising me like a brand of soap. There is nothing in the book to warrant these extravagant, full-paged notices which are appearing in The Times, World and other papers throughout the country.

I have received many cables from Balfour and others while in Washington, all of them being parts of the record.

Lord Reading called Gordon today in some excitement and asked him to come to the Embassy. He had a despatch from his Government concerning our agreement as to placing our man power on the Western Front.[8] I advised Reading, through Gordon, not to ask for an appointment with the President until tomorrow and not to see him until after he had received a letter from me which I will write today and which will become a part of the record. This letter will explain the controversy which has arisen.

[7] That is, Arthur Douglas Howden Smith, *The Real Colonel House* (New York, 1918). It was published by the George H. Doran Co.
[8] D. Lloyd George and A. J. Balfour to Lord Reading, April 9, 1918.

Two Letters to Joseph Patrick Tumulty

Dear Tumulty: [The White House, c. April 10, 1918]

I do not want to be drawn into this.[1] I think the agitation against teaching the German language is ridiculous and childish, but I would have to write a considerable essay to put my views in the right light and I would like to know if you can think of a proper and courteous way in which I could reply to questions of this sort without getting involved.   The President.

[1] Wilson enclosed Carl Eben Stromquist to WW, April 4, 1918, TLS (WP, DLC). Stromquist, Professor of Mathematics at the University of Wyoming and a former instructor and preceptor at Princeton University during Wilson's presidency of that institution, requested Wilson's "personal view as to whether a universal elimination of the German language from our high schools and colleges is advisable and would be of any aid in the successful prosecution of the war or in any other way would be advantageous to the country."

Dear Tumulty: [The White House, c. April 10, 1918]

Of course, Mr. Brady either was misunderstood or he went much further than he was justified in going.[1] I did not say that motion pictures would do more than any single thing to win the war. That would be ridiculous. But it is true in the sense explained in this memorandum in the extract from the Acting Secretary of War's letter that moving pictures have been permitted in the camps on Sunday.[2] I do not believe that there is any sufficient objection to this if the pictures are proper in themselves, and this method of handling the matter suggests itself to me, if you approve of it and are willing, namely, in a letter to Bowlby you correct, as at my request, the overstatement of Mr. Brady and then send him the quotation from the Acting Secretary of War's letter.

The President.

TL (WP, DLC).
[1] Wilson was responding to the White House Staff to WW, c. April 10, 1918, T MS (WP, DLC). This memorandum summarized the later portions of a lengthy correspondence between Wilson and the Rev. Dr. Harry Laity Bowlby, most of which is attached to the memorandum in WP, DLC. Bowlby, Princeton 1901, was at this time general secretary of the Lord's Day Alliance of the United States. He and his colleagues were much exercised over alleged violations of the Sabbath in military training camps, in particular the showing of motion pictures on Sunday. In his most recent letter (H. L. Bowlby to WW, April 5, 1918, TLS [WP, DLC]), Bowlby had asserted that William Augustus Brady, president of the National Association of the Motion Picture Industry and chairman of its committee to cooperate with the Committee on Public Information, had publicly made approximately the following remarks: "He made the clean-cut statement that you told him a few days ago that you believed the motion pictures would do more than any one single thing to win the War, and that Sunday motion picture shows had the approval of the Federal Government. He urged the Committee [of the New York State legislature] to be as broad-minded as the President of the United States and tried in every conceivable way to leave the impression that you were for the legalizing of the Sunday motion picture show business."
[2] In response to a request from Wilson (WW to B. Crowell, March 6, 1918, CCL [WP, DLC]), Crowell had made the following comment: "I desire to state that the policy of the War Department with regard to Sunday amusement is, with the exception of danc-

ing, that any form of Sunday amusement that is properly supervised by the division authorities and sent out by the Commission on Training Camp Activities, is to be encouraged. It is found from actual experience that where such innocent amusements are discouraged by local authorities, the physical and moral welfare of the troops of such division training camps has suffered." B. Crowell to WW, March 18, 1918, TLS (WP, DLC).

To John Sanford Cohen

Personal.

My dear Major Cohen: [The White House] 10 April, 1918

I know you will pardon my delay in replying to your letter of April first.[1] There are certain things that refuse to be postponed and I have to follow the line of most imperative demands on my time.

I thank you sincerely for the frank candor and earnestness of your statement about the Senatorial race.[2] Through Mr. Woolley and others, whom I have seen, the whole situation has been laid before me very fully.

And I think that you will bear me out in the statement that my course with regard to the situation is justified by all the circumstances. The circumstances are these: Mr. Harris has openly entered the race. I have the utmost confidence in him. Everything that he has done has justified that confidence. Nobody would excuse me for not standing by a man I believe in, and I think it must be the common judgment that to divide the field would be folly. I did not suggest Mr. Harris's candidacy. I would not feel at liberty to direct the course of events in any way, but when a man I so thoroughly believe in is the first to get into the field, I must in candor say to all my friends that it is the worst conceivable strategy to allow any doubt to remain as to the support he is to get and to leave the question open whether somebody else is not either now or eventually to be substituted for him.

I am sure you will understand that I am taking this very direct way of putting the case merely because I haven't time to elaborate it. I know I can depend upon your knowledge of politics and your keen appreciation of facts to write between the lines I have dictated all the shadings and modulations which they lack, and I hope you will take it as an evidence of my very sincere respect for you that I thus lay bare my whole thought before you.

Cordially and sincerely yours,   Woodrow Wilson

TLS (Letterpress Books, WP, DLC).
    [1] It is missing.
    [2] Cohen had undoubtedly objected to Wilson's support of William J. Harris, as had been suggested in WW to E. T. Brown, March 29, 1918.

From Gutzon Borglum

New York, April 10, 1918.

Have just received a letter from Marshall[1] suggesting a conference regarding certain allegations contained in my confidential
report to you. Kindly let me know if you wish me to aid him in this
matter.   Gutzon Borglum.

T telegram (WP, DLC).
[1] That is, H. Snowden Marshall.

To Gutzon Borglum

The White House, Apr 11 18

Hope you will render Marshall any and every assistance he asks
for   Woodrow Wilson

T telegram (G. Borglum Papers, DLC).

From the Diary of Colonel House

[New York] April 10, 1918.

Up to one o'clock today the President had not made an appointment with the British Ambassador. Reading is leaving for Chicago
at five o'clock and Frank Polk and Gordon are having nervous
prostration over it. I have tried to calm them, saying the President
would certainly see Reading, but that he was irritated because it
was necessary and that he would delay it as long as possible. This
proved to be true for he saw Reading at two o'clock.

They had what Reading considered only a fairly satisfactory conference. He sent for Gordon immediately and with his help framed
a cable to his Government explaining the President's attitude. He
is to give Gordon a paraphrase of this cable to send me and it will
be attached to the diary. Reading is using Gordon as liaison officer
between himself and me in exactly the way he used Wiseman. This
indeed, was our understanding when I insisted that Wiseman should
go to England, to which Reading strongly objected until I proposed
the plan of using Gordon in his stead.

Lord Reading to Arthur James Balfour

Washington. April 10th, 1918.

No. 1526. Very urgent. Very secret,

Your telegrams Nos. 2017 and 2049.[1]

I have just seen the President and have placed substance of your communications and views before him. We had some conversation about request made by you on March 30th and my report of his compliance with it. I found President rather disinclined to answer specific points although he was emphatic in his assurances to me that whatever it was possible for him to do to help the Allies in present situation would assuredly be done but that he had to consult his military advisers and be guided by them as to details. He informed me Secretary Baker was on the High Seas travelling home and that immediately upon his arrival President thought it would be advisable for me to see Secretary Baker with President.

President showed extreme reluctance to express any decided view on questions raised in your telegrams and I drew the inference that he wished to avoid saying anything which might be reported to or used in London or Paris until he had had the opportunity of conferring with Secretary of State for War (group undecypherable) present discussions in Europe and knew General Pershing's views. In my opinion President did not wish even to appear to give a decision without waiting for arrival of Secetary of State for War. Consequently I did not press for any further answer and have no doubt I took the right course notwithstanding great urgency of matter as represented by you. I have no doubt but that President will act in accordance with my original reports to you. I expect but do not know that his military advisers see objection to brigading of so many infantrymen and machine gun units with British and French Divisions because they fear this will retard as it probably must formation of an American Army and American Divisions. President will form his own conclusions after he has heard Mr. Baker and will issue instructions accordingly.

I beg of you not to regard this report as indicating a change of view of President. I see nothing to indicate although I agree that I am not able to give you a definite confirmatory statement.

It is highly important that nothing of my conversation with President or my inference from it or views that I express to you should leak out.

Misunderstanding should be left to be cleared up by President Wilson direct with General Pershing doubtless with the assistance of Secretary Baker and it may be General Bliss. Forgive this warning. I give it for reason that otherwise President's task would be rendered more difficult if he wished to act after concluding, if he did conclude, that there had been some misapprehension in General Pershing's mind but I need not dilate upon importance of this aspect to you.[2]

T telegram (W. Wiseman Papers, CtY).
[1] A. J. Balfour to Lord Reading, April 9, 1918 (second telegram of that date), and n. 1 thereto.
[2] Lord Reading to A. J. Balfour, April 10, 1918, T telegram (FO 115/2461, p. 173, PRO):
"My tel. No. 1526.
"I am convinced that representations to same effect as yours and Prime Minister's to me had reached President before I saw him today from American sources, including I believe Secretary Baker.
"President placed much reliance upon Supreme War Council and said their decisions would have greatest weight with him. I infer that he means to lean upon the Council to support him if he has to override views of Pershing."

To Robert Lansing, with Enclosures

My dear Mr. Secretary,   The White House. 11 April, 1918.

This affair excites my deep sympathy and indignation, as I have no doubt it does yours. Is there no chance of our sending assistance which will serve to protect these people in the future? I should heartily approve of doing so, and after all considerable interests are affected,—the whole future power of Germany on the western coasts of Africa.   Faithfully Yours,   W.W.

Perhaps England could spare a ship of sufficient force.

WWTLI (SDR, RG 59, 763.72/9594, DNA).

ENCLOSURE   I

Monrovia. April 10, 1918.

German submarine now in harbor Monrovia. Commander sent President Liberia[1] following letter this morning: "Sir: I have not the wish to do unnecessary damage to the Liberian people being sure that you were driven into the war against your true interest therefore I send you back those prisoners I made beating your armed ship PRESIDENT [HOWARD]. In the same time I want to draw your attention to the fact that the capital of Liberia is at present helpless under German guns. Like many other allies of England and France you are not being supported by them in the moment of the most critical danger. If the wireless and cable station[s] of Monrovia do not at once cease their work I shall regret being obliged to open fire on them. If you wish to avoid this you will have to send on to me a boat under a flag truce and declare that you consent to stop them yourself. Gercke,[2] servant, Gercke, Kapitan Lieutenant and Commandant S.M.U. Kreuzer U." Liberian Government has not yet given its final answer to these demands but in any case it looks as if the wireless and cable stations at Monrovia will be put out of commission accordingly. This is probably the last message I will be able to send the Department. It is urgently requested that assistance be sent at earliest possible moment.   Bundy.[3]

[1] Daniel Edward Howard.
[2] Not further identified.
[3] Richard Carlton Bundy, Secretary of Legation and Chargé d'Affaires at Monrovia.

E N C L O S U R E   I I

Monrovia. April 10, 1918.

Liberian Government agreed to stop operation of wireless and cable stations and in reply to it's communications Commander of submarine makes following demands:

"Extreme urgence, dernier ultimatium. Have the honour to acknowledge the receipt of your answer to my note from this morning. Being sure of your earnest good will to comply with my demands I will not open fire on the cable and wireless stations which I was in the act of doing when just in time your boat was sent out. I am glad to be able to do so because my gun fire might have hurt innocent people. In answer for this I must put to you the following demands: 1, the French flag is to be removed from its place shown to your commissioners; 2, fire is to be set on all houses belonging to the wireless and cable stations, the apparatus of each stations to be destroyed; 3, one and two to be executed within one hour after your commissioners have reached the shore. I have the honor to be, sir, your obedient servant, Gercke, Kapitan Lieutenant and Commandant S.M.U. Kreuzer U."

Liberian Government has not yet given its final answer to these demands but in any case it looks as if the wireless and cable stations at Monrovia will be put out of commission accordingly. This is probably the last message I will be able to send the Department. It is urgently requested that assistance be sent at the earliest possible moment.   Bundy.

E N C L O S U R E   I I I

Monrovia April 10, 1918

Liberian Government's final reply to demands of submarine commander were considered unsatisfactory by him. At about four this afternoon submarine bombarded French wireless station rendering it inoperative. As result bombardment two Liberian person killed and two wounded. Submarine is now engaging merchant steamer off Monrovia, result as yet not known. No public disorder. Believe submarine will return to complete demolition of cable and wireless station.   Bundy.

E N C L O S U R E   I V

Monrovia, Liberia. April 10, 1918.

Until now, eleven p.m., no naval assistance having reached Monrovia the Secretary of State[1] has just expressed, to Allied representatives, the opinion as representing public sentiment, that the republic of Liberia has not yet received that aid which has been counted upon in such a crisis as confronted the government today.
                                            Bundy.

TC telegrams (SDR, RG 59, 763.72/9594, DNA).
 [1] Charles Dunbar Burgess King.

From Robert Lansing, with Enclosure

Returned with comment
that paper contained
nothing new RL 4/12/18

My dear Mr. President: Washington April 11, 1918.
I have received a communication from the French Ambassador—a translation of which I enclose. I have not made any reply but do not find anything in the facts presented which influence me to change our present policy relative to Japanese intervention in Siberia. Will you be good enough to let me have your opinion in regard to these representations of the French Government?
                Faithfully yours,   Robert Lansing.

TLS (SDR, RG 59, 861.00/1464½, DNA).

E N C L O S U R E

Translation

Embassy of the French Republic to
the United States.

Mr. Secretary of State,   Washington, April 8, 1918.

Referring to the notes which I have previously had the honor to address to Your Excellency on the subject of a Japanese action in Siberia, and in particular to that of the 14th of last month.[1] I deem it my duty to let you know that fresh and highly important information on that question has just come to me from my Government.

The French Naval Attaché at Tokyo[2] received word from the Japanese General Staff that by reason of the murder of three Japanese merchants in Vladivostock by Maximalists[3] or Russian brigands it had been decided to land two companies of seamen at that port.

On the other hand, according to the same information the Bolshevik troops which drove back the Russian general Semenoff have been reinforced first by four thousand prisoners and two guns and quite recently by five thousand nine hundred prisoners armed with 24 machine guns and 10 field guns. Six trains carrying prisoners to the East passed through Chita between the 28th of March and the 2nd of April. The Cossacks and Chinese troops on the border could not withstand an attack.

There were 1800 prisoners at Irkoutsk in the early days of March; they now number 6000 and more than 10,000 are on the way to that city. One thousand cars, a large quantity of rifles and ammunition and military automobiles have also been brought there.

According to a Russian officer 60 trains of prisoners from the West are now on their way to Irkoutsk. One carrying arms has just arrived there. Arrangements have been made to organize two army corps consisting of Austro-German prisoners.

The Japanese General Staff looked as ready to act as ever to our naval attaché; but public opinion seems to be wavering and opposition to the expedition grows as the resistance to be met looms more serious. As for the Government it still holds its decision contingent on the United States Government's adhesion and promise of financial and industrial support.

In the opinion of the Minister of Foreign Affairs of the Republic[4] these reports are worthy of very earnest consideration. The Japa-

[1] The Enclosure printed with RL to WW, March 18, 1918.
[2] R. Brylinski.
[3] That is, Bolsheviks.
[4] That is, Stéphen Jean-Marie Pichon.

nese, with their excellent means of obtaining intelligence and clear headedness furnish us with data which are considered by my Government to be extremely grave. Consequently the longer the intervention which continues to be the one effective mode of action is delayed, the more difficult will it be of execution, while its purpose will be thereby impaired.

The various reports at hand indicate that Japan regards it as its duty to start today in Vladivostock an action of a personal character in the defense of its own interests, without any guarantee to the Allies or Russia; this would seem to be a departure that may draw it away from us and nearer to the Germans.

Nothing final has yet happened however, and encouragement from the United States would make it possible to carry out the plan, with its attendant pledges and guarantees which the British Ambassador and I have taken the liberty of most urgently commending to the approval of the United States Government.

The American, French and Italian Ambassadors assembled at Vologda[5] are under the impression that the Maximalists themselves might be induced to accept the Japanese intervention which the Ambassadors admit is necessary to combat Germany and make a reorganization of Russia possible. The Maximalists' call on the allied military missions for their aid in reconstituting a Russian army[6] is from that viewpoint, a significant symptom, notwithstanding the precautions and reservations with which the suggestion ought to be received. After consultation the three Ambassadors with the assistance of their military advisers and of Captain Garstin of the British Army[7] drew up on the 3d of this month an official statement the text of which was no doubt directly sent to Your Excellency but which, for greater safety, I deem it my duty to reproduce hereinbelow. That paper, of a very confidential character, runs as follows:

"The three Ambassadors have unanimously found: 1st that Japanese intervention is more than ever necessary to combat Germany;

2nd, that it will only work its full effect if it bears the character

---

[5] That is, David R. Francis, Joseph Noulens, and Pietro Paolo Tomasi, Marchese della Torretta, the Italian Chargé d'Affaires.

[6] For accounts of the informal and inconclusive negotiations between Trotsky and the Allied military representatives in Moscow upon which this statement is based, see Kennan, *The Decision to Intervene*, pp. 112-23, and Ullman, *Intervention and the War* pp. 135-36. A good summary is Ullman's: "He [Trotsky] made no single or comprehensive request for assistance. Rather, he seems to have more or less thought out loud about the possibilities of co-operation; so eager were his listeners—particularly [Jacques] Sadoul—for such a course that they amplified and elaborated Trotsky's vague conjectures into concrete proposals." *Ibid.*, p. 136.

[7] Dennis Garstin, a cavalry captain serving at this time as an assistant to R. H. Bruce Lockhart.

of an inter-allied participation and if the Bolshevik Government is prevailed on to accept it, as grave risks would otherwise be taken;

3d, that allied personalities who have access to Trotsky are under the impression that he could probably be induced to accept Japanese intervention.

4, that the Ambassadors have deemed it expedient to maintain, by reason of those facts, the adhesion on principle given by the Head of Missions and military attachés to cooperation in organizing the Russian Army against Germany with the reservation that final adhesion will be put off until the drafts of decrees shall have been examined.

Informal negotiations will be entered into with a view to obtaining guarantees as to the true disposition of the Bolshevik Government toward the Allies.

These guarantees will consist in the acceptance of Japanese intervention and the granting to the Allied citizens and subjects of at least the same advantages, privileges and indemnities granted by Russia to German subjects by the Brest Treaty of Peace."

On the other hand the detailed reports received from Col. Pichon by the Minister of Foreign Affairs of the Republic show that a Siberian Government which would restore order with the desired help of Japanese troops could easily be constituted. According to that high officer Russian opinion abroad and even in Russia has made considerable headway in that direction and would quite cheerfully accept the coming of the Japanese if preceded by a categorical declaration of the Allies and accompanied by an American representation.

There is no doubt that a cooperation of the United States even though it were purely nominal in the contemplated action would assume in the eyes of the Russian a capital importance as being the token of the absence of any intention that did not harmonize with their interests. To the Japanese it would stand as the best confirmation of that American approval without which the Mikado's Government, until it just now took the purely local measure at Vladivostock where it acted furthermore in concert with the English, has refused to take any broad action.

The events that are unfolding along our front are continually showing how timely such a diversion would prove in every respect, for from all the information that comes to us it appears that the Central Empires which are preparing a renewed effort against our troops are in position to draw from the Eastern front several hundred thousand men if they foresee no danger on that side. Now no such danger can come to them from the demobilized Russian troops or the Russian people who thrown on their own resources will remain absolutely passive whereas they might be led to react if they felt that a powerful military force stood ready to come to their assistance. The experience of the first few months has shown to Russia what she was to expect from the Germans and there is ground for a hope that she would rally if tangible succor were extended to her.

It seems to my Government, in any event, that the attempt should be made by all means and I am instructed by it again to point out to Your Excellency the importance and urgency of immediately adopting measures to which, owing to the existing circumstances, the American Ambassador to Russia has just adhered. From all that we hear they will be adopted without a doubt if President Wilson so wills, and the Government of the Republic would be most grateful to him if he would, taking these new considerations into account, consent to reexamine the question with a view to the earliest possible solution.

Be pleased to accept etc.   Jusserand

T MS (SDR, RG 59, 861.00/1464½, DNA).

From Edward Riley Stettinius

Dear Mr. President: Washington, D. C. April 11, 1918

I received yesterday the official announcement of my appointment as Second Assistant Secretary of War, and I hasten to thank you for the confidence which the appointment implies and to assure you that I will do everything in my power to prove worthy of that confidence.

Since I have been in Washington I have frequently wished that I could pay my respects to you, but loaded as you are with such a weight of care, I have been reluctant to even suggest that you give a moment of your time to me. I would of course consider it an honor if I were permitted to thank you in person, for your trust in me, and to pledge you my loyalty.

Your obedient servant, Edw R Stettinius.

ALS (WP, DLC).

From William Cox Redfield

My dear Mr. President: Washington April 11, 1918.

In view of the report of the Senate Committee,[1] I think I should place in your hands the enclosed correspondence.

The house of J. H. Williams and Company is my own old concern with which I was actively connected for twenty years. The difficulties under which they have labored in connection with the forgings for the Liberty and other motors for our airplane program are familiar to me.[2] They are sufficient in themselves to have caused many weeks of delay.

The trouble with tolerances, mentioned in the last paragraph, is also a familiar and costly fault. In this connection, as the matter has been one I have from time to time been discussing with Dr. Stratton, who is a member of the Advisory Board for Aeronautics, I venture to hand you copy of letter I have sent him today commenting on the facts.[3]

There is also sent confidential copy of letter from Mr. A. A. Landon to Mr. H. E. Coffin of October 18, 1917 commenting then upon the situation in connection with the aircraft program.[4]

The whole difficulty in this motor delay has been one with which for many years I have been familiar. It arises from the fact that the men in authority behind these motors were not manufacturers but engineers. I think I can say from my own general knowledge of the situation that there is no reason why, if this matter had been in the hands of trained producers, the motor should not have been out in quantities weeks ago.

On the other hand there is every reason to believe that if and when the changes can be stopped and quantity production insisted upon and rigidly adhered to, the motors can be turned out in any needed quantity and that the general result, if this is done, will be if looked at over the whole period from the inception of the motor to its close, one of which American industry can justly be proud.

Yours very truly,   William C. Redfield

TLS (WP, DLC).

[1] The Senate Committee on Military Affairs, on April 10, released a brief report on aircraft production as part of its ongoing investigation of the War Department. While commenting favorably upon the Signal Corps' training schools and on the production of training airplanes, the report was very critical of delays in the production of the Liberty engine and of combat airplanes. It recommended that oversight over the production of aircraft and engines be removed entirely from the Signal Corps and placed in the hands of a single executive officer, appointed by the President and responsible to him. This officer should be assisted by a "corps of the best aircraft engineers and designers possible to obtain, both European and American." Somewhat paradoxically, the committee also recommended that "no man who has any near or remote interest in a company manufacturing airplanes or engines should be permitted to act as advisor or be in authority." Senators Morris Sheppard, Henry L. Myers, and William F. Kirby submitted a minority report which defended the Signal Corps and its aircraft program and said that much had been accomplished in a very short time in the face of great difficulties. 65th Cong., 2d sess., Senate Report 380, Parts 1 and 2. The full text of both reports appeared also in the *New York Times*, April 11, 1918.

[2] Redfield here refers to James Harvey Williams to WCR, April 9, 1918, TLS (WP, DLC), also enclosed in Redfield's letter.

[3] WCR to S. W. Stratton, April 11, 1918, CCL (WP, DLC).

[4] Archer A. Landon to H. E. Coffin, Oct. 18, 1917, TCL (WP, DLC). Landon, vice-president of the American Radiator Co. and a member of the Aircraft Production Board, expressed concern that the board was purely advisory in nature and had no power to

get things done. He believed that only an organization directly responsible to the Secretary of War or the Secretary of the Navy, or to both, with real power to implement its recommendations, could carry out an effective program of aircraft production.

From the Diary of Colonel House

April 11, 1918.

The Archbishop of York, ex-President Taft, Senator Root, Presidents Lowell and Mezes came to lunch today. The discussion during the main part of the meal was largely about the Civil War, its causes and the attitude of Great Britain and her statesmen toward the belligerents. Interesting as it was, I was compelled to break in when luncheon was over in order to start the discussion for which I had called them together. I wished to harmonize the divergent views of Taft, Lowell[,] Root and the British group with the President's as how best to prevent future wars.

I read them an extract from the President's letter on this subject[1] as well as a letter from Lansing.[2] There was general disagreement with Lansing. Root agreed with him as far as he went but thought he left the matter in a state where it is now and was before the war. Lansing's idea is that it is only necessary to democratize the world, and that the democracies will not war upon one another. This is a fallacy which I made clear by recalling recent wars in which democracies have engaged. I cited the Fashoda incident which a few years ago brought Great Britain and France to the verge of war. The only thing that prevented it was the menace of Germany in the background.

None of them altogether agreed with the President. They thought he did not go far enough. The final conclusion was that Root should draw up a memorandum embracing three proposals:

1. That every nation was interested in war, no matter how small or in what quarter of the Globe.

2. That some machinery should be set up during peace times through which, at the threat of war, a conference of nations could be held for the purpose of making an attempt to stop it.

3. Some machinery establishing a court or bureau of arbitration to which cobtroversial [controversial] matters might be referred.

The Archbishop was to receive a degree at Columbia University and was compelled to leave before we had finished our conference.

If this war should end today it would leave but three first class powers in the world: Great Britain, Germany and the United States, and if any two of these powers should suddenly war with one another, it would practically be impossible to stop them. Therefore, in working out a plan for a league to enforce peace, or a similar organization, it is necessary to take into consideration this possibility.

I am trying to keep the threads of this subject all in my hands so that nothing will be done contrary to the President's wishes, and no agitation started that might ripen into a controversy.

[1] WW to EMH, March 22, 1918.
[2] RL to EMH, April 8, 1918, *FR-LP*, II, 118-20.

To Otto H. Butz[1]

My dear Mr. Butz: The White House 12 April, 1918

I appreciate very highly the courtesy of the officers and directors of the Chicago Society of the Friends of German Democracy in sending me the beautifully engrossed copy of the resolutions passed at the mass meeting of March fifth, at Orchestra Hall, Chicago.[2] Such action is indeed heartening and reassuring.

You may be sure, too, that I sympathize and shall cooperate with every effort to see to it that the loyal residents of the United States of German birth or descent are given genuine proof of the sincerity of our institutions. It distresses me beyond measure that suspicion should attach to those who do not deserve it and that acts of injustice and even of violence should be based upon the suspicion. The way to honor and vindicate the free government of the United States is to use in all circumstances the machinery of justice and never to permit excesses of passion which can only discredit a free people.
            Cordially and sincerely yours,   Woodrow Wilson[3]

TLS (ICHi).
    [1] President of the Chicago branch of the Friends of German Democracy.
    [2] "A message of greeting and protestation of loyalty upon the part of the audience was sent President Wilson by unanimous vote." *Chicago Daily Tribune*, March 6, 1918.
    [3] This letter, in whole or in part, was widely printed in the newspapers.

To Louis de Sadeleer

My dear M. Sadeleer: [The White House] 12 April, 1918

The sad news borne by your letter of April ninth[1] grieves Mrs. Wilson and me most deeply. It is with the keenest regret that we learn of the death of your son. It must be a great consolation to you that since the beginning of the war he has devoted himself with such single-hearted loyalty to the cause of his country and of mankind, but I know that even the pride you must feel in him does not suffice to remove the tragical sorrow, and Mrs. Wilson joins me in expressing the sincerest sympathy.
                    Cordially yours,   Woodrow Wilson

TLS (Letterpress Books, WP, DLC).
¹ It is missing, but it told of the death of his son, Étienne de Sadeleer, killed at Amiens, France, on March 26 by a bomb dropped from a German airplane. *New York Times,* April 5, 1918, and June 30, 1918, VI, 15.

To Edward Riley Stettinius

My dear Mr. Stettinius: [The White House] 12 April, 1918

Thank you very much for your letter of yesterday, and allow me to assure you that it gave me a great deal of pleasure to have an opportunity to show my confidence in you.

I shall look forward with pleasure to some early opportunity of meeting you, for I like to have the personal touch of the men that I am working with, and feel very much cheated sometimes because circumstances make it so difficult for me to have it.

Cordially and sincerely yours,   Woodrow Wilson

TLS (Letterpress Books, WP, DLC).

To William Schley Howard¹

My dear Mr. Howard: [The White House] 12 April, 1918

Your letter just received disappoints me very seriously indeed and I very much regret it.²

Sincerely yours,   Woodrow Wilson

TLS (Letterpress Books, WP, DLC).
¹ Democratic congressman from Georgia since 1911.
² It is missing, but it informed Wilson that Howard had decided to enter the Georgia primary contest for the Senate seat then held by Thomas W. Hardwick. Howard had leaked the news of his decision to the press on April 11 and had officially announced it on April 13. *Atlanta Constitution,* April 12 and 14, 1918.
Howard had had an interview on this subject with Wilson at the White House at 4:30 p.m. on March 29. Wilson had tried to dissuade Howard from entering the primary, undoubtedly on the ground that his doing so would divide the anti-Hardwick vote and thus permit that Senator to remain in office. For the only account of the interview, see WW to W. S. Howard, April 20, 1918, n. 1.

To Simon Julius Lubin

My dear Sir: [The White House] 12 April, 1918

After you were kind enough to send me the papers which I requested you would send me at our interview, I again took the matter up, as I did after Mr. Bell's visit, and I must frankly say that it seems to me that the Federal Government is doing everything that it can along the very lines of your own suggestions. There is no legal authority for such internment as you suggest except in the case of alien enemies, and the proportion of alien enemies among the class referred to is, of course, very small.

I can only again assure you of the cooperation of the Federal Government in every way that it is possible and legitimate that it should cooperate, for our interest is no less keen and active than is yours and that of those associated with you.

With much respect,   Sincerely yours,   Woodrow Wilson

TLS (Letterpress Books, WP, DLC).

To Joseph Edward Davies

Personal

My dear Davies: [The White House] 12 April, 1918

Indeed, the fight in Wisconsin was a good fight and I honor you for the spirit in which it was conducted.[1] It grieves me that we are to lose you here in Washington. I was looking forward with so much satisfaction to the part that you might play in the Senate, but I must not let regret play any part in connection with our association with one another. You may be sure that you will not be for a moment forgotten by any of your friends here and that we shall follow you with affection.

Personally, I do not feel that Lenroot was at all a satisfactory choice. I think his early record, as indicated by his votes on the McLemore resolution, the armed neutrality matter, and the rest, showed a very serious weakness, and there is no telling at what crisis such a weakness may come out, but I accept the result like a sport and shall hope that he will disappoint my fears.

All join me in warmest regards to you all. Do let me hear from you occasionally, and let me know what you are doing and planning.
                Cordially and faithfully yours,   Woodrow Wilson

TLS (Letterpress Books, WP, DLC).
[1] In the special election held on April 2, Irvine L. Lenroot was elected to the Senate with 163,980 votes. Davies received 148,714 votes; the Socialist candidate, Victor L. Berger, 110,487.

To Stockton Axson

Dear Stock: The White House 12 April, 1918

The "Educational Secretary" of the Southern Sociological Congress, Mr. J. E. McCulloch,[1] has written me telling me of the meeting which is to be held at Birmingham, Alabama, beginning next Sunday, the fourteenth, and continuing four days, at which he

In the frontline trenches of the Rainbow Division, March, 1918

Marshal Ferdinand Foch

Alfred Milner, 1st Viscount Milner

David Franklin Houston

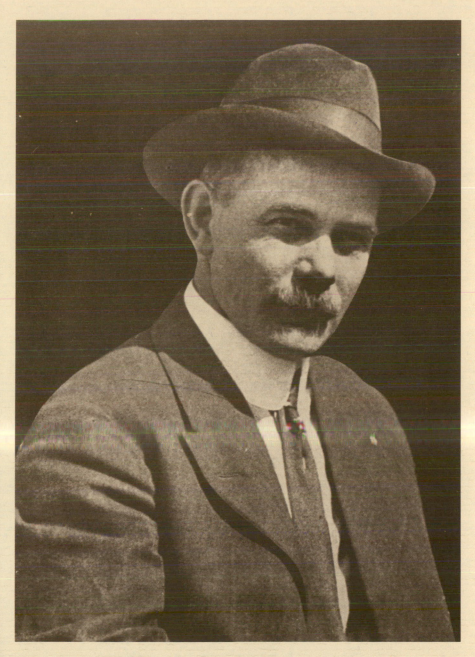

Gutzon Borglum

The National War Labor Board

The War Cabinet

Carrie Clinton Lane Chapman Catt

understands that you are to be one of the speakers as the representative of the Red Cross. He has asked me to send a message to the Congress, and I would so much rather send it by you than by anybody else that I am going to ask if you will not be kind enough to convey my warm personal greetings to the Congress and express my very sincere interest in the important conferences it is holding and my confident hope that the best sort of cooperation in the great common aims of the country at this time may issue out of those conferences.   Affectionately,   Woodrow Wilson

TLS (WC, NjP).
    [1] The Rev. James Edward McCulloch, a Methodist minister. The Southern Sociological Congress had been organized in 1912 under McCulloch's leadership as an agency for the discussion of southern urban and industrial problems and to promote social reform and religious liberalism. E. Charles Chatfield, "The Southern Sociological Congress: Organization of Uplift," *Tennessee Historical Quarterly*, XIX (Dec. 1960), 328-47, and "The Southern Sociological Congress: Rationale of Uplift," *ibid.*, XX (March 1961), 51-64.

From Robert Lansing

Dear Mr. President: Washington April 12, 1918.

I too have been very much concerned about the Liberian situation.

We communicated promptly with the British and French Governments and the Navy got in touch immediately with Admiral Sims. A despatch received yesterday from Mr. Page states that the Admiralty has informed Admiral Sims that assistance has been dispatched to Monrovia.[1] The Navy Department is of the opinion today that a British squadron has probably already arrived at Monrovia.

I am today asking the British and French Governments what protection they would be disposed to accord Liberia in the future. The British and French are undertaking to patrol the Western coast of Africa and it would seem as if they should be able to include Liberia in their patrol.

Admiral Benson advises me that it would be possible for Admiral Caperton to send a ship to Liberia but that there will be difficulties in maintaining a ship permanently owing to the question of coal supply. I shall not fail to keep you advised of the replies of the British and French when they are received.

With assurances of respect, etc., I am, my dear Mr. President,
                    Faithfully yours,   Robert Lansing.

TLS (WP, DLC).
    [1] WHP to RL, [April 11] 1918, *FR-WWS 1918*, 1, I, 742.

From Benedict Crowell, with Enclosure

Dear Mr. President: Washington. April 12, 1918.

Inclosed please find the preliminary report of the Committee on Aircraft Investigation.

Very truly yours,   Benedict Crowell

TLS (WP, DLC).

E N C L O S U R E

The President: Washington, April 12, 1918.

Your Committee appointed to make an investigation of the manufacturing program, distribution of contracts, and progress of work in the matter of aircraft and aircraft motors and accessories, and to submit any recommendations that may be suggested to the Committee in the course of its investigation, submits the following preliminary report:

There are two phases of the problem which has been submitted to us; first, the condition of work upon contracts already placed for aircraft, aircraft motors, and accessories, deliveries upon which have, as is widely known, been delayed, and the causes which lead to such delay; second, the inherent faults in the organization which need immediate correction to prevent a continuance of the present conditions.

In a later report we propose to embody our criticisms and comment in regard to the delays which have occurred in deliveries under existing contracts. Data bearing on this subject are still being collected. The Committee has called to its assistance engineers of prominence. Causes which have led to delay in deliveries are being run down. Such criticisms as we have to make and detailed information as to the status of work now on order will be contained in such later report. We think that some plain and inherent faults in organization call for prompt and decisive action. We are so convinced of this that we hope these faults will be corrected, as far as possible, by executive action without incurring the necessary delay of awaiting legislation. We are accordingly submitting this preliminary report, which has to do only with present and future conditions.

Aircraft are used by the two arms of the service,—the Army and the Navy. It is the belief of your Committee that eventually it will be desirable to make of the aircraft service a separate department entirely distinct from the Army and the Navy; but it is not believed that the time is yet ripe for this very radical change.

Proportionately, the demands of the Navy for aircraft are quite small compared with the demands of the Army. The Navy had an organization for production and construction at the time of our entrance into the war more nearly approximating a war footing than had the Army. It has therefore been able to handle its aviation program with an immediate success which the Army has found it impossible to achieve. For these reasons it is the opinion of the Committee that the situation as relates to the Navy had best be left alone.

In the Army, matters of aviation have been handled by the Signal Corps, with the result that there suddenly fell upon this quite minor division of the service a tremendous burden for which it was illy equipped. There was to be developed a new art for our country, and there were available very few men who had had any experience whatever in aviation and very little advanced scientific knowledge of the subject. There were many problems to be undertaken; such as the procurement of airplanes in large quantity; and the organizing of a division of the service to use these airplanes and to provide the facilities required, such as training schools, aerodromes, etc.; and all of this had to be carried on at a time when to accomplish it the Signal Corps had to be built up and augmented more than one-hundredfold.

There are two distinct problems in the air service, the first of which is the procurement and production of aircraft; the second of which is the handling of these machines for military purposes. It is our belief that the first of these can best be handled at this time by a civilian head. We are of the opinion that in the course of time, when courses in aviation will be a part of the military training at West Point, there will be available in the Army abundant material for the organization of a department capable of attending to all of the details of aircraft designing and production; but we believe that in this present emergency it is far better to put this department of engineering, procurement, and production into the hands of a civilian of industrial training and experience and in close touch and sympathy with the industrial field.

Such a civilian should be of broad industrial experience, a business man accustomed to doing big things in a big way, and he should be clothed with absolutely dictatorial powers. The appropriations made for the extension of the aviation service should be spent under his direction, as far as relates to the question of the purchase of aircraft, and the general appropriation for aviation purposes should be divided in such a way that a distinct portion of it is allotted for this purpose and a distinct portion of it allotted to the Signal Corps for training camps, aerodromes, and other more strictly military purposes. It is suggested that a proper title for this executive would be Administrator of Aviation.

Under his charge should be the entire engineering and experimental work, as well as the procurement and production of apparatus. He should have control of the present Equipment Division of the Signal Corps. The Administrator should have power to employ experts wherever they can be found, to request from the proper military authorities the assignment from the active military service of such men as may be needed in the engineering and experimental division from time to time, to employ foreigners, and to pay such men, except military officers, such compensation as in his judgment is proper, and without statutory limitation. The very best engineering and technical talent in the world should be at his command, and should not be asked to serve at personal sacrifice. Ordinarily speaking, men in these callings are not men of great means.

It is expected that this Administrator would provide himself with a greatly strengthened engineering and experimental organization. One of the great troubles heretofore has been the lack of direct and immediate contact with France and England on the part of the engineering and experimental organization, and it is of fundamental importance that this should be remedied. He should have power to arrange to have a revolving engineering and experiment board, part of which should always be in France and England, keeping abreast of all advances in the changing art of producing aircraft and keeping their colleagues in the United States in full touch with the progress of events and with the faults and advantages of such aircraft and motors as are sent by us abroad.

He should have further power to arrange that under direction of the Inter-Allied War Council, transmitted through the General Staff, the production program of this country shall consist of completed aircraft or of motors and parts to be supplied to our allies for assembling in machines to be constructed abroad, or of both.

The Administrator should have no connection or interest in any concern in any way connected with aviation or the production of airplanes; but he should not be limited in securing assistants from concerns so engaged. The reason for this latter provision is that the number of men available for this service in this country is extremely limited, and practically all of them have connections with manufacturing concerns engaged in airplane work.

To accomplish all of this it is perhaps necessary to procure legislation; but we believe that this change is so vitally needed that the President would be justified in the use of any power which he may possess to put it into effect immediately, as far as possible,

and continue during the period necessary to get the proper legislation if such be required.

The present Aircraft Board exists under a law which gives it no
executive power, and the sole function which it can exercise at
present is to submit suggestions and recommendations. It has been
believed by many people who have been interested in this subject,
but who have been insufficiently informed, that this Aircraft Board
possessed powers which were never given to it, and it has been
therefore subject to a good deal of criticism for occurences over
which it had not control. It may be retained, if desired, in an advisory
capacity to the Administrator. In such case the Administrator should
be its Chairman.

To summarize our plan briefly, it is as follows:

I.

The General Staff of the Army shall originate the whole aircraft
program; that is, shall determine what general type and quantity
of airplanes are needed in the future for the service. To this end
there should be created in the General Staff a section on aviation,
and there should be a similar section in the General Staff abroad.

II.

There shall be created an organization under the title of Aviation
Administration, either in the War Department or directly account-
able to the President as may be determined, in charge of an Administrator who shall have very full authority. To the Administrator
shall come the requisitions from the General Staff. He shall have
power to employ the necessary subordinates, who shall not, for the
present, be subject to Civil Service rules and who may be obtained
by him in this country or from any foreign country. He shall have
under his control the engineering and experimental work involved
in the design and production of aircraft. He shall be empowered to
direct the making of all purchases and have charge of production.

It may of course be necessary to more elaborately define the
powers of the Administrator than in this brief memorandum, but
he should be given as complete power as is possible.

III.

If the Aircraft Board is continued, the Administrator should become its Chairman.

IV.

The present Equipment Division of the Signal Corps shall be placed under the control of the Administrator. The other divisions of the Signal Corps shall not be disturbed by this plan.

V.

If the plan requires legislation, it is recommended that, pending the action of the Congress, it be put into effect, as far as can be done, by the President. The need is very urgent.

Respectfully, H. Snowden Marshall
E. H. Wells
Gavin McNab
Committee on Aircraft Investigation.

I concur in the conclusions herewith presented except that my personal opinion is that the Aircraft Board should be abolished; this without reflection on its personnel, which is the very highest. The law is unworkable. It provides a deliberative, advisory body without authority or executive power. Under the plan suggested by us it would be useless; but that would not insure its being harmless. One cause of the present difficulties is that deliberation has been out of proportion to execution,—to production. There has been too much authority without ability and too much ability without authority. It is difficult to translate thought into action and action into machinery, but this is impossible with executive authority paralyzed by large advisory councils.

However, I recognize that this is a matter which should be determined on the advice of the Administrator of Aviation, if such shall be appointed.   Respectfully,   Gavin McNab

TS MS (WP, DLC).

Tasker Howard Bliss to Robert Lansing and Others

Number 85 CONFIDENTIAL.   Versailles. April 12th [1918].

For Secretary of State, Secretary of War and Acting Chief of Staff.

Paragraph 1. At a meeting of the military representatives April 8th, 1918, joint note number 21 was adopted, expressing the opinion of the military representatives in substance that, for the present, military forces could not be diverted to Allied Naval activities in the Adriatic, and have called on the Allied Naval Council for complete data on the project so that a thorough study can be made and plans prepared should project prove feasible and circumstances later permit its execution. The note was based on project for Naval activities in the Adriatic, submitted by Allied Naval Council, and requiring substantial military aid for its accomplishment. No action by American Government required.

Paragraph 2. The Allied Naval Council and the military representatives Supreme War Council at joint meeting March 23, 1918 adopted a report concerning Allied intervention at Archangel and Murmansk expressing briefly the following opinions: From a military point of view military resources are not available for expeditions to either points; from Naval view point use of the transports or men of war for Archangel expedition would be severely felt both in anti-submarine warfare and in transportation; that all possible steps should be taken to destroy stores at Archangel to prevent their falling into enemy's hands; that Naval steps being taken with respect to Murmansk be continued in order to retain the place for the Allies as long as possible. No action by American Government required.

Paragraph 3. The Secretary of War en route home has with him the draft of a joint note proposed by British and dated March 29th intended to be submitted to military representatives on the subject of "The situation in the Eastern Theater" with special reference to Japanese in Siberia.[1] Consideration of the note was urged by the British. It was adopted as joint note number 20 by the British French Italian military representatives after departure of Secretary of War from Paris. The American military representative informed his colleagues that his last information was to effect that this matter was subject of diplomatic negotiations by his government which hoped that matter would not be pressed. General Bliss therefore declined to take part in the action of his colleagues but said that he would forward their action for the information of his government. On arrival of the Secretary of War compare the following with original proposed draft in his possession.

Paragraph 4. Subparagraph A. In Secretary of War's draft omit all of paragraph 1 excepting first sentence. In the first sentence omit words "Under Bolshevik control" and add words "Unless there is an immediate inter-allied intervention in that country."

Subparagraph B. In Secretary of War's draft omit in first sentence of paragraph two the words "And which will be facilitated wherever Bolshevism has had time to prepare the ground."

Subparagraph C. In Secretary of War's draft add to first sentence of paragraph 5 the words "With the eventual assistance of Czech and other *new element* which can be organized on the spot." Add to the end of paragraph 5 the sentence "The military representatives are of opinion that such intervention should have an international character."

Paragraph 5. My colleagues state that the essential object of the note signed by them is to make clear a military aspect of the situation which was not considered when joint note number 16 was adopted February one eight.[2] This aspect is the military danger resulting from unchecked German influence in fostering Pan-Islamism in Persia Afghanistan and Mohammedans of India. The British apprehend this in near future with result that their military efforts must be diverted from Europe to India to prevent disruption of empire.   Bliss.

TC telegram (WDR, RG 407, World War I Cablegrams, DNA).
[1] Joint Note No. 20, printed as an Enclosure with NDB to WW, April 25, 1918.
[2] See T. H. Bliss to H. P. McCain, Feb. 19, 1918, Vol. 46.

From the Diary of Josephus Daniels

April Friday 12 1918

At Cabinet. WW said in [if] House cited George Creel for contempt he would go up to the House as his attorney & say "It's me you are after. Here I am. Be brave enough to go after me"[1]

Gregory: Said at Bridgeport the Judge sent for every German who would not subscribe & after he talked to them awhile, they gener'ly took bonds

[1] Creel had delivered a speech in Washington on April 8 before the National Conference of American Lecturers. The *New York Times*, April 9, 1918, quoted Creel as making, among other controversial remarks, the following statement: "There was a question, when we went to war, of preparation. We had not prepared, and I shall always be proud, to my dying day, that there was no rush of preparation in this country prior to the day the President went before Congress and said: 'We are driven to accept a state of war by the aggressions of the German Government.' For, to have prepared, to have held out offers of peace with one hand and attempted a conciliation with the other, and all the while have been preparing for war, would have been to give the lie to what we said, namely, that we would not engage in war unless we had exhausted every recourse at our command."
Creel's alleged remarks evoked denunciations of him in both houses of Congress and calls for his resignation or dismissal from office. The *New York Times*, in an editorial on April 11, called for his removal. Creel later claimed that he had been misquoted, but the *New York Times* stated that its quotation had come from the official report of the meeting made by a professional shorthand reporter employed by the National Conference of American Lecturers itself. *Ibid.*, April 16, 1918.

From Lord Reading

My dear Mr. President   Washington April 13th/18

On my return from Chicago this morning I found a telegram from Mr. Balfour asking me to convey to you his high appreciation of the speech which you made at Baltimore on April 6th. Mr. Balfour adds that it has been received with great enthusiasm by our people.

He also expresses to me the opinion, which I should like to repeat, that you chose a particularly opportune moment to remind Germany and Austria of the inexhaustible resources of America and of her determination to carry on the war until German militarism is defeated.

Believe me, my dear Mr. President

Yours with the highest respect   Reading.

ALS (WP, DLC).

From Gutzon Borglum

My dear Mr. President: Washington, D. C. April 13, 1918.

I have just had a talk with Mr. Marshall over the phone. At his suggestion I shall see him in New York next week and shall tell him when the Government is prepared to appoint a Federal Grand Jury with a prosecutor to investigate the matters my report brought before you, I shall be glad to put before them the sources of the evidence, produce witnesses, etc., for the charges contained. There has been so much falsehood, definite, organized departmental conspiracy to misrepresent *me to you*, my motives, and discredit my report that I must tell you that I shall not permit information, that I have been at such pains and expense to secure and upon which my own honor and credit now stands, to be released in a manner that can be vissiated or destroyed without proper judicial hearing. The "World's" statement this morning' is unfounded and false. There has been no investigation of the charges I have made in my report and there could be in consequence no report made upon such charges.

It's been very unfair to me that I have been obliged to establish my own organization and with my own resources made my investigation. What your reason has been to leave me in this unpleasant position unsupported I do not know. However, I have not understood it in any other than a complimentary way, but I have often needed counsel with you and personal conference and I think it has been an error in the large usefulness that I could be that I am not able to talk to you.

Have you heard of *Lt. Col. H. M. Byllesby*?[2] There is a gentleman by that name in the Signal Corps. I have never met nor seen him but I have heard about him all through the period of my investigation as a strange, forceful, independent character, incorruptible— unattached, and from the Middle Northwest, who towered above his associates. I took it upon myself to investigate him and I find he is a man with a remarkable history and great integrity and constructive ability. I know no more about him but such a man you need at the head of this aeronautic establishment.

                    Yours sincerely and faithfully,   Gutzon Borglum

I shall of course gladly give Mr. Marshall any assistance I can.

TLS (WP, DLC).
    [1] "Wilson Receives Aircraft Report," New York *World*, April 13, 1918. This brief account of the submission of the preliminary report of the Marshall committee to Wilson included only the following remarks on Borglum: "The committee's findings developed no suspicion of graft or profiteering, such as was charged in the report of Sculptor Gutzon Borglum, recently made public. Mr. Borglum, it is understood, submitted no proof to back up his sensational conclusions."
    [2] Henry Marison Byllesby, at this time serving at the headquarters of the Chief Signal Officer in Washington.

From Ripley Hitchcock

Dear Mr. President: New York, N. Y. April 13, 1918.

    May I express our profound appreciation of your letter of April ninth, consenting to sign the sheets of the Documentary Edition of your History? May I assure you that we shall do everything in our power to secure for the Red Cross the largest possible returns?
    I have the honor to be,
                    Very respectfully yours,   Ripley Hitchcock

TLS (WP, DLC).

From Edward Nash Hurley

Dear Mr. President: Washington April 13, 1918.

    I am heartily in accord with the Director General of Railroads' letter to you of March 25, relative to restricting additional industrial development in New England and other Eastern territory which is already so congested.[1] In the establishment of additional shipyards, as well as in letting new contracts for equipment, instructions will be given to scrupulously observe your recommendation.
                    Very truly yours,   Edward N. Hurley

TLS (WP, DLC).
    [1] Wilson had sent Hurley a copy of the letter summarized in WW to B. M. Baruch, March 27, 1918, n. 1.

From Fred William Mueller[1]

Dear Mr. President: Detroit, Michigan, April 13th, 1918.

Again, upon my own behalf and in behalf of our large constituency, I desire to thank you most sincerely for your graciousness and kindness in permitting an interview with you recently as representing the loyal patriots in the ranks of German Methodism.[2]

I am endeavoring to convey to our people your kindly attitude toward them and appreciation of their peculiar relation to this world war, and for them I desire again to express our deepest gratitude to you and the government in not contemplating to abolish the use of the German language in their houses of worship and in their literature.

Permit me to assure you, Mr. President, that these churches and especially our literature are being used to the fullest extent to arouse the latent elements of patriotism to aggressive action, to which our people are responding readily and beautifully.

I also know that we have an opportunity of creating patriotism in the ranks and file of that German contingent in our country beyond our direct church lines and which cannot be successfully reached excepting through the medium of a German periodical.

Furthermore, I was very glad to note that you made a distinction between some foreign speaking secular papers and the religious periodicals as to their value in the assimulating process which ought even more rapidly to be going on in our country, and I desire again to assure you that German Methodism with its institutions and its literature, as a distinct americanizing and evangelizing factor in the life of our country, will be putting forth its best efforts to make a commensurate contribution to that which is highest and noblest in our country's welfare.

Assuring you that our people are daily remembering their President in their supplications, and hoping that victory might soon come to us on the high principles as you have set them before the world, I am   Very respectfully yours,   F. W. Mueller.

TLS (WP, DLC).
[1] District Superintendent of the Methodist Episcopal Church in Ohio and Michigan and associate editor of *Der Christliche Apologete*, a Methodist periodical.
[2] At the White House on March 20. See J. W. Hamilton to WW, March 12, 1918, n. 6, Vol. 46.

David Lloyd George to Lord Reading, with Enclosure

[London, April 14, 1918]

Following from Prime Minister.
Most Secret.

I think you may still have to overcome a good deal of opposition especially at your forthcoming Conference with the President and Mr. Baker. I am, therefore, sending you a memorandum which sets forth quite dispassionately the military situation and the reasons why the immediate brigading of American troops with Allied and especially British units is imperatively necessary. It has been prepared under the direction of the General Staff. The contents must be kept secret.

T telegram (W. Wiseman Papers, CtY).

E N C L O S U R E

I believe this memorandum will give you the facts necessary to convince the President and Mr. Baker. We can do no more than we have done. It rests with America to win or lose the decisive battle of the war. But if it is to be won America will have to move as she has never moved before and the President must overrule at once the narrow obstinacy which would put obstacle in the way of using American infantry in the only way in which it can be used to save the situation. If she fails disaster is inevitable. I want you to get that into the President's mind. The figures speak for themselves and irresistably point to no other conclusion. Can you get Colonel House to put his back into this business. If he does I feel assured all will be well.

Begins: The enemy's plan for victory is now clear. It is to destroy the British army. He has adopted this method partly in accordance with the axiom that the essence of his offensive is to concentrate overwhelming forces against a portion of the enemy force, in this case the smaller of the two armies opposed to him. But he has done so also because he believes that if he succeeds the war is at an end so far as the continent of Europe is concerned. He thinks that if the British army can be defeated, neither the French nor the Italian will continue the war, because he will be able to face them with the alternative of certain defeat or the acceptance of his terms. In this view he is probably correct.

The Germans may have hoped to inflict a decisive defeat on the British army with their first overwhelming blow and to separate

what remained of it from the French by the capture of Amiens. If
they did, they have failed in their first objective. The battle has
therefore entered upon its second phase. They are now trying to
defeat us by attacks further North. In this phase also they have
had considerable success and further attacks on a large scale are
imminent for which fresh German reserves are available which
have not yet taken part in the battle. The results of this second
phase are still undetermined. If the Germans fail however to produce a decision during this second phase, there will certainly be a
third and decisive phase in which after refitting all their divisions
they will once more launch against the British army an attack not
less violent than that which they delivered in the first phase of the
battle.

The real significance of this can only be realised when we consider the question of reserves. The Germans began the battle with
196 divisions of 9 battalions of 850 men each. They had 400,000
trained men for use as drafts in depots. There are probably another
100,000 men fit for offensive operations who can be combed out
for replacement purposes from the Russian front, or they can bring
over 15 to 20 complete divisions, some good, some bad, which can
be used in some capacity or other on the Western front. The German
losses to date are estimated at 250,000. It has therefore been possible for them to refit all their divisions and they will be able to
continue to do so for some considerable time. In point of fact since
the battle began the number of their divisions has risen from 196
to 201 by transfers from other theatres of war.

The British began the battle with 48 British divisions of 10 battalions of 1000 men each, 10 Colonial divisions of 13 battalions of
1000 men each, and 2 Portuguese divisions. Since then 1 division
has been transferred from Italy. They had in depots in France
30,000 men, and in England 140,000 men—a total of 170,000.
There are also a number of men being brought back from the
Eastern theatre which cannot exceed 45,000 and in addition there
are some drafts to replace Colonial casualties also on their way. The
British losses to date have been not less than 200,000. The number
of men in reserve are thus insufficient to remake all the British
divisions up to strength. In any case in order not to be left without
any pool from which to feed the divisions now fighting in the North,
or in attacks now impending, we have been unable to use up all
our reserves in order to refit all the divisions used up in the first
phase of the battle. We have therefore had to reduce 5 divisions to
skeleton cadres.

Thus since the battle began the number of German divisions has
risen from 196 to 201, the number of British divisions has fallen

from 58 to 53. As a result of the operations of the second phase already in sight we shall have to reduce a further 6 divisions to skeleton cadres, while the Portuguese divisions have ceased to have any fighting value, a total reduction of 13 divisions. If the Germans therefore go on concentrating against us, as they certainly mean to do, it is a mathematical certainty that within a very short time they can reduce the British army to less than 30 divisions, while the fighting strength of the German army will not be reduced at all, if it has not actually increased. According to the German plan as it now stands revealed, the third phase of the battle would take the form of another tremendous attack on the British army thus reduced to nearly half its original size, with the whole strength which Germany and her allies could muster with the object of overwhelming it by numbers and forcing it into the sea.

Needless to say the French army would not allow this to happen without exerting itself to the utmost. But there are very great difficulties in the way of their supporting the British army with their whole power. The French have already taken over an additional 40 miles of front, of which 26 are due to the lengthening of the total allied lines. If they go to any distance North of the Somme, their supply becomes extremely difficult and clashes with the British supply arrangements, for, now that the St. Just Amiens line is under enemy fire all French supply must go by routes already fully occupied by British supply. On the other hand, the enemy has the great advantage of fighting on interior lines and of an immensely superior railway system behind his front. He is therefore able to threaten all parts of the Allied front from Rheims to the Flanders coast far more rapidly than the Allies can concentrate against him.

It is not the purpose of this paper to enter upon the strategic problems which now confront the Allies. Its object is to show the significance of a persistent attack by the enemy on the British army, and the conclusion which inexorably follows therefrom. The German command, if it cannot destroy the British army in battle, is bent on reducing it to impotence by forcing division after division out of existence, because there is no infantry with which to refit them. Even therefore if the British army succeeds in withstanding the terrific strain of attacks by forces at least twice as great as its own in all three phases of the battle, the position of the Allies as a whole will ere long be in dire peril. The total number of their divisions has already fallen from 166 to 153. By the end of the third phase it will certainly have fallen to 130. Yet the Germans will still have a fighting army of at least 200 divisions, though they will then have exhausted all the fresh drafts they have accumulated. They will (then) be in a position to deliver a knockout blow to the Allied forces as a whole if they still refuse a German peace. The fundamental problem therefore is how to restore all the divisions of the British army to the fighting line and maintain them there.

There can be little doubt that victory or defeat for the Allies depends upon the arrival of the American infantry. Until the American infantry arrives the skeleton divisions will remain skeleton and useless in the field. As it arrives they will spring into life and take their part in the war once more. For the moment infantry and machine gunners are the only troops which matter for the wastage of infantry is out of all proportion to that of the artillery and other services. Barring disaster it will not be impossible to keep the latter up to strength. The real fact is that the Allies have the necessary reserves of sufficiently trained infantry to make it impossible for the Germans to succeed. But these reserves are now largely in America. If the American reserves arrive in time it will be possible to recreate the British divisions which now only exist as cadres for want of men, and so build up that reserve which is essential if the Allies are to withstand the attack in the third phase of the battle. The time, however, is very short. The third phase is likely to begin as soon as the divisions used in the first attack have been rested and refitted. No other reinforcements are in sight by then. Unless American infantry is already brigaded with allied units in considerable numbers by that time it is difficult to see how the German attack can be withstood. Ends.

T MS (W. Wiseman Papers, CtY).

To Marrette Applegate Broussard

[The White House] 15 April, 1918

May I not express my profound sympathy with you in the death of your husband.?[1]   Woodrow Wilson.

T telegram (Letterpress Books, WP, DLC).
[1] Senator Robert F. Broussard had died on April 12.

To George Creel, with Enclosure

My dear Creel: The White House 15 April, 1918

I know you will read this letter with very much the same feelings that I read it. It expresses my own judgment, as I need hardly tell you.   Cordially and faithfully yours,   Woodrow Wilson

ENCLOSURE

From Thomas Francis Logan[1]

Personal.

My dear Mr. President: Washington, D. C. April 13, 1918.

May I write a word or two with respect to Mr. George Creel?

Most of my time in recent years has been given to advisory work for corporations, and, since the war began, I have tried to help the government itself. But I have kept in touch with newspapers and magazines, eight or nine of which I still represent, as well as with business institutions. From the standpoint of both, I have had occasion to observe very closely the splendid work done by Creel, as chairman of the Committee on Public Information.

I think that I, probably better than anyone else in Washington, know the sentiment of the big business interests; and I can testify to the wholesome influence that Creel's work has had upon them. Through his work, moreover, the newspapers themselves, consciously or unconsciously, have achieved a larger vision. The attacks that are made upon him now are so unjust, and they evidence so clearly the spirit that catches upon a single word to make a political argument, that I felt constrained to give expression to my own knowledge that these criticisms are unjust and unfounded and that they do not represent the view of the country or of men who have opportunity and take the time to study conditions in Washington.

Mr. Creel's work has been one of the most helpful influences in the war. You couldn't have found another man who could have put the same zeal, intelligence and loyalty into the task. I have not been thrown very much in contact with him, but I have had ample opportunity to observe the wholesome results which he has been obtaining.

At times, when the uninformed are very vocal, those who are informed remain silent, and wrong impressions are created. Mr. Creel needs no support with you, but it may interest you to have an impartial outsider's view.

Faithfully yours,   Thomas F Logan

TLS (G. Creel Papers, DLC).
    [1] Washington correspondent of the *Philadelphia Inquirer* and of several magazines.

To Thomas Francis Logan

My dear Mr. Logan: [The White House] 15 April, 1918

That was a fine and generous letter you wrote me about Creel and I appreciate it deeply. It expressed my own judgment of Creel, but it was certainly a generous impulse which led you to write it and characteristic of your feeling for justice.

Cordially and sincerely yours,   Woodrow Wilson

TLS (Letterpress Books, WP, DLC).

To Frank Duffy

My dear Sir: [The White House] 15 April, 1918

Your telegram of April twelfth conveys a most welcome message.[1] The action taken by the United Brotherhood of Carpenters and Joiners of America in their regular quarterly session at Indianapolis does them the highest credit and speaks a spirit of patriotism which I am sure will meet with the applause and approbation of all public-spirited men.

Cordially and sincerely yours,   Woodrow Wilson

TLS (Letterpress Books, WP, DLC).
[1] It is missing, but it was W. L. Hutcheson and F. Duffy to WW, April 12, 1918, printed in *The Carpenter*, XXXVIII (May 1918), 32. It informed Wilson that the General Executive Board of the United Brotherhood of Carpenters and Joiners of America, meeting at their regular quarterly session at Indianapolis, wished to congratulate the President on the establishment of the National War Labor Board and to declare their "hearty accord" with the principles upon which it had been founded. They said that their union would fully cooperate with the board.

To Lord Reading

My dear Mr. Ambassador: [The White House] 15 April, 1918

Thank you very much for your kind note of April thirteenth, sending me Mr. Balfour's very kind message about my speech recently made at Baltimore. I appreciate his kind estimate of it most highly and hope with all my heart that it will serve some useful heartening purpose.

I am, my dear Lord Reading,

Cordially and sincerely yours,   Woodrow Wilson

TLS (Letterpress Books, WP, DLC).

To Gutzon Borglum

My dear Mr. Borglum: The White House 15 April, 1918

I am afraid that you have for some time been under a serious misapprehension. You call my attention to the fact that you were not supplied with suitable expert assistance in the investigation which you, of your own motion, undertook of the aircraft production.

You will remember that at the beginning you wrote to me saying that you feared and believed that there were very serious efforts not only, but serious bad practices, in the aircraft production, and after consulting with the Secretary of War I wrote you that if that was your impression, you were, of course, at liberty to examine any evidence that was in our possession. I never at any time constituted you an official investigator. I merely gave you the right to look into the matter of your own motion, and I am sure that the letter which the Secretary of War provided you with he gave you with the same purpose and idea. We have wished at every point to assist you and to make possible for you what you wished to do, but we have at no time regarded you as the official representative of the administration in making the investigation. If I had so regarded you, I would, of course, have supplied you with such assistance as you feel you have lacked.

You will understand, of course, that I write this in the most cordial way and only because it is evident from your last letter that you have been laboring under a misapprehension.

I hope that you will be willing and that you feel that it is your duty to put at the disposal of those whom I have constituted official investigators all the evidence that may be in your possession.

Cordially and sincerely yours,   Woodrow Wilson

TLS (photostat in G. Borglum Papers, DLC).

From Robert Lansing, with Enclosure

My dear Mr. President: Washington April 15, 1918.

I have received the enclosed letter of the 3d from Ambassador Fletcher and I thought it was important that you should see it. After reading will you kindly return it to me for my files?

Faithfully yours,   Robert Lansing

TLS (SDR, RG 59, 711.12/77½, DNA).

ENCLOSURE

Henry Prather Fletcher to Robert Lansing

PERSONAL AND CONFIDENTIAL

Dear Mr. Secretary: Mexico, April 3, 1918.

I think I should amplify for your confidential information, some of the impressions which I set forth in my despatch number 838 of March 13th, with reference to the attitude of the Carranza Government.[1] That there has been a gradual change for the worse in our relations with Mexico since the export embargo went into effect, is very apparent. Upon my return from Washington, this changed attitude on the part of the Carranza Government was particularly noticeable. Our export and import restrictions, the enemy lists, and all our war measures, seem to have aroused the particular resentment of President Carranza and the men of his Government. As you will have noticed from my telegrams and reports to the Department on the subject of the negotiations, Carranza's attitude has been anything but conciliatory. He and the men about him have nothing but complaints of the attitude of our Government. They constantly refer to the fact that we do not allow them to bring from the United States the gold which has accumulated to their credit;[2] that they cannot secure arms and ammunition to pacify the country, while the bandits and the rebels seem to be supplied from our side of the line. Border difficulties have again sprung up, and the crossing by our troops into Mexican territory in pursuit of marauding bands is also resented and complained of.

I think there are a number of explanations for the unsatisfactory state of our relations with Mexico. Much, I think, is traceable to German intrigue, which we know, from intercepted instructions from the German Government to Von Eckhardt, has as its object the fomentation of difficulties between the two countries wherever possible; the anti-American newspaper propaganda financed by the Germans is not only not discouraged by the Carranza Government, but materially assisted in many ways, and, I am reluctantly coming to believe, is approved in high quarters.[3] The failure of the Carranza Government to secure financial assistance in the United States is also a factor; banditry and opposition to the Government is prevalent throughout the country, and it is possible that President Carranza, finding the consolidation of his power and the pacification of his country much more difficult than he had anticipated, is not averse to keeping an anti-American sentiment alive for interior political reasons.

I am convinced that the Mexican Government and the great bulk of the Mexican people generally, would rejoice at a German victory. This fact has been particularly apparent since the Germans began their recent great offensive in France.

I have not been able to satisfy myself that the Mexican Government has received financial assistance from German sources,[4] nor do I believe that German intrigue is wholly responsible for the present unsatisfactory relations between Mexico and the United States.

Foreigners who came to Mexico prior to the present Carranza regime and who are almost exclusively responsible for such material development and progress as Mexico enjoyed up to that time, seem to be identified, in the minds of the revolutionary party now in control of the government, absolutely with the Diaz regime, and they are execrated accordingly. This feeling finds expression in the Querétaro Constitution, and has inspired the recent petroleum decree.[5] The whole trend of recent events seems to indicate that the Mexican Government will attempt, in some way or other, to annul or abrogate foreign private property rights in Mexico, and as such rights are held by the nationals of the allied countries and neutral nations, in great measure, much, I think, will depend upon the outcome of the present Great War. If the Mexican Government believes that it can safely venture upon the expropriation of the property of foreign individuals and corporations in Mexico, I think we should be prepared for some attempt in this direction. In this connection, I doubt very much that the protest which I have made in pursuance of the Department's instructions, as to the effects of the petroleum decree of February 19th, will have a deterrent effect.[6] Everything seems to indicate that the Mexican Government is determined to force this issue.

The sympathy and assistance which the revolution in all its stages, and particularly the Carranza party, has received at the hands of President Wilson, seems not to have had the slightest effect on Carranza and his group. The patience and forebearance which we have consistently shown them has, I fear, been misconstrued. Our prestige, and with it that of our allies, has declined to the danger point where Carranza, in the light of what his press here terms his "repeated" diplomatic successes in his dealings with the United States, may precipitate a serious crisis in our relations.

Heretofore I have felt confident that I could keep the Mexican question from distracting our attention and efforts from the Great War, because I felt that the Carranza Government would appreciate and reciprocate our friendly disposition and would not care or dare to provoke difficulties with the United States, but I think I would be failing in my duty if I did not bring to your notice the present unsatisfactory trend of affairs.

I am, my dear Mr. Secretary,

Very sincerely yours,   Henry P. Fletcher

TLS (SDR, RG 59, 711.12/77½, DNA).

¹ H. P. Fletcher to RL, March 13, 1918, printed as an Enclosure with RL to WW, March 27, 1918.

² About which, see WW to RL, April 18, 1918 (first letter of that date), n. 1.

³ For a discussion of German propaganda efforts in Mexico during the war, see Katz, *The Secret War in Mexico*, pp. 446-53.

⁴ About this subject, see H. P. Fletcher to RL, March 13, 1918, n. 1, cited in n. 1 above.

⁵ Carranza had issued a decree on February 19 which levied new taxes on titled surface oil lands, rental fees, and royalties. More important, it required landowners and holders of concessions to register their holdings within three months by submitting titles and leases to the Mexican Department of Industry, Commerce, and Labor for verification. Following this provision, they could file formal claims to their holdings. This provision was in effect an implementation of Article XXVII of the Mexican Constitution of 1917 (about which see n. 2 to the extract from the Diary of Chandler P. Anderson printed at March 8, 1917, Vol. 41). A translation of Carranza's decree is printed in *FR 1918*, pp. 702-704.

⁶ For the text of Fletcher's note of protest and for related documents, see *FR 1918*, pp. 704-15.

From George Wylie Paul Hunt

My dear Mr. President: Phoenix, Arizona April 15, 1918.

Your confidential letter of the 29th ultimo was awaiting me upon my return from Washington, and with it I am glad to consider the matter of Captain Wheeler's appointment closed. I quite agree that any attempt to remove Captain Wheeler from the Army now would probably not be to the best interests of the Nation. I have never questioned his physical bravery or his patriotism through the very limited scope that he would view patriotism.

I understand that Captain Wheeler has sailed to France. There, under our splendid organization, he can undoubtedly render a real service. Certainly he cannot do the harm that would result in his continued presence as sheriff in this State. But I have already taken up too much of your time on this subject.

It is, of course, a source of keen regret to me that I was unable to see you while in Washington, but realize the task that is yours must necessarily almost eliminate visitors from the provinces. I hope for better fortune next time.

Very respectfully yours,   Geo. W. P. Hunt

TLS (WP, DLC).

From George Horace Lorimer

My dear Mr. President: Philadephia April 15, 1918
    We have had a very genuine desire to serve the country to the limit of our ability in the Saturday Evening Post, and it is a great pleasure to know that you feel that we have, in some measure at least, measured up to our responsibility.
    With thanks for your very kind and cordial letter, believe me,
                              Yours sincerely,   Geo. H. Lorimer

TLS (WP, DLC).

From Benedict Crowell

My dear Mr. President: Washington. April 15, 1918.
    I am inclosing copy of a telegram from General Pershing,[1] recommending that the title be conferred upon General Foch of Commander in Chief of the Allied Armies in France. The War Department recommends that you approve this proposition.
                              Very truly yours,   Benedict Crowell

TLS (WP, DLC).
[1] J. J. Pershing to B. Crowell, April 15, 1918, T telegram (WP, DLC).

From the Diary of Josephus Daniels

                                        1918 Monday 15 April
    Mrs Baker[1] was going to Cleveland and two men behind her were talking & one expressed very vigorously the hope that the ship on which the Secretary of War was returning would be sunk. She was so indignant she resented it & told them who she was. His name was Wm. E. Lamb, a Chicago lawyer, and bitter Republican partisan.
    I went to see the President about it & he thought he ought to be punished if seditious and should be brought here by the Attorney General and given the 33rd degree and then the story of his comment given to the public so he would be forever damned by the people.
    Mayo came & urged that he go abroad with the fleet & Benson opposed. We already have 5 & Mayo would supersede Sims. I saw the President & he agreed not to send
    "Fear I will come out of the war hating English"

[1] That is, Elizabeth Leopold (Mrs. Newton D.) Baker.

To Benedict Crowell

My dear Mr. Secretary: The White House 16 April, 1918

As I told you over the telephone a few minut[e]s ago, I am in entire accord with Mr. Clemenceau and Mr. Lloyd George in the action of bestowing upon General Foch the title of Commander-in-Chief of the Allied Armies in France, and beg that you will cable to the proper authorities the cordial acquiescence of this Government in the action.

Cordially and sincerely yours,   Woodrow Wilson

TLS (B. Crowell Papers, OCIWHi).

From Benedict Crowell

My dear Mr. President: Washington. April 16, 1918.

According to your telephonic instructions, we have to-day cabled your confirmation of the action of Mr. Clemenceau and Mr. Lloyd George in conferring on General Foch the title of Commander-in-Chief of the Allied armies in France.[1]

Very respectfully,   Benedict Crowell

TLS (WP, DLC).
[1] In H. P. McCain to T. H. Bliss, No. 47, April 16, 1918, TC telegram (WDR, RG 407, World War I Cablegrams, DNA).

To Henry Fountain Ashurst

My dear Senator: [The White House] 16 April, 1918

That was a brilliant and, so far as it concerned me, an exceedingly generous speech which you delivered in the Senate the other day[1] and I cannot deny myself the pleasure of sending you this line of admiration and sincere personal appreciation.

Cordially and sincerely yours,   Woodrow Wilson

TLS (Letterpress Books, WP, DLC).
[1] Ashurst had spoken on April 11 in support of the Overman bill. He compared Wilson's request for legal authority to reorganize governmental departments and agencies with Abraham Lincoln's assumption of extralegal powers in the early days of the Civil War, which Congress had ratified *ex post facto*. Ashurst hailed Wilson as the spokesman and statesman of the Allies. He pointed out that, as commander in chief of the army and navy, the President possessed undisputed power over the destinies of all members of the armed forces. Ashurst therefore ridiculed the stand of those who argued that Wilson could not be trusted with the power to alter the organization and functions of governmental departments and agencies. *Cong. Record*, 65th Cong., 2d sess., pp. 4969-72.

To Sarah Louise Winston Stone

My dear Mrs. Stone: [The White House] 16 April, 1918

May I not convey to you my deepest and most sincere sympathy?[1] Your loss is indeed a tragical one and I am sure that all hearts will go out to you in this day of your loneliness.

Cordially and sincerely yours,   Woodrow Wilson

TLS (Letterpress Books, WP, DLC).
[1] William Joel Stone had died of a cerebral hemorrhage on April 14.

To Lee Slater Overman

My dear Senator: [The White House] 16 April, 1918

You are a splendid fighter. I am following your present generous and able course in pushing the bill with appreciation and admiration, and wanted to give myself the pleasure of sending you at least this line.

Cordially and sincerely yours,   Woodrow Wilson

TLS (Letterpress Books, WP, DLC).

To Cleveland Hoadley Dodge

My dear Cleve: The White House 16 April, 1918

Please forgive me for not answering your letter of April eighth sooner.[1] The fact is that Mrs. Wilson and I were greatly tempted. Mrs. Stokes is very generous and her place would be ideal for our use in the summer, but, alas, the more we discuss it the more clear it becomes that it is my duty to be here and not anywhere else. I may run away for a few days at a time, but at this crisis of things it would be inexcusable of me to create any additional inconveniences in communicating with headquarters here.

Will you not express to Mrs. Stokes our very warm and cordial appreciation of her generosity and thoughtfulness of our comfort and pleasure, and may I not thank you, my dear fellow, for the full letter and plans?

I am distressed to hear that you are limited at all by your health. Do, I beg of you, take care of yourself. It would be a great distress to all of us who love you if you did not get back your health to the old point of robustness.

Mrs. Wilson and all join me in the most affectionate messages.

Affectionately yours,   Woodrow Wilson

TLS (WC, NjP).
[1] C. H. Dodge to WW, April 8, 1918, ALS (WP, DLC). Dodge informed Wilson of the offer by Helen Louisa Phelps (Mrs. Anson Phelps) Stokes of the use of her country house at Noroton Point, near Stamford and Darien, Conn., as a summer White House.

From Samuel Gompers

Sir: Washington, D. C. April 16, 1918.

About ten days ago, Honorable Charles A. Douglas, soon after his return from Mexico, had a conference with me, in which the situation in Mexico and the relations between that country and the United States were fully discussed. Judge Douglas, you know, is the representative of the Government of Mexico in the United States in a legal capacity. The conference was participated in, not only by the Judge and the undersigned, but by the executive committee of the Pan-American Federation of Labor.

The accompanying document is a summary of Judge Douglas' statements and also expresses the opinions of the conferees in regard to the subject matter of the helpful work which the Pan-American Federation of Labor may be enabled to perform in the service of the United States and the Latin-American countries and, particularly, Mexico.[1]

While Judge Douglas is the representative of the Mexican Government in the United States, in a legal capacity, I am confident that he is whole-heartedly and loyally American and his utterances to President Carranza, in the conference held with him, were interesting and pointed.

When I saw published in the newspapers in Washington, a dispatch from El Paso, Texas of April 10th, that Mexican troops were marching to the border; that an American patrol had been fired upon; that the United States Army officers are on the alert to meet any attack—it perturbed me to a great extent but it seemed to me imperative that the entire subject matter of the conference with Judge Douglas and the Committee of the Pan-American Federation of Labor, and the undersigned, should be presented to you, which I now do, in person.[2]

The American Federation of Labor, as you know, has in the past been of some assistance in re-establishing better relations than existed, at a few of the critical periods in the relations between the Government of Mexico and the United States and I am constrained to believe that the subject matter presented herein can be helpful again to meet, not only the immediate situation, but in the development of the best possible relations—first, with Mexico, and soon thereafter, with all the Pan-American countries.

Respectfully and sincerely yours,   Saml. Gompers
Chairman, Conference Committee
Pan-American Federation of Labor.

TLS (WP, DLC).
[1] A typed, unsigned memorandum by Charles Alexander Douglas (Gompers Letterbooks, AFL-CIO-Ar). Douglas devoted the principal part of his memorandum to an

account of a long interview with Venustiano Carranza in Mexico City, in which he urged the Mexican President to abandon neutrality and enter into an alliance with the United States and the Entente countries. Carranza replied that he would consider the suggestion. Douglas also had an interview with General Pablo González, "the coming man of his country," who declared emphatically that Mexico should "come out for the Allies."
    [2] At 4:45 p.m. on April 16.

From John Albert Sleicher[1]

My dear President: New York April 16, 1918
    I find the enclosed in the "Oregon Voter."[2] I am writing to ask if the statements it makes in reference to your endorsement of the Non-Partisan League are true. I desire to make some comment on the matter and before doing so, would like to be assured that the statements are justified.
                        Sincerely yours,   John A. Sleicher.[3]

TLS (WP, DLC).
    [1] Editor of *Leslie's Illustrated Weekly Newspaper*.
    [2] "Wilson With League?," Portland *Oregon Voter*, April 6, 1918, clipping (WP, DLC). This brief news item stated that organizers for the Nonpartisan League were "whispering the information confidentially 'that President Wilson is behind the League.' " "To support this," it continued, "they are exhibiting copies of a letter from President Wilson to Congressman Baer expressing his sympathy with the purposes of the league." For the correspondence referred to, see J. M. Baer to WW, Feb. 7, 1918, and WW to J. M. Baer, Feb. 18, 1918, both in Vol. 46.
    [3] "Won't you answer this letter for me and say that I have never endorsed any organization; that the most that I did in the letter to Congressman Baer referred to was to commend such purposes as professed by this league and to which Mr. Baer called my attention. Any citizen would do that. I said nothing about the organization itself." WW to JPT, c. April 19, 1918, TL (WP, DLC).

From Gutzon Borglum

My dear Mr. President: Washington, D. C. April 16, 1918.
    Your letter of yesterday has just been given to me.
    I have reviewed our entire correspondence and in the face of the full authority you had requested the Secretary of War to clothe me with to go to the bottom of every situation, etc., etc., I confess a grievious misapprehension exists.
                        Very sincerely yours,   Gutzon Borglum.

TLS (WP, DLC).

William Phillips to Robert Lansing

[Washington] April 16, 1918.

To: The Secretary.
Subject: Defense of Liberia.

The accompanying telegrams show that the French have offered to

1. Erect sand bag defense around cable and wireless buildings,
2. Land guns, gunners and am[m]unition at Monrovia.

Liberia has declined all French assistance except to permit "machinery inside wireless buildings to be covered with sand bags."

The French Ambassador this morning gave me the same information. He told me, however, that the French forces to be landed were Singalese. The Singalese look down upon the negro, and friction, therefore, might easily occur between the Liberians and the Singalese. In these circumstances it is somewhat natural for the Liberians to refuse Singalese help.

In the circumstances I cannot but feel that the responsibility for the protection of Liberia should fall upon the United States and that we should send a vessel to remain in Liberian waters for the present. Liberia is our ward; she looks to the United States for everything, and French and British protection will not, I think, be appreciated by the Liberians or negroes in this country. Admiral Benson told me that a ship could be detached from Admiral Caperton's fleet for duty at Monrovia.   W Phillips

TS MS (SDR, RG 59, 763.72/10493, DNA).

From the Diary of Josephus Daniels

April Tuesday 16 1918

Cabinet. Navy had asked about taking Swan island[1]—little islands which nobody claims—so we could take over the radio controlled by fruit Co. Not very far from Colon. He [Woodrow Wilson] disliked the idea of claiming territory, or taking it. It would smack of doing what Austria had done but would be nothing like it, but would hate to put Americans on with radio without protecting them. Am to look into it

National Research Council wished an Executive Proclamation setting forth what they should do.[2] Houston objected that they wished to take over existing agencies of government and said it would not be wise.

[1] Two small islands in the Caribbean Sea, about 110 miles off the coast of Honduras.
[2] George Ellery Hale, the chairman of the National Research Council, had sent the proposed Executive Order to Wilson on March 26. The order defined the agency's existing role as the promoter and coordinator of scientific research in the United States both for military and civilian purposes. Wilson had forwarded the order to Daniels on April 12 for the consideration of the Council of National Defense. After some modification, the order was issued on May 11. See G. E. Hale to WW, March 26, 1918, TLS, and WW to JD, April 12, 1918, CCL, both in WP, DLC. For the order as issued, see the *Official Bulletin*, II (May 14, 1918), 1, 3.

From William Benjamin Munson[1]

Dear Sir: Denison, Texas. April 17th, 1918.

I beg pardon for offering the following suggestion, as probably you have already considered something of the kind, if not it may be possible that you would consider it worthy of adoption, as it might end the war.

Have Edison or some capable inventor invent and have manufactured a large number of bombs carrying fagots that would burn upon explosion and scatter flames sufficient to set fire to ripened grain fields. Have them ready before the coming harvest in Germany. Send a fleet of air craft to the most productive wheat fields of Germany within reach, and reduce their wheat crop to ashes.

Absolute secrecy would be necessary, hence I am writing to you personally. It is a harsh measure but any thing that will end this war will be a blessing to the world.

If you think the suggestion worthless, destroy this letter.
Yours very truly,   W. B. Munson

TLS (WP, DLC).
[1] Civil engineer, contractor, lawyer, rancher, banker, and businessman; chairman of the Liberty Loan bureau of the Denison War Council.

From Samuel Reading Bertron

My dear Mr. President: New York April 17, 1918.

Last night a prominent American, a resident of Paris for many years and representing our Chamber of Commerce there, who has just returned to this Country, dined with me. He stated that the French Nation's reverence and respect for you was something beyond expression and that if the French people could elect you as President of France the vote would be unanimous. He stated that the same feeling existed in England. In other words, that your position was pre-eminent in those Countries, as well as here. This is certainly a wonderful position for an American President to maintain throughout the civilized world and should be most flattering to you. Of course it carries with it corresponding responsibilities.

I do hope that your health will enable you to continue this great work to a victorious ending.

Recently I made a speech to the Press Association of Connecticut on the anniversary of our entering into war, and I was deeply impressed with the importance of the press in winning the war and I think, if you will permit me to say so, that it would be a very useful thing if you could give half an hour to representatives of the press once in a while.

Please believe me,   Faithfully yours,   S R Bertron

TLS (WP, DLC).

Arthur James Balfour to Lord Reading

Handed me by Lord Reading
Apr 19/18 RL

Washington, April seventeenth 1918.
Paraphrase of a telegram from Mr. Balfour to Lord Reading
dated April 15th 1918.

Please see instructions sent to Moscow respecting proposed policy in Russia.[1]

The position in Russia is still causing great anxiety to the British Military authorities, who are of opinion that the Russian situation must be considered as a whole. The greatest danger at present is that the Germans may be able to transfer to France further divisions from those still in Russia. They still have about forty divisions in the East which they are slowly withdrawing, and it will be possible to continue the movement of German troops to the West Front as long as Russia remains in her present state of disintegration and disorganisation. To prevent this transfer of German troops the only effective means would be the creation of some definite and important pro-ally force in Russia, but it may perhaps already be too late to create such a force.

There is in the meantime grave danger that a considerable amount of supplies of all sorts will be available for Germany from Russian sources. It appears that the quantities of grain actually seized in the south were not very large but if these districts remain in German occupation during the next few months it will no doubt be possible for Germany to obtain large supplies from them.

In the West Siberian district round Omsk there are huge food resources and in addition large stores are available at Petrograd, Moscow, Archangel and Vladivostok. It may certainly be stated that if all these resources pass into German hands the enemies power of resistance would be prolonged for an indefinite time.

Further, the German plan now clearly includes a design to cause trouble in India and if a successful effort to this end should be made the result would necessarily be the diversion of strong British forces while the reputation and prestige of the Allies would suffer in the Mussulman theatres of war. With this purpose in view the enemy are preparing to penetrate Persia and we believe Turkestan also. In order to advance on these lines they must obtain control in the Caucasus districts and to do this they are depending partly on the action of the Turks against the Armenians and Russians and partly on direct action across the Black Sea and from South East Russia. To prevent this we can do something by direct armed intervention in Persia but, in order to prevent the enemy from reaching Turkestan across the Caspians, it is also necessary that local action should be taken in Trans Caucasia.

There is finally the serious risk that, if disorder in Russia continues the rapidly increasing number of people who suffer from it will be driven to prefer even intervention by the enemy to the continuance of present conditions. This feeling has already had its effects in Finland and in the Ukraine and our information indicates that it is growing stronger all over Russia.

A bold and determined policy is required in the face of all these dangers. The presence of Allied Forces at ports such as Archangel, Vladivostok and Murmansk would be of some use in preventing the seizure by Germany of the stores in these towns but the whole problem is much larger than this. Our military advisers are unanimous in thinking that we cannot possibly hope to set up at the present moment any military force in Russia which would be really effective, at any rate by Russian effort alone, and unless such a force exists it is impossible to carry out any of the main purposes of our policy. Even assuming that the Soviet Government could, by their own efforts, call a new army into being, it is most uncertain that this army would be employed to fight or impede the enemy. The object of the Soviet Government is to produce a world wide social revolution, not to gain a military victory, and they might very well consider that their main object would be more easily obtained by encouraging peaceful penetration by the Germans than by resisting the German Army.

We are advised moreover that there is a large proportion of the Russian people, stated by some observers as more than half, who regard intervention by the Allies as their only hope of rescue from domination by Germany on the one side and from anarchy on the other, and are therefore passionately desirous of such intervention. Trotsky himself has given indications that he is inclining to this view but he seems reluctant to take so decisive a step as to request intervention. There seems from the point of view of the Allies to be no other course leading to safety and I request therefore that you will urge the United States Authorities to send instructions to the American Agents at Moscow to make use of every possible argument with a view to persuading the Russian Authorities to give their consent to intervention by the Allies on the lines indicated in my telegram to Mr. Lockhart. Owing to the geographical position such intervention must, from the very nature of the case, be principally Japanese, but we should wish to associate with the Japanese representative units from the other Allied Countries and especially if possible from the United States.

T MS (WP, DLC).
[1] He probably refers to the two telegrams to Lockhart, cited in Ullman, *Intervention and the War*, pp. 160-61.

Three Letters to Robert Lansing

My dear Mr. Secretary,   The White House. 18 April, 1918.

I have gained from other sources the same impressions that Mr. Fletcher here expresses. It is a serious situation.

No doubt the gold export difficulty lies at the bottom of a great deal of it. I suggest that, as soon as possible, you have a conference with the Governor of the Reserve Board about possible alterations or modifications of our present uncompromising position.[1]

Faithfully Yours,   W.W.

WWTLI (SDR, RG 59, 711.12/78½, DNA).
[1] Wilson, in a proclamation issued on September 7, 1917, had imposed an embargo on the export of coin, bullion, and currency to all foreign countries. *FR-WWS 1917*, 2, II, 943-45. However, the Federal Reserve Board did permit the export of gold by special license. For example, during the period January 1 to August 20, 1918, licenses were granted for the export to Mexico of $22,393,051 in gold. W. P. G. Harding to WW, Sept. 14, 1918, TLS (WP, DLC). See Emily S. Rosenberg, "Economic Pressures in Anglo-American Diplomacy in Mexico, 1917-1918," *Journal of Interamerican Studies and World Affairs*, XVII (May 1975), 130, 146.

My dear Mr. Secretary,   The White House. 18 April, 1918.

I would very much value a memorandum containing *all* that we know about these several *nuclei* of self-governing authority that seem to be springing up in Siberia. It would afford me a great deal of satisfaction to get behind the most nearly representative of them, if it can indeed draw leadership and control to itself. A summary of what we know (stripped of the confusions of the cables) would be a most welcome thing as a support to my judgment in the premises.   Faithfully Yours,   W.W.

WWTLI (SDR, RG 59, 861.00/1602½, DNA).

My dear Mr. Secretary,   The White House. 18 April, 1918.

I quite agree that it is of capital importance that an armed vessel of the United States be sent to Monrovia, if there is one that can be spared for the purpose, and I would be very much obliged if you would be kind enough to suggest such an arrangement to the Secretary of the Navy and seek his advice in the matter.[1]

Faithfully Yours,   W.W.

WWTLI (SDR, RG 59, 763.72/10492, DNA).
[1] A typed memorandum attached to the above letter reveals that Joseph C. Grew took up the matter with Franklin D. Roosevelt on April 18. Roosevelt agreed to send a naval vessel to Monrovia immediately. *U.S.S. Raleigh*, a cruiser, arrived at the Liberian capital on May 7 and spent two days there. *FR-WWS 1918*, 1, I, 745.

To Herbert Bayard Swope

My dear Swope: The White House 18 April, 1918

In reading the memorandum you were kind enough to send me under date of the sixteenth,[1] and which I have just had time to return to, I get the impression that the facts you set forth are old facts. They are certainly facts which have been called to my attention before and which I thought were in a fair way to be altered.

My own feeling is that the publication of such things produces no substantial result except to encourage those who are trying to make the impression (an impression which, of course, spreads to the other side of the water) that we are not and will not be prepared to push the present programme. May I not suggest that you take no further steps in the matter until I have had an opportunity of conferring with the Secretary of War, whom I have always found ready and prompt to correct every condition that was shown to be wrong or detrimental to the efficiency of the service?

In haste

Cordially and sincerely yours,   Woodrow Wilson

TLS (received from Bruce Gimelson).
[1] H. B. Swope to WW, April 16, 1918, TLS (WP, DLC). Swope discussed in detail serious problems and delays in the mass production of artillery. As his prime example, he described the apparent determination of the Ordnance Department to develop a specifically American version of the thoroughly tried and tested French seventy-five millimeter field gun, an effort which Swope said was costly, time-consuming, and unnecessary. He suggested that Wilson initiate an investigation of the ordnance program similar to the one under way of the aircraft program. He also asked Wilson whether he, Swope, should write an article for his newspaper based on the information which he had gathered. He pointed out that if he did not do so soon, some other less friendly journalist would.

To John H. Beckmeyer[1]

My dear Mr. Beckmeyer:　　　　[The White House] 18 April, 1918

I warmly appreciate the telegram of April seventeenth which you were kind enough to send me on behalf of the mass meeting which assembled to consider the Mooney case.[2] I have certainly tried to do all that it was my privilege to do and am confident that Governor Stephens will be disposed to do the utmost justice.

Sincerely yours,　　Woodrow Wilson

TLS (Letterpress Books, WP, DLC).
  [1] Member of Local No. 68 of the International Association of Machinists and a representative of the International Workers' Defense League, an organization based in San Francisco which provided legal assistance to radicals.
  [2] J. H. Beckmeyer to WW, April 17, 1918, T telegram (WP, DLC).

To Ruth Smith McKelway

My dear Mrs. McKelway:　　　　[The White House] 18 April, 1918

The news of your husband's death has come to me a very great shock.[1] I had not heard of his illness. I esteemed him most highly and valued him as a friend, and shall feel, now that he has gone, that I have lost something that I very much valued, his friendship and counsel.

Cordially and sincerely yours,　　Woodrow Wilson

TLS (Letterpress Books, WP, DLC).
  [1] Her husband, Alexander Jeffrey McKelway, had died of heart disease on April 16.

To Samuel Reading Bertron

My dear Mr. Bertron:　　　　[The White House] 18 April, 1918

It was certainly generous of you to write me your letter of yesterday with its cheering quotation from your friend just returned from Paris, and I thank you most gratefully.

There are many difficulties in the way of my seeing the newspaper men, the chief being that I am dependent in every interview upon the discretion and good will of the least discreet and friendly member of the conference, and that has made it very difficult for me to talk as frankly as I should like to talk with the general body of correspondents down here, but it is not a matter which I have finally closed my mind about by any means.

Cordially and sincerely yours,　　Woodrow Wilson

TLS (Letterpress Books, WP, DLC).

To Daniel Hoffman Martin[1]

My dear Mr. Martin: [The White House] 18 April, 1918

Your letter of April sixteenth[2] disturbs me. I am very sorry that you took the step of obtaining a year's relief from your duties as pastor in the expectation of receiving some assignment to governmental work. If you had consulted me beforehand, I would have earnestly advised you against such a step, for this reason: There are, greatly to the credit of the country be it said, hundreds of offers of this sort made to me by many men of the finest capacity, and yet we are not able to place them because, as a matter of fact, the ranks are at present full. I should be at a loss to think of any assignment which I could give you which would afford you means to support your family.

Your offer is most honorable and creditable to you, but I am bound in fairness and kindness to state to you the facts. I hope sincerely that it is not too late to reconsider your recent action.

Cordially and sincerely yours,   Woodrow Wilson

TLS (Letterpress Books, WP, DLC).
[1] Pastor of the Fort Washington Presbyterian Church in Manhattan since 1913; prolific author on religious subjects.
[2] It is missing. He had written from 509 Third St., N.W., Washington.

From Robert Lansing

My dear Mr. President: Washington April 18, 1918.

The question of the necessary relief of interned enemy aliens and their families, and those non-interned enemy aliens who have been thrown out of employment as a result of the war, has become an important and pressing one, not only from the humane point of view of preventing distress and, in some cases, actual starvation, but also from the aspect of maintaining this considerable element in the country in a safe state of mind. It must be considered that many enemy aliens have been thrown out of employment as a result of the water front and zone restrictions, etc., no less than on account of the sentiment of employers throughout the country. The Government has been unable to assume any responsibility for the position into which such enemy aliens have been placed and as a result they are often dependent on charity or on such relief as they may be able to obtain.

Formerly this relief was afforded by various organizations which solicited subscriptions from German subjects or kind-hearted Americans of German origin, but there has been no means of preventing the use of this money, collected under the guise of relief, for propaganda purposes. It has therefore seemed advisable to establish a system by which this entire relief work could be controlled by the Government.

An arrangement has now been made with the Swiss and Swedish Legations, in charge respectively of German and Austro-Hungarian interests in this country, under which certain committees, chosen by the Legations and recognized by the Department, are to undertake the investigation of cases, the collection of funds and the disbursement thereof to deserving enemy aliens and their families, under the direct supervision of the Legations and the Department, to which regular accounting is to be made. These committees, in various parts of the country, are to be composed of American citizens who may be interested in the work and whose loyalty is unquestioned. But in order that their activities may not be misunderstood by the country at large, it seems essential that some authoritative statement be made, indicating that the Government appreciates the necessity of rendering such assistance and therefore approves of the activities of those committees that are organized under the patronage of the Swiss and Swedish Legations in the solicitation, collection, and distribution of funds for the purpose stated, as being in the interests of the nation.

I therefore venture to bring this matter to your attention and to request an expression of your views as to the manner in which these facts can best be brought to the notice of the country, if you approve in principle of such a course.

With assurances of respect, etc., I am, my dear Mr. President,

Faithfully yours,   Robert Lansing

TLS (WP, DLC).

From Howard Earle Coffin

Dear Mr. President: Washington April 18, 1918.

I feel that the work I am best fitted to perform in helping to lay the industrial foundation for the construction of aircraft has been largely accomplished. The reorganization of the machinery for carrying out this great undertaking is a matter which I believe is engaging your attention.

In order that you may be without any embarrassment in enlisting such executive talent as the future developments in this new art may call for, I place in your hands my resignation as Chairman of the Aircraft Board, to use as your good judgment dictates.

I trust you will believe that the incentive which moves me in this course is solely a desire to be helpful. No publicity will be given to my action in this regard except as you yourself may desire.

Sincerely yours,   H. E. Coffin.

TLS (WP, DLC).

William Bayard Hale to Joseph Patrick Tumulty

My dear Mr Secretary   New York April 18th 1918

I am obliged to you for the letter of April ninth.[1] The matter is one which I was sure (even before the President in the letter said so) must be causing him concern. You say that The President greatly deplores recent acts of lawlessness, and that he "would like to know the best means of protecting innocent men from mob violence." The President might spare a couple of minutes for the following suggestions:

A SUGGESTION AS TO HANDLING ENEMY ALIENS
Respectfully submitted to The President.

Should not the task (certain to grow ever greater and more delicate), of the oversight and regulation of Enemy Aliens be definitely organized under a *single special authority*?

If it has been expedient to have a Custodian of Enemy Alien *Property*, is it not advisable to have a Warden, (or Custodian, Director, Commissioner, Surveyor, Guardian, or What-you-may-callhim) of Enemy Alien *Life*?

Besides co-ordinating the work of various agencies now engaged in registering Aliens, regulating their movements, and administering internment camps, this Authority could make a swift, but careful, study of existing statutes bearing upon the treatment of Enemy Aliens, and of sympathizers with them, and develope and recommend measures desirable for copeing with the problem. It would, naturally, do several other things—but I pass to the main point:

The main point is that the creation of such a special authority would be a *proclamation to the country that the Administration is fully appreciative of, and is vigorously dealing with, the problem of resident enemies, and enemy sympathizers*—a problem which it recognizes as a special one, like that of Food, Fuel, Railroads, and Enemy Property.

Would not knowledge of the fact that The President had taken special cognizance of this problem go, of itself, a long way toward allaying disorder throughout the country? Would it not go a very long way indeed to discourage extra-lawful activities—give the country somewhat dramatic notice that the *Government at Washington is fully master of the situation, proposes to remain so, and needs no assistance from rioters?* On the counter-hand, this Warden, or Commissioner, could initiate a thorough campaign to instruct the several millions of Teutonic subjects and their sympathizers, that while (1) they will be guarded against unlawful violence, they (2) will be held to strict, rigid, and scrupulous responsibility to law.

The Warden, or Commissioner, could be the means of impressively communicating to the froward the absolute necessity of never-nodding discretion of act and word;—or informing them of the humane sentiments of The President, but of the imperative necessity he is under to prosecute the war to a successful finish, without annoyance from the disloyal and unsympathetic. Surely there are extremely few who deliberately plot against the Government. Surely the interior peace can be kept by firm, plain and dispassionate expression of the mind of The Executive, such as his special Commissioner could reiterate in word and illustrate by deed—thus, at the same time repressing unpatriotic acts and utterances at home, and removing all ground for the unfortunate animadversions which, one cannot but fear, have probably been made abroad as to the lawless tendencies of occidental civilization.

I feel, dear Mr Tumulty, that The President might recognize the above as really a practical suggestion.

With high regards   Yours sincerely   Wm. Bayard Hale

TLS (WP, DLC).
¹ Tumulty's letter to Hale, written at Wilson's request, is missing. See W. B. Hale to WW, April 6, 1918, n. 5.

John Lord O'Brian¹ to Thomas Watt Gregory

Washington, D. C. April 18th, 1918.

MEMORANDUM FOR ATTORNEY GENERAL:

I respectfully suggest the following reasons which might be well embodied in a public statement for the purpose of reassuring the people, quieting their apprehension and preventing so far as possible the spread of mob-violence, evidence of which is now appearing in all parts of the Country.

1. We are now on record as a nation against similar brutality in Belgium, in German prisons camps and elsewhere.

2. Lawless and brutal oppression will surely result in reprisals to the detriment of our own men in the field.

3. Up to the last week there have been grave defects in the Federal laws, essential for preservation of order and vigorous punishment of seditious crimes. With the passage of the Sabotage law,[2] the law relating to internment of dangerous women alien enemies[3] and the expected early passage of certain amendments of the Espionage Law[4] and the passage of the Passport Bill,[5] the Federal statutes will be substantially adequate to deal with the present situation.

4. The existence of war does not decrease the responsibility resting upon local officials, but on the contrary greatly intensifies it. The administrative of the machinery [administrative machinery] of the Federal Government manifestly cannot reach all parts of the country and every hamlet and country-side has a body of state law and has its duly elected local officials charged with the responsibility of administering that state law and protecting life and property. These officials must realize the responsibility which rests upon them for preserving property and protecting life.

5. Existing laws are being enforced rigorously and successfully. Juries show no disposition to release defendants charged with seditious crime and instead of courts and juries being lax in the performance of their duties, they have in almost all parts of the country shown a same patriotic desire to aid in the impartial and vigorous administration of justice.

6. With the aid of Government and State officials and a very large body of private citizens organized for the purpose of watching out for offenders against the cause of the Government, this country is being policed more thoroughly and successfully than ever before in its history.

7. The public must not credit too readily the exaggerated stories of enemy activity, now in general circulation, and most of which are unfounded. To spread these stories invites hysteria and disorder, affects the confidence of the people both in the enforcement of law and in the vigorous prosecution of war; and distinctly aids in the cause of the enemy by disintegrating public sentiment. An example of this type of story is the frequently repeated assertion that vast quantities of ammunitions have been destroyed, factories damaged by fires, etc. It is the consensus of opinion, both of the leaders of the fire insurance business and of the Government officials in charge of this, that substantially no fire losses of this character during the past year have been caused by enemy activities within this country. The recent story of the faulty manufacture of gas masks is without foundation.[6] Likewise the story that since we entered the war ammunition has been shipped out of this country for German use. The widely circulated stories of ground glass and poisonous substances alleged to have been found in food almost invariably disappear on investigation. It is safe to say that in 97% of the reports of such

instances the complaint is unfounded. Circulation of stories of this character by the over-credulous have the direct result of weakening the morale of our people and promoting the cause of Germany.

8. Animated by the American instinct for fair play, the President directed in his first proclamation that so long as an enemy alien behaved himself he should be unmolested both in his life and occupation.[7] This action was also in accordance with the dictates of international law, which confer upon an alien enemy a distinct status and give him certain rights of protection so long as he conforms to the law of the place of his residence. This war is one for American principle and for the sanctity of long recognized standards raised by international law. Any act of such oppression directed toward an alien enemy is an act which discredits the good name of America and its motives in this war.

Respectfully,   John Lord O'Brian

TLS (WP, DLC).

[1] At this time special assistant to the Attorney General for war work.

[2] Wilson, on April 20, signed into law this measure "to punish the willful injury or destruction of war material or of war premises or utilities used in connection with war material." 40 *Statutes at Large* 533.

[3] Wilson had signed this bill on April 16. It extended to include women the power which the President already possessed to control, deport, or intern male subjects or citizens of enemy nations. 40 *Statutes at Large* 531.

[4] These amendments were embodied in H.R. 8753 which was enacted on May 16 as what came to be known as the "Sedition Act." It extended the punishable offenses of the Espionage Act of June 15, 1917 (40 *Statutes at Large* 217) to include the obstruction of the sale of bonds of the United States or the making of loans to or by the United States. More important, it provided heavy fines and/or imprisonment for anyone who should "willfully utter, print, write, or publish any disloyal, profane, scurrilous, or abusive language about the form of government of the United States, or the Constitution of the United States, or the military or naval forces of the United States, or the flag of the United States, or the uniform of the Army or Navy of the United States, or any language intended to bring the form of government of the United States, or the Constitution of the United States, or the military or naval forces of the United States, or the flag of the United States, or the uniform of the Army or Navy of the United States into contempt, scorn, contumely, or disrepute or . . . willfully utter, print, write, or publish any language intended to incite, provoke, or encourage, resistance to the United States, or to promote the cause of its enemies, or . . . willfully display the flag of any foreign enemy, or . . . willfully by utterance, writing, printing, publication, or language spoken, urge, incite, or advocate any curtailment of production in this country of any thing or things, product or products, necessary or essential to the prosecution of the war in which the United States may be engaged, with intent by such curtailment to cripple or hinder the United States in the prosecution of the war . . . [or] willfully advocate, teach, defend, or suggest the doing of any of the acts or things in this section enumerated . . . [or] by word or act support or favor the cause of any country with which the United States is at war or by word or act oppose the cause of the United States therein." Moreover, the Act provided that any employee or official of the United States Government who committed any disloyal act or uttered any unpatriotic or disloyal language, or criticized the army, navy, or flag of the United States "in an abusive and violent manner" should be at once dismissed from the service. Finally, the Act gave the Postmaster General explicit authority to return to the sender all mail addressed to anyone whom he considered to be in violation of the provisions of the Act. 40 *Statutes at Large* 553.

[5] H.R. 10264, enacted on May 22. It empowered the President to control the exit and entry of aliens from and to the United States and the use of passports by American citizens. 40 *Statutes at Large* 559.

[6] See WW to TWG, March 25, 1918, and WW to WGM, March 28, 1918.

[7] See n. 1 to the Annual Message on the State of the Union printed at Dec. 4, 1917, Vol. 45.

Arthur James Balfour to Lord Reading

[London] 18 April 1918.

[No. 2303] I am sending following at the request of War Cabinet.

Further consideration of military problem before Allies has driven us to conclude that if we are to win the war we must treat Europe and Asia as a single front for the purposes not of command but of strategy. Germans are still transferring divisions from East to West. Since my last telegram[1] four more have been located making total of 205. Our military advisers calculate that Germany could bring across another 15 divisions of which half would be kept for offensive operations half for holding the line. For reasons which will be obvious to you from my previous telegram it is imperative to stop this process if we possibly can and nothing will do this save German anxiety in regard to East.

Moreover taking a longer view even if we successfully hold up German attacks there is but a small chance of our being able to make a successful offensive in the West so long as that is the only front from which Germany has to fear attacks and so long as she can draw upon Asia for her supplies of food and raw material. Nor in view of that absolute and ruthless power now in hands of General Staff can we reasonably expect an internal revolution or a genuine desire to make a just peace unless Germany is threatened not merely with military stalemate in the West but with defeat or at least complete restoration of an effective blockade. From this point of view also it is essential that we should once more bring pressure on the Central Powers from the East.

There is also another factor. There is no doubt that Germany is trying to weaken us by reducing Middle of East [the Middle East] and through it India to same condition of disorder as she has reduced Russia. She hopes to do this by Pan Slav or Turanian[2] propaganda backed by Turko German military force. Their agents are already endeavouring to stir up Persia Turkestan and Afghanistan. Turks have now captured Batoum and if they take Kars as seems probable they will be masters of Caucasus and their road towards Central Asia and India will be open. Unless this movement is checked it is bound to have far reaching effects.

From every point of view therefore it has become matter of greatest urgency to recreate an effective allied front in East. In our judgment only hope of doing this lies in resuscitating Russia. If we could bring about a national revival in Russia such as freed Russia from despotism of Napoleon very great results might ensue. It must not be forgotten that Russian situation differs from all historical precedents in that almost its whole manhood has been trained in

arms and has had actual experience of modern warfare and that
there are thousands of trained men and officers including Generals
of greatest ability now in country. If necessary national spirit could
be roused it would be possible to create an army armed and supplied
from stores now at Archangel and Vladivostock in a short space of
time. It would certainly be possible to create situation which would
compel Germany to withdraw or reinforce divisions now scattered
throughout vast territories she is at present occupying.

It seems to us that if this national revival is to take place Allies
must actively help to bring about it and that they ought therefore
to unite upon a policy which has for its object allied intervention
in order to free Russia from all forms of foreign control. It is of
course essential that Allies should avoid taking sides in Russia itself
for local politics are now so bitter that which ever side we took we
should make its opponents our enemies. On the other hand Bolshevist Government is de facto Government of Russia and it seems
to us impossible to go behind it provided it will actively co-operate
with us in fighting Germany. Of late a very significant change has
come over attitude at any rate of its M.F.A.[3] Trotsky towards Allies.
For sometime past he has begun to show signs that he recognises
that co-operation with Allies in a war to free Russia from German
domination is the only hope either for Russia or revolution or possibly for maintenance of his own power. Opinions differ as to Trotzsky's honesty but he is evidently a man of decision and of late,
whatever may be motives, he has not only curbed anti ally tone of
Bolshevist Press but he has approved of allied co-operation at Murmansk and has suggested that British naval officers should assist
in restoring discipline in Black Sea Fleet. We have only just heard
that he has now definitely invited "Allied Governments to submit
to him at earliest possible opportunity a full and proper statement
of help which they could furnish and of guarantees they are prepared to give. If conditions are satisfactory (?) he considers conclusions of an agreement both necessary and desirable."[4] We consider that we ought immediately to avail ourselves of this opportunity
to offer de facto Govt of Russia an allied intervention in order to
fight Germans so enabling Russian people to recover their independence. This offer ought to be of course accompanied by a declaration of complete disinterestedness in Russian internal politics
and with guarantees as to evacuation of Russian territory by allies
as soon as war is over. If Trotzsky backs out we shall at least know
where we are with Bolshevists. If he accepts it advance of allied
forces into Russia with consent and co-operation of de facto Government is bound to transform whole situation in East.

As to form of intervention it is clear that if any considerable military force is to be employed it must be Japanese. It is equally clear that an intervention of Japan alone might throw large classes in Russia into the Germanys arms. The only course open to us therefore is to offer an intervention in which all the Allies effectively participate but of which Japan provides most military strength. We should be prepared to make a naval demonstration at Murmansk and Archangel which would hold ports as bases and serve as rallying points for anti German forces. We should be prepared also to give such assistance as is possible to Russian forces in Trans Caucasia (gr. undec) we can establish communication through Persia which largely depends on support of Bolshevist elements in that region. But important measure would be advance of an allied force predominantly American Japanese through Siberia. We should be ready to send a British detachment and probably also French and Italians but allied character would have to be supplied mainly by American contingent. We think that American force should consist largely of technical Corps specially air detachments mechanical transport railway troops and signal units together with medical units and in addition one complete division. As it would probably have little or no fighting to do for some time this division could complete its training in Siberia. Finally we should render available great accumulation of war materials at ports for re-arming of Russian army.

Will you please see President as soon as you can and ask him if he will agree to:

    1.   A.   A simultaneous proposal on the part of America and Great Britain to Bolshevist Government for allied intervention on lines laid down including undertaking to withdraw all allied forces at conclusion of hostilities.

    B.   Americans sending above contingent to Far East.

If he agrees to this as a general policy there remains the question of approach to Japanese. According to this plan Japan would enter as part of a joint allied intervention. She would be ?? gr om. "not" pleased by allied declaration and she would probably have to use some of her troops in European Russia as well as Asia in conjunction with Russian and allied forces. In return we think that she should be given military command of allied expedition though a mission from each Ally including a strong propaganda detachment should be attached. We think that this proposal for allied intervention should be made to Japanese as soon as possible and pressed on the ground that it is necessary in order that Alliance of which Japan is a member may win victory. If we put it to her in this way she cannot easily refuse though she will not greatly like it.

You will of course realize that problem is one of pressing importance. It is in no sense alternative to sending of American infantry

to Europe urgency of which grows every day more vital. It is com-
plementary to it. We cannot afford delay in beginning to bring
pressure on Germany's Eastern flank. Without this it is not easy to
see either how our blockade measures can be kept effective or how
peace is to be reached through conclusive defeat of enemy's forces.
First and most important step however in carrying out of this policy
is to obtain whole hearted concurrence of President. Until we are
assured of this we do not propose to approach our Allies.

T telegram (Reading Papers, FO 800/222, PRO).
   [1] A. J. Balfour to Lord Reading, April 17, 1918.
   [2] Balfour apparently used the word rather loosely to encompass the areas which he
discusses in the balance of this paragraph.
   [3] That is, Minister of Foreign Affairs. Actually, Trotsky was now Commissar for War;
Georgii V. Chicherin had become Commissar for Foreign Affairs.
   [4] Balfour was quoting from a telegram from R. H. Bruce Lockhart, sent from Moscow
on April 13 and received in London at 7:15 p.m. on April 18. For a discussion of its
context and significance, see Ullman, *Intervention and the War*, pp. 160-61.

Lord Reading to David Lloyd George

                                        Washington. 18th April 1918.

No. 1686. Following for Prime Minister.
Very Urgent and Very Secret.
Your telegrams No. 2017 and 2049 and my telegram No. 1526.[1]
I have just returned from long interview with Secretary Baker.
We had some discussion about the history of the brigading of American infantrymen with British and French troops which is now
relatively of so little importance that I do not repeat it. In substance
there was no difference between us.
When however we got to your telegram to me of 20th March No.
1828[2] which contained the first mention of 480,000 infantrymen
and machine gun units in the four months April to July he said
that although there had been discussion about 120,000 monthly at
the Supreme Council and otherwise, there was no decision of the
Supreme Council at Versailles that this number should be sent
although there was a decision that infantrymen and machine gun
units should be shipped from America in preference to other units
during the present emergency.
I then informed him of my conversation with the President of
30th March, see my telegram No. 1360 to you,[3] which reported my
interview with the President, and called Secretary Baker's attention
to the conversation in Paris between General Hutchinson [Hutch-
ison] on the one side and Mr. Baker and General Pershing on the
other. Mr. Baker said that he had become aware that there was a
difference of opinion as to the result of this interview; that he had

dictated a memorandum of which a copy had been sent to General Hutchinson or Whigham,[4] and that he had now asked General Pershing to cable his view. It would be well for you to cable me the text of Secretary Baker's above mentioned note.

It did not seem of importance that we should attempt further at this moment to elucidate what had actually happened at the interview reported in your telegram No. 2017. It was of importance to know definitely what is now regarded as the course to be pursued by the American Administration. I referred to the secret memorandum contained in your telegram of April 14th.[5] which we read together and discussed. I said it was a document of the utmost gravity to which of course he assented. He wondered whether it was necessary to go so far as to fix the number of infantrymen and machine gun units to be shipped during the next four months. I impressed upon him that it was imperative that you should know whether this number could be depended upon during the period of four months while you would be training new men. He observed that before those four months were over the Germans might attack the Americans and they might themselves be in need of the reinforcements of infantrymen or other replacements and that it seemed difficult for them to pin themselves down definitely to the 480,000 infantrymen for this reason and proposed that we should leave matters to be decided as to the later months by the then circumstances. I replied that the four months programme ought to be a definite plan; he said no hard and fast programme could be made and that it must be subject to variation. I said that if as might happen in war other emergencies arose later the plan could then be reconsidered by the light of the new circumstances and decided by the Supreme Council at Versailles or the Commander in Chief of the Allied Armies, whichever was the proper authority.

He then assented to this view, making the further condition that when circumstances permitted these infantrymen should be withdrawn and take their place in the American Army. I said we had always understood that, as was shown by the published references of yourself and Mr. Balfour, and I raised no difficulty provided they were only withdrawn when the crisis was passed and circumstances permitted the change. He agreed and proposed that he should draw up a memorandum which he would submit to the President and me. I expect to receive it tomorrow and will communicate its terms to you, and which I shall only accept if it embodies what I consider to be the results of our interview and no objection is raised by you.

I summarize these briefly as follows:

(1) That the 480,000 men consisting of infantry and machine gun units should be shipped at the rate of 120,000 a month in each of

the months of April May June and July to be brigaded with French and British divisions.

(2) That in the event of an emergency this programme may be subject to revision of the Supreme Military Council or of General Foch whichever is the right authority to decide it (and upon which I should like information).

(3) When the emergency has passed and circumstances permit it these men should be withdrawn from the French or British divisions and placed with the American Army.

Generally Secretary Baker means to be helpful but I think is a little impressed by the difficulties which may be created by the high military command. I purposely discussed the problem with him first as it seemed wiser not to have arguments between him and me in the presence of the President unless this course became imperative. I shall await the memorandum which he will discuss with the President before he submits it to me and provided it does not whittle away the effect of the arrangement made between the President and me except by addition of points (2) and (3) I shall accept it without appealing to the President. Otherwise I shall go direct to the President.

Please cable at once if you see any ground for objecting to a memorandum on the lines stated.

As I was leaving Secretary Baker said he hoped that we should not be too tender about the carrying out of arrangements as to infantrymen etc inasmuch as it might well happen again that it was desirable to send a ship off at once without waiting for further infantrymen when there might be room for one or two hundred other soldiers who could be useful although they were not infantrymen. He instanced the case of the "Kronprinzessin Cecile" which had sailed with 3100 infantrymen and having room for another 200 who were not at the moment available. The ship was not to be detained and consequently 200 men not infantrymen were shipped. I assured him that that was not the spirit in which we should regard any arrangement arrived at between us but I did hope that they would not hesitate to take the most drastic measures to secure the shipment of 120,000. I said that no question could arise between the heads of Governments as to the carrying out of an agreement. What was to be feared was that high military authorities might find difficulties in carrying it out. He agreed that this might happen and therefore he wished to record the arrangement in a document. My impression is that he wishes to keep to my understanding of the President's decision whilst not making it too difficult for the Military Commanders to accept.   R.

T telegram (Reading Papers, FO 800/224, PRO).
    [1] No. 2017 is A. J. Balfour to Lord Reading, April 8, 1918, T telegram (Reading Papers, FO 800/224, PRO). For the other two telegrams, see A. J. Balfour to Lord Reading, April 9, 1918, and Lord Reading to A. J. Balfour, April 10, 1918.
    [2] D. Lloyd George to Lord Reading, March 29, 1918.
    [3] Lord Reading to D. Lloyd George, March 30, 1918.
    [4] Maj. Gen. Sir Robert Dundas Whigham, Deputy Chief of the Imperial General Staff.
    [5] D. Lloyd George to Lord Reading, April 14, 1918, and its Enclosure.

To Claude Motley Jones[1]

My dear Mrs. Jones: [The White House] 19 April, 1918

It is with deep and genuine grief that I have heard of the death of your distinguished husband. I had formed so high a personal regard for him and so sincerely valued his counsel in public matters that his death has come to me as a personal grief. I hope I may convey to you my profound and heartfelt sympathy.

Cordially and sincerely yours,   Woodrow Wilson

TLS (Letterpress Books, WP, DLC).
    [1] Mrs. William Atkinson Jones, whose husband had died of a paralytic stroke on April 17.

To Albert Sidney Burleson

My dear Burleson: [The White House] 19 April, 1918

Mr. Gompers handed me the enclosed the other day.[1] It is, as you will see, a translation from the New York Volks Zeitung. I take the liberty of calling your attention to it because if this publication is going through the mails, this particular thing must have escaped the attention of the department.

Always   Faithfully yours,   Woodrow Wilson

TLS (Letterpress Books, WP, DLC).
    [1] The Editors have been unable to find this enclosure.

From Newton Diehl Baker

MEMORANDUM for The President: Washington. April 19, 1918.

Prior to March 28, 1918, various negotiations had been entered into between the British Government and the United States with reference to the transportation of American troops by Great Britain, in addition to those possible to be transported in American tonnage, and on that date the arrangement substantially stood that Great Britain had agreed to transport the full personnel of six (6) complete divisions (American Army standard size of division) in such a way

as not to interfere, by the use of ports or otherwise, with the con-
tinuity of the American program of shipping in its own tonnage its
troops at a rate not less than two (2) complete divisions per month.
On the 28th of March, 1918, the permanent military representatives
with the Supreme War Council adopted unanimously a joint note
reviewing the military situation in Europe proceeding from the
German concentration and attack, expressing the opinion that "it
was highly desirable that the American Government should assist
the Allied Armies as soon as possible by permitting, in principle,
the temporary service of American units in Allied Army corps and
divisions, such reinforcements must however be obtained from other
units than those American divisions which are now operating with
the French, and the units so temporarily employed must be eventually returned to the American Army."[1]

In execution of the foregoing, the permanent military advisers
recommended that "until otherwise directed by the Supreme War
Council, only American infantry and machine gun units * * * be
brought to France, and that all agreements and conventions hitherto made in conflict with this decision be modified accordingly."[2]
This joint note was submitted to the Supreme Military Council,
and the President approved it in the following language:

"The purpose of the American Government is to render the
fullest cooperation and aid, and therefore the recommendation
of the military representative with regard to the preferential transportation of American infantry and machine gun units in the
present emergency is approved. Such units when transported
will be under the direction of the Commander-in-Chief of the
American Expeditionary Forces and will be assigned for training
and use by him in his discretion. He will use these and all other
military forces of the United States under his command in such
manner as to render the greatest military assistance, keeping in
mind always the determination of this Government to have its
various military forces collected as speedily as their training and
the military situation will permit, into an independent American
Army, acting in concert with the armies of Great Britain and
France, and all arrangements made by him for their temporary
use, training, and service will be made with these ends in view."[3]

Thereafter, March 30, Mr. Lloyd George dispatched to Lord Reading a cable directing him to present to the President urgently the
view of the British Government that for a period of four (4) months
American infantry and machine gun units should be preferentially

[1] See NDB to WW, March 28, 1918.
[2] *Ibid.*
[3] See *ibid.* and WW to NDB, March 29, 1918.

transported, and setting up an estimate of the combined capacity of British and American shipping for such transportation aggregating 120,000 troops per month. The arguments by way of inducement for this consisted of a discussion of the available reserves in Great Britain and the length of time necessary to prepare them for replacement use with the existing British divisions. In the language of Mr. Lloyd George's dispatch, he directs Lord Reading to urge that "as the American regiments arrive in France their battalions should be brigaded with the British or French divisions on the same basis as that planned for the infantry of the six (6) divisions," and refers to the recommendation of the military representatives with regard to the preferential shipping of infantry and machine gun units, and concludes: "In the case of the above 120,000 troops, just as was agreed in that of the six (6) divisions, battalions as soon as trained can be re-formed in regiments and sent to General Pershing as he may require.["]4

Thereafter a study of the shipping possibilities was made, and by direction of the Chief of Staff of the War Department the determination of the President with regard to the stimulation of our dispatching of troops was conveyed to the Supreme War Council under date of April 5, which determination covered the shipping of 91,000 troops monthly, beginning April 1, in American transports, British-loaned transports, and British liners; in addition to which Great Britain was to carry 29,000 troops per month, aggregating the total of 120,000. Certain arrangements with regard to cargo tonnage were also set forth in that dispatch, a copy of which was handed to the British and French Ambassadors in the United States and a copy sent to General Pershing.

At a meeting in Paris between General Pershing, Sir Robert Whigham, General Hutchinson, and me, the question was raised as to how many troops of those to be transported were to be trained with the British, and an agreement was reached satisfactory to all present, covering only the troops transported in the month of April, of which 60,000 infantry and machine gun personnel were assigned for training with the British; the other 60,000 to be transported in the month of April to be otherwise disposed of by General Pershing; and leaving the question of troops to be brigaded and trained with the British, out of those transported in May, June, and July, to be subsequently disposed of by General Pershing on the theory that he would either continue this basis of division and assignment if the situation continued to justify it, or modify the distribution as the exigencies of the situation require.

4 See D. Lloyd George to Lord Reading, March 29, 1918.

Lord Reading, by the direction of Mr. Lloyd George, desires to have definite assurance that the program of 120,000 American troop personnel per month will be maintained for four months, and that the recommendation of the Versailles permanent military representatives with regard to the preferential shipment of infantry and machine gun personnel will be adhered to throughout that period.[5]

By the action of the President upon the joint note of the permanent military representatives, the United States is committed to the preferential transportation in the present exigency of infantry and machine gun personnel. The recommendations of the permanent military representatives, however, stipulated no time for the continuance of that preference, nor do they stipulate numbers.

I recommend that I be authorized to say to Lord Reading:

"Pursuant to the direction of the President and in conformity with his approval of the joint note of the permanent military representatives at Versailles, the United States will continue, throughout the months of April, May, June, and July, to supply for transportation both in its own owned and controlled tonnage, and in that made available by Great Britain, infantry and machine gun personnel. It is hoped, and on the basis of study so far it is believed, that the total number of troops transported will be 120,000 per month. These troops when transported will, under the direction and at the discretion of General Pershing, be assigned for training and use with British, French, or American divisions as the exigencies of the situation from time to time require; it being understood that this program, to the extent that it is a departure from the plan to transport and assemble in Europe complete American divisions, is a concession to the exigencies of the present military situation and is done in order to bring into useful cooperation at the earliest possible moment the largest possible number of American personnel in the military arm most needed by our Allies.

"It being also understood that this statement is not to be regarded as a commitment from which the Government of the United States is not free to depart when in its view the exigencies upon which the concession is made no longer require it; and also that the preferential transportation of infantry and machine gun units here set forth as a policy and principle is not to be regarded as so exclusive as to prevent the Government of the United States from including in the troops carried by its own tonnage from time to time relatively small numbers of personnel of other arms as may be deemed wise by the United States, as replacements and

[5] See Lord Reading to D. Lloyd George, April 18, 1918.

either to make possible the use of a maximum capacity of ships
or most efficient use of the infantry and machine gun units transported, or the maintenance of the services of supply already organized and in process of construction for the American Army
already in France.

"These suggestions are made in order that there may be neither
any misunderstanding either of the intention of the United States
or misconstruction of the execution of that intention, and they
are not stipulated as indicating any intention on the part of the
United States, until the situation has in its judgment changed,
to depart from as full compliance with the recommendation of
the permanent military representatives as the nature of the case
will permit."

T MS (WP, DLC).

From Robert Wickliffe Woolley and Matthew Hale, with Enclosure

Dear Mr. President: Washington April 19, 1918.

With great respect we beg to submit that in our opinion the
Administration's entire production program is threatened by an
alarming labor situation. Ships, transportation, guns, munitions,
food, fuel, all alike, are irretrievably linked to this underlying factor.

Labor unrest is increasing to a threatening extent.

Strikes are more numerous than at any previous time.

Competitive bidding for labor by government departments and
government contractors is flagrant and on the increase. Government boards establish diverse standards.

Officers of labor unions confess to finding it increasingly difficult, and frequently impossible, to hold their men.

At certain points serious shortage of skilled labor is offset by a
similar surplus at other points.

The creation of various wage boards, including your recent appointment of the Taft-Walsh board, has effected a judicial machinery which, when brought into proper relation, will be of great value.
It is in danger, however, of failing of its full usefulness if not supported by coordinate administrative machinery. Today there exist,
in addition to the bureaus of the Department of Labor, labor sections
in the War Industries Board, the Shipping Board, the Navy and
War departments, and the Fuel Administration, all acting independently of each other. There are also certain sections of a projected labor administration as outlined by the advisory board under
former Governor Lind. The majority of these sections, however, are

still uncreated. To meet this condition, we beg to respectfully suggest:

a) *The appointment by Secretary Wilson, with your approval, of a Director General of Labor.* Secretary Wilson may then place upon the Director General full responsibility for the organization and administration of appropriate machinery. The Director General must have administrative ability of a high order, and must approach the problem with imagination, insight, and rare human sympathy.

b) *The creation by the Director General of Labor of the administrative machinery necessary.* Recommendations for this have already been made by the advisory board under Governor Lind.

c) *The temporary loan to the Director General of Labor,* from funds placed at your disposal by Congress, of moneys adequate to meet the expenses of the labor administration until Congress shall have appropriated for its support.

d) *The issuance of Executive Orders* by the Secretaries of War and Navy, Chairmen of the Shipping Board and War Industries Board, the Fuel Administrator, and other agencies, placing under the Director General of Labor all agencies in their departments dealing with the labor problem.

For the post of Director General of Labor we submit the name of Mr. Justice Brandeis.   Faithfully yours,   R. W. Woolley
Matthew Hale

TLS (WP, DLC).

E N C L O S U R E

ADDENDUM TO LABOR LETTER, APRIL 19, 1918.

I. WAGE POLICY.

Today the Government is by far the largest employer of labor. Wages are fixed by different departments on the basis of their own situation and without following any general policy. They are frequently fixed without consultation with the officials of other departments responsible for the labor policy in these departments. For example:

1. a) A ship-building adjustment board has fixed the wage to be paid in all shipyards throughout the country. The Shipping Board frankly state that these wages were fixed above the going rates because it was necessary to draw men from other employments to ship building. The Shipping Board state that they purposely fixed a rate which might disturb the labor situation in the localities because of the pressing need

for securing ship workers. This constituted the wage policy for the Shipping Board.

b) The unions have since made a demand upon the Navy Department to bring the wages of navy yards up to the wages in ship yards. The navy yards are raising their maximum rates to the ship yard rates.

c) The unions have now made a demand upon the War Department to raise the rates in arsenals to the ship yard rates. This demand is under consideration.

d) The unions have now demanded of the War Department that the wages in the Remington Arms Company be raised to the ship yards rate. The Remington Arms is the key industry in the key munitions city of New England.[1]

Result:

Organized labor has a definite policy which is to raise the wages in industry to the ship yard rates. This is contrary to the wage policy of the Shipping Board. If it is desirable from a national point of view that the ship yard rates should be above other rates, all production departments should be so advised. If it is desirable, on the other hand, that the rates of all war industries shall be standardized, all departments should be so advised.

2. The National Adjustment Commission, appointed by the Shipping Board, War Department and Labor Department, adjusted a longshore difficulty in San Diego on a basis of say 65¢ per hour; the Navy at the same time adjusted a similar difficulty at the same location on the basis of 70¢ per hour. The figures are given from memory, the facts are correct.

3. Overtime. The Ship Building Adjustment Board in certain cases is allowing two and one half times for overtime; the War Department is going on the basis of the conditions in the locality, which in some cases is double time and in some cases time and a half. Organized labor cannot understand the difference.

4. The Railway Adjustment Board is now fixing wages for 2,000,000 men. They state that the wages fixed by the Ship Building Adjustment Board make their problem many times more difficult. The latter are fixing wages in machine shops without consultation with the War and Navy Departments, at the same time the War and Navy Departments are fixing wages in machine shops without consultation with either the Ship Building Adjustment Board or the Railway Adjustment Board.

II. CONDITIONS OF LABOR.

1. Eight-Hour Day. The Taft-Walsh board avoided the question of the uniform eight hour day, leaving it where it was. The eight-hour law is variously interpreted by the Navy and by the Army.

The result is unrest, because organized labor does not understand. Example: In an ordnance shop, the workers on repeat work making parts of guns are on a basic eight hour day; the workers making the tools and jigs, which is a more skilled trade, are not on the eight hour day basis. This is in accordance with the law, but is obviously not a sound policy. Certain work as to which the eight hour law does not apply is being put on the eight hour hasis [basis] by the Government.

III. EMPLOYMENT.

There is continuous flagrant drawing of labor by one department from another, and by Government contractors from other Government contractors. Examples:

1. A representative of the Department of Labor was sent into North Carolina to secure common labor for the Army and Navy at Hampton Roads. He secured 300 laborers and had them on the platform to take to Hampton Roads at Government expense. Two hundred of the 300 were taken away from him on the platform by an agent of a Government contractor who offered a slightly higher wage.

2. Government contractors are sending agents into Hampton Roads to take labor out of Hampton Roads at the same time that the Government is trying to bring labor in there.

3. A contractor for one procurement department took a carload of laborers to New London. When they left the car more than two-thirds of them were taken away by a contractor for another procurement department in the same town who offered a fraction of a cent higher wage.

IV. ADJUSTMENTS OF STRIKES.

When a strike occurs in a munitions plant, the production department sends a representative to adjust it; the Department of Labor sends a representative to adjust it. Where the two adjustors cooperate the results are satisfactory. In many cases they have different ideas, and there is no one to force them to work on the same basis. In general, a contractor prefers to follow the advice of the adjustor from the production department. The labor involved will follow the advice of the adjustor whose ideas are more generous to them in the particular instance, which in some cases is one and in some cases the other.

T MS (WP, DLC).
[1] New Haven, Conn.

From Henry Burchard Fine

My dear Tommy   [Washington] April 19th, 1918

Having found myself in Washington this afternoon almost un-expectedly, I have come here in the hope that by some favoring chance I might have the pleasure of exchanging greetings with you. But I find you too deeply engaged, and so must content myself with this note. I should have the temerity to try again, but must be back in Philadelphia again this evening.

My special errand in Washington was, with Hibben, to call upon Col. Bradley at the War College,[1] in order to learn from him what would be the most approved course for dealing with the problem of the military preparation of our students. There had occurred to us the plan of a course of study similar to that at West Point and we desired to learn his opinion of that. And we wished also to make him realize the difficulty in these war times in keeping boys at their studies who ought to be kept at them, and to give him our opinion that the only effective way of accomplishing this would be to give such students as should take an approved course of study some sort of status as men enlisted in their country's service, though inactive, as reserves. We found Colonel Bradley kindly disposed toward both the plan and the suggestion.

Thanks to your kindness I shall soon have the opportunity as member of the Board of Visitors at Annapolis to get into touch with the problem of the educational training of young men for the Navy.

With the kindest regards to Mrs. Wilson, as ever,

Affectionately Yours,   Henry B. Fine

ALS (WP, DLC).
    [1] John Jewsbury Bradley, at this time chief of the training branch of the General Staff.

To Robert Lansing

My dear Mr. Secretary: [The White House] 20 April, 1918

I have your letter of the eighteenth about the necessary relief of interned enemy aliens and their families and those enemy aliens not interned who have been thrown out of employment as a result of the war, and am very glad to learn of the arrangement which has now been made with the Swiss and Swedish Legations in that matter. I think that perhaps the best way of making the arrange-ment public and giving it the proper standing and dignity would be for you yourself to issue a brief statement and make a special request of the Associated Press through Mr. Noyes, its President here, to carry this statement and give it the prominence which we ought in mere justice and right to give it.

Cordially and sincerely yours,   Woodrow Wilson

TLS (Letterpress Books, WP, DLC).

To Lee Slater Overman

My dear Senator: [The White House] 20 April, 1918

Thank you for your letter of yesterday.[1] I am heartily obliged to you for consulting me about the Court-Martial Bill, as perhaps I may call it for short.[2] I am wholly and unalterably opposed to such legislation, and very much value the opportunity you give me to say so. I think it is not only unconstitutional, but that in character it would put us nearly upon the level of the very people we are fighting and affecting to despise. It would be altogether inconsistent with the spirit and practice of America, and in view of the recent legislation, the Espionage Bill, the Sabotage Bill, and the Woman Spy Bill, I think it is unnecessary and uncalled for.

I take the liberty, my dear Senator, of expressing myself in this emphatic way because my feeling is very deep about the matter, as I gather your own is.

It is admirable the way you have been handling these important bills and I thank you with all my heart for standing by the bill which bears your name without any compromise of any kind. The efforts at amendment are not sincere in purpose and would only injure the bill, and injure it, I am afraid, by intention.

It gives me the greatest satisfaction to tell you how much I have appreciated what you have been doing.

Cordially and sincerely yours,   Woodrow Wilson

TLS (Letterpress Books, WP, DLC).
[1] It is missing.
[2] S. 4364, introduced by George E. Chamberlain on April 16 and referred to the Committee on Military Affairs. The bill provided that anyone, whether an American citizen or the citizen or subject of a foreign nation, who was found to be obstructing the American war effort by word or action in numerous specified ways was to be considered a spy and therefore subject to court-martial by either army or navy authorities and to the death penalty, or other punishment determined by the court-martial, if convicted. The full text of the bill appears in the *New York Times*, April 17, 1918.
Wilson's letter condemning the bill was printed in the *New York Times*, April 23, 1918. The same story reported that Senators Borah and Brandegee had attacked the measure as unconstitutional and that Brandegee wished to have it taken from the Military Affairs Committee and referred to the Judiciary Committee. Another article in that issue printed the text of a letter from Thomas W. Gregory to William Gordon, Democratic congressman from Ohio, written between April 19 and 22, in which the Attorney General revealed that the bill had been drafted by Assistant Attorney General Charles Warren and sent by him, together with a supporting memorandum, to Chamberlain on or about April 8. Gregory added that Warren's action became known to him

only on April 18, that he strongly disapproved of it, and would not have permitted it had he known that it was contemplated. Warren "resigned" his position on April 19. *Ibid.*, April 20, 1918.

Chamberlain announced on April 23 that he was withdrawing the bill and stated that Wilson's opposition made it pointless to attempt to pass it, since a veto was certain if it passed. *Ibid.*, April 24, 1918.

To William Schley Howard

My dear Sir: [The White House] 20 April, 1918

My attention has been called to a recent communication by Mr. Holloman to the Atlanta Constitution concerning our recent conversation at the Executive Office in the interview which you sought with me.[1] Mr. Holloman, of course, had no direct knowledge of that conversation and his version of it conveys a very false impression, no doubt unintentionally on his part, but the impression it conveys is so false that I write to ask whether it is or is not your intention yourself to correct that impression.

                              Very truly yours,   Woodrow Wilson

TLS (Letterpress Books, WP, DLC).

[1] James Arthur Holloman, "Wilson Hands Off in Georgia Fight," *Atlanta Constitution*, April 17, 1918. Holloman, the Washington correspondent of the *Atlanta Constitution*, wrote of Howard's interview with Wilson as follows:

"Several days ago [March 29] Congressman Howard had a long interview with President Wilson in which the Georgia situation was gone into thoroughly. Neither the president nor Mr. Howard will discuss what transpired at that conference, but I am reliably informed the facts are as follows:

"Howard told President Wilson that a great majority of the people of Georgia were loyal to his administration and to his war policies and resented the misrepresentations of them by their junior senator [Hardwick], but that he was sincere in believing that Harris, who had been promoted as the Wilson candidate, in Georgia, was not the choice of the rank and file of the Georgia loyalists. He told the president of his own desire to enter the race. To this the president replied that he felt very kindly to Chairman Harris, the latter had always been loyal to him and faithful as a government department head, but that as between two loyal democrats he would take no stand, as the results of his having taken a stand in state contests, two or three of which he named, including Georgia, at which time Hardwick was nominated, had not been entirely satisfactory or pleasing to him.

"In this connection Howard informed the president if he was irrevocably committed to Harris, and should express to the democrats of Georgia, in a statement, the hope that they might elect Harris, that although he did not speak to Harris he would show the measure of his loyalty and his regard for his president's wishes by going on the stump for Harris in Georgia in order to encompass the defeat of Hardwick. The president replied that he hoped Howard would not enter the race, but in the event he should do so, as between two good loyal men in opposition to Senator Hardwick, he would not attempt to inject himself into the situation.

"It is reported that Howard left the matter in this shape and notified the president that he had decided to enter the race the day prior to the issuance of his formal announcement."

To Howard Earle Coffin

My dear Mr. Chairman: [The White House] 20 April, 1918

I quite understand and very sincerely appreciate the motives which have led you to submit to me your resignation as Chairman of the Aircraft Board, but I am going to take the liberty of withholding action upon it because the Secretary of War and I are in the midst of considering questions of reorganization. We do not in the least underestimate the valuable services which you and your associates in the Board have performed, and we want to effect the best possible coordination, in which we can all pull in the same harness.   Cordially and sincerely yours,   Woodrow Wilson

TLS (Letterpress Books, WP, DLC).

To Henry Burchard Fine

My dear Harry: The White House 20 April, 1918

I am heartily sorry to have missed you when you were here. That day was not only very full, but I had the ill luck to burn my hand in the British tank which called on me early in the afternoon and was a little bit out of commission for the time being.[1] Let me know beforehand next time you come down and we can get together.

   In haste   Affectionately yours,   Woodrow Wilson

TLS (WC, NjP).
[1] Wilson, on April 19, had burned his hand on the exhaust pipe of a British tank which was in Washington as part of a campaign to promote the sale of Liberty bonds. The accident occurred as Wilson was alighting from the tank after a ride around the White House grounds. *New York Times*, April 20, 1918.

From Robert Somers Brookings

My dear Mr President: Washington April 20, 1918.

You are doubtless familiar with the proposed action of the War Trade Board looking to the increase of our available ocean tonnage. The War Trade Board has notified me of their intention of so curtailing the importation of hides and leather (and probably wool) that when their action is made public it will doubtless lead to immediate speculation in the articles affected with the result of a runaway market.

The price of clothing has already advanced to a point where I am in daily receipt of letters from state and national retail organizations urging the Government to take some action with a view of stabilizing cotton and wool fabrics. The present estimate of the

Government needs for wool this year is so large a proportion of all that is on hand, and all that will be raised during the year as to make it vitally important for us to control the entire crop, and we are now negotiating with the Wool Growers' Association (who represent the producers), the wool dealers and woolen manufacturers looking to an agreement which will not only stabilize the price of wool, but the manufactured products as well.

We are also negotiating with the hide and leather trade in hopes of bringing about a similar situation in the hide, leather and leather products industry.

The negotiation with cotton manufacturers to which your attention was recently called still continues with good prospects of reaching a satisfactory result.

I am simply giving you this information in advance and hope soon to be able to submit for your consideration an agreement or understanding with these various interests which will meet with your approval. The prices of cotton, wool and leather products largely involve the cost of living, and necessarily in turn involve the great problem of labor wage. The labor wage and cost of living are inseparable. It is probably our most important economic problem.

I understand that Great Britain has so stabilized the cost of living (with a fixed price on standard shoes and clothing for the laboring class) as to establish a more or less basic relation between the cost of living and the scale of wages, in preparation for the inevitable competition between nations after the war. It is perfectly evident that unless we make some effort in this direction we will soon find our values (including wages) established on a basis that will practically destroy the great advantage which our raw materials and merchant marine should give us in competing for the world's trade after the war.

As a Trustee of the Carnegie Peace Foundation, I made a special study for several years before the war of colonial differential tariffs and their influence upon the three great industrial nations, Germany, Great Britain and the United States. As a result it is a conviction with me that a permanent peace must provide for a greater equality of trade opportunity between the nations, which of course means increased competition.

If you could give me, Mr President, for my guidance (and, of course, in confidence if you wish) an expression of your views regarding this important problem, I am sure it will prove most helpful.   Respectfully yours,   Robt. S. Brookings

TLS (WP, DLC).

From Albert Shaw

Dear Mr. President: New York April 20, 1918.

I was discussing the Overman bill with Dr. Frederick A. Cleveland[1] at the Cosmos Club the other day (you know Dr. Cleveland's work as an expert in public accounting, budget making and administrative efficiency), and I was much impressed by the vigor of his views. I asked him to write me a letter giving his argument for the Overman bill; and, with a little sub-editing, I have made his letter into what seems to me a very effective article for the May number of the "Review of Reviews" which is just now going to press.[2]

Dr. Cleveland adheres strongly to the views you set forth in "Congressional Government." He was much interested when I told him of the opportunity you gave me so long ago to read parts of the manuscript of that book as you were writing it.

As for my own views, I was in doubt and "on the fence" for a little time after the Overman bill was introduced; but I have come to believe that the principles of the measure are sound, and that you should at once have the opportunity to make the adjustments you find to be best in the Administrative machinery.

I greatly hope that in consequence of new legislation, it will be possible for you to take a good many permanent steps in the direction of those logical relationships between the two branches of government, the lack of which is going to hurt us much more now than in times past, because it has become necessary for government to expand its functions so greatly.

It occurs to me that just at this moment, with the Overman bill pending, you might like to glance over Dr. Cleveland's vigorous letter, and so I am taking the liberty to enclose advance proofs.[3] I also slip in a galley proof of editorial notes of my own in support of the measure.[4]

The war situation has left for us no alternatives of policy. I accept, therefore, most cheerfully and completely, your decisions regarding the sending of as many men as possible to help build up the Allied reserves. My views which I had expressed to you before, regarding the relative importance for the year 1918 of the financial, shipbuilding, agricultural and supply features of our program, were expressed in the light of European conditions as understood by us several months ago.[5] It is plain that we have now to push *all* parts of the program, and I think the country is ready to respond with a wholly new spirit of devotion and enthusiasm.

You have rendered the common cause an immense service by securing unity of command under General Foch. Undoubtedly Schwab[6] is the right man to help Hurley build ships; and the War

Department business seems to be straightening out very rapidly. I hope that upon the foundations laid for the aviation program there may soon appear results that will literally scrape the skies.

As ever,   Faithfully yours,   Albert Shaw.

TLS (WP, DLC).
    [1] At this time secretary of the Industrial Service and Equipment Co.
    [2] Frederick A. Cleveland, "Making Democracy Efficient: The Overman Bill as an Opportunity," *American Review of Reviews*, LVII (May 1918), 500-502. Cleveland suggested that the Overman bill, with a few amendments, provided the opportunity to create in the United States the kind of efficient and responsible cabinet government which Wilson himself had advocated many years earlier in *Congressional Government* and other writings.
    [3] That is, of the article just cited.
    [4] "As to the Overman Bill" and "Making Democracy Efficient," *American Review of Reviews*, LVII (May 1918), 460. These brief editorials reiterated the argument set forth in Cleveland's article.
    [5] See A. Shaw to WW, Dec. 8, 1917, Vol. 45.
    [6] Hurley had appointed Charles Michael Schwab, president and chairman of the board of directors of the Bethlehem Steel Corporation, as Director General of the Emergency Fleet Corporation on April 16. *New York Times*, April 17, 1918, and Edward N. Hurley, *The Bridge to France* (Philadelphia, 1927), pp. 135-39.

Lord Reading to David Lloyd George

Washington [April 20, 1918], R. 650 p.m. April 21st, 1918.

Very urgent. Following for Prime Minister:

Last night Secretary Baker, after long consultation with President, submitted a memorandum to me substantially in terms set out hereunder. I considered it this morning with Generals Bridges, Hutchinson and Maclachlan who accompanied me later to Secretary Baker's office. Eventually and after I had had some further conversation with Baker upon various points I took the document to submit to you and (sic) upon the understanding that I should bring before him any objections you wished to raise. Following is text of memorandum.

Beginning of "D."

Pursuant to direction of the President and in conformity with his approval of joint note of permanent Military representatives at Versailles, United States will continue throughout the months of April, May, June and July to supply for transportation, both in its own and controlled tonnage and in that made available by Great Britain, infantry and machine gun personnel. It is hoped, and on the basis of study so far it is believed, that total number of troops transported will be 120,000 per month. These troops when transported will, under direction and at the discretion of General Pershing, be assigned for training and use with British, French, or American divisions as exigencies of the situation from time to time require; it being understood that this programme to the extent that it is a departure from plan to transport and assemble in Europe complete American divisions, is made in view of exigencies of present military situation and is made in order to bring into useful cooperation at the earliest possible moment largest number of American personnel in the military armament needed by the Allies.

It being also understood that this statement is not to be regarded as a commitment from which Government of United States is not free to depart when exigencies no longer require it; and also that preferential transportation of infantry and machine gun units here set forth as a policy and principle is not to be regarded as so exclusive as to prevent Government of United States from including in troops carried by its own tonnage from time to time relatively small numbers of personnel of other arms as may be deemed wise by United States as replacements and either to make possible use of a maximum capacity of ships or most efficient use of infantry and machine gun units as such transported or maintenance (sic) of sources of supply already organised and in process of construction for American army already in France.

These suggestions are made in order that there may be a clear understanding of intention of United States and of mode of execution of that intention and they are not stipulated as indicating any intention on the part of United States, until situation has in its judgment changed, to depart from as full compliance with recommendation of Permanent Military Representatives as nature of the case will permit. (End of D.).

I told Secretary Baker that I had hoped document would contain a definite undertaking to transport 120,000 infantrymen and machine gun units whereas there was no definite commitment and a reservation was made to include relatively small numbers of personnel of other arms. Secondly, we should have (? group omitted "liked") discretion to have been exercisable by Supreme Military Council or General Foch. To first, Baker replied that if there should be more shipping available they hoped to send more troops but that there were small numbers of personnel of other arms of which they must keep (? liberty) to ship in their own tonnage and, secondly, that United States Government could not be asked to part with discretion as to assigning of its own troops for training and use with divisions of other armies (? or its) own army should it in an emergency require infantrymen but that General Pershing's discretion would doubtless be influenced by views of Council and General Foch. I did not think we could use pressure upon these points at this moment.

My view is that we should accept document as presented. I think President means to hold to his original undertaking whilst giving effect to some objections raised by Pershing so as to make it more easily acceptable by latter. I shall send you further observations tomorrow.[1]

T telegram (W. Wiseman Papers, CtY).
[1] This telegram was circulated to the King and the War Cabinet.

Jesse Richardson Hildebrand[1] to Joseph Patrick Tumulty

Press Room The White House
Memorandum for Mr. Tumulty: April, 20 [1918].

Herewith is a copy of a letter, similar to a number received by The Star, relative to the forthcoming production here at popular prices of "The Birth of a Nation."[2]

There is considerable feeling among colored people here about this picture and leaders of the colored folk insist that it is hurting the Liberty Loan and the Red Cross subscriptions among colored people, and otherwise causing discontent.

These letters have not been printed, because agitation would increase the feeling. The office suggested that I refer the matter to you because, if you deemed advisable, an informal request from the White House to Mr. Griffith probably would result in a suspension of exhibitions of the film in war time.

Very truly,   J R Hildebrand[3]

TLS (WP, DLC).
[1] Reporter and feature writer for the Washington *Evening Star*.
[2] Henry Jenkins to the Washington *Evening Star*, c. April 20, 1918, TCL (WP, DLC).
[3] "I have always felt that this was a very unfortunate production and I wish most sincerely that its production might be avoided, particularly in communities where there are so many colored people." WW to JPT, c. April 22, 1918, TL (WP, DLC). Plans for the showing of *The Birth of a Nation* were apparently canceled; there are no advertisements for it in the entertainment sections of the *Washington Post* during April, May, and June 1918.

Gavin McNab to Edward Mandell House

My dear Colonel House: San Francisco, April 20, 1918.

I regret very much that I did not have an opportunity to meet you when in the East. I very much wanted to speak to you about a matter, very dear to my heart.

Do you not think that it is unwise for the President to write political letters like that Wisconsin one?[1]

The President is not only the head of the Nation at probably its greatest crisis, but he is the leader of the whole world. On him, more than on any man in history, perhaps, depends the future of civilization. Does it not occur to you that, under these circumstances, the President can depend on the general feelings and knowledge of the people and their appreciation of his lofty character and noble purposes, and that, if these are not sufficient to insure him support, it is idle to attempt to obtain such support by personal appeal in individual instances?

Considering the majestic position the President occupies, it seems to me a loss of proportion and a sacrifice of dignity to enter any state contest personally. I may liken it to a jarring note in the sacred music of a great Cathedral choir.

The opponents of the President are anxious to find something through which they can thwart and injure him for partisan purposes. They have been afraid to engage in this openly. This Wisconsin act was the most welcome thing to them: it gave them their only opportunity.

Hayes, the National Republican Chairman, was here the other day and gave a banquet. He, and his associates, made free use of this letter of the President, which William Kent, former Congressman and now Tariff Commissioner, used very adversely to the President in the Wisconsin campaign through clever construction. Using this letter and the Kent construction of it, they were able to work upon the prejudices of many people and secure their attendance at the banquet—some people who, otherwise, would not have been there.

I find that this is being extensively used throughout the West in the charge that the President is not above crude partisanship during the war. I wish very much that this were not so.

Like yourself, I have the deepest and most unselfish regard for the President: his nobility—his magnificence of character—his supreme leadership. I wish that the Party leaders would not impose upon his good nature in individual instances and drag him from his pedestal into local issues.

I realize, Colonel House, that it would be very unfortunate if the next Senate and House should go adversely to the President. I recognize that the great principles on which our people must progress to a higher civilization are dependent on the execution of the President's great purposes.

I cannot share the optimism that seemed to permeate the National Committee when I was in Washington.

I hope the people will give the President the majority of his faith. But some things that the National Committee does, while acting with the best intentions, to me cheapen the situation. I am doubtful of the wisdom of some of the things the National Committee did in relation to the Wisconsin affair, though of course, they acted according to best judgment at the time: we can always see better after things are over. For example:

After the Wisconsin election, the National Committee issued a proclamation which, to me, was lacking in force and dignity under the circumstances—we having been defeated.[2] I should have thought that, before issuing a statement of this kind, the President's immediate advisors in Washington should have been consulted. I doubt whether this was done. But proclamations are too important to be issued hastily or on the spur of the moment. I mention it here so that those, close to the President, may consider the advisability of holding conferences with the National Committee before further action, and before statements are issued.

After the President's letter, these pronunciamientoes of the Committee were naturally, by poorly informed people, associated with the same transaction.

I firmly believe, Colonel House, that, by proper measures, both the Senate and the House, this autumn, can be returned, favorable to the President, but I am very sure that it cannot be so done on the lines of the Wisconsin campaign.

I believe that the President should depend upon the people-at-large without reference to personal effort or endeavor beyond the discharge of his mighty duties. However, it is the duty of every man who believes in the President and his work for mankind to take practical measures along lines of broad-gauge intelligence to assist in producing this result. This can, and must, be done.

Knowing your profound love for the President and your patriotism, I am therefore expressing my feelings and convictions.

With kindest regards, I am

Yours very sincerely,   Gavin McNab

I am sending this for your information. E.M.H.

TLS (WP, DLC).
[1] That is, WW to J. E. Davies, March 18, 1918. For assessments of the significance of this letter in the Wisconsin senatorial election, see Seward W. Livermore, *Politics Is Adjourned: Woodrow Wilson and the War Congress, 1916-1918* (Middletown, Conn., 1966), pp. 117-21, and Herbert F. Margulies, *Senator Lenroot of Wisconsin: A Political Biography, 1900-1929* (Columbia, Mo., 1977), pp. 244-47.
[2] The Democratic National Committee had issued a statement on April 3 in which it charged that Lenroot had fought the senatorial primary campaign on the issue of "loyalty" to the United States and then, following the advice of the Republican National Committee, had reversed himself by courting the La Follette and pro-German vote within the Republican party during the election campaign against Davies. Davies, in contrast, had deliberately spurned the pro-German vote and had stood consistently for "100 per cent Americanism." The complete statement is printed in the *New York Tribune*, April 4, 1918.

From Edward Mandell House

Dear Governor: New York. April 21, 1918.

I have a cable from Sir William saying that he has arrived and that as soon as he can get a line on the situation he will cable fully. We should have some interesting news in a few days.

I sincerely hope that the newspapers have [ex]aggerated the accident you had on the tank. I have been trying to get Grayson on the telephone today in order to ask about you.

Affectionately yours,   E. M. House

TLS (WP, DLC).

From Robert Wickliffe Woolley and Matthew Hale

Dear Mr. President: Washington April 21, 1918.

We beg to report that, in obedience to your request,[1] we conferred today with Secretary Wilson as to the suggestion that he be authorized to appoint at the earliest possible moment a Director General of Labor and left with him a copy of our letter to you.

It was a pleasure to find he was in hearty accord with the idea and that he dwelt upon the importance of selecting for the place an outstanding figure in our national life whose breadth of vision and human sympathy are unquestioned.

With great respect, we are

Faithfully yours,   R. W. Woolley
                    Matthew Hale

TLS (WP, DLC).
[1] Conveyed orally, when Wilson saw Woolley at the White House at 5 p.m. on April 19.

From Anita Eugénie McCormick Blaine

Chicago, Ills., April 21, 1918.

In a school of which I am a trustee[1] an incident has brought up the question of what the school attitude should be toward pupils who have any sympathetic leaning toward Germany and toward pupils who are not with the war because of conscientious objections to war. Should both or either type be excluded from a school during the period of the war? I am not putting the question with a negative cast. Any cleavage between the forces for and against the war seems desirable. I am only wanting my responsibility to that part of the community so far as it goes to be in the line of what the government would approve. The pupils are of high school age and below. The influence of the school of the community in which there are many families of German origin should have a bearing on the question; two, and it seems important enough even to ask you this if you feel that you can give me light on this question I shall not consider that I may use it except as a guide for my own vote unless you say that I may be quoted. If you can send a reply may it be by telegraph, as the question is urgent.   Anita McCormick Blaine.

T telegram (WP, DLC).
  [1] The Francis W. Parker School in Chicago, a private school founded by Mrs. Blaine in 1901.

From Jessie Woodrow Wilson Sayre

Dearest, dearest Father,   Siasconset Mass. April 21, 1918

Here we are in Siasconset, Frank and I, having a very happy little *Easter* vacation, a vacation which Frank needed. He is spending most of it *studying*, but our long rambles over the moors every afternoon are freshening him up. I, strangely enough, was not even tired, in spite of the long siege with the children. I believe my little visit with you all[1] was such a tonic that even Frankie's 105° degrees of temperature couldn't bowl me over except for the first minute. I don't suppose, Ive had time to write that the chickens both had tonsilitis—in succession—and so prevented, temporarily, having their tonsils removed. But they have only postponed it, little rascals!

Incidentally we are seeing about the house and garden for the summer. I wish to add again, minutely, to the food supply. I had dreamed of sending you the *first* proceeds of last year's garden but, alas, though good to eat it was not good enough to *look* at, and I didn't send it.

This dear old island makes me look forward with pleasure to the summer again—*if only*—I weren't so far away from you all. I wish I could ask Cousin Helen or somebody to come and stay with me but it wouldn't do to ask *her*, for her conscience would stand in the way and she wouldn't feel it was enough of a duty. I wish I could persuade her that I *need* someone to walk around and play with and help me take care of all my summer family. Your permission to suggest it would help but I'm afraid I'm being very, very selfish to ask such a thing.

Frank sails the end of June, probably, and we are hoping to deposit the household here about the 15th of June. (Please excuse my illegible writing; my hands are cold, for S'conset has not warmed up to the promise of spring *yet*)

I can't tell you what my lovely little visit to you all meant to me. It is a constant joy to remember! I will write Edith very soon. Please give her my dearest love, and to yourself a whole heart full of devotion,   Adoringly Jessie

ALS (WP, DLC).
  [1] Mrs. Sayre had spent the weekend of March 23-24 at the White House.

Lord Reading to David Lloyd George

Washington. 21st April 1918.

Following for Prime Minister. Personal and Very Secret.

I very earnestly hope that you will not ask me to raise objection to the Memorandum of which I sent you text yesterday. I am fully alive to the extreme necessity of getting these troops but it would be a mistaken policy to try to amend the text for I am sure that no better result will be obtained. The document is formulated to carry out the President's view as originally indicated to me and is contrary to General Pershing's view as related in the second and third paragraphs of your No. 2017. Observe particularly the beginning of the Memorandum. As cabled to you it is, save for comparatively unimportant alteration of some words and the addition of the words "as such" (explained later herein) as presented to me by Secretary Baker immediately after his consultation with the President. If a conflict of opinion should hereafter be raised between the civil authorities here and the American Military authorities in France this document would afford an explanation of the action of the civil authorities, of some of the circumstances that led to their decision and the conditions they thought right to insert. Although the document is longer and fuller of qualifications than I like it provides in substance (save as regards relatively small numbers of personnel of other arms carried by American tonnage) for the shipment of 120,000 infantrymen and machine gun units per month for four months.

The words "as such" were introduced by Secretary Baker to meet my objection that as originally worded the "most efficient use" might be to form complete divisions with all other arms. He said these words were not introduced with that intention and in order to limit the meaning he inserted somewhat hurriedly words "as such" before "transported." These words are probably more intelligible and excusable with this explanation but they certainly make bad reading.

Secretary Baker repeated that if there are more good ships available they will be able to send more infantrymen but he objects to the slow ships proposed by us. I have discussed this question with Graeme Thompson and with his assistance am taking it up and will report later.   R.

T telegram (Reading Papers, FO 800/224, PRO).

To Anita Eugénie McCormick Blaine

My dear Mrs. Blaine: The White House 22 April, 1918

I value your telegram of April twenty-first and your courtesy in consulting me.

I am just now very deeply concerned about the treatment which is being accorded those people throughout the country who do not show an active sympathy with the purposes and the prosecution of the war but who take no active measures to oppose or impede it and whose offense is merely one of opinion. I feel that we should in our treatment of such people vindicate in every way our claim that we stand for justice and fairness and highminded generosity. Of course, if any such person is dangerous to the Government or to the community in which he or she lives, that is another matter and should be brought to the attention of the representatives of the Department of Justice, but I have a very great passion for the principle that we must respect opinion even when it is hostile, and I should feel, as I think you do, that we ought to be very careful to vindicate that principle.

Cordially and sincerely yours,   Woodrow Wilson

TLS (Anita Eugénie McCormick Blaine Papers, WHi).

To Lee Slater Overman

My dear Senator: [The White House] 22 April, 1918

I am taking the liberty of sending you the enclosed because I think that both the letter and its enclosure may interest you.

Doctor Shaw and I were fellow-students at the Johns Hopkins years ago, and I learned there to have a very real confidence in his character and public spirit.

May I ask that you let me have his letter again when you have read it?   Cordially and sincerely yours,   Woodrow Wilson

TLS (Letterpress Books, WP, DLC).

To Albert Shaw

My dear Shaw: The White House 22 April, 1918

Your letter of April twentieth with its enclosures has interested me extremely, and I want you to know how it cheers me to feel that what we are doing now has the full approval of your own judgment, because I value your judgment. I have taken the liberty of letting Senator Overman see Doctor Cleveland's letter and your editorial comments. I am sure he will be stimulated by them.

In great haste

Cordially and sincerely yours,   Woodrow Wilson

TLS (A. Shaw Coll., NjP).

To William Benjamin Munson

My dear Sir: [The White House] 22 April, 1918

I have received your letter of April seventeenth and take the liberty of saying that I have been greatly shocked by the suggestion which it contains. I should feel that to act upon such a suggestion would be to emulate the spirit which we have so condemned in the Germans themselves. I cannot believe that after mature consideration you would feel that the course you have suggested should in fact be acted upon.   Very truly yours,   Woodrow Wilson

TLS (Letterpress Books, WP, DLC).

To Robert Somers Brookings

My dear Mr. Brookings: [The White House] 22 April, 1918

Thank you for your letter of April twentieth.

I imply from what you say in the opening paragraph of your letter that the War Trade Board is not likely to act in the matter of curtailing the importation of hides and leather (and probably wool) until the negotiations which you kindly detail to me are completed and the matter of prices adjusted as well as the circumstances permit.

I entirely approve of the course you are pursuing in trying to come to an understanding with the wool and leather and cotton manufacturing people that will be fair to the public and standardize prices. I wish I were wise enough to give you a suggestion, as you express the wish that I would, but, unfortunately, I know so much less about the matter than you do, and my mind is barren.

Cordially and sincerely yours,   Woodrow Wilson

TLS (Letterpress Books, WP, DLC).

To Arthur Everett Shipley

My dear Mr. Shipley: [The White House] 22 April, 1918

It was exceedingly gratifying to me to receive your kind letter of April fifth. I realize the extraordinary honor which Cambridge University has done me in conferring the honorary degree *in absentia*, and am very much touched and moved by it, for I do not feel that I have done anything to deserve it except what any other man with the opportunities I have had would have done.

It is deeply distressing to me to hear of the effects the war has wrought upon the colleges and the University, and I hope with all my heart that in the days to come there may be influences and sources of strength enough to build them again into their old energy and influence.

With kindest regards,

Cordially and sincerely yours,   Woodrow Wilson

TLS (Letterpress Books, WP, DLC).

Two Letters from Joseph Patrick Tumulty

The White House.

Memorandum for the President: 22 April 1918.

Henry Ford asked his representative to see me to say that he did not wish his name considered in connection with the re-organization of the Aircraft Board;

That Colonel Deeds was a competent man and that he should be kept;

That he considered that Potter[1] represented the Wall Street point of view, that he had personally made an investigation of the Curtiss plant in Buffalo and that it was not up to standard.

I thought you ought to have this information.

The Secretary

I hope there may be an opportunity of conveying to Mr. Ford my thanks for this message.   The President.

[1] William Chapman Potter, at this time a member of the firm of Guggenheim Brothers of New York and chief of the aviation equipment division of the Signal Corps.

Dear Governor: [The White House] April 22, 1918

Senator Poindexter has made a speech in the Senate today attacking Mooney and the I.W.W. Senator Phelan asks if he may be permitted to read to the Senate your letter of January 22d to Governor Stephens.[1]   J.P.T.

Yes W.W.

TL (WP, DLC).
[1] That is, WW to W. D. Stephens, Jan. 22, 1918, Vol. 46.

From Robert Lansing, with Enclosure

My dear Mr. President: Washington April 22, 1918

In compliance with your request of April 18th, I am sending you a memorandum which gives you all the information, so far as we now have it, regarding the various movements for self-government in Siberia. Two of the members of the so-called Government of Autonomous Siberia are known to Mr. Boris Bakmeteff as honest and capable men; these are Mr. Oustrougoff,[1] an official of the Ministry of Ways and Communications under the Provisional Government, and Mr Stahl[2] who was active in politics at that time.
                          Faithfully yours,   Robert Lansing.

TLS (SDR, RG 59, 861.00/1664½, DNA).
[1] L. A. Ustrugov.
[2] Aleksei Fedorovich Staal, lawyer and public prosecutor in Moscow under the Provisional Government.

ENCLOSURE

MEMORANDUM   Washington April 22, 1918.
Subject: *Movements for autonomy in Siberia.*

There have appeared three movements for autonomy in Siberia.
1. The Siberian Provincial Assembly which first met at Tomsk in January.
2. The movement in Harbin which centers around General Horvath.
3. The Military venture of Semenoff to put down the Bolsheviki, which has no clear political purpose but which is supported in funds and munitions by Japanese, British and by Russians who back Horvath.

1. The Department has been trying to get clear information about what may be called the "Tomsk" movement ever since it was first reported by Mr. Francis when a delegation appealed to him in January. The attached telegram from Harbin,[1] badly garbled, is the most detailed statement yet obtainable. The movement is weak in

leadership but the Consul reports that it has undoubted popular support.

The merit of this movement would seem to lie in its claim to represent the Zemstvos, municipalities, and cooperative societies of Siberia, as well as numerous national and social bodies.

2. General Horvath's movement claims the support of several influential Russian liberals but its impetus is wholly from outside of Russia; it has no mandate from any body or section of the population within Russia. General Horvath himself, for many years head of the Chinese Eastern Railway, is a survival of the old regime, a man of statesman-like view who is puzzled as to how anything but the monarchial idea can satisfy in the mind of Peasant Russia the void created by the sudden elimination of the Tsar—The Little Father. He is a typical Russian Colonial Administrator of the best type. Any movement headed by him might be expected to be open to the charge of "Counter Revolutionary."

3. Colonel Seminoff is a young Cossack officer who started an independent attempt to produce order by opposing the Bolsheviki. His force is a miscellaneous collection of soldiers, Buriat Cossacks, and officers—not more than 1,000 men. General Horvath has recently proclaimed General Pleshkoff[2] Commander-in-chief of all Russian forces in Siberia and, on paper, Semenoff is now acting under him. There is no evidence that Pleshkoff has been able to accomplish anything tangible as yet.

The French government has received an appeal from the Tomsk movement similar to that received by this Department, and which is attached to this memorandum.[3] It appears that the French Consul at Irkutsk however, has telegraphed he is not yet satisfied with the outlook, (April 13), and that the Russian Ambassador at Paris, Mr. Maklakoff, has advised against doing anything at present. Mr. Boris Bakhmeteff, the Russian Ambassador here, seems to be of the same opinion although he regards both the Tomsk and Horvath movements as encouraging indications. He seems to know all of the men whose support is claimed by Horvath but knows only two of those who are stated to be definitely committed to the Tomsk movement.

The suggestion has been made that so long as the Bolsheviki are not antagonized by the Allies, they and the Austrian prisoners-of-war who are joining them in Siberia may be regarded as co-belligerents with us against autocracy. This also suggests what are the facts about prisoners-of-war. In the whole Russian Empire there are at most 80,000 German soldiers and 1,300,000 Austrian soldiers. Of these, only about 10,000 Germans and 80,000 Austrians are in Siberia. The reported influence of Germany over these prisoners-of-war seems to be greatly exaggerated. Recent telegrams show that practically all the Germans want to go home. The Austro-Hungarians on the other hand are joining the Bolsheviki. There is no indication however, that the arming of prisoners is extensive. The Austro-Hungarians are reported to be dismissing their own officers. When we had charge of German-Austrian interests our representatives reported numerous instances of disaffection among the Austro-Hungarians—both officers and men—towards their own government.

It would appear therefore that with some adjustment of leadership, a coalition of 1. and 2. above, might offer some promise of gaining popular support.   Basil Miles

TS MS (SDR, RG 59, 861.00/1664½, DNA).
    [1] C. K. Moser to RL, April 12, 1918, *FR 1918, Russia*, II, 119-21. Moser described briefly the history, objectives, and leadership of the Tomsk movement or "Government of Autonomous Siberia."
    [2] He cannot be further identified.
    [3] Peter Derber [Petr Iakovlevich Derber] to RL, n.d. but received April 6, 1918, *ibid.*, pp. 101-102. Derber, the prime minister of the Government of Autonomous Siberia, set forth the same list of objectives for his regime given in the telegram cited in n. 1 above.

From Henry French Hollis

Dear Mr. President: [Washington] 22 April, 1918

I have received from a friend in Rhode Island the enclosed bill[1] which passed the Rhode Island Senate unanimously and the Rhode Island House with only a few votes against it. I feel quite sure that both Rhode Island Senators will vote for the Suffrage amendment. My friends wanted this Act called directly to your attention as a very hopeful sign from a conservative State like Rhode Island.
                          Sincerely,   Henry F. Hollis

TLS (WP, DLC).
    [1] State of Rhode Island and Providence Plantations, *S 152 . . . Resolution Relating to Certain Measures now Pending in Congress*, c. Jan. 1918, printed resolution (WP, DLC). It requested the United States senators from Rhode Island to vote for the equal-suffrage amendment to the Constitution.

From William Kent

My dear Mr. President: Washington April 22, 1918.

While in St. Paul at the meeting of the Nonpartisan League, I learned of a dangerous situation in connection with attempts of the State administration to suppress meetings of the League. I met many of the leaders in the movement, and feel certain that it is economic, and along the lines of constructive democracy, and as stated in my telegram to you,[1] that those most interested are entirely loyal to the Government. I wish also to state that they have a confidence in you as a leader in constructive democratic thought that would warm your heart if you could realize it.

There is in Washington an old time friend who has not been connected with the League movement, but who is expert in civic matters, and has a deep-seated public sense and sense of justice. He tells me that the situation is becoming unbearably acute, and that, on a charge of disloyalty, the State Committee on Safety is guilty of high-handed persecution and political tyranny.

I do not wish to worry you with the detail of this situation, but suggest that it is of such national importance that the Administration should be cognizant of the facts. I sincerely hope that you may suggest someone to take up the investigation of this question, in which event I shall be glad to render any assistance in my power, and my Minnesota friend, who is here for a short time, has wonderful facility for getting next to the situation.

Yours truly,   William Kent

TLS (WP, DLC).
    [1] It is missing.

From Theodore Newton Vail

Dear Mr. President: New York April 22, 1918.

The demands of the country and the public upon the service of the Bell Telephone System are calling for our utmost efforts.

We have contributed to the service of the country in the Army, Navy and in other departments of the Government, many of our most highly trained experts and experienced officials. We expect to contribute many more.

The places of these men have, of course, to be filled by those of less training and experience which makes it necessary to keep a closer supervision over our whole organization and for this we need the services of Mr. H. B. Thayer,[1] now with the Aircraft Board, but long associated with this Company in high executive positions and among other duties is President of Western Electric Company, Incorporated, the Manufacturing Company of this System.

We feel that Mr. Thayer can be better spared from this position than he can from our service, having the service to the country as a first consideration.

I, therefore, take the liberty of asking your favorable consideration to his resignation.   Very respectfully yours,   Theo. N. Vail

TLS (WP, DLC).
    [1] Harry Bates Thayer.

Shane Leslie[1] to Joseph Patrick Tumulty

Dear Mr Tumulty,   Washington April 22, 1918

Pardon my presumption and tear up my plan,[2] though it is worth remembering that Rochambeau brought Dillon's Irish Brigade to America.

Whatever plan follows the passing of Home Rule must be the President's, and we Nationalists must follow whatever indications he gives to us. Without him we should not be getting Home Rule, and it is his due to command the Irish sentiment in the world.

Yours very sincerely   Shane Leslie

ALS (WP, DLC).

[1] Anglo-Irish author and poet. Born John Randolph Leslie, he adopted the name Shane and became a Roman Catholic convert while an undergraduate at King's College, Cambridge. He had come to the United States early in 1916 as an unofficial representative of John Redmond. Although Leslie was an advocate of home rule for Ireland, he had close ties to the British embassy in Washington and served as an unpaid anti-German propagandist. See Arthur Willert, *The Road to Safety: A Study in Anglo-American Relations* (London, 1952), pp. 90-92.

[2] Leslie's plan was explained briefly in another letter to Tumulty of April 22, obviously written earlier in the day. He suggested that Wilson "raise a legion from the exempted Irish in America, similar to the Polish legion." "I find," he continued, "that Lafayette brought over a regiment of Irishmen under Dillon in the Revolution. Could not this loan be repaid with such an Irish regiment by Mr Wilson[,] trained and enlisted under the American flag (with a promise of citizenship to all who returned) and brigaded either with the American or French troops in France? Once in France they could draw on voluntary enlistments from Ireland and enable the British Government to withdraw the Conscription proposal which at present promises relief only to the German." S. Leslie to JPT, April 22, 1918, TLS (WP, DLC).

Tumulty had immediately communicated with Leslie—perhaps by telephone—to tell him that this "plan" would be unacceptable to Wilson.

To Edward Parker Davis

My dear E.P.:   [The White House] 23 April, 1918

Thank you for your note about the hand,[1] but please don't worry about it. It was very painful and it is extremely inconvenient to do without the hand's assistance, but it is coming along all right, the doctor thinks, and he hopes that I will not be a great while without its use.

Mrs. Wilson (to her own surprise, I think) enjoyed her day in Philadelphia, and was greatly impressed by the parade.[2] She was very sorry to miss you and Mrs. Davis.

In great haste   Affectionately yours,   Woodrow Wilson

TLS (Letterpress Books, WP, DLC).
[1] It is missing.
[2] Mrs. Wilson had attended a Liberty Loan parade in Philadelphia on April 20.

From Scott Ferris

My dear Mr. President: Washington, D. C. April 23rd, 1918.

I am anxious that you have before you the exact status of the pending general Leasing Bill, which has to do with relief for the oil claimants on the public domain. I have in mind your keen interest in the matter and have felt that I should keep you advised of the very important turn matters have taken in reference thereto.

You will recall that your three Departments of Interior, Navy and Justice, made recommendations for the adoption of the so-called Swanson Amendment. I tried to get that adopted, but was unsuccessful. The majority of the committee adopted the views of the oil men, who were here 50 or 60 in number, and who had presented the matter at very great length before the Committee, and who were insisting on having some 15 or 20 far-reaching amendments adopted by the committee.

So that you may have the matter before you, the so-called Swanson Amendment is as follows:

"That any claimant who, either in person or through his predecessor in interest, entered upon any of the lands embraced within the Executive order of withdrawal dated September 27, 1909, prior to July 3, 1910, honestly and in good faith for the purpose of prospecting for oil or gas, and thereupon commenced discovery work thereon, and thereafter prosecuted such work to a discovery of oil or gas, shall be entitled to lease from the United States any producing oil or gas well resulting from such work, at a royalty of not less than one-eighth of all the oil and gas produced therefrom, together with an area of land sufficient for the operation thereof, but without the right to drill any other or additional wells; Provided That such claimant shall first pay to the United States an amount equal to not less than the value of one-eighth of all the oil and gas already produced from such well: And provided further, That this act shall not apply to any well involved in any suit brought by the United States, or in any application for patent, unless within 90 days after the approvsl [approval] of this act the claimant shall relinquish to the United States all rights claimed by him in such suit or application: And provided further, That all such leases shall be made and the amount to be paid for oil and gas already produced shall be fixed by the Secretary of the Interior under appropriate rules and regulations."

This amendment having been voted down by the Committee, I offered a modified form of the Swanson Amendment which I thought would be acceptable to you. It is as follows:

"Provided, That any claimant who, either in person or through his predecessor in interest, entered upon any of the lands embraced within the Executive order of withdrawal dated September twenty-seventh, nineteen hundred and nine, prior to July third, nineteen hundred and ten, honestly and in good faith, for the purpose of prospecting for oil or gas, and thereupon commenced discovery work thereon, and thereafter prosecuted such work to a discovery of oil or gas, shall be entitled to lease from the United States the producing oil or gas well or wells resulting from such work at a royalty of not less than one-eighth of all the oil and gas produced therefrom, together with an area of land sufficient for the operation thereof, but without the right to drill any other or additional wells, and no wells shall be drilled on lands subject to the terms of this act within six hundred and sixty feet of any such leased well, without the consent of the lessee thereof: Provided, That where the President shall determine that it is to the public interest the Secretary of the Interior may lease the remainder of any such claim to the claimant, upon such terms and conditions as he may prescribe: Provided further, That all such claimants shall first pay to the United States an amount equal to not less than the value of one-eighth of all the oil and gas already produced from such well or wells: And provided further, That this act shall not apply to any well involved in any suit brought by the United States or in any application for patent, unless within six months after approval of this act, the claimant shall relinquish to the United States all rights claimed by him in such suit or application."

This amendment was likewise voted down. They have incorporated other and numerous amendments in the bill which were suggested by the oil men. The bill as it now stands and as it was reported on yesterday, April 22nd, goes far beyond the so-called Swanson Amendment or any other relief that yourself, the Navy, the Interior or Department of Justice have ever agreed to.

I am enclosing herewith a copy of it,[1] as it has been perfected by the Committee, so that you may have it before you.

I have felt it my bounden duty to file a minority report, oppose the majority action of the committee, feeling that it would be the wish of yourself and your three Cabinet members who have given great attention to this matter, to do so, and furthermore that it is in the interest of common justice that these lands be not grabbed up by a lot of oil claimants and speculators, and make a farce out of the leasing bill.

You will recall, I spoke to you about this the other day when I was down there, and as I understood you then, and as I have understood you all along, the Swanson Amendment was the very outside relief that you were willing to accord these so-called oil claimants.

With great respect, I am

Very sincerely yours,   Scott Ferris

TLS (WP, DLC).
    [1] 65th Cong., 2d sess., S. 2812, Committee Print, April 22, 1918, printed bill (WP, DLC). As Ferris indicates above, this document reproduced the text of the bill as amended by the House Committee on Public Lands.

From Harry Augustus Garfield

Dear Mr. President: Washington, D. C. April 23, 1918

In reply to the question asked in your letter of the 18th instant[1] whether anything can be done to regulate the prices of oil, I beg to advise that action limiting price be postponed until further developments concerning Mexican oil, unless, of course, a runaway market develops.

It is true that quoted prices of crude oil have advanced since last August from 15¢ to 75¢ per barrel and that bonuses paid by the independents have advanced the prices still more, but neither Mr. Requa nor Mr. Naramore of the Bureau of Mines,[2] think a runaway market exists at present. Present prices of crude seem to be warranted by the heavy demand and fear of a still greater shortage because of the withdrawal of Mexican oils.

The following statements are set forth at length in the accompanying papers:[3]

(1) There is an actual shortage of domestic oil. We are drawing heavily on our reserve stock of oil and will be compelled to do so to a still greater extent if the Mexican oil is cut off.

(2) The problem, therefore, is to find more oil. This means drilling new wells.

(3) Prices are not too high to stimulate new wells, although the old wells would continue to pump if prices were lower.

(4) The payment of bonuses or premiums of from 10¢ to 50¢ above the quoted prices seems to justify the above statements.

Cordially and faithfully yours,   H. A. Garfield.

TLS (WP, DLC).
    [1] WW to H. A. Garfield, April 18, 1918, TLS (Letterpress Books, WP, DLC).
    [2] Mark Lawrence Requa, general director of the Oil Division of the United States Fuel Administration, and Chester Naramore, chief petroleum technologist and head of the Petroleum Division of the Bureau of Mines.
    [3] M. L. Requa to H. A. Garfield, April 23, 1918, and W. J. Harris to WW, April 17, 1918, both TLS (WP, DLC).

From John Skelton Williams, with Enclosure

Dear Mr. President: Washington April 23, 1918.

I thank you for your note of the 20th instant.[1]

I am most reluctant to intrude further upon your valuable time to discuss the railroad fuel situation, but the problem is such an exceedingly important one to the Railroad Administration that, in the absence of the Director General, I trust you will pardon me for bringing before you certain aspects of the case and some facts which may possibly be worthy of your attention.[2]

The plan which you suggested to Dr. Garfield and to the Railroad Administration at the White House conference on April 3rd[3] would have afforded a very happy solution, and was entirely workable. I am satisfied that it can still be carried out if the Fuel Administration, instead of seeking to find objections, should address themselves with equal earnestness to overcoming whatever difficulties they may think lie in the way.

If, however, the Fuel Administration should refuse definitely to carry out the plan first suggested by you at the White House conference on April 3rd, it will mean, as far as I am able to judge, an unnecessary cost for coal to the Railroad Administration of somewhere from $100,000 to $200,000 per day.

The plan you outlined was eminently practicable. I had already on March 19th had a conference with the President of a large bituminous coal company who had agreed to furnish the Railroad Administration with

4,000,000 tons of fuel coal

and to accept therefore such price as might be <i>determined by the Director General</i> as being fair and equitable, if the old policy should be carried out.

A week later, having thus paved the way for negotiations with other operators, I called a conference in Washington of some ten or fifteen coal operators from the Pennsylvania and West Virginia fields, and it was at this conference that a distinctly selfish spirit was developed on the part of certain operators who opposed the suggestion of concessions to the Railroad Administration, and their spokesman openly threatened to use his "influence" with the Fuel Administration to prevent the Railroads from obtaining the advantages always enjoyed theretofore. The operators, on leaving the meeting, promptly called on Dr. Garfield. I subsequently learned from Dr. Garfield himself that they had slightingly alluded to my appeals to their patriotism in behalf of moderate profits, and the record shows that they then and there began an active propaganda in the newspapers and through other means to wipe out the concessions the Railroads had always had as to fuel, and which they need now more than ever.

The day following my conference with the operators Dr. Garfield promptly brought the subject up at the White House conference (March 27th) and has issued circulars or orders which have aided the operators materially in their fight to maintain the maximum price. I assume that he feels that he is fully justified in all he has done.

Mr. President, I cannot resist the conviction that Dr. Garfield is permitting himself, however unconsciously, to be influenced by the specious and insidious arguments which have been urged upon him by some operators, more in their own behalf than for the common good. I do not, of course, for a moment suggest that the Fuel Administrator is willingly co-operating with the operators for the purpose of enabling them to make greater profits at the public expense, but this is precisely the effect which is being produced.

Statements just received for the two first months of the year, January and February, indicate that our railroads have been compelled to pay for those two months not far from $20,000,000 *additional* for locomotive coal—beyond what they paid in the corresponding months a year ago. This increased cost is at the rate of *more than $100,000,000 per annum.*

I am taking the liberty of attaching hereto a brief memorandum regarding the several conferences held between the Fuel Administrator and the Director of Purchases of the Railroad Administration, which immediately followed the conference at the White House on April 3rd, at which were discussed your very clear and comprehensive suggestions for the solution of the fuel problems.

I also enclose data showing the large percentage of the coal mines in all of the leading coal producing States, which, according to the reports of the Federal Trade Commission, have been making a net profit of $1.00 per ton *and more* on their output. In normal times a profit of 10 cents per ton is generally regarded as satisfactory.

Respectfully and faithfully yours,   Jno Skelton Williams

P.S. If the President should direct a reduction in coal profits from $1 to, say, 50¢ per ton, with the understanding that these profits simply come out of the operators, and are not to affect the profits of the miners, I believe that instead of demoralizing the miners it would have the opposite effect upon them; would make them more contented and less likely to strike or to demand an increase in wages already the highest ever paid. I also believe such a reduction in profits per ton would stimulate operators to increase production so as to keep close to their present big *total* earnings.

Therefore, I think it reasonable to conclude that a material reduction in the large profits *per ton* which are now being received by the coal operators instead of reducing the output of coal would be more apt to lead to a material increase in the production. JSW.

TLS (WP, DLC).
[1] WW to J. S. Williams, April 20, 1918, TLS (Letterpress Books, WP, DLC).
[2] While continuing to serve as Comptroller of the Currency, Williams was now also director of the Division of Finance and Purchases in the United States Railroad Administration.
[3] See the extract from the Diary of Josephus Daniels printed at April 3, 1918.

E N C L O S U R E

MEMORANDUM.

RELATING TO SUGGESTIONS OFFERED BY THE PRESIDENT
IN CONNECTION WITH THE RAILROAD FUEL QUESTION

Under the proposition suggested by the President at the White House conference on April 3rd, the railroads were to be given the opportunity of contracting for their fuel supply on the best terms they could get below the maximum price; roads were to provide the car supply for their own fuel and were to have the privilege of taking substantially the entire output of a mine if this should seem desirable, but in placing their orders in any particular region they were to give the operators generally in that region the opportunity of participating in the railroad contract at the reduced rate, and these mines were thereupon to receive a larger or more constant supply of cars. It was also understood that certain essential industries could be given certain preference in the matter of coal supply, but the coal cars generally were to be distributed as evenly and as equally as possible to all mines.

The day after this suggestion was offered, April 4th, Mr. Baruch of the War Industries Board, Dr. Garfield and myself and several others met to thrash out the plan suggested by the President. Dr. Garfield in a preliminary way explained that the Fuel Administration was well posted as to mining costs and proceeded to explain in detail how accurately and how scientifically the costs per ton were arrived at, in collaboration, as I understood it, with the Federal Trade Commission.

The Fuel Administrator argued earnestly against the plan which had been suggested at the White House conference the preceding day. Nothing was accomplished and we adjourned to meet the following morning, April 5th.

At the second conference at which Mr. Baruch was also present, Dr. Garfield raised questions as to the legal authority of the railroads to give a preferential car supply for locomotive fuel to obtain a concession in price. It was thereupon suggested that this aspect of the case be submitted to members of the Interstate Commerce Commission who were experienced in such matters, and arrangements were made for a conference at the Interstate Building the following morning, April 6th, which was attended by Interstate Commerce Commissioners Harlan[1] and Woolley, Mr. Baruch, Dr. Garfield, Mr. Hines,[2] assistant to the Director General, one of Dr. Garfield's assistants, Mr. Spencer[3] of our Purchasing Committee and myself.

Dr. Garfield presented fully his side of the case and the views of the Railroad Administration were also briefly stated.

Commissioner Harlan made a very clear and comprehensive statement which apparently removed any doubt which Dr. Garfield may have had as to the legality of the plan proposed, and an understanding was reached by all present, which it was hoped would solve the question.

This agreement was briefly set forth in a letter which I wrote the same day, April 6th, immediately after the conference, to the Director General, in which I said:

"Dr. Garfield has at last agreed that the Director General may negotiate with coal operators in all fields except those expressly reserved for by-products ovens, coking, and other metallurgic purposes and may engage to give these operators, in exchange for reduced prices on fuel, whatever car supply he may deem it expedient to allot them, and that this arrangement may be made either with individual operators in the unreserved fields, or with groups of operators in those fields.

"The understanding is that all coal cars not needed for railroad fuel, or for the war industries where priorities may be given, shall be distributed as evenly and as equitably as possible throughout the various coal regions and to the various operators in each region."

This brief extract correctly sets forth the agreement reached, at the conference Saturday, April 6th. It was also agreed at the same time that representatives of the Fuel Administration and of the Railroad Administration should meet for the purpose of mapping out the areas containing by-product and other special coal mines from which locomotive fuel was not to be bought.

The above extract from my report on the agreement to the Di-

[1] James Shanklin Harlan.
[2] Walker Downer Hines.
[3] Henry Benning Spencer, vice-president of the Southern Railway System, at this time director of the Division of Purchases and Stores of the United States Railroad Administration and chairman of its Central Coal Committee.

rector General was read by me at the White House conference Wednesday, April 10th, and Mr. Baruch, who was present, substantially confirmed this version as the understanding which we all had agreed to.

At the White House conference April 10th, it was explained that the matter of delimiting the areas from which locomotive fuel could be obtained was still in progress but that these areas had not been finally defined.

Despite the agreement which had been reached on Saturday, April 6th, and the adoption unanimously of the plan which had been suggested by the President, Dr. Garfield at the White House on April 10th still argued against it and read a long letter setting forth his objections. In the course of the discussion the President suggested an additional or alternative plan, namely, that the railroads should be permitted to purchase railroad fuel from all available mines at a net profit to the miner of 10¢ per ton, which it was pointed out was in normal times regarded as a very fair profit. The President suggested that we consider both plans and endeavor to put either one or the other of them into effect.

The following day, April 11th, another conference was held at Dr. Garfield's office at which were present, Dr. Garfield, Mr. Baruch, several members of the Railroad Purchasing Department, and three of Dr. Garfield's representatives, Mr. Calloway, Mr. Morrow and Dr. Hannald.[4]

It was at this meeting that Dr. Hannald threatened that if the Railroad Administration should undertake to purchase coal from the operators at a profit of 10¢ per ton, coal operators including Dr. Hannald himself, would become the "enemies" of the President and the Administration and he predicted dire results to follow the adoption of any such plan.

Dr. Hannald's vigorous opposition to a 10¢ per ton profit suggested to me to enquire what the current profits really were and I asked Dr. Hannald if he knew the cost of producing coal per ton at the mines. He replied that he did. I enquired of him what coal was costing at the mines in the fields referred to. He replied that he did not know. I reminded him that he had just stated that he did know, and to this he answered that he knew the cost at his own mines but *not* at the mines of others. We then asked him to state the price coal was costing at his mines as we thought it would be well to know just how much profit his mines were making, net,

[4] Alfred Woodward Calloway, president of several coal companies, at this time director of the Bureau of Bituminous Coals and Coke in the Distribution Division of the Fuel Administration, and John DeLorma Adams Morrow, general director of the Distribution Division of the Fuel Administration. "Dr. Hannald" was probably Fred C. Honnold, secretary of the Illinois Coal Operators Association.

in view of his vigorous opposition to a 10¢ profit. He replied that he was not willing to state what his coal was costing, and when I appealed to Dr. Garfield, the latter refused to insist upon his representatives divulging the real cost of coal per ton, and explained Dr. Hannald's reluctance to give figures by saying that the "coal operators objected to letting each other know what their costs were." When I looked around to find the other "operators" who might misuse such information, Mr. Calloway, another assistant to Dr. Garfield, spoke up and remarked that he also was a coal operator.

Frankly, I was much surprised that Dr. Garfield who, at the first conference on April 4th, had taken such pains to tell us how accurately his office worked out or analyzed the cost sheets of the coal mines, should now approve of one of his representatives refusing to divulge to the Chairman of the War Industries Board and Director of Purchases of the Railroad Administration the cost of coal mining in a certain field on the ground that another one of his representatives who was present at the conference to assist in reaching an adjustment of the problem would learn the secret of the cost of coal!

The reports as to large profits which are being gathered in by coal operators are fully confirmed by the latest investigations of the Federal Trade Commission, whose reports regarding the cost of mining and net profits for the months of November and December, 1917, I have been able to secure and from which I draw the following facts:

In central Pennsylvania, apparently the second largest coal mining district in the United States, 65.7% of the coal produced was mined on a basis to yield $1.00 per ton or more.

The principal mining district in southwest Virginia showed that 91.7% of the mines were earning the same large profits.

The Pocahontas district of West Virginia showed that 51.3% of the coal output was bringing a net profit of $1.00 or more. Another large district in the same State reported 94.6% of its coal netting $1.00 or more.

The largest district in Ohio showed about 60% was being mined at 75% per ton and over, some of it yielding over $1.00 per ton.

In the Elkhorn district of Kentucky 89.1% showed profits of $1.00 or more.

The largest coal district in Illinois showed that 90% of the coal was being mined at a profit of 75¢ and over per ton—about 20% bringing $1.00 or more.

In Alabama the Cahaba field showed 31% of the output netting $1.00 or more, 27% from 75¢ to 99¢ per ton, and 30% from 50¢ to 74¢ per ton.

The Arkansas mines showed 88% yielding $1.00 per ton profit or over.

In Maryland 45% of the coal from Georges Creek reported $1.00 per ton and over.

In the Montana mines 73% was being sold at a profit of $1.00 or over, while in the Raton mines of New Mexico the entire output was yielding $1.00 and over per ton.

The financial articles in the daily newspapers are containing from day to day comments upon the fabulous earnings of the coal companies. In the Washington Post of the 18th instant reference is made to a certain coal company in Pennsylvania with a capital of $5,000,000, whose earnings for 1917 are estimated at from $8,000,000 to $10,000,000[.] From a morning newspaper of the 16th instant I take the following:

> "Coal stocks are being picked up without attracting much attention. * * * The situation is such that these companies can no more help making bonanza earnings than can the petroleum companies."

Does it seem fair that the coal operators who are making in one year, in some cases, 100% on their capital stock, or as much as they were formerly accustomed to make in ten years, should now be permitted to levy an extra tax upon the railroads for locomotive fuel, and should refuse to accede to them the reduction in price which they have always been only too ready to grant in times gone by for the large and steady orders which the railroads were able to give, but that they should exact from these roads the full maximum price permitted by the Government or that the Fuel Administrator should step in and forbid the railroads to make contracts with the operators for fuel at prices which some operators are willing to accept?

The needless extra cost of $100,000 to $200,000 *per day* which the position taken by the Fuel Administrator is imposing upon the Railroad Administration seems to me, as I am sure it does to the President and to the Director General, wholly indefensible.

T MS (WP, DLC).

Shane Leslie to Joseph Patrick Tumulty

Confidential

Dear Mr. Tumulty,   Washington April 23 1918

Not to trouble you any further, this is how matters stand. Last night Lord Reading sent for me on the Irish question. Confidentially, I found his views just and sagacious and perfectly in line with the President's general sentlment [sentiment] as to self-determination. As I am not in any official service I spoke frankly.

I told him that the President would never deign to supplicate or bargain for Irish Home Rule, that he was above diplomacy and that it was up to England to smooth the path of the President on her own initiative. But I repeated your private feeling that it was a mistake to enforce Conscription before Home Rule in Ireland, which he recognised himself. I then frankly told him the substance of what I had gathered from six Archbishops in the last fortnight, varying from a feeling that it was not fair to them or the President to complicate the Irish question at this moment to a downright expression that England was adding insult to injury. Lord Reading then gave me to understand that Home Rule was certain and immediate, and that he had done his share from this side. "The Prime Minister has given his word," he said. "May I tell Mr Tumulty that the Prime Minister will keep his word?" He nodded, a just and hard pressed man, but fully realising that the President alone can hold and wield the Irish sentiment in the world.

I am your obedt servant   Shane Leslie

TLS (WP, DLC).

Arthur James Balfour to Lord Reading

URGENT. Personal.   [London] 23rd April. 1918.
    Your telegram of April 22nd.[1]
Please explain to Colonel House that in my view situation is entirely altered by apparent willingness of Trotski to invite allied assistance against German aggression. Allied troops would be able to traverse Siberia at great speed provided that Russians are friendly and if joined by Bolshevists and other Russian contingents would certainly constitute such a menace to Germans in East that latter could hardly withdraw further divisions and might even be compelled to strengthen the forces already there.

T telegram (Reading Papers, FO 800/223, PRO).
    [1] It is missing in all collections.

To Josephus Daniels

My dear Daniels: The White House 24 April, 1918
    Thank you for your letter of yesterday with its extract from the New York Times' summary of the financial condition of the Stand-

ard Oil Company of Indiana. It will be very useful to Garfield and me.

In haste

Cordially and faithfully yours,   Woodrow Wilson

TLS (J. Daniels Papers, DLC).

To Harry Augustus Garfield, with Enclosure

My dear Garfield: The White House 24 April, 1918

I know that you will welcome the enclosed item as part of the subject matter of the difficult question of determining oil prices.

Cordially and faithfully yours,   Woodrow Wilson

ENCLOSURE

From Josephus Daniels

My dear Mr. President: Washington April 20, 1918.

Understanding that the matter of price fixing with respect to petroleum products may be shortly brought to your attention, I am transmitting below extract from article recently published in the New York Times on the financial status of the Standard Oil Company of Indiana which it is believed you should have before you:

"The balance sheet of the Standard Oil Company at the end of 1917 indicates the most prosperous year this concern ever had, with earnings in the neighborhood of $43,800,000, after allowing for depreciation. The surplus increased $36,608,931, which was equal to the full par value of the stock, and $6,600,000 over. It is understood that the company reserved about $17,000,000 for the Federal war taxes, and set aside an unusually large amount to cover depreciation. The expansion of its business, present and in prospect, was indicated by the increase of $10,500,000 in the construction account. These items show the strong position of this, the largest producer of gasoline in the country, and to make the picture more powerful in outline, it may be cited that the accumulated surplus at the end of the year was $89,845,000 equal to nearly three times the par of the stock."

Sincerely yours,   Josephus Daniels

TLS (H. A. Garfield Papers, DLC).

To Henry French Hollis

My dear Senator: [The White House] 24 April, 1918

Thank you for sending me the resolution of the Rhode Island Senate. It is fine to see how well this cause is going, and I am sure you knew it would cheer me to learn this item.

I couldn't catch your eye the other night at the theatre to share with you the enjoyment of "Nothing but the Truth."[1]

Cordially and sincerely yours,   Woodrow Wilson

TLS (Letterpress Books, WP, DLC).
[1] A three-act farce by James Montgomery, which starred William Collier. Wilson saw it at the Belasco Theater on April 22. For a review of both the plot and the performance, see the *Washington Post*, April 22, 1918.

To Thomas Watt Gregory

[The White House]
My dear Mr. Attorney General: 24 April, 1918

The enclosed letter, I must say, appeals to me.[1] Will you not be kind enough to have the circumstances looked into in order that we may be sure whether there is or is not something that we could do? It may be that this is one of the many instances we have been concerned about recently in which the distempers of the time are being taken advantage of to work gross injustice.

Cordially and faithfully yours,   Woodrow Wilson

TLS (Letterpress Books, WP, DLC).
[1] W. Kent to WW, April 22, 1918.

To Theodore Newton Vail

My dear Mr. Vail: [The White House] 24 April, 1918

I dare say you are right about the choice which Mr. Thayer should make, and yet I concede it with the greatest reluctance because I have very much valued Mr. Thayer's services and have very much admired his spirit in accepting a position on the Aircraft Production Board which has, I know from members of the Board, profited by his advice. I yield to your judgment and his with great reluctance but in the confidence that it has been arrived at in the general interest.   Cordially and sincerely yours,   Woodrow Wilson

TLS (Letterpress Books, WP, DLC).

To Harry Bates Thayer

My dear Mr. Thayer: [The White House] 24 April, 1918

It is with genuine regret that I see you sever your connection with the Aircraft Production Board,[1] and I yield to your desire to do so only because it is so clear that your own conviction is the same as Mr. Vail's that you can render more effective service to the general cause in your other work.

May I not express my sincere appreciation of the self-sacrifice which led you to accept appointment on the Aircraft Board and my admiration of the spirit of your labors since you have been a member of it?   Cordially and sincerely yours,   Woodrow Wilson

TLS (Letterpress Books, WP, DLC).
  [1] H. B. Thayer to WW, April 22, 1918, TLS (WP, DLC).

To Scott Ferris

My dear Mr. Ferris: [The White House] 24 April, 1918

Thank you very much for your letter with the information about the present status of the General Leasing Bill. I am heartily glad that you are going to put in a minority report and hope that you will fight for all you are worth for its adoption by the House.

I think that the substitute which you yourself proposed for the Swanson amendment, while not exactly what we suggested, would meet with general acceptance, and I am very glad to trust your judgment in that matter because of your thorough familiarity with the whole controversy and with the dangers involved in concessions.   Cordially and sincerely yours,   Woodrow Wilson

TLS (Letterpress Books, WP, DLC).

To Horace Mather Lippincott[1]

My dear Mr. Lippincott: [The White House] 24 April, 1918

I have your letter of the twenty-second[2] and have looked with the greatest interest through the paper to which you call my attention, entitled "Some Particular Advices for Friends and a Statement of Loyalty for Others."[3] I have always entertained the highest respect for the principles and for the character represented by the great Society of Friends, and I think it is true that upon occasions of manifest national danger and exigency the members of that Society have seen the path of patriotic duty and followed it. The arguments used in this paper which you submit to me are certainly most cogent and convincing, and I am sure that their earnest patriotism and clear purpose of resisting intolerable evil will constitute the strongest possible appeal to the convictions as well as the sentiments of all members of the Society.

Cordially and sincerely yours,   Woodrow Wilson

TLS (Letterpress Books, WP, DLC).
[1] Alumni Secretary of the University of Pennsylvania, author of numerous works on the University of Pennsylvania, the history of the Philadelphia area, and Quakers.
[2] It is missing.
[3] It is also missing.

From Robert Lansing, with Enclosure

My dear Mr. President: Washington April 24, 1918.

I enclose a letter which I received last evening from the Serbian Minister relative to the present effort being made in the Senate to have Congress declare a state of war between this country and Bulgaria and Turkey.

My own view is that it would be a mistake to do this. There is no evidence that the Bulgarians are employing their troops on the western front and I believe one of the reasons for their not doing so is that it would bring them in conflict with the American forces.

However, in view of the letter of the Serbian Minister I would like your opinion as to what course should be pursued.

Faithfully yours,   Robert Lansing.

E N C L O S U R E

Lioubomir Michailovitch[1] to Robert Lansing

Dear Mr. Lansing,   Washington, April 23th 1918.

The debate which to-day has been started in the Senate on the opportunity of a declaration of war by the United States against Bulgaria and Turkey[2] prompts me to write to you a few words, to request you to take into consideration the following ideas, which I am communicating to you as to a friend of my people.

There is no need to specially point out how great the hardships of the Serbian Army have been during this protracted war. The Serbian Army is ready now, as ever, to sacrifice itself to the end, but it is necessary to keep up its moral[e] and to encourage it in the struggle. The entry into the war of the United States and the material help which is extended to the Serbian Government have encouraged both the Serbian Army and the people. In the present most trying situation the declaration of war to Bulgaria and Turkey would be of immense moral influence upon the Serbian Army and the people, because it would mean that the United States will really take part in the solution of the Balkan question and apply the principles for which it entered the war.

Such a solution would also be of great influence upon the people in Austria-Hungary, which to-day are inspired by a revolutionary spirit, a fact which is necessary to be taken into serious consideration, if we desire to weaken the military strength of our common foe.

Finally, the French, English and Italian troops on the Salonica front would greet such an action with great enthusiasm, because it would contribute to the weakening of the moral[e] of the enemy troops.

I am also convinced that such a decision would be most welcome in all allied quarters, which would see in it the determination of the United States to col[l]aborate to the end in the solution of the actual problems, military as well as political.

The moral strength of your country is of the greatest importance. It is as much encouraging to all the Allies as it is dangerous to our enemies. In the present decisive moments it should be taken advantage of, because it will be as important as are the lives of the sons of your Great Republic.

For these reasons I beg to request Your Excellency to use your great influence that the question of the declaration of war to Bulgaria and Turkey be settled in a way which would be greeted with enthusiasm by the Serbian people and by—

faithfully and sincerely yours,   L. Michailovitch

TLS (WP, DLC).
[1] Or Ljubo Mihajlović.
[2] Senator William H. King of Utah, on April 2, had introduced S.J. Res. 145 which declared that a state of war existed between the United States and Bulgaria and Turkey. The resolution was at that time referred to the Committee on Foreign Relations. The debate on April 23 was upon S. Res. 229, introduced by Senator Frank B. Brandegee of Connecticut on April 22, which called upon the Foreign Relations Committee to give prompt consideration to S.J. Res. 145 and report on it to the Senate. The debate, largely along party lines, was inconclusive, and no action was taken on either the resolution or the joint resolution. *Cong. Record*, 65th Cong., 2d sess., pp. 4427, 5403, 5472-78.

From Edward Mandell House

Dear Governor: New York. April 24, 1918.

Reading was with me today. Balfour has sent an entirely new proposal regarding Russia[1]—one that I think you will approve. Reading is asking for an appointment tomorrow in order to discuss it with you.

I hope your hand is steadily improving. It looked pretty bad to me from the pictures taken when you were attending the funeral of the Chilean Ambassador.[2]

Affectionately yours,   E. M. House

TLS (WP, DLC).
[1] The plan set forth in A. J. Balfour to Lord Reading, April 18, 1918. Reading gave a paraphrase of this message to Lansing (T MS, SDR, RG 59, 861.00/1653, DNA) on April 25. Reading also saw Wilson at the White House at 2 p.m. on the same day and discussed this memorandum with him. There is no copy of the memorandum in WP, DLC.
[2] Wilson attended the funeral of Santiago Aldunate in St. Matthew's Roman Catholic Church in Washington on April 22. Aldunate had died of apoplexy on April 17. *Washington Post*, April 18 and 23, 1918.

From John Skelton Williams

Dear Mr. President: Washington April 24, 1918.

In connection with the discussion at the White House this afternoon, I think the following facts may be of interest:

A circular was sent out by the Railroad War Board in the latter part of December, 1917, to all railroads, for the purpose of ascertaining the status of railroad contracts for fuel and the extent to which the railroad requirements for coal for the ensuing year, 1918, had been covered by contracts.

When these returns were compiled some weeks ago they showed that the railroads of the country had contracted for approximately 66,000,000 tons of coal for delivery during the calendar year 1918.

The total estimated requirements of all the railroads of the country for the calendar years are approximately 166,000,000 tons of coal, so that they entered the new year with only about 40% of their coal requirements covered, and leaving approximately 100,000,000 tons of coal still to be purchased.

An analysis of these contracts shows that the prices at which the 66,000,000 tons of coal were contracted for averaged approximately 36.1¢ per ton *below* the maximum prices which were fixed by the Government some six or eight months ago.

Since the Government took over the railroads on January 1st, they have been buying coal, generally, only for temporary requirements, pending the establishment of a definite policy by the Railroad Administration.

The Regional Director at Chicago[1] telegraphed the Director General some weeks ago that he could make a number of contracts for coal at a saving of twenty-five cents or more per ton, if authorized to insure the preferential car supply, but when he was authorized to go ahead he reported that the operators claimed that under instructions from the Fuel Administration they were prevented from contracting for more than 65% of their output. This prevented the making of the very advantageous contracts which were in contemplation.

The returns which we have before us do not show precisely what proportion of the contracts for the 1918 fuel referred to above were negotiated after the maximum prices were fixed by the Government last summer, but the figures show the ability of the roads to secure their fuel on large contracts not only at prices below the inflated figures which prevailed in the earlier part of 1917, but also at prices materially *under* the more limited figures which were established as "maximum" prices later on by the Fuel Administrator if permitted to do so.

If the railroads should be given a free hand at this time to make contracts for their necessary fuel and should place orders for, say, 100,000,000 tons at an average reduction of 36.1¢ from the maximum Government prices, the entire saving on the twelve months supply of, say, 160,000,000 tons, on this basis, would be $59,570,000.

When the operators are making, as is shown by the reports of the Federal Trade Commission, more than $1 per ton net on such a very large proportion of their entire output, does not the statement which Dr. Garfield made at the White House conference this afternoon, that the maximum reduction he had thus far been able to get the operators to consent to was *five cents* per ton, furnish strong proof of their narrowness or illiberality?

Dr. Garfield stated that notwithstanding the fact that the operators were only willing, as yet, to consent to a reduction of five cents per ton, he proposed that the reduction should be ten cents. I think it can be clearly shown that a reduction of fifty cents per ton can be made in many mines and yet leave the operators a profit several times as great per ton as the average profits in the pre-war period.

I shall as requested have the honor of submitting to you, in a few days, a memorandum relative to the increased operating costs of the railroads arising from the advance in the cost of materials and the possible additional increase due to the advance in wages.

Respectfully and faithfully yours,   Jno. Skelton Williams

TLS (WP, DLC).
¹ Richard Henry Aishton.

Samuel Gompers to Joseph Patrick Tumulty

Dear Mr. Tumulty: Washington, D. C. April 24, 1918.

As you know I had the honor of a conference with the President on the Afternoon of Tuesday, the sixteenth instant. I submitted to the President a number of important matters, one particularly dealing with the international political, as well as the labor situation in Mexico. With the memorandum upon the subject I handed the President a letter.[1] He said he was glad to get both.

My associates who are familiar with Mexican conditions, inform me that the representatives of the workers in Mexico and the United States could be exceedingly helpful in establishing better relations than now exist. That work, to be most effective should begin as soon as possible and thereby prevent, if it can be prevented, any more acute state of affairs to develop.

More than likely the President did not deem it necessary to make a reply, and yet I should like to have a word from him as to his views upon the memorandum I left with him. Will you kindly find opportunity to bring it to the President's attention and let me have a word as soon as convenient?[2]

Of course, I might have written to the President direct, but I do not want to even seemingly be impatient for I really am not. I know in a measure the great responsibilities resting upon him and the many duties he has to perform. If you can, however, without taking up more than a minute of his time being [bring] the subject to his attention, I will appreciate it.

Thanking you, I am

Very truly yours,   Saml. Gompers.

TLS (WP, DLC).
    [1] S. Gompers to WW, April 16, 1918.
    [2] "The fact is I have not written to Mr. Gompers about this matter because my own judgment had been puzzled about it and I had not come to a conclusion. Please tell him that I am going to reply as soon as I have a clear judgment about the matter." WW to JPT, c. April 25, 1918, TL (WP, DLC).

To John Henry Jowett

My dear Doctor Jowett: [The White House] 25 April, 1918

Your letter of April twenty-fourth has touched me very much.[1] I value most sincerely your generous words about myself and, while I am deeply sorry that you are leaving America, where your services have been of the most useful and distinguished sort, I am glad you are taking away an intimate knowledge of our people which will enable you to interpret them to those who have not always understood them on the other side of the water. One of the most difficult things I have attempted is to convince foreign ministers and foreign peoples that the purposes and ideals of the people of the United States are indeed unselfish and altruistic. I am sure you are convinced of that fact, as I am, and my great pleasure in expressing such purposes has been derived from the confidence that I was really and truly speaking for my people.

You carry with you, my dear Doctor Jowett, my earnest good wishes, and my prayers for your safety and success in all highest things will follow you.

Cordially and sincerely yours,   Woodrow Wilson

TLS (Letterpress Books, WP, DLC).
[1] It is missing. However, Jowett told Wilson that he was leaving the Fifth Avenue Presbyterian Church in New York to assume the pastorate of the Westminster Congregational Chapel in London. See the *New York Times*, April 15, 1918.

To Georges Roth[1]

My dear Captain Roth: [The White House] 25 April, 1918

I am more than willing that you should translate into French my "Life of George Washington," and am very much complimented that you should wish to do so.[2] I shall take pleasure in asking the publishers of the book to communicate with you in regard to the matter.

With the best wishes,

Cordially and sincerely yours,   Woodrow Wilson

TLS (Letterpress Books, WP, DLC).
[1] Captain in the French army, at this time serving with the French mission to the American Expeditionary Force; formerly a Lector in French at Gonville and Caius College, Cambridge University.
[2] *George Washington, Fondateur des États-Unis* (1732-1799), trans. Georges Roth (Paris, 1927).

From Newton Diehl Baker, with Enclosure

Dear Mr. President: Washington. April 25, 1918.

I enclose the paper referred to in General Bliss's cablegram[1] as one brought back to this country by me. It deals with the situation in the eastern theatre and is a mere expression of opinion by the Military Representatives, and does not call for any action on your part. None of the actions suggested for you to take with regard to the numbered resolutions of the Permanent Military Representatives has any bearing upon this paper or upon the Japanese situation.

The cablegram of General Bliss suggested that certain words and phrases be substituted in the paper brought home by me, and the substitutions have been made in the copy herewith transmitted, so that you have the paper before you in the final form in which it was brought up for consideration before the Military Representatives. Respectfully yours, Newton D. Baker

TLS (WP, DLC).
[1] That is, T. H. Bliss to H. P. McCain, April 12, 1918. The document printed as an Enclosure is the revised version of Joint Note 20.

E N C L O S U R E

SECRET

THE SITUATION IN THE EASTERN THEATRE

29 March, 1918.

1. The Military Representatives after a careful consideration of all the factors involved, are of the opinion that no serious military resistance to Germany can be expected from Russia unless there is an immediate inter-Allied intervention in that country.

2. The objects which the enemy have in view in the East are the following:

    (a) To supplement the inadequacy of food supplies from the Ukraine by supplies from Western Siberia which contains large quantities of wheat, butter, fats, etc.

    (b) To get access to raw materials such as the oil and minerals of Caucasia, the cotton of Turkestan, etc.

    (c) Generally speaking to utilize the reaction after Bolshevism in order to organize as large a part of the Russian Empire as possible as a friendly State, enabling him not only to draw upon its economic resources, but to transfer to the West a great part of the 47 Divisions which Germany still maintains on the Eastern Front.

    (d) To utilize relatively small German military forces, in conjunction with Turkish troops, and with the native Moslem populations, in order to secure control of the whole of Transcaucasia, and of Northern and Central Persia, with the object both of threatening the flanks of the British forces in Mesopotamia, and of inciting the Afghans to attack India. The gravity of this menace to the whole British position in the East would, they assume, compel the British Government to divert large forces from other fronts or even frighten it into concluding peace.

    (e) To send German and Turkish Agents, or even small bands,

into Turkestan, either by railway from Samara or by steamer from Baju to Krasnovedsk, in order to stir up Pan-Turanian propaganda and secure a new sphere of German-Turkish influence and control which might even embrace Chinese Turkestan and the Moslem population of Southern China. From Turkestan, as well as from Persia, they might hope to work up an anti-British agitation in Afghanistan.

3. The objects of the Allies are:
   (a) To reduce to the narrowest possible limits the area from which Germany can draw supplies of food, raw materials or labor.
   (b) To check German military and political penetration into Caucasia, Persia and Turkestan.
   (c) Generally to prevent the creation of a state of affairs which will enable the Germans to withdraw their remaining Divisions from the Eastern to the Western Front.

4. The general method by which these objects can be attained is to give effective military support to every element of the Russian people that is willing to organize itself on lines which will enable it to resist German penetration, and to every nationality or element in the non-Russian regions of the Russian Empire, or in Persia, which is prepared actively to oppose the advance of the enemy or to reject his intrigues.

5. In Siberia that support can only be given effectively by the Japanese, with the eventual assistance of Czech and other *new elements* which can be organized on the spot. The extent to which political difficulties connected with a Japanese advance into Siberia can be overcome by securing an initial invitation from some provisional nucleus of Government in Siberia, by the presence of Allied Missions at Japanese Headquarters, by proclamations addressed to the Russian people explaining clearly the objects of the operation or by a definite statement on the part of Japan of the reward she expects for her efforts and sacrifices, are political questions which the Military Representatives must leave to the Governments represented on the Supreme War Council. They would wish, however, to point out that their conception of the Japanese advance is not that of an Army of invasion, but that of a mobile base or nucleus of regular armed force affording moral, material, and if necessary military support to mobile Russian detachments and commissaries moving in advance and on both flanks. The military representatives are of opinion that such intervention should have an international character.

6. To be of any substantial service the advance, of which the Japanese forces will form the nucleus, should extend as far West

as possible, at least to Omsk or Cheliabinsk, but preferably as far as Samara, where it would control not only all Siberia, but also the railway to Turkestan, and the waterway of the River Volga, and afford a line of access to elements of resistance in the Caucasus, and, if the command of the Caspian Sea be secured, also to Northern Persia.

7. It is always possible, if the movement of reorganization in Siberia, of which the Japanese forces are to form the nucleus, is successful, that it may give impetus and strength to any movement of resistance to the Germans in European Russia, whether originally started by the Bolsheviks, or in any other way. In that case the knowledge that the improvised armies of the Russian National uprising, will be stiffened by the regular forces of Japan, will compel the Germans to retain a large Army in the East, and may have a very depressing effect on German public opinion.

8. With regard to the situation in Persia and Trans-Caucasia the Military Representatives are convinced that the ultimate consequences of the success of the enemy's manoeuvres in this region may be of the very gravest character and involve a most serious drain upon the military resources of the British Empire. The forces immediately engaged will, however, be relatively quite small on each side, and should be furnished without difficulty by the British force in Mesopotamia and by the British Army in India. The Military Representatives must insist, however, on the supreme importance of rapidity of action in this region. Failure on the part of Allied detachments to forestall a pro-German coup d'Etat in Teheran, or to prevent a band of a few hundred Germans and Turks reaching Afghanistan may create situations which it will require large armies to cope with afterwards. Rapidity of action may not only secure the position in Persia and Afghanistan, but may still enable the Armenians and other elements of resistance in Transcaucasia to check the advance of the weak and ill-organized Turkish forces.

9. The Military Representatives lay stress in this connection, upon the desirability of improving the whole system of communications in that region. The Bagdad-Hamadan route should be developed in its maximum capacity, by light railway or cable line, alternative routes into Persia should be developed, and the railway from India through Mushki pushed ahead to enable British troops to secure Eastern Persia, and, from Meshed, exercise an influence over Turkestan.

T MS (WP, DLC).

From Robert Wickliffe Woolley

Dear Mr. President: Washington April 25, 1918.

I left Secretary Wilson on Sunday last with the distinct impression that he considered Justice Brandeis preeminently the man for the post of Director General of Labor and that it would be difficult to find another anything like as well equipped for undertaking this important and delicate task. The names of Mr. Endicott,[1] Judge Alschuler, of Chicago,[2] and others were discussed but doubts were expressed as to all.

Since Sunday I have gone somewhat into the probable attitude of the members of the Supreme Court and venture to suggest to you that it is possible to obtain the consent of the Chief Justice and his fellow conservatives to the drafting of Justice Brandeis. It seems that when the late Justice Lamar asked Chief Justice White if he thought the Court would approve of his serving on the Mexican Commission the latter replied in the negative, then added: "But, each member of this Court is his own master and should decide such a question for himself." The result was that Justice Lamar served.

As you doubtless know, the Chief Justice and Justice Brandeis have become warm friends; they walk to and from the Capitol together nearly every day. Justice Holmes and the Chief Justice are also very intimate and entertain like views as to the sanctity of the Supreme Bench. I have known for some time that the winning of the war has become a passion with the Chief Justice; he considers that anything else is of minor importance as compared with it. Therefore, it occurred to me that Justice Holmes, who is also deeply interested in the outcome of the war, might be willing to undertake the task of convincing the Chief Justice of the propriety of consenting to the drafting of Justice Brandeis for the period of the war to fill a position upon the successful administration of which victory itself may depend. Accordingly, I asked Mr. Felix Frankfurter, one of Justice Holmes' closest friends, to come to my office today for a conference. He enthused over the idea, saying: "You may depend upon me to deliver Holmes." Mr. Frankfurter then said the situation had entirely changed since you last thought of drafting Justice Brandeis[3]—that the Chief Justice's attitude toward Justice Brandeis and your Administration had undergone a complete change and that he felt confident he would welcome the opportunity for the Supreme Bench, by lending one of its members, to do something big to help win the war.

If you approve, I shall be glad to ask Mr. Frankfurter to see Justice Holmes. He stands ready to act. He has just returned from Chicago, where he went for Secretary Wilson to confer with Judge Alschuler, and assures me the latter would not do at all for the post of Director General of Labor.

With kindest regards and great respect, I am,

Faithfully yours,   R. W. Woolley

TLS (WP, DLC).
   [1] That is, Henry B. Endicott.
   [2] Samuel Alschuler, judge of the United States Circuit Court of Appeals for the seventh judicial circuit.
   [3] To serve on the Mexican-American Joint High Commission in 1916. See L. D. Brandeis to WW, Aug. 14, 1916, Vol. 38.

From Robert Lansing, with Enclosures

MOST CONFIDENTIAL:

My dear Mr. President: Washington April 25, 1918.

I enclose for your information a memorandum on Baron Goto, the newly-appointed Minister of Foreign Affairs of Japan,[1] together with two telegrams from Ambassador Morris which were received last January reciting interviews which he had had with Baron Goto, then Minister of Home Affairs in the Terauchi Cabinet.

I feel a measure of anxiety in this change of Government as possibly you may upon reading carefully Mr. Morris' telegrams.

Faithfully yours,   Robert Lansing

TLS (WP, DLC).
   [1] Alarmed by the demand of Foreign Minister Ichiro Motono for an immediate military expedition into Siberia and by the news of the Japanese landing at Vladivostok on April 5, the government of Premier Masatake Terauchi forced the resignation of Motono on April 10. Baron Shimpei Gotō was appointed as his successor on April 23. Morley, *The Japanese Thrust into Siberia*, pp. 136-56.

E N C L O S U R E   I

MEMORANDUM

Baron Goto, newly appointed Minister for Foreign Affairs of Japan.

Baron Shimpei Goto, ex-Minister of Communications and ex-President of Imperial Railways; born 1856 in Iwate-ken; studied medicine both in Japan and Germany; was chief of the Nagoya Hospital. Subsequently appointed junior Director of the Sanitary Bureau, Home Office; was arrested on charge of implicity in the notorious Soma scandal[1] but was acquitted. Appointed as Sanitary Commissioner at the time of the Japan-China War, and then re-entered the Sanitary Bureau as its Director. Was singled out '97 by the late Viscount Kodama,[2] newly appointed Governor-General of Formosa, as Director of the Civil Administration Bureau which he had continued to occupy till his transfer to the Presidency of South Manchuria Railway in '06, and the Ministerial chair in '08. Once combined the office of Deputy-President of the Colonial Bureau, Cabinet, cr. '10. Retired from the posts in August, '11 and again held them in the 3d Katsura Cabinet; formed the Doshikai with late Prince Katsura,[3] but left it in '13. Minister for Home Affairs in the Terauchi Cabinet.   F.P.L.[4]

TI MS (WP, DLC).
[1] The case concerned the poisoning of a member of the Sōma family in 1892.
[2] Gentaro Kodama.
[3] Prince Taro Katsura had been appointed Premier for the third time in 1912. Early in 1913, in an effort to shore up his shaky government, he formed, with the assistance of Gotō, a new political party, the Rikken Doshikai (Constitutional Fellow Thinkers' Association). Katsura was soon forced to resign but the new group survived and, by absorbing many members of the older parties, soon became one of the major parties of Japan. See Robert A. Scalapino, *Democracy and the Party Movement in Prewar Japan: The Failure of the First Attempt* (Berkeley and Los Angeles, Cal., 1953), pp. 192-97.
[4] Frank Pruit Lockhart, assistant chief of the Division of Far Eastern Affairs in the State Department.

ENCLOSURE II

(STRICTLY CONFIDENTIAL)   Tokio Jan. 10, 1918.

Further replying to your telegram of December 15, 5 p.m. Investigation indicates that the peace group in the present Government has been recently gaining strength. The leading representative of this group is Baron Goto, Home Secretary. He was educated in Germany and is suspected of strong German sympathies. On January 8th, accompanied by his son-in-law[1] as interpreter, he called upon me remaining two hours. I had known him previously only in the most formal way and I am informed by British Ambassador that in his experience of five years a visit of the character by a leading member of the Government is unprecedented.

Professor Ross[2] who had been lunching with me was present during the last part of visit and the conversation was largely on conditions in Russia. At the very end and in the presence of Ross the Baron turning to me and speaking with great earnestness and in Japanese, his son-in-law interpreting, stated: that the late Emperor was not only born King but also divinely inspired statesman, that he had impressed upon those around him certain principles to guide Japan in the future, the most important of which was that Japan should at all times avoid war and seek peace; that unfortunately when the present war began the Government then in power, in order to divert attention from domestic problems, involved this Government in the war; that the United States and Japan were the only two nations now involved which occupied a similar and *unusual* position in that they were both apart from ancient controlling race conflicts and national jealousies of Europe, that Japan like the United States was a peaceful nation, unaggressive and without territorial ambitions; that for these reasons they could take a dispassionate view of the war situation; that newspapers had utterly misrepresented this country in picturing her as warlike and aggressive; that what she desired now was peace and that he hoped that the United States, as a peace loving nation, would understand and sympathize with this desire. He stated that although he was expressing only personal views he could assure me that these views were fully shared by the Prime Minister Count Terauchi.

Using presence of Major Henry J. Horn[3] of the American Red Cross Mission to Russia as the occasion, I had today another interview with Goto, he again coming to the Embassy with his son-in-law. The interview opened with a summary by Major Horn of railroad conditions in Russia. I had interpreter read in Japanese that portion of the President's message[4] just received relating to Russia; when this was concluded the Baron stated that he did not think it necessary to repeat to me Japan's attitude *of* Russia; that Japan had no desire to take any aggressive action in Shughrue[5] but desired friendly relations with Russia, above all things, because Japan had a peculiar responsibility for the peace of Asia; but that more important to him was immediate peace in the world; that he and the Prime Minister felt that such peace was now possible and was most desirable. He again emphasized peculiar aloofness of the United States and Japan from the European complications; all the others he continued had selfish interests involved; in this respect he referred particularly to England; her attitude towards the issues of the war could be best represented by a very *crossed* (crooked?) line while America's attitude since she entered the war could be represented by a perfectly straight line; the last speech of Lloyd George[6] was for instance much more moderate than previous speeches. I inquired in what particular. He then sighted [cited] earlier statements of intention to crush Germany as compared with the last statement of Great Britain's war aims. This change he attributed to the President's leadership. I then asked whether he and the Prime Minister had in mind any action looking to attainment of the immediate peace which they so much desired. He replied that to make a beginning was full of difficulties as was evident from their reports of Paris Conference, that the United States now holds control of that situation, that Great Britain in trying to crush Germany was spent (interpreters exact words) and that the war could continue only so long as America willed it. He realized that this country could not alone initiate peace proposals by [but] that the United States was in a position to take the (∗) and that he felt convinced that England would even further moderate her terms.

At this point I referred to the President's message and told him I would send a Japanese translation to him at once and would greatly appreciate an opportunity to hear his views and those of the Premier on the terms there stated after they had carefully read it. This closed the interview.

I comment on these interviews as follows.

First. All the circumstances indicate that these conversations while informal were semi-official and carefully planned in advance. Second. It is entirely possible that the Baron is acting as medium for Germany. Third. I am inclined to infer that Germany is making well directed drive at Japan and is urging pressure upon the United States, which if unsuccessful will be followed by an effort for a separate peace with Japan. Fourth. I am in a position to continue this conversation by showing continued interest and thus possibly obtain additional information as to German channels of communication. Fifth. I have discussed these conversations with the British Ambassador who fully associates himself with the conclusions I have stated and desires to report to his Government but awaits my consent. I beg to request your advice as to the advisability of continuing the conversation with Goto and also ask authorization for the British Ambassador to report to his Government and request your further instructions.   Morris.

[1] Yūsuke Tsurumi, an aide to his father-in-law.
[2] Edward Alsworth Ross, Professor of Sociology at the University of Wisconsin. Ross was just returning from a six-month tour of Russia. Edward Alsworth Ross, *Seventy Years of It: An Autobiograpy* (New York and London, 1936), pp. 150-66.
[3] Henry John Horn.
[4] Wilson's Fourteen Points Address, printed at Jan. 8, 1918, Vol. 45.
[5] Siberia?
[6] About which, see British embassy to WW, Jan. 5, 1918, Vol. 45.

ENCLOSURE III

Tokio Jan. 22, 1918.

(STRICTLY CONFIDENTIAL)

My January 10, midnight.

At a third conversation with Baron Goto at his request on the evening of the 19th we discussed the President's message. He expressed admiration for ideals, emphasized again Great Britain's exhaustion, and believed Germany much stronger in consequence of Balkan situation and Russian collapse. He expressed the opinion that peace could be attained with few compromises if Alsace-Lorraine were to remain under German sovereignty, otherwise he feared the war would last for years which, as a practical man, he deeply deplored and he asked for an expression of my opinion as to America's determination to continue. I referred again to the President's message, its moderation, justice and determination, as expressing exactly the position of the United States. He appeared distressed and disappointed and concluded the conversation with the statement "It will be a long, long war." While repeated questions failed to elicit the source of his convictions as to the German attitude rumors are persistent here and believed by some of my colleagues that Germany has been in communication with prominent Japanese through Swedish channels.   Morris.

T telegrams (WP, DLC).

From Robert Lansing, with Enclosure

Handed me by the Prest.
4/27/18 RL.

Dear Mr. President: Washington April 25, 1918.

The French Ambassador has presented us a note, a copy of which I beg to enclose, containing a message from Mr. Noulens,[1] the French Ambassador in Russia. Mr. Jusserand was particularly anxious that you should see Mr. Noulens' message.

With assurances of respect, etc., I am, my dear Mr. President,
Faithfully yours,   Robert Lansing

TLS (R. Lansing Papers, NjP).
[1] That is, Joseph Noulens.

E N C L O S U R E[1]

Jean Jules Jusserand to Robert Lansing

Mr. Secretary of State: Washington. April 23, 1918.

My Government has just forwarded to me a telegram from the Ambassador of France to Russia who, under the impression made on him by the more and more alarming advance of German enterprises in that country, is led by the series of facts that have lately come to his knowledge, to the conclusion that a Japanese intervention bearing an interallied character has become an urgent necessity. I deem it my duty, owing to the gravity of the facts reported by Mr. Noulens to transmit hereinbelow to Your Excellency the substance of his message.

"In spite, so telegraphs Mr. Noulens, of the protest of the People's Commissioners and in violation of the provisions of the Brest Litovsk Treaty, the Germans are still broadening their action and are advancing in every direction. Their soldiers have already passed beyond Karkoff and Odessa, in the South. In Finland they are extending to the White Guards an assistance which is but the first step toward a protectorate that would isolate Russia from the rest of Europe. They have possessed themselves of nearly all the Black Sea fleet and the Helsingfors that has sought temporary refuge at Kronstadt can hardly escape their clutches.

In control of the Southern provinces and Black Sea ports, they are now using the Finnish guards in cutting off the communications of Russia with the Entente Powers. If the allied contingents are not reinforced as I have repeatedly asked they should be, there is ground to fear that raids like that which was recently intended to blow up the Kem bridge will eventually be successful and that German-Finnish forces will occupy Kem and Kandaladja where a sub-marine station could be established that would singularly hamper navigation to Arkhangel.

But the German schemes are not confined to that. From a Social view point, the Bolshevik propaganda is giving too much concern to the Central Empires for them not to find the means of bringing about the downfall of the People's Commissioner and setting up their own authority at Petrograd and Moscow by occupying those two capitals. Information that I recently forwarded to you shows how, under cover of the Ukrainians and Finns, this two-fold contingency might at any moment become an accomplished fact.

If the Germans succeed in overthrowing the Maximalist rule, the succeeding government will be all the more devoted to them as they would stand before the majority of the Russian people in the prestige not only of conquering soldiers but also of true liberators.

Japan's military action, brought into play as soon as possible with the assistance and in the name of the Allies can alone thwart the schemes of the German Government in Eastern Europe. It would be important to complement such an intervention by the unavoidable landing, which may be urgent, of an interallied body of troops at Mourmansk and Arkhangel. The group of Czechs which has not yet been sent on to the Far East might render valuable service in that respect.

In order to offer the required guarantees to the Entente Powers as well as to Russian opinion, the Japanese intervention should bear an interallied character which of course implies the consent of the United States. Again it must be borne in mind that Japan has reserved to itself the right to intervene on its own initiative on the day when its interests are threatened."

Your Excellency will perhaps share my view that considering the importance of these data and the gravity of the events that may be foreseen in the very near future, it might be advisable to place before the President of the United States the foregoing résumé of our Ambassador's telegram.

Be pleased to accept, Mr. Secretary of State, the assurances of my highest consideration.   Jusserand

TCL (R. Lansing Papers, NjP).
    [1] This document is a translation of J. J. Jusserand to RL, April 23, 1918, TLS (SDR, RG 59, 861.00/1967, DNA).

From Robert Lansing, with Enclosure

My dear Mr. President: Washington April 25, 1918.

The enclosed telegram from Mr. Page in London, and the telegram received yesterday at the White House from Fort Morgan, Colorado,[1] present a problem which is I think worthy of careful consideration. Will you please indicate your wishes as to what reply I should make to the London dispatch.

                                    Faithfully yours,   Robert Lansing

TLS (WP, DLC).
    [1] J. F. Weibright *et al.* to WW, April 24, 1918, T telegram (WP, DLC). The signers, who claimed to represent numerous other signers of their petition, protested against the proposed visit of the Mayor of Dublin (or of "any anti-draft delegation") to the United States and requested that Wilson urge the British government to refuse passports to the Mayor's group. If the group was permitted to sail, the telegram continued, it should not be allowed to land on American soil.

E N C L O S U R E

                                    London. April 24, 1918.

9687. Confidential. It is reported that the Lord Mayor of Dublin[1] intends to proceed to the United States with a view to placing before the President, on behalf of the Irish nationalists and Sinn Feiners, a protest against the application of conscription to Ireland as provided in the military service act which has just passed Parliament.

I learn from the Foreign Office that the Lord Mayor has not yet applied for a passport but that if he does apply he will receive one as Foreign Office feel it would be well for him to go to America and learn for himself the views of Americans with regard to the attitude on conscription taken by the disaffected element in Ireland. There is a strong probability attendant Seamen's and Firemen's union will refuse to take the Mayor but an intimation from the British Government that they favor his journey will doubtless remove this obstacle.

Present conditions incline me to the opinion that it would be advisable for the Mayor to make the journey and I should be glad of an expression of your views for my confidential guidance as well as explicit instructions whether his passport should be visaed.

Page.

T telegram (WP, DLC).
    ¹ Laurence O'Neill.

From Edward Mandell House, with Enclosure

Dear Governor: New York. April 25, 1918.

I am enclosing a cable which has just come from Sir William and which I know you will read with as much interest as I have.

Have you any suggestions as to an answer to this and is there any particular information you would like to have him obtain?

Affectionately yours,   E. M. House

TLS (WP, DLC).

ENCLOSURE

London, April 24, 1918.

No. 580. Following for Col. House from Sir William Wiseman:

I have now seen the British General Staff, Prime Minister, Balfour, Milner and others, who have given me freely all their information, but I still find it difficult to form an opinion on the military situation because it is more complicated than at first appeared and depends on technical military questions such a[s] topographical strength of positions and employment and assembling of reserves. Certainly the British Staff is badly rattled or the situation is exceedingly grave. The general atmosphere in London is better than I expected. The public has become hardened to crises and, not understanding the military situation, probably underrates the gravity of the position.

(a) Military situation: The great battle was evidently long and carefully prepared by the Germans. Our people think it was the sole object of the Germans to crush the British Army but it seems to me that they may have still a plan to attack the French at some later stage and force their way to Paris. The Allies and the Germans started battle with about equal numbers, but the German interior lines, better railway communications, unity of command (operating as single unit) gave them a great strategic advantage which they counted on and used. German plan apparently is to use 200 divisions and to keep them up to strength by reserves from their depots, by further withdrawal from Russian front and by normal recruiting of young men. Possibly also by Austrian help. They know that the Allies have not sufficient reserves to keep up their divisions; and if they keep on hammering at them with one great attack after another the time will come when the Allies are reduced to perhaps 120 or 130 divisions and the Germans still have their 200. They then hope to be able to concentrate at some strategic point and overwhelm one of the armies by weight of numbers. They contemplate continuing the offensive for months if necessary until this happens. The morale of the German troops appears excellent and owing to their success up to now their morale has improved while that of the Allies has naturally somewhat diminished. It may be fairly described as a "battle of reserves," and the side which can bring up the most reserves will win. Personally I think the Germans have made a mistake in trying to crush the British rather than the French Army, but they may have reckoned on being able to drive the British back into the sea, and upon the fact that the French would not care to uncover Paris by heavy counter attacks to help the British. It is no good enquiring at this stage why the Allies were not better prepared for this blow. Those who support the Supreme War Council say it is the fault of Haig and Petain for not creating a mobile reserve. The Robertson school, on the other hand, say it is because the British were forced to take over too much of the line and politicians dissipated troops in expeditions in other parts of the world and did not handle the man-power of the country as the soldiers advised.

It is of course of the very highest importance that American infantry should be rushed over as quickly as possible during the next two or three months. If they are arriving on time and taking their places in the line, the British Staff will use up their last man and hold on with the greatest tenacity, encouraged by the knowledge that the Americans are coming. If, on the other hand, there is any delay in the arrival of the American infantry, I fear it might have a disastrous effect on the morale of our military leaders and troops. If the Germans pursue their policy of hurling attack after attack against us and we are able to withstand it, they will, of course, exhaust themselves and be in a most perilous position just at the time when the American forces in France have reached sufficient numbers to enable us to turn on the exhausted Germans and crush them.

Everything then depends on whether the Allies in general and the British in particular, can hold out against these attacks for another three months, after which the Germans should be exhausted. The British Army has undoubtedly borne the whole brunt of the attack so far and is battered and shaken. In case of further German success we should have to abandon some of the Channel ports which would, of course, be most serious as it would hamper supplies to the Army and facilitate U-boat operations against American convoys.

(b) An unfortunate difference of opinion has arisen between General Pershing and H. M. Government. The British Staff maintain they must have at least 250,000 American infantry to fill divisions which have been knocked out and if they do not get them they cannot hold the German attacks. Pershing is willing to let them have 72,000 and after that to reconsider position. British say this is not practicable as they must make their dispositions ahead and can entirely deplete their reserve only if they are assured of 250,000. This dispute is causing a good deal of bad feeling as H. M. Government thinks General Pershing is adopting a narrow and selfish view in face of a very grave crisis. Unless Pershing has information which satisfies him that H. M. Government is exaggerating danger of the position I think his decision is unwise. Fortunately, Milner is keeping his head and is a great strength in the situation. He sends his regards to you and hopes to work very closely with you.

(c) It is most important from every point of view that America should not fail to send the full 120,000 infantry per month. I understand during April not more than sixty thousand will arrive. The Shipping Controller here says there is ample tonnage available for more than the 120,000. If so, it will surely be possible to embark that number. What I want to make clear is that all Europe believes the fate of the battle depends on American troops arriving in time and that the Germans apparently have calculated on the Americans being late.

(d) Please telegraph me quite fully your observations on this message and any further points regarding military situation on which I may be able to obtain information for you.

(e) Since writing above I have had further long interview with Milner. He has come to a fairly satisfactory agreement with General Pershing which settles the difficulty described in paragraph (b).

T MS (WP, DLC).

Edward Mandell House to Sir William Wiseman

[New York] April 25th 1918.

CXP 601

Following for W. from Tabriz [House]:

Many thanks for your No. 580. Dent [Reading] lunched with me yesterday and after summing up everything we were entirely satisfied with the situation as far as the sending of troops is concerned. Dent thinks tonnage may be found for as many as 200,000 per month and we both believe that Angus [the President] will sanction the sending [of] as many as can be transported until a sufficient number is sent over to make the front safe.

It is important that Upton [H. M. Government] accept in good faith and without question Angus' repeated assurances in regard to the sending of troops. I have impressed this upon Dent and he understands.

Dent read me Craig's [Balfour's] cable about the new plan regarding Brown [Russia], and I heartily approved.[1] It is what I had in mind from the beginning.

With Schwab at head of shipbuilding, Ryan in charge of aircraft production and general reorganization of army supplies under Baruch and Stettinius, everything is moving ahead rapidly and satisfactorily. If the enemy can be held until midsummer his ultimate crushing defeat is certain.

Please remember me kindly to Lord Milner and say that his assumption of the War Office has heartened us greatly.[2]

T telegram (E. M. House Papers, CtY).
  [1] "Lord Reading called at 11.45. . . . The Ambassador had an extensive budget to go through. The most pressing matter was Russia. His Government believe that it is possible now to get Trotzky and his associates to agree to an understanding by which the Allies could send a force into Russia and compel Germany to reform an army on the Eastern Front. He seemed gratified to learn that I thoroughly endorsed the plan which Mr. Balfour outlined in a very long cable. He instructed Reading to present the plan to me first before taking it to the President, because I was responsible for the President's refusal to consent to the Japanese going into Russia without an invitation from Russian sources." House Diary, April 24, 1918.
  [2] Lord Milner had become Secretary of State for War on April 18.

From Joseph Patrick Tumulty

Dear Governor: The White House. April 25, 1918.

I have been asked by the representative of one of the Chicago papers—the Tribune—if I would let them know the total amount of your subscription to the Third Liberty Loan. Personally, I think this is no one's business, and I think also that the purpose of the question is possibly to embarrass. I thought, however, that I should let you know of the inquiry.[1]   J.P.T.

TL (WP, DLC).
[1] "You are quite right about this. It is nobody's business how much my subscription to the Loan is. I wish you would simply decline this request. We certainly owe nothing to the Chicago Tribune." WW to JPT, c. April 25, 1918, TL (WP, DLC).

Daniel Willard to Joseph Patrick Tumulty

My dear Mr. Tumulty: Baltimore, Md. April 25, 1918

Just a word to tell you of the real satisfaction I felt when reading in the papers this morning the announcement of the appointment of Mr. J. D. Ryan as head of the Aircraft Board. The appointment of Mr. Ryan to that position, and of Mr. Schwab as the active manager of the Shipping Board, means as much, I really believe, to the cause of the Allies as the winning of a battle.

I have known both of these gentlemen more or less intimately for many years, and I am confident there is no man in the United States who can do more with the shipping problem than Mr. Schwab can and will do, nor is there any man better fitted by broad experience and executive capacity to head the Aircraft Board than Mr. Ryan. These two appointments will not only inspire confidence in the minds of all, but, better still, the confidence so inspired will, I am sure, be fully justified. It is most encouraging to see men such as Messrs. Ryan, Schwab, Stettinius and McRoberts[1]—not to mention others—actively identified with the war program.

With best wishes for your continued good health, I remain,

Sincerely yours,   D Willard

TLS (WP, DLC).
[1] That is, Col. Samuel McRoberts, vice-president of the National City Bank of New York, at this time chief of the procurement division of the Ordnance Department.

Allen W. Ricker to Edward Mandell House

Dear Col. House: New York April 25th, 1918.

In compliance with your request I am putting the substance of our conversation of last evening in the form of a letter.

Shortly after [the] election I noticed that President Wilson had carried a number of Republican states. I took the time yesterday to go over the election returns given in the World Almanac for 1917.

I found that the President's popular majority over Mr. Hughes, to be precise is, 582,952.

The combined majorities of Republican candidates for Governor or United States Senator total 1,001,516. In other words,—the Republicans had a majority for their state tickets of over a million while President Wilson had a majority over Mr. Hughes of nearly 600,000.

As I pointed out to you last evening, no such intelligent discrimination on the part of the voters has ever occurred in the history of these United States.

WHY?

I believe that three-quarters of a million votes were given Mr. Wilson which under other circumstances would have been cast for the socialist candidate. In addition, the President received the vote of the former populists in states like Kansas and Nebraska. I know this situation quite well because in my early boyhood days I was prominently identified with the Populist Party. I served four years as state secretary of that party in Iowa.

Kansas gave the President a majority of 37,000 while at the same time the republican candidate for Governor had 162,000. The attitude of the members of the Non-Partisan League is likewise interesting. I know this organization thoroly because I helped to organize it and I am on the inside so to speak.

North Dakota gave Mr. Wilson a majority of 1,735 while at the same time it gave Gov. Frazier,[1] the Non-Partisan League candidate running on the Republican ticket, a majority of nearly 70,000.

Minnesota is even more remarkable. The League was organized in the western half of the state. Hughes carried Minnesota by a majority of 392 while the Republican candidate for Governor had a majority of 153,000, and so I might go through the important states which contributed to the President's election.

The President owes his election to the votes of radicals, progressives, members of organized labor, organized farmers,—in brief,—the intelligent producers and workers of the nation.

When war was declared, the people classified above were immediately the President's severest critics. Participation in the war was repulsive to us. We did not and could not understand. It took time and events to justify the President's war message.

I maintain that time and events have justified the President and that the people who were his bitter enemies one year ago, but had been his best friends in 1916, are now about to become his best friends again.

We now see clearly that our REAL enemies, the enemies of progress and social justice, are getting ready to function in the Republican Party.

The Republican business men of the north are sore because they

have been taxed and made to give up actual money for the prosecution of the war.

We understand now that the President is our real friend and that
what he is trying to do is what we all want. In view of these facts,
the radicals, and I make that term cover a multitude of people,—
the very heart and soul and conscience of this country, are ready
again to support the President as they did in 1916.

If I am right about this, and I am sure I am, is it not now time
for us to get together and stop prosecution and persecution of the
people that the President most needs? The radicals should not be
punished for views and opinions freely expressed a year ago because
they no longer hold those views and opinions.

I have had a heart to heart talk with Mayor Hoan of Milwaukee
for example, who is in the city. Mayor Hoan is pro-war. Everybody
in Milwaukee knows his position. Hoan a loyalist carried Milwaukee
by a bigger majority than Berger who was running as a disloyalist.
Hoan tells me that if the socialist candidate for Senator had been
County Attorney Zabel,[2] he would have been elected,—that Berger
was not the strongest, but the weakest candidate they had.

I am ready to do and I will do anything in my power to consumate
what I have outlined above. I believe the attitude of the administration toward the radicals should be modified. That's all that is
needed to bring them in line.

The Non-Partisan League will probably elect a dozen Congressmen, perhaps more, in Republican states.

The socialists will also elect some,—certainly here in New York
and in Wisconsin.

These Congressmen will all stand behind the President and his
policy and they may be of vital need in the next Congress. I would
not of course expect and it would not be desireable for any public
declaration to be made by anyone in the administration, but the
attitude of the administration toward the radicals may be changed
without declarations and I am in a position to interpret this attitude
effectively.

Thanking you for your kind interview and your frankness to me,
I am,   Sincerely yours,   A W Ricker

I believe what Ricker says is largely true. E.M.H.

TLS (WP, DLC).
  [1] Lynn Joseph Frazier.
  [2] Winfred C. Zabel, District Attorney for Milwaukee County.

Lord Reading to Arthur James Balfour

Washington. April 25th, 1918.

No. 1833. Very urgent and secret.

Your tel. No. 2303 of April 18th.

I had interview with President today and laid before him the proposals of the War Cabinet. He desired me to say that of course he would reconsider the whole problem viewed by the new light upon it.

1. He was anxious that situation should be closely watched to see that we were not lead into a trap by Trotzsky. U.S.G. was daily expecting arrival of person in charge of documents which were alleged to prove conclusively that Trotzsky and Lenine were in the pay of the German government.[1] The U.S.G. would not allow the text to be cabled and did not yet know except generally what the documents contained. Of course it was not intended to publish them or their effect for the present. Their relevancy in new phase of situation is to show the necessity for extreme care. Further he said that his information seemed to show that Trotsky's position in the government was no longer as powerful as in past and consequently he suggested that Lockhart should be asked for further information hereon.

2. Your proposal regarding American force with the addition of one complete division could not in any event be carried out because of lack of shipping. Pacific had been denuded except for essential purposes. The sending of a division with all stores and supplies and other units mentioned in your telegram could only be effected by the subtraction of shipping employed in the Atlantic. He thought a regiment could be sent but no considerable force.

3. A favourable opportunity was in his judgment now presented of ascertaining Japan's views upon her intervention with the co-operation of American and Allied contingents, as Viscount Ishii, the new Japanese Ambassador, will arrive in Washington tomorrow (April 26th). You will remember Ishii was here last autumn and made very good impression upon the President and U.S.G. President suggested that immediately upon Ishii's arrival a conference should take place between Ishii, Lansing, Baker and myself. I demurred to this proposal as your immediate object was to ascertain whether President would concur in your proposals before submitting them to our Allies, and I thought it would obviously be for you to take matter up yourself having regard to your earlier discussions with Japanese Representative in London. The President wished to ascertain from Ishii what effect Motono's resignation would have upon Japanese policy. Eventually he agreed that it would be better for Lansing to sound Ishii of course without disclosing your pro-

posals or Trotsky's invitation. The President seemed to doubt whether Japan would intervene at all and more particularly if she was to be accompanied by American and Allied contingents. He then requested me to see Lansing and to submit a paraphrase of our telegram to him, and generally to inform him of the interview between the President and me and its results. I pressed upon him the extreme urgency of the matter for the purpose of preventing the further diversion of German troops from the East and he agreed that no time should be lost.

4. My impression of the President's attitude is that he doubts the practicability of the proposal, more particularly as he seems to think that the Japanese would not undertake it; but his attitude is different from that hitherto adopted and is more favourably disposed.

5. I then had interview with Lansing, explained your proposal and gave him a paraphrase of the telegram.[2] He thought that Trotszky's attitude made a considerable difference in the position and was more favourably inclined to cooperation than I have yet seen him. He proposed to sound Ishii generally on intervention, taking special care not to disclose either your proposal or Trotszky's request. He suggested that after he had seen Ishii I should meet Ishii and him; but I pointed out that you had not yet consulted the Allies and that objection might be taken by the French. In any event, I said that I should wish to consult you first. My own view, as I am sure will be yours, is that the subject should be dealt with by you in London.

6. Lansing said you had similar information about Lenine and Trotszky, and was anxious that it should not be published by you. I promised to transmit his view and observed that it was obvious you would not do so at present.

7. I must now await the result of the interview with Ishii and will communicate immediately it has taken place.

T telegram (FO 115/2446, pp. 8-11, PRO).
[1] That is, the Sisson documents, about which see D. R. Francis to RL, Feb. 13, 1918, n. 1, Vol. 46. Sisson, who had left Russia on March 4, sailed from London for New York on April 25, carrying the documents with him. He arrived in New York on May 6. Kennan, *Russia Leaves the War*, pp. 443-45.
[2] "PARAPHRASE OF A TELEGRAM FROM MR. BALFOUR TO LORD READING," April 25, 1918, T MS (SDR, RG 59, 861.00/1653, DNA), a paraphrase of A. J. Balfour to Lord Reading, April 18, 1918, No. 2303.

From Edward Mandell House, with Enclosures

Dear Governor: New York. April 26, 1918.

Here are two important and interesting cables from Sir William.

I am glad he is able to give more hopeful news regarding the Front. As for the Irish question, I doubt the wisdom of making any statement at this time, though I wish something could be done to improve that situation.

Affectionately yours,   E. M. House

TLS (WP, DLC).

ENCLOSURE I

[London] April 25, 1918.

583. Following for Col. House from Sir William Wiseman:

(a) Political situation:

There will be no serious criticism of H. M. Government during present battle, but afterwards there is certain to be a big outburst, and in my opinion, Lloyd George will have to go. The most probable alternative would be some form of national party under the Speaker of the House of Commons.[1]

Irish situation is extremely difficult. In order to conscript older and comb out younger men H. M. Government considered it necessary to conscript Ireland. It is not intended to put conscription into operation until the new Home Rule bill is passed, based on Sir Horace Plunkett's report,[2] but Irish agitators pretend to think this is only a trick and are organizing most powerful resistance to conscription, the most serious feature of which is the part taken by the Irish Church. H. M. Government is in the serious difficulty that they can not avoid conscripting Ireland without going back on their pledge given to men in England, whom they are now taking under the new draft. Moreover, I understand there is evidence that the Sinn Feiners have been actually financed by Germany. Nationalists intend sending a deputation to the President to seek his support. It occurs to me that this might be forestalled by taking some opportunity of publicly expressing his view along the line that he is glad that Sir Horace Plunkett's conference has recommended a form of Home Rule and that H. M. Government intends to legislate accordingly, and feels sure now that her national aspirations having been satisfied Ireland will not fail to do her part with the other democracies.

(b) I understand that the International News Service has been definitely reinstated by H. M. Government, but not by the French. How do they feel?

(c) It is probable that Prince Arthur of Connaught will shortly proceed to Japan on special mission, and travel via America. I presume there would be no objection, and that he could have an interview with the President.

(d) I have had an interesting talk with Arthur Henderson. I think he is too occupied with his personal grievance to be an effective factor.

(e) I have just seen Crosby, who returns to Washington next week. Among other things he will urge that General Pershing should be supported by civilian advisers.

(f) Have just seen Sir Horace Plunkett, who is very pessimistic. He intends to cable you. Quite apart from my idea, which of course I did not discuss with him, he is very anxious for some statement from the President.

[1] James William Lowther, Conservative M.P. for the Penrith division of Cumberland-shire, Speaker of the House of Commons since 1905.

[2] That is, Plunkett's report on the Irish Convention, about which see E. Drummond to W. Wiseman, April 2, 1918, n. 1.

ENCLOSURE II

[London] April 26, 1918.

587. *Very Urgent.*

Following for Col. House from Sir William Wisemen:

(a) Have just seen a Colonel of Divisional Staff returned today from the battle. He gives very encouraging account. The Fifth Army disaster was the fault of the General[1] and even there the troops themselves fought well. Everywhere else troops have confidence in their leaders and are fighting splendidly. His own Division fought eleven consecutive days and men are not discouraged. Rawlinson,[2] whom he saw yesterday, is now confident as to ultimate result though he still expects much strenuous fighting. The Germans are disappointed with the results to date and may find themselves in a very dangerous position unless they can keep up overwhelming superiority of numbers. British Army pleased at Foch's appointment. Quite realize they may have to give up some of the Channel ports but that would not by any means be decisive. The Germans are fighting well and discipline and staff work magnificent, but men show signs of flinching at continuous frontal attacks. Battle will depend on numbers and no one seems to know the extent of the German reserves or how many Austrians can be brought over. He thinks there is, as usual, more confidence at the Front than in London.

(b) The feeling in London amongst officials as well as public fluctuates according to reports from the Front. Today position seems better. British are holding latest attack better than others and the French are reported to have safely got into position with their reserves well placed.

(c) I will cable more fully later as regards Ireland. Meanwhile I am anxious about the position of the President. Both sides intend to try to bring him into the controversy. On reflection, he could not quite make the statement I suggested because it is not absolutely certain that H. M. Government will legislate on Sir Horace Plunkett's recommendation. My idea was that he might somehow express his view before either side pressed him to do so, thereby adopting a better stand.

I do not see how he can altogether keep out of it. Ambassador Page here is foolishly advising H. M. Government to take strong measures. The action of the Church of Ireland is in the long run likely to cause anti-clerical feeling in all democratic countries. It is a long time since the Church has taken such a direct hand in an acute political situation.

T MSS (WP, DLC).
    [1] Lt. Gen. Sir Hubert de la Poer Gough.
    [2] Gen. Sir Henry Seymour Rawlinson, former British military representative to the Supreme War Council, who replaced Gough as commander of the Fifth Army on March 27.

Edward Mandell House to Sir William Wiseman

[New York] April 26th 1918.

CXP 602 Following for W. from Tabriz [House]:

Your 583 and 587[1] are received. It is a perfect joy to be in such intimate touch as we now are through you. Angus [the President] and I not only deeply appreciate your cables, but we feel that they make intelligent action possible.

Our War Office has just received word from France saying a new plan regarding troops has been devised and accepted by Upton [H. M. Government], Cutler [the French government] and our Staff as being more satisfactory than the one agreed upon. Details have not yet come.

I doubt the advisability of Angus making any statement on the Irish situation unless something can be worked out which will be proper and helpful.

T telegram (E. M. House Papers, CtY).
    [1] The two preceding Enclosures.

From Robert Somers Brookings

My dear Mr President: Washington April 26, 1918.

I herewith enclose copy of statement given to the press which fully explains the wool situation.[1] I am glad to be able to report that, although we were many millions of dollars apart both with the wool dealer, whose large holdings we are taking over, and the wool grower, whose entire wool clip for this year is being controlled, after numerous meetings with the organizations representing these two interests, we unanimously agreed upon terms which, although saving the Government and the public many millions of dollars was accepted by the dealers and growers as being satisfactory to them. The grower was comforted in accepting a lower price than he had expected by the knowledge of the fact that the sepculator [speculator] could no longer stand between him and the value of his product.

As you know, both the Secretary of Agriculture and Mr Lever have been strongly of the opinion that it was not wise to fix prices on agricultural products, and they were both somewhat concerned regarding our proposed taking over of the wool clip. When I explained to them both at luncheon yesterday, however, all of the facts, they expressed themselves as being perfectly satisfied that the situation absolutely required the Government to take the action which it has.

Now, while for some reasons, Mr President, we would prefer this to be made a matter of proclamation by you, upon the other hand, as the actual requirements of the Government enable us to do this, not only by agreement, but by the power to commandeer if we find it necessary, I have thought it best to work along those lines and relieve you entirely of any personal connection with it, as the fixing of a price on an agricultural product without enabling legislation would be a new diversion, and, knowing the agricultural classes (or rather their representatives in Congress) as we do, a proclamation by you might involve you in numerous applications for other agricultural proclamations.

I can only say in conclusion that the results of these numerous wool meetings confirm me in the opinion that we can accomplish much by reasoning and an appeal to patriotism.

The press of other business has prevented Mr Baruch from attending these meetings. I have explained to him all the details, however, so that as he has frequent need of meeting you personally, he may be able to give you any additional information you would like. Of course, I am always at your command.

Respectfully yours,   Robt. S. Brookings

TLS (WP, DLC).
[1] "Press Announcement," c. April 26, 1918, T MS (WP, DLC).

From Lee Slater Overman

My dear Mr. President: [Washington] April 26, 1918.

I thank you for your esteemed favor enclosing letter from Dr. Shaw, together with an article by Dr. Frederick A. Cleveland, which I am herewith returning to you as requested. I have read Dr. Shaw's letter and the article with a great deal of interest.

The reform urged by Dr. Cleveland was included in your letter to me some two years ago when I succeeded in passing an amendment through the Senate, but which was lost in conference.[1] If something is not done along this line, sooner or later we will have a bureaucracy in this country which is really as bad as an autocracy, in my judgment.

I have confidence that the bill will pass tomorrow or Monday without amendment. The Hoke Smith amendment exempting the Interstate Commerce Commission and the Federal Trade Commission will be very close. I am surprised at some of the democrats who will vote for it. But we will win out. I might have brought this bill to a conclusion sooner, but by delay we have succeeded in bringing some to our support which we would have lost if a vote had been taken some week or so ago.

I know the people of this country are with you in this great fight, and I am sure those who oppose you in days to come will feel the effects of the steam roller.

History will undoubtedly record that your ability, statesmanship and vision have never been excelled by mortal man.

Very sincerely yours,   Lee S. Overman

TLS (WP, DLC).
[1] Overman apparently refers to an amendment which he offered on January 24, 1917, to H.R. 18542, an appropriations bill. The amendment permitted the President, when Congress was not in session, to reorganize governmental agencies. Under the threat of a point of order against this amendment, Overman reworded it to permit the President to make recommendations to Congress for the reorganizations of agencies at the beginning of its next regular session. *Cong. Record*, 64th Cong., 2d sess., pp. 1891, 1896.
The Editors have not found any communication from Wilson to Overman concerning this or any similar legislative action.

From William Lea Chambers

My dear Mr. President: New York April 26th, 1918

I have just completed a Mediation Conference here in which I hope for a successful settlement of a long pending controversy that, at times, threatens seriously interruptions of traffic in the Buffalo Terminals of the New York Central Railroad. It was not a controversy concerning wages and conditions of service, but of seniority rights, and, as to whether the contract in that yard should be held by the Switchmen's Union of North America or the Switchmen of the Brotherhood of Railroad Trainmen.

Recent adjustments, so happily arrived at between the Director General of Railways and Representatives of the Transportation Labor Organization, will greatly relieve the burden of work heretofore conducted by the Board of Mediation. At least this is my hope as well as my opinion, as these adjustments provide ample machinery for the final settlement of controversies (in case mediation fails) through the abritrament [arbitrament] of Boards of Arbitration, which, by the terms of the agreements, will continue at least throughout the war period.

Under these conditions, and especially if the Overman Bill passes, which seems to be now assured, you will probably find it convenient, in the rearrangement of Government work among the different Departments, Commissions, Boards, etc. to assign certain other duties to the Board of Mediation, and I wish at this time to express to you my personal, as well as my official, desire, to be of every possible service to you.

With this purpose in view may I not ask that you appoint a time when it will be convenient to you for me to present some views bearing upon this subject which I think will be of interest and probably aid you?

I expect to be in Washington from next Monday for some days and it is hardly necessary for me to say that I will hold myself in readiness to answer any call you may make upon me.

Sincerely yours,   W. L. Chambers[1]

TLS (WP, DLC)
[1] "Won't you be kind enough to explain in a little note to Judge Chambers how pressed I am at present, and say to him that I would greatly value a compact memorandum from him with regard to the matters he has in mind, since I want to have all such things assembled before acting under the power that will probably be conferred upon me?" WW to JPT, c. April 29, 1918, TL (WP, DLC).

From Anita Eugénie McCormick Blaine

My dear Mr. President: [Chicago] 26th April 1918

Your letter so kindly sent in answer to my telegram came after we had reached our policy for the school.

I want to tell you what that was and if that does not seem to you to come within the principles you are upholding for our country, I want to ask that you say so.

The policy has not been announced and if you think we have done unjustly or unwisely it would be my wish to reopen the question and review it in the light of your belief. What we have done is this:

We considered our school as an influence in the community and decided that it was right to have it a unit back of the government, a part of the country, doing its utmost in this struggle.

First we limited our consideration to High School pupils—feeling that no younger could be taken as independent thinkers.

We concluded that in the High School, if we do our utmost to know that the pupils understand the issues, it is a service to them that we put the question as a choice between what the United States is doing and being and what Germany is today.

If, knowing that, children of thinking age choose Germany, we have thought that it is well for them to feel that they do not belong to that school community for the time of the war.

It would no doubt be because of parents' attitudes. Even so we have thought it would be better for them to feel the separation of that for the time being and, if there are such pupils, let them withdraw under our platform of cooperation with the United States— not as an expulsion but as a choice.

But if any pupil theoretically or religiously, although with our country, disbelieves in fighting, we should let him do his kind of service regardless of his conscientious opinion about war.

I do not think we shall lose a pupil, but only emphasize to ourselves and to them the understanding by each of the whole matter and that it is something worth understanding.

But that is the working out of the principle. The question is, is the principle right and with what our country is doing? We have thought it was letting the school have the privilege of feeling that it is standing for the United States in the struggle—with all that that would mean to each pupil.

Within that, we could more surely promote the abhorrence of hatred, vindictiveness, injustice and all the qualities that Germany is showing today and uphold the ideals of the United States in this war, as you, in leading, have put them there, high and fine and clear, a sacred possession forever—so that generations to come may grow by that heritage in living up to it—the heritage of giving our all in this war because our ideals called for it—wanting nothing— accepting nothing but the duty and the privilege of helping and giving and defending.

This is only one school—but it is one that wants to do just right to the children if it can find the way and to do right to them is a vital matter.

So it seems again worth asking your view of the light we have reached—whether it seems to you to be light or darkness?

If you think we are not taking the course that an American school should take, would you send me a telegram at once?

If you think our decision is right, I can wait for an answer or more gladly, to save you trouble, do without one.

I am   Yours very sincerely   Anita McCormick Blaine

ALS (WP, DLC).

David Franklin Houston to Joseph Patrick Tumulty

Dear Mr. Tumulty: Washington April 26, 1918.

It was very thoughtful of the President to express his appreciation of the potatoes recently sent to the White House. I shall let those who have been working to discover how to store potatoes so as to prevent loss by decay know of the President's appreciation.

I may say for your information that the country produces about 80,000,000 bushels of sweet potatoes. Sweet potatoes have a higher nutritive value than Irish potatoes and on the average a larger quantity can be produced per acre. It is difficult, however, to store them satisfactorily. Unlike most other commodities, they require warm storage. The Department experts have been conducting experiments to determine how they can best be conserved. The potatoes sent to the White House show that through the Department's method of storage the loss by decay is less than one-half of one per cent. We shall take pains to make the results known especially throughout the South.   Faithfully yours,   D. F. Houston

TLS (WP, DLC).

To Robert Wickliffe Woolley

My dear Woolley: The White House 27 April, 1918

Just a note to say go slow, please, in the matter of Justice Brandeis. I admire and trust him as much as you do, but I am not convinced that it would be wise to choose a member of the Supreme Court just at this juncture. I am going to give the matter a little further thought.

            Cordially and faithfully yours,   Woodrow Wilson

TLS (R. W. Woolley Papers, DLC).

To William Mann Irvine

My dear Irvine: [The White House] 27 April, 1918

You evidently have a most delightful idea of the Presidency of the United States if you think that it would be possible for me to come down and carry out the very attractive programme you suggest to me in your letter of the twenty-fourth.[1] It is no more possible to me than to go to Europe in an aeroplane, but I am very glad that you think it is and am heartily and unaffectedly obliged to you for thinking of me when you had such delightful plans to suggest.

When I can do things of that sort, the war will be over and, I hope with all my heart, my public duties also.

Mrs. Wilson appreciated very much Mrs. Irvine's letter[2] and regrets as much as I do that such pleasures are denied us.

Cordially and sincerely yours,   Woodrow Wilson

TLS (Letterpress Books, WP, DLC).
    [1] It is missing. It probably referred to the forthcoming celebration of the twenty-fifth anniversary of Mercersburg Academy and of Irvine's headmastership. Wilson had participated in ceremonies there on June 3, 1903, which marked the tenth anniversary. See WW to E. R. Craven, May 27, 1903, n. 1, Vol. 14.
    [2] Camille Hart Irvine's letter to Mrs. Wilson is also missing.

To Robert Somers Brookings

My dear Mr. Brookings: [The White House] 27 April, 1918

Thank you for your letter of yesterday about the wool arrangement. I am very glad you are working along the lines that you have so successfully followed and think the statement you have made of the matter is entirely luminous and ought to clear the matter up to the general public.

I greatly appreciate the motives which have led you to leave me out of the matter, at any rate for the time being.

Cordially and sincerely yours,   Woodrow Wilson

TLS (Letterpress Books, WP, DLC).

Two Letters from Robert Lansing

My dear Mr. President: Washington April 27, 1918.

I have attached a note to the Roumanian Chargé d'Affaires, replying to a communication we received from him announcing the union of Bessarabia with Roumania.[1] The American Minister at Jassy has also asked for instructions on the same subject.[2] It is proposed to telegraph him the text of our reply to the Roumanian Chargé d'Affaires.

Will you be kind enough to let me know whether the reply which I have attached meets with your approval?[3]

Faithfully yours,   Robert Lansing

TLS (SDR, RG 59, 763.72119/1653, DNA).
[1] N. H. Lahovary to RL, April 20, 1918, TLS (SDR, RG 59, 763.72119/1637, DNA).
[2] C. J. Vopicka, to RL, April 18, 1918, T telegram (SDR, RG 59, 763.72119/1606, DNA).
[3] RL to N. H. Lahovary, April 27, 1918, TL (SDR, RG 59, 763.72119/1653, DNA). Lansing reaffirmed the "purpose" of the United States Government "to use its constant efforts, in any final negotiations for peace, to see to it that the integrity of Roumania as a free and independent nation is adequately safeguarded." "This government views with favor," he continued, "any measure that will assure the realization of this purpose."

My dear Mr. President: Washington April 27, 1918.

The attached telegram from the Allied Ministers at Jassy, dated April 16th, which has been received through Paris,[1] indicates that the Roumanian Prime Minister[2] appears to base his confidence in the victory of the Central Powers on the information given him at Bucharest according to which the United States is said to have undertaken that Austria-Hungary shall have her hands left free as regards the Balkans.

I suggest that a categorical denial be issued stating that this Government has undertaken no negotiations whatever with Austria-Hungary and would not consider for a moment any proposal to abandon the Balkans to either of the Central Powers.[3]

Faithfully yours,   Robert Lansing

TLS (WP, DLC).
[1] W. G. Sharp to RL, April 20, 1918, T telegram (SDR, RG 59, 763.72119/1603, DNA). This telegram embodied the text of the joint telegram of April 16; it is printed in FR-WWS 1918, 1, I, 769.
[2] That is, Alexandru Marghiloman.
[3] RL to C. J. Vopicka, May 3, 1918, T telegram (SDR, RG 59, 763.72119/1603, DNA). "The Government of the United States," Lansing wrote, "has not and will not commit itself to a policy which denies the rights of small nations and recognizes in Austria-Hungary a supremacy which it does not and ought not to possess. The United States entered this war in opposition to this idea of the primacy of the strong over the weak, and it will never relinquish its purpose to maintain the full sovereignty of small nations which the great nations seek to subordinate and control."

From Edward Thomas Taylor

My dear Sir: Washington, D. C. April 27th. 1918.

On February 3rd. last I took the liberty of writing you asking you to grant an audience to a small committee of Colorado oil operators in relation to the pending oil leasing bill.[1]

On February 4th. you very kindly wrote me clearly showing the impropriety of your conferring with the oil men on the measure, but also very kindly saying that you would be very glad to receive any memoranda that anyone interested may wish to lay before you, or to consult with the committees and members of the two Houses.[2]

As you are undoubtedly aware, the members of the Public Lands Committee of the House are not in accord upon this measure. After five weeks hearings and an exhaustive consideration by the Committee, nearly all of the Committee are not in accord with the position of Hon. Scott Ferris, the Chairman, and have authorized and instructed me as the ranking member of the Committee, to report the bill to the House as they have agreed to it. I will of course follow the Committee's instructions and prepare and report the bill, and Mr. Ferris will prepare a minority report. I will not go into details as to the procedure in the House, or in Conference. But the result will be, either one of three things will, I fear, happen, viz:

That there will be no bill passed, as has several times heretofore happened; or a bill may be passed that you would feel constrained to disapprove; or possibly a bill might be passed that the West would feel was unjust to hundreds of thousands of people who are perfectly honest and innocent in their interests in oil investments.

Our country, especially California, sorely needs a vast increase of oil production, and to obtain it we need the prompt passage of some sane and fair oil bill. I am exceedingly anxious to assist in every possible way towards the passage of a bill, and I have for that purpose yielded to many provisions that are impracticable, unworkable, harsh, and utterly unwise, and unnecessary. But I cannot assent to provisions that will absolutely prevent instead of increasing production, and work an unwarranted hardship upon possibly a hundred thousand people in Colorado alone, and prohibit further development, and meet the unqualified disapproval of my state.

I have not yet reported the bill to the House, because I feel that this legislative situation is, under present conditions, not only very unfortunate, but utterly unnecessary; and for that reason I would appreciate the courtesy very much if you will grant me personally, a brief interview on this subject, with the hope of obtaining your approval of a course of procedure that I feel would meet the approval of the Committee, and Mr. Ferris, and the House, and insure the prompt passage of the bill.

Trusting that you may feel warranted in granting this request,[3] I have the honor to remain,

Very sincerely and respectfully yours,   Edward T. Taylor.

TLS (WP, DLC).
  [1] E. T. Taylor to WW, Feb. 3, 1918, TLS (WP, DLC).
  [2] WW to E. T. Taylor, Feb. 4, 1918, TLS (Letterpress Books, WP, DLC).
  [3] Apparently Wilson did not see Taylor at this time.

From Hans Froelicher[1]

My dear Mr. President: Baltimore, Maryland April 27, 1918

I am addressing you in a matter of very grave concern to me.

By action of the Trustees of Goucher College[2] my connection with the College will terminate at the close of the present academic year. President Guth[3] gave as the reasons for this action my alleged negative attitude towards the war activities at college. He declined to enter into details on the ground that the Trustees had the undoubted right to dismiss whom they chose without trial or stating of reasons. I can therefore neither deny nor concede the allegations.

I wish to have my Americanism judged by the record of my life as a man and as an American citizen during the thirty years spent in Baltimore as an instructor at Goucher College, and more especially by the article written by me in support of your candidacy as President in 1916.[4] I believe indeed that my dismissal is due to my outspoken approval of your acts and utterances before and since we entered the war. In admiration and in somewhat of awe I have seen you invest in ever more austere and worldmoving causes the same lofty spirit of humanity and justice, the same courage and steadfastness of purpose which you once applied to what seem now questions of minor concern. In small things and large I have found myself in agreement with you, and I and mine have been, and are American to the core.

I would not otherwise think of addressing you and offering my services to the government in whatsoever service I may be fitted for. To the end of securing an appropriate position I ask respectfully your intercession in my behalf. I enclose a brief statement of data of my life and my special preparation.[5]

Very respectfully yours   Hans Froelicher

TLS (WP, DLC).

[1] Professor of German Language and Literature and of Art Criticism at Goucher College (formerly the Woman's College of Baltimore). He had been born, reared, and educated in Switzerland and received the Ph.D. degree from the University of Zurich in 1888. He had come to the United States in 1888 as Associate Professor of French Language and Literature at the newly opened Woman's College of Baltimore. He switched to German language and literature in 1890 and added art criticism in 1895. He became an American citizen in 1897 and was active in the civic affairs of Baltimore. He had taught Margaret Wilson and Jessie Wilson Sayre during their years at the Woman's College of Baltimore.

[2] The name of the college had been changed in 1910 to honor the Rev. Dr. John Franklin Goucher, a founder and, from 1890 to 1908, president of the institution.

[3] William Westley Guth.

[4] Froelicher had issued a statement on October 27, 1916, in which he criticized German Americans who supported Hughes in order to defeat Wilson and expressed his support of Wilson for the "positive good" he had done "for the country and for humanity." *New York Times*, Oct. 28, 1916.

[5] Not printed.

Jessie Woodrow Wilson Sayre to Edith Bolling Galt Wilson, with Enclosure

Dear dear Edith,   Cambridge Mass. [c. April 28, 1918]

I am overwhelmed by the news given me in the enclosed letter. Dr. Froelicher is one of the most upright honorable and finest men I know and it seems incredible that he could be treated in such a manner by President Guth. He is not young any more and the difficulties of beginning life all over again are immense. It is because we, Margaret and I, loved him so much that I send this on to you to ask your advice in the matter. He never was a German so he would not be debarred from government service, would he? Could Father, at least, write him a letter of confidence and appreciation that would help him on his feet again? I don't suggest any thing but I am very much grieved and [it] would help so much if it is possible

Your dear letter, so full of love and direct news was such a joy and I repay it by being even more of a nuisance! I *hate* sending things but my heart is so in this that I can't help it. And I have still another matter to turn to you about or rather to report to you, a most ominous account of matters in Spain, first hand—but—one thing at a time.

The children are convalescing steadily. We went out in the sunshine today, and Francis is quite himself again. Eleanor, too is recovering poise.

Ever devotedly to both my dear people in Washington,

Lovingly Jessie

E N C L O S U R E

Frances Mitchell Froelicher[1] to Jessie Woodrow Wilson Sayre

Dear Jessie   Balto. Md. April 26, 1918

Today Dr Guth called Dr Froelicher to his office and announced to him that his term of service at Goucher College would terminate with this academic year! The alleged reason being his attitude towards the war. It is the most unbelievable piece of injustice and ingratitude that I ever heard of. My husband is writing to your Father, in whom he has never lost faith for a moment, and whom he has followed in his great diplomacy with admiration and sympathy.

We sent the letter thru you to insure its personal delivery to our

President. Will you read the letter and then send it to your Father. This has all come very suddenly into our lives and I have not the heart to write you any more tonight. I know this cruel war has brought it[s] many trials to you too. Someday perhaps I may have the pleasure of introducing your little folks to our Betty Froelicher and Hans Froelicher III

In the old affection   Yours Frances Mitchell Froelicher

ALS (WP, DLC).
¹ Mrs. Froelicher had met her husband at the University of Zurich, where she had studied for, and received, the Ph.D. degree, the second granted to a woman by that institution. She had taught German at the Woman's College of Baltimore from 1888 to 1890 and from 1895 to 1901. She had also, before her marriage in 1888, spent the year 1887-1888 as a Reader in Anglo-Saxon at Bryn Mawr College and might have known Wilson and Ellen Axson Wilson at this time.

From Newton Diehl Baker, with Enclosure

My dear Mr. President: Washington. April 29, 1918.

I enclose a copy of a confidential memorandum received by me to-day from General Pershing.

Clearly, General Pershing, Lord Milner, and Sir Douglas Haig have had a conference and agreed among themselves upon a plan for the shipping of American troops which differs widely from the arrangement we worked out with Lord Reading, and is very much more favorable to the early building up of complete American divisions.

Lord Reading called on me to-day with a copy of the same agreement, which had been transmitted to him by Lord Milner. Lord Reading said that he was mystified and disturbed at the modification which had been made in the plans. I told him, however, that I felt he and I were too far from the situation to see this as clearly as those in Europe and that so far as I was concerned I felt it my duty to cooperate to carry out the arrangement which plainly seemed wise to Lord Milner and General Pershing.

The modification really is not so serious when one remembers that the total number of infantry and machine gun units which would have been shipped under this program is as great as we could in any case have ready for shipment by the last of July, while the increased tonnage made available will carry over artillery and other personnel, making total shipments of troops by the last of July very much larger than were contemplated in the memorandum submitted by Lord Reading to which I made reply a week ago.

Respectfully yours,   Newton D. Baker

TLS (N. D. Baker Papers, DLC).

E N C L O S U R E

Received at the War Department April 25, 1918, 10:53 P.M.
From London To The Adjutant General, Washington. Number 961,
April 24th.

Paragraph 1. For the Chief of Staff and Sec. of War. Confidential.
The following memorandum regarding shipment of American troops
has been agreed to as indicated: "London April 24th 1918. It is
agreed between the Secretary of State for War, representing British
Government, and General Pershing, representing the United States
Government, that for the present American troops be sent giving
preference in the following order: A: That only the infantry, machine gun, engineer and Signal troops of American divisions and
the headquarters of divisions and brigades be sent over in British
and American shipping during May for training and service with
British Army in France up to 6 divisions and that any shipping in
excess of that required for troops be utilized to transport troops
necessary to make these divisions complete. The training and service of these troops will be carried out in accordance with plan
already agreed upon between General Sir Douglas Haig and Gen.
Pershing, with a view at an early date of building up American
Divisions. B: That the American personnel of the artillery of these
divisions and such corps troops as may be required to build up
American corps organizations follow immediately thereafter, and
that American artillery personnel be trained with French material
and join its proper division as soon as thoroughly trained. C: If,
when the program outlined in paragraphs A and B is completed,
the military situation makes advisable the further shipment of infantry, etc. of American divisions, then all the British and American
shipping available for transport of troops shall be used for that
purpose under such arrangements as will insure immediate aid to
the Allies, and at the same time provide at the earliest moment for
bringing over American artillery and other necessary units to complete the organization of American divisions and corps. Provided
only combatant troops would be necessary A and B be followed by
such service of the rear and other troops as may be considered
necessary by the American Commander-in-Chief. D: That it is contemplated American divisions and corps when trained and organized shall be utilized under the American Commander-in-Chief in
an American group. E: That the American Commander-in-Chief
shall allot American troops to the French or British for training or
train them with American units at his discretion, with the understanding that troops already transported by British shipping or in-

cluded in the 6 divisions mentioned in paragraph A are to be trained with the British, details as to rations, equipment and transports to be determined by special agreement."

Paragraph 2. The plan seems to meet the situation as it appears at present and leaves shipment of service of the rear troops and other necessary contingents for our own determination as may be required. It also provides for and is understood to cover the question of bringing over artillery with very little delay to complete our divisional and corps organizations. There now seems to be a real desire on the part of Sir Douglas Haig and Lord Milner to do this as early as practicable.

Paragraph 3. Memorandum of agreement between Sir Douglas Haig and General Pershing. "*Advance* American troops arriving in France for service with British be disposed of as follows: American divisions will be allocated for training as agreed upon by the respective staffs to English cadre divisions. The training staffs of the English divisions to be at disposal of the American regiments for instruction in English rifle, Lewis machine guns, gas precautions and details of various kinds. As soon as approved by the American divisional commanders each American regiment will be attached to each 3 brigades of the English Division. The American battalion will be commanded by its own officers and will work as a part of the English brigade. The staff of the American regiment will be attached to the Staff of an English Brigade for instruction. In next stage the American regiment (3 battalions) under its own commander will be attached as a brigade to an English division. Finally the American regiments will be grouped into a division under their own commander. The Field Marshal will be prepared when this stage is reached to place the artillery of an English division, up to six divisions at present, at disposal of the Commander in Chief United States Army, until such time as the United States divisional artillery arrives or the British cadre divisions are made up to full strength."

Paragraph 4. It is confidently asserted by the British shipping authorities that the shipment of personnel by both British and American shipping can be very much expedited which if possible of accomplishment will enable us without doubt to bring over whole divisions and all other personnel necessary for organization of units and for various other service. In connection with this it should be remembered that England has Irish conscription question on her hands. Number of British troops will probably be sent to Ireland to enforce conscription. The possible political effect on American troops of Irish origin fighting under British flag even temporarily should not be lost sight of. This only emphasizes the desirability of our organizing American units as such and uniting them into an American Army at earliest possible date.

Paragraph 5. The following estimate as to troops transportation from United States is made up by the British "British ships: April 60,000, May 130,000, June 150,000, total 340,000. American ships: April 58,000, May 70,000, June 70,000, total 198,000. Grand total 538,000. To the end of July it is thought that a total of 750,000 can be provided for."   Pershing.

TC telegram (WP, DLC).

From Newton Diehl Baker

Dear Mr. President: Washington. April 29, 1918.

General Bliss, although retired (64 years of age), has been called back into actual service, as you know, and continues to hold the office of Chief of Staff; he is also our Permanent Military Representative on the Supreme War Council at Versailles. As Chief of Staff, his rank is "General." He has been wearing the insignia of that rank, but now feels that he should surrender the office of Chief of Staff so as to make possible the permanent designation of another to perform those duties. Should this course be taken General Bliss will of course revert to his rank of Major General, which would mean taking off two of his four stars and otherwise altering his insignia and the obvious evidence of his military status. So far as the American soldiers are concerned this would be a matter of no special moment, but I feel quite sure that the British, French, and Italian military men, who surround the Supreme War Council at Versailles and number some hundreds, would find it very difficult to understand that this great reduction in rank was not in some sense disciplinary, and it might even suggest to those who could not be made to understand the facts some loss of confidence in General Bliss by his own Government and, consequently, less weight for his counsels in the Conference.

I find that under the law the President has the right to nominate, subject to the confirmation of the Senate, any officer of the Army to brevet rank for distinguished service in the theatre of operations, and I have little doubt that the Senate would confirm General Bliss in such brevet rank if you would make the nomination. It might, however, be unwise to send the nomination in without my having first canvassed the Senate Committee and discovered their attitude to the suggestion, and I am writing this to learn whether this course would meet with your approval, and also whether you prefer to have me consult the Committee privately on the matter, as I can very easily do.

Should you approve this plan and it be carried out, General Bliss will have the rank of "General" only so long as he remains on detail to the Supreme War Council; it would not affect his permanent rank on retirement, which would in any case be that of "Major General," as the rank of "General," which was created last year for the Chief of Staff and the supreme commander of our Expeditionary Force, retains to the office and not to the man, and expires as to any individual when he ceases to occupy one or the other of those relations.   Respectfully yours,   Newton D. Baker

TLS (N. D. Baker Papers, DLC).

From Robert Lansing

My dear Mr. President: Washington April 29, 1918.

I had an interview yesterday (Sunday) afternoon with Viscount Ishii. We spent an hour discussing various questions relating to the Far East, particularly the Siberian situation. It is most gratifying to find that the Japanese Government agree fully with our point of view and that they do not see at present the military compensation for the danger of uniting the Russian factions to resist intervention and of throwing them into the arms of Germany.

Viscount Ishii said that the menace to Japan was a Germanized Russia and that intervention might increase rather than decrease it. I said to him that he had previously told me of the attempts Germany had made to enter into an agreement with Japan and that I had no doubt a fourth attempt would be made on the basis of a division of Siberia between them. He replied, "We cannot trust them. They seize the profits of an agreement and then they break it at once. We never will trust them. Germany would take Western Siberia and then drive us out of eastern Siberia even if we desired it, which we do not. Our national life would be next." He went on to say that the danger had not yet taken definite form; that he felt the Bolsheviks were still distrustful of Germany and would oppose German agents unless we did something to make them hostile to us; that many rumors had been received but no actual proofs to show the Germans were influencing the actions of the Soviets in Siberia; and that he felt that the wiser course was to wait until we knew the truth and could base action on something more substantial than the reports which we had thus far received.

I then said to him, that assuming the necessity or advisability of intervention I would like to know what his views were as to Japan's attitude toward participation by the United States or of the Allies in the expedition. He replied that he could speak without hesitation so far as he was personally concerned and that was that it would be most welcome; that he believed his Government would hold the same opinion; and that it was evident that the presence at least of troops of the United States, Japan, and China would go far to remove the suspicion of the Russians as to the purpose of territorial conquest which might be inferred if Japan acted alone. I suggested to him to obtain authority from his Government to say this. He said that he would.

After speaking of the five several routes of advance against China from the west and the possible line of defense which would have to be taken, he answered, to an inquiry of mine, that including reserves Japan could put in the field 400,000 men and that fully 250,000 could be sent at once into Siberia if it was necessary. He also said that he did not think that it would be practical to go much further west than Irkutsk because of the difficulties of keeping open the line of communication. He said that he thought the southern routes to China from the west could be guarded by Chinese troops and he believed eight divisions would be sufficient to do this.

I told him that not being a military man I felt incompetent to judge of the possibilities, but that it seemed to me that the chief purpose of intervention at this time would be to threaten German domination over western Russia to such an extent that no German troops could be withdrawn to take part in the battles in Flanders; that it was as essential to Japan as it was to the United States that Germany should not be victorious in France for if she was she could turn a large part of her force eastward and become mistress of Siberia; and that a German Siberia would be a grave peril to Japan, as he must know.

With these statements Ishii agreed and said that he was prepared to advise his Government to act in conjunction with the United States in defeating Germany's purposes by any means which seemed practicable.

My interview with the Ambassador was in every way satisfactory. He is most frank and evidently desirous to do only what is entirely acceptable to this Government; and he assured me that is the wish and purpose of his Government.

Ishii is applying to you for an audience at your convenience. Permit me to suggest that it be granted as soon as possible and that at the formal reception you say to the Viscount as a spontaneous thought that you wish that he and I would remain with you after the formal presentation for a conference upon matters of vital and immediate importance. This I know is a little unusual but I feel that the Ambassador would be highly complimented and at the same time this vexatious business as to intervention in Siberia could be definitely settled or at least discussed. I would take pains to express to him after we left you the unusual mark of consideration shown him, a favor on your part which would have a wonderfully good effect on our relations with Japan.[1]

Faithfully yours,   Robert Lansing

TLS (WP, DLC).
[1] Wilson received Ishii for the formal presentation of his credentials as Ambassador at noon on April 30. For an account of the discussion which took place during this meeting, see Lord Reading to A. J. Balfour, May 1, 1918, and K. Ishii to S. Gotō, April 30, 1918.

From William Bauchop Wilson

My dear Mr. President: Washington April 29, 1918.

I had an interview with Messrs. Robert W. Woolley and Matthew Hale at which they gave me a copy of a letter they had jointly addressed to you on April 19th relative to the appointment of a Director General of Labor.

I find upon examination of the communication that the basis for the suggestion is laid down in the following declarations:

"1. Labor unrest is increasing to a threatening extent.

"2. Strikes are more numerous than at any previous time.

"3. Competitive bidding for labor by government departments and government contractors is flagrant and on the increase. Government boards establish diverse standards.

"4. Officers of labor unions confess to finding it increasingly difficult, and frequently impossible, to hold their men.

"5. At certain points serious shortage of skilled labor is offset by a similar surplus at other points."

Messrs. Woolley and Hale have been grievously misinformed relative to the first, second and fourth of these declarations. Labor unrest is not increasing. On the contrary it is very much less than during last year. Strikes are not more numerous. There has never been a time within my knowledge when there were fewer serious strikes than at present, notwithstanding the fact that it is that period of the year when strikes are usually most numerous. There is not a solitary strike in the shipbuilding, packing house, lumber, steel, transportation, telegraph, telephone or oil industries of the country, only one small strike in the coal industry, and a few strikes of very minor importance in the textile industry, metal trades, munition factories, and all the other productive enterprises.

The speech made by you to the Convention of the American

Federation of Labor last November[1] had a wonderfully beneficial effect. Every mediator, every employment official, every field officer of the Department of Labor, in addition to a corps of speakers trained for the purpose, have been carrying the message to the workers of America that this is their war for the preservation of their institutions, to enable the masses of the people to continue working out their own destiny in their own way, unimpeded by the mailed fist of the German Kaiser or any other autocrat on earth. Every great labor leader in the country from Samuel Gompers on through the list has been carrying forth the same kind of message. As the rank and file grasp the importance to democracy of the conflict now being waged, the influence of these officials of labor unions has increased instead of being diminished, and the effect is very apparent in our mediation work. One year ago sixty per cent of all the labor controversies handled by the mediation division of the Department had reached the strike stage before they were brought to our attention. At present less than thirty per cent reach the strike stage, and the percentage is rapidly diminishing.

There has undoubtedly been a great deal of competitive bidding for labor by government departments and government contractors, a policy which this Department has persistently sought to change. The need for military supplies has made the mobility of labor an important factor in military operations. The impulse of every department, board and industrial establishment has been to secure the labor required to increase their productive capacity without regard to its effect upon the industrial situation or the priority claims of others. That condition is rapidly being remedied through the centralization of the responsibility for the mobilization of labor in the Employment Service of the Department of Labor and its Division of Public Service Reserve. There is still considerable waste resulting from different agencies dealing with the labor supply. For instance, there is a shortage of bricklayers in Washington, Baltimore and Norfolk. Recently this Department brought into each of these places bricklayers from Illinois, Indiana and Ohio, their transportation being paid by the War Department. Yet within the past two weeks a representative of the Air Nitrates Corporation of Sheffield, Alabama, has been in Baltimore, Norfolk and Washington for the purpose of recruiting bricklayers for their Sheffield plant, instead of securing them from localities where there is a surplus. There are other instances of a similar nature. We are at present negotiating with the different departments and boards a proposition that they discontinue advertising for workmen and include in their

---

[1] It is printed at Nov. 12, 1917, Vol. 45.

contracts a provision that the contractors refrain from advertising and that all of the movement of labor be handled through our Bureau of Employment. The suggestion is receiving the sympathetic consideration of the War Department and the Shipping and War Industries Boards.

There has been a shortage of skilled laborers in some localities, particularly in the shipbuilding industry, because of the rapidity with which their organization was created. This Department, however, has registered a working reserve of 250,000 skilled men for shipbuilding purposes, with a classification of their respective qualifications, which has enabled us for the past two months to supply skilled and unskilled workmen in the proportion required, securing them from industries least affected by the war program. As the war needs increase the dilution of skilled labor must increase. That can only be overcome by a comprehensive system of intensive shop training to rapidly supply the needed skill. The Department is seeking an appropriation from Congress for the organization of a division or bureau for the purpose of handling labor dilution and training, securing as far as possible the cooperation of manufacturers in their shops and the consent of the trade unions to such modification of their apprenticeship rules as may be necessary to meet the conditions confronting us.

The working out of a satisfactory method of labor adjustment has been no easy task. Last June after numerous conferences I developed a plan which seemed to be satisfactory to the Council of National Defense and the representatives of employers and employees. One of the sections provided that in every contract hereafter made by the government which may require or involve the employment of laborers or mechanics, there shall be included the following stipulations: That wages of persons employed upon these contracts shall be computed upon a basic day rate of eight hours work, with overtime rates to be paid for at not less than time and one-half for all hours work in excess of eight hours; that whenever a labor dispute arises in any establishment under contract with the government which the employers and the employees or their representatives are unable to mutually adjust and a strike or lockout seems imminent, the matters in dispute shall be submitted to an adjustment commission for adjudication and work shall be continued pending its decision; that every contractor and subcontractor shall agree to accept and abide by the decisions of the labor adjustment commission, and every worker accepting employment in any plant within the jurisdiction of the adjustment commission shall do so with the definite understanding and agreement that he will accept and abide by its decisions.

I am fully convinced that if a provision of this kind could be written into the contracts hereafter let, it would make the decisions of the National War Labor Board, recently created, thoroughly effective and keep industry in motion without conscripting either the properties or the workers.

The representatives of labor insisted that a clause should be included making union wages and conditions in existence in the vicinity in June, 1917, the basis of all awards made by the adjustment board. The Council declined to include that provision and the plan was abandoned. It was deemed inadvisable to adopt any adjustment plan that did not have the support of the leaders of labor.

Since then a number of industrial sections have been organized in different departments and boards with their own labor adjustment machinery, having no connection with each other and consequently no common policy. The result has been to some extent a diversity of standards, but it has not been as great as might have been expected under the circumstances due to the fact that the representatives of the workers have naturally presented for the consideration of each board the highest wage rates paid elsewhere, while the employers have just as naturally presented to the board the lowest rates paid.

There has been considerable justification for the action of the different departments and boards because Congress has not been convinced of the necessity of furnishing this Department with ample funds to do the work. As you will recall, when the question of creating a Labor Administrator was brought to your attention on January 4th, last, your judgment was that all of these activities should be headed into the Department of Labor. Immediately thereafter I proceeded to work out a plan of organization for the administration of a national war labor program which would bring us into immediate touch with the labor sections of the different departments and boards. I am sending you a copy of a chart showing the plan as finally adopted.[2] Your generous allotment of $825,000.00, plus the appropriation from Congress, has enabled us to put the Employment Service promptly on an effective basis. Our Housing and Transportation Bureau is rapidly developing plans for handling the housing problem when Congress makes the necessary appropriation. The creation of the National War Labor Board, with Messrs. Taft and Walsh as Chairmen, we hope will result in a unification of the adjustment policies of the government. We are unable to proceed with the organization of the other divisions until Congress has appropriated the funds for that purpose. Even our funds for the adjustment service are reaching a very low ebb.

[2] Not printed.

Under all of these circumstances it does not seem to me that a labor director, such as is contemplated in the letter of Messrs. Woolley and Hale, would in any manner help in the solution of the problem. I have very competent assistants handling the adjustment, housing and employment divisions, and have no doubt that able assistants can be secured to handle the other divisions as soon as sufficient finance is made available. What we need in addition, and what I have been trying to get for sometime, is a competent man who can take charge of the coordination of our activities with those of the other departments.

I shall be very glad to discuss the whole subject matter with you further at your convenience.

Faithfully yours,   W B Wilson

TLS (WP, DLC).

From Edward Mandell House, with Enclosure

Dear Governor: New York. April 29, 1918.

One of the ablest men the British have yet sent over is Major General Hutchinson who expects to return this week.

Hutchinson tells me that Secretary Baker suggested that you might want to see him and, in view of this, the British Ambassador may ask whether you would care to talk with him for a few minutes.[1]

He is in the closest possible touch with Generals Robertson, Haig and Wilson and it might be of some service to see him and give him your point of view direct. He told me in confidence that he was practically certain that the Lloyd George Government would go within a few weeks, and that General Robertson would be returned as Chief of Staff.

Affectionately yours,   E. M. House

TLS (WP, DLC).
[1] Wilson saw Gen. Hutchison at 6 p.m. on May 3.

E N C L O S U R E

London, April 27, 1918.

591. Following for Col. House from Sir William Wiseman:

Most grateful for your telegram 602 of the 26th.

(a) I am sending you a message from Sir Horace Plunkett, but send you these notes of my own in advance. Sir Horace Plunkett regards the problem solely from an Irish, as distinguished from a general political, point of view, and does not fully take into consideration H. M. Government's dilemma, described in my telegram No. 583 of the 25th, paragraph a.[1] Also he does not refer to the difficulty of reconciling claim of Ulster to self determination. His position, however, is a sensible description of the problem from an honest Irish point of view.

(b) H. M. Government is unofficially representing to the Vatican the danger of the Church taking an active part in anti-conscription movement.

(c) Russia: Lockhart, who has always been a keen supporter of Trotsky, now seems to think the latter is losing his influence.

An interesting observation from well-informed Austrian quarters is that peace with Russia has heartened the Austrian people to continue the struggle in the West, and if Eastern Front is even partially recreated the Austrian morale, which is very weak, might break down altogether.

I have a long cable from Sir Horace but I cannot get it in shape to send to you tonight. E.M.H.[2]

T telegram (WP, DLC).
  [1] Enclosure I printed with EMH to WW, April 26, 1918.
  [2] EMHhw.

From Charles Richard Crane

Dear Mr President   [New York] April 29 1918

The Non-Partisan League movement in the Dakotas and Minnesota seems to be growing and may need a little chaperoning. I have been in the way of hearing something about it and, if you should care to look into it pretty soon, I suggest that you you [sic] have Colver come to see you. He has been in touch with it from the beginning and can best summarize its activities.

The foundation of the movement is Scandanavian—not at all Bolshiviki—but quite determined to bring about many perfectly legitimate economic changes by democratic processes—election and legislation.

The men in the movement absolutely trust you, can be easily lead but, as Scandanavians, cannot be driven an inch. It is very interesting and quite worthy of a little sympathetic regard.

                    Yours sincerely   Charles R. Crane

ALS (WP, DLC).

From Thomas Joseph Mooney

San Francisco, California, April 29, 1918.

As you have taken an interest in justice being done in my case I wish to assure you that no attempt will be made with my consent to interfere by calling strikes May first. I have telegraphed the labor organizations reported to have called protest strike for May first asking them to call off that strike and to continue with the nationally important work on which they are engaged. I have read your letter to Governor Stephens and shall do nothing and allow nothing to be done in my behalf which will weaken the force of your appeal.

Thomas J. Mooney.[1]

T telegram (WP, DLC).
[1] Wilson asked Tumulty to read this telegram over the telephone to William B. Wilson and Thomas W. Gregory and ask their advice as to an answer. The former suggested that Tumulty merely acknowledge receipt of Mooney's telegram and say that it would be brought to the President's attention. Gregory concurred and added that he did not believe that the President could "afford" to reply personally. Woodrow Wilson then instructed Tumulty to follow W. B. Wilson's suggestion. Three typed memoranda attached to the above telegram in WP, DLC.

From Robert Wickliffe Woolley

Dear Mr. President: Washington April 29, 1918.

I beg to thank you sincerely for your note regarding my suggestion as to Justice Brandeis. In making it I was mindful of what you said to Mr. Hale and myself of the "master and servant" decision and of the importance of his remaining at his post.

My thought was that the present term of the court would end in about thirty days, that Justice Brandeis was undoubtedly up on his work, and that he would gladly consent to be drafted until October, by which time he would have the work of the Director General of Labor so well organized that it could with safety be turned over to an able successor to be selected meanwhile. I regret that I did not make myself clear on this point and hasten to assure you that I would not think of proceeding unless you should so direct.

With kindest regards and great respect, I am,

Faithfully yours,   R. W. Woolley

TLS (WP, DLC).

John Joseph Pershing to Peyton Conway March and Newton Diehl Baker

Received at the War Department Washington, D. C. April 29, 1918.
From GHQAEF. To The Adjutant General, Washington
Number 1020 April 29th. Confidential. For the Chief of Staff and Secretary of War.

Realizing that the President approves of unity of command of the Allied forces and that the principle is now accepted by the Allies in France, recommend for consideration the extension of the principle to the Italian Army. General Foch has the confidence and even the affections of the Italians, grateful for his energetic help after their disaster last autumn. It is suggested that the President might with propriety make an appeal to the Italian Government to complete the unity of command of all the Allied armies by placing its army under the same control. No one is so qualified to make this request; no one would be listened to with such respectful attention. This suggestion coming from France or Great Britain might excite suspicion; coming from the President only the highest motive touching the general good would be ascribed. It seems possible that the Italian cabinet is already willing to take this step if it felt able to protect itself from hostile criticisms in the Italian parliament and the Italian opposition press. This protection would be amply furnished by the fact that the suggestion came from the President. Both the Italian Government and the people would see in his action only a desire to serve the common cause. Should the President not wish to make the recommendation directly to the Italian Government the next best solution would then be to communicate his view to the French and British Governments and authorize them to present it to the Italian Government. I am making these recommendations on my own initiative and have consulted no one. Its realization would strengthen us with the Italian Government and would have a happy effect in France and Great Britain.
                                                                    Pershing.

T telegram (WP, DLC).

From Edward Mandell House, with Enclosures

Dear Governor: New York. April 30, 1918.
    Here are two more cables which will interest you.
                          Affectionately yours,   E. M. House

TLS (WP, DLC).

London, April 28, 1918.

No. 596 and 597. Following for Col. House from Sir Horace Plunkett:

(a) On my sole responsibility I wish to send you fuller information about the Irish crisis than you could gain from censored press or official sources. I do so because the Irish people, more united than ever before and incited by their Church to resist the British authority, are about to submit their grievance to the President. Even if their envoy is not given a passport the case is sure to be presented through Congress or direct to the President by the political and ecclesiastical organizations in touch with Ireland. In that case he might think well to avert possible diplomatic and domestic embarrassment by expressing his opinion upon the issues raised in some appropriate manner. He might thus have an opportunity to relieve if not to save an Irish situation far more dangerous than the British Government realize, and conceivably be the means of bringing the Irish at home and abroad into full co-operation with the Allies.

(b) The crisis was precipitated by the introduction of conscription at a time when the attainment of Home Rule seemed imminent. During the lengthy sittings of the Convention the Sinn Fein movement, which had rapidly grown in power since the executions after the rebellion, exercised increasing pressure upon the Nationalist delegates, a minority of whom, together with the members of the Roman Catholic Hierarchy, demanded the status of a self-governing dominion such as Canada, Australia or South Africa. Even the moderate Nationalists, a majority of the party has put on record their preference for the Dominion status; but they had won over the Southern Unionists to a liberal measure of self-government by agreeing to a constitution which was not inconsistent with Federal principles. It was understood that the Cabinet would present a bill to Parliament based on this agreement and do their best to get it passed quickly into law and put into operation. The Ulster Unionists, who held out for exclusion, would, it was hoped, have come in perhaps under protest. The establishment of a Parliament for undivided Ireland would then, I think, have been accepted as being in the circumstances a reasonable settlement of the Irish question.

(c) Unhappily, just when the Convention reported, military situation necessitated a big draft of older men in Great Britain and this the Cabinet considered impracticable without taking power to extend to Ireland the compulsory service which had been in operation for two years in the rest of the United Kingdom. This decision, which I personally think most unwise, played into the hands of the extreme anti-British party in Ireland. Today all the Nationalists have been compelled to join in the organized resistance to conscription. Under clerical influence women will make the passive resistance very effective, and I doubt whether any considerable levy can be effected without bloodshed, with untold consequences in the United Kingdom and abroad. Organized labour is equally determined. The country now demands settlement which will abolish supreme authority of the Imperial Government over military service.

(d) The moral justification put forward by the Catholic Church, and therefore likely to be widely repeated in America, is as follows:

Ireland claims and expects the President to support her right of self-determination. She demands the full status of a self-governing dominion. The acts constituting the dominions give them certain naval and military powers and control over conditions of military service, yet the dominions have all supported the Empire voluntarily with their blood and treasure. Trust, satisfy her political aspirations and she will do likewise. The Irish Parliament is long overdue, and to accompany the concession of Home Rule for Ireland with conscription by England is a tyrannical act.

(e) This claim for dominion status demanded by the Sinn Feiners as the nearest approach to complete independence has given fresh strength to the Federalist idea. Activity of the Catholic Church against conscription has hardened the opposition to Home Rule in England and Ulster, which now asserts its right of self-determination and its claim to exclusion. The new Irish demand for military powers, not even asked for in former attempts for settlement, is objected to on the further ground that they could not be conceded to English, Scottish and Welsh Parliaments which are expected by many to be established immediately after the war. I hear it said that with so much pro-German activity in Ireland and among American Irish a concession which might open Irish harbours to enemy submarines would involve grave military risk.

(f) The foregoing will show that after a long, earnest and hopeful attempt to settle the Irish question in the interest of both our war effort and peace aims, the Government feel compelled to take a course which revives the difficulties in a new and aggravated form. I have placed the situation before you because it may be presented to the President in such a way as to enable him to bring his powerful influence to bear upon it. If he could first win all but the extreme Irish by expressing sympathy with their reasonable political aspirations and noting with gratification the readiness and anxiety of the British people to meet their wishes, he might possibly make a statement on some such lines as follows:

The Irish people have a duty to the cause of Liberty for which the democracies of the Empire and of the Republic of France, of Italy and Belgium are fighting together. If in this war for the safety of democracy and liberties of small nations, Ireland plays the part which all her history indicates, which her kinsmen and friends in the United Kingdom and throughout the Empire are by their example calling upon her to play, there will be a general desire that her reasonable aspirations should be satisfied. On the other hand, if she stands out of this war for civilization, she may alienate the sympathies of the world.

You will believe me that I would not have cabled this were not the situation gravely critical.

E N C L O S U R E   I I

London, April 29, 1918.

596. Following for Col. House from Sir William Wiseman.

(a) I have postponed Paris trip in order to accompany the Prime Minister and Milner to Supreme War Council meeting at Abbeville on Wednesday. I should be in Paris on Thursday night. Chief purpose of Supreme War Council is for the Allies to agree on recommendations to the United States Government regarding the best use of American force especially the plan referred to in your telegram 602 of the 26th.[1]

(b) Milner bids me tell you that he is much encouraged by your message and by the knowledge of your sympathetic cooperation.

TC telegrams (WP, DLC).
[1] EMH to W. Wiseman, April 26, 1918.

Allen W. Ricker to Edward Mandell House

Dear Col. House: New York April 30th, 1918.

I think you will be interested in reading copies of two letters I have sent to Solicitor Lamar since I saw you. After a glance at them, please return them for my files.

I have been unable to do business for the last few days because I have had a stream of socialists coming to my office to talk over the situation.

Here is one thing I did not tell you. If I can get the proper encouragement I want to make a trip to see Debs. There are three men in this nation who have a bigger personal following than any other of our citizens. The first of course is the President; second— Roosevelt; third—Debs.

The radicals will follow Debs as they will follow no other man. I believe I can swing Debs over if I can spend a couple of days with him. With Debs won over, the case is made.

Scott Nearing[1] was in to see me this morning, and Nearing is about the hardest of all, but Nearing agreed with me absolutely and promised to write me a letter in support of our program.

I have information from Massachusetts that the Fin[n]ish [?] Organizations will line up with us and that will swing the state of Mass.

My advices from Chicago are also encouraging.

Will be glad to report progress as often as you like or when events of importance occur.   Sincerely yours,   A W Ricker

TLS (WP, DLC).
  [1] Sociologist and lecturer at the Rand School of Social Science; chairman of the People's Council of America for Democracy and Peace (about which see n. 3 to the extract from the Daniels Diary, printed at July 13, 1917, Vol. 43).

A Translation of a Telegram from Viscount Kikujiro Ishii to Baron Shimpei Gotō

Washington April 30, 1918

Number 228. Today I met the President and had a conference with him and the Secretary of State. At the outset, the President expressed his gratification that, in spite of various irresponsible rumors, Japan and the United States completely agreed on the question of the Siberian intervention. Then he said that he would be the first to approve Japan's intervention, provided that she sends a large force to Siberia, effectively diverting the German army, and having thereby a great influence on the western front, and provided that the benefit produced by this activity is larger than the possible danger of letting the Russian people slip into Germany's clutches.

The President asked my opinion of approximately how many troops Japan could send to Siberia. I answered that I could not give him the number of the troops available for this purpose because I did not know how many among 450,000 Japanese soldiers in both the active army and the ready reserve could be sent for tasks other than the main one of defending the Japanese home islands, Formosa, and Korea. Then I asked in return, if—as I had thought that the American government as well as the public had deemed the question of the Siberian intervention settled for the time being—the American government had found it necessary to reconsider the question now. The President said that both he and the Secretary of State had not changed their view on the problem. Although the attitude of his government had not altered, he continued, Britain and France had proposed the intervention on several occasions. According to the President, these governments have never ceased to insist strongly that nothing but the Siberian intervention could prevent Germany from shifting its about 470,000-man force from the front in Russia to that in France in response to the increase of the forces sent from the United States. The President explained that, although the American government had not changed its attitude, he thought that it was his minimal duty to those governments to study every possibility, and that this was the reason why he requested the Secretary of State to ask for the Japanese government's reaction to the possibility of the United States' adding a small force to the Japanese army in the event of a Siberian intervention.

The Secretary of State entered the conversation, saying that he would discuss the matter from the same perspective as that of the President. He said that, even if the United States sent its soldiers to Siberia, it now lacked the means to transport troops in the Pacific area and asked whether Japan could help the United States a little in this respect. In reply, I repeated what I told the Secretary of State the other day, which was that the question of a Siberian intervention would arise in Japan only if the German armed forces appeared as a real threat in the eastern part of Siberia, and that this problem was totally different from one of sending troops deep into Siberia, effectively influencing Germany's military position in western Europe. I added that, since I recognized that the United States Government had not changed its attitude since the day before, I considered its question about lending the means of transportation in the event that the Siberian intervention would be necessary as merely a hypothetical one, but that I would consult the Imperial government about its reaction to it anyway. Therefore I request you to reply to it. The Secretary of State referred in the conference to a report from the United States Ambassador in Russia who had dispatched a detective to Irkutsk to confirm rumors about the German prisoners of war in Siberia. According to this report, he said, these prisoners of war had not only been armed but had conspired with the Bolsheviks to arrest and kill their own superiors, the German officers. At this point the conference ended, for the President had another appointment.

Hw telegram (MT 16384-13, pp. 105-110, JFO-Ar).

Two Letters to Robert Lansing

My dear Mr. Secretary: The White House 1 May, 1918

Before approving the enclosed message,[1] I would very much like to know whether there are not some serious complications involved in this case. Are we sure that Bessarabia is willing and that the union is one which we should wish in any case to advocate and approve?[2]

Cordially and sincerely yours,   Woodrow Wilson

TLS (SDR, RG 59, 763.72119/1653, DNA).
    [1] See RL to WW, April 27, 1918 (first letter of that date), n. 3.
    [2] As it turned out, the message to the Rumanian government was not sent. Phillips informed Lansing on May 6, 1918, that the Allies had decided not to answer or even to acknowledge the Rumanian communication, lest an acknowledgement might be interpreted as an approval of Rumania's action. Phillips suggested, and Lansing agreed, that the United States should also avoid any comment on the matter. W. Phillips to RL, May 6, 1918, TLS (SDR, RG 59, 763.72119/1637, DNA).

My dear Mr. Secretary: The White House 1 May, 1918

I thank you for the enclosed.[1] I think a categorical denial such as you suggest[2] is desirable and entirely justifiable.

Cordially and faithfully yours,   Woodrow Wilson

TLS (SDR, RG 59, 763.72/13412, DNA).
    [1] See RL to WW, April 27, 1918 (second letter of that date), n. 1.
    [2] *Ibid.*, n. 3.

To Edward William Pou

My dear Mr. Pou: The White House 1 May, 1918

I am afraid you will think I am always running to you,[1] but I beg you to believe, and I feel sure you will believe, that I do so only when the matter seems of critical importance.

My plea now is that it is of vital importance that the Passport Bill (H.R. 10264), which has been favorably reported to the House by the Committee on Foreign Affairs, should be acted upon quickly as possible, in order that we may control exits and entrances across the Mexican border.

May I not say that at one of the regular weekly meetings of intelligence chiefs (a confidential meeting, of course) it developed that there is reason for grave apprehension arising out of conditions on the coast of Mexico and at Chapultepec? The military intelligence officers report that there are now under construction at Chapultepec new wireless stations which will undoubtedly be capable of communicating directly with Nauen. The work is being done, it is said, by Germans, under the direction of a German expert. By reason of these new means of communication it has become immediately important that every precaution should be taken to close the border against the transmission of information which would be used by these wireless towers when completed. Mexico, it is believed, now already receives wireless messages directly from Germany.[2]

Apparently, there is more disquiet and anti-American feeling in the northern provinces of Mexico at present than there has been for many months past, and there have been many signs in recent months of an increasing pro-German attitude on the part of the officials of the Carranza Government in the Tampico oil district; also, a serious situation has developed threatening a very important portion of the world's supply of oil. German agents are active at Tampico in agitating the laborers along I.W.W. lines, and the results may be very serious.

Cordially and sincerely yours,   Woodrow Wilson

TLS (E. W. Pou Papers, Nc-Ar).
  [1] As chairman of the Rules Committee of the House of Representatives.
  [2] The German government had considered plans for an extensive radio network in Central and Latin America as early as 1916. In May 1916, the German Minister to Mexico, Heinrich von Eckardt, had urged the Foreign Office in Berlin to establish direct radio and telegraphic connections between Mexico and Germany. As a result, a receiving station under the control of the Mexican government had been built at Ixtapalapa, which had begun operation in April 1917. In addition, the German secret service seems to have had a secret receiver of its own in the house of one of its agents.
  In late 1917, work was begun, under the supervision of a German engineer who had worked at the station at Sayville, Long Island, on a transmitter at Chapultepec. Although this transmitter began operation in July 1918, due to technical problems its broadcasts could not be received in Nauen directly but had to be transmitted via Spain. For a detailed discussion, see Katz, *The Secret War in Mexico*, pp. 416-22.

To William Kent

My dear Mr. Kent: [The White House] 1 May, 1918

Pardon my delay in replying to your letter of April twenty-second about the situation in the Northwest with regard to the Nonpartisan League. My attention has frequently been called to the situation and it has given me a great deal of concern, but every time I approach it, it becomes evident that there is nothing that can be done by federal authority and nothing that can be done in restraint of the state authorities. I am afraid it is a situation which will have to work itself out, much as I should like to take a hand in working it out.

In haste   Sincerely yours,   Woodrow Wilson

TLS (Letterpress Books, WP, DLC).

To Ida Minerva Tarbell

My dear Miss Tarbell: [The White House] 1 May, 1918

I have your letter of April twenty-seventh[1] and will be very glad to have you use the following words on the "News Letter" which you expect to distribute upon the arrival of the delegates to the first annual conference of the Woman's Committee of the Council of National Defense on May thirteenth next:

"The work which has been undertaken by the Woman's Committee of the Council of National Defense has my warm approval and support. Already what the Committee has been able to accomplish has been most encouraging and has exceeded the first expectations of those who were instrumental in constituting it. Many barriers have been broken down, many new ties of sympathy and cooperation established, and a new spirit of cooperation and of devotion to a common cause aroused,—circumstances which are not only of the greatest immediate service to the nation but which promise many fine things for the future. I hope that the conference to be held on May thirteenth, fourteenth and fifteenth will be fruitful of the finest results."

Cordially and sincerely yours,   Woodrow Wilson

TLS (Letterpress Books, WP, DLC).
    [1] Ida M. Tarbell to WW, April 27, 1918, TLS (WP, DLC).

To William Harryman Rapley[1]

My dear Mr. Rapley: [The White House] 1 May, 1918

What you tell me about the forthcoming production of "Out There"[2] at the New National on Monday night, May thirteenth, interests me very greatly,[3] and Mrs. Wilson and I will certainly make a special effort to be present.

I am sorry to say, however, that it is really out of the question for me to attempt to compose a speech for Mrs. Fiske's use.[4] I have always suffered a singular disability in things of this sort. I can write a speech only when I can myself have an audience, and anything else I attempt is as dry as a bone. Mrs. Fiske would not be willing to repeat it.[5]

Sincerely yours,   Woodrow Wilson

TLS (Letterpress Books, WP, DLC).
    [1] Owner and director of the New National Theater in Washington.
    [2] A play by John Hartley Manners about a Cockney woman's attempt to get to the front to contribute her share to Allied victory. The performance in Washington, which would feature a dozen of the leading stars of the stage, was to be the opening of a three-week tour of sixteen major cities in the East and the Midwest for the benefit of the

American Red Cross. Since all participants on the tour were to donate their services, it was expected that the performances would raise $1,000,000 through the sale and auction of tickets and auctions of autographed programs and pictures of the stars. See the *New York Times*, April 22, 1918.

³ W. H. Rapley to WW, April 29, 1918, TLS (WP, DLC).

⁴ Minnie Maddern (Mrs. Harrison Grey) Fiske, leading actress famous for her character roles.

⁵ Instead of reading an address by Wilson, Mrs. Fiske delivered an appeal for the Red Cross at the end of the play. Wilson and Mrs. Wilson attended the performance, which raised $18,000 for the Red Cross.

A Telegram and a Letter to Anita Eugénie McCormick Blaine

[The White House] 1 May, 1918

Frankly, I think it would be wise to reconsider the policy and not set up such distinctions too deliberately.

Woodrow Wilson.

T telegram (WP, DLC).

My dear Mrs. Blaine: The White House 1 May, 1918

I am sure that you understood my telegram of this date. I feel that it is very dangerous to raise questions of loyalty unnecessarily, though I believe in raising them very emphatically when it is necessary. I am afraid that we are getting in a suspicious attitude towards people who are not really disloyal but merely unreasonable. We never know until a crisis like this how many of them there are in the country, and yet upon reflection it is evident that most of them do very little harm.

Cordially and sincerely yours,   Woodrow Wilson

TLS (Anita M. Blaine Papers, WHi).

To Albert Sidney Burleson

My dear Burleson: The White House 1 May, 1918

The two letters enclosed were sent me by House.¹ They are, as you will see, addressed to him. I wish you would read, ponder and inwardly digest them. The Pearson's Magazine letter made a special impression on me.²

Be kind enough to let me have them back when you have read them.   Cordially and faithfully yours,   Woodrow Wilson

TLS (WP, DLC).
¹ A. W. Ricker to EMH, April 25 and 30, 1918.
² Probably Ricker's letter of April 25.

Two Letters to Newton Diehl Baker

My dear Mr. Secretary: [The White House] 1 May, 1918

The enclosed case of the court-martial at Camp Dix, New Jersey, of Joseph C. Robinson, First Lieutenant, M.R.C.,[1] 312th Infantry, has given me pause, at any rate with regard to accepting the recommendation for a modification of the sentence.[2] Cases of this sort are so grave that I would like your opinion as to whether we are justified in remitting any part of the verdict of the court-martial.

            Cordially and faithfully yours,   Woodrow Wilson

[1] The Army Medical Reserve Corps.
[2] Dr. Robinson was charged with having contributed to and hastened the death of a soldier through gross neglect of duty. According to a statement by the War Department, Robinson had incorrectly diagnosed the ailment of Pvt. Wardell C. Van Tassell, a recruit at Camp Dix, and had failed to furnish proper medical relief. Dr. Robinson was sentenced to be dismissed from the army and to serve one year's imprisonment at hard labor. *New York Times*, July 12, 1918.

My dear Mr. Secretary: [The White House] 1 May, 1918

I wish with all my heart I could help in the matter of truck gardens at the camps,[1] but I am afraid that they wouldn't fall under the terms, "Security and Defense." The men on the Hill are counting on me to be a bit strict in my interpretation of the appropriation. I wish that it were less restricted. If you disagree with me about this, don't hesitate to say so, because this is not a confident opinion.

            Cordially and sincerely yours,   Woodrow Wilson

TLS (Letterpress Books, WP, DLC).
[1] NDB to WW, April 29, 1918, TLS (WP, DLC). Baker wrote that the War Department was eager to begin the experiment of having truck gardens at several army camps to be maintained by men under detention. In order to purchase the necessary seeds, tools, and machinery, he asked Wilson for $100,000 from his special emergency fund.

To Charles Richard Crane

My dear Friend: [The White House] 1 May, 1918

Thank you for your note about the Nonpartisan League. I have been giving a good deal of attention to the circumstances connected with the activity of that body and shall look into it still further along the lines you suggest.

It is always a pleasure to hear from you.

In great haste

            Cordially and faithfully yours,   Woodrow Wilson

TLS (Letterpress Books, WP, DLC).

To the Norman Foster Company

My dear Sirs: [The White House] 1 May, 1918

I am very much obliged to you for your courtesy in reminding me of my accident policy in connection with my recent burn.[1] So soon as the burn is healed, I will send you a memorandum of the circumstances and rely upon your judgment as to what benefits I am entitled to under the policy I hold.

Sincerely yours,   Woodrow Wilson

TLS (Letterpress Books, WP, DLC).
[1] N. Foster to WW, April 25, 1918, TLS (WP, DLC). Foster was president of the Norman Foster Co., an insurance company of Trenton, New Jersey.

From George Lewis Bell

San Francisco, Calif., May 1, 1918.

In connection with federal prosecution of industrial workers of world in Sacramento president Simon J. Lubin of our state immigration commission was subpoenaed before Federal grand jury. On account of his hesitancy to divulge subject matter of my conference with you last summer as confidential emissary of eight western governors[1] through some leak in grand jury charges and allegations are being publicly made that Lubin is disloyal and blocking government in these prosecutions. I have just had conference with United States attorney Prestons[2] who desires to be in possession of all facts in order to examine charges therefore he asked me to telegraph you for permission to disclose and discuss with him confidentially matter of my mission and conference with you also Lubins conference with you on March twenty nine and supplementary correspondence.[3] May I have such permission from you by telegram tonight if possible address Two Hundred Fifteen Underwood Building.[4]   George L. Bell.

T telegram (WP, DLC).
[1] About this matter, see WW to JPT, July 20, 1917, n. 1, Vol. 43, and the memorandum by G. L. Bell, printed at July 25, 1917, *ibid.*
[2] That is, John White Preston, United States attorney for the northern district of California.
[3] See S. J. Lubin to WW, March 29, 1918.
[4] "Atty General to advise Preston that the President thinks it unwise to establish a precedent of bringing confidential conferences with the President into Court." White House memorandum dated May 3, 1918, T MS (WP, DLC). TWG to JPT, May 4, 1918, TLS (WP, DLC), informed Tumulty that Gregory had followed Wilson's instructions.

Two Letters from Newton Diehl Baker

My dear Mr. President: Washington. May 1, 1918.

I present you herewith the court martial proceedings in four cases occurring in the American Expeditionary Forces in France, each of which involves the imposition of the death penalty by shooting to death with musketry.[1]

These cases have attracted widespread public interest, and with the papers are numerous letters and petitions urging clemency, most of which are of that spontaneous kind which are stirred by the natural aversion to the death penalty which humane people feel. Many of them are from mothers of soldiers whose general anxiety for the welfare of their sons is increased by apprehension lest exhaustion or thoughtlessness may lead their boys to weaknesses like those involved in these cases which the newspapers have described as trivial and involving no moral guilt, with the consequence that sons whose lives they are willing to forfeit in their country's defense may be ingloriously taken for disciplinary reasons in an excess of severity. Many of the letters are from serious and thoughtful men who argue that these cases do not involve disloyalty or conscious wrongdoing, and that whatever may have been the necessities of military discipline at other times and in other armies, the progress of a humane and intelligent civilization among us has advanced us beyond the helpful exercise of so stern a discipline in our Army in the present war.

I examined these cases personally, and had reached a conclusion with regard to the advice which I am herein giving before I had seen any of the letters or criticisms.

The record discloses the fact that the Divisional Commander, the Commander in Chief, General Pershing, the Chief of Staff, General March, and the Judge Advocate General concur in recommending the execution of the penalties imposed. The Judge Advocate General limits his concurrence to the technical statement that the proceedings in the cases are regular, and expressing regret that a more adequate conduct of the defense of the several men concerned was not provided, concurs in the recommendation of General Pershing. As I find myself reaching an entirely different conclusion, and disagreeing with the entire and authoritative military opinion in case, I beg leave to set out at some length the reasons which move me in the matter.

The cases must be divided into two classes, and I will deal first with the two young men convicted of sleeping while on duty; namely,

---

[1] Baker probably meant that he was now presenting a summary of the court-martial proceedings or records.

Private Jeff Cook and Private Forest D. Sebastian, both of Company G, 16th Infantry.

These cases are substantially identical in their facts. The accusations were laid under the 86th Article of War, which reads: "Any sentinel who is found * * * sleeping upon his post * * * shall, if the offense be committed in time of war, suffer death or such other punishment as a court-martial may direct."

In both cases a Corporal inspecting along a front line trench found these young men standing in the proper military position, leaning against the trench, with their rifles lying on the parapet of the trench within easy reach of their hands. Each man had his head resting on his arm, and his arm resting on the parapet. The offenses were committed, in the Sebastian case on the night of November third and fourth, and in the Cook case on or about the fifth of November. In both cases the testimony was exceedingly brief, and showed that the night was dark and cold, that the soldiers had their ponchos and other equipment on, and in one case it was a fair inference that the poncho was drawn over the ears and trench helmet in such a way as to make it difficult for the soldier to hear the approaching steps of the Corporal. In each case the Corporal laid his own rifle upon the parapet, and took that of the soldier, carrying it away with him, and instructed the other sentinel, the men being posted in this outpost duty in twos, to shake the soldier and tell him to report to the Corporal for his gun. In each case the Corporal shamed the soldier for his neglect of duty, and pointed out to him the fact that not only his own life but those of others were at stake, and that he should be more zealous and alert. In neither case does either the Corporal or the fellow-sentinel swear positively that the accused was asleep, but I confess that on all reasonable grounds, taking the circumstances into consideration, it seems to me entirely likely that both men were asleep; but it is important to note that in neither case had the accused stepped away from his proper military post to sit down or lie down; both being found standing at their posts of duty in what is admitted to have been a correct military position, and if they were asleep their heads literally nodded over on to their arms without any intentional relaxation of attention to their duty so far as can be gathered from any of the surrounding circumstances.

These soldiers are both young. Sebastian enlisted into the Regular Army by volunteering on the 18th of April 1917, having had no previous military experience, his age at that time being 19 years and 6 months. He was, therefore, slightly more than 20 at the time of the alleged offense. Cook enlisted on the 11th of May 1917, without previous military experience, his age at that time being 18 years and 11 months. He was, therefore, at the time of the alleged offense, slightly under 20 years of age.

From the testimony it appears that both of these young men had been posted as sentinels doing what is called Double Sentry Duty, going on duty at four P.M., and remaining on duty until six A.M., with relief at intervals by other sentinels during the night, but with no opportunity to sleep during the night because of there being no place where they could secure sleep. It further appeared that neither of them had slept during the day before after having spent the previous night on gas sentinel duty, although both had tried to sleep during the day preceding the night of the alleged offenses but found it impossible because of the noise. In both cases the Commanding Officers of the soldiers who forwarded the charges and recommended trials by general courts martial added to his endorsement as extenuating circumstances the youth and failure of the soldiers to take the necessary rest when off duty on the first occupation of trenches.

It is difficult to picture to the eye which has not seen it the situation in which these young soldiers were placed. In the month of November the section of France in which these soldiers were stationed was cold, wet and uncomfortable in the extreme. No sort of shelter of any confortable kind could be provided near the trenches, because it attracts enemy observation and fire. Throughout one long night they performed duty as gas sentinels, dut[y]ing the next day, when they perhaps ought to have sought more rest than they did seek, they found it difficult to secure any sleep because of the noise and discomfort of their surroundings. As a consequence on the night of the alleged offenses they had reached the place at which exhausted nature apparently refused to go further, and without any intentional relaxation of vigilance on their parts they dozed in standing positions at their posts of duty.

I am quite aware of the gravity of this offense, and of the fact that the safety of others, perhaps the safety of an army and of a cause, may depend upon such disciplinary enforcement of this regulation as will prevent soldiers from sleeping on sentinel duty; and yet I cannot believe that youths of so little military experience, placed for the first time under circumstances so exhausting can be held to deserve the death penalty, nor can I believe that discipline of the death sentence ought to be imposed in cases which do not involve a bad heart, or so flagrant a disregard of the welfare of others, and of the obligation of a soldier, as to be evidence of conscious disloyalty.

In both of these cases the reviewing Judge Advocate[2] quotes with

[2] First Lt. Paul C. Green.

approval some observations of General Upton who in his work on military policy[3] points out that action taken by President Lincoln in the early days of the Civil War pardoning or commuting sentences in cases of death penalty led to the need of greater severity at a later period in the interest of discipline; but the cases which General Upton had in mind were cases of desertion in the face of the enemy involving cowardice, and cases of substantially treasonable betrayal of the nation, and I can see no persuasion in them as an example. Rather it would seem to indicate that the invocation of this opinion of General Upton indicates a feeling on the part of the reviewing Judge Advocate that while these particular cases might not be deemed on their own merits to justify the death sentence, that, nevertheless, as a disciplinary example such action would be justified. I am not, of course, suggesting that any of the military officers who have reviewed these cases would be willing to sacrifice the lives of these soldiers even though innocent; but I do think that if these cases stood alone no one of the reviewing officers would have recommended the execution of these sentences; their recommendations being, in my judgment, soldierly and in accordance with the traditions of their profession, and based upon a very earnest desire on their part to save the safety of their commands, and the lives of other soldiers; but, nevertheless, to some extent influenced by the value to the discipline of the Army of the examples which their execution would afford.

I have not sought to examine the learning of this subject, and, therefore, have not prepared a history of the death penalty as a military punishment; but I think it fair to assume that it arose in times and under circumstances quite different from these, when men were impressed into armies to fight for causes in which they had little interest and of which they had little knowledge, and when their conduct was controlled without their consent by those who assumed to have more or less arbitrary power over them. Our army, however, is the army of a democratic nation fighting for a cause which the people themselves understand and approve, and I had happy and abundant evidence when I was in France that the plain soldiers of our Expeditionary Forces are aware of the fact that they are really defending principles in which they have as direct an interest as anybody, principles which they understand, approve and are willing to die for.

I venture, therefore, to believe that the President can with perfect safety to military discipline pardon these two young men; and I have prepared and attached hereto an order which, if it meets with

[3] Emory Upton, *The Military Policy of the United States*, ed. Joseph P. Sanger (Washington, D. C., 1904).

your approval, will accomplish that purpose, and at the same time, I believe, upon its publication further stimulate the already fine spirit of our army in France. Such an order as I have here drawn[4] would be read by every soldier in France and in the United States, and coming from the Commander in Chief would be a challenge to the performance of duty, quite as stimulating as any disciplinary terror proceeding from the execution of these sentences. In the meantime, public opinion in this country would, I believe, with practical unanimity approve such action on your part.

In the cases of Stanley G. Fishback and Olon Ledoyen, the charges are substantially identical in that each of them is accused under the 64th Article of War of having "wilfully disobeyed any lawful command of his superior officer." The facts show that on the 3rd day of January 1918, these two young men in broad day light in the theatre of war, at a place back of the actual line, were directed to bring their equipment and fall in for drill. Each refused, whereupon they were warned by the lieutenant who gave the order not to persist in their refusal on the ground that grave consequences would ensue. They were not warned that the penalty of disobedience was death; but were advised earnestly to comply. Both persisted in their refusal. Each gave as his reason for refusing that he had been drilled extensively the day before, that they had gotten cold, the weather being extremely severe, and that they had not yet recovered from the effects of that exposure.

Both plead guilty at the trial.

It is perfectly obvious that this order ought to have been obeyed. It was a proper military order, and it seems to me inconceivable that such obstinate refusal on so trivial a matter could have been made with any consciousness that the death penalty was the alternative. Nevertheless the disobedience was wilful, undisciplined and inexcusable, and it ought to be punished with a suitable punishment.

The Judge Advocate General in reviewing these cases limits himself again to the technical correctness of the proceedings; but in a subsequent memorandum he called the attention of the Chief of Staff to the fact that four cases of sleeping on post arising in the same Regiment at approximately the same time resulted in acquittal of the accused on substantially the same evidence as that recited in the Sebastian and Cook cases above reviewed, and that in six cases similar offenses committed elsewhere in France had led to

[4] It is missing in WP, DLC. However, separate orders approved by Wilson on May 4 confirmed Cook's and Sebastian's sentences but granted them full and unconditional pardons and returned them to active duty. The order affecting Cook was printed in the *Official Bulletin*, II (June 20, 1918), 5.

very moderate penalties. The Judge Advocate General says in this memorandum: "In addition to the foregoing, the study in this office reveals a number of cases which have come in from France where men have been convicted of wilful disobedience of orders under circumstances which do not distinguish them as to the locus of the offense from the cases of Fishback and Ledoyen, who were sentenced to death. The sentences in the cases referred to run from a few months to several years' confinement."

In other words, the Judge Advocate General reviewing generally the state of discipline in the Army in France, and the steps taken to enforce it, reaches the conclusion that up to the time of the trial of these cases the offenses of which these soldiers were convicted had been regarded as quite minor in their gravity. The Chief of Staff in commenting upon this memorandum of the Judge Advocate General is able from his own recollection to add that the wilful disobedience cases lately tried in France did not occur in the actual theatre of war, making at least that much of a distinction. But the case still remains one in which suddenly a new and severe attitude is taken without the record disclosing that any special order had been made notifying soldiers that the requirements of discipline would call upon courts martial thereafter to resort to extreme penalties to restore discipline.

Both Ledoyen and Fishback are young. The record shows that Ledoyen enlisted on the 3rd of February 1917, without previous military experience, his age at that time being 18 years and 1 month. Fishback enlisted on the 17th of February 1917, without previous military experience, his age being 19 years and 2 months. Each of them at the time of the commission of the alleged offenses was, therefore, less than 20 years of age.

The record in the Fishback case shows that there had been previous shortcomings on his part in the matter of obedience. That is to say, he had once failed to report for drill for which he was required to forfeit 15 days pay; a second time failed to report for drill, penalty not stated; and a third time failed to report for fatigue duty, for which he was sentenced to one month at hard labor and to forfeit two-thirds of his pay for two months. He seems, therefore, to have found it difficult to accommodate himself to the discipline of the life of a soldier, and his offense hereunder reviewed is aggravated by this previous record.

By a very extraordinary coincidence this record discloses the fact that these two soldiers were members of a company commanded by Captain D. A. Henckes.[5] It is from the Captain of his company

---

[5] David A. Henkes, not Henckes.

that the soldier most immediately learns discipline and obedience. The Captain sets the example, and inculcates the principles upon which the soldier is built. Now, this particular Captain Henckes, although for many years an officer in the Regular Army, was himself so undisciplined and disloyal that when he was ordered to France with his command, he sought to resign because he did not want to fight the Germans. Born in this country, and for twenty years an officer in its Army, under sworn obligation to defend the United States against all her enemies, domestic and foreign, he still sought to resign; and when the resignation was not accepted, and he went to France, the Commander in Chief was obliged to return him to this country because of his improper attitude toward the military service, and his country's cause in this war. He was thereupon courtmartialed, and is now serving a sentence of twenty-five years in the penitentiary for his lack of loyalty and lack of discipline.

I confess I do not see how any soldiers in his company could have been expected to learn the proper attitude toward the military service from such a commander. I do not suggest that the short-comings of Captain Henckes be made an excuse for their disobedience, but these mere youths can hardly be put to death under these circumstances, and I, therefore, recommend that the sentence in each case be commuted to one involving penal servitude under circumstances which will enable them by confinement in the Disciplinary Barracks at Fort Leavenworth to acquire under better conditions a wholesomer attitude toward the duty of a soldier. Orders accompanying this letter[6] are drawn for your approval which will carry out the recommendation here made.

In view of the fact that both Fishback and Ledoyen had been previously guilty of minor offenses as disclosed by the record the penalty suggested is three years confinement.

Respectfully submitted,   Newton D. Baker

[6] They are missing.

My dear Mr. President: Washington. May 1, 1918.

After conferring with you several days ago about the possibility of sending an American military unit to Italy, I sent a confidential cablegram to General Bliss, stating the whole case, and asking for an expression of his views. Incidentally, I pointed out to General Bliss the danger of our creating expectations of further forces which it would be difficult for us to meet, and proposed as one solution of the problem that we get the British or French, or both, to brigade some of the American troops which we are sending for training with them with their divisions in Italy. I have just received a cablegram from General Bliss which reads as follows:

"In my weekly letter to you dated April twentieth which left Brest on Transport 'America' I stated that General Giardino[1] had represented to me on April eighteenth the view of the Italian Government about sending American military units to Italy. He said they did not expect a large unit; but only a brigade, or even only a regiment. They propose to put them in training behind the lines near the Swiss frontier. I told General Giardino I did not favor dispersion of our military efforts, but that I would write you sympathetically about suggestion of sending small unit solely for moral effect if it should prove possible. Danger is that demand would follow for more troops. This morning had interview with Italian civil representative with War Council, and he stated that his view is that we should send at first a small unit, and then establish a base in Italy with a view to having eventually a large force there. I told him emphatically that I did not believe my Government would send any troops except upon distinct understanding that it would be a small unit for moral effect, and not to be followed by others. I think your proposition is the only practicable solution. Let British or French, or both, send some of the Infantry that we are loaning them to be brigaded with their divisions now in Italy, relieving equivalent number of British and French troops that can be sent North. I think this plan would be gladly accepted by the British and French and do for the Italians all we can do. Number of troops sent to Italy should be small, not more than one or two regiments. Personally, I do not favor sending troops to Italy, because of the certain demand that will be made for more. The trouble in Italy is not so much the morale of the Army as it is the morale of the country at large. The common people will soon be complaining that more Americans are not coming in order to relieve them from the burden of war, and the final moral effect may be bad instead of good."

If this meets with your approval I will cable General Pershing, asking him to suggest to General Foch or General Petain and to Sir Douglas Haig the sending of some American troops to be brigaded with their several divisions in Italy, explaining to General Pershing that our object is the appearance of American soldiers on the Italian Front under circumstances which will not create expectations of further forces at the present time of a kind which would be created if an independent American force made its appearance there.   Respectfully yours,   Newton D. Baker

TLS (WP, DLC).
[1] That is, Lt. Gen. Gaetano Ettore Giardino, Italy's representative on the Supreme War Council.

From John Skelton Williams

Dear Mr. President: Washington May 1, 1918.

I am taking the liberty of handing you with this a statement which has just been prepared for the press, regarding the advances which the Director General of the Railroad Administration has made to the railroads of the country in the past thirty days, and which will probably be of interest to you.[1]

The aggregate amount advanced thus far, you will note, is $90,614,000.

I think you may credit the Director General with having already saved from insolvency, by timely aid, many important railroad systems, including, among others, such important lines as the New York Central, the New York, New Haven & Hartford, the Baltimore & Ohio, and others.   Respectfully and Faithfully yours,
                                                    Jno. Skelton Williams

TLS (WP, DLC).
[1] The enclosure is missing. The statement is printed in the *Official Bulletin*, II (May 2, 1918), 3.

Lord Reading to Arthur James Balfour

Washington. 1st May 1918.

No. 1951. Secret. Viscount Ishii was presented to the President yesterday and later called upon me but the visit was formal only. Secretary Lansing informed me today that the President and he and Viscount Ishii after presentation had some discussion about intervention.

(1) Viscount Ishii said the Japanese were ready to make intervention if they could be satisfied that the effect would be beneficial to the common cause but from their reports they feared the consequence would be to make the Russian population hostile to Japan and to drive them into better relations with Germany.

(2) If intervention occurred it would be first for the protection of East Siberia up to Irkutsk. The Japanese had not contemplated going further and to use Secretary Lansing's words in relating the conversation to me "they required to be satisfied (a) that the military advantage of intervention would be sufficient to compensate for the risk they would incur and (b) that it would produce a sufficient diversion to cause the Germans to move troops from West to the East."

(3) The Japanese had an army of 250,000 ready with 200,000 reserves. Their General Staff did not think this force sufficient to

warrant attempting to advance as far as Chiliabinsk or the Ural mountains unless they were advancing through a friendly country with the assistance instead of the hostility of the population.

Viscount Ishii thought the ways into China might be guarded by the Chinese but nevertheless the Japanese forces available would be insufficient to protect the railway unless the population helped. (4) Generally, Secretary Lansing produced the impression and indeed stated that Viscount Ishii's view was practically identical with the American. Lansing added very confidentially that Ishii had said they would very gladly welcome American cooperation if intervention took place.

(5) I told Lansing that you welcomed the discussion taking place at Washington. I explained to him as I did at the time of demurring to the proposal that I thought it right to consult you before assisting in the negotiations with Ishii here and that you had answered as above stated.

(6) I informed him that I should be paying a return visit to Viscount Ishii this afternoon and should talk with him upon intervention, and pressed upon Lansing that time was slipping by and that in any event there should be an answer to the questions I had submitted on your behalf to the President. Lansing wished to confer with me again & afterwards together with Ishii.

(7) I called on Ishii. I told him that I feared according to reports we had received that intervention by the Japanese alone would be likely to rouse hostility of the Russians but that our reports as to probable results in the event of intervention of Japanese with contingents of allies and Americans were more favourable than the American reports. He repeated to me substantially all that Lansing had told me and in particular said that he had had reports since his arrival here from Tokio which showed that the Bolsheviki Government was making more insistent demands for the withdrawal of the Japanese troops from Vladivostock. I told him that the Bolsheviki Government seemed to have turned towards the Allies latterly and instanced the better tone of the Press [,] Murmansk co-operation and Trotsky's request to us in regard to Black Sea Fleet. He doubted Trotsky's good faith and stated that since his arrival he had received reports from Tokio to the same effect as the American and which pointed to the probability of the Russians turning to Germany for assistance against the Japanese even if supported by Allies and Americans. He added that in his own opinion there should be no objection to contingents of Allies and Americans joining the Japanese if intervention should be decided upon but he would not commit his Government to this view.

(8) My impression is that the Japanese are not at present favourably

disposed to go further than Irkutsk although they would be ready to consider the matter in any change of circumstances. He stated that their General Staff was of opinion that the Japanese soldiers were not fitted for a campaign to Chiliabinsk or the Ural and they had to be supplied with special food which a single railway line rendered difficult of accomplishment.

(9) We arranged to exchange any information of importance and agreed to renew our conversations very soon.

(10) Although I am not able to express definite views I do not regard the prospect of the intervention we wish as very hopeful. I cannot rid myself of the impression that the Americans are glad to find a reason for delay and I am inclined to think that Ishii's arrival will help them rather than us.

T telegram (FO 115/2445, pp. 412-15, PRO).

From Robert Lansing

My dear Mr. President: Washington May 2, 1918.

I spent nearly two hours this afternoon with the Senate Committee on Foreign Relations in regard to the King resolution for a declaration of a state of war with Turkey and Bulgaria. From what Senator Hitchcock had told me and from the impression I gained in the first few minutes of the conference today I found that all of the Republicans and many of the Democrats on the Committee were predisposed to reporting favorably the King resolution.[1]

In view of the situation I thought it best to state that the question was one of expediency, that I was not present to advise but to consult with the Committee as to the wisdom of a declaration such as the one proposed. I made it clear that neither you nor I sought to influence improperly Congressional action, that the responsibility for the declaration of a state of war lay with Congress and they could not avoid the responsibility, and that the Executive branch of the Government could go no further than lay the facts before them and give opinions when asked. This attitude seemed to make the supporters of the resolution very cautious.

The Committee asked me whether it was considered expedient by the British, French and Italian Governments for us to declare a state of war with these two allies of Germany. I told them that I did not know but that I was willing to inquire if they wished me to do so.

I emphasized the fact that the whole problem was one of policy based upon the proposition of winning the war, that I was not there to advocate a particular course of action but to elucidate to the

Committee the situation as far as I was able, and that it was only a question of whether a declaration of war would be more helpful or more injurious to our cause.

As a result of this conference with the Committee it was arranged that I should obtain the views of the Allied Governments as to the advisability of a declaration by us of a state of war with Turkey and Bulgaria together, or with Bulgaria alone. Until this information is obtained there will be no action.

In view of the very evident majority in the Committee favoring a declaration against both Turkey and Bulgaria I suggest the sending of the enclosed telegrams to London, Paris, and Rome, and to the War Council at Versailles.[2]

Will you be good enough to consider these telegrams and to indicate your wishes in the matter?

I have agreed to confer again with the Committee when I know more definitely the views of our cobelligerents, expressing the opinion that it would take at least ten days to obtain these views.

Faithfully yours,   Robert Lansing.

TLS (SDR, RG 59, 763.72/10115b, DNA).
[1] See n. 2 to the Enclosure printed with RL to WW, April 24, 1918.
[2] RL to WHP (the same to Paris and Rome), May 2 [3], 1918, T telegram (SDR, RG 59, 763.72/9799a, DNA); RL to W. G. Sharp (for Bliss), May 2 [3], 1918, T telegram (SDR, RG 59, 763.72/9799b, DNA). Lansing informed Page (and others in the separate telegrams) that there was a strong movement in Congress for declarations of war against Turkey and Bulgaria, or against either of them. The action of the United States would be based primarily upon expediency, and the American government wanted to know whether the Allied governments and the Supreme War Council thought that such declarations of war would contribute materially to the defeat of the Central Powers.

From Newton Diehl Baker

Dear Mr. President: [Washington] May 2, 1918.

By arrangements which I made in Europe, General Bliss writes me a weekly letter which he entrusts to some officer returning to the United States for personal delivery. I enclose his letter of last week,[1] which left France quite recently and contains some very interesting comments which you may care to glance over. It will also serve to show you the sort of discussions which go on among the military men in the Supreme War Council.

On page 8 General Bliss gives his views on the question of the Japanese intervention. He told me in Versailles that he felt embarrassed, being one of the military advisers, to sit into the conference on this subject when he knew that you regarded it as more political than military, and that he was equally embarrassed in refusing to participate in the discussions, since refusal by one nation's representative to discuss one question might be a precedent for similar action by others, ultimately disintegrating the Council. I told him that I felt certain that we should not take the attitude that we would not discuss the military aspects of any proposal, but that you wanted him not to concur in recommendations of a political character, as those questions are plainly reserved for the Supreme Council itself. This he perfectly understood and regarded as the only wise course.

I would be glad if I might have this letter back for my continuing file of his letters.   Respectfully yours,   Newton D. Baker

CCL (N. D. Baker Papers, DLC).
  [1] The Editors have been unable to find this letter.

From George Creel, with Enclosure

My dear Mr. President: Washington, D. C. May 2, 1918.

I am very much distressed to hear of your indisposition, and trust that it is quite temporary.

I have just finished with the Lithuanian National Council, and I have rarely met a more remarkable body of men. I attach the address that they had intended for personal delivery to you today. A word from you is all that is needed to put this powerful body behind us absolutely. Will it be possible for you to receive them tomorrow, and if not, may I beg a letter in answer to this address that will get the confidence of Lithuanian aims and aspirations.[1]

                    Respectfully,   George Creel

TLS (WP, DLC).
  [1] Wilson received the Lithuanian National Council, a group of twenty people, at the White House on the following day at 2:30 p.m. The Rev. J. J. Jakaitis of Worcester, Massachusetts, read the following address.

E N C L O S U R E

From the Lithuanian National Council

Mr. President:

The Lithuanian National Council, for itself, and on behalf of nearly 1,000,000 Lithuanians who have sought refuge from autocracy in the free and enlightened environment of the United States, pledges you the loyal support and lasting affection of the Lithuanians of America. Perhaps the most tangible evidence of our loyalty to the country and to yourself is to be found in the fact that in the great army which we are now sending to Europe to "make the world safe for democracy" are to be found more than 25,000 Lithuanians, by far the greater percentage of whom responded to your call by volunteering to make the world, with the bayonet where need be, a decent place to live in.

For centuries Lithuania has longed to be an independent nation. For centuries she has been ground between the millstones of imperialism, Russia and Germany, but the unyielding kernel of national aspiration has refused to disintegrate. Today it sends forth its shoots searching for encouragement and assurances of a hardy and durable growth.

To Poland has been vouchsafed, in the Thirteenth Condition of your program for the world's peace, such assurances and guarantees as Lithuania would fain apply to herself and for which she petitions. Lithuania formally declared her independence December 11, 1917, in consonance with that desire of small nations "to determine their own allegiances and their own forms of political life." She has been abandoned by Russia with whom she would not, if she could, renew her former coercive connection. She revolts at the idea of a resumption of the old personal union with Poland, and better obliteration than Prussian domination. Independence and autonomy, free of alien influences, are those things for which she has declared and for which she strives.

You have precisely stated, Mr. President, that "this war had its roots in the disregard of the rights of small nations["] and of nationalities which lacked the union and force to make good their claims, and you have declared that "covenants must now be entered into which will render such things impossible for the future; and those covenants must be backed by the united force of all the nations that love justice and are willing to maintain it at any cost."

The Lithuania of today possesses the union, but she still lacks the force, unaided and unencouraged, to make good her claims. One of the first tasks with which she finds herself confronted is to rid the land of German influences and German propaganda. Once that has been achieved the stabilizing of national status will speedily follow, for we are confident we possess those attributes and racial characteristics which make for sound government.

No single factor would more result in stiffening Lithuania's resistance to German control than an assurance on the part of the United States, voiced by our President, that when she shall have proved her capacity for self-government Lithuania will be guaranteed permanent independence. As the Allied Powers in Europe followed the example of the United States in recognizing the Chinese Republic, so will they follow the United States in extending assurances and guarantees to Lithuania, for the United States under your leadership, Mr. President, means the world under the leadership of the United States.

Upon the practical considerations which urge the extension to Lithuania of assurances and guarantees similar to those which have been accorded to Poland, we shall not dwell. Rather do we respectfully refer the President to the memorandum prepared by us and submitted to the State Department on April 27th, in which the question is more lengthily discussed.[1] But to this ancient of nations and infant of republics, bounded on the east by chaos and on the west by despotism, the importance of being assured that Lithuania's independence will be recognized, and her territorial integrity guaranteed, cannot be overestimated.

We respectfully ask your favorable consideration of our request, and we pledge anew our loyalty to, and our faith in the cause which you champion.

T MS (WP, DLC).
[1] Julius J. Bielskis, secretary, Lithuanian National Council, to the State Department, April 26, 1918, TLS (SDR, RG 59, 860M.01/77, DNA).

From John Dennis Ryan

Dear Mr. President.   New York [c. May 2, 1918]

I am most grateful for the expression of your confidence in me shown by your approval of my selection as Director of Aircraft Production of the Army.

I hope to prove myself worthy of it and assure you I have never felt as strong a desire to do anything else in a way to prove my selection to be a good one.

I have just enough knowledge of the work now to realize its responsibilities but I am hopeful that they can be met.

Very respectfully,   John D. Ryan

ALS (WP, DLC).

From Robert Somers Brookings

My dear Mr President: Washington May 2, 1918.

While the Price Fixing Committee is recognized as a Committee of the War Industries Board, you have, in the creation of this committee, placed upon it responsibilities and given it authority which by necessity compels it to function more or less independently. It is probably only a question of time when all departments of the

Government (including the Railroad Administration) will have recourse to the Price Fixing Committee for such help as it is best constituted to render.

As Chairman of the Price Fixing Committee, I assume that you expect me to keep informed regarding all matters of price fixing as they have developed in other countries, and to prepare and submit to you from time to time such important price fixing policies as the welfare of the nation and of those associated with us in the war would seem to necessitate.

We have now control of the wool situation and will soon have control of hides and leather, and negotiations for cotton products control are progressing favorably. These three industries clothe our people, and, I am told by Mr Frayne that there is no one element which causes more discontent and is a greater stimulus to strikes for advanced wages than the constantly advancing price of shoes and clothing.

With the control of the above named industries, it would be a simple matter for the Government to assume control of a trade mark for all clothing and shoes, presumably "LIBERTY" (the Liberty shoe, the Liberty suit of clothes, the Liberty tailor suit for women, the Liberty shirt, etc. etc.). Both the material and the finished product of these articles would be made under specifications furnished by the Government which would insure the very best value for cost, and would be made subject to Government inspection only by the most responsible mills and manufacturers. They would cover only such clothing and shoes as the laboring class or the working people would require. They would cover, however, the greatest possible value in quality for price charged, and would be made and sold in such quantities as to reduce the cost to the consumer at prices very, very much below the prices now in vogue and still rising.

As you probably know, the British Government has already put into effect a system of this kind. They have gone somewhat further in guaranteeing to the laboring man his loaf at a price which, while upon the one hand forces a loss upon the national treasury, upon the other assists in fixing a basic labor wage which in its far reaching influence more than justifies the loss.

The present high price of shoes and clothing has a very little relation to the cost of raw material. The whole nation has simply been stimulated to feel that everybody is justified in getting a war profit, and so the manufacturer and dealer have competed with each other to see who can get the most of it and the consumer is paying the price. Between the press and the sentiment of the country Liberty clothing and Liberty shoes would almost immediately be so well known in every village and hamlet of the country, with the Government's approved retail stamped price on each article, that profiteering would be impossible.

I believe all this can be worked out practically by agreement as we have the wool problem. In discussing this with woolen cloth manufacturers, they were in perfect sympathy with some such scheme, and suggested that Liberty cloth (of staple shades and patterns) would be made in such large quantities that, like most staples, it should bear a relatively small percentage of profit. As the garments would be manufactured and retailed in the same large way, the cost of production and distribution would be reduced to a minimum.

It seems to me that some such action as this would be highly appreciated by the great mass of our people and add to the present popularity of the Administration.

Pardon me, Mr. President, for trespassing upon your time with so lengthy a communication, but I feel it is of sufficient importance to justify submitting to you for your approval and criticism.

　　　　　　　　　　Respectfully yours,　Robt S Brookings

TLS (WP, DLC).

Lord Reading to Arthur James Balfour

　　　　　　　　　　　Washington. May 2nd, 1918.
　　No. 1963. My telegram No. 1951.
1. I should have added that Viscount Ishii said Japanese Govt. would be prepared to make declaration of disinterestedness.
2. He drew attention to the statements in the Press that Trotsky was seeking to raise an army to resist the Imperialistic Aims which threatened them from the East and said this attitude confirmed his reports of the policy of Bolsheviski Government.
3. In the absence of contradiction of this statement attributed to Trotsky it will be difficult to convince either Japanese or U. S. Govt. that he will be favourably disposed to intervention.
4. Secretary Lansing told me that Trotsky had stipulated that if he did request assistance of Allied or Japanese his request must in no circumstances be published and therefore it would really be of no value. Have you information upon this?

T telegram (FO 115/2445, p. 416, PRO).

A Memorandum by Ferdinand Foch[1]

[May 2, 1918]

Very confidential

A statement of General Foch at the Superior War Council,
held at Abbeville, May 2, 1918.

I have been selected as commander-in-chief of the allied armies
by the Governments of the United States, France and Great Britain.
It is impossible for me, therefore, not to consider that at this, the
most perilous moment of the greatest battle in the war, I have a
right to state my views as to how American Infantry should be sent
to France.

Fully aware of the heavy responsibility resting on me at the time
when the greatest German offensive threatens both Paris and our
communications with England by way of Calais and Boulogne, I
want it to be clearly understood that each of the Governments
should assume, on its part, the share of responsibility belonging to
it.

In my conscience, I deem it of absolute necessity that there arrive
monthly from America in France, during at least the months of
May, June and July, by right of priority, 120,000 American infantrymen and machine gunners. I even consider that, if tonnage
allows it, as we have been led to understand it may, it would be
highly desirable that this number be surpassed. For the greater the
amount of American infantry able to appear, without loss of time,
on the battlefields, the more rapid and decisive will be the success
of the allied armies.

It is in fact necessary to well understand that the characteristic
of the last enemy offensive has been to cause losses in infantry and
machine guns out of all comparison with such losses as occurred
during the last three years of the war. The British army's losses in
infantry have surpassed in an unexpected measure all those which
had been previously suffered. It is the same with the French proportionately to the part they have borne in the battle. And it is
inevitable that, in the coming weeks, the infantry losses will go
increasing. The troops which must be recuperated without a moment's loss are therefore infantrymen and machine gunners; the
more so that the resources in infantry and machine gunners which
the Germans have still in their depots are estimated at between 5
and 600,000 men; while the British depots are almost empty and
the French ones will remain without resources until August next.

I most categorically ask the Superior War Council, composed of
the Allied Governments, to decide on this request and to be so good
as to have it submitted to the President of the United States.

I would not have it thought that I fail to take into consideration the observations of General Pershing who desires to bring over to France, as soon as possible, the complements that will allow him to perfect the formation of the great American army of which he is the chief and which we await with our most earnest wishes. But, on the one hand, my request can only cause a delay of a small number of weeks, and on the other, my imperious duty as a soldier and commander-in-chief obliges me to declare that, when the greatest German army is prosecuting the greatest offensive in this war before Amiens and before Ypres, so slight a postponement cannot be taken into consideration, when the issue of the war itself may depend upon a success of the enemy before the two afore-mentioned objectives.

After the enormous losses which it has suffered with splendid valor, the British army has just had ten of its divisions suppressed, and in order to definitively stop the German armies, it is not enough to replace them: new forces in *infantry* and machine gunners are necessary to us *without any delay*. If one remembers that the American troops will need, on landing, some rapid supplementary instruction, the urgency of the contemplated decision becomes even more apparent.

Let each of the interested Governments, at this hour the gravest of all, be inspired only by its duty towards the great cause of which we are all the servants.

I have stated the measures which, as commander-in-chief of the allied armies, I feel bound to submit to the Governments of the United States, France and Great Britain: it pertains to those Governments to decide.

T MS (WP, DLC).
[1] Jusserand presented this memorandum to Wilson on May 8.

From the Diary of Colonel House

May 2, 1918.

Secretary McAdoo spent the entire morning with me. The particular subject of his conversation was the direction of the railroads. He claims the President is constantly hampering his management by permitting collateral branches of the Government to interfere. The President apologizes each time he goes to him, but, nevertheless, continues the practice. At one time he had his resignation written out to hand the President but his wife persuaded him out of it. His latest difficulty is with the coal situation. He believes the railroads should have a preferential rate as they have always had.

I will not go into his arguments but there is considerable merit in what he says. He declares that the money the railroads have to pay in addition to what they would have to pay if let alone does not go toward reducing the price of coal to the general consumer, but goes into the pockets of the coal operators. He thinks, as indeed I do, that the solution would be for the Government to take over the entire coal production and pay the owners a reasonable price per ton above the cost of production. McAdoo wanted my advice as how best to approach the matter with the President, and how far he should go toward pushing him to a conclusion. What he wished to say was that he would not sustain before the people such a decision as that which they are about to make and, therefore, he would be compelled to offer his resignation.

I suggested that he leave off the part about his resignation. That, I thought, went by inference, and it was better not to say it unless he was determined to do so. I argued with him from the President's viewpoint, telling him the President had no thought of interfering with his direction of the railroads, but he did not consider a solution of the coal question contrary to McAdoo's wishes, interference. I thought there was a feeling in Washington, which the President shared, that he, McAdoo, had an insatiable desire for power. He flushed at this, and said if that was the feeling he had better resign. I soothed him by saying the feeling was natural, since the field of his activities was so large that it must necessarily cause antagonisms.

He spoke of the influence of Secretary Baker with the President, and he thought Baker antagonistic to him. The matter has come to this, the President will have to yield to McAdoo's insistent demand for more power or depose him. I have a feeling that he will yield because McAdoo has unquestionably done good work and there is no one else on the horizon at present who could command such confidence. I am undetermined whether to write the President and warn him of the coming storm, or let him weather it himself. I dislike interfering in every situation that arises, and in this instance it has to do with his personal, as well as his political, family.

To Solomon Bulkley Griffin

My dear Mr. Griffin: The White House 3 May, 1918

Thank you very much for thinking of me in connection with your conversation with Doctor Davis.[1] Frankly, I hesitate to see Doctor Davis. I can never see anyone privately and to have it known that I was interviewing Doctor Davis would, I am afraid, in some quarters create the impression that I was trying to learn something that would give me a personal advantage strategically over the Kaiser. I am not expressing my meaning very well, but I am sure you will catch it. I am sure the Secretary of State would be very much interested to see Doctor Davis if he expects to be in Washington soon.   Cordially and sincerely yours,   Woodrow Wilson

TLS (MSCV).
¹ Griffin's letter is missing. Arthur Newton Davis had been William II's dentist for fifteen years and had returned to New York from Berlin in February 1918. He tells his story in Arthur N. Davis, *The Kaiser as I Know Him* (New York and London, 1918).

To Edward Nash Hurley, with Enclosure

My dear Hurley: [The White House] 3 May, 1918

I have been very much interested in what you tell me¹ of the extraordinary record made in getting the steamship TUCKAHOE ready for launching, and I beg that you will be kind enough, when you attend the launching, to read the enclosed letter addressed to the workmen and the staff of the New York Shipbuilding Company.
          Cordially and faithfully yours,   Woodrow Wilson

¹ E. N. Hurley to WW, May 2, 1918, TLS (WP, DLC). Hurley informed Wilson that, with the launching of *Tuckahoe* on May 5, 1918, the New York Shipbuilding Company at Camden, New Jersey, was going to break all records for speed in the construction of steamships of a particular class. The previous record, established by a shipyard in Seattle, stood at fifty-four days, but *Tuckahoe* would be launched only twenty-seven days after the laying of her keel. Hurley asked Wilson to express his appreciation of the achievement of the workers and the staff in a letter which Hurley would read at the launching.

E N C L O S U R E

To the Workmen and Executive Staff of the New York Shipbuilding Company

My dear Friends: [The White House] 3 May, 1918

I want to congratulate you on the extraordinary record you have made in your work on the steamship TUCKAHOE. I wish I could be present in person to express to you the feeling that I have that we are all comrades in a great enterprise and that you have played your part with extraordinary devotion and skill, eliciting not only my admiration but I am sure the admiration of all who will learn of what you have accomplished. I congratulate you and bid you Godspeed.
          Cordially and sincerely yours,   Woodrow Wilson

TLS (Letterpress Books, WP, DLC).

To Edward William Pou

My dear Mr. Pou: The White House 3 May, 1918

You are always generous and helpful and I thank you warmly for your letter of yesterday.[1] Undoubtedly you know the best way to handle H.R. 10264, the Passport Bill, and I am more than willing to trust entirely to your judgment.

Thanking you again for your very great generosity in cooperating.

Cordially and sincerely yours,   Woodrow Wilson

TLS (E. W. Pou Papers, Nc-Ar).
[1] It is missing in both the Pou and Wilson Papers.

To John Dennis Ryan

My dear Mr. Ryan: [The White House] 3 May, 1918

Thank you very warmly for your note. You may be sure that my designation of you as Director of Aircraft Production expressed a very real and genuine confidence in both your ability and your character. I have not the slightest fear that you will not in every respect make good, and I shall look forward with pleasure to every opportunity of cooperating with you.

Cordially and sincerely yours,   Woodrow Wilson

TLS (Letterpress Books, WP, DLC).

To Newton Diehl Baker

Confidential.

My dear Mr. Secretary: The White House [May 3, 1918]

Thank you for your letter of the first about sending men to Italy. General Bliss's message about the matter seems to me singularly just and comprehensive in its appreciation of the many things involved, and I hope that you will take the action which you suggest, namely, ask General Pershing to suggest to General Foch, or General Petain, and to Sir Douglas Haig, that some of the American troops be brigaded with their several divisions in Italy with the explanation that our hope is that American soldiers may appear on the Italian front under the circumstances which will not create the expectation that we can send further forces at the present time or an independent American force at a later time.

Cordially and faithfully yours,   Woodrow Wilson

TLS (N. D. Baker Papers, DLC).

To Robert Somers Brookings

My dear Mr. Brookings: [The White House] 3 May, 1918

I have read with a great deal of interest the suggestion contained in your letter of yesterday, but before forming a judgment about it I would like to suggest these questions:

First, would we not be in danger by adopting such a course of putting the manufacture of the standardized goods too exclusively in the hands of the large manufacturers and making it difficult for the smaller factories to avail themselves of the government standards?

Second, would it be feasible to carry out the process of inspection and oversight without creating a very large and expensive machinery of inspection?

These practical questions answered, I could see my way very much more clearly.

In necessary haste
                Cordially and sincerely yours,   Woodrow Wilson

TLS (Letterpress Books, WP, DLC).

To Jessie Woodrow Wilson Sayre

My dear little Daughter: [The White House] 3 May, 1918

I know you will pardon me for sending you a dictated letter about a matter of business.

I had a talk the other day with the Secretary of War about the Y.W.C.A. work on the other side about which you wrote to Edith and think that I was able to point out to him just the error of fact into which you think the department fell.[1] He took the correspondence away with him and promised to look into it. He is so clearheaded and just that I am sure he will do the best he can to think it out, and he will know some of the circumstances on the other side which we do not know.

We were all delighted that you and Frank got a little outing at Nantucket.

We are all well. My burnt hand is slowly getting well. I don't mean that there have been any setbacks; I mean merely that it takes a long time for new skin to form and to get my hand released from dressings and bandages. Now I am going about like a hotel waiter with a white glove over the bandages on my left hand, feeling as if I ought to be handing something to somebody! We get very interesting news at irregular intervals of Margaret's success on her singing tour and are very impatient to have her back. She ought to be in Atlanta by now, I think, with the Browns.

In haste, with dearest love from us all,

Your devoted   Woodrow Wilson

TLS (Letterpress Books, WP, DLC).
  ¹ Jessie W. W. Sayre to EBW, April 25, 1918, ALS (WP, DLC). The point at issue was whether the Y.W.C.A. should carry on its work in France independently or in subordination to the Y.M.C.A. and the American Red Cross. See NDB to WW, May 11, 1918.

From Edward Mandell House, with Enclosures

Dear Governor: New York. May 3, 1918.

I am enclosing a copy of a cable from Sir William on the Russian situation.

I am also enclosing a copy of a letter from Frazier which I think will interest you.   Affectionately yours,   E. M. House

TLS (WP, DLC).

E N C L O S U R E   I

London, May 1st, 1918.

602. Following for Col. House from Sir William Wiseman:

(a) I am sending following not to suggest any immediate action, but merely to inform you of my conclusions after discussing with all particularly concerned here.

(b) There are four courses open to the Allies:

1. To take no action, but await developments. This is open to two very strong objections. First it enables the Germans to withdraw more troops and guns from the Russian front; secondly, it enables the Germans to organize Russia politically and economically for their own advantage and gives them undisputed access to grain, oil and fat supplies in Siberia and valuable metal supplies in the Urals. Also it enables them to sustain Austrian morale by telling them that the war is over in the East and that they have only to help in the West to secure complete German victory.

2. Allied intervention at the invitation of the Bolshiviki. This would probably be the most desirable course. Various Allied missions to come from Archangel and Southern Russia, giving whole proposition the character of Inter-Allied movement rather than solely Japanese. From Vladivostock the main military force would come, consisting in the first place of about five Japanese divisions accompanied by Allied missions and a few Allied troops, to be fol-

lowed by very much larger Japanese force. This would meet Bolshevik force which they would help organize and could, it is thought, easily penetrate to Chiliabinsk as the first stage of operation. This would deny all Siberian resources to the Germans and threaten the re-creation of a formidable Eastern front.

This program, however, depends upon an invitation from Trotzky, and I begin to doubt whether this is feasible. If Trotzky invites Allied intervention Germans would regard it as hostile act and probably turn his government out of Moscow and Petrograd. With this center lost the best opinion considers whole Bolshevik influence in Russia would collapse. No one knows this better than Trotzky and for this reason he probably hesitates. The only chance would be if Trotzky would be prepared to abandon Moscow and retire along Siberian railway to meet the Allied force, calling upon all loyal Russians to rally to him and save the revolution from German reactionary intrigues.

3. If we decide Trotzky will not or cannot invite us, we might find Kerensky and other members of the original republican revolution and get them to form a Government Committee in Manchuria and do what Trotzky will not do. Many think this would be the signal for the rising of all elements that are best in Russia. It would have the advantage that Kerensky's is the Government still recognized and we could deal with him through his Ambassadors in Washington and elsewhere.

4. The only other scheme is for Allied intervention without the invitation of any party in Russia and possibly against the wishes of the Bolsheviki. This is urged as a last resort by our military people and the French, but has of course its disadvantages.

(c) It is certain that nothing can be done without the wholehearted cooperation of the President. I believe the Japanese are influenced by two considerations: First, they are genuinely afraid of German domination of Siberia, eventually threatening their position in the Far East. Also strong party in Japan really want to do their part in helping the Allies and see in Japanese advance towards Eastern front an opportunity for the Japanese to play a glorious part in the world war. Far-seeing Japanese statesmen also foresee an opportunity of friendly cooperation with America, which might go far to solve Japanese-American problem. Those who know them best maintain that anything they solemnly undertake before the whole world, they will strain their utmost to carry through for the sake of their own prestige if nothing else.

The situation in Russia is constantly altering, but it is fairly clear that the Russian people are not satisfied with the German peace, and are afraid of the sinister activities of the Germans towards restoration of the old regime.

I repeat that one of the chief advantages we might expect from intervention would be the very depressing effect which the re-creation of an Eastern front would have on the Central Powers, particularly Austria. Everybody here is emphatic as to value of time, as the Germans seeme to be moving rapidly.

E N C L O S U R E   I I

Arthur Hugh Frazier to Edward Mandell House

Strictly Confidential.

Dear Mr. House: Paris. April 11, 1918.

The day before yesterday I had a long talk at Versailles with General Studd[1] an old friend of mine upon whom I rely for confidential and sometimes unpalatable information. His duty at the Supreme War Council since its creation was to study out possible German offensives and the corresponding measures for countering them.

I remember as far back as December when I took General Pershing out to Versailles for the first time that General Studd shewed us the map room and pointed out how the Germans could make a thrust in the neighborhood of Cambrai with 96 divisions in March. Studd told me that his section had worked out a plan for resisting this offensive indicating quite clearly where the reserves were to be placed; this plan he said had been communicated several weeks ago to both the British and French Headquarters but apparently no attention had been paid to it as the reserves were not where they should have been with the result that the combined Franco-British armies fell back 60 kilometres instead of 3 or 4 as my friend anticipated they would have to; I gathered that he thought both Haig and Petain equally to blame.

It should not be forgotten that this particular sector was taken over quite recently by the British from the French although the British protested at the time that it would weaken their lines of communication which run parallel to the front from the Channel ports.

Studd thought the situation very serious and felt that unless we hastened the despatch of troops across the Atlantic the war would end by the summer or before by the defeat of the Allies.

Respectfully yours,   Arthur Hugh Frazier.

T MSS (WP, DLC).
[1] Brig. Gen. Herbert William Studd, chief of staff of the British section in the Supreme War Council.

From William Gibbs McAdoo

Dear Governor,   White Sulphur, W. Va. May 3. 1918

The presiding officer of the Liberty Loan meeting at Houston Texas embarrassed me very much by mentioning my name for the Presidency in 1920.

I thought you might be interested in reading the brief extract from my speech (which I enclose)[1] showing how I disposed of it.

I shall be on hand Tuesday. Am very tired as I had an unusually strenuous trip.

Nell joins in dearest love of you Edith & Helen.

Affectionately Yrs   W G McAdoo

ALS (WP, DLC).

[1] "Extract from Speech Made by Secretary McAdoo at Houston, Texas, April 15, 1918," T MS (WP, DLC). McAdoo stated that the successful prosecution of the war demanded the subordination of all personal interests and the development of a unity of purpose which would spurn politics and private ambitions. He said that he would have "infinite contempt" for anyone who would take advantage of any aspect of the war to promote his own selfish interests, and he declared categorically that he had no ambition for public office. All that he desired was the confidence of the American people and the opportunity to do his present job as best he could. As to the presidential election in 1920, McAdoo concluded: "In my humble judgment, as things stand today and as they may stand in 1920, there is only one man in America who deserves the great and exalted office of the Presidency, and he is holding that office now."

From William Phillips

Dear Mr. President: Washington May 3, 1918.

The Secretary left before I had an opportunity to ask him whether a decision had been reached in regard to the proposed visit to the United States of the Lord Mayor for Dublin.

The accompanying telegram from Ambassador Page[1] says that a passport will probably be issued him. I should be very grateful if you would kindly indicate your views.

With assurances of respect, etc., I am, my dear Mr. President,

Faithfully yours,   William Phillips

TLS (WP, DLC).

[1] It is printed as an Enclosure with RL to WW, April 25, 1918, third letter of that date.

From Theodore Marburg, with Enclosure

Dear Mr. President: Baltimore, Md. May 3, 1918

I have the honor to enclose copy of letter from Viscount Bryce. You will be the judge of whether you desire any further message to be sent to him.

I am, with great respect,

Yours sincerely,   Theodore Marburg

TLS (WP, DLC).

E N C L O S U R E

James Viscount Bryce to Theodore Marburg

London, S.W.

My dear Mr. Marburg: (Undated; received May 1, 1918)

Thank you for your letters of Mar. 12 and Mar. 21,[1] which are most welcome, and for the copy of President Wilson's letter to you.[2] It seems to me that my letter which you showed to him must have failed to convey what I really meant. I fully agree with the President's view that the time has not come to discuss (i.e. to discuss publicly) the formal constitution of a "league to enforce peace." We can't tell till the war comes to an end what the conditions will be, whether a league will have to be formed to resist a still menacing Germany, or one into which a better Germany, "renewed in the spirit of its mind," may be admitted as a partner.

I have the fullest confidence in the President's earnestness in this great enterprise for which he has done so much. But there are so many difficult problems to be solved in constituting any League, whosoever may be its members, that it seems to me that the best jurists and diplomatists and historians ought to be studying these problems now, in concert, quite privately, but with the knowledge of their governments. They should be working out alternative plans to be placed at the disposal of the Government when the end of the war comes. These things cannot be extemporized. Hence I should have liked to see five of your best and five of our best minds brought together to work out a scheme or schemes which should be available for our Governments, the difficulties having been all considered and grappled with in advance. Of course no *action* is possible yet. But the best action is that which has been prepared for in advance.

I am,   Very truly yours,   Bryce

P.S. I must not forget to thank you for the valuable and carefully thought out Tentative Draft Convention which your Private Study Group has prepared.[3] I am studying it with care and hope to send you some criticisms, or rather observations, on the comparatively novel and very important proposal for an International Council. Your Group has rendered great service whatever happens. Though I trust Germany will be defeated, still even if she remained undefeated and formidable, ought not the League, which must in that event be formed by the Allies to resist her in the future, to be not merely a defensive one of Great Powers against her, but one which should try to draw in the minor States, offering them the benefits of Arbitration and Conciliation? The next difficulty would be Armaments. These could not be reduced in face of a still menacing Germany. Pray kindly continue to keep me informed of your action.

I am,   Very truly yours,   Bryce

TCL (WP, DLC).

[1] T. Marburg to J. Bryce, March 12 and 21, 1918, both printed in Latané, *Development of the League of Nations Idea*, I, 417 and 418-20. In his first letter, Marburg informed Bryce that he had forwarded Bryce's letter of February 8 to Wilson, and he enclosed Wilson's reply. For the correspondence between Marburg and Wilson on this matter, see T. Marburg to WW, March 5, 1918, and WW to T. Marburg, March 8, 1918, both in Vol. 46.

In his letter to Bryce of March 21, Marburg expressed his disappointment that Wilson had failed to approve Bryce's suggestion for the appointment of a combined group of British and American experts to work out the details of a practical plan for a league of nations. Without Wilson's support, Marburg pointed out, Bryce's plan would lack the necessary authority and would have to be abandoned. Marburg then went on to summarize the progress which the American government and various European governments had made toward developing a detailed concept for the organization of a league. He said that the most important practical step would be the formation of a council at Versailles, which could well be the beginning of a permanent league. However, Marburg concluded, unless the Allies won the war, it would be impossible to establish the kind of league which was now being considered. Without a thorough defeat of Germany, the league would lack the overwhelming military power to implement the fundamental idea of compelling nations to submit to inquiry before going to war.

[2] WW to T. Marburg, March 8, 1918, Vol. 46.

[3] For a summary of this document, see n. 5 to the memorandum by W. H. Taft, printed at March 29, 1918.

From Joseph Patrick Tumulty

Dear Governor: The White House 3 May 1918.

In the Borglum matter which now seems to be greatly exciting the Senate, there is a great deal of misapprehension as to what his status really is under your letter.[1] This afternoon I have looked through the correspondence between you and Mr. Borglum, and I am sure the whole thing would make a fine impression upon the country if it could be given out *with a copy of the report made by Mr. Marshall, Mr. McNab and the other gentlemen who are the members of the Committee.* If it were not for the mystery surrounding the letter which you gave Borglum, I am sure he would have no standing at all with the country. Our attitude of seeming indifference has done a lot to bolster up the charges which Borglum has freely made.

I notice a disposition on the part of the newspapers who have gone into this whole matter, to come to the defense of General Squiers and those associated with him. But we have given them no facts upon which they can base any "counter offensive." Representatives of papers like the Springfield Republican, the Chicago Daily News, and the Christian Science Monitor, are those who have been in to see me.   Sincerely yours,   J. P. Tumulty

TLS (J. P. Tumulty Papers, DLC).
¹ That is, WW to G. Borglum, Jan. 2, 1918, Vol. 45.

From Newton Diehl Baker

My dear Mr. President: Washington. May 3, 1918.
I hand you herewith the final report of the Marshall-McNab-Wells committee to investigate aircraft.¹

This report with its exhibits is of course an extremely careful and helpful document, and if you consent I would like to have it for Mr. Ryan, General March, and General Kenly² to read, so that they may profit by its conclusions and statements.

The report states on page 24, in dealing with the subject of charges of improper conduct: "We can not leave this subject without stating that we should be greatly surprised if any such charges would be sustained on full investigation. The impression that has been left in our minds of the personnel of the Government officials and contractors engaged in this work is that they were honest, patriotic, and zealous." These observations are made expressly excluding, however, the charges made by Mr. Borglum, which were exhibited to the Committee and by them returned to Mr. Crowell³ with the statement that the Committee could not adequately investigate them since it had no power to summon witness and compel testimony and the production of books and papers. The Committee believes that such an investigation ought to be made, because of the gravity of the charges made by Mr. Borglum.

Since the matters referred to by Mr. Borglum were in fact investigated by the Senate Committee before I went to Europe, I had assumed that there was an absence of proof or a determination of innocence which disposed of that matter. Yesterday, however, in the Senate a very angry and heated debate again took place on this subject, and statements were made by Senators that there was evidence of criminal misconduct in connection with the aircraft program. The debate centered around the charges made by Mr. Borglum, and the opinion was freely expressed that an adequate investigation of them was necessary. I feel that the situation is one of enough gravity to require prompt and adequate action. I have hesitated whether to advise the whole matter being placed in the hands of the Attorney General and investigated through a grand jury, or the formulation of a Court of Inquiry through War Department channels. The latter course has some advantages in that being composed of military men its sessions would be so conducted as not to disclose information valuable to the enemy, which of course is always a danger in discussing this sort of a subject. I believe it would be possible to constitute such a Court so as to command public confidence, and it would have full power to summon witnesses and compel testimony, and upon the basis of its findings punishment could be made to follow by immediate court-martial of all persons found guilty of any offense, so far as such persons are connected with the Military Establishment; and civilians could then be brought before grand juries for indictment and punishment.

I am having the Borglum reports to you[4] carefully digested by a member of the Judge Advocate General's Corps, so as to extract in the form of a précis the sort of instructions which could be given to such a Court if one were assembled. If you have during my absence, in dealing with this question formed a judgment as to the course of action best to follow, I will be very glad to act at once in accordance with your direction. If you have not had occasion to consider the subject from this point of view, I will be very glad to speak with you about it at your early convenience. It seems to me that it would be a matter of considerable gravity to have this subject longer debated in its present status, and I am anxious to seek the most convincing method of showing that the War Department is as anxious as anybody else to discover and punish wrongdoers, although I am not unaware that military considerations make it necessary for this inquiry to be conducted in such a way as not to convey to our enemy information which would be of value to him.

Respectfully yours,   Newton D. Baker

TLS (WP, DLC).
  [1] "REPORT OF COMMITTEE ON AIRCRAFT INVESTIGATION APPOINTED MARCH 15, 1918,"
TS MS (WDR, RG 60, Hughes Aircraft Investigation Reports, DNA). This report, twenty-nine pages in length, surveyed the progress, or lack of it, in the production of combat aircraft in the United States since April 1917. Foolish and grossly optimistic predictions about the possibility of rapid production had created expectations, both in the United States and abroad, the report said, which simply could not be realized. There had been delays in the program on account of the scarcity of skilled labor, a failure to coordinate the supply of parts from subcontractors to the major producers, the fact that the tech-

nology of the aeronautical industry was in constant flux, and, most important, "the lack of technical knowledge and manufacturing experience necessary to the design and production of aircraft in this country." These difficulties and deficiencies had been largely overcome, and the outlook for steady and increased production of combat aircraft was good. The committee found no evidence of fraud in or deliberate obstruction of the aircraft program; moreover, the report concluded, any person who said that such deliberate obstruction had existed should be given an opportunity to prove such charges.

Accompanying the report are forty exhibits. Eight of these were copies of Borglum's letters to the President, including Borglum's preliminary report of January 21, 1918 (about which see n. 1 to the Enclosure printed with G. Borglum to WW, Jan. 24, 1918, Vol. 46). Other exhibits were copies of letters to and from Borglum. The balance of the exhibits consisted of odds and ends of little importance.

[2] Maj. Gen. William Lacy Kenly, former chief of the Air Service of the A.E.F., since April 26, 1918, director of the Division of Military Aeronautics in the War Department.

[3] These "charges," whatever they were, are missing in all files and collections.

[4] Baker presumably referred to Borglum's letters to Wilson, all of which have been printed in this series.

From Gutzon Borglum

My dear Mr. President   Washington, D. C. May 3rd, 1918.

Yesterday I returned to Washington to correct instantly some misstatements due to misunderstanding, made on the floor of the Senate, regarding my inquiry together with certain false charges as to motive or monetary interest in my investigation.

I also informed the Senators that I was a student of aerodynamics and in every way that I can I shall continue to aid its development and use for this war, and tried to make it clear to the Military Committee *my interest* was *to get planes*, of some kind, *built* and *delivered* to our Army.

I have promised the Senators to carefully assemble all my evidence and bring it properly before them.

It is with respect and alarm that I see the present chart of "reconstruction" in the aero-department.

Yours sincerely,   Gutzon Borglum

TLS (WP, DLC).

Charles Spalding Thomas to Joseph Patrick Tumulty

Dear Joe   Washington 5/3/18

The "Borglum" episode is assuming large proportions, because of his exploitation by certain Senators on the other side, and principally because the N. Y. Times has taken him up and is giving him daily editorial notice.

After phoning you yesterday, Borglum had an informal conference with some members of the Military Affairs Committee, and the charges and statements he makes are very broad, although his facts are so far very meager.

We may be compelled to give him a hearing & as he claims to have several letters from the President (which I do not believe) and as the Marshall Committee has all the papers relating to the Indiana episode which presumably are with the President,[1] and as he claims he informed the President long ago of everything he is now exploiting[,] some Member of the Committee should talk with the President, get such documents as he may let us have and enable us to dispose of this fellow finally. I am troubling you about it only because it is thought that as I have already discussed aviation with the President I can best take it up with him. If the latter should prefer for any reason to talk with some other Member of the Committee it is perfectly agreeable to me.

Sincerely &c   C S Thomas[2]

ALS (WP, DLC).
    [1] About which, see NDB to WW, Feb. 1, 1918, Vol. 46 (first letter of that date).
    [2] "Dear Governor. I would like to say a word to you about this matter. Yours Tumulty." JPT to WW, c. May 3, 1918, ALS (WP, DLC).

Tasker Howard Bliss to Robert Lansing and Others

Versailles. May 3rd [1918].

Number 103 For Secretary of State, Secretary of WAR and Acting Chief of Staff. Very Confidential.

Paragraph 1. Supreme War Council met for its fourth session at 2:30 pm May 1st and adjourned at 4 pm May 2nd. Following is the summary of business transacted.

Paragraph 2. First subject taken up was the shipment and employment of American troops, the French Government requesting amendment of agreement made between General Pershing and Lord Milner in London so as to provide for exclusive shipment of Infantry and machine gun units not only in May but also in June.[1] After considerable discussion subject was referred to a committee consisting of Lord Milner, General Foch and General Pershing with instructions to draft a form of resolution and submit it at 5 pm. In order to communicate with London for information regarding it, reports of sub-committee were delayed until the next day session when their drafts were considered. After impassioned appeals by Mr. Lloyd George, Mr. Clemenceau and General Foch a modified form of General Pershing's proposal was adopted, the essential point of which is:

Subparagraph A. Allied transportation facilities to be used for transportation of American troops, preference being given to Infantry and machine gun units, as far as consistent with the necessity of building up an American army for training and service with French and British armies subject to provision that they are to be formed into divisions and corps at discretion of American Commander in Chief after consultation with Commander in Chief of Allied armies in France.

Subparagraph B. During May Infantry and machine gun units of six divisions to be transported and any excess tonnage available applied to transportation of such troops as American Commander in Chief may desire.

Subparagraph C. This program to be continued in June, provided British Government furnishes transportation for minimum of 130,000 men in June; that first six divisions Infantry go to British for training and service and those brought over in June to be allocated for training by American Commander in Chief.

Subparagraph D. If British Government transports more than 150,000 in June, excess shall be Infantry and machine gun units and situation shall be reviewed early in June with a view to determining program for July.

Paragraph 3. In view of the reinforcement Allied forces at Salonika by newly formed Greek divisions, British Government desired to withdraw 12 battalions of their troops from Salonika front. Supreme War Council decided that it should be possible to do this but that no transfer should be made without consultation with Commanding General Allied armies there.[2] The Supreme War Council agreed that a French and a British General officer should be despatched forthwith to Salonika where in association with the General commanding the Italian forces at Valona[3] they will confer with Commanding General of Allied armies on this question, to arrange with him for the immediate withdrawal of Allied battalions.

Paragraph 4. The Executive War Board established by resolution number 13 of the Third Session Supreme War Council was dissolved: The main duties having already been transferred to General Foch.

Paragraph 5. Mr. Orlando on behalf of Italy agreed to extension of the powers of General Foch over the Italian troops in France under conditions of Beauvais agreement, April 3rd.[4] He agreed to General Foch's exercising over the troops on the Italian front coordinating powers granted to him over British and French by agreement at Doullens March 26th.[5]

Paragraph 6. Formal acceptance was given to joint notes number 19 to 24, inclusive, of the military representatives.[6] Joint note number 20 relating to Japanese question was not signed by American military representative but was transmitted by me to Washington.

Paragraph 7. Joint note 25[7] passed by military representatives on April 27 expresses the following conclusions: "That there is everything to be gained by securing the transportation of Czech contingents from Russia; and that, as the greatest rapidity can be ensured by using Archangel and Murmansk, all Czech troops which have not yet passed east of Omsk on Tran-Siberian railroad, should be dispatched to these two ports."

Subparagraph A. The Supreme War Council approved the aforesaid joint note, the British Government undertaking to arrange as far as possible for transportation of Czech troops already at Vladivostok or on their way there, and to request Russian Government to concentrate other Czech troops at Murmansk and Archangel; French Government retaining general charge of Czech troops until embarked.

Paragraph 8. The Supreme War Council considered report of Allied Naval Council, third *April*, April 26 and 27, and agreed that transfer to Corfu of Italian dreadnaughts would be desirable to free French bay for Allied naval forces in Aegean sea and urged the Italian Government to comply with the least possible delay.

Paragraph 9. Documents by mail.   Bliss.

TC telegram (WDR, RG 407, World War I Cablegrams, DNA).
    [1] For the text of which, see J. J. Pershing to H. P. McCain, April 25, 1918, printed as an Enclosure with NDB to WW, April 29, 1918 (first letter of that date).
    [2] Louis Guillaumat, Commander of the Army of the Orient.
    [3] Vlonë or Vlona, etc., a seaport in southern Albania. The Italian general there was Giacinto Ferrero.
    [4] For the text of which, see T. H. Bliss to P. C. March, April 3, 1918.
    [5] *Ibid.*
    [6] Joint Note 19, dated March 27, 1918, concerned a plan for supporting the Italian army in the event of an enemy offensive on the Italian front. See T. H. Bliss to P. C. March, April 20, 1918, and its enclosure, TLS and T MS (WDR, RG 407, World War I Cablegrams, DNA). Joint Note 20 is printed as an Enclosure with NDB to WW, April 25, 1918. About Joint Note 21, see T. H. Bliss to RL *et al.*, April 12, 1917. Joint Note 22, dated April 18, 1918, concerned coal for Italy. T. H. Bliss to H. P. McCain, No. 94, April 19, 1918, TC telegram (WDR, RG 407, World War I Cablegrams, DNA). Joint Note 23, dated April 18, 1918, concerned the disposition of Belgian railroad workers and locomotives. *Ibid.* Joint Note 24, dated April 18, 1918, concerned proposed measures to assist the importation of American locomotives into France. *Ibid.*
    [7] The full text of Joint Note 25, dated April 27, 1918 (T. H. Bliss to P. C. March, May 4, 1918, with enclosure, TLS and T MS, WDR, RG 120, Records of the American Section of the Supreme War Council, 1917-1919, File No. 335-1, DNA) follows:
    "1. The Permanent Military Representatives, having regard to the discussions that have taken place on the subject of the transportation of Czech contingents from Russia and after examining the present position of those contingents, are of opinion:
        "i. That there is everything to be gained by securing their transportation at the earliest possible date.
        "ii. That as the greatest possible rapidity can be ensured by using Archangel and Murmansk, all Czech troops, which have not yet passed East of Omsk on the Trans-Siberian Railway, should be despatched to these two ports.
    "2. Furthermore, while these troops are waiting to be embarked, they could be profitably employed in defending Archangel and Murmansk and in guarding and protecting the Murman railway. Similarly, Czech troops which have already proceeded East of Omsk could eventually be used, as recommended in Joint Note No. 20, para. 5, to co-operate with the Allies in Siberia."

An Appeal to the American People

[May 4, 1918]

PROCLAMATION

Inasmuch as the War Fund of 1917, so generously contributed by the American people to the American Red Cross for the administration of relief at home and abroad, has been practically exhausted by appropriations for the welfare of the men in our military and naval forces, and for those dependent upon them, and for the yet more urgent necessities of our Allies, military and civilian, who have long borne the brunt of war;

And, inasmuch as the American Red Cross has been recognized by law and international convention as the public instrumentality for war relief;

And, inasmuch as the year of our own participation in the war has brought unprecedented demands upon the patriotism and liberality of our people, and made evident the necessity of concentrating the work of relief in one main organization which can respond effectively and universally to the needs of humanity under stress of war;

And, inasmuch as the duration of the war and the closer and closer cooperation of the American Red Cross with our own Army and Navy, with the governments of our Allies, and with foreign relief organizations, have resulted in the discovery of new opportunities of helpfulness under conditions which translate opportunity into duty;

And, inasmuch as the American Red Cross War Council and its Commissioners in Europe have faithfully and economically administered the people's trust;

NOW, THEREFORE, by virtue of my authority as President of the United States and President of the American Red Cross, I, WOODROW WILSON, do hereby proclaim the week beginning May 20, 1918, as "Red Cross Week," during which the people of the United States will be called upon again to give generously to the continuation of the important work of relieving distress, restoring the waste of war, and assisting in maintaining the morale of our own troops and the troops and peoples of our Allies by this manifestation of effort and sacrifice on the part of those, who, though not privileged to bear arms, are of one spirit, purpose, and determination with our warriors.

IN WITNESS WHEREOF, I have hereunto set my hand and caused the seal of the United States to be affixed.

Done in the District of Columbia, this 4th day of May, in the year of our Lord One Thousand Nine Hundred and Eighteen, and of the Independence of the United States of America, the One Hundred and Forty-second.   WOODROW WILSON

By the President:
    Robert Lansing
        Secretary of State.

Mimeographed MS (WP, DLC).

To William Phillips

My dear Mr. Phillips: The White House 4 May, 1918

It is plain to me that there is no way in which we can head off the Lord Mayor of Dublin, though I think his visit is most unwise from every point of view. We can only follow the best course we can devise amongst us when he gets here. If he knew how little he was going to get out of the trip, he would stay at home!
                            Faithfully yours,   Woodrow Wilson

TLS (SDR, RG 59, 841.00/76, DNA).

To Albert Sidney Burleson

My dear Burleson: The White House 4 May, 1918

May I not add the enclosed letter from Ricker of Pearson's Magazine to the one I sent you yesterday?[1] It would look as if these men were really in earnest.
    In haste   Faithfully yours,   Woodrow Wilson

TLS (A. S. Burleson Papers, DLC).
    [1] These letters are missing in all collections known to the Editors.

To Newton Diehl Baker

My dear Mr. Secretary: [The White House] 4 May, 1918

I am in entire agreement with you about the cases of Private Jeff Cook, Forest D. Sebastian, Stanley G. Fishback, and Olon Ledoyen, and have taken pleasure in signing the orders which you were kind enough to have drawn up for me.
    May I not thank you for your very full and convincing letter?
                Cordially and sincerely yours,   Woodrow Wilson

TLS (Letterpress Books, WP, DLC).

From Newton Diehl Baker, with Enclosure

My dear Mr. President: Washington. May 4, 1918.

I enclose a message from General Pershing, which has just come, giving the details of the agreement adopted by the Supreme War Council, May 2, at Abbeville. I understand you have already received the accounts of that conference, sent by Mr. Frazier. In view of the fact that General Pershing, General Foch, and General Haig conferred and finally recommended this agreement, it would seem to be an authoritative determination of the questions which have been troubling us and now to have the concurrence of Mr. Lloyd George, Mr. Clemenceau, and Mr. Orlando, which relieves us from any possible embarrassment due to a misunderstanding of our execution of the resolution of the Permanent Military Representatives at Versailles.

I confess I was very favorably impressed by the position taken by General Pershing and his bearing throughout the interview, and am glad to see it result in an agreement which apparently has the general concurrence.

Respectfully yours,   Newton D. Baker

TLS (WP, DLC).

ENCLOSURE

From Paris To The Adjutant General, Washington.
No. 1042 May 3rd. Confidential.
For the Chief of Staff and Secretary of War.

Following agreement adopted by Supreme War Council May 2d at Abbeville. Will cable more in detail later. "It is the opinion of the Supreme War Council that, in order to carry the war to a successful conclusion, an American army should be formed as early as possible under its own commander and under its own flag. In order to meet the present emergency it is agreed that American troops should be brought to France as rapidly as allied transportation facilities will permit and, that as far as consistent with the necessity of building up an American army, preference be given to infantry and machine gun units for training and service with French and British armies; with the understanding that such infantry and machine gun units are to be withdrawn and unite with its own artillery and auxiliary troops into divisions and Corps at the discretion of the American Commander in Chief after consultation with the Commander in Chief of the allied armies in France.

Subparagraph A. It is also agreed that during the month of May preference should be given to the transportation of infantry and machine gun units of 6 divisions, and that any excess tonnage shall be devoted to bringing over such other troops as may be determined by the American Commander in Chief.

Subparagraph B. It is further agreed that this program shall be continued during the month of June upon condition that the British Government shall furnish transportation for a minimum of 130,000 men in May and 157,000 men in June with the understanding that the first 6 divisions of infantry shall go to the British for training and service, and that troops sent over in June shall be allocated for training and service as the American Commander in Chief may determine.

Subparagraph C. It is also further agreed that if the British Government shall transport an excess of 150,000 men in June that such excess shall be infantry and machine gun units, and that early in June there shall be a new review of the situation to determine further action." Pershing.

T telegram (WP, DLC).

From Newton Diehl Baker

Dear Mr. President: Washington. May 4, 1918.

I enclose you a copy of a statement made by a Lieutenant Commander of the Navy with regard to the success of the Liberty engine.[1] You will, I am sure, be pleased to find this testimonial to the success of that engine, in view of the fact that one still hears serious people express grave apprehensions on the subject.

Respectfully yours,   Newton D. Baker

TLS (WP, DLC).
[1] Lt. Commander Arthur Kennedy Atkins, U.S.N., to Col. Henry Harley Arnold, U.S.A., May 4, 1918, TCL (WP, DLC). Atkins summarized the navy's experience with the Liberty engine in several test flights and stated that its performance had been "eminently satisfactory." In no case had a flight been interrupted by engine failure, and flyers and mechanics agreed that the Liberty 12 was an excellent engine. Atkins concluded that, although future experience would undoubtedly suggest minor improvements, there was every indication that the Liberty engine would be entirely successful.

From Emil Carl Wilm,[1] with Enclosure

My dear Mr. President: Newton, Mass., May 4, 1918.

I wish to express to you my personal appreciation and gratitude for your splendid statement of attitude towards "the loyal residents of German birth or descent," published recently.[2] Nothing else will do so much to gain the affection and support of German Americans, the vast majority of whom are without question at heart loyal to American institutions and ideals.

I take the opportunity to add that, although hoping to the last against America's participation in the war, and although sometimes harboring misgivings regarding the purity of the war aims of some of the allies, I have been able, after a severe struggle, and largely owing to your own successive utterances, to take up a firm and final attitude, and am doing all I can, especially among Americans of German descent, to further American efforts in the war. I am mailing you herewith a copy of a Declaration of Principles which I have caused to be published, through the Associated Press, and which has been signed by prominent scholars in all parts of the country.

I am, my dear Mr. President, with all esteem,

Very sincerely yours, E. C. Wilm

TLS (WP, DLC).

[1] Professor of Philosophy at Boston University.
[2] See WW to O. H. Butz, April 12, 1918.

ENCLOSURE

At this, the first anniversary month of America's entrance into the world war, and after the ideals and aims of the war have been clarified and matured by a year's earnest discussion and stern practical endeavor, it seems fitting that Americans of German descent should state their convictions and sentiments on the great issues involved in the world conflict. Therefore, we, the undersigned, persons of German birth and members of American college and university faculties, hereby make the following Declaration of Principles, the support of which we urge upon our German-American fellow-citizens, everywhere:

We view with abhorrence and condemn without reservation the part which the German Imperial government had in provoking and permitting the present world conflict; we disavow and disown the doctrine, subversive of international security and future peace, that international covenants may be set aside whenever it is to the interest of any nation to do so; and we condemn unqualifiedly, as unworthy of the German nation, the various acts of violence in disregard of such international covenants; finally, we express our firm adherence to the political principles and ends for which the United States has entered the war, the vindication of international right, the self-determination of nations, the discrediting of militaristic and imperialist, and the substitution therefor of liberal and democratic ideals and principles of government, and we pledge our unalterable loyalty, our material support and our influence until these ends shall have been attained.

Printed statement (WP, DLC).

From Peter Golden

New York, May 4, 1918

At a mass meeting of 15,000 Irish Americans of Greater New York, held in Madison Square Garden, New York, on May 4th, the following resolutions were passed unanimously:

WHEREAS, Conscription has been passed for Ireland by the British parliament without consulting the Irish people and altogether against their will and as this is not only a violation of every right the Irish people possess but is a direct violation of the principle of national self-determination for which President Wilson says the American people are fighting, and

WHEREAS, Conscription in Ireland in the present temper of the people may lead to a condition which we shudder to contemplate, and which may threaten the very life of the race. Be it

RESOLVED, By this mass meeting of Irish Americans assembled in Madison Square Garden, on May 4th, representing not alone the people of Greater New York but the Irish people of Philadelphia, Baltimore, Washington, Boston, New Haven, Bridgeport, Newport, Syracuse and other eastern cities whose representatives are present, that we extend our utmost sympathy and support to the united people of Ireland in what appears to all to be an effort to avert the extermination of their race. We call upon President Wilson and the Senate and Congress of the United States to use their influence to have this action by the British parliament reversed and that we ask Irishmen and women everywhere to rally to the support of their motherland and aid her in her fight against extinction.

Peter Golden,   Secretary, Irish Progressive League.

T telegram (WP, DLC).

From John Paul Cooper[1]

Mr. President: Rome Georgia May 4th, 1918.

I ask leave to bring to your notice an indication of the extent of the reflex action, by which the Liberty Loan has itself aroused, even created, that patriotic feeling, to which appeal has been made for its support.

Three out of four of the men employed on my farm have bought these bonds. Two of these, unprompted, gave as the chief consideration the fact that they "would like to help in this war."

I can believe that this sentiment, spontaneous in these negro men, will seem to you important, as another evidence, coming this time from the absolute circumference, and no doubt of more value, because of its humble source, showing how entirely the Nation is stirred.   Respectfully,   J P Cooper

TLS (WP, DLC).
  [1] Farmer, merchant, and banker of Rome, Ga.; chairman of the Third Liberty Loan organization of Floyd County.

From Howard Earle Coffin

Darien, Ga., May 4, 1918.

Charges of dishonesty have been made against the Aircraft Board which demand the fullest inquiry. I request and urge that an official inquiry be had in order that the reputations of innocent men may not be ruined.   Howard Coffin.

T telegram (WP, DLC).

From George Creel, with Enclosure

My dear Mr. President,   Washington, D. C. May 4, 1918

The attached letter from Mr. Bullard is informative and somewhat amusing. I also enclose an account of recent Texas outrages[1] that may have bearing upon the statements that you intend to write.[2]
                                        Respectfully,   George Creel

  [1] "A Roman Holiday in Texas," *Nonpartisan Leader*, VI (April 29, 1918), 3; "Small Bore Editor Gloats over Atrocity," *ibid.*, pp. 3-4; and "True Story of the Horror," *ibid.*, p. 4, clippings (WP, DLC). All three articles dealt with a recent incident of mob violence against organizers of the Nonpartisan League. The first article reported that four organizers of the league were arrested on charges of vagrancy in Mineola, Texas, on April 4, 1918. They were subsequently taken from prison by a mob, driven to the woods, and severely beaten with "blacksnake" whips. The second article reprinted an editorial from the *Greenville* (Tex.) *Banner*, which strongly supported the action of the citizens of Mineola, gleefully described the violence inflicted on the organizers, and presented the incident as proof that "Americanism" was not to be tampered with around Mineola. The third article consisted of detailed statements of the incident by three of the four victims.
  [2] Wilson and Creel had obviously been discussing the advisability of a statement by Wilson denouncing mob violence.

E N C L O S U R E

Arthur Bullard to George Creel

Petrograd Office, Gorokhovaia 4, apt. 14.

My dear George: 18/5/February, 1918.

The President's third Message[1] has just arrived. We succeeded better than before in getting the text published in the newspapers, and so are not driving quite as hard on the posting. We will, however, distribute about one-quarter million handbills here in Petrograd, and I have ordered the Moscow Office to print and distribute in their district, as they did with the second Message.[2]

The second Message is still going strong, and has a much broader popular appeal than this third Message, which is more especially addressed to Germany and Austria. We are, therefore, making our principal drive on No. 3 on German and Hungarian translation, which we plan to get to all the Prisoner of War Camps in Russia, and as many as possible over the line.

I am enclosing the English text of our first Russian "Red White and Blue Book."[3] I had it under way before Sisson came over, and was expecting to run it as a serial in one of the Moscow papers, but the present press regime is too rigorous, and so we decided to bring it out as a pamphlet. I am also enclosing the first proof. A few condensations will bring it down to 32 pages and it will look quite flossy for Russia, when we get the red and blue ink on the cover.

The translation of the "How the war came to America"[4] is in its last revision and will be our second "Red, white and blue book."

The ABC Book[5] has been held up because the authoress has an artistic temperature of 102 in the shade. I am afraid that we will have to find an other one.

I am sending herewith a letter to Lee[6] in regard to our business organization. It will either make him laugh or curse. Every time I think of it it gives me a fit. There is no possibility of getting the right kind of a business manager here.

It is the one and original topsy-turvy land. To day's news is that Germany has declared war on Russia and that Trotsky sent back a despatch telling the Kaiser to quit his kidding.

We've got the only job that is really worth doing here. "In the beginning was the Word." And we are certainly shooting that into them.   Good luck,   Arthur B.

TLS (WP, DLC).
  [1] That is, Wilson's message to a joint session of Congress of February 11, 1918, printed at that date in Vol. 46.
  [2] That is, the Fourteen Points Address, printed at January 8, 1918, Vol. 45.

3 Arthur Bullard, *Letters of an American Friend*, a pamphlet of twenty-four pages, which expressed America's friendly interest in the democratic progress of the Russian people and explained the principles of American democracy. See the *Complete Report of the Chairman of the Committee on Public Information, 1917, 1918, 1919* (Washington, 1920), pp. 220, 222-23, and 251.

4 [Arthur Bullard and Ernest Poole] *How the War Came to America*, Red, White and Blue Series, No. 1 (Washington, 1917).

5 A book for Russian primary school children, which the C.P.I. had planned to issue and distribute as a gift from American to Russian school children. Although three thousand advance copies were eventually printed, they were never sent out, and the project was soon abandoned. See *Report of the Chairman of the C.P.I.*, pp. 226-27.

6 Clayton D. Lee, head of the division of business management of the C.P.I.

Carl William Ackerman to Edward Mandell House

Pontarlier (Berne) May 4, 1918

3249. For Colonel House. "Venture to submit survey of conditions in enemy countries to show possibility of another crisis Germany which may be influenced again by America's attitude.

Several things indicate Germany is preparing political maneuvers to begin as soon as military authorities convinced that decision is impossible in France. If high command compelled to stop attacks, chief preoccupation will be to avoid responsibility so they cannot be accused of failure. There are obviously only three ways of halting offensive: One, by German victory; two, by Allied victory which would maintain unbroken front; three, by German *source*. From Reichstag and newspaper comment it seems to be fairly certain that high command while not giving up hope for first are beginning to question its possibility. They cannot permit second because they have definitely promised peace and victory this year by means of offensive. They are undoubtedly considering possibility of third. They will attempt to have outside power advance peace suggestions at psychological moment to save them.

Many evidences that a certain reaction is developing among people as a result of offensive. Public is becoming nervous. Please note, for example, inspired answer to rumors that offensive is lagging because of shortage of horses; because of growing losses; because of lack of transportation and rations. These apprehensions, from my experience in Germany during Verdun and the Somme, only develop when public begins to doubt possibilities of success. I emphasize indirect effects of offensive on German people because there is every reason to believe that enemy public cannot stand strain of prolonged battle as well as Allies. Our object, if we hope for break within Germany, should be to force enemy to drag out offensive and withhold from enemy everything which gives him excuse to stop, without his stopping becoming a public and unquestionable evidence of defeat.

In addition to effect of offensive the food situation also contributes to possibility of crisis. Difficulties for year not passed in either Germany or Austria. It has been officially stated both in Berlin and Vienna that only possibility for continuation of present rations is help from the Ukraine and Roumania but troops having great difficulty pacifying Ukraine.

The DEUTSCHE ZEITUNG states another obstacle to Ukraine food is high prices and that it was agreed to pay Ukraine farmers four hundred and six marks per ton for rye and four hundred eighty seven marks per ton for wheat without transportation. Since Germany pays German agrarians only two hundred seventy and two hundred ninety marks per ton for rye and wheat respectively objection of agrarians comprehensible. Considering open acknowledgment of enemy that everything depends on Ukraine, I feel it highly to our interest to postpone and delay agreements and shipments between Germany and Ukraine in every possible way. Scarcer the food, greater the difficulty for Government to quiet German public.

From political standpoint Chancellor advises Prussian election reform[1] for one principal reason; effect upon United States. Effect upon German people is only secondary to German Government. German Government apparently wishes to exhibit bill as evidence of reform so that when next peace move is launched American cooperation can be expected. German Government undoubtedly still believes United States will talk peace and retire from war if it has a good excuse; if there is evidence that Germany has changed.

Apparently Germany hopes some outside power will initiate peace move. Germany expected to use Vienna and Czernin's address in February was planned for this purpose but failed. Now Germany looks for Vatican or some European neutral to make suggestions.

Considering these indications and possibility of another crisis in Berlin between electoral reform advocates and conservatives; between the Fatherland party and the Jewish and Catholic political leaders and press, I venture to suggest that United States first let it be understood definitely but privately and unofficially that United States will not be interested in any peace maneuvers unless officially and directly from Berlin; second, prevent the enemy from placing responsibility upon any other persons or conditions than her own leaders and mistakes if she cannot break through in France; third, if possible delay shipments of grain from Ukraine.

Most promising way of interfering with enemy plans and preventing peace move at present, which would be against our interests, is for United States to take the initiative, not in a peace move, but in public address of statement with following objects: One, to show our unyielding determination to support our Allies and bear

the future burdens; two, express public confidence in our Allies.
We have not done this as much as we might have. It is human for
nations, as for a man to desire public expression of sympathy and
support in periods of great stress and suffering. Before we entered
the war England was the great power to which all Allies looked
when suffering under invasion. Each time Russia, Roumania, Servia, Belgium, France, in early days, and to certain extent Italy,
looked to London for strength. Today Allies look to Washington not
only for military assistance, financial help and moral support, but
for public confidence and strength. I do not think we should ad-
vertise what we are doing but we might emphasize the principal
reasons for our fighting and assure Allies we will bear the brunt of
future attacks and repeat what we said a long time since: We cannot
make peace with an un-representative German Government. This
may forestall Germany's maneuver. Our chief emphasis from today
should be upon our determination. The more strength we and our
Allies exhibit the greater will be the reaction in Germany from the
offensive and from lack of food and from political disagreements.
If we appear weary or inclined to peace when Germany is worn out
there will be no reaction in Germany. Ackerman."

Stovall.

T telegram (WP, DLC).
  [1] That is, reform of Prussia's three-class suffrage law, about which see the Enclosure
printed with RL to WW, Nov. 12, 1917, Vol. 45. The law had come under increasing
attack during the war from Social Democrats, Progressives, and the left wing of the
National Liberal party. Throughout 1916 and 1917, both Bethmann Hollweg and William
II had repeatedly promised a reform of the Prussian election system. In November 1917,
Hertling introduced a bill in the lower house of the Prussian Diet, which called for the
adoption of the Imperial equal-suffrage system by Prussia. However, the Conservative
majority in the lower house strongly opposed the notion of universal equal franchise
and suggested instead a system of plural voting based on wealth, age, income, and
social standing. Thus, at the second reading of the bill on April 30 1918, Hertling
suggested a compromise. He reiterated his firm support of equal suffrage, but, at the
same time, advocated the adoption of precautionary measures, which he did not specify,
against its "radical" consequences and harmful effects. See the *New York Times*, May
1 and 3, 1918. For a detailed discussion, see also Reinhard Patemann, *Der Kampf um
die preußische Wahlreform im Ersten Weltkrieg* (Düsseldorf, 1964).

From Edward Mandell House

Dear Governor: New York. May 5, 1918.
    The Italians want very much to celebrate the day that Italy en-
tered the war and the Ambassador and others are hoping that you
may be willing to do something to call attention to May 24th.
    Mr. Hughes is President of the newly formed Italy-America So-
ciety and he will write you a letter tomorrow on the subject. The
letter will be private and merely for the purpose of learning your
wishes.
    There is a feeling among the Italians that Italy has been sadly

neglected and the purpose of the Ambassador and of the Society is to stimulate some interest among our people. They do not think they can do this unless you in some way countenance it.

Lansing was present at the conference yesterday when we discussed the matter and will give you further information.

I saw John D. Ryan yesterday and was cheered with what he had to say in regard to airplanes. He believes if he has a free hand as to production that by January 1st planes will be coming in almost as fast as they can be taken abroad. He is very decided as to the necessity for complete control, and if he does not get it I do not believe he will continue to serve. He thinks the Overman Bill gives you complete authority to do what you like in the matter, and he hopes you will let him go at the work unhampered. He believes that eventually, but not now, it should be a department to itself—just as it is in other belligerent countries.

I do not believe you could have chosen a better man.

Affectionately yours,   E. M. House

TLS (WP, DLC).

From Grosvenor Blaine Clarkson, with Enclosure

My dear Mr. President: Washington 5 May, 1918.

I have the honor to hand you herewith a copy of a memorandum that I have prepared at the request of the Secretary of War for submission at the Council meeting tomorrow, Monday, morning.

It is my earnest and wholly impersonal hope that some of the ideas advanced in this memorandum may be realized in fact, even though I may not be here when they do come to fruitage.

A good many persons believe the Council to be moribund. In view of that belief, which a very considerable pride in the Council causes me to resent, do you not think that I would be justified in outlining discreetly to a few of the more capable editorial writers of the country, many of whom I know well, some of the work that would logically fall under the Council in the future? And if I were permitted to do that, might I also feel at liberty to disclose to them for their private knowledge the contents of your letter to me of March 26? I really feel that we have reached a point where it would [be] well in a measure to revive the Council in the public mind, lest it be separated too far from the public memory.

Faithfully yours,   Grosvenor Clarkson

TLS (WP, DLC).

ENCLOSURE

A memorandum to the Council of National Defense and the Advisory Commission on further plans for future work for the Council and Advisory Commission, submitted by Grosvenor B. Clarkson, Secretary of the Council and of the Advisory Commission.

6 May, 1918.

On March 22, 1918, I gave the President a memorandum on the past and future functions of the Council of National Defense and its Advisory Commission.[1] That memorandum is attached hereto as part of this record.

On March 26, 1918, I received the following letter from the President:

My dear Mr. Clarkson: THE WHITE HOUSE 26 March, 1918.
Mr. Forster has handed me your letter of March twenty-second and the accompanying memorandum on the past and future functions of the Council of National Defense, and I have given both a very careful reading.

I am very much impressed by your discussion of the subject and find myself in substantial accord with you. Indeed, it has been my hope and expectation all along that the investigating and advisory functions of the Council of National Defense would proceed in the fullest vigor, because they are perhaps needed now more than ever and I cannot foresee any situation in which they would not be needed and would not be of the highest value. The War Industries Board is practically now under its reorganization divorced from the Council of National Defense. By my recent letter to Mr. Baruch, I have practically made it a direct administrative agency and, indeed, I so regard it, feeling that I am very much indebted to the Council of National Defense for having created the board in the first place and made it ready for such separate and independent uses.

I shall be very glad to keep your suggestions in mind, and want to thank you very sincerely for your generous references to myself in your letter.   Cordially and sincerely yours,
(Signed) Woodrow Wilson.

Mr. Grosvenor Clarkson,
Council of National Defense.

Copies of the foregoing correspondence were transmitted by me to all members of the Council and Advisory Commission and on April 17, 1918, I received the following letter from the Chairman of the Council:

[1] It is printed as an Enclosure with G. B. Clarkson to WW, March 22, 1918.

Dear Mr. Clarkson: April 17, 1918.

I have read with interest your letter of the 17th and the documents which accompany it.

You are quite right in your feeling that this is the time for the Council to plan carefully and intelligently for the future, and I hope that you and Mr. Gifford can prepare a rather specific proposal to that end, which may be made the basis of discussion at an early meeting of the Council.

With best personal wishes,   Cordially yours,
                          (Signed) Newton D. Baker.

Mr. Grosvenor Clarkson,
    Council of National Defense.

In this memorandum I shall make eight specific suggestions for new work to be undertaken by the Council.

First, industrial reconstruction (in broad terms, the re-conversion of industry from the war-time basis back to the peace-time basis) and the re-absorption into the industries of labor employed in the services of the United States.

For the purpose of being concrete—or as concrete as one can be in dealing with a new national problem—I have confined myself to only two aspects of reconstruction. I should like, however, to develop at least tentatively the general theme.

It is elementary that after the war America will not be the same America. Already she has in many directions broken with her past and she is being hourly transformed. The metamorphosis is going on as much in the thought of the country as it is in the structure; the same thing will be true in the period after the war. New conditions and relationships create new problems for nations as well as for individuals; and, let me add, the change will be as great in the thought and ideals of the nation as it will be in its strictly material problems, whether these be military, commercial, or those having to do with labor. Let us grant that we shall gain military success. Let us then not fall into the danger-trap of allowing the material effects of such success to overshadow consideration of the higher values which give a nation its life. The civilized world today, as we know that world, may be said to be one great altar of sacrifice. If that is not true now, it certainly will be true if the war continues for another year. It is our duty in any adequate intellectual conception of the task to see to it that the gains to the moral as well as to the material well-being of the nation shall square with the sacrifice. A little reflection will convince one that this aspect of reconstruction is the fundamental aspect and that upon it must be predicated all successful plans in this direction.

A year ago we were a great lazy democracy. Lincoln said, "A fat hound won't hunt." That sentence illumines our national disease. The transformation from the condition is already under way. Soon the spirit of the nation will be a burning flame. There will be sloughed off the scales fostered by a love of luxury and the loose and sentimental and boastful thinking that have been our curse in the last generation. Out of the turmoil and the sacrifice will come discipline and orderly living and thinking; and, therefore, with sequential and irresistible logic will come demands for new conditions of living commensurate to the new ideals. Again I repeat, here is the fundamental reconstruction to which the American Government should address itself and only herein can be found the policy which shall be the groundwork of any enlightened organization for reconstruction. History records but few fruitful governmental agencies that did not have a firm and penetrating policy at the base. Raising the framework for the task is merely a matter of mechanics in organization and the proper method can in all probability only be arrived at by a first-hand study of European methods on the part of a carefully selected American commission which shall conduct its investigations with due regard to the ever-present danger of carrying the European analogy too far. In the meantime the Council and Advisory Commission should accumulate all of the literature bearing upon this question and form it into a working library.

Even with the appointment of such a commission as I have suggested, it is probable that at present we can only feel our way in the organization of machinery to handle these problems. It may be that as the war nears its end and as the issue between autocracy and democracy becomes ever sharper and more terrible, the civilized world will demand that immediately at the war's close all reconstruction of the world's affairs be based upon the dictum of Lincoln that no man is good enough to govern any other man without that other man's consent, to the end of approaching the proper readjustment of national, inter-national, and racial relationships. I offer this thought not for the purpose of injecting idealism in a discussion where undue accent of it does not belong, but to emphasize anew that none of us can now see the end of the road and that therefore all plans for reconstruction should be builded so as to permit of flexibility of action and even of minor policy at any given time. The main thing now is to come to concrete thinking and study of the entire problem.

Even to outline all of the foreign organizations for reconstruction would take too much space and would be outside the immediate purpose of this memorandum. However, the commissions and committees under the British Ministry of Reconstruction are now ap-

proximately ninety in number and fall into fifteen groups, as follows:

    I.   Trade development, under which grouping are five com-
mittees dealing with general aspects and nine dealing with
specific phases of the situation.

    II.   Finance, with two committees.

    III.   Raw materials, with six committees.

    IV.   Coal and power, with two committees and four subcom-
mittees.

    V.   Intelligence, with two committees.

    VI.   Scientific and industrial research, with two research boards,
five standing committees, seven research committees, four
inquiry committees, and three provisional organization
committees.

    VII.   Demobilization and disposal of stores, with eight com-
mittees.

    VIII.   Labor and employment, with two committees.

    IX.   Agriculture and Forestry, with four committees.

    X.   Public administration, with six committees.

    XI.   Housing, with four committees.

    XII.   Education, with eight committees and commissions.

    XIII.   Aliens, with two committees.

    XIV.   Legal, with three committees.

    XV.   Miscellaneous, with three committees.

To visualize what Germany is doing along reconstruction lines
there may be cited the work of the Imperial Ministry of Economics,
formerly the fourth division of the Imperial Ministry for the Interior.
The Imperial Ministry of Economics was created on October 21,
1916, and in November of 1916 there was coordinated with it the
organization responsible for the German reconstruction policy since
August, 1916. This was the office of the Imperial Commissary for
Transition Economy. Under the Imperial Commissary operates a
Transition Economy Parliament of two hundred and fifty members,
divided into twenty-one subcommittees dealing with finance (composed of fifteen of Germany's greatest bankers); transport; iron and
manganese ores; lead, antimony, zinc, tin, nickel, copper, chrome,
wolfram, and molybdenite ores; cotton, wool, matting fiber; silk,
rags and worn fabrics; fodder, bread, corn, meat, and livestock;
vegetable and animal oils and fats; resins; skins, hides, leather, and
tanning materials; rubber; cocoa, coffee, rice; coal; and, lastly, py-
rites and phosphates. It is said that the best commercial thought
of Germany is enlisted in these committees. The Imperial Commissary further deals with the tasks of bringing back soldiers to
civil life; of caring for the disabled and providing necessary work

for them; of eliminating women and children from the labor market and of bringing into force again the protective labor laws that have been partially repealed. With regard to capital, the duties of this office are to utilize and to extend production to the uttermost and to exercise the strictest economy; to lay up reserves of capital for the peace period; to create credit on the security of real and personal property; to offer credit to urban property owners and shipping companies; to revive trade; to improve the currency, and to make liquid the capital locked up in war loans. The Imperial Secretary of the Interior had divided the problems into three main branches: Labor questions, the creation of credit, and the provision of raw materials. It was from the first apparently the intention that while requisite changes would be brought about by legislative and administrative action, the cooperation of all who were affected would be organized and utilized—that is, a large advisory body of specialists would review the problems of currency, shipping, finance, trade, industry, and so forth.

Nowhere has the philosophy underlying reconstruction been more vividly stated than by Mr. Lloyd George in the following remarks that he addressed to the executive committee of the British labor party which in June, 1917, presented to the Prime Minister resolutions approved in the Manchester conference dealing with demobilization, restoration of trade union conditions, and so forth:

There is no doubt that the present war presents an opportunity for the reconstruction of the industrial and economic conditions of this country such as has never been presented in the life of the world. The whole state of society is more or less molten. You can stamp upon that molten mass almost anything so long as you do so with firmness and determination. * * * There is no time to lose. I firmly believe that what is known as the after the war settlement is the settlement that will direct the destinies of all classes for some generations to come. The country will be prepared for bigger things immediately after the war than it will be when it begins to resume the normal clash of selfish interests. I believe the country will be in a more enthusiastic mood, in a more exalted mood, for the time being in a greater mood for doing things; and unless the opportunity is seized immediately after the war, I believe it will pass away, far beyond either your ken or mine, and perhaps beyond our children's

I am not afraid of the audacity of these proposals. I believe the settlement after the war will succeed in proportion to its audacity. The readier we are to cut away from the past, the better are we likely to succeed. * * *

Think out new ways of dealing with old problems. Don't always be thinking of getting back to where you were before the war. Get a really new world.

I may point out that the chairman of the Republican National Committee is quoted in the newspapers of May 4th as saying that one of the three main things that the Republican party stands for at this time is "a sane preparedness now for the great problems of reconstruction."

Second, a central bureau for the compilation and safeguarding of statistics necessary for the proper planning and prosecution of all phases of the war programme.

Third, a central bureau to examine and report on all inventions which are now variously sent for examination to the Naval Consulting Board, the National Research Council, the National Advisory Committee for Aeronautics, the General Staff, and the Interior Department. It is essential that such a bureau shall be warmly responsive to the ideas and plans of inventors; in short, that it shall be intelligently human and receptive. I need not rehearse here what the lack of such a bureau has cost America over a long period of years.

Fourth, a central repository for the national records. No such repository now exists under the Government. Even in the War Department I understand there is no such repository. The waging of this war is so essentially made up of economic and industrial elements that there is being accumulated a priceless fund of material which should be made available, not only for the next generation, but for this generation, and which should be properly concentrated and cl[a]ssified for immediate and easy examination. This is of course primarily a matter for expert statistical control, to use the apt phrase of the Director of the Council, than whom probably no one in the United States is better qualified to speak of such matters. After the Civil War some three million dollars were spent in work of this nature but it was never done in such a sufficiently qualified way to justify the expenditure.

Fifth, a central bureau for the examination of and report on all new ideas of federal administration. It is elementary that some such bureau should exist under the Government to be in effect a clearing house for new national problems and systems of government, and the need for which may, and probably will increase as the war goes on.

Sixth, a division of information to direct, in peace as well as in war, a campaign to teach the people of the country how to think intelligently on economic questions, and particularly on new economic questions as they arise.

Seventh, a central secret service division, to direct all secret service matters having to do with the civilian population. Several years previous experience in the investigation of criminal cases for the Government, together with an intermittent study, extending over a period of four years, of secret service matters in connection with the enforcement of the Customs Administrative Act, have convinced me of the need for such a central division, particularly when engaged in a war with the Imperial German Government.

Eighth, a bureau which shall be a point of contact for the American Negro and his problems, such a bureau to be headed by a Negro citizen of the United States. Nowhere in the framework of our society is there any problem so poignant and so baffling as that presented by the colored race in America. Where else can the consideration of human rights over all other rights be more properly dealt with than in a council of national defense? I cannot imagine anything more fitting than that the Council and its Advisory Commission should give heed to this most human of questions of our national life.

Finally, I suggest the immediate and complete divorce of the War Industries Board from the Council of National Defense. The present situation is confusing to the public and to the two bodies alike, and such a separation would, in my judgment, bring about more efficient and fruitful administration for both the Board and the Council.

CC MS (WP, DLC).

From William Gibbs McAdoo

White Sulphur Springs, W. Va., May 5, 1918.

Have developed a sore throat with a little temperature this evening. Doctor thinks can leave tomorrow night. Very sorry. Will see you Tuesday. Nell joins me in greatest love for you all.

W. G. McAdoo.

T telegram (WP, DLC).

To William Gibbs McAdoo

The White House May 6 1918

Sincerely sorry to hear that you are not well and beg that you will stay as long as necessary really to get well All unite in loving messages to you both and congratulations on the success of the loan   Woodrow Wilson

T telegram (W. G. McAdoo Papers, DLC).

To Edward Mandell House

My dear Friend: The White House 6 May, 1918

I am sure you understand why I have not been sending you more frequent notes. I haven't had the use of my hand, and my notes are generally run off on my own typewriter when I happen to think of them and not when I sit down for formal dictation.

I am sorry that you have been annoyed by the articles about yourself.[1] Knowing you, I am not surprised, however, that you are. At the same time, those that I have been able to read, and I have read a good many of them, are certainly written in an excellent spirit and, while I have known in reading certain passages that you would squirm, on the whole I think the writer has tried to treat you fairly and he certainly has treated you in the most friendly spirit. We just have to grin and bear it when these things happen.

Won't you be kind enough to put the enclosed from the Lithuanian National Council in Mezes' hands?[2] It was brought to me by a very earnest group of men who made a very considerable impression on me.[3] They evidently dislike Russia and Prussia with almost equal intensity, though the balance dips a little towards Prussia, whom they fear as well as dislike, and their desire for independence is genuine and intense. I made them a non-committal speech in which I expressed little more than sympathy, which I genuinely feel.

I am afraid if this hot weather keeps up, you will be driven away northward. I am praying for some interval when you can come down and see us.

The hand is getting to feel almost normal, though I still have to keep a bandage on it and it is of only half use to me, but it is healing up beautifully.

All join in affectionate messages.

Affectionately yours, Woodrow Wilson

WWTLS (E. M. House Papers, CtY).
[1] EMH to EBW, May 5, 1918, ALS (WP, DLC). House complained to Mrs. Wilson about the publicity which he had received in connection with the serialization of Arthur D. Howden Smith's *The Real Colonel House*, which appeared in twenty-six installments in the New York *Evening Post* from April 8 to May 7, 1918. The articles, House maintained, had driven him "near to drink," and he resented that he had been "advertised, misquoted and hung on a limb for the public to gaze at." For an example of how Smith's articles were advertised, see the New York *Evening Post*, April 6, 1918.
[2] It is printed as an Enclosure with G. Creel to WW, May 2, 1918. The copy which Wilson sent to House is still in the House Papers.
[3] That is, when he received the members of the Lithuanian National Council at the White House on May 3, 1918.

To Newton Diehl Baker

My dear Baker: The White House 6 May, 1918

Thank you for sending me the full text of the message from General Pershing, giving the details of the agreement adopted by the Supreme War Council, May second, at Abbeville. Personally, I agree with you in thinking the agreement entirely satisfactory and as having been arrived at by just the right sort of conference in the right way. I hope that this will dispose of further indefinite discussions of the particular views of any single government.

Cordially and faithfully yours,   Woodrow Wilson

TLS (N. D. Baker Papers, DLC).

To Theodore Marburg

My dear Mr. Marburg: The White House 6 May, 1918

Thank you very much for sending me a copy of Lord Bryce's letter to you of recent date.

I do not know that there is any special message I can suggest to Lord Bryce. I am always disinclined to differ with his views, because I have learned to respect his judgment and to suspect that I may be wrong when I disagree with him, but I cannot escape the conviction that to occupy ourselves now with the development of a working organization for a League of Nations would be a mistake, strong as the arguments are which Lord Bryce urges. The thing could not be done privately, as he suggests. No international conference of men of the stamp that would be necessary in this great undertaking can be held in a corner or without public knowledge, and we would start a discussion of the very thing which ought not now to be discussed, a discussion in the field where jealousy and competitive interest is most likely to block the whole business.

Cordially and sincerely yours,   Woodrow Wilson

TLS (WP, DLC).

To Charles Spalding Thomas

My dear Senator: [The White House] 6 May, 1918

You were kind enough to consult me the other day about the wholesale charges in regard to the production of aircraft which have been lodged by Mr. Gutzon Borglum. I take the liberty of writing you this letter in order to say more formally what I said to you then informally, namely, that every instrumentality at the disposal of the Department of Justice will be used to investigate and pursue charges of dishonesty or malversation of any kind, if the allegations made by Mr. Borglum are considered worthy of serious consideration, and I sincerely hope that the matter will be treated as one for searching official investigation by the constituted authorities of the Government. Only in this way can the reputations of those whose actions have been perfectly regular and blameless be protected and the guilt, if there is any, definitely lodged where it should be lodged.   Sincerely yours,   Woodrow Wilson

TLS (Letterpress Books, WP, DLC).

To Jessie Woodrow Wilson Sayre

My dear little Girl: [The White House] 6 May, 1918

I am sincerely distressed about what you tell me of the way in which Doctor Froelicher has been treated. I hardly know what to do except write him a letter expressing my confidence in him, which I shall, of course, do. I have half a mind to write to Doctor Guth to the same effect, though I do not know whether that will be particularly helpful to Doctor Froelicher or not.

If anythings turns up down here which would give me a chance to help Froelicher, of course I will do it, though I do not think it would be wise to say that to him, because it might raise hopes that I never could fulfill.

I know you will pardon a dictated letter. We all send you a heart full of love, and are so delighted that the children are getting all right again.   Lovingly,   Father

TLS (Letterpress Books, WP, DLC).

To Hans Froelicher

My dear Doctor Froelicher: [The White House] 6 May, 1918

I am very much distressed to hear of the action of the Trustees of Goucher College in the matter of your connection with the college. I feel that through my daughters I can almost claim you as a personal friend, and I have learned through them to have the utmost confidence in you. I should be willing at any time to place the fullest confidence in your patriotic attitude towards our own Government, and I feel that I cannot do less at the present time than express to you thus directly my personal feeling towards you.
           Cordially and sincerely yours,   Woodrow Wilson

TLS (Letterpress Books, WP, DLC).

To William Westley Guth

My dear President Guth: [The White House] 6 May, 1918

I hope that you will not think I am taking an unwarranted liberty if I express my surprise and concern that the Trustees of Goucher College should have determined to dispense with the services of Doctor Hans Froelicher and that the reasons should apparently be a lack of confidence in his loyal attitude towards the Government of the United States. I have known so much of Doctor Froelicher through my daughters, and have formed so favorable an impression of him by direct contact with him, that I am sure that if any such impression on the part of the Trustees exists, it must be based upon some cruel misunderstanding.

I beg that you will believe I am prompted to write this letter only by genuine regard for a man whom I very much esteem and without the least desire to thrust my counsel, uninvited, into the deliberations of the authorities of the college. Perhaps my personal interest in the college would be a sufficient justification in the eyes of the Trustees.[1]   Sincerely yours,   Woodrow Wilson

TLS (Letterpress Books, WP, DLC).
[1] The president and trustees of the college reversed their decision; Froelicher remained in his post until his death in 1930. He also served as acting president of Goucher College in 1929-1930.

To Howard Earle Coffin

[The White House] 6 May, 1918

Your telegram received. You may be sure I shall cooperate in every way to prevent what you rightly foresee might happen. The Department of Justice will cooperate to the utmost in seeing that all charges are probed and the truth got at.

Woodrow Wilson.

T telegram (Letterpress Books, WP, DLC).

To William Bauchop Wilson

My dear Mr. Secretary: The White House 6 May, 1918

Thank you very much for your letter to me about your interview with Messrs. Woolley and Hale. I instinctively felt when they laid the matter before me that they were stating it a good deal too strongly and I entirely subscribe to the conclusions of your letter. I think that you have at every turn handled the matter just as well as it was possible to handle it, with a great deal of discretion and vision, and of course there was nothing in what Woolley and Hale said that involved any doubt on that point. They were merely misinformed as to the troubles that were occurring.

Cordially and sincerely yours,   Woodrow Wilson

TLS (received from Mary A. Strohecker).

From Robert Somers Brookings

My dear Mr President: Washington May 6, 1918.

Answering yours of the 3rd would say:

First: When I mentioned these articles being made only by the most responsible mills and manufacturers, I did not intend to classify them especially as to size. As a matter of fact, any reliable small manufacturer would be permitted to make a Liberty article, and, as he would receive, through the influence of the Government, his materials at the same price as the large manufacturers, it would in a sense be a protection rather than a disadvantage to him. As a matter of fact, however, the Liberty article would be so staple and sold on such a small margin of profit that the small manufacturer would probably avoid it. We find in most industries, including steel, that in order to compete with the large manufacturers the small concern selects the greater refinements of the industry and avoids the staples, thus securing maximum value for the relatively large *personal* equation which enters into his business.

Second: As I did not wish to discuss this matter to any extent with others or enter into any details until I had received some sort of a tentative expression from yourself, the question of method of inspection has not been determined. I might say roughly, however, that I had no thought of its becoming in any way a financial burden to the Government. We could doubtless draft a form of affidavit required from those who manufacture the Liberty article by which, for example, the foreman of a factory makes affidavit that he has absolute knowledge of the facts and swears that the product of the factory in Liberty goods for the week or month ending ——— have conformed in every way to Government specifications. With specifications carefully drawn, and a knowledge of the fact that the article would, from time to time, be inspected, we would probably secure a standard of quality not possible under present trade conditions. In any event, the comparatively small expense incident to Government inspection could properly be contributed by the manufacturer and charged in the cost of producing the article. In a word, about the only thing the Government does is to originate the scheme and induce the interested industries to carry it out along the lines suggested. I have only mentioned this to Mr Rosenwald and one or two others who are familiar with the clothing and shoe trade, and was encouraged by their rather enthusiastic reception to submit it to you. It is barely possible, when we get into the details, that we may find difficulties which are not now apparent. However, it may grow into a very large and important matter, and, while it involves the Government in no money, it involves it in the use of its good name and a principle which entitles it to the most serious consideration.

Of course this whole problem is necessarily placed before you in very tentative shape, and your approval of the general principle only is now involved. Its development will be conditioned upon its practicability after we have thoroughly investigated the details.

Respectfully yours,   Robt. S. Brookings

TLS (WP, DLC).

From Samuel Huston Thompson, Jr.

Dear Mr. President: Washington May 6th. 1918.

Several days ago I went to Quantico—thirty miles south of here—with the intention of acting as a sort of back ground for John D. Rockefeller Jr. who was to make a speech at the dedication of the new Y.M.C.A. hut. Mr. Rockefeller was taken sick and was unable to speak so I was thrust forward in his place and had to make the main address. I only had about ten minutes to prepare myself before sentence was pronounced, but an inspiration flashed across my mind and saved me. It was in the nature of the subject I selected — "The Commander in Chief." For twenty minutes I told them all I knew about you. Never have I had such an appreciative audience.

When I finished and the affair was over the boys crowded around me and wanted to know more about you. Many of them said in a wistful way "how we would like to see him.["]

It occurred to me that if you could drop in on this camp and the other camps nearby when you have some leisure—if such is ever the case—that it would greatly stir their national pride and patriotic spirit and when they go abroad they would pass the word along to the other boys that they had seen you. I want our men "over there" to visualize America in the personality of their Chief.

You know how necessary it is for the normal mind in human affairs to centralize its ideal in a human personality just as in religion the human mind reverts to a spiritualized personality. You are the one around whom we all radiate and you have well earned the right.

What better proof than in a letter from my brother Marshall[1] from Scotland where he says: "Every Englishman or Scotchman who has expressed himself to me, and I may add every Australian or New Zealander, seems to have the highest admiration in fact almost veneration for our President. They all recognize him as the wisest statesman and the great man of the world. He has indeed reached the pinnacle of fame."

     With affectionate regard. Huston Thompson.

  P.S. This letter does not call for an answer and I want to spare you the time and trouble.

  It may interest you to know that Marshall has been made secretary for the Y.M.C.A. in charge of all educational matters in Scotland.

ALS (WP, DLC).
 [1] That is, Alexander Marshall Thompson, Princeton 1893, a lawyer of Pittsburgh.

From Matthew Hale

Dear Mr. President: Brunswick, Georgia, May 6, 1918.

  Yesterday in "Everybody's Magazine" I read a poem which I am taking the liberty of bringing to your attention.[1] It seems to me that it summarizes in poetry the spirit that you have been breathing into our people in regard to the war. I wish that more people felt the way you do—that a grim determination to use force does not necessarily mean the abandonment of our spiritual side. The editorial from the front page of the "Manufacturers Record"[2] and the column also taken from that magazine[3] seems to me as devilish in their influence on our people, as the poem from "Everybody's" is inspiring.   Very sincerely yours, Matthew Hale

TLS (WP, DLC).
 [1] Allen Crafton, "In Time of War I Sing," *Everybody's Magazine*, XXXVIII (May 1918), 30; clipping, WP, DLC.
 [2] It is missing in WP, DLC. However, it was "The Struggle Is Unto Death!" *Manufacturers Record*, LXXIII (April 25, 1918), 39. The editorial stated that America faced the choice of either spending millions of lives and billions of dollars to defeat Germany overwhelmingly or being destroyed and enslaved by Germany. It then continued: "This nation must fight; fight as never before in its history; fight with the utmost power of an awakened, burning, living hatred of the accursed thing we fight; fight not German militarism only, but fight all Germany; fight not to make the world safe for democracy, but fight for infinitely more than democracy—fight for our existence as a nation; fight to save our women and children from the brutish beasts who have saddened millions unto worse than death; fight unto death the power that, with a hatred infinitely greater than its hatred to Belgium and France, would enslave us; fight, fight and fight with all the enraged, death-defying power of a nation that slumbered long, but which now knows that either it must conquer or it must die."
 [3] It, too, is missing. The Editors have been unable to determine what article Hale enclosed. There are several articles and editorial notices in the *Manufacturers Record* of April 25 and May 2, 1918, which fit Hale's description.

From Newton Diehl Baker

My dear Mr. President: Washington. May 6, 1918.

I have just received from Major General George O. Squier, Chief Signal Officer, a request for the appointment of a Court of Inquiry to investigate charges more or less currently made hinting at disloyalty, corruption, and graft in the development of the Army aircraft program. So far, such charges, although made in responsible places by responsible men, have lacked definiteness, and have not, so far as my attention has been brought to them, dealt with any specific instances, nor have they been supported by any evidence. These charges are, however, of a kind which can be investigated thoroughly, and I desire to constitute a board for their investigation.

A Military Board, in my opinion, because of its broad powers, should be ordered in lieu of the Court of Inquiry which has been requested. The field of inquiry of this board may include an examination into all of the charges and accusations made with reference to any matter or thing in which this Department is concerned, or any charge against any military officer, or accusation or charge against any civilian employe of this Department in connection with his conduct regarding any matter concerning this Department and any accusation or charge against the Aircraft Board. This board will have the power to compel the attendance of witnesses and their testimony, and to require the production of all necessary books and papers. It is of the highest importance to assure the country whether the men who have been engaged in this work have been upright and have known no other impulse than loyalty to their country and zeal for its welfare.

If this course meets with your approval, I will immediately submit to you the names of those officers whose qualifications, both as to experience and character, seem to me to be appropriate for the constitution of a tribunal whose judgment will be final in the opinion of the country.

                         Respectfully yours,   Newton D. Baker

TLS (WP, DLC).

From Thomas James Walsh

My dear Mr. President: Washington. May 6, 1918.

I am moved to address you, by reason of the deep concern I feel in consequence of the determination, as the morning papers advise us, to entrust the investigation of culpability in connection with the air-craft measures to the War Department. I hope very sincerely that, as is not infrequently the case, the report is erroneous.

The War Department has no such trained force at its command for the work as has the Department of Justice. The public demand, so far as there is a demand, is for the punishment of any one who may have been actuated by criminal or disloyal motives, private citizen or public officer, civilian or member of the military forces. So far as any civilian culprit, at least, is concerned, any action by the War Department must be supplemented by the Department of Justice before he can be reached.

But it must be borne in mind that the Department of War is itself, in some measure, involved. If the investigation should not offer any victim to appease the wrath which has been aroused or which will be aroused, or simulated, the caluminous will be busy acclaiming the proceeding as a whitewashing affair. It seems to me exceedingly unwise to invite such criticism, even if the prospect of it should not constrain some of the investigators to incline to a conclusion they might not otherwise reach. As between the two departments mentioned, I feel that any inquiry instituted should be under the direction of the Attorney General with a view to civil and criminal proceedings. Of course, there may be governing considerations of which I have no knowledge.

But I am convinced that the wise course is to have a *public* investigation, before the Military Affairs Committee. A secret investigation by the Department of Justice would be open to some of the objections that might be made, as above advanced, to an inquiry by the War Department. It is true that it is often desirable not to disclose in advance what might be produced at a trial, but it often transpires that a preliminary hearing is helpful. The insurance hearing, in which Justice Hughes had a conspicuous part,[1] not only was no obstacle to a recovery of the moneys appropriated or misapplied, but brought out evidence which probably would not otherwise have been available.

Under the circumstances confronting us, I am confident that, unless there is peril in it to our military operations, and I can not conceive how there can be, full publicity should attend any investigation that may be conducted, and that it ought not to be under either the direction or control of the War Department.

Very truly yours,   T. J. Walsh

TLS (WP, DLC).
  [1] About which, see the news report printed at Nov. 12, 1905, n. 3, and WW *et al.* to J. J. McCook and C. B. Alexander, Dec. 29, 1905, n. 1, both in Vol. 16.

From Samuel Gompers

Sir: Washington, D. C. May 6, 1918.

I feel it my unescapeable duty to present to you certain facts in regard to conditions in Porto Rico in the form of charges against Arthur Yager, Governor of Porto Rico.[1] These charges, signed and specified by Santiago Iglesias, President of the Free Federation of Workers of Porto Rico, show that Governor Yager has been derelict in cooperating with national war policies; that he has not performed his duties as an administrator with impartiality and equity to all; that he has knowingly or unknowingly used the high power of his office to interfere with constructive efforts of Porto Rico's workers to better their conditions of life and work, and that his policies and acts have been at complete variance with those high ideals and standards of human welfare and value that are essential to democratic institutions. A statement has been made out to accompany these charges describing conditions in Porto Rico and embodying documentary evidence proving the charges.

The agricultural workers who are now on strike in the sugar plantations of Porto Rico have been denied political, legal, and industrial justice. The United States government, which is now in a war against the principles of autocracy and denial of human right, cannot longer remain responsible for a condition in territory over which it has jurisdiction, which is totally at variance with the ideals and institutions for which our government and nation have declared.

The situation in Porto Rico, which is inducing and leading the working people to the verge of a revolution, is being used to the discredit of our Republic in Spanish speaking countries. The story of injustice in Porto Rico has already been carried to the Spanish speaking people of North and South America, and even to Europe. The people of those countries value the declarations of our government and our people by the results they are able to achieve.

I feel very keenly that a condition ought not longer to remain which I am sure you, and all other right thinking citizens, would not approve or sanction if the facts were known. I therefore, am bringing to your attention the following charges and supplementary information in order that steps may be taken to remedy a situation which is totally at variance with the desires of our people and which is being used to discredit the high aims and desires of our Republic.

Conditions in Porto Rico have in years past been presented to you personally and to various governmental agencies, especially to the Federal Commission on Industrial Relations. It is my purpose at this time not only to make charges against Governor Yager, but to suggest that a commission ought to be sent to the Island to make an investigation and a report with recommendations. The evil that exists there is in the main economic. For years, the workers of Porto Rico have been underfed, practically starving. Something practical ought to be done to better such a condition among workers in an Island rich in many valuable products. A practical effort ought to be made to give these people of Porto Rico the real opportunity which democracy implies, and with which I know you have the most sincere and practical sympathy.

Respectfully,   Saml. Gompers.

TLS (WP, DLC).
  ¹ S. Iglesias to S. Gompers, Dec. 11, 1917 (two letters of the same date), TCL (WP, DLC). Iglesias discussed at length several recent examples of Yager's alleged complicity with the vested interests of Porto Rico and his hostile policy toward labor. In particular, Iglesias mentioned the Governor's veto of a compulsory workmen's compensation bill; his failure to accept a joint resolution by the legislature of Porto Rico to sell a plot of land to the Free Federation of Workers for a nominal sum for the purpose of building a labor temple; and his refusal to order an investigation into the labor practices of the Guanica Centrale, a huge sugar trust, which allegedly employed its workers under inhuman conditions, shipped them to a plantation in the Dominican Republic by deceitful means, and treated them like slaves.

Lord Reading to Arthur James Balfour

No. 2031. VERY URGENT.   Washington. May 6, 1918.

Secretary Lansing told me today that the President had delayed sending an answer to the questions to your tel. dated the 18th April[1] as he did not wish to reply in the negative but nevertheless he was convinced that the moment was not opportune or that a sufficient military advantage would be gained. Consequently he could not at present concur in your proposals.

The Bolshevik Govt. has demanded the recall of U. S. Consul at Vladivostock[2] and has probably also asked for recall of British and French Consuls on the ground that discovery has been made of plans hostile to the Bolshevik Govt. Mr. Lansing also said that he understood that the Bolshevik Govt. were asking or intended to ask for the withdrawal of British troops from Murmansk. Further the Bolshevik Govt. would not permit the use of cypher messages from U.S.G. to their representatives in Russia. Generally the view here is that the Bolshevik Govt. wishes to pick a quarrel with the U.S.G.

This new development does not encourage the President to believe in Trotzsky's good intentions towards Allies. If this news had not arrived this morning I am convinced the President's answer to you would have been the same. He remains unconvinced that the balance of advantage and disadvantage is in favour of action at present.

T telegram (FO 115/2446, pp. 19-20, PRO).
  [1] A. J. Balfour to Lord Reading, April 18, 1918.
  [2] John Kenneth Caldwell.

To Newton Diehl Baker

My dear Mr. Secretary: The White House 7 May, 1918

I would be very glad to have Mr. Ryan, General March, and General Kenly read the accompanying report,[1] and anybody else whom you think it desirable to show it to.

My own view, strengthened by a comparison of views with some of the gentlemen on the Hill, is that it would not be wise to have the investigation of Mr. Borglum's charges undertaken by the War Department, because, as one of them has suggested, it would be made to appear that the War Department was in some degree an interested party inasmuch as the reputation of some of its officers was involved; and before I received your letter accompanying the report of the aircraft investigation I had committed myself to certain Senators to the effect that the inquiry ought to be instituted by the Department of Justice.

Of course, this does not dispose of General Squier's request. I dare say that he is entitled, for the sake of his reputation, to any process of inquiry which is necessary to put his conduct in the right light, though it may be that he will feel that if the inquiry conducted by the Department of Justice does not touch him, in the event he will be sufficiently vindicated.

Cordially and faithfully yours,   Woodrow Wilson

TLS (N. D. Baker Papers, DLC).
  [1] That is, the final report of the Marshall-McNab-Wells committee.

To Samuel Gompers

My dear Mr. Gompers: [The White House] 7 May, 1918

You must have wondered why I have not sooner written you about the subject matter of our recent interesting conference concerning Mexican matters and the possibility of adopting means which would bring about a better understanding. It has been only because I wanted to give the matter mature consideration and be reasonably certain that I was making the right answer to your suggestion. I have fortified my judgment by talking with a number of men whose practical opinions I value, and I find that they have the view which I was inclined to form myself and now believe to be the right view, namely, that it would probably be unwise to have any action taken by the Government itself which would give an official character to such a conference between the representatives of labor in the United States and the representatives of labor in Mexico, as you suggested. This does not mean, however, that a conference between the representatives of labor in the two countries is not highly desirable. I think that it is. It only means that in my judgment it should be brought about without consultation or arrangement with either government and as an independent action on the part of the representatives of labor in both countries. I think that this would give it added, not lessened, force, and inasmuch as it would be a spontaneous movement of friendship from both sides, it ought to have a very important and persuasive moral affect.

May I not thank you for having let me see the enclosed synopsis of the view of Judge Douglas? I have read the paper with thoughtful attention.

Cordially and sincerely yours,   Woodrow Wilson

TLS (Letterpress Books, WP, DLC).

From Edward Mandell House

Dear Governor: New York, May 7, 1918.

I am delighted to hear that your hand is getting better. Some day soon I shall hope to see "your own handwriting."

As to the book that Smith is writing, I am reminded of the halcyon-days when McCombs was hailed as the greatest man in the world and was compared, at a banquet which I attended, to Alexander, Caesar and Napoleon.

I am happy over the way you are handling the aircraft investigation. It would not surprise me to see Borglum land where he wants the others sent. I am sure the turn has come in the aircraft situation and that before the end of the year, everyone will realize that a great undertaking has been successfully accomplished.

We are going through now exactly the same phase that they went through in England, and only a year ago.

The shipping problem has also turned the corner and there is nothing left, as far as I can see, to worry over except the ordnance, and that is not important since we can get sufficient in France and England. I hope all this makes you as happy as it does me.

Affectionately yours,   E. M. House

TLS (WP, DLC).

From Joseph Patrick Tumulty

                                                    The White House.
MEMORANDUM for the President: May 7, 1918.

Mrs. William Kent telephones to ask for an appointment for herself, Mrs. Wainwright and Mrs. Wiley[1] to see the President at his
earliest convenience to show the President a poll taken by them on
the suffrage bill, and to ask the President's help in lining up certain
doubtful Senators.

Dear Governor:

Mrs. Kent and her colleagues represent the National Women's
Party, the militant branch of the suffrage movement. Mrs. Catt,
Mrs. Gardener and the women of the other branch have been cooperating with the Administration in a most loyal way. It strikes
me that Mrs. Kent and her friends may be seeking certain notoriety
in asking for this appointment, and if it meets with your approval,
I will advise them that it is impossible for them to see you owing
to the pressure of other business, but that if they will send a memorandum I shall lay it before you.   J.P.T.

Approved W.W.

TL (WP, DLC).
    [1] Elizabeth Thacher (Mrs. William) Kent, "chairman" of the congressional committee
of the National American Woman Suffrage Association; Evelyn Wotherspoon (Mrs.
Richard) Wainwright; and Anna Campbell Kelton (Mrs. Harvey Washington) Wiley,
members of the National Woman's party.

From Thomas Riley Marshall

My dear Mr. President: Washington. May 7, 1918.

I have been thinking of seeking an interview with you upon a
subject which lies very close to my heart and which I think is of
vast moment to the American people. On mature deliberation, however, I have concluded to put the subject briefly in writing in order
to save you much time.

Throughout America today, under the Children's Bureau, there
is going forward the work of weighing and measuring and examining all children under six years of age. Statistics show that 300,000
of them die every year, and that, humanly speaking, with proper
advice, attention and care, one-half of this number can be saved.
This work is being done gratuitously all over the Republic and is
a very serious strain upon charitably disposed people.

When we are urged to subscribe the last dollar we have for Liberty
Bonds and to go in debt for more, to contribute to the Red Cross,

the Y.M.C.A. and the Knights of Columbus, then to buy tickets for every allied enterprise of interest to every kind hearted man and woman in America, I am quite sure you will understand that real sacrifices are being made by the people. The only question is whether they can keep it up.

Mrs. Marshall and other good women here in Washington are spending three hours a day three days of each week in the making of this health census under the auspices of the Washington Diet Kitchen. When this census is completed it will be about as valuable as a last year's bird's nest unless some plan is devised to follow it up to see that proper care and attention are given these children. It is doubtless true that throughout America where local self government still reigns, if it does anywhere, the duty is incumbent upon a locality to look after its children but in the City of Washington there is neither an autocracy nor a democracy. The District government can make no appropriation for the carrying on of this work without the consent of the Congress and the Congress is too much interested in the boll weevil and San Jose scale to appropriate for children. Nothing but your strong hand and forceful and emphatic approval of some appropriation to follow up this work will avail.

Have I put the subject so as to appeal to you? If so, will you touch the secret springs that will remedy this evil.

Very sincerely and cordially yours,   Thos. R. Marshall

TLS (WP, DLC).

From Richard Crane, with Enclosure

My dear Mr. President: [Washington] May 7th, 1918

I am enclosing a memorandum on Russia prepared by Professor Masaryk of Prague, who has just arrived in this country after a year in Russia. Professor Masaryk is recognized of Bohemians all over the world as their leader and father considers him the greatest living authority on Central Europe. This memo. was received by father just as he was leaving Washington and as he was most anxious to have it reach you as soon as possible he asked me to transmit it.

Faithfully yours   Richard Crane

ALS (WP, DLC).

E N C L O S U R E

PRIVATE AND CONFIDENTIAL. LETTER FROM PROFESSOR T. S. MA-
SARYK TO CHARLES R. CRANE.

April 10, 1918.

1. The Allies should recognize the Bolshevik Government (de facto, the de jure recognition not to be discussed); President Wilson's message to their Moscow meeting[1] was a step in this direction; being on good terms with the Bolsheviks the Allies can influence them. (I know the weak points of the Bolsheviks, but I also know the weak points of the other parties—they are not better nor more able).

2. The Monarchic movement is weak; the Allies must not support it. The Cadets and Social Revolutionists organize themselves against the Bolsheviks; I do not expect great success of these parties. The Allies expected that Alexjeff and Kerniloff[2] at the Don will have a great success; I did not believe it and refused to join them, though invited by the leaders. I say the same about Semenoff etc.

3. The Bolsheviks will maintain the power longer than their adversaries suppose; they will die, as all other parties, on political dilettantism—it is the curse of ts[a]rism, that it did not teach people to work, to administer. The Bolsheviks have been weakened by their failure in the peace negotiations and in the land questions, but on the other hand they are gaining sympathies, learning to work, and because of the weakness of the other parties.

4. I would think a Coalition government of the Socialist parties the left of the Cadets included could after some time gain the general support. (The Bolsheviks of course included).

5. A lasting democratic and republican government in Russia will exercise (through the Socialist and democrats) a great pressure on Prussia and Austria; that is the reason why the Germans and Austrians are against the Bolsheviks.

6. All small nations in the East (the Fin[n]s, Poles, E[s]thonians, Lethons,[3] Lithuanians, Bohemians, Slovaks, Romanians, etc.) need a strong Russia, else they be at the mercy of the Germans and Austrians. The Allies must support Russia at any rate and by all means. After conquering the East the Germans will conquer West.

---

[1] WW to the Fourth All-Russian Congress of Soviets, March 11, 1918, Vol. 46.
[2] That is, Gen. Mikhail Vasil'evich Alekseev, Chief of Staff to Nicholas II, 1915-1917, Supreme Commander (March-May 1917), and Chief of Staff to Kerensky (September 1917); and Gen. Lavr Georgievich Kornilov, former Commander in Chief of the Russian armies (August-September 1917), who had been killed on April 13, 1918. Alekseev and Kornilov had been the founders of the anti-Bolshevik Volunteer Army in early 1918.
[3] That is, Latvians.

7. An able government could induce the Ukrainians to be satisfied with an autonomous republic, forming a part of Russia; that was the original plan of the Ukrainians themselves, only later they proclaimed their independence. But an independent Ukrainia will be in fact a German or Austrian province; the Germans and Austrians follow with the Ukraine the same policy as with Poland.

8. It must be remembered that the South of Russia is the rich part of Russia (fertile soil, Black Sea-Donetz Basin etc.) the North is poor; Russian politics will gravitate towards the South.

9. The Allies must have a common plan respecting Russia; how to support her.

10. The Government of the Allies must not leave their functionaries in Russia without directions: in other words, the single Governments must have a clear plan respecting Russia.

11. The Japanese, I hope, will not be against Russia; that would suit the Germans and Austrians; on the contrary the Japanese should fight with the Allies, the chasm between Japan and Germany would be widened.

12. Nowhere in Siberia (15th of March-April 2nd) have I seen German and Austrian armed prisoners; in Siberia there is no greater anarchy than in Russia.

13. The Allies must fight the Germans and Austrians in Russia:
(a) Organize a company buying the grain (wheat etc.) and selling it where there is want of it: in doing so the Germans will be prevented from getting the grain. But the Russian (Ukrainian etc.) peasant will not sell his corn for money because it is useless to him, he wants manufactures, boots, clothes, soap, iron, implements, etc. As the Germans and Austrians have no manufactures the Allies have the best opportunity to occupy the Russian market. The plan requires only energy and organization, the capital put in the business will be returned.
(b) German and Austrian agents will flock into Russia—the necessary counter action must be organized (American etc. agents must bring samples—perhaps small (travelling) expositions of choice wares; illustrated catalogues Etc.)
(c) The Germans influence the Russian Press, not only by their special journalistic agents, but the German prisoners of war write in the various papers all over the country (not only in the big cities.) To some extent our Bohemian prisoners work against it, but the whole work must be organized.
(d) The Russian railways must be supported; without railways there will be no army, no industry etc.
(e) The Germans bought Russian securities to control in the future the industry.
(f) It is known that the Germans influenced the prisoners of war

(for instance preparing the Ukrainians prisoners for the Ukrainian army etc.)

(g) I succeeded in organizing in Russia out of our Bohemian and Slovak prisoners a corps of 50,000 men; I agreed with the French Government to send it now to France. The Allies can help to transport the army; they are excellent soldiers as they proved in the renewed offensive last June.

We can organize a second corps of the same amount; that must be done to prevent our prisoners returning to Austria, where they would be sent against the Allies to the Italian or French front.

The Allies agreed to procure the necessary means. In France we have a smaller corps also, partly sent from Russia partly formed of refugees; and I hope to form one in Italy too.

The political significance of a whole Bohemian army in France is evident; and I must acknowledge that France understood the political meaning of the matter from the very beginning and supported our national movement by all means. Minister Briand, was the first statesman who publicly promised to our nation the help of France and it was he who succeeded in inserting the Note to Wilson the explicit demand that the Czecho-Slovaks must be liberated.[4] (The Czecho-Slovaks are the most western Slav barrier against Germany and Austria.[)]

Under given circumstances 100,000—even 50,000 trained soldiers count.

14. My answer to the oft repeated question, whether there can be formed a Russian army: It could be formed in 6-9 months, say one million. The Red Guard is of no use and the Bolsheviks have already invited officers to join their army as instructors. (Railroads necessary for the army.)

Note: Today's Advertiser April 11th. brings this news:

(Clipping from Japan Advertiser)
Volunteers Drop Arms.

Slovaks Corps going to France intercepted by Trotzky.
Nokusai Vestnik Service.
Moscow, April 5.—As the result of an understanding between M. Trotzky and the French Ambassador, a corps of Slovak and Tschen volunteers who were leaving for France surrendered their arms to the authorities of the Soviets. The officers have been discharged with the exception of General Diterichs,[5] who was accompanying the corps to France.

---

[4] That is, in the reply of the Allies to Wilson's peace note of December 18, 1916, printed in W. G. Sharp to RL, Jan. 10, 1917, Vol. 40.

[5] Mikhail Konstantinovich Dietrichs, former Quartermaster General of the Russian army, who had been appointed by Masaryk as the Chief of Staff of the Czech corps in Russia.

This very favorable: the corps is going to France, they need not have their rifles as they will be armed in France; the officers mentioned are the Russian officers, who joined our army.[6]

TCL (WP, DLC).
    [6] An edited version of this memorandum is printed in Thomas G. Masaryk, *The Making of a State: Memories and Observations, 1914-1918*, ed., Henry Wickham Steed (London, 1927), pp. 192-95.

Shane Leslie to Joseph Patrick Tumulty

Confidential

Dear Mr Tumulty,   Washington May 7 1918

Some leading Sinn Feiners in this country have given some of us an understanding that Freedom or free institutions in Ireland should or would be followed by placing the weight of Ireland in the Allied scales. At this juncture federal proceedings against any of their number would be unwise.

                    I remain your obedt. servant   Shane Leslie

TLS (WP, DLC).

Arthur James Balfour to Lord Reading

[London, May 7, 1918]

No. 2788. I have had under review situation in Mexico as it appears in light of recent tels: from yourself and H. M. Representative in Mexico.[1] You are well aware that H.M.G. have for many months had strong grounds for believing that German influence over Carranza has been used to bring about ultimately

1. War between U. S. and Mexico for the purpose of diverting to a Mexican campaign troops which would otherwise be available for Western front and

2. Interruption of supply of oil for allied fleets. H.M.G. believe these are real dangers.

Germans would have much to gain and little to lose by serious attempt to impede flow of men and oil to Europe at present juncture. To this end they are doubtless making most of military situation in Europe[2] and misrepresenting it to our prejudice. On the other hand Carranza might well hesitate before challenging a conflict with U.S.G. at a moment when they have a large army in process of formation.

Possibly greater danger lies in provocation by unscrupulous German agents of some grave incident such as massacre of U. S.

citizens in hope of exciting Press of America[3] to such an extent as to necessitate despatch of large punitive expedition.

There is sufficient risk in situation as to cause me considerable uneasiness in absence of fuller knowledge of President's views and intentions.

It has been suggested that best means of counteracting offensive measures on the part of Carranza would be to give active support to revolutionary leaders and possibly to encourage a diversion on the part of Guatemala but I am loth to take any action which might run counter to President's policy.

As not only large British interests are involved but those of Allies I should be glad should you see no objection if you would take any opportunity of discussing question in all its bearings with President and of endeavouring to ascertain his views.

T telegram (FO 115/2413, pp. 411-12).
[1] Herbert Ashley Cunard Cummins, British Chargé d'Affaires in Mexico City.
[2] "France" in A. J. Balfour to Lord Reading, No. 2788, May 7, 1918, T telegram (FO 371/3244, pp. 187-88, PRO).
[3] "public opinion in America" in *ibid*.

To Charles Evans Hughes, with Enclosure

Personal.

My dear Mr. Hughes: The White House 8 May, 1918

Your letter of May sixth about the celebration of the twenty-fourth of May, the date of the entrance of Italy into the war, has interested me very much, and I will be very glad indeed to do what I can to cooperate in marking the day in some special way.

The way that would first occur to me would be to issue a proclamation requesting the general celebration of the day, or its general observance, in some dignified way, but when I reflect upon the possible feeling of the other nations who are associated with us in the war and whose entrance into it has not been celebrated in any particular way, I feel that, on the whole, that course would not be wise.

I understand that you are going to preside at the meeting which the Italy America Society is planning for the twenty-fourth, and I take pleasure in enclosing a letter which I would be very much obliged if you would be kind enough to read to those then assembled. I shall direct that the Italian flag be displayed on all public buildings on that day, and I shall try through the Bureau of Public Information to spread as widely as possible the suggestion that the day be marked in the several communities of the country in some special way.   Very sincerely yours,   Woodrow Wilson

E N C L O S U R E

To Charles Evans Hughes

My dear Mr. Hughes: The White House 8 May, 1918

Will you not convey to those assembled on the twenty-fourth of May this expression of my regret that I cannot be present in order to express in person my feeling of admiration for the great Italian people who are engaged with us in the great struggle now going forward for securing the rights of free men? The friendship of America for Italy has always been deep and cordial. We have welcomed to this country with a very genuine welcome millions of Italians who have added their labor and genius to the richness of American life, and this new association with the Italian people in a struggle which has given to men everywhere the sense of community of interest and comradeship of right more intensely than they ever had it before, will serve to strengthen that friendship still more and crown the many happy recollections of the association of the two countries in thought and feeling. I am sure that I express the sentiment of the whole country when I thus express my admiration for Italy and my hope that increasingly, in the days to come, we may be enabled to prove our friendship in every substantial way.   Sincerely yours,   Woodrow Wilson

TLS (C. E. Hughes Papers, DLC).

To Newton Diehl Baker

My dear Baker: The White House 8 May, 1918

I dare say that it will be possible, will it not, to let the Attorney General have copies of Borglum's so-called reports and of the Marshall report, for the guidance of those to whom he has assigned the duty of looking into the charges of malfeasance? If this can be arranged without putting your force to the trouble of making copies, I would be very much obliged.

Cordially and faithfully yours,   Woodrow Wilson

TLS (N. D. Baker Papers, DLC).

To Robert Lansing, with Enclosure

My dear Mr. Secretary: The White House 8 May, 1918

I send you the enclosed letter from Mr. Louis Marshall merely to ask your opinion as to whether it would be possible to extend the limit referred to for the sake of the Jews outside of Poland.

Faithfully yours,   Woodrow Wilson

E N C L O S U R E

From Louis Marshall

Dear Mr. President: New York May 4, 1918.

It is only because of imperative necessity that I venture to present to you facts, which I am confident will arouse your sympathy, on behalf of the Jews of Poland, Lithuania and Courland, now dwelling in territory in German and Austrian occupation.

Since 1914 there have been in the United States three societies organized by Jews, engaged in the collection of funds for the relief of their co-religionists in the war zones. They are the American Jewish Relief Committee, of which I have the honor to be the President, the Central Relief Committee and the Peoples Relief Committee. These societies have but one distributing agency, known as the Joint Distribution Committee, of which Mr. Felix M. Warburg, of Kuhn, Loeb & Company, is the Chairman. Since our country entered into the war the relief funds intended for the Jews of Poland in the occupied districts, have been distributed through a committee formed in Holland, with the sanction of the Dutch Government, and the moneys forwarded to this Dutch organization, with the sanction of the State Department, have been distributed through the consular representative of the Dutch Government in Warsaw.

From time to time the War Trade Board has granted licenses specifying the amount which may be forwarded from here for Polish relief for distribution through the agency indicated. These orders, as I am informed, have been made after consultation with the State Department. In December, 1917, the War Trade Board fixed the amount that might be sent at $500,000 monthly. In January there was an increase to $600,000, and in February a further increase to $800,000. Of this last amount the Joint Distribution Committee was permitted to forward $600,000, the other organizations which were to share in the privileges, through lack of funds, being able to send but $200,000. The total amount which the Joint Distribution

Committee was thus enabled to send during the months of February and March, 1918, was approximately $1,100,000.

On March 18, 1918, the State Department notified the War Trade Board that, under your instructions, the total amount thereafter to be sent monthly to Poland was to be limited to $300,000. Of this sum $100,000 were to be used exclusively for individual remittances and $200,000 for general relief. The latter sum has been apportioned between the Joint Distribution Committee and the Polish Victims Committee. Owing to the fact that the funds available to the latter organization do not exceed from $25,000 to $30,000 monthly, the right to send the remainder of the $200,000 has been accorded to the Joint Distribution Committee.

It is believed that this reduction of the amount that may be sent to Poland is due to the promulgation of an order by the War Trade Board to the effect that hereafter no relief funds may be sent into Lithuania or Courland, and that the reason for this order lies in the fact that information has been received by the State Department that Germany is seeking to establish an independent government in Lithuania, that the inhabitants of Lithuania have declared themselves in favor of the German project, and are actually contributing funds to enable it to carry on war. The same conditions are said to exist in Courland.

It is obvious that the unfortunate Jews of Lithuania and Courland, who are entirely destitute of the most elemental necessaries of life, who are actually starving, could not possibly make contributions to Germany. Indeed, Germany may be regarded as their most virulent foe. Nor is it conceivable that any of the inhabitants of Lithuania would, except under duress, pay tribute to Germany. In their abject poverty and misery, the Jews of Lithuania and Courland have nobody to look to for help but their brethren in America. If the latter are not permitted to afford succor in this extremity of woe, the extermination of the greater part of these innocent sufferers, men, women and children, is likely to ensue.

However shocking the alternative, I can assure you that if the best interests of our country can only be promoted by the withholding of relief from these victims of oppression, as loyal American citizens we would recognize it as our duty to submit to consequences without a murmur, but we earnestly implore you to cause such further investigation to be made into the condition in which these unfortunates find themselves, to the end that we may be enabled, under such safeguards as can be devised, to continue our ministrations to their needs.

Very sincerely yours,   Louis Marshall

TLS (SDR, RG 59, 860C.48/83, DNA).

To William Bauchop Wilson, with Enclosure

My dear Mr. Secretary: The White House 8 May, 1918

I have no hesitation in accepting the enclosed list, which I return
to you, though I must confess to some regret that we could not use
from the other list at least Mr. Matthew Hale and Mr. Henry Ford.
Henry Ford's attitude towards his own employees has been so widely
known to be generous and disinterested that I don't think any
suspicion of partiality would attach to him, and I assume that the
same is true of Mr. Matthew Hale, but if in your judgment these
two gentlemen cannot with advantage to the general plan be substituted for any two of those whom you suggest, I am perfectly
content to abide by your judgment.

Cordially and sincerely yours,   Woodrow Wilson

TLS (LDR, RG 174, DNA).

E N C L O S U R E

From William Bauchop Wilson

My dear Mr. President: Washington May 7, 1918.

Referring to paragraph (d) of the report of the War Labor Conference Board,[1] which provides:

"The members of the National Board shall choose the umpire
by unanimous vote. Failing such choice, the name of the umpire
shall be drawn by lot from a list of 10 suitable and disinterested
persons to be nominated for the purpose by the President of the
United States,"

I have given careful consideration to a number of names that have
been presented for the position of umpire, and of those suggested
the following list seems to me to best conform to the description of
suitable and disinterested persons: James H. Covington, Charles
C. McChord, V. Everit Macy, Julian W. Mack, Henry Suzzallo, John
Lind, William R. Willcox, Walter Clark, Rowland B. Mahany and
Hywel Davies.[2] I am inclosing herewith a brief memorandum relative to each.[3]

Among the names which have been brought to my attention are
Secretaries Lane and Redfield and Mr. Justice Brandeis. I have
assumed that their official duties would make it impossible for them
to devote their attention to this work.

Messrs. H. B. Endicott, Matthew Hale, Louis Kirstein, J. Frank
McElwain, William O. Thompson, Henry Ford and A. A. Landon[4]
are each large employers of labor, and while excellent types of men
who might be very properly agreed upon, in case selection is to be

made by lot the possibility that they might be considered as interested has to be guarded against. That statement would apply to Mr. John B. Lennon,[5] who was for twenty years Treasurer of the American Federation of Labor.

Messrs. Emory R. Buckner, Leon Marshall and E. W. Lewis[6] are each clean-cut, upstanding men, but are not sufficiently well known to give general assurance of their courage and fairness. Judge Alschuler has done a splendid piece of work in the packing house industry, and he should not be taken away from the work which he has now well in hand.

I have not asked any of these men whether or not they would accept, but will be glad to do so if you decide upon their selection.

Faithfully yours, W B Wilson

TLS (WP, DLC).

[1] It is printed as Enclosure II with WBW to WW, April 4, 1918.

[2] Persons not hitherto identified in this series were Julian William Mack, a judge on the United States circuit court and chairman of the section on the compensation of soldiers and sailors and their dependents of the committee on labor of the Council of National Defense; and Walter Clark, Chief Justice of the Supreme Court of North Carolina since 1903.

[3] The enclosure is missing.

[4] Persons not heretofore identified were Louis Edward Kirstein, vice-president of William Filene's Sons Co. of Boston, and director of several other retail companies in Boston and Rochester; James Franklin McElwain, president of the W. H. McElwain Co., shoe manufacturers, and chief of the shoe, leather, and rubber division of the Quartermaster Bureau of the War Department; William Ormonde Thompson, president of the American Cotton Oil Co., former member of the board of arbitration for the New York cloak industry, and former counsel for the United States Commission on Industrial Relations; and Archer A. Landon, vice-president of the American Radiator Co. of Buffalo and, much earlier, president of the associated labor unions of Detroit.

[5] At this time a mediator for the Department of Labor.

[6] Persons not hitherto identified were Emory Roy Buckner, former assistant district attorney for New York County, and Leon Carroll Marshall, chairman of the Department of Political Economy of the University of Chicago, chief of the section on industrial service of the Council of National Defense, secretary of the Advisory Council of the Department of Labor, and director of industrial relations for the Emergency Fleet Corporation.

To Herbert Clark Hoover

My dear Mr. Hoover: The White House 8 May, 1918

A good deal of embarrassment and dislocation in the administrative business of the Government has been caused by the transfer of clerks and specialists of one sort or another from the older and longer established departments to the new instrumentalities which have necessarily been created or greatly enlarged since this country entered the war, and I take the liberty of calling your attention to the fact, because it has often happened that employees of the older departments have been drawn away by offers of considerable increases of pay, to the very serious embarrassment, and sometimes to the serious weakening, of the departments which they were induced to leave. All this has been a very natural process. There have in fact not been trained men enough to go around, but I thought I might venture to speak of this to you, because I was sure your judgment would agree with mine that this process ought to be avoided wherever it is avoidable, and the new activities recruited from outside Washington. I write, therefore, to beg for your cooperation in seeing that we all act as a single family in this matter and restrain our subordinates from poaching in each other's preserves wherever it is possible to restrain them.[1]

Cordially and sincerely yours,   Woodrow Wilson

TLS (H. Hoover Papers, HPL).
[1] Wilson wrote the same letter, on the same day, *mutatis mutandis,* to H. A. Garfield, TLS (H. A. Garfield Papers, DLC); and to W. J. Harris, J. D. Ryan, B. M. Baruch, V. C. McCormick, and E. N. Hurley, all TLS (Letterpress Books, WP, DLC).

To Samuel Huston Thompson, Jr.

My dear Thompson: [The White House] 8 May, 1918

You are kind enough to say in your letter of May sixth that you don't want me to take the trouble to reply to it, but I would be missing a pleasure if I did not, because that letter has warmed my heart mightily and brought me very great encouragement and I must at least send you this scanty line of warm appreciation that you should remember to cheer me up in this way.

Cordially and sincerely yours,   Woodrow Wilson

TLS (Letterpress Books, WP, DLC).

To Herbert Welsh[1]

My dear Mr. Welsh: [The White House] 8 May, 1918

I have your letter of May sixth enclosing the letter to you from Mr. William R. Bricker.[2] What Mr. Bricker proposes interests me very much and I need hardly say has my cordial approval. I believe that by such means a vast deal of the unjust suspicion which has rested upon some classes of our fellow-citizens may be effectually removed and their genuine loyalty and devotion brought into high relief.   Sincerely yours,   Woodrow Wilson

TLS (Letterpress Books, WP, DLC).
[1] Philadelphia artist and publicist; president of the Indian Rights Association, a leader of the movement for municipal reform in Philadelphia, and an advocate of universal peace through international arbitration.
[2] H. Welsh to WW, May 6, 1918, enclosing W. R. Bricker to W. Welsh, May 6, 1918, both TLS (WP, DLC). Bricker, a lawyer and real estate agent of Philadelphia and a

member of the advisory council of the Friends of German Democracy, informed Welsh that, upon Welsh's request, he had consulted several of the larger German-American societies of Philadelphia about their participation in a loyalty meeting which was to be held under the auspices of the Friends of German Democracy on May 15. The societies which Bricker had approached had told him that, since America's entry into the war, they had deliberately kept a very low profile in order to avoid adverse criticism of their activities. However, Bricker continued, they would welcome an opportunity to break their silence and speak out in loyal support of the government if they could be assured that the government would approve. If such approval could be secured, Bricker concluded, it would help greatly in arousing enthusiasm for the war among a large and influential group of citizens who had so far been perfectly loyal but not very outspoken. In forwarding Bricker's letter to Wilson, Welsh asked Wilson to lend his support to the proposed meeting and the participation of the German-American societies of Philadelphia.

To Thomas Riley Marshall

My dear Mr. Vice President: [The White House] 8 May, 1918

You are always considerate and I appreciate your motive in writing me your letter of yesterday instead of seeking an interview about the very important matter which it concerns, at the same time that I regret having missed the pleasure of seeing you.

I appreciate the vital importance of the subject to which you call my attention and will seek to find out what channels I can best act through in trying to bring the matter to the favorable attention of the Congress.

In haste, with warm regard,

Sincerely yours,   Woodrow Wilson

TLS (Letterpress Books, WP, DLC).

To Albert Sidney Burleson

My dear Burleson: The White House 8 May, 1918

I am in warm sympathy with what the Vice President proposes in the enclosed letter, but I don't know how to go about acting in the matter because I don't know what committee of the House would have charge of it. Would it be the District Committee?

Cordially and faithfully yours,   Woodrow Wilson

TLS (A. S. Burleson Papers, DLC).

To John Sharp Williams

My dear Senator: The White House 8 May, 1918

Thank you for your letter of May sixth.[1] I have the same sympathy with the Bohemians that you have and you may be sure I will speak sympathetically to them if I have the opportunity.

In great haste   Faithfully yours,   Woodrow Wilson

TLS (J. S. Williams Papers, DLC).
  [1] J. S. Williams to WW, May 6, 1918, TLS (WP, DLC).

To Grosvenor Blaine Clarkson

My dear Mr. Clarkson: [The White House] 8 May, 1918

Thank you very much for your letter of May sixth [fifth] with its enclosures. I have read the enclosures with real interest and shall be glad to take counsel concerning the suggestions they contain.

Cordially and sincerely yours,   Woodrow Wilson

TLS (Letterpress Books, WP, DLC).

From Charles Richard Crane

Dear Mr President   Washington, D. C. May 8 1918

I hope you can set aside a little time for a talk with Professor Masaryk. He is the wisest and most influential Slav of our day and probably only a Slav of such dimensions could fully understand and sympathize with what you are trying to do. I believe that he could materially aid you in a technical way with your world program. Otherwise I should not ask you.

With affectionate messages
Yours always sincerely   Charles R. Crane[1]

ALS (WP, DLC).
  [1] "Dear Tumulty: Mr. Crane's son sent me a memorandum which had been prepared by this gentleman which I read with the closest attention. I wish you would tell Mr. Crane this and tell him that I do not think I ought to attempt an interview unless something material can be added to what the memorandum contained. The President." WW to JPT, c. May 10, 1918, TL (WP, DLC). Tumulty read this message to Richard Crane, who passed it on to his father.

From William Gibbs McAdoo, with Enclosure

My dear Mr. President: Washington May 8, 1918.

I send you herewith copy of a letter I have just sent to Senator Simmons. Nothing is more imperative than new revenue legislation at this session of the Congress. I have been unable to take up the matter before. The War and Navy Departments and the Shipping Board have been changing their estimates so often that I have been unable to keep up with them, and I also felt that it was necessary to get the Liberty Loan out of the way before considering the question of new taxation. As I understand it, Congress is anxious to avoid new revenue legislation at this time, but it is unescapable. Unless this matter is dealt with now firmly and satisfactorily, we shall invite disaster in 1919. I think it will be necessary for you, at the proper time, to deliver a special message to the Congress on the question of new revenue legislation.

The way in which the estimates are climbing is appalling, but we must find a way, if possible, to meet the situation.

I am feeling better today and hope to get out Friday,

Affectionately yours,   W G McAdoo

TLS (WP, DLC).

E N C L O S U R E

William Gibbs McAdoo to Furnifold McLendel Simmons

PERSONAL.

My dear Senator: [Washington] May 8, 1918.

I have just read with great regret the statement attributed to you in the New York Sun of May 6, to the effect that there would be no new revenue legislation at this session of the Congress. I hope that you were incorrectly quoted. In view of the large additional estimates which I understand will be submitted by the War and Navy Departments and the Shipping Board, to say nothing of other branches of the service, and in view of the position of the Treasury, nothing is more imperative than new revenue legislation at this session of the Congress. I am preparing a memorandum on the subject for Mr. Kitchin and shall be glad to send you a copy as soon as it is completed.

I am sorry to be laid up at my house with a very bad throat, and that the Doctor has ordered that I shall not see anyone at present; otherwise I should ask you to come up. I hope to see you soon.

With best wishes, I am

Cordially yours,   [W G McAdoo]

CCL (WP, DLC).

From Newton Diehl Baker, with Enclosure

Dear Mr. President: Washington. May 8, 1918.

I enclose a letter from General Bliss and have made a copy of the first portion which I wanted to read to the French Ambassador, so that you need not return this until it is entirely at your own convenience. I am sending it because of the discussion of the Dutch situation.   Respectfully yours,   Newton D. Baker

TLS (WP, DLC).

ENCLOSURE

Tasker Howard Bliss to Newton Diehl Baker

Dear Mr. Secretary: Versailles. April 27, 1918.

On Thursday night, and again on Friday morning, I received an urgent request from General Foch to go to his Headquarters in order to have a conference on Friday night with himself and General Pershing. I left here at noon and it required six hours to make the trip which ordinarily could be done in 2½. The roads were encumbered with countless ammunition and supply motor trains, hospital trains, etc., all moving toward the battlefield. I had taken a very round-about way, much further to the West than on any of the previous trips I have made to General Foch's Headquarters, but it seems impossible at this stage of the game to get beyond the region of moving troops and supply trains.

The Conference illustrated one of the peculiarities of the French mind. Their military men seem unwilling to act except upon a definite agreement drawn up in black and white, with every "i" dotted and every "t" crossed, and then signed. General Foch has noted that the Resolution of the Supreme War Council, approved by our President, relating to the sending of American infantry, says that this movement is to continue only while the emergency demands it. General Foch is convinced that the emergency will last until at least the end of July. The object of his Conference was to get General Pershing to accept this view and to agree that American infantry should have precedence, to the exclusion of all other units, until at least that date. As this was a matter which concerned General Pershing alone, I said nothing. After a long discussion without, apparently, getting anywhere, General Foch appealed to me as to what the Military Representatives meant when they prepared the Joint Note in regard to the movement of American infantry. I replied that they meant just what the Resolution said, to-wit: that in view of the existing emergency American infantry should have precedence in transportation to France, with the assumption that this movement would continue as long as the emergency continued. I said that so far as I could see he and General Pershing were in substantial accord except as to a mere form of words which did not in reality amount to anything; that he, General Foch, wanted General Pershing to agree that the emergency would last to at least a fixed date, which General Pershing was unwilling to do because no one could tell what might happen to-morrow that would relieve the emergency; that, he, General Pershing, agreed that the movement should continue as long as the emergency existed; in other words, that General Pershing was, in reality, more liberal in his view than General Foch demanded, because General Pershing's attitude was that the movement should continue as long as the emergency lasted, even if it lasted longer than the month of July; and that he, General Foch, had secured an understanding with General Pershing that went even further than General Foch had asked. The Conference broke up with, apparently, that general understanding.

The two principal things that have occupied the attention of the Military Representatives during this past week are the following:

(1½) The British War Cabinet has asked the Military Representatives for its recommendation as to the attitude that should be taken by Great Britain with respect to Holland in view of the following. It appears that Germany has made the following demands on Holland, through their Minister at the Hague:

(1)   New boots, clothes, etc., taken from Holland by prisoners transferred from Germany to be allowed to pass the frontier more freely;

(2)   Civilian goods to be given free transit over the Limberg railway into Belgium;

(3)   Holland to recognize the right of Germany to transport every class of commodity in accordance with the terms of the Rhine Convention;

(4)   The transit, without any restriction, of sand and gravel to Belgium, via Lobith to be resumed. Germany to be prepared to send up to 200,000 tons a month and 250,000 tons a month to be exported from Holland to Belgium;

(5)   Troops and ammunition to be given free passage over the Limberg Railway.

It is said that the German Minister has not communicated the 5th demand as yet, because he is opposed to the policy which dictates this demand. It appears that the first two demands have been accepted. The British War Cabinet wants to know whether

Holland should be advised by the Allies (1) to submit to the German demands, or, (2) to resist even to the point of war. We are to decide to-day on the following suggested opinion of the Military Representatives:

"The Military Representatives having considered the above question are of opinion that:

  (i) The interests of the Allies are best served by Holland remaining neutral.

  (ii) The vital interests of the Allies are:

    (a) To prevent large quantities of material such as rubber, food, fats, etc. from falling into German hands;

    (b) To prevent any part of the coast of Holland which can be used in any way as naval bases from being made available for German naval enterprises.

"With these conditions in view the Military Representatives are of opinion that Holland should be advised not to go to war with Germany unless the Central Powers attempt to violate that part of Holland which lies west of the New Holland Water line of defenses and inundation which stretches from LOEVESTEIN on the MAAS through UTRECHT to MUIDEN."

The second thing that we have been considering is the utilization of the 45,000 to 60,000 Czech troops in Russian and Western Siberia who were on their way to ports of Eastern Siberia. The general view of the Military Representatives is that it is still possible to make arrangements with the Russian Government by which these troops (who will not fight with Russia but who will fight with the other Allies against Germany) shall be transported to Archangel and Mourmansk, thence to be carried by water to the Western Front. Personally, I think that now the question has been put up (by the British Government) the above is about the only answer that we can make, although I doubt whether much material result will come from it.

Later: After a prolonged discussion this morning the Military Representatives decided that it was not appropriate for them, at this juncture, to adopt a Joint Note to the four Governments on the Dutch question put up to us by the British War Cabinet. We agreed on a presentation of the "pros" and "cons" in a statement addressed to our British colleague, General Sackville-West.[1] This presentation of "pros" and "cons" leads to the natural inference that it is better under present conditions for the Allies, if Holland can preserve her neutrality and have it respected by Germany, even though the latter makes use of the Limberg Railway. If the British Government, after receipt of the letter from General Sackville-West chooses to take the matter up through diplomatic channels with the other Governments (she may have already done so, but we do not know it), she will do so. I shall advise you later of the terms of General Sackville-West's letter.

We are looking forward to your return to France according to the desire expressed by you while here.

Sincerely yours,   Tasker H. Bliss.

TLS (WP, DLC).
¹ Maj. Gen. Charles John Sackville-West, the British military representative on the Supreme War Council since April 11, 1918.

From Newton Diehl Baker, with Enclosure

Dear Mr. President: Washington. May 8, 1918.

I enclose a dispatch which has just come from General Pershing, and which is the last chapter of the conference and agreement about the shipment of troops.

The second paragraph of General Pershing's dispatch I am sure will surprise you, as General Pershing was not in favor of sending troops to Italy when I talked to him about the matter. Apparently, however, the concurrence of Mr. Clemenceau and Mr. Lloyd George, with Mr. Orlando's representations, overcame his feeling in the matter. My own disposition in the situation is to acquiesce in whatever arrangements they feel necessary to make there, because the maintenance of Italian morale is of course of the very greatest importance, and we on this side are never quite in possession of all the information they have over there as to either the need for stimulation of morale or what what [sic] will suffice to do the stimulating. In the meantime, I sent General Pershing a cablegram a day or two ago, suggesting the brigading of some of our troops with British and French divisions in Italy as a possible answer to the whole question. I have not had any reply from him on that subject, and do not know whether the dispatch I am enclosing was sent before or after he received my cablegram.

Respectfully yours,   Newton D. Baker

TLS (WP, DLC).

ENCLOSURE

Received at the War Department, Washington, D. C.,
May 7, 1918, 6:23 A.M.

From GHQAEF To The Adjutant General, Washington.
Number 1064, May 6th, Confidential.
For the Chief of Staff and Secretary of War.

Paragraph 1. Reference conference of Supreme War Council at Abbeville May 2nd, agreement between Lord Milner and myself seems to have displeased the French notwithstanding their previous approval in February of our sending 6 divisions for training with the British. London agreement was principal question of discussion at Supreme War Council. French insisted upon commitment for jurisdiction for exclusive infantry program and would not accept condition London agreement that infantry would be continued for *June* should situation still appear critical. British were entirely satisfied with London agreement and were willing that decision regarding June program be left until later. After rather warm discussion between the French on one side and the British and ourselves on the other, Mr. Lloyd George proposed to guarantee to transport 130 thousand in May and 150,000 in June by British tonnage alone. As this offered opportunity for great increase arrival American troops and arrangement for May was already made, seemed wise to accept British guarantee and extend Infantry program for infantry of 6 divisions during June and my memorandum was drawn accordingly. Mr. Lloyd George later proposed that shipment of extra personnel in excess of 150,000 by British shipment for June should be infantry on condition that British should assist us in July to make up other deficiencies caused thereby to which I agreed. This latter promise by British was not part of my memorandum but was agreed to verbally. The conference ended in good feeling and satisfaction all around and will have good effect on Allies. Also it is believed that question is now settled definitely.

Paragraph 2. Reference conference with Secretary of War regarding sending small number of troops to Italy, had conference with Mr. Orlando and outlined proposed plan of sending not more than one regiment to begin with and possibly gradually increasing number during succeeding four or five months up to a division, upon the condition that the Italians furnish transportation which Mr. Orlando thinks can be done. The Italians are immensely pleased over the prospect and the proposition is cordially approved by Mr. Clemenceau and Mr. Lloyd George. Am awaiting cable from Mr. Orlando in regard to transportation before taking any further action.

Paragraph 3. Had further conference at Abbeville with Mr. Clemenceau, Mr. Lloyd George and Mr. Orlando on the subject of pooling supplies, and a military man of business experience has been selected by each government to meet on May 6th to outline plans. The suggestion seems to appeal to all concerned. Believe that considerable can be accomplished although it may not be *possible* to extend it as far as would be desirable. Believe the plans offer no serious obstacles. It simply means that each army will share surplus supplies with other, and that general stock will be regulated not by each army for itself but by this executive committee for all. Will keep advised routine work as matter progresses.

Pershing.

T telegram (WP, DLC).

From Robert Lansing, with Enclosure

My dear Mr. President: Washington May 8, 1918.

You have undoubtedly read the enclosed message from General Bliss giving the opinion of the Supreme War Council that we should declare war against Turkey but not at present against Bulgaria. From the fact that it is signed by Sackville-West I assume that it represents in substance the views of the British Government. As you have also seen the Italian Government favors a declaration against both, and I have been unofficially advised that the French Government holds the same view. I think that we may assume, therefore, that all the Entente Powers favor a declaration against Turkey, but that Great Britain thinks that it would be wise to delay action against Bulgaria and that is also Bliss' opinion.

In considering these replies I think that we should observe the failure to recognize the humanitarian side of the question. Thousands of Armenians and Syrians are being kept alive today by the distribution of supplies purchased through funds sent to our missionaries in Turkey, which amount to one or two millions of dollars a month. If a state of war is declared that relief will come to an end, our missionaries will be expelled or interned and the great missionary properties will be confiscated. I am not arguing the undesirability of a declaration but only pointing out the consequences which appear to have been ignored, possibly through ignorance, by the Supreme War Council and the Governments which have given their opinion. Their point of view seems to have been entirely military and their opinion based practically on the encouragement of resistence by the Georgians, Caucasians and others to the Turkish advance in the Caucasus and upper Euphrates. Whether that is sufficient aid in winning the war must be decided.

In any event the time has arrived when a definite policy for or against a declaration against the Turks must be formulated as the Senate Committee will expect guidance in regard to the resolution before them. Furthermore I think nothing can be gained now by delay in reaching a decision.

In regard to our attitude toward Bulgaria Great Britain seems disposed to have us postpone action until we have seen the effect upon that country of a declaration against Turkey. I see the possible strategic advantage to be gained by such a course, but I am not at all sure that the Committee will, and I am not at all sure that British diplomacy is now more adroit than it has been previously in dealing with the Balkan situation.

It has been my impression that the chief advantage to be gained by declaring war against the two Governments which we are considering was the effect that a declaration against Bulgaria would have upon the Greeks and Serbs; and that the peculiar reason for a declaration against Turkey was that war against a Christian nation without war against a Moslem nation would cause general criticism in this country and possibly could not be prevented in view of the temper of the Senate. Undoubtedly the presence of the Bulgarian Minister[1] in this capital has been one of the principal reasons for the present agitation, and I do not think that we can ignore it.

I think that I should add that an argument against any declaration has undoubtedly weighed with some of the Committee in that neither Turkey nor Bulgaria have committed acts of war against this country since the declaration against Austria-Hungary. In view of this fact, what plausible reasons could be urged for a change of policy at the present time? In this connection would not it be said with reason by Germany that we had not declared war against Turkey or Bulgaria because we hoped to separate them from the Central Powers and that having failed in our diplomacy we had abandoned the effort and purposed to coerce them? This might possibly encourage the Germans and subject us to their ridicule.

As I expect any day to be asked to appear again before the Senate Committee and tell them of the views of the other Governments and of the War Council, I would like to be advised what I shall say to them.

The following courses seem open:

1. No declaration against either country on the ground that we could not declare war against Bulgaria without declaring against Turkey, and that to declare against Turkey would be to remove the protection and relief which we have furnished to thousands of refugees in Turkey.

2. A declaration against Turkey alone, on the ground that it would

encourage the resistence in the regions of the Caucasus, and would constitute a threat to Bulgaria which would bring her to terms.

3. A declaration against Turkey and a severence of diplomatic relations with Bulgaria which would emphasize the threat as to the future.

4. A declaration against both Turkey and Bulgaria on the ground that every nation which is an ally of Germany should be classed as a foe.

I do not include as an alternative a declaration against Bulgaria alone because I think that the Committee would be radically opposed to that action.

If you would be good enough to indicate the attitude which you think that I should take with the Committee I would be greatly obliged.   Faithfully yours,   Robert Lansing

TLS (WP, DLC).
    ¹ Stephan Panaretoff.

ENCLOSURE

Paris May 7, 1918

3825. The following is the reply of General Bliss to your 3831: "Immediately after receipt by me of the State Department telegram 3831, I submitted the subject of it in conference to my colleagues and after careful consideration we agreed to the following joint recommendation."

One. In reply to the question submitted by the American military representative at the instance of his Government as to whether it would be advisable for the United States to declare that a state of war exists at the present time between the United States and both the Ottoman Empire and Bulgaria or either of them, the majority representatives after considering the subject from a military standpoint agree to the following joint recommendation.

A. An immediate declaration that a state of war exists between the United States and the Ottoman Empire is desirable through their representatives.

B. In view of the moral effect upon Bulgaria of the above action, it is advisable to oppose a declaration that a state of war exists between the United States and Bulgaria until it shall have been found impossible by diplomatic negotiation to detach the latter country from her alliance with the Central Powers, but a limit should be placed upon the time allowed her for consideration of this subject, to be immediately followed by a declaration of a state of war should she within that time limit fail to take satisfactory action.

C. It is distinctly understood, however, that no situation resulting from a declaration of the existence of a state of war between the United States, on the one hand, and Ottoman Empire or Bulgaria or both of, on the other, shall be allowed to divert any American troops from the western front which is in need of, and will be in need of, every man that the United States can send to it until the situation on that front is radically changed.

Two. Although it is imperative that the United States permit no diversion of the assistance desired by the Allies on the Western front, the military representatives are of opinion that the following military advantage would result from the action recommended above:

One. The moral effect and influence on the peoples of these countries that would follow such a declaration, in the case of the Ottoman Empire and subsequently if necessary in the case of Bulgaria, showing the Allies to be really in unison in every theater of the war.

Two. The fact that this declaration would enable the United States to participate in the eastern theater and cooperate there with her Allies, should opportunity offer; which she cannot do under present conditions and which the necessity for legislative action might prevent her from doing in their opinion, should the declaration be left until the emergency presents itself.

Three. Those elements of the peoples of the middle east who, owing to the uncertainty of the situation, are now hesitating to put forth strong efforts against the Turks will be encouraged to throw in their lot decidedly with the Entente Powers when they find that the vast potential power of the United States is now to be opposed to the Government of the Ottoman Empire. Signed by Generals (?), Sackville-West, Serpigo *Bilant*,[1] and Bliss.   Sharp.

T telegram (WP, DLC).

[1] That is, Gen. Emile Eugène Belin, former First Assistant Chief of Staff of the French army, who had been appointed as the French military representative on the Supreme War Council on April 19, 1918, and Gen. Count Mario Nicolis di Robilant, former commander of the fourth Italian army, now Italy's military representative on the Supreme War Council.

From Joseph Patrick Tumulty

Dear Governor: The White House. 8 May 1918.

Mrs. Catt was in to see me this morning. She is greatly worried about the suffrage situation and asked me to send the following telegram to Senator James, which I am reluctant to do without your consent:

"It is absolutely necessary that you be not paired on the suffrage amendment."

They also informed me that Senator Martin is using every influence possible to defeat the amendment.

Sincerely yours,   J P Tumulty

TLS (WP, DLC).

From Elizabeth Thacher Kent

My dear Mr. President: [Washington] May 8, 1918.

The vote on the Suffrage Amendment will probably come up in The Senate on Friday of this week.

We need sixty-four votes.

We have, definitely and openly pledged, fifty-three votes—of which twenty-five are Democrats and twenty-eight Republicans.

Besides these, there are five Democrats and six Republicans of whose votes we are very hopeful. If every one of these men votes for the amendment it will pass, *but almost all the other Senators have declared themselves opposed.* You see this leaves no margin of safety.

I should like to talk over the situation briefly with you and should be very grateful if you could give five minutes to Mrs. Richard Wainwright, Mrs. Harvey W. Wiley and myself. As this may not be possible I enclose our poll for your consideration.[1]

We feel that only at your behest will this measure of justice pass at this time—this measure which you have so finely included in our war aims.   Yours sincerely,   Elizabeth T. Kent.[2]

TLS (WP, DLC).
  [1] Not printed.
  [2] "Dear Tumulty: Please say to Mrs. Kent that I have been keeping in touch with this situation as closely as possible and am doing everything that is open to me to do. The President." WW to JPT, c. May 9, 1918, TL (WP, DLC).

From Julio Betancourt

Sir: Washington, D. C. May 8th, 1917 [1918].

Because I know that the war affairs now entirely absorb the time and attention of Your Excellency, I have refrained from requesting the audience which some days ago Your Excellency kindly granted me, and respectfully write these lines in compliance with the special injunction from my Government of begging Your Excellency to be so good as to use his high authority in order to secure the ratification by the Senate of the pending Treaty between Colombia and the United States.

To-day this great Nation has invested Your Excellency with absolute power,[1] and Colombia expects that nothing will be able to prevent the fulfilment of that most noble purpose Your Excellency has several times shown of obtaining the approval of the Treaty.

After such an act of justice is performed, my Government will do everything that may be of advantage to the interests of the two countries, and the illustrious name of Your Excellency will be for ever blessed by the Colombian People.

Accept, Sir, the renewed assurances of my highest consideration.

Julio Betancourt.

TLS (WP, DLC).
[1] Betancourt undoubtedly referred to the Overman bill (S. 3771) which, after its adoption by the Senate by a vote of sixty-three to thirteen on April 29, had been referred to the House Judiciary Committee on May 1 and had been ordered favorably reported by a vote of fifteen to one on May 7. See *Cong. Record*, 65th Cong., 2d sess., pp. 5765-66 and 5919, and the *New York Times*, May 8, 1918.
The Overman bill was reported to the House on May 9 (H. Report 545), was debated on May 13 and 14, and was passed by a vote of 294 to two on May 14. Wilson signed the bill on May 20, 1918. See *Cong. Record*, 65th Cong., 2d sess., pp. 6298-99, 6441-68, 6500-25, and 6765. For the origins of the Overman bill and a summary of its major provisions, see WW to L. S. Overman, March 21, 1918, n. 1.

From William Dudley Haywood and Others

Chicago, Ills., May 8, 1918.

In reply to a wire received from Senate Judiciary Committee, dated May 3rd in confirmation of our telegram of the same date, we beg to submit, herewith, a statement of our attitude and the attitude of the I.W.W. toward the Walsh bill.[1] We have been compelled to reply [rely] for our information about this measure entirely upon press reports, none [some] of which have come to our attention. Have published the text of the bill but all have stated unequivocally and many have quoted the authors of the bill to the effect that the measure was aimed at the I.W.W.[2] This is the ground and the only ground of our protest. We have no objection on any ground to any measure however drastic which merely aims to prevent acts of violence or destruction of whatever character, for there is probably no organization in this country which has more frequently or positively declared its opposition to such tactics than the I.W.W. We are sending a pamphlet by mail entitled On The Firing Line, consisting of extracts from the report of the general executive board to the 1912 annual convention,[3] also a copy of resolution on the same subject recently adopted by the same board.[4] In addition we might refer to similar declaration published in hundreds of official bulletins and newspapers and to the report of the industrial relations commission wherein we were commended for our orderly strike methods. We deplore and oppose violence not only because it is wrong but because it is futile it is not the working man's weapon. Please remember that this organization was conceived in the travail of the Cripple Creek strike which was so thoroughly investigated by Carroll D. Wright, then U. S. Commissioner of Labor, and the lessons labor learned there are not easily forgotten.[5] It is true that we have been repeatedly accused by the public press of all kinds of violent acts. This is bad enough but it has been tolerated because we realized that they were inspired by selfish interests but the thought is intolerable that the government should pass any law, no matter what is [its pre]text for the avowed purpose of slandering this organization before the public. More than three hundred principal officers are already under indictment on this very charge of violence in four federal cases and we are now seeking vindication before a Chicago jury. The passage of proposed bill will be followed by hundreds or thousands of other arrests and prosecutions. Wouldn't it be fairer and more American to await the determination of some of the cases already pending before more oppressive measures are attempted. Does not the government owe us this much in justice, if not in gratitude. It is easily proven that we harvested a large percentage of last year's crop and the Food administration is even now asking our assistance for the coming season. We are mining a large percentage of the country's copper and iron; we are loading [ships] carrying large percentage of our troops and munitions; are playing an important part in ship and submarine construction and not a single one of our employers has complained of the slightest want of fidelity. It is true that we have been involved in strikes in the copper and logging industries but even in these our position has been approved by the president['s] Mediation Committee. We are speaking in behalf of over 200,000 members and their immediate families

Wm. D. Haywood, General Secretary Treasurer;
    I.W.W.;
Fred Hardy, Secretary, G.R.U.;[6]
Maurice Bresnan, Secretary Treasurer,
    Agricultural Workers;
Fred Hegge, Secretary Treasurer, Metal Mine Workers;
Paul Baker and C. Chestnut, committee, Marine
    Transport Workers.
W. T. Nef, Secretary Treasurer, Construction
    Workers.[7]

T telegram (WP, DLC).
    [1] This bill (S. 4471), which was approved by a subcommittee of the Senate Judiciary Committee on April 30 and introduced in the Senate by Senator Walsh on May 2, outlawed any association or organization which, in time of war, advocated, defended,

used, or threatened to use force, violence, or physical injury to persons or property for the purpose of bringing about governmental, social, industrial, or economic change in the United States. Any person engaged in the activities of such an unlawful organization would be punished by imprisonment for up to ten years and a fine of $5,000. The Senate Judiciary Committee reported the bill favorably on May 6, 1918, and the Senate passed it on the same day. *Cong. Record*, 65th Cong., 2d sess., pp. 5933 and 6082-91. See also the *New York Times*, May 1, 1918.

The bill was referred to the House Judiciary Committee on May 29, 1918, which reported it favorably on August 19, 1918 (H. Report 758). However, the House failed to take any action on it. See *Cong. Record*, 65th Cong., 2d sess., pp. 7222 and 9238.

[2] See, for example, the editorial in the *New York Times*, May 2, 1918.

[3] It is missing in WP, DLC. However, it was Industrial Workers of the World, *On the Firing Line: Extracts from the Report of the General Executive Board to the Seventh Annual Convention of the Industrial Workers of the World* . . . (Spokane, Wash., [1912]).

[4] It is missing.

[5] See Melvin Dubofsky, *We Shall Be All: A History of the Industrial Workers of the World* (New York, rev. edn., 1975), pp. 36-56.

[6] The General Recruiting Union of the I.W.W.

[7] Walter T. Nef, former general secretary-treasurer of the Agricultural Workers' Organization, one of the I.W.W.'s strongest unions. The Editors have been unable to add anything to the identification of the other signers of this telegram.

Lord Reading to Joseph Patrick Tumulty, with Enclosure

Private.

Dear Mr. Tumulty,   Washington 8th May, 1918.

I have received some copies of the Irish Convention Report from London, and at Sir Horace Plunkett's request I am sending one to the President.[1] I thought it might also interest you to read the Report, and I am sending you one herewith.

Yours sincerely,   Reading

TLS (WP, DLC).

[1] It is missing in WP, DLC. For a summary of the report, see E. Drummond to W. Wiseman, April 2, 1918, n. 1.

E N C L O S U R E

In view of the present situation of Irish affairs, and the combined necessity of effecting a settlement of the issue of self-government with securing the further co-operation of Ireland in the war, I wish to submit the following proposal.

As I understand, President Wilson has more than once intimated quite unofficially to London his wish to see an Irish settlement. I suggest that, with the assent of the London Cabinet, President Wilson should send to Ireland an unofficial representative to privately interview the leaders of Public opinion there, with a view to informing them that if they would be willing to pledge themselves to do what they could towards getting Ireland to rally to the further support of the war if given a reasonably satisfactory measure of self-government on the lines of the Majority Report of the Irish Convention President Wilson would undertake, privately and un-officially, to use his good offices with the Government of Great Britain in favour of the establishment at the earliest possible mo-ment such a measure of self-government, with the understanding that the question of raising more troops for the war from Ireland should be left to the discretion of the new Irish Parliament and Government.[1]

T MS (WP, DLC).
    [1] This document was a copy of a telegram from Plunkett to Wilson.

To Helena de Rosen Paderewska[1]

My dear Madame Paderewska: [The White House] 9 May, 1918

I am afraid you must have got the impression that I had forgotten my interesting interview with you, by which I was very much moved and impressed, but I assure you that that is not the case. I have delayed writing to you only because I was in great doubt what I ought to do concerning your suggestion about the proclamation of a Polish Day.[2] I am sorry to say that I have been forced to the conclusion, after consulting many persons whom I regard as wiser than myself, that it would not be wise to proclaim an official Polish Day. In view of the many national elements of which our population is composed and by which it is enriched, and of the many contro-versial matters which have sprung up, not only with regard to the question of Polish enlistments but with regard to similar matters affecting their nationalities, I believe that it would be wisest to leave action in these matters entirely to private initiative. You will prob-ably have observed that there is a very strong movement among Americans of Bohemian origin in this country to take some active part against the Central Powers, and questions are arising with regard to their wishes very similar to those which have arisen with regard to the very admirable and commendable purposes of the Polish people.

You will believe, I am sure, my dear Madame Paderewska, that this decision does not mean that my sympathy is not strongly en-listed. I am merely uttering a hard-headed practical judgment and hope that further consideration of the matter will convince you that the conclusion is inevitable.

                    Cordially and sincerely yours,   Woodrow Wilson

TLS (Letterpress Books, WP, DLC).
    [1] Wife of Ignace Jan Paderewski.

[2] Wilson had received Mme. Paderewska at the White House on February 27, 1918. Referring to Mme. Paderewska's conversation with Wilson, James C. White, the director of the Associated Polish Press, informed Tumulty on April 25, 1918, that Mme. Paderewska would prefer the designation of an official Polish Day during the week of May 6 to May 11. The purpose of such a day, White said, was to raise funds for the 12,000 soldiers of the Polish army in France and their dependents in the United States. J. C. White, memorandum, [April 25, 1918], T MS (WP, DLC).

On April 26, 1918, White wrote to Tumulty that Mme. Paderewska had suddenly realized that the period which she had originally selected would not allow her sufficient time to organize the fund drive efficiently. She now requested the designation of the entire week of June 1 to June 8 for her activities. J. C. White to JPT, April 26, 1918, TLS (WP, DLC).

Tumulty presented White's communications to Wilson on the same day. Wilson told Tumulty that he would personally write to Mme. Paderewska, and asked that, in the meantime, Tumulty inform White that the President would not consider it wise to accede to Mme. Paderewska's request. WW to JPT, c. April 26, 1918, TL (WP, DLC).

To Samuel Gompers

My dear Mr. Gompers: [The White House] 9 May, 1918

I realize the seriousness of the charges which you have conveyed to me made by the Free Federation of Workers of Porto Rico against Governor Yager, and am taking the matter up with the Secretary of War in order that I may have his judgment as well as my own with regard to an investigation of the matter.

Cordially and sincerely yours,   Woodrow Wilson

TLS (Letterpress Books, WP, DLC).

To Newton Diehl Baker

My dear Mr. Secretary: [The White House] 9 May, 1918

These papers concern serious matters. Personally, I do not believe that there is any real case against Governor Yager as these papers present, because I have learned to have very little confidence in Iglesias, who seems to be the formulator of the charges, but I would very much like your judgment as to whether it would be wise to act upon Mr. Gompers' suggestion as to the sending of a commission of inquiry to Porto Rico to look into all these matters and report to us.   Cordially and faithfully yours,   Woodrow Wilson

TLS (Letterpress Books, WP, DLC).

To Josiah Oliver Wolcott

My dear Senator,   The White House. 9 May, 1918.

Will you forgive the leader of your party if he begs that you will vote for the suffrage Amendment?

I am writing this letter on my own typewriter (notwithstanding a lame hand) in order that it may be entirely confidential and may not in the least embarrass you if you should find that you cannot yield to this very earnest request.

A crisis has come such as the world never faced before. In that crisis the world depends upon the United States. Unless the Administration is sustained throughout the war by real friends it cannot meet that responsibility successfully. The next Congress must be controlled by genuine dependable friends; and we may lose it,—I fear we shall lose it,—if we do not satisfy the opinion of the country in this matter now.

That is the whole argument. I am deeply anxious,—the issues involved are so tremendous! They are so tremendous as to justify this ardent appeal for your support.

Faithfully Yours,   Woodrow Wilson

WWTLS (received from Daniel F. Wolcott).

To Joseph Patrick Tumulty, with Enclosure

Dear Tumulty: [The White House, c. May 9, 1918]

Here is one of the most touching letters I ever received, and I think that it ought not to go unnoticed, it is so beautiful an evidence of the new feeling of the Philippines towards us. I feel confident that Judge Bardin would not object to publicity being given to the incident.   The President.

TL (WP, DLC).

E N C L O S U R E

From James Alfred Bardin[1]

Sir: Salinas, California May 1st, 1918.

A few days ago Jesus Y. Garcia, a stranger in this community and a native of the Phillipine Islands, died at the county farm. He was a leper and of course was restrained of his liberty and for months he was left alone.

After his death and burial there was found among his few effects, the following will, written in a good hand on a portion of a magazine page. It's existence was not suspected until found.

"Monterey County Hospital.

I give and bequeath one hundred forty dollars and ninety-five cents ($140.95) to the government of the United States in order that President Wilson, with power larger and greater than mine, might succeed in bringing everlasting peace.

J. Y. Garcia,

March 24, 1918.
I am sorry that I could not find any flag of the United States of America, in order that I might place it over my heart when I close my eyes,—J.Y.G."

Today his grave has been covered with flowers. A flag staff has been erected there and a beautiful silken American flag waves above the mortal remains of this one of America's adopted children, who loved this country because this country had been kind and just to the land of his birth.

Every penny this patriot has left behind, while only a pittance, will in due season be forwarded to you to be applied towards the consumation of the ideals that so deeply appealed to this lonely, unhappy Filipino.   Respectfully yours,   J. A. Bardin

TLS (WP, DLC).
¹ Judge of the Superior Court of Monterey County, California.

To James Alfred Bardin

My dear Judge Bardin: [The White House] 9 May, 1918
The facts recounted in your interesting letter of May first have touched me very deeply. I wish that the poor fellow who left the little sum of money might be accessible to a message from me, but since he is gone I can only express to you the deep feeling which the incident has caused, a feeling of gratitude that the simpler people, as well as the better informed, in the Philippines should have acquired in this short time such a friendly sentiment towards this country.

I shall not know exactly what to do with the money, but you may be sure I shall try to apply it to the objects that Garcia had in mind.
Cordially and sincerely yours,   Woodrow Wilson

TLS (Letterpress Books, WP, DLC).

To Eugene Meyer, Jr.

My dear Mr. Meyer: [The White House] 9 May, 1918
Thank you for your note of yesterday.¹ You may be sure that it gave me real pleasure to have an opportunity to express in some definite way my confidence in you, and I am very glad indeed that

you are finding it possible to serve as a member of the Board of Directors of the War Finance Corporation.

With the best wishes,

Sincerely yours,   Woodrow Wilson

TLS (Letterpress Books, WP, DLC).
    [1] It is missing.

To Lord Reading

My dear Mr. Ambassador: The White House 9 May, 1918

I am very much obliged to you for your courtesy in sending me a copy of the report of the proceedings of the Irish Convention which Sir Horace Plunkett was thoughtful enough to wish me to have. I shall look forward with a great deal of interest to examining it.   Cordially and sincerely yours,   Woodrow Wilson

TLS (Reading Papers, Eur. F. 118/90, IOR).

To Thomas James Walsh

My dear Senator: [The White House] 9 May, 1918

Finding that the letter to you of which I spoke in our interview yesterday had not yet received my signature and been posted,[1] I have not thought it worth while to send it to you because it merely repeats what I told you yesterday as to my judgment in the matter of the aircraft investigation, and our talk was very much more satisfactory than a letter could be.

I am sending this, therefore, to make a formal acknowledgment of your letter of the sixth and to say how I appreciated the opportunity of going into the matter more fully with you.

Cordially and sincerely yours,   Woodrow Wilson

TLS (Letterpress Books, WP, DLC).
    [1] Wilson's letter was not saved.

From John Crepps Wickliffe Beckham

Personal.

My dear Mr. President: [Washington] May 9, 1918.

Your note, asking me to support the Suffrage amendment in the Senate,[1] has just been delivered to me, and such a request coming from you adds more to the difficulty of my position on that subject than anything else that has happened in connection with it.

Your leadership of our party and of the Nation in these critical times makes it an extremely hard matter for me to refuse any request you might make of me. I believe you are aware of the fact that no member of the Senate has recognized your leadership, especially in all war measures, more than I have done, and that I have in practically every instance stood for all measures that would give you an absolutely free hand as Commander-in-Chief to deal with the great problems which are constantly before you.

In the matter of Woman Suffrage, however, I do not see either a party question or a war question, and great as is my respect for your opinions on all matters, I cannot see this as you do. In the first place, I am very much opposed to any federal action on suffrage questions, and believe that they should be left entirely to state control. In the second place, I have such deep seated convictions against Woman Suffrage that I cannot under any circumstances vote for it. I may be somewhat old-fashioned and behind the times in this matter, but I cannot help it, and I feel that I would be untrue to myself if I should vote contrary to those convictions. I have stated in any number of instances in answers to letters, telegrams, and in personal interviews that I would vote against this amendment, and I have not undergone any change of opinion since those statements were made.

It is, of course, a source of sincere regret to me that I am unable in this instance to comply with a request of yours, and yet I feel sure that you can fully and generously appreciate the position in which I am placed.

With great respect, I am

Very sincerely yours, J.C.W. Beckham

TLS (WP, DLC).
[1] It is missing.

From George Creel, with Enclosure

My dear Mr. President: Washington, D. C. May 9, 1918.

I enclose a cable sent recently to the London Times by Henry Hall. Acting under my blanket instructions, to the effect that censors should not pass matter purporting to give your views, the whole cable was killed with the exception of the opening paragraph.[1]

I think it best for you to tell me whether the action expresses your wishes. Respectfully, George Creel

TLS (WP, DLC).
[1] He meant the opening sentence of the text as printed below.

ENCLOSURE

Times.
London.

News that Lord Mayor O'Neill, Dublin, to start for America lay before President Wilson Irish Conference statement on conscription aroused very little interest official circles. President would probably not receive O'Neill, any such mission unless Dublin Mayor was presented by Lord Reading and clearly understood mission agreeable to British Government. It was made clear while House contemplates no departure existing policy refrain from anything that could be interpreted as interfering slightest degree with manner solution Irish question. Moreover if O'Neill came and were received would find President Wilson unswerving in his belief that conscription is only fair truly democratic method raising armies. President Wilson has warmest sympathy for Irish and tis well known Washington that he hopes to see Ireland given fullest possible measure autonomy before provisions new man power act applied but if this done those who resist conscription by force will forfeit his sympathy. Of course idea of an Irish appeal to Wilson has fired imagination many Americans but everybody recognizes that from practical point view nothing can come of suggestion and one-ills mission would only serve embarrass President. In Government circles here there is growing expectation that Lloyd George will insist immediate passage bill self government Ireland embodying majority report Irish Convention and immediately inforce same regardless Ulster opposition or Carson's threats. Today thanks to Balfour, Northcliffe, Reading, American Government and people thoroughly convinced sincerity British war aims and whereas formerly very large influential section American opinion was frankly suspicious of Great Britain and believed she sought her own aggrandizement this war there now exists implicit confidence that England like America is fighting only crush power German military autocracy and establish four fundamental principles laid down by President Wilson his address Congress February eleven. Fourth these principles is directly applicable Ireland and unquestionably Ireland was one of small nations which Wilson had in mind when said "That all well defined nations applications shall be accorded utmost satisfaction that can be accorded them without introducing new or perpetuation old elements discord and antagonism." Should England refuse apply this principle self determination to small nations Ireland both President Wilson and American people will have grave doubts sincerity Great Britain this war. No one of course doubts for single moment sincerity Great Britain's efforts defeat Germany or her willingness fight to last man, last penny crush Prussianism but cannot be made too clear that from American point view defeat German military power is merely preliminary to establishment of "new international order under which reason, justice and common interests mankind shall prevail." Position President Wilson occupies today as spokesman democracy renders natural certain degree of speculation in Ireland elsewhere as how he would deal Irish problem if fates had placed burden upon his shoulders. Principles which President Wilson would apply are so clear so obvious that his attitude hardly matter speculation at all and can be almost stated as matter of assured knowledge. Since February three, nineteen six, when Wilson first publicly toasted as future President United States[1] have been close student the man his works. An acquaintance eight years has ripened into admiration my part confidence on his. I may fairly say that as far his foreign policy concerned President has shown me inside his mind. I have heard him talk with unsuppressed emotion of Ireland's past woes as belonging to world dead gone and I feel free express my belief what President Wilson would do and would like see done especially as have never discussed Irish question with him. President Wilson believes that if British statesmen will look critically upon existing system Government applied Ireland they will see that old familiar form which seemed so natural has altered aspect and when examined with fresh awakened minds reveals itself as sinister and repugnant to democratic ideals. He believes that autonomy for Ireland looked upon frankly by men willing comprehend its true character will assume aspect of things believed in of rights long cherished by Englishmen themselves stuff of their own convictions. President Wilson would not hesitate apply Ireland principles laid down Virginia Bill of Rights which he looks upon as very cornerstone Government by consent Governed and is landmark by which his policy towards self determination small nations will always be guided. Virginia Bill Rights lays great stress fact that majority community has indubitable unalienable *indefeasible* right to reform alter form their Government such manner as judged most conducive public weal. It goes without saying that there could be no thought in President's mind separating Ireland from British Empire any more than separating one of forty-eight states from American Union. But there would be most generous recognition nationalist not separatist aspirations. Leaving with Imperial Parliament all questions succession crown and military naval matters Ireland would be granted complete autonomy with Irish Parliament elected on universal man woman suffrage basis. Full fiscal autonomy would be included on grounds that responsibilities must be assumed along with privileges. Fact that Ireland would perhaps not able become self-supporting not vital matter because United States stands ready lend money self-governing Ireland on same terms she lends Great Britain Canada. Unquestionably if President Wilson were handling situation rights Ulster minority would be most carefully safeguarded but any refusal accept rule majority any attempt offer resistance enforcement law would be dealt with firm hand. Finally a small representation Ireland would be left Imperial Parliament only if twas intended extend system representation self-governing dependencies to Canada, Australia, South Africa, all which would be entitled larger representation than Ireland note censor if in doubt please submit Whitehouse Sunday Ten.

HALL

T MS (G. Creel Papers, DLC).
　[1] See Colonel Harvey's speech proposing Wilson for the presidency printed at Feb. 3, 1906, Vol. 16.

From Edward Mandell House

Dear Governor:　　　　　　　　　　　　New York. May 9, 1918.

If the Senate investigates the aircraft management, they will do it in a spirit of hostility to the Administration, and they will splash all the mud around that they can. This will hearten the enemy, which the Senate does not mind so long as some political capital against you may be made.

It has occurred to me that the Senate investigation might be killed if you would have Gregory appoint Hughes to undertake an investigation. If made honestly it can do no harm.

I spoke to Frank Cobb about it and he is enthusiastic in his approval. I also had Gordon speak to Gregory and he, I think, is willing if it can be done. He will talk with you tomorrow.

There is another point and that is if you use Taft, Root, Hughes and other republicans as you are doing, people will begin to understand that there is some reason why Col. Roosevelt is not available. I have been doing my best to help bring about a [s]chism between such republicans as Taft, Root and Hughes on the one hand and such republicans as Sherman, Brandegee, Penrose and their ilk on the other, and it looks as if it might be done. I take it you saw what Root said in his speech yesterday[1] and which Mann echoed in the House.[2]

Affectionately yours,　E. M. House

TLS (WP, DLC).
　[1] Root had addressed the annual meeting of the National Security League at the Metropolitan Opera House on May 8, 1918, and had called for the abandonment of party

politics and the unity of all loyal citizens in support of the government. He said that, although he had been a Republican all his life and was proud of the splendid loyalty with which the G.O.P. had rallied behind a Democratic administration, party affiliations were of little consequence in the present crisis. Referring to the forthcoming congressional elections, Root continued: "There is one great single predominant qualification for an election to that Congress, and that is a loyal heart. I don't care whether a man is a Democrat, or a Republican, or a Progressive, or a Socialist, or a Prohibitionist, or what not, he must have a loyal heart or it is treason to send him to Congress." In the twenty or thirty districts where a division of a loyal majority would permit the election of a pro-German candidate, Democrats and Republicans and all loyal men should get together, agree upon the loyal candidate who was most likely to carry the district, and unite on him without regard to party. The one crucial task, Root concluded, was to win the war and to elect people who would represent the driving power of the American people that was behind Congress and the administration. *New York Times*, May 9, 1918.

² James Robert Mann, Republican congressman from Illinois and the House minority leader, had appeared on the floor for the first time after a long illness on May 8, 1918, to impress upon his colleagues the need for an end to partisanship and to warn against an overly critical attitude toward the conduct of the war. The country had to realize, Mann said, what a tremendous task the departments of the government had undertaken in raising a great army and navy. He pointed out that it was only natural that, in the process, certain mistakes had been made, and he continued: "We must have patience. We must not be too hurried in our judgment. We must not condemn too quickly where mistakes have occurred. . . . In the war there is no partisanship. We stand as a united country and a united people, unwilling to let bickerings at home affect our determination to win abroad." *Cong. Record*, 65th Cong., 2d sess., pp. 6218-19.

From the Diary of Colonel House

May 9, 1918.

It has been an interesting day on the telephone. It seems that the French Ambassador saw the President about the Foch statement at the Supreme War Council, a copy of which Lord Reading sent me and is among my papers. Jusserand "got nowhere" with the President, so the matter stands just where it was before. I had advised Reading to let Jusserand go to the front in this matter because I thought he, Reading, had pushed the President almost to the point of annoyance. However, when I found that Jusserand was not equal to the task, I advised Reading through Gordon, to see Secretary Baker and press it upon him. I gave the arguments to be used, and Reading greedily seized upon the suggestion. He is to see Baker at once.

A Translation of a Telegram from Jean Jules Jusserand to the Foreign Ministry

Washington, without date,
received May 10, 1918.

Nos. 573-574. I talked with Mr. Wilson about the question of Japanese intervention in Siberia. I found him less positive in his opposition but still not resolved to act.

I explained, in accord with your last telegrams, the grave motives which have caused us to want to separate ourselves entirely from the Bolsheviks and, consequently, to abandon altogether the idea of an appeal coming from them in order to justify in Russian eyes the projected action. The President has not formulated any opinion on this subject. Once again it is necessary to know, he said, if this intervention which, according to the probabilities, will be rather limited, would cause enough worries to the Germans to lessen their pressure in the West. He repeated to me once again that he had not obtained positive assurances on this question from his military advisers (my telegram No. 359).[1]

He persists in evaluating much less than we the strength of the Japanese army: 200,000 regulars and 300,000 reserves. These are the figures given by Viscount Ishii.

I refrain from recapitulating the arguments which I used. The department knows them since they are its own. I have always insisted on the fact that no other remedy has been proposed by anyone; that the most influential Russians, originally hostile to its execution, now recommend it, and one could hope that, thanks to the precautions adopted, the "inter-Allied" expedition would be well received by the population, in which case it would be easy to advance very far into the interior. As I have already indicated, the divergence of views between England and ourselves is a great encouragement to Mr. Wilson and his government in this abstention.

Jusserand.

T telegram (État-Major de l'Armée de Terre, No. 4 N 46, FMD-Ar).
[1] J. J. Jusserand to the Foreign Ministry, No. 359, received March 20, 1918, T telegram (État-Major de l'Armée de Terre, No. 4 N 46, FMD-Ar).

To George Creel

My dear Creel: The White House 10 May, 1918

You were quite right in suppressing Hall's telegram. I am very much distressed that he should have attempted to send anything of the kind. He, of course, had no authority to do so and he goes much beyond the limits usually observed even in such matters.

Faithfully yours,   Woodrow Wilson

TLS (G. Creel Papers, DLC).

To Thomas Watt Gregory

My dear Gregory: [The White House] 10 May, 1918

Do you think that I ought to make any reply at all to the enclosed?[1]

Cordially and faithfully yours,   Woodrow Wilson

TLS (Letterpress Books, WP, DLC).
[1] That is, W. D. Haywood *et al.* to WW, May 8, 1918.

From Joseph Patrick Tumulty

Dear Governor: The White House. 10 May 1918.

I hope by this time you have read the disclosures showing Borglum's connection with an aeroplane company, which are contained in the attached article by Dave Lawrence.[1]

The opinion of those with whom I have discussed the matter is that Borglum has destroyed himself. I have been asked the question whether the Snowden-Marshall report showed any proof of any irregularities approaching graft. I think it would complete the whole business if we could give out a summary of the report,—of course holding back those parts which are purely confidential. The country at this time would accept any statement from you, or even a resume of the report. I am afraid that if we withhold the Snowden-Marshall report, inferences unfavorable to us will be drawn.

Sincerely yours,   J. P. Tumulty

TLS (J. P. Tumulty Papers, DLC).
[1] David Lawrence, "Borglum Charged with Using Confidence of the President to Promote Aero Company," *Washington Times*, May 10, 1918, clipping (J. P. Tumulty Papers, DLC). The article included several sworn statements which indicated that Borglum had told officials of the Dodge Manufacturing Co. of Wisconsin that he could and would use the investigative powers which Wilson had allegedly given him to procure aircraft plans and technical data from the government for the use of the company and that he would use his influence with Wilson to alter the personnel of the Aircraft Board so as to favor his own commercial projects. Lawrence's article also appeared in the New York *Evening Post*, May 10, 1918.

To Joseph Patrick Tumulty

Dear Tumulty: The White House [c. May 10, 1918].

I am quite willing that my correspondence with Borglum should be given out, but as to the report made by Mr. Marshall's committee, it is exceedingly voluminous and detailed, and the summary report which preceded the detailed one is of rather an intimate character recommending the reorganization which I have now effected but also recommending a person to head the new organization. The report, as a matter of fact, is not now in my possession. It is in

Baker's possession, through whom I effected the reorganization. I think Borglum is sure to make an ass of himself when he tries to make good.   The President.

TL (J. P. Tumulty Papers, DLC).

To Joseph Patrick Tumulty, with Enclosure

Dear Tumulty: [The White House, c. May 10, 1918]

The enclosed letter, which I have just received from the Secretary of War, bears upon the matter of where the Snowden Marshall report is now. It is out of my hands and I doubt if anything in it bears directly upon this matter of Mr. Borglum's complicity in promotions, etc.

Perhaps someone in the Attorney General's department could tell you whether there is anything pertinent in it. I do not think that there will be any such feeling as you fear, provided it is known that these reports are in the hands of the Attorney General and that anything they disclose will be dealt with.   The President.

TL (J. P. Tumulty Papers, DLC).

E N C L O S U R E

From Newton Diehl Baker

My dear Mr. President: Washington. May 10, 1918.

Your note of the eighth with regard to the Borglum and Marshall reports reaches me this morning.

Immediately after your request to the Attorney General to look into the Borglum charges, I transmitted to him the Borglum report. I also sent him, as soon as it reached me from your office, the Marshall report, and I have placed in his hands some of the secret service reports with regard to Borglum's activities, which have accumulated in this Department.

I am now going over the rather voluminous papers and correspondence which is here, with the view of placing immediately in the hands of the Attorney General every item of information or suggestion which can serve in any way to facilitate or expedite his inquiry.   Respectfully yours,   Newton D. Baker

TLS (J. P. Tumulty Papers, DLC).

From David Franklin Houston

Sir: Washington May 10, 1918.

Pursuant to the provisions of the Act of March 1, 1911,[1] the United States has acquired title to large quantities of land within the States of Virginia, West Virginia, New Hampshire, and Maine. Section 11 of that Act provides that the lands so acquired shall be permanently reserved, held, and administered as national forest lands under the provisions of section 24 of the Act of March 3, 1891, 26 Stat. 1095, 1103, and Acts supplemental to and amendatory thereof.

It is believed that, in designating these lands as specific National Forests, notice of the boundaries thereof should be given by proclamation. Such action will charge the public with knowledge of the Forest boundaries, and greatly facilitate the administration and protection of the Government owned lands therein.

I have the honor, therefore, to submit herewith for your consideration and execution the drafts of three proclamations establishing the Natural Bridge, Shenandoah, and White Mountain National Forests, and showing the boundaries of each Forest on the diagram attached to the corresponding proclamation.[2]

Respectfully,   D. F. Houston.

TLS (WP, DLC).

[1] This act, among other provisions, authorized the Secretary of Agriculture to purchase forest lands necessary to the protection of the watersheds of navigable streams and to designate these lands as national forests. 36 *Statutes at Large* 961.

[2] These proclamations, signed by Wilson on May 16, 1918, are in 40 *Statutes at Large* 1779-81.

From Robert Lansing

Returned by hand May 10/18 RL

My dear Mr. President: Washington May 10, 1918.

I feel that the time has arrived when it is wise to assume a definite policy in relation to the various nations which make up the Austro-Hungarian Empire.

The ill-considered disclosure of the "Sixtus letter" by M. Clemenceau[1] has compelled the Emperor and Government of Austria-Hungary to take a position in regard to Germany which makes further peace approaches to them well-nigh impossible, while their attitude toward Italy will be, as a result, generous in order to influence the latter country to withdraw from the war, and so release Austrian troops for the front in Flanders.

Like all these questions arising at the present time I think that they should be considered always from the standpoint of winning the war. I do not believe that we should hesitate in changing a policy in the event that a change will contribute to our success provided it is not dishonorable or immoral.

In the present case it seems to me that the pertinent questions are the following:

1. Is there anything to be gained by giving support to the conception of an Austria-Hungary with substantially the same boundaries as those now existing?

2. Is there any peculiar advantage in encouraging the independence of the several nationalities such as the Czech, the Jugo-Slav, the Roumanian, &c, and if so, ought we not to sanction the national movements of these various elements?

3. Should we or should we not openly proclaim that the various nationalities subject to the Emperor of Austria and King of Hungary ought to have the privilege of self-determination as to their political affiliations?

4. In brief, should we or should we not favor the disintegration of the Austro-Hungarian Empire into its component parts and a union of these parts, or certain of them, based upon self-determination?

It seems to me that the time has come when these questions should be answered.

If we are to check the effect of the possible bribe of territory which will doubtless be offered to Italy, is not the most efficacious way to offset this inducement to declare that the aspirations of the subject nations of Austria-Hungary should be determined by the people of those nations and not by the power which has compelled their submission? Italy in such circumstances will undoubtedly consider the possibility of obtaining far greater concessions than Austria-Hungary can offer. She will therefore remain true to the common cause. Furthermore the revolutionary spirit of the nationalities concerned would be given a new hope. Unquestionably a revolution or its possibility in the Empire would be advantageous. Ought we or ought we not to encourage the movement by giving recognition to the nationalities which seek independence?

I have no doubt that you have been, as I have, importuned by representatives of these nationalities to give support to their efforts to arouse their fellow-countrymen to opposition to the present Austrian Government. This importunity is increasing. What should be said to these people? Some answer must be made. Should we aid or discourage them?

I do not think in considering this subject we should ignore the fact that the German Government has been eminently successful

in the disorganization of Russia by appealing to the national jealousies and aspirations of the several peoples under the Czar's sovereignty. Whether we like the method or not, the resulting impo-
tency of Russia presents a strong argument in favor of employing
as far as possible the same methods in relation to Austria's alien
provinces. I do not think that it would be wise to ignore the lesson
to be learned from Germany's policy toward the Russian people.

I would be gratified, Mr. President, to have your judgment as to
whether we should continue to favor the integrity of Austria or
should declare that we will give support to the self-determination
of the nationalities concerned. I think that the time has come to
decide definitely what policy we should pursue.

Faithfully yours,   Robert Lansing

TLS (R. Lansing Papers, NjP).

[1] From February to June 1917, Charles of Austria-Hungary had engaged in sporadic
efforts to feel out the French government on the prospects for a peace settlement. He
used as his chief emissary Prince Sixtus of Bourbon-Parma, who was of French nationality and had fought in the Belgian army and was a brother of Empress Zita. The
principal document of this negotiation was a letter from Charles of March 24, 1917,
addressed to Sixtus but intended for the eyes of President Poincaré. The letter was
actually quite noncommittal, but it did contain an assertion by Charles that he would
support, "by every means" and by exerting all his personal influence with his allies,
France's "just claims regarding Alsace-Lorraine." *New York Times*, April 12, 1918. As
several commentators have pointed out, the significance of this phrase depends entirely
upon exactly what Charles meant by the word "just." The "Sixtus Letter," as it came
to be called, was communicated in confidence by the French government to its British
and Italian allies. The negotiations came to naught because of Italian demands for
territories then controlled by Austria-Hungary.

Georges Clemenceau, on April 8, 1918, in the midst of a propaganda exchange with
Count Czernin as to whether France or Austria had been the first to make peace
overtures, publicly declared that a letter existed, written by Charles, which stated that
French claims to Alsace-Lorraine were justified. Three days later Clemenceau made
public the text of the Sixtus letter. *Ibid.*, April 9 and 12, 1918. This revelation set off a
furor in the Allied nations and the Central Powers. The Austrian government frantically
denied the authenticity of the document, although it was in fact genuine. In any event,
it had the effect of binding Austria-Hungary more closely than ever to Germany by
making it nearly impossible for Austria-Hungary to initiate any further moves for a
separate peace.

For a brief discussion of the Sixtus affair of 1917, its revelation in 1918, and the
significance of both events, see Arthur J. May, *The Passing of the Hapsburg Monarchy,
1914-1918* (2 vols., Philadelphia, 1966), I, 486-91; II, 630-36.

From Robert Lansing, with Enclosures

My dear Mr. President: Washington May 10, 1918.

I have had copies made of the memorandum I sent you April
22nd,[1] regarding the different movements for self government in
Siberia, and of the telegram from Peking, dated April 10th, and am
sending them to you with a later telegram from the Consul at
Harbin, dated April 20th. I have added this later telegram because
it transmits a petition for support by the Allied Governments from
the "Russian Far Eastern Committee," a political organization with-

out party lines, which apparently constitutes a fourth Anti-Soviet movement. The Committee signifies its willingness to work for a coalition with members of the Tomsk movement, but looks to leadership to the Horvath faction;[2] its members would seem to be local Bourgeois from Eastern Siberia and China.

For the moment the Horvath movement has taken the form of a re-organization of the Chinese Eastern Railway administration, in which the board of directors will be composed of Horvath's associates and supporters, together with two Chinese. While this measure is avowedly administrative, it is believed to be primarily political, and to aim at constituting a government for Siberia with the same personnel, following on military successes achieved with the assistance of the Allies or of Japan alone.

Colonel Semenoff, who may now be considered practically as an outpost of the Horvath movement, is reported to be receiving additional munitions and supplies, including armored cars, from Japan. His immediate objective is Karymskaya, where the Amur Railway joins the Trans-Siberian.

Faithfully yours,   Robert Lansing.

TLS (WP, DLC).
   [1] It is printed as an Enclosure with RL to WW, April 22, 1918.
   [2] About these groups, see the document cited above.

E N C L O S U R E   I

COPY OF TELEGRAM FROM PEKING,
Dated April 10, 5 p.m.

Confidential. Referring to my cable of (*) and the (?) The American Government in holding back in the matter of intervention in Siberia is borne out by recent reports from there, particularly British Military Attaché and Major Fitz-William, British army.[1] Following is a summary of the situation as it appears from here:

There is no evidence of a concerted plan on the part of the Germans to control Siberia through the prisoners nor could such an attempt succeed. Earlier reports about armed prisoners were exaggerated; most of these reports came from one source in Irkutsk. A great many Austrian prisoners have become international socialists and have thrown in their lot with the Russians. Most German prisoners desire to return to Europe. In case of need, Bolsheviks will make use of technical knowledge of German officers, but the latter could not control unless Russian people should be driven into the arms of Germany through some fatal mistake.

Intervention can do good only if supported by the (#) from there.

Intervention in support of a group superimposed from above would badly upset things for the Allies. Semenoff has no backing in Russia though at present (advised) by Kuroki,[2] Japanese officer. Any advance would put him in a helpless condition dependent entirely upon outside force. Extent of Ussuri Cossack organization not know[n] here but other Cossacks generally stand with workmen. Only reactionaries want intervention at all costs, even in the last report [resort] by Japan alone. The so-called Siberian autonomous government organized at Tomsk, members of which addressed President Wilson from Vladivostok by telegraph April sixth,[3] might possibly get sufficient backing in Siberia to warrant Allied support.

It is believed the Allies, particularly the United States, will have it in their power to take action which will save Russia and Siberia from German dominion and keep up the spirit of the other Slavic nationalities in Europe; economic rather than military action will now accomplish this. Russian population needs clothes and manufactured goods; workmen need food held by peasants. The immediate creation of a Russian trading corporation which would import needed goods from the United States and Japan and would exchange for grain and supply same in cities all through local Russian and Siberian committees absolutely on condition that order be first restored so that the beneficial use of materials assured; this policy if announced to the people will gain their immediate adhesion. Restoration of railway traffic, policing by local guards with only potential support by international force. If the policy of economic support to Siberia and restoration of railway traffic is put in the foreground, it is believed that other matters will take care of themselves. Should intervention come first there is danger that it will be understood to be in favor of reaction and capitalism, and will alienate the people permanently.

The financial support required for the economic program would be much smaller than military action would require; it would give assurance of ultimate effective military action against Germany. Economic support as primary action, military support in the background, made effective where local anarchy requires, would appear safe policy.   Reinsch.

[1] The "British Military Attaché" was probably Maj. David Stephen Robertson, then stationed in Peking. The Editors have been unable to further identify Maj. Fitz-William.
[2] That is, Capt. Shinkei Kuroki.
[3] Peter Derber to RL, n.d. but received April 6, 1918, *FR 1918, Russia*, II, 101-102.

ENCLOSURE II

Harbin, April 20, 1918.

Russian Far Eastern Committee for the active defence of their country and the creation of a Constitutional Assembly, declaring itself a political organization without party lines, has asked the Consulate to forward to the Government of the United States its petition for the support of the Allied Governments. The Committee proposes as follows: Negotiation: one. The restoration of order Siberian Russia by disarmament. Overthrow of Bolsheviks as (?) to anarchy and responsible and for treacherous peace with Germany. Two. Measures for the (*) of military force to oppose Bolsheviks and restoring the army and navy, to annul peace and reestablish action in accord with Allies. Three. Cooperation with all parties for the earliest possible formation of special government for Siberia and Far East leading up to Constitutional Assembly. Immediate tasks declared are to restore authority of local Zemstvos and municipal councils, securing civil liberty to population, restoring economic finances through immediate reestablishment of transportation *dalevsky*, food assistance where required.

Committee states it will work for coalition with members Siberian Government previously reported my telegram April eleventh,[1] without regard for party lines but looks for leadership to Horwarth faction. Following is personnel for Committee: From Harbin, Alexandrof, lawyer; Klulaeff, merchant, mine owner; Kaido, notary, insurance manager; Spitzen, editor, orator; Koloboff, general militia railway zone. From Peking: Brandt professor oratory; from Tronavostok, Merkfuglogzatezsky, retailer, from Habarovsk, Lichoihoff, chairman Bourse Committee; from Irkutsk, Schelkounoff, chairman Bourse Committee; Monomakoff, mining engineer, chief Irkutsk mining district; from Stratensk, Renicker, merchant; from Chita, Tatinkoff, mine owner; Dobitoff, banker; from Blagoviestschensk, Permykin, Chairman Lvoff member provincial Zemstvos, Chairman Miners Food Committee; Zkytzeff (?), Olenin, geology, expert prototypes, *Nvhhs*, oratory, captain army.[2]

Hundreds refugees from Blagovestchensk arrived yesterday having come overland Tsiowiharh in pitiable condition bringing, however, 8,000,000 rubles in gold from State Bank and deposited here with Russian Asiatic Bank. They report horrible stories of Bolsheviki atrocities similar to Belgium. Far Eastern Committee requests Allied consuls appoint commission one delegate from each consulate to sit with Committee and take sworn testimony refugees. Telegraph instructions.   Moser.

T telegrams (WP, DLC).

¹ C. K. Moser to RL, April 12, 1918, printed in *FR 1918, Russia*, II, 119-21.

² With the single exception of "Lichoihoff," who was K. T. Likhoidov, a conservative financier, the Editors have been unable further to identify any of the persons mentioned above.

From Newton Diehl Baker

My dear Mr. President: Washington. May 10, 1918.

Mr. Jusserand and Lord Reading have both called upon me with reference to the expressions of their Governments in the matter of the preferential shipping of Infantry and Machine Gun units.

There seems to be confusion as to whether the statement of General Foch [w]as made before or after the formal written agreement drawn up by General Foch, Lord Milner and General Pershing as a committee and subsequently approved by the members of the Supreme War Council present at Abbeville. I told both Mr. Jusserand and Lord Reading that it seemed to me quite inadmissible for us here to reach any sort of agreement at variance with the formal written and signed agreement transmitted to us as representing the common belief of the military commanders; that if we undertook to depart from that program General Pershing might well feel disturbed and might come to the belief that so definite an agreement ought not to have been varied by the action of civilians without reference to him.

I, therefore, suggested that if General Foch felt that the agreement made did not really meet the exigencies of the military situation the best course would be for General Foch spontaneously to send for General Pershing, go over the military situation with him, and get General Pershing to agree to whatever modification is proper. We would then have a complete understanding between General Pershing and General Foch, and no possible holdback on General Pershing's part due to a feeling that his Government was not relying upon his judgment.

Mr. Jusserand believes that the wisest course, and told me that he was going to suggest to Mr. Clemenceau that he suggest to General Foch that he send for General Pershing and work out just what they want in a discussion between two military commanders, with full opportunity to weigh from personal observation the military needs.   Respectfully yours,   Newton D. Baker

TLS (WP, DLC).

From Albert Sidney Burleson

My dear Mr. President: Washington May 10, 1918

I return herewith the letter of the Vice-President. I think there will be but little difficulty in accomplishing what he suggests in his letter. The District Appropriation Bill is now pending before the Committee on the District of Columbia, and a paragraph could be embodied therein, under the heading of the Health Department, providing an appropriation for the support of a division or bureau of Infant Hygiene, and such powers as it might be desired to delegate to the said bureau or division and authorization for the expenditure of money to be appropriated therefor could be expressed in a few words in connection with the item making the appropriation.

If you desire it, I will undertake to see Mr. Brownlow, one of the District Commissioners, and have the matter brought to the attention of Hon. John Walter Smith who will be, I am quite sure, only to[o] glad to meet the wishes of the Vice-President, especially if it were known that you are interested.

                    Sincerely yours,   A. S. Burleson

TLS (WP, DLC).

From George V

Dear Mr. President   Windsor Castle May 10th, 1918.

I am glad to think that my cousin, Prince Arthur of Connaught, will have the pleasure of paying his respects to you on his arrival in America en route to Japan, as Head of a Mission, with which I have entrusted him, when he will convey to you the assurances of my sincere friendship & goodwill.

The British people join with me in offering our warmest greetings to the Army of the United States, on the occasion of the landing of its several units on our shores. I have been fortunate personally to see some of the Regiments & to meet many of their Officers, & I am always impressed by their splendid spirit & keenness to take their place in the battle front.

The visits paid from time to time to this country by Colonel House, have enabled me to become intimately acquainted with him, & to appreciate his high character, sound judgement & friendly regard for this country. I have also not failed to realise his devotion to you & his earnest desire to be the faithful exponent of your wishes & aspirations with regard to the conduct of the War, into which our

two Nations are throwing their fullest energy. I hope before long
we may have an opportunity of welcoming him here again.

With my heartfelt good wishes for yourself & the American people
I remain   your sincere friend   George R.I.

ALS (WP, DLC).

From Benjamin Ryan Tillman

My dear Mr. President: Washington, D. C. May 10, 1918.

Nothing could pain me more than being unable to comply with
any wish of yours.

I find myself unable, however, to vote for the Suffrage Amendment because I am pledged in advance to vote against it. I know
in voting against it I will truly represent the people of South Carolina. When the women of South Carolina want the vote the men
will give it to them.

Respectfully and sincerely,   B. R. Tillman

TLS (WP, DLC).

From Edwin T. McCoy[1]

My dear Mr. President,   Tuscon, Arizona. May 10th 1918.

Attached hereto are copies of correspondence with the War Department with reference to the commissioning of Mr. Harry C.
Wheeler as Captain in the Signal Corps.[2]

It appears that the War Department refuses to consider that Mr.
Wheeler's admittedly illegal actions in connection with the Bisbee
deportations of last July and subsequent suspension of constitutional rights and guarantees disqualify him as an officer unless he
has been convicted in a criminal court and that the failure of the
authorities, state or Federal, to proceed against him has relieved
him of liability, which view cannot be accepted by this committee
without appeal to you.

This committee and the labor organizations in Arizona have opposed Mr. Wheeler's appointment on the ground that a man who
for months ignored his oath of office and legal obligations and not
only violated the laws of Arizona but all the principles of decency
and humanity, which charge is confirmed by the evidence secured
by your Mediation Commission,[3] cannot reasonably be expected to
have any higher regard for his obligations as an officer in the U. S.
Army.

In your telegram to Governor Campbell at the time of the deportations you deplored the actions of the citizens in taking the law into their own hands,[4] but in this case it was Mr. Wheeler, himself, Sheriff and chief peace officer and Chairman of the Local Exemption Board, who organized and directed this arbitrary, unlawful and unjustifiable denial of constitutional rights and guarantees to approximately two thousand citizens of the Warren District.

Either Mr. Wheeler's actions in this affair were a bold and patriotic move in a great emergency and worthy of approval and commendation or his arbitrary and unlawful conduct was not justified, which fact is established by the evidence secured by your Mediation Commission, and should receive the condemnation of responsible authorities and governmental departments. In this case his appointment to a position of honor and trust in the Army of the United States appears to be an endorsement of his actions.

Under these conditions Mr. Wheeler's ability and services, no matter how great, most certainly cannot compensate for the distrust in the sincerity of purpose of the Government to maintain the legal rights of workingmen and women at this time when action by themselves to maintain such rights, which involves suspension of work, must be waived in the interest of uninterrupted prosecution of the war, which this appointment must create.

The War Department having definitely refused to take any action toward the removal of Mr. Wheeler the matter is respectfully presented to you for consideration and final determination.

Assuring you of the whole and united support of the labor organizations of Arizona and of the individual members thereof, I am,   Very truly yours,   E. T. McCoy

TLS (WP, DLC).
[1] Of Bisbee, Ariz., a member of the Legal Rights Committee of the Arizona State Federation of Labor.
[2] E. T. McCoy to WW, March 9, 1918, TC telegram (WP, DLC); B. Crowell to E. T. McCoy, March 14, 1918; E. T. McCoy to B. Crowell, March 24, 1918; B. Crowell to E. T. McCoy, April 2, 1918; E. T. McCoy to B. Crowell, April 15, 1918; B. Crowell to E. T. McCoy, May 2, 1918; and E. T. McCoy to B. Crowell, May 10, 1918, all TCL (WP, DLC).
[3] See W. B. Wilson *et al.* to WW, Nov. 6, 1917, Vol. 44, and the report of the President's Mediation Commission printed at Jan. 28, 1918, Vol. 46.
[4] See WW to T. E. Campbell, July 12, 1917, Vol. 43.

A Proclamation

[May 11, 1918]

A PROCLAMATION.

WHEREAS the Congress of the United States, on the second day of April last, passed the following resolution:

"Resolved by the Senate (the House of Representatives concurring), That, it being a duty peculiarly incumbent in a time of war humbly and devoutly to acknowledge our dependence on Almighty God and to implore His aid and protection, the President of the United States be, and he is hereby, respectfully requested to recommend a day of public humiliation, prayer, and fasting, to be observed by the people of the United States with religious solemnity and the offering of fervent supplications to Almighty God for the safety and welfare of our cause, His blessings on our arms, and a speedy restoration of an honorable and lasting peace to the nations of the earth";

AND WHEREAS it has always been the reverent habit of the people of the United States to turn in humble appeal to Almighty God for His guidance in the affairs of their common life;

Now, therefore, I, Woodrow Wilson, President of the United States of America, do hereby proclaim Thursday, the thirtieth day of May, a day already freighted with sacred and stimulating memories, a day of public humiliation, prayer and fasting, and do exhort my fellow-citizens of all faiths and creeds to assemble on that day in their several places of worship and there, as well as in their homes, to pray Almighty God that He may forgive our sins and shortcomings as a people and purify our hearts to see and love the truth, to accept and defend all things that are just and right, and to purpose only those righteous acts and judgments which are in conformity with His will; beseeching Him that He will give victory to our armies as they fight for freedom, wisdom to those who take counsel on our behalf in these days of dark struggle and perplexity, and steadfastness to our people to make sacrifice to the utmost in support of what is just and true, bringing us at last the peace in which men's hearts can be at rest because it is founded upon mercy, justice and good will.

IN WITNESS WHEREOF I have hereunto set my hand and caused the seal of the United States to be affixed.

Done in the District of Columbia this eleventh day of May, in the year of our Lord Nineteen hundred and eighteen and of the independence of the United States the one hundred and forty-second.   WOODROW WILSON[1]

By the President,
    Robert Lansing
        Secretary of State.

Offset copy (WP, DLC).
[1] There is a WWsh draft of this document in WP, DLC.

To Joseph Patrick Tumulty

[The White House, c. May 11, 1918]

Please get in touch with the State Department and the Committee on Public Information and tell them that the following is in response to the dispatch from Rome, numbered 1582, May sixth, 4 P.M.:

"I am sure that I am speaking for the people of the United States in sending to the Italian people warm fraternal greetings upon this the anniversary of the entrance of Italy into this great war in which there is being fought out once for all the irrepressible conflict between free self-government and the dictation of force. The people of the United States have looked with profound interest and sympathy upon the efforts and sacrifices of the Italian people, are deeply and sincerely interested in the present and future security of Italy, and are glad to find themselves associated with a people to whom they are bound by so many personal and intimate ties in a struggle whose object is liberation, freedom, the rights of men and nations to live their own lives and determine their own fortunes, the rights of the weak as well as of the strong, and the maintenance of justice by the irresistible force of free nations leagued together in the defense of mankind. With ever increasing resolution and force we shall continue to stand together in this sacred common cause. America salutes the gallant Kingdom of Italy, and bids her Godspeed.   Woodrow Wilson."

The President.

TL (WP, DLC).

To Joseph Swagar Sherley

My dear Mr. Sherley: [The White House] 11 May, 1918

I take the liberty of writing to call your attention to a matter which seems to me of capital importance in connection with the effective conduct of the war. I mean the sum for National Security and Defense which has been placed at my disposal during the past fiscal year. I think that it is of the utmost importance that a similar fund should be put at my disposal for the next fiscal year, though in my judgment it need not be so large as the last appropriation for that purpose. I think that a sum of half the amount, namely $50,000,000, would be abundant.

I think you and your colleagues in the Committee on Appropriations are familiar with the objects for which I have used the appropriation, but perhaps you will permit me to summarize them.

I have used considerable sums for the maintenance of the Food Administration, the Fuel Administration, and the War Trade Board, and for the maintenance of the proper agencies for the allocation of labor, a matter of the utmost importance and no little difficulty during this time of the general dislocation of labor throughout the country. For these objects it seems to me that the fund is no longer necessary, inasmuch as their administration has been now quite thoroughly organized and is susceptible of being maintained by definite appropriations assigned to their use in the usual manner. Of course, this method of appropriation is very preferable to any other.

Besides these objects, I have spent very large sums for the repair of ships owned by alien enemies which we took possession of immediately after our entrance into the war and which, as you know, had been deliberately damaged in the most serious way by their own crews; for the providing of temporary accommodations for the newly-created services connected with the war; for advances to the regular departments for services regularly appropriated for when it seemed unwise in the circumstances to wait until the appropriations, which would certainly be made, could be acted upon by the Congress; to provide additional facilities for the Civil Service Commission, in order that it might more nearly meet the exceptional demands of the time for clerical aid; for miscellaneous expenses connected with the very serviceable action of the Council of National Defense; and for labor matters of many sorts, investigation, mediation, the settlement of strikes, and many objects arising from time to time and impossible to foresee or calculate for beforehand. Most of these matters, also, may now be taken care of in the regular way, though similar occasions for the immediate expenditure of money may no doubt arise on a smaller scale than before.

There remain the uses for such a fund which I may perhaps characterize as continuing but incalculable beforehand. I refer to the conduct of many necessary investigations in connection with the determination of the prices which the Government is to pay and which the governments associated with us in the war are to pay;

To indispensable secret service and to confidential uses abroad;

To the very large necessities of record and information;

To the maintenance of instrumentalities both on this side of the water and the other which are doing admirable work in informing public opinion both here and there of the real aims of America, of the progress she is making in the conduct of the war, of the real facts with regard to all the larger aspects of our policy;

And to the service and guidance of all sorts of patriotic movements in the United States which appeal to the Government for its assistance, for materials wherewith to conduct their work.

Besides these things which can now be stated, the experience of the past year convinces me that there are many occasions which will arise which I cannot now even conjecture which will make it necessary that I should have a free fund at my disposal.

May I not say a word of special emphasis with regard to the work which the Committee on Public Information is doing? Mr. Creel in conducting this work is in a very special sense my personal representative. I have kept in close touch with the work that he is doing, and it has at all times been based in large part upon my advice. It has been admirably done and I think it very likely that nobody, not even those most intimately connected with the Government, are aware of the extent, the variety and the usefulness of that work or of the really unusually economical manner in which it has been accomplished, so far as the expenditure of money is concerned. I should feel personally crippled if any obstacle of any kind were put in the way of that work.

It is really impossible to outline what that work is, but if the Committee would like to know, I am sure they would derive pleasure as well as discover a most unusual and interesting piece of work if they would personally examine it.

Cordially and sincerely yours,   [Woodrow Wilson][1]

CCL (WP, DLC).
  [1] There is a WWT outline of this letter in WP, DLC.

To Joseph Taylor Robinson

My dear Senator: [The White House] 11 May, 1918

There is a matter, small in one sense but very great in another, in which I am deeply interested and to which I hope you will permit me to call your attention. An item proposed to the Appropriations Committee of the House of Representatives for the establishment and maintenance of a bureau of child welfare in the District was omitted in the Committee's recommendation to the House, but I think that it is of vital importance. It involves only the sum of $17,560, and I cannot think of any money that would be better spent.[1] I am, therefore, taking the liberty of asking if I may interest you to see that it is included in the bill as it passes the Senate.

For fear this matter had not been called to your attention otherwise, I felt that perhaps I might take the liberty of speaking of it myself.

　　With warm regard,　　Sincerely yours,　　Woodrow Wilson

TLS (Letterpress Books, WP, DLC).
　¹ Wilson's letter was based upon the detailed budget and rationale for the proposed Bureau of Child Welfare in the District of Columbia given in L. Brownlow to A. S. Burleson, May 10, 1918, TLS (WP, DLC).

From Thomas Watt Gregory, with Enclosure

Dear Mr. President:　　　　　　Washington, D. C. May 11, 1918.

　　At the close of an especially strenuous day I find my brain in such an addled condition that I am not at all satisfied with the enclosed suggestion of a form of letter to Judge Hughes in regard to the aircraft production investigation.

　　After giving the matter more mature thought I am still of the opinion that it is desirable to follow the course suggested to you on yesterday. In case you conclude to write this letter, will you not promptly notify me so that I can write a personal letter to Judge Hughes?　　　　　　Faithfully yours,　　T. W. Gregory

TLS (WP, DLC).

E N C L O S U R E

　　You have doubtless noticed the very serious charges of dishonesty made in connection with the production of aircraft.

　　Because of the importance of this branch of the military service I feel that these charges should be thoroughly investigated with as little delay as practicable, in order that the guilty, if there are such, may be promptly and vigorously prosecuted, and that the reputations of those whose actions have been attacked may be protected in case the charges are groundless.

　　I have requested the Department of Justice to use every instrumentality at its disposal to investigate these charges. With the approval of the Attorney General, I ask you to act with him in making this investigation. I feel that this is a matter of the very greatest importance, and that you will not hesitate to contribute your services in studying and passing upon the questions involved.

　　　　　　　　　　　　　　Sincerely yours,

T MS (WP, DLC).

From Thomas Watt Gregory

Dear Mr. President: Washington, D. C. May 11, 1918.

I have just received yours of the 10th, accompanied by copy of a wire to you of May 8th, signed by William D. Haywood and others (all of them, I assume, being members of the I.W.W. organization). You ask if I think you should make any reply to the telegram.

You doubtless know that I did not ask for the passage of the Walsh bill. I know of its provisions in a general way only.

Haywood and a number of other I.W.W. leaders are now on trial in the United States District Court at Chicago; the evidence is sensational and very convincing, and to the effect that these people have been teaching sabotage in its most outrageous form, and have deliberately attempted to interfere with various Government endeavors immediately connected with the prosecution of the war. I believe the Government is developing an excellent case and I expect to procure convictions.

Under these circumstances, I do not think it would be well for you to reply to this telegram. Would it not be as well to let Secretary Tumulty send a reply stating that the telegram had been received and referred to you for consideration?

I herewith return the telegram you enclosed, having kept a copy for my files.   Faithfully yours,   T. W. Gregory

TLS (WP, DLC).

From Jesse Holman Jones[1]

My dear Mr. President: Washington, D. C. May 11, 1918.

We are confidently counting upon you to speak in New York, either Saturday evening, the 18th, or Sunday evening, the 19th, at the Hippodrome. I believe this to be the best place for the meeting.[2]

It seems in every way appropriate for you to speak on this occasion, and a message from you at this time will be good for us all, not alone in this country, but throughout the world.

I venture to suggest the following programme: Go to New York on Friday with Mrs. Wilson, theatre on Friday evening, golf Saturday morning, review the Red Cross parade Saturday afternoon, (and by the way, we are having fifteen hundred parades on Saturday, and expect that five million people will participate in them), theatre Saturday evening, and speak at Red Cross meeting Sunday evening.[3]

We want to complete arrangements for the meeting and can as well have it Sunday as Saturday. In fact if it is just the same to you, we will have it Sunday evening. Our thought was to have Mr. Cleveland Dodge, or Mr. Taft, preside at the meeting, and to have the Star Spangled Banner sung by some noted singer, and perhaps one other short speech, depending entirely upon the length of your message.

This is merely a suggested programme. We will make definite arrangements for the meeting after hearing from you.

Colonel House and Dr. Grayson will do the rest.

Sincerely yours,   Jesse H. Jones

TLS (WP, DLC).
[1] Banker of Houston, at this time Director General of Military Relief for the American Red Cross.
[2] The meeting was to open the second wartime fund-raising drive of the American Red Cross.
[3] Wilson's speech is printed at May 18, 1918.

From Robert Lansing, with Enclosures

My dear Mr. President: Washington May 11, 1918.

Lord Reading called again this morning and presented me with the enclosed telegrams which he had received from Mr. Balfour in relation to intervention in Russia.

I pointed out to Lord Reading that the problem had really become two problems in that intervention in western Russia in no way involved the racial difficulty which had to be considered in regard to Siberia. I further told him that intervention at Murmansk and Archangel would receive far more favorable consideration on our part than intervention in Siberia, for the reason that we could understand the military advantage of the former but had been unable, thus far, to find any advantage in sending troops into Siberia. I also said that the communications which had been received from Trotsky as to his favorable attitude toward intervention might apply only to the northern part and not to the Far East and that I had some doubts as to how far the reported invitation for intervention would go even if it was made by the Bolsheviks, and, therefore, it seemed to me advisable that that should be thoroughly understood in case the purpose of inducing an invitation persisted.

He asked me if you would not express your views as to whether it was not advisable, in any event, to secure an invitation from Trotsky, or from the Bolshevik authorities and I told him I would ask you.   Faithfully yours,   Robert Lansing

TLS (WP, DLC).

E N C L O S U R E   I

Handed me by Lord Reading
May 11/18 RL

Washington. May 11th, 1918.

PARAPHRASE OF TELEGRAM[1] FROM THE BRITISH
REPRESENTATIVE AT MOSCOW TO MR. BALFOUR.
May 7th, 1918.

I was to-day told by the Minister of Foreign Affairs that the position at Murmansk was now most critical, owing to the published report of speeches made at Murmansk by Admiral Kemp[2] and by American and French officers: the Russian Government was warned on May 6th by the German Ambassador that Germany would be obliged to take steps which would be most serious in their result for the Russian Government, unless the Allied forces were withdrawn.

The Minister of Foreign Affairs added that he would not, without seeing Lenine, tell me what course of action the Bolshevist authorities would pursue, but he thought that the Allied Forces at Murmansk should either be withdrawn or largely increased.

He also informed me that a protest had been made by the Bolshevist Government against the proceedings of the German authorities in the Crimea, and that they had received a reply to the effect that the Germans had been obliged to take steps in self-protection against the Black Sea fleet, owing to the fact that the fleet had made an attack upon a Ukranian town. It is not yet known exactly what has happened to the fleet, but a portion of it is thought to have succeeded in escaping from Sebastopol. A position is now being reached at which it is impossible longer to avoid a definite decision. In my opinion there seems to be only one possible course of action, that is, to make urgent military preparations for landings at the earliest possible date at Archangel, Murmansk and in the Far East. When it has been possible for the Allies to reach an understanding among themselves as to this and to instruct their representatives in Moscow to put before the Bolshevist authorities collective proposals as to intervention, I have little doubt that such proposals will be accepted. It is, in any event, necessary to push forward intervention with the greatest possible rapidity.

The necessity of this course is agreed upon by all the military representatives in Moscow, and I am sure that if arrangements could be made for co-operation in the Far East between the United States and Japan we should be able to remove the not unnatural suspicion which is felt by Russians of all classes in respect of Japan, and to induce the present Government to agree to Allied intervention.

I was also told by the Minister of Foreign Affairs that the Government was much agitated by reports received from the Ukraine and that it was possible that a break with Germany might take place at any time as a result of the German proceedings there. A secret meeting was held yesterday night by the small Council of People's Commissioners, at which there was a discussion of the question of peace or war.

This afternoon I am to see the Minister of Foreign Affairs again and he is to give me further information as to the above Conference.

T MS (WP, DLC).
  [1] A. J. Balfour to Lord Reading, May 10, 1918, No. 2875, T telegram (FO 115/2446, pp. 41-42, PRO). It repeated R. H. B. Lockhart to A. J. Balfour, May 7, 1918, No. 163.
  [2] Rear Admiral Thomas Webster Kemp, commander of the British naval squadron in the White Sea.

E N C L O S U R E   I I

Handed me by Lord Reading
May 11/18 RL

Washington. May 11th, 1918.

PARAPHRASE OF TELEGRAM[1] FROM MR. BALFOUR
TO LORD READING—MAY 10TH, 1918.

In recent reports from our representative at Moscow you will have noticed a most important change in the attitude of Trotsky, as described in these telegrams, and an even more noticeable alteration in Mr. Lockhart's estimate of the position. The embarrassment in which Trotsky now finds himself is caused by his belief, for which there is only too much foundation, that the Allies even if asked to intervene would not be ready to give him help for a long time, while Germany is in a position to make an immediate attack. His enemies would be able to crush him completely before his friends had been able to put even one division ashore in the Far East.

In this situation would not the President be ready to make confidentially such political and military arrangements with Japan as would ensure that the intervention contemplated would be effectively carried out the moment that a decision to intervene had been reached.

I feel sure that America will sooner or later be convinced that intervention is necessary. Either an invitation will be given to her by the Bolshevik authorities or else so grave a danger will arise from the absorption of Russia by the Germans that vigourous measures will become unavoidable, whether an invitation is extended or not. If the President is still in doubt whether the psychological moment has been reached, as I fear is the case, I earnestly trust that he may in any event take measures to ensure that when this moment arrives the best possible use may be made of it without delay.

It should be borne in mind that, in order to secure the desired invitation from the Bolshevik Government, we can follow no better line than to convince them that such an invitation will be accepted and acted upon the moment we receive it.

T MS (WP, DLC).
    [1] A. J. Balfour to Lord Reading, May 10, 1918, No. 2871, T telegram (FO 115/2446, pp. 37-38, PRO).

From Robert Lansing

My dear Mr. President: [Washington] May 11, 1918.

I have received your letter of May 8, 1918, enclosing a letter from Mr. Louis Marshall concerning the possibility of extending the limit of relief remittances for the sake of the Jews outside of Poland and hasten to say that I am now gathering certain data on this subject, which I trust will enable me in a few days to express a careful opinion, as you request.

With assurances of respect, etc., I am, my dear Mr. President,
                    Faithfully yours,   Robert Lansing

CCL (SDR, RG 59, 860C.48/68a, DNA).

From Atlee Pomerene

Dear Mr. President: Washington, D. C. May 11th, 1918

In reply to your note[1] asking me to support the suffrage amendment; I need not say to you, if it were possible I would be glad to do it, if only because you ask it.

I have favored Woman Suffrage for fifteen or twenty years. Three times within five years I voted for it in Ohio and three times it was overwhelmingly defeated by popular vote—the first time by more than 87000, the second time by more than 180000, and the third time after the Woman Suffragists quietly laid their plans and succeeded in having a law passed conferring upon women the right to vote at Presidential elections, on a referendum it was defeated by over 140000.

Believing as we do in representative Democracy can I openly defy this expression of my constituents and vote for a resolution which will deprive them of the right of determining this question for themselves, and thereby give Nevada with a voting population of about one third of your majority in Ohio in 1916 the right to say, by a mere majority of her legislature that Ohio shall have woman suffrage whether the majority of her voters want it or not?

Surely if I took this course I could not claim to be representing my State. Rather I would be misrepresenting it. This is to me a very serious matter. I cannot overlook the fact that I have a commission from a state with a population of more than 5000000 people— as many as are within the limits of ten of the smaller states and as long as I can sense their wishes they shall be a law unto me.

Believe me when I say, it is with a feeling of very keen regret that I find myself unable to comply with your request.

Very sincerely   Atlee Pomerene

ALS (WP, DLC).
[1] It is missing.

From Duncan Upshaw Fletcher

My dear Mr. President: [Washington] May 11th, 1918.

Your personal note of the 9th instant was duly received.[1] I have not felt impressed that the situation was so serious as you indicate. It is unnecessary to say that I have the highest respect for your views and I thank you for writing to me.

My convictions, however, on the subject of the proposed Constitutional Amendment have always been so deep set and fixed that I have not hesitated to announce them and I feel bound by them.

Numerous inquiries I have answered in the most positive and definite terms and with more or less details as to reasons.

I recognize the times are abnormal and even critical and that it is essential that the administration be sustained by "real friends." I have endeavored to do my part in that regard and I mean to continue but in this matter I feel so bound by my conscience & judgment and so absolutely committed that, regretting, as I do, that I cannot conform to your wishes, I am obliged to persist in the position heretofore firmly taken.

Faithfully Yours,   Duncan U. Fletcher.

ALS (WP, DLC).
[1] It is missing.

From Franklin Knight Lane

My dear Mr. President: Washington May 11, 1918.

Here is a letter that Congressman Bankhead, author of H.R. Bill 11047, the purpose of which is the elimination of adult illiteracy, has written me, and also a copy of a letter that I recently sent to Senator Hoke Smith and Representative Sears, the Chairmen of the Senate and House Committees on Education, in this connection.[1] I think it very important that action be gotten on this bill if possible.

Would you feel like interesting yourself enough to write a letter, or to see someone in the House who can speak for you, and suggest that special consideration be given to it?

Cordially and faithfully yours,   Franklin K Lane

TLS (WP, DLC).
[1] The enclosures were returned. However, the second was F. K. Lane to W. J. Sears, March 12, 1918, printed in 65th Cong., 2d sess., House Report No. 418. Lane outlined the great scope of the problem of adult illiteracy in the United States, which had been forcibly brought to the government's attention by the need for military manpower. There were over 4,600,000 illiterates in the country who were twenty years of age or more. There were some 700,000 men of draft age who could not read or write in English or any other language. Lane urged the passage of a measure to make a start at solving this problem. H.R. 11047, introduced on March 26, required the Commissioner of Education "to devise methods and promote plans for the elimination of adult illiteracy in the United States." It was reported out of the Committee on Education on March 27. However, no further action was taken upon it during the second session of the Sixty-fifth Congress. *Cong. Record*, 65th Cong., 2d sess., pp. 4109, 4180.

From Richard Crane

My dear Mr. President: At the Executive Office, May 11, 1918.

Father would like to see you some time Monday afternoon, if possible, to tell you why he is most anxious to have you see Professor Masaryk. He also wished to have me explain to you that the memorandum of Professor Masaryk, which I sent you last week, was made in answer to a series of questions put to him by our Ambassador in Tokyo, the substance of which was cabled to the State Department. This memorandum does not, in Father's opinion, cover the field in the way that it should be presented to you.

Furthermore, Professor Masaryk's position as the leader of the Bohemian race, as well as a recognized authority on racial and political conditions in Austria-Hungary, makes it especially desirable, in view of recent developments in regard to these questions, that he be given an opportunity to see you.

Sincerely yours,   Richard Crane

Please tell Mr. R. Crane (on the 'phone) that it is not possible for me to do this to-day and that I am so pressed just now that I *must* postpone it. W.W.

TLS (WP, DLC).

From Newton Diehl Baker, with Enclosure

My dear Mr. President: Washington. May 11, 1918

This very specific information will interest you and I think will give you pleasure. It really is the concrete answer to many current doubts and queries. The figures (gross) vary from the half million which I announced the other day because of some troops shipped but not arrived in France when General Pershings study was made
                              Respectfully,   Newton D Baker

ALS (WP, DLC).

E N C L O S U R E

Received at Washington D. C. May 11, 1918. 9.57 A.
To the Adjutant General, Washington.
No. 1086 May 10th Confidential.
For the Chief of Staff.

Paragraph 1. In order that the War Department may be fully informed as to the present disposition of our forces in France and of the assistance now being rendered the Allied armies by these forces, the following summary is given.

Subparagraph A. On March 19th, two days before the German offense began, there were in France 296,819 officers and men, of which 167,672 were combatant troops, represented by 4 combat divisions, 1 replacement and one depot division and ond [one] regiment of Infantry—colored troops—serving with the French.

Subparagraph B. At present there are in England and France, 466,412 officers and men, of which 290,765 are combatant troops. To these should be added 21,912 en route from ports of debarkation giving a grand total of 488,224. The combatant troops are represented by the following complete divisions: 1st, second, 3rd, 26th, 32nd, 41st, 42nd, and 77th and the following incomplete divisions: 5th, 28th, 35th, 82nd and 93rd. There are also 203 brigades of heavy coast artillery, the 74th Gas and Flame Engineers, 4 regiments of Cavalry and certain special troops giving a total of 290,765 officers and men.

Subparagraph C. Organizations serving in American divisional sector are: first division, second division, 26th division, 42nd division, 1 brigade Heavy Artillery. A total 4,100 officers, enlisted men 98,989. These organizations are tactically under the French Corps Sector Staffs, but for administration, replacement and supply are under our own first corps headquarters.

Subparagraph D. The first division is in the Picardy battle near Montididier; the second division holding a sector near Verdun, but troops withdrawn within a few days (being replaced by a used French division) and take position on the Picardy front; the 26th division is holding a sector north of Toul and the 42nd division is holding a sector near Luneville. The 32nd division which, because of the present emergency, has been reconstituted from a replacement to a combat division, will shortly enter the line in a quiet sector and relieve further French troops. Divisions being approximately double the strength in infantry of a French division we are taking over a length of front in proportion to the strength of our troops, thus relieving double the number of French divisions from the line for participation in the Picardy battle.

Subparagraph E. The infantry and machine gun units of the 77th division which have arrived from British area are receiving preliminary training preparatory to entering the line by battalions in British brigades for initial trench training. The 35th and 82nd divisions are now arriving and will undergo training with the British preparatory to entering the line under the same condition as the 77th division. We have sent to the British the following auxiliary troops: 4 regiments railroad Engineers, 1 regiment pioneer Engineers, 1 battalion Forestry Engineers, 1 telegraph battalion Signal Corps and six Base Hospitals; also 9,826 officers and men of the Air Service (4 aero squadrons being at the front).

Subparagraph F. The French have had turned over to them 4 negro regiments, of the 93rd division, approximately 5,500 motor mechanics, 6 machine shop truck units and 80 sections of the United States Ambulance Service.

Subparagraph G. To accomplish the above, the aero squadron service of supply has contributed every available unit not absolutely essential to continue the operation of our supply service.

Subparagraph H. The following organizations are now undergoing training: the 3rd division; the 5th division, less its artillery which has not yet sailed; the 41st division (depot) which is composed of necessary personnel only *for instruction* and administration of newly arriving replacements; heavy artillery, consisting of 31st and 32nd artillery brigades, which arrived during the past month and are in training and the 54th heavy artillery regiment which has been designated as a replacement for these brigades; the artillery of the 77th division. Total for training and replacements officers 5,500, enlisted men 101,600.

Subparagraph J. Service of supply troops total 140,049. Combatant troops attached to service of supply include 4 cavalry and two infantry regiments, 1 Engineer regiment and two ammunition trains. Total 16,885.

Subparagraph K. Troops with the British in training 34,334, of which 27,960 are infantry, the rest special units. Troops in service with the British 11,410, *all* of which are special units, giving a total of 45,744.

Subparagraph L. Troops with the French in training 8,199, *all* infantry. Troops with the French in service 12,234, *all* of which are special units. Total 20,423.

Subparagraph M. Recapitulation. In service. Serving with American sector of the line 103,089; service of supply troops 140,049. Combatant troops used in service of supply 16,885; serving with the British 11,410; serving with the French 12,234; total 283,667. In training. In American training areas, including aviation, 133,534; with British forces 34,334; with French forces 8,199; total 176,067. En route from ports of debarkation to join American Expeditionary Forces and British Expeditionary Forces, 21,812; sick and detached 6,678; making a grand total of 488,224.

Subparagraph N. In addition to the assistance being given to the French and British in the form of infantry and special troops, as has been enumerated herein, our troops are actually holding 35 miles of the front line. The significance of these facts can be better appreciated with [when] it is realized that this is more than double *the* front held by the Belgian Army and more than the front held by the British during the first year of the war.   Pershing.

T telegram (WP, DLC).

From Newton Diehl Baker

My dear Mr. President: [Washington] May 11, 1918.

I return herewith the carbon copies which you gave me the other day, and which were sent by your daughter Mrs. Sayre. To them are attached copies of cablegrams from Mr. H. P. Davison of the American Red Cross to Major Perkins,[1] Chief of the Red Cross in Paris, and from Major Perkins to Mr. Davison in reply.

From these cablegrams it appears that the Y.W.C.A. is already actively cooperating with the Red Cross on nurses and Red Cross employees, and also cooperating with the Y.M.C.A. in some forms of military work, but that the total of Y.W.C.A. personnel at present in France amounts to only forty persons.

Apparently two thoughts are in the minds of the Y.W.C.A. women, (1) that they will be able to greatly enlarge their work among the French munition workers, and (2) that as the American Army increases the number of women employees, telephone operators, etc., there will be a distinct field for Y.W.C.A. work as distinguished from that now conducted by the Y.M.C.A. among our male military personnel.

As to the second of these possibilities, it is only fair to say that there is no determination on the part of the War Department at present largely to increase the militarized female personnel of our Army in France. The French make an extensive use of women in clerical positions, and as drivers of trucks and ambulances. The British have formed a large corps which they call the Women's Auxiliary Army Corps, made up of uniformed and militarized women who drive trucks, do storage warehouse work, clerical service, orderly service in hospitals, and in various other ways replace men in the services of supply. This is so extensive that I can well understand the need for an independently organized recreational service for them; but our own Army, at present, presents no parallel, and only a few hundred women will be sent over, these being largely used at General Headquarters which will always be in cities where ready-made facilities for recreation are abundant, and where Red Cross activities are already carried on.

With regard to the first of these fields of extended activity; namely, munition workers among the French civilian population, it is clear that an opportunity does exist for valuable service, and I can see no reason why any work which the Y.W.C.A. desires to undertake in that field might not well be separately organized and independently recognized by the government.

To the extent that the Y.W.C.A. proposed to carry on its work with the American Army it seems quite clear that it would be wiser for them to continue as they are at present in cordial cooperation with the Y.M.C.A., and the Red Cross, rather than to set up an independent agency. This view, I feel sure, would be shared by General Pershing who is anxious to limit the officially recognized agencies associated with his Army to the fewest possible number.

Will you be good enough to have these suggestions conveyed to Mrs. Sayre, and ask whether there is any further consideration she would like to have me give the subject?

Respectfully yours,   [Newton D. Baker]

CCL (N. D. Baker Papers, DLC).
¹ James Handasyd Perkins, vice-president of the National City Bank of New York.

Albert Sidney Burleson to Joseph Patrick Tumulty

My dear Mr. Tumulty: Washington. May 11, 1918.

The regular aerial mail service will be inaugurated at Washington on May 15th. The airplane with the first dispatch of mail will leave Polo Field at 11:30 a.m.[1]

I take pleasure in transmitting herewith a permit to the field to witness the initial flight.

Sincerely yours,   A. S. Burleson

TLS (WP, DLC).

[1] The Post Office Department, using army aircraft and pilots, began daily (except Sunday) mail service between New York, Philadelphia, and Washington on May 15. The Wilsons were at the airfield in Potomac Park to see the departure of the first flight from Washington to Philadelphia at 11:47 a.m. Poor visibility forced the pilot to land only thirty miles away in Maryland. However, the three other flights from Philadelphia to New York, New York to Philadelphia, and Philadelphia to Washington, were completed successfully. *New York Times* and *Washington Post*, May 16, 1918.

Newton Diehl Baker to John Joseph Pershing

[Washington] May 11th [1918].

No. 1297-R. The following from the Secretary of War: "The President asked me to say to you that he has been much impressed and disturbed by representation officially made to him here by French and British Ambassadors showing the steady drain upon French and British replacements and the small number of replacement troops now available. He feels that you on the ground have full opportunity to know the situation and fully trusts your judgment as to how far we ought to give additional priority to infantry and machine gun units, in view of the fact that such troops seem to be the most immediately serviceable and urgently needed. The Abbeville agreement, of course, provides less priority for infantry and machine gun units than was recommended by the Supreme War Council, but with shipping at present in prospect will result in practically 120,000 infantry and machine gun units, Signal Corps, and Engineer Corps per month during May and June. It has been suggested to the President that General Foch may reopen this subject with you and the President hopes you will approach any such interview as *systematically* [sympathetically] as possible, particularly if the suggestions as to replacements which has [have] been presented to him is as critical as it seems." In this connection, for your confidential information, there is now left in the United States, excluding three divisions at ports of embarkation, 263,852 infantrymen of sufficient training for overseas service, so that unless the acceptance untrained infantrymen is desired, there is a practical limit to the extent to which the infantry and machine gun program can be carried. The number quoted above troops augmented during this month by some 200,000 men but of course these men should not be sent abroad without at least three months' training. March.

McCain

CC telegram (WDR, RG 120, Records of the American Expeditionary Force, AGO, Confidential Telegrams, DNA).

From Edward Mandell House, with Enclosure

Dear Governor:　　　　　　　　　New York. May 12, 1918.

Here is a cable which has just come from Sir William. While interesting it is in some ways disturbing.

When I was in Paris I saw that Pershing needed someone to help him do the things that were not strictly military but were more or less diplomatic. I talked with him frankly about it and he seemed to realize the need and asked my advice as to what was best to do. He has too much on his shoulders.

Pershing knows as well as we do that the Roosevelt-Wood crowd are trying to push him out, and he is also conscious of your desire and that of the entire Administration that he should succeed.

I hope Sir William is mistaken in believing that he and Bliss are at outs for while Bliss has not great initiative, he has the saving quality of good sense and Pershing would not go far wrong if he advised with Bliss and they acted in unison. Bliss also has the quality of getting along with others.

I learn from Gregory that you thought well of the Hughes suggestion. The more I think of it the more certain I am that it would be a wise move. I am sure the country will receive it with great applause.

I am hoping that you have found it possible to arrange to come over on Friday. I am looking eagerly forward to seeing you.

Affectionately yours,　E. M. House

TLS (WP, DLC).

ENCLOSURE

London, May 11, 1918.

Following for Col. House from Sir William Wiseman:

Following are my observations on the present situation:

(a) The morale of the British Army is excellent; in fact marvelous considering recent reverses. Morale of the French Army I hear is also splendid. Morale of American troops could not be better; it has improved since you were here in December. The American troops engaged have distinguished themselves, and everyone recognises that there is no better fighting material. Size of the American Expeditionary Force is, however, growing far too large for the present Staff and organization.* This is beginning to constitute a serious problem which needs early attention. Morale of the French civilians has improved as a result of the German offensive. Clemenceau's position is strong, and even those who do not like his methods recognize that he is the right man for the emergency.

(b) Position of the Supreme War Council at Versailles is unsatisfactory. I feel that this body properly constituted and used might be the solution of many difficulties. In the meantime they are doing very useful work, but no one pays any attention to their recommendations. Bliss feels this situation keenly. He has achieved a considerable success and represented America with distinction and dignity. Unfortunately he and Pershing do not get on well together.

(c) Military Situation: I have seen a report of Versailles by Wilson, Foch and Bliss, which accurately foretold present German offensive and made recommendations to meet it, which were not carried out. I therefore assume these same soldiers are as accurate in their appreciation of the present situation about which they are entirely in agreement. Their views are approximately as follows: The situation is very grave. If we succeed in frustrating German plans it will be by nothing but the magnificent heroism of tired troops fighting against great odds. The Germans are not dissatisfied with results of the offensive so far. They are deliberately inspiring in the Press a contrary view. German troops are fighting well and on the whole succeeding as fast as their General Staff could reasonably expect. They are engaged in the first phase of their great offensive, which is to hammer us out of prepared positions into the open or hastily prepared positions, and to destroy our reserves and tire our Armies. In this phase the actual territory gained is of secondary importance. If this succeeds, the second phase will be to bring up further reserves and attempt to obtain a decisive victory. They would have the choice of striking for the Channel ports and cutting off a large portion of our Army in the northeast corner of France or splitting up the British and French Armies and seizing Paris.** The nature of their railway communications is especially favourable for this alternative scheme, which also prevents us from massing troops

*This I think is true. [Text footnotes by E.M.H.]
**This largely agrees with McNally's cable #3271 from Berne[1] which I inclose.

in either place, because we cannot know until the last moment whether they will strike north or south. The first phase may well continue during May and part of June, and the second phase may not develop until July or August. The German prisoners I saw, recently captured, prove that they have good material in good condition in their lines. I give you these facts in detail because a most unfortunate situation has arisen regarding American cooperation. Briefly I will recapitulate it.

(d) In December last it became clear that an American Army could not be created in time to meet the great offensive, but that American infantry could play a very decisive part. It was therefore agreed that the infantry of six divisions should come over at once to be brigaded with the British and French. Later the whole situation was reviewed with much care, and as far as I can see with much skill, by Versailles. On March the 21st. in joint note No. 18, unanimously agreed on (Bliss and his whole Staff cordially agreed) it was recommended in view of the emergency that the idea of creating an independent American Army should be postponed for a time and nothing but infantry and machine gunners should be sent, and these as rapidly as possible to be used in whatever way it was considered best by the Allied and American commanders. This note was, I understand, approved by Secretary Baker during his visit. Unfortunately it was not acted upon. Later Reading made his arrangement with the President and Secretary Baker of which you are aware. In the meantime Milner assumed office and considered it was of the first importance that any arrangement should be approved by General Pershing. He feared that Pershing would object to the Baker-Reading agreement. He therefore sent for Pershing and made his agreement without consulting the French Government or the Generalissimo. The French Government objected but it was decided to consider the matter at the Supreme War Council at Abbeville. At the first meeting it was clear that Pershing stood by himself in direct opposition to all the other authorities present. Foch and Clemenceau wanted to force an issue. Lloyd George and Milner considered it of supreme importance to avoid open disagreement with Pershing. I confess that I shared their view and hoped, after hearing the very grave statements of the French and British Staffs and of the Generalissimo, Pershing would agree. He appeared, however, entirely unaffected by their arguments, and therefore Lloyd George worked out with him the Abbeville agreement in spite of Foch's protest, and everybody knowing perfectly well that it was an unsatisfactory compromise.

(e) The position now is that the Allied Governments have formally accepted this agreement, and it would, therefore, appear absurd to reopen the discussion; in fact, they are not likely to do so. Let us consider the difference between the Abbeville agreement and what might be done. By the Abbeville agreement the French and British will get the infantry from six divisions, or about 95,000 men, in May and the same in June. If, on the other hand, we do what Foch wants and strain our tonnage resources, we could undoubtedly bring considerably more than double that number of infantry in the time.*** On the one hand, therefore, you put in, say 400,000 reserves at the most critical stage of the battle and delay creation of American Army for two or three months; and, on the other hand, you take the responsibility of saying that Pershing is right and everybody else is wrong and that less than 200,000 infantry are sufficient for the emergency. It should not be forgotten that the main features of these discussions are known to the British and French Armies, and that a strong and generous line adopted by the President at this moment, accompanied by a suitable message of determination and encouragement, would mean a great deal to the soldiers who are enduring, and will have endured, a terrible strain.

It is unnecessary to state that General Pershing is quite honest in his opinion. He is obsesssed with two ideas: one, the creation of an autonomous American Army and, two, that the Allies are making use of the present emergency to get American reinforcements into their Army. He spoke at some length at Abbeville and the objections he made were purely political; in fact, his remarks would have been more suited to a civilian head of a government rather than to a Commander-in-Chief in the field. At the same time one cannot help sympathizing with his position; he is much overworked and un- derstaffed and is called upon to discuss, indeed to decide, questions which should clearly be determined by civilian authorities. I gather it is Pershing himself and his immediate Staff who feel so strongly about this question, and that his views are not unanimously shared by the American Army, but this, of course, is only hearsay, and I cannot vouch for its truth. I believe he is considerably influenced by certain American residents in Paris whom we have discussed.

(f) I have tried to give you fairly both sides of the case, and cannot help feeling that there is more to be said for Pershing's point of view than the Allies care to admit. I doubt if the German Army can secure another success as great as they did at the beginning of the battle. At the same time the stakes are too big to take chances, and

***It would certainly seem safer to stick to the plan you, Reading & Baker worked out

we had better have too many than too few infantry at this critical stage. I think the present would be an excellent opportunity for the President to

(g) address the American people on the situation, giving a message of encouragement to all our Armies in the field, a message of warning to the peoples at home to stand solidly together and face a great trial and say that he has had an appeal from the Allies to rush American assistance into the battle;† that this is not a time for half measures nor is that an American characteristic, and the American people are prepared to make the high sacrifice of delaying for a time the creation of their autonomous Army in order to fling themselves at once into the fight. In this way and in no other way can America win the battle for the world.

I have not shown this cable to anyone or consulted them as to suggestions which I have ventured to make just as if I were talking to you.

(h) Sir Horace Plunkett wanted to know if you have received his cable[2] and whether you have any observations to make. I think it is generally felt that it is impossible to enforce conscription in Ireland without giving Home Rule first, but that places the Government in the dilemma I have already described.[3]

(i) I propose sailing on Wednesday.[4] Will you cable me your views generally so that I can have a final talk with mutual friends before leaving.

† If you think well of this would not your Red Cross address here be a good opportunity.

TC telegram (WP, DLC).
  [1] P. A. Stovall to RL, May 7, 1918, T telegram (SDR, RG 59, 763.72/9918, DNA).
  [2] The Enclosure printed with Lord Reading to JPT, May 8, 1918.
  [3] That is, H. Plunkett to EMH, April 28, 1918, printed as an Enclosure with EMH to WW, April 30, 1918.
  [4] That is, May 15.

Lord Reading to Arthur James Balfour

Washington. May 12, 1918.

No. 2137. Your tel. No. 2871 of May 10.[1]

Intervention.

1. There is an undoubted hardening by U. S. Administration against intervention in Siberia caused by (a) reports which reach them from Russia (b) scepticism as to military advantage to be gained (c) the Japanese Ambassador's statements as to the position taken by his Government and already reported by me to you (d) confirmation by the Japanese Ambassador of the President's view

that any intervention which brings the Japanese into Siberia will meet with hostile action both from the Bolsheviki Government and Soviets and the Russian people.

2. In effect the President holds the opinion which nothing seems to shake that the advantages which might be gained by Japanese American and Allied intervention will be far outweighed by the disadvantages which he thinks must inevitably follow. As I have told you for some little time I have been convinced that this is the definite view of the President and although the French Ambassador thought as I informed you that the President was slightly more favourably disposed than my opinion indicated, M. Jusserand has informed me that he has now arrived at a conclusion entirely corresponding with mine. He was very discouraged by an interview he had had with Secretary Lansing after which M. Jusserand came to see me.

3. I thereupon saw Secretary Lansing. As to last paragraph of your telegram No. 2871 I have continuously and immediately kept both State Department and President fully informed of most of Lockhart's telegrams and only do not give paraphrases when I have felt it inadvisable. Secretary Lansing rarely gives me documents but he tells me generally the effect of the reports received by the State Department concerning Siberia and Russia. At my visit to him yesterday I pressed to obtain an answer to the questions and suggestions in your telegram No. 2871 of which I gave him paraphrase except last paragraph.[2]

4. As regards Japanese intervention he gave me clearly to understand that the President was against America joining with Allies and Japanese for an intervention in Siberia. He closed the door although he did not bolt it. I think this best describes the situation. He repeated that the President thought the moment inopportune and that he was unconvinced that there was military advantage to be gained. Moreover the President still thought the effect of such intervention would be to make Russia more friendly to Germany and that it would be better to leave Germany to the difficulties she was herself creating in Russia. I pressed upon him that these difficulties did not seem very serious at present inasmuch as Germany was transferring divisions from Russia to the West and that Trotzsky had no disciplined organized and well equipped force to oppose to the Germans. I again made reference to the change of attitude of Trotzsky as reported to you by Lockhart. Secretary Lansing said that according to their reports there was perhaps some indication of Trotzsky turning to the Allies for cooperation and assistance at Murmansk. Secretary Lansing said that there was a sharp distinction to be drawn at any rate in the view of the U. S.

Administration, between intervention by America and the Allies to protect Murmansk and Archangel and the intervention with the assistance of Japan into Siberia. He certainly led me to believe that the President would be ready to cooperate with the Allies in the intervention in the North which should take place without the assistance of Japan. Secretary Lansing thought that there was danger of confusion in speaking of intervention without distinguishing between these two different propositions. I asked what they would be prepared to do to assist in the North. His answer was that there were great difficulties as to shipping more especially to provide food and such supplies as could not be found at Archangel or Murmansk. In the result I promised to ascertain what our views were upon this subject and how and to what extent we and the Allies would be ready to send further troops to Murmansk and Archangel. I observed that we had had to seek support of U. S. infantrymen in France as we were so hard pressed for troops but I would enquire from you.

5. Viscount Ishii tells me that his Government has informed him that it will be quite ready to consider any proposition put forward by the Allies and America for their cooperation with Japanese forces in intervention in Siberia. He says he has no doubt his Government would agree but that the proposal must come of course from the Allies and America. He also says that the Russians are strongly against intervention by Japanese according to the reports received by them.

As long as the American attitude is unfavourable I think Viscount Ishii will adopt the same attitude but I still think the Japanese Government would take a more favourable view of the situation if the American Government showed an inclination to join in intervention.

6. I have postponed visit to President and shall wait till I get your answer as to Murmansk and Archangel suggestions particularly as there is nothing pressing except Mexico. There is no doubt State Dept. is well aware of the happenings in Mexico. I shall not discuss your telegram of May 7th on Mexico with the State Department but shall wait till I see the President.

T telegram (FO 115/2446, pp. 248-52, PRO).
¹ A paraphrase of this telegram is printed as an Enclosure with RL to WW, May 11, 1918 (first letter of that date).
² "I presume that you keep State Department and President fully informed of Lockhart's telegrams."

ADDENDA

Four Letters to Richard Ludwig Enno Littmann[1]

My dear Dr. Littmann,   Princeton, N. J. 1 February, 1906.

I fear that I must have seemed to you very ungracious in not having replied sooner to your letters.[2] They have interested me deeply. I have been deeply pleased to learn of your gratifying success; and I have entirely approved of your course in consenting to attach yourself to the German expedition. It was the only wise, indeed the only sensible, thing to do. But you know the many and very far-reaching changes we have been making here, and I have allowed myself to become almost selfishly engrossed in them, to the exclusion of everything else. I know that you will understand, and that you will not doubt my warm interest both in your work and in your personal fortunes.

I send you these lines to convey my most cordial greetings, to wish you the best possible success and a happy return to Princeton, and to say that I expect to propose to the Board of Trustees at their March meeting an arrangement as to your rank and remuneration here that will, if they accept it, make you feel both permanent in your tenure and much more comfortable in the matter of salary.

I think that you know that I cannot pledge the Board in matters of this kind, but I hope to nominate you to a full Professorship, and to suggest $2,500 as your salary. I shall be very happy if these proposals are accepted, and I shall confidently expect them to be favourably acted upon.

Hoping that I may have the pleasure of hearing from you again,
With warm regard,
Cordially and sincerely Yours,   Woodrow Wilson

[1] Identified in n. 2 to the entry from Wilson's diary, Jan. 11, 1904, Vol. 15.
[2] R. L. E. Littmann to WW, Sept. 19 and Nov. 24, 1905, Vol. 16.

My dear Professor Littmann,   Princeton, N. J. 10 July, 1909

I need not tell you that we have kept you in mind here at Princeton ever since you felt obliged to leave us, and have always kept alive the hope that some day you would be willing to return. I am now in a position to ask you if you will not come back to us and accept a Professorship in your chosen field at a salary of three thousand dollars a year; and I would urge the invitation upon you most earnestly and cordially. There is no one else we would care to have here to handle the materials Mr. Garrett and others have put at our disposal, and I hope with all my heart that you will feel at liberty and also inclined to accept. I know that all my colleagues would join very cordially in the invitation, did they know I was writing. Mr. Garrett, Professor Butler, and Dean Fine do know that I am sending this invitation and are very eager to have you come. I beg that you will give it your most favourable consideration.

    With warmest regard,
            Faithfully and sincerely Yours,   Woodrow Wilson

                                          Lyme, Connecticut,
My dear Professor Littmann,   26 August, 1909.

    Thank you for your letters of the fourth and fourteenth of August.[1] They bring me a real dissapointment. We had set our hearts on having you back at Princeton, where so much work in your line waits to be done and where we are unwilling to have anyone else but yourself do it. But I understand perfectly the grounds of your decision and how imperative the duty to remain in Strassburg seems to you. You may be sure that I have not a word of criticism to utter.

    I am only deeply sorry. I believe that a great opportunity awaits you on this side of the water, and that there is no better place at which you could avail yourself of it than at Princeton. I hope that the opportunity will not slip by and that some not too distant future time may find you free to make the choice.

    I am away from Princeton; but I am sure that all my colleagues (especially Fine and Butler and Mr. Robert Garrett) will feel that I bring them very bad news when I have the opportunity to tell them that you cannot come. I am sure, too, that they would wish me to include them in my messages of warmest regard and best wishes.

            Cordially and faithfully Yours,   Woodrow Wilson

WWTLS (received from Thomas Fischer).
    [1] R. L. E. Littmann to WW, Aug. 4, 1909, Vol. 19; Littmann's letter of Aug. 14, 1909, is missing.

My dear Professor Littmann: [Trenton, N. J.] November 9, 1911.

    It was very delightful to hear from you.[1] I was sincerely disappointed when I knew you had been in Princeton and I had not had the pleasure of seeing you. I recall very often our delightful association at Princeton and wish very heartily so great a space of earth and sea did not hold us apart. Pray, let me know the next time you come to America and I will make a point of seeing you. I cannot help feeling that you would have been happier in Princeton and I want to express my warm hope that you will have the greatest success and happiness in your work at Stras[s]burg.

            Cordially and sincerely yours,   Woodrow Wilson

TLS (received from Thomas Fischer).
    [1] Littmann's letter is missing.

INDEX

NOTE ON THE INDEX

THE alphabetically arranged analytical table of contents at the front of the volume eliminates duplication, in both contents and index, of references to certain documents, such as letters. Letters are listed in the contents alphabetically by name, and chronologically within each name by page. The subject matter of all letters is, of course, indexed. The Editorial Notes and Wilson's writings are listed in the contents chronologically by page. In addition, the subject matter of both categories is indexed. The index covers all references to books and articles mentioned in text or notes. Footnotes are indexed. Page references to footnotes which place a comma between the page number and "n" cite both text and footnote, thus: "418,n1." On the other hand, absence of the comma indicates reference to the footnote only, thus: "59n1"—the page number denoting where the footnote appears.

The index supplies the fullest known form of names and, for the Wilson and Axson families, relationships as far down as cousins. Persons referred to by nicknames or shortened forms of names can be identified by reference to entries for these forms of the names.

All entries consisting of page numbers only and which refer to concepts, issues and opinions (such as democracy, the tariff, and money trust, leadership, and labor problems), are references to Wilson's speeches and writings. Page references that follow the symbol Δ in such entries refer to the opinions and comments of others who are identified.

Two cumulative contents-index volumes are now in print: Volume 13, which covers Volumes 1-12, and Volume 26, which covers Volumes 14-25. Volume 39, covering Volumes 27-38, is in preparation.

INDEX